WITHDRAWN

A HISTORY OF THE
GREEK AND ROMAN WORLD

A HISTORY OF THE GREEK AND ROMAN WORLD

BY

G. B. GRUNDY
M.A., D.Litt.

FELLOW AND TUTOR OF CORPUS CHRISTI COLLEGE, OXFORD
AUTHOR OF "THUCYDIDES AND THE HISTORY OF HIS AGE," ETC.

WITH TWO MAPS

METHUEN & CO. LTD.
36 ESSEX STREET W.C.
LONDON

A HISTORY OF
THE GREEK AND
ROMAN WORLD

G. B. GRUNDY
M.A., D.Litt.

FELLOW AND TUTOR OF CORPUS CHRISTI COLLEGE, OXFORD
AUTHOR OF *THUCYDIDES AND THE HISTORY OF HIS AGE*, ETC.

First Published in 1926

WITH TWO MAPS

METHUEN & CO. LTD.
36 ESSEX STREET W.C.
LONDON

PRINTED IN GREAT BRITAIN

PREFACE

SUCH works as I have hitherto published on ancient history were written without any limitation of the space which might be devoted to them. In writing the present work I have been subject to limitations which the present price of production imposes on authors and publishers, limitations which must necessarily affect the performance of a writer who has never previously worked under conditions which tend to reduce the history of a period so long as that covered by the present work to a dry annalistic compilation. Every writer would wish to avoid such a result ; and different writers might take different ways of attaining this end. For myself, I have adopted that method which I have used for many years in the teaching of history, the emphasising of the story of those events and institutions which had lasting effects on the lives and history of those races with which I have been concerned. Circumstances of ephemeral consequence I have treated briefly, or, perhaps, omitted altogether, even at the expense of having to pass over a dramatic story. I have felt that it is possible that some of those who make use of a work covering so much historical ground may wish to confine their reading to certain sections of it. In order to provide for that contingency I have, at the risk of repetition, mentioned more than once in the course of the history certain considerations which have an important bearing on various contexts.

No attempt has been made to write a history which shall be, to use an expressive German word, *tendenziös*, that is to say, designed at the outset to prove the goodness or badness of certain abstract ideas or concrete forms in political and social life. I have not attempted to prove that the Athenians were early Victorian Liberals, nor that the abler Roman statesmen belonged to the Prussian school. If any condemnation has been passed on any institution or individual, it is founded on the facts of their existence judged by that standard of good and evil which is known to every man.

Limitations of space have hampered me most when I have expressed views which are not in accord with those expressed by standard writers on the subject, in that I have been unable to cite all the reasons which I had for differing from them. Moreover, the tradition of ancient history as accepted in this country is sown with difficulties which the teacher discovers for himself in the course of his teaching, or, if not, his abler pupils discover for him. For those difficulties I have tried to find some solution. But I have avoided controversy, even if I have not avoided controversial matter.

There is one thing which I would point out to anyone who reads this book, that the evidence for views expressed on one page of it is not concentrated on that page, but is largely resident in the story of the development of earlier or later events.

The method which I have adopted in my last chapter dealing with the history of the Roman Principate may seem strange, because it is not customary in the writing of history on the usual chronological lines. But the whole history of that century and a half was so moulded by the work of one great man, Augustus, that I feel that its story is best told by following the developments of the individual institutions which he founded.

In spelling I have throughout adopted the Latin forms of Greek names, simply because they are to British readers more familiar than the Greek forms.

To two friends, Mr. Michael Holroyd and Mr. A. J. Jenkinson, of Brasenose College, Oxford, I have submitted two chapters of the work, those on the Fourth and Third Centuries B.C. I have every reason to be grateful to them for their help, which has been most valuable to me. At the same time they are in no way responsible for all the views expressed in those chapters.

My colleague, Dr. F. C. S. Schiller and Mr. C. S. Hignett, of Hertford College, have very kindly read through some of the proof-sheets and have suggested important modifications.

G. B. GRUNDY

Beam Hall, Oxford
October, 1925

CONTENTS

CHAP.		PAGE
I	THE SECOND MILLENNIUM BEFORE CHRIST, 2000–1000 B.C.	1
II	THE FIRST TWO CENTURIES OF THE FIRST MILLENNIUM BEFORE CHRIST, 1000–800 B.C.	31
III	THE EIGHTH AND SEVENTH CENTURIES BEFORE CHRIST, 800–600 B.C.	54
IV	THE SIXTH CENTURY, 600–500 B.C.	87
V	THE FIRST HALF OF THE FIFTH CENTURY, 500–450 B.C.	112
VI	THE SECOND HALF OF THE FIFTH CENTURY, 450–400 B.C.	167
VII	THE FOURTH CENTURY, 400–300 B.C.	222
VIII	THE THIRD CENTURY, 300–200 B.C.	280
IX	THE SECOND CENTURY, 200–100 B.C.	345
X	THE FIRST CENTURY, 100–31 B.C.	394
XI	THE EMPIRE, SOMETIMES CALLED THE PRINCIPATE, 31 B.C.–A.D. 138	451
INDEX		531

MAPS

ANCIENT GREECE

THE DEVELOPMENT OF THE ROMAN EMPIRE, B.C. 218—A.D. 100

At End of Volume

GRUNDY: "HISTORY OF THE GREEK AND ROMAN WORLD"

List of Errata

p. 1, l. 10 : for "is" *read* "are."

p. 79, last line but one : for "second" *read* "first."

p. 218, l. 6 : after "commander" *insert* "of."

p. 373, l. 2 : for "magistrates" *read* "consuls."

p. 432, l. 9 : *insert* full stop after "Syria."
       l. 30 : for "Carrhe" *read* "Carrhae."

p. 436, l. 18 : after "It was with" *insert a line omitted from the MS.*, "a comparatively small number of troops drawn from."

p. 441, last line but 2, for "empire" *read* "Empire."

p. 442, l. 1 : for "empire" *read* "Empire."

p. 443, l. 6 : after "than" *insert* "of."

p. 485, l. 33 : *omit* "Tiberius."

p. 495, l. 9 : for "illigitimate" *read* "illegitimate."

p. 506, l. 31 : for "north-west" *read* "north-east."

A HISTORY OF THE GREEK AND ROMAN WORLD

CHAPTER I

THE SECOND MILLENNIUM BEFORE CHRIST, 2000–1000 B.C.

TO any nation of modern times that part of the story of the ancient world is of special interest which deals with those races whose character and institutions form either wholly or in part the foundation of the polity under which it lives. In the case of the nations of modern Europe and their kinsmen in other parts of the world the civilisations which sprang up in the region of the Mediterranean form not merely the basis of their institutions, but have been responsible for the most fundamental ideas upon which the life of the modern State and of the modern individual is founded. It would be a task beyond the powers of any single historian to tell the whole tale of their development from the dawn of Mediterranean history to the present day; and he who would attempt to deal with the story can only attain some measure of success if he confines himself to certain chapters of it limited in matter to a certain period. Thus for those who live under the modern western civilisation the limitation to the Mediterranean area is a natural one, whereas the limitation in respect of time is artificial, imposed by the powers and interests of the author.

CIVILISATION

The period from about 1000 B.C. to A.D. 138 is that in which the institutions which have affected the Western World of the present day grew to their prime. That events and circumstances existent before that period affected the earliest growth of Mediterranean civilisation is admittedly the case, since all institutions are the products of an evolution as old as the human race. But if the civilisations of Greece and Rome form the foundation of the modern polities of the Western World, then it must further be admitted that the story of the ages prior to 1000

B.C. is as yet too little known for it to be possible to say precisely how large or how small is the debt which those institutions which formed the earlier of the two Mediterranean civilisations, that of Greece, owe to them.

These two civilisations were of a type which is without parallel in the history of the world. In its earliest development that of Rome was independent of that of Greece, though they both originated under very similar general conditions. The greatest civilisations of the rest of the ancient world, those of Egypt, the Euphrates region, India and China, came into being in lands of unusual fertility, where men were not hard put to it for the sheer necessaries of existence, and had the means and the leisure to evolve those standards of comfort which lead to the realisation of a form of life in which the barbaric animal element in human nature is subordinated to an ordered and peaceful association. But those of Greece and Rome sprang up in countries where life had to be won from the soil by hard work, and where the earth did not always respond to the labour bestowed upon it. This was more the case in Greece than in Italy; and with the Greek it was the direct cause of those migrations which brought him into close contact with the nations dwelling around him. In like manner, though owing to somewhat different circumstances, the Roman came not merely to know but to rule the other nations of the Mediterranean world; and it was to such intercourse that the civilisations of Greece and Rome were due. For the Greek first, and the Roman later, came by this means to discover that the life which he lived was not the only form of life which men could live : that there were other peoples in the world living lives of a different type containing elements which, even if they did not actually adopt them, suggested to them modifications in their own way of living. Thus they gradually evolved civilisations due to intercourse, as contrasted with those of the oriental world which sprang from ease of life. It is not merely surmised, it is known, that they were influenced in definite ways by the older civilisations of the Euphrates and the Nile; but this definite influence is limited to factors which, though important, form but a small element in the institutions of the two great Mediterranean peoples.

It is probable that there will always be certain marked differences in development between civilisations of intercourse and those due to ease of existence; but it is not to that cause only that the differences between the Mediterranean civilisations and those of the Near East are due. The independence in the development of the former is to be attributed to the fact that the Mediterranean area is cut off from the rest of the world by physical barriers of a very formidable character.

The Mediterranean Region

It is difficult for those who live in the age of steamships and railways, when the Mediterranean itself has become perhaps the greatest sea highway in the universe, and when its surrounding lands have been linked with the external world on all sides save the south by railways, to realise the isolation of this Mediterranean area in ancient times. Of the two exits by sea, the Strait of Gibraltar on the west led into an ocean which only the most reckless would face in the ships of those days. The Pillars of Hercules were a fable to most of the dwellers on that inland sea, and were to all of them the limit of all certain geographical knowledge. The Bosphorus led into that inhospitable sea which the Greek with propitiatory euphemism called the Euxine, a maritime cul-de-sac in any case, and surrounded by peoples whose habits were not encouraging to the peaceful penetration of the trading stranger beyond its immediate shores. As to the lands round the Mediterranean, the lines of communication with the outside world were few, and for the most part difficult. Spain, a land of difficult passage, afforded no outlet except to the fabled and dreaded ocean. Up the Rhône valley, through Gaul, lay the one easy line of communication with the external world ; but it led into a land of barbarism from which neither ideas nor institutions could be borrowed by those on the road to civilisation. Then came the Alps, continued down to the east side of the Adriatic by the Julian Alps, and that Pindus range which with its branches cuts off Greece from the rest of the Balkan peninsula. The Hæmus and the Rhodopé ranges formed parallel barriers stretching from the Italian Alps to the Euxine, so much so that never in the Greek age and only late in the Roman did the region of the lower Danube become well known to the peoples on the shores of the Mediterranean.

The peninsula of Asia Minor has always been a debateable land between Europe and Asia. In actual fact the mass of the Armenian mountains, together with the Anti-Taurus and Taurus ranges, have at most periods of the history of the world been the real and most effective barrier between Eastern and Western civilisation. On the east shore of the Mediterranean Syria belongs, and has always belonged, to the East rather than to the West, though it is essentially a Mediterranean region cut off from the great Euphrates basin by the north extension of the Arabian desert. As far as land communications are concerned it is singularly isolated from the rest of the world. On the north the double barrier of the Taurus and the Amanus ranges reduced the line of communication with Asia Minor to a mere thread which passed through the needles' eyes of the Cilician and the Syrian Gates. To the south and east it was shut in by the desert. Only to the north-east was there any easy communication with the outside world, at the point where the Upper Euphrates approaches most nearly to the Mediterranean coast. Had not the great kingdoms of the Euphrates and the Nile respectively been mutually jealous and apprehensive of its possession by a formidable and hostile power, it might have played but a small part in the history of the Near East. With Semitic tenacity its inhabitants resisted all attempts to occidentalise it. Neither Jew nor Phœnician would accept Hellenism, though they imbibed unconsciously some of its spirit. They remained orientals endowed with a Western energy.

Egypt was both physically and ethnically a land alone, with a civilisation which bore no resemblance to those which sprang up on the north shore of the Mediterranean, and presented great contrasts to that which had its home in the Euphrates basin. Neither the country itself nor its polity can be classified as belonging to any type existent in any other part of the world at any period of history. Before the days when improvements in ship architecture and the growth of experience in navigation facilitated communication with it by sea, it was by nature one of the most isolated countries of the world. Surrounded on three sides, east, south and west, by desert, and only open on the north to a sea which in that part did not afford any sheltered waters such as might be the nursery of early navigation, it presented difficulties of external communication which deterred its neighbours from frequent intercourse with it, and secured it from attack save from either some reckless band of semi-pirate adventurers who were attracted by its wealth, or had been driven into exile by some ethnic commotion elsewhere, or from the successive Euphrates monarchies when at the zenith of their power, or from those " blameless " Ethiopians who used the middle Nile Valley as an avenue for invasion. Its Mediterranean relations were as paradoxical as itself. Till the time of Alexander the Great western civilisation represented by Hellenism had had no traceable influence on its life. The Egyptian found the Greek useful as a mercenary, and later tolerated him as a trader. But even the Ptolemies could never hellenise Egypt. The Greek city flourished luxuriantly on the soil of Asia Minor under Alexander's successors, but could never take real root on that of Egypt. The institutions of the conquered absorbed those of the conqueror. Such, too, had been the experience of those who conquered the land before Alexander, and such has been the experience of those who have conquered it since. The fellaheen of Egypt have been the most successful passive resisters in history.

Thus Egypt has remained outside the Mediterranean world, though geographically part of it. But the real paradox of its position among the Mediterranean lands and peoples is not perhaps that, though in them, it was not of them, but that, though not of them, it became the most important factor in their life during that long period in which first Greek, and later Græco-Latin civilisation, dominated large parts of the shore of that sea. The greatest factor in life is means for its maintenance ; and to the successive authors of these two civilisations Egypt was of the utmost importance in this respect at the times at which their power and influence were dominant. The Greeks coveted the land ; and on one famous occasion Athens made an ill-advised attempt to conquer it. Otherwise, after a period in which they played the part of soldiers of fortune in the pay of Egyptian kings, the Greeks were contented with peaceful penetration as traders. As a source of food supply Egypt was at all times important, and in some ages critically important, to that Greek world which from very early times was unable to grow grain sufficient to feed its population. The more Rome flourished, the more dependent did Italy become on Egypt for its daily bread ; and, the greater the dependence, the more averse did Rome become for political reasons to taking over the direct rule of the country,—one more paradox in the history of this land of paradoxes.

The physical characteristics of North Africa, a fringe of fertile land backed by the wide Sahara, are too well known to need description. They emphasise the isolation of the Mediterranean region.

The last millennium before Christ brought so many changes into the distribution of the population of the lands round the Mediterranean that it is very difficult to recall the ethnography of South Europe in the dark millennium which preceded it. The historian feels himself on very unsafe ground in dealing with the subject ; and the ground is least safe in those lands the population of which was destined to play the most important part in later history.

Of Spain it is fairly safe to conjecture that the population was throughout of that stock to which, from its prevalence in that country, the name Iberian has been given. It was a dark-haired race which seems at that period to have extended northwards up the west coast of Europe as far as the Lower Rhine, and also to have been the aboriginal population of the British Isles.[1] It seems to have stretched eastward as far as the Rhône,

[1] In speaking of the ethnography of the extreme west of Europe I am merely giving the conclusions which seem to me to be most in accord with the main evidence. That evidence has been summed up in Mr. Rice-Holmes' book, " Cæsar's Conquest of Gaul," to which I would refer any reader who wishes to follow a detailed discussion of that important ethnographical question.

where it came into contact with that Ligurian race which formed the earliest traceable population of North Italy. This latter race seems also to have penetrated west of the Rhône, and to have been mingled with the Iberians in the district between that river and the Pyrenees. Inasmuch as the Celts, one branch of whom conquered Gaul, and settled in large numbers in Spain, were, according to the universal testimony of ancient writers, a fair-haired race, while the modern French are dark-haired, save in those districts into which Norsemen or Germans penetrated, it seems certain that the Celtic invaders of Gaul, the Galli of Roman authors, were a conquering minority, which in the course of centuries lost type by becoming merged with the race it had subdued and had originally kept in servitude. To Cæsar, whose attention was absorbed in the Celtic military caste which opposed his conquest, the subordinate Iberian element was out of the picture, unless, as may be the case, the term Galli as used by the Romans included the whole population of Gaul, Celtic and non-Celtic, without distinction. But to the Roman a people in the position of servitude to a race dwelling among them might be left out of account in any definition of nationality, just as the slaves of Italy would have been ignored in reference to the Roman or Italian nationality of that peninsula.

The earliest references to Gaul in the writings of antiquity refer to a period when the Celts were already a dominant race in that region. The date of their invasion is quite unknown. In the period before 1000 B.C. that Ligurian race which has been already mentioned held the greater part of Italy north of the Apennines. Etruscan, and later, Celtic invaders, gradually drove them into the fastnesses of the north-west Apennines and Western Alps, but the Celtic invasion belongs to the next millennium, and of the date of the Etruscan invasion nothing is known. The Veneti, a people of Illyrian stock, may have held the north-east plain of Italy even before the second millennium ended. Their name is connected with an amber trade which is at least as old as the dawn of Greek navigation in the Adriatic. Whether the Etruscans were already in the north part of peninsular Italy before 1000 B.C. is a question on which there is no evidence worth calling such. The riddle of the origin of this most tantalisingly mysterious people will come into consideration in reference to the evidence of Greek authors as to the early population of the Ægean region. In the south-east of the peninsula another offshoot of the Illyrian race had settled at some early period. The rest of the south of Italy and the middle belt of the peninsula were at the close of the millennium inhabited by tribes akin to the Romans and speaking languages closely akin to Latin.

Of the great islands of the Western Mediterranean Sardinia

THE SECOND MILLENNIUM BEFORE CHRIST

was peopled by an Iberian race, and the basic population of Sicily was also Iberian, while the inhabitants of Corsica were probably of Ligurian kin. Of the smaller islands Malta shows traces of an embryonic civilisation which had a home also in other regions of the Western Mediterranean.

In the second millennium B.C. the ethnography of Greece and of the Ægean is a subject which admits of many theories, but no finality. Within the lifetime of men who are not yet old amazing discoveries have been made with regard to these obscure ages which preceded the historic period in Ægean history; but, being undocumented, or affording only documents which cannot as yet be interpreted, the finds hitherto made by the archæological explorers are like streaks of sunlight piercing the cracks in a shutter of a darkened room. Most of the dark age of Greek history still remains dark; and from the little which has been established by evidence many and different conclusions have been drawn even by those expert explorers to whose energy and insight the discoveries are due.[1]

Historians who flourished in that age of sceptical history which fell within the later half of the nineteenth century were wont to treat lightly those traditions of the Dark Ages of Greece which survived in the fifth and later centuries before Christ, and were preserved for the modern world in the works of Herodotus, Thucydides, and other Greek writers. They were treated contemptuously as myths, and, with that would-be precision at which contempt always aims, they were denominated sun-myths, a term which conveyed to the reader a wealth of undiscovered meaning into which he did not further inquire. The

[1] Of books accessible to English readers the translations of Schliemann's works, and the great book of Sir Arthur Evans on the discoveries at Gnossos, give the original views of the two great protagonists in the realms of discovery. Dr. Schliemann's original views have been much modified by further consideration of his evidence both in its own light, and in the light of further discovery. Apart from the work of the explorers themselves two very useful summaries of the evidence and theories emanating from it have been made by English authors: (1) "Handbook of Homeric Study," by Henry Brown, S.J. (Longmans, 1905); (2) "The Discoveries in Crete," by Ronald M. Burrows (John Murray, 1907). These give an excellent account of the evidence and the questions involved at the time at which they were written. In a later and very excellent work, "The Ancient History of the Near East," by H. R. Hall (Methuen), there is a very sane discussion of the problems presented by the evidence so far obtained. Those who would read rather divergent views stated concisely might do well to read "Histoire de l'Antiquité," i. (Javan.), by Eugène Cavaignac (Paris: Fontemoing et Cie, 1917). Neither here nor elsewhere in this volume will any attempt be made to give a complete bibliography of this or any other subject which may be touched upon. The author will confine himself to the mention of works which he has used in the past and found useful.

8 A HISTORY OF THE GREEK AND ROMAN WORLD

present age, though not perhaps less inherently sceptical, has learnt to be more cautious in its criticism of ancient authors, taught by the fate of those critics of forty years ago who were far more prolific in their creation of myths than the historians whom they attacked either were or could have been. The great discoveries of recent years have tended to confirm rather than cast doubt upon the truth of those traditions which Herodotus and Thucydides found prevalent among the Greeks of the fifth century; for it is obvious that these authors found them in existence. The sea power of Minos was a reality. That which has been discovered at Troy is confirmatory of the general legend of the Trojan War. The Homeric poems preserved the legend of the latter; but that the former should have survived through a thousand years of oral tradition, a millennium of chance and change in Greek life, is one of the most remarkable instances which can be cited of the permanence of tradition among an illiterate people.

CRETAN CIVILISATION

When the second millennium before Christ opened it was Crete, not the mainland of what was afterwards Greece, that was the centre of the Ægean world. That island was the home of a brilliant civilisation which was already old when the millennium began. The discoveries in Crete go back to the Neolithic Age, centuries before the civilisation attained its zenith, to a time before Homer as long as that which has elapsed since his reputed death. Truly the world is very old; and those ages of which the story has been preserved in history are but a fraction of the lifetime of the human race. Archæological discovery alone can never provide detailed history, unless, as in Egypt and the Euphrates region, it produces a large mass of epigraphic evidence; and the Cretan pictographs from Gnossos, even if they could be interpreted, are few and brief, and may be no more than catalogues of stores and other property. But the sites of Crete do afford distinct evidence of epochs in the life and civilisation of the island, and of catastrophes which separated these epochs from one another. Between layers of remains sinister of disaster are other layers which throw considerable light on the life of the periods intervening between these catastrophes; and, furthermore, the discovery of objects emanating from Egypt, that ancient home of accurate chronology, enables explorers to date the various strata of the deposits. Thus those who have made an intimate study of Cretan archæology on the spot have been able to produce reasonable evidence of the duration and character of the larger epochs in the story of this civilisation; and, though not always in agreement on minor points, are sufficiently in agreement on the larger questions involved to make their conclusions probable.

To one who would trace the outlines of the development of that Mediterranean civilisation of which the peoples of modern Europe are the heirs the so-called Minoan period in the Ægean is important in two respects. The ethnographical question as to the ultimate fate of that race which created and developed that civilisation known in its early stages as Minoan, and in its later as Mycenæan, is not one which can be ignored in any consideration of the origin or origins of some of the most striking features of the Greek genius. Did the race die with its civilisation, and the civilisation die with the race ? Or did one or both survive by a slender thread of existence into the great period of Greek history, and contribute to the glories of attainment in various departments of life which are associated with that period ?

Excavations in Crete have shown that the great period of its civilisation was preceded by a Neolithic Age extending back into an undateable past. The long period of development which succeeded the Neolithic Age in the island and in the neighbouring parts of the Ægean has been divided chronologically [1] into three main divisions, Early, Middle, and Late Minoan, in each of which three sub-divisions may be recognised. The success of attempts to arrive at some definite date for the various epochs is dependent, as has been said, upon the discovery of objects which can be associated with some definite period in Egyptian history.

To the third sub-period of the Early Minoan belong objects which are imitations of Egyptian originals dating from the sixth dynasty. The second sub-period of the Middle Minoan was at any rate partly synchronous with the twelfth dynasty. The third sub-period of the Late Minoan produced objects which show relations with Egypt from 1587 onwards. But in the previous, or second, sub-period of the Late Minoan, which lasted till about 1500 B.C., the palace at Gnossos was destroyed ; and the centre of this civilisation was transferred to Mycenæ on the mainland of Greece. It is then that the Minoan question becomes of critical importance in relation to Greek history.

Of the authors of this Cretan civilisation several negative, but few positive, facts are known. It seems quite certain that they did not belong to that Indo-European family of nations from which the Greeks, Romans, and the majority of the races of modern Europe are descended. All that is known of the earliest races traceable in Europe and West Asia renders it most improbable that these Cretans came from either of those continents ; and it is therefore conjectured that they came from North Africa.

[1] See Evans, " Classification of the Successive Epochs of Minoan Civilisation " (B. Quaritch, London, 1906).

The pictures which the Gnossians drew of themselves on the walls of the palace at Gnossos tend to support this conjecture. Identity of civilisation suggests, but does not prove, identity of race; and arguing on the basis of civilisation it is at any rate probable that the islands of the Ægean contained at the time a kindred population. As far as the mainland of Greece is concerned the great centres of this civilisation at Mycenæ, Tiryns, Sparta, and elsewhere, were probably founded by migrants from Crete early in the second millennium before Christ. It is further conjectured that about 1500 years before Christ descendants of those migrants attacked the home country and destroyed Gnossos, thus transferring the centre of the civilisation to the mainland. But so far as the exploration of prehistoric Greece has gone, it leads to the far more startling conjecture that these migrants from Crete who founded Mycenæ and other centres found on the Greek mainland a population akin to themselves which occupied the whole of the Peloponnesus, and at least that part of North Greece which is east of the Pindus Chain and south of Thessaly. Even in Thessaly it seems to have occupied the northern fringe of the Pagasætic Gulf, though recent exploration has shown [1] that the greater part of the land was occupied by a race whose culture was of a totally different type to that of Gnossos and Mycenæ, and whose civilisation was far more backward. To those who have studied Greek history in the past this is a most startling theory in that it tends towards conclusions which completely upset the views hitherto held with regard to the origin of those Greeks who produced the civilisation which culminated in the fifth century before Christ. It seems as if this non-Indo-European race which produced this Minoan and Mycenæan civilisation did not disappear from the stage of world history when Gnossos was destroyed and when, later, Mycenæ fell into the hands of new comers of another race. It becomes then of importance to consider what features in that early civilisation may have survived and contributed to that new civilisation which developed in the Greek world in the first half of the last millennium before Christ. There seems to be no doubt that the wealth and splendour of Gnossos and of the cities which later sprang up on the Greek mainland were due to trade. The power of Minos is represented in later tradition as a sea-power which put down piracy in the Ægean. This must have given a great impetus to trade and navigation; and though, when this power fell, piracy once more flourished, as it

---

[1] See Wace and Thompson. Sir Arthur Evans is inclined to think that there was a Greek-speaking race, in Arcadia at any rate, at the time when the Cretan migrants invaded Peloponnese. Further exploration may solve the question. In the present state of the evidence it is insoluble.

THE SECOND MILLENNIUM BEFORE CHRIST 11

always did in the Ægean when there was no naval power sufficiently strong to check it, yet the very survival of the Minos tradition at a time more than a thousand years after the Cretan sea-power had vanished, shows that the population of the shores of the Ægean had learnt from these early Cretans a lesson in navigation and trade which they never forgot.

The other great feature of Cretan civilisation is the development of art. It begins with geometrical design, that mechanical draughtsmanship which is a common feature in decorative art of the early peoples of the world. The Cretan cannot claim any particular genius for having discovered that a spiral might be drawn by twisting the Cretan equivalent for a piece of string round a peg, or that a straight line might be produced mechanically by straightening the edge of a piece of wood, or even that combinations of straight lines might produce triangles and other patterns. It was when in the later days of his civilisation the Cretan became a freehand artist that he showed his genius on the walls and pottery of his Cretan cities. His fondness for bright colours is also very marked ; and, though his colours are of a crudity due largely to limitations in the production of colouring matter, yet they are no more brilliant and no more crude than the colours with which the artistic Greek of the fifth century overlaid even his marble sculptures.

In later days the Hellenic invaders of Greece from the north showed no such skill. From which of these two sources then did the Greek of the middle of the first millennium develop the great art of the fifth century ?

It has already been said that the traditions of the prehistoric past preserved by Greek authors have been confirmed rather than refuted by the discoveries of the last fifty years ; and the moral conveyed by that fact is that those which have not been confirmed cannot be treated as old wives' tales, or as the invention of the authors who set them down. Even the much-abused Herodotus has to be taken seriously. The modern author can hardly arrive at the truth by assuming that an ancient author was guilty of romance. Of the ethnography of prehistoric Greece Herodotus has a quite definite view which is largely confirmed by fragments of Greek tradition preserved in other authors.[1]

[1] For Herodotus' tradition of the Pelasgi, see Hdt. i, 56, and i, 146 ; ii, 56 ; vi, 136-40 ; vii, 94, 95, 161 ; viii, 44, 73, etc. Among other passages in Greek authors which throw light on the Pelasgic question are : Hellanikos, " Frag," 28 and 29 ; Hom. " Il." ii, 681 ; " Il." xvi, 23, x, 428 ; " Od." xix, 170-7 ; Dion. Halic. i, 18 ; Thuc. iv, 109.
The connection of the Pelasgic name with Argos is implied again and again in the tragedians of the fifth century.
A full discussion of the Pelasgic question is not possible in a work of the scope of the present ; but this may be said,—that Herodotus' account

It is thus clear that, though he gives more information than can be found elsewhere, he is following largely a tradition prevalent in the Greek world of his day. He says that the aboriginal population of Greece was known by the general name of Pelasgi. He further implies that these Pelasgi were a non-Hellenic people, and definitely states that the Ionian Greeks of his day were Pelasgic in origin, that is to say were non-Hellenic. This was a bold statement for a historian to make to an Athenian audience in the fifth century; but perhaps the times were such that the Athenians did not object to a widening of the ethnic gulf which separated them from the loathed Dorian as represented by Sparta and Corinth.

It is noteworthy [1] that in Greek tradition of the historic period the Pelasgic name is peculiarly associated with those parts of Greece in which remains of the age called Mycenæan have been discovered in the last half-century, a fact which obviously suggests the identity of these Pelasgi with the Mycenæan migrants from Crete. Could that identity be established, then the Herodotean conjecture that these Pelasgi were non-Hellenic would be proved. It would be optimistic to expect that such a proof will some day be forthcoming; but the amazing nature of the discoveries made in the last fifty years makes it possible to cherish at least the hope that something further may be discovered which may either prove or disprove the very embarrassing suspicion that that branch of the later Greek race which was most responsible for all that is associated with the idea of Greek culture was not merely non-Hellenic, but did not even belong in origin to the Indo-European family of nations. That such a

of this people, which has been attacked as not merely mistaken but inconsistent, is, when the various items are pieced together, perfectly consistent, whatever view may be taken as to the truth of it.

His position is: (1) That the aboriginal population of Greece were called by the name of Pelasgi; (2) that the Pelasgi spoke a " barbarous " tongue, i.e. were not Hellenes; (3) that the autocthonous peoples of Greece, the populations of Attica and Arcadia, must have been Pelasgic; (4) that (arguing probably from the Attic population) the Ionian Greeks were Pelasgic; (5) that, though these populations had in his day dropped the Pelasgian name, there were still on the shores of the Propontis a people who retained the name, and that within something like the historical period Pelasgi, called by that name, had been in Attica, Samothrace, and Lemnos.

[1] See Prof. Ridgway in the " Journal of Hellenic Studies," 1896. The paper referred to was anything but well received by the editors of that journal, and by many who read it after publication. But, though much, especially of the latter part of it, is fanciful, and has never obtained acceptance, there are certain elements in it which have come to stay in the minds of those who have studied Greek history in the last twenty-seven years.

THE SECOND MILLENNIUM BEFORE CHRIST

suspicion is not ungrounded is certainly the case.[1] The theory of the non-Indo-European origin of the Ionian branch of the later Greek race involves the assumption that the Mycenæan language was supplanted by the language of the Hellenic conquerors. But if the Hellenic conquerors were, like the Achæan element in them, fair-haired [2] then the mass of the population of Greece in the fifth century, which was black-haired, was descended from the non-Hellenic element in the early population of the country, just as the mass of the population of modern France shows that it originated in an Iberian rather than a Celtic or other element in its ancestry. Still, even so, there are other instances in world history in which a conquering minority has imposed its language on a conquered majority.[3] But on the Ionian question another theory has been put forward to the effect that the race which founded Mycenæ and other centres on the mainland found a Greek-speaking race already there even as far south as Peloponnese.[4] A difficulty in accepting the theory arises from the fact that it would be necessary to

[1] If M. Eugène Cavaignac (" Histoire de l'Antiquité ") may be taken as representing the views of French students of Ancient History, then the French School refuses even to entertain the suspicion. French scholars in the classical department of learning have always shown themselves very conservative in their treatment of ancient evidence, which, if a fault, is a fault on the right side. But the conservatism which shuts its eyes to the consequences of recent discovery tends to an unscientific treatment of history. It is somewhat astounding, for instance, that M. Cavaignac should not have weighed the evidence of Messrs. Wace and Thompson with regard to the proto-Achæans of Thessaly, and the considerations which Professor Ridgeway (op. cit., " J. H. S." 1896) has drawn from the Homeric evidence, before assuming that the civilisation known as Mycenæan was Achæan in origin. The Hellenic origin of the Ionian Greeks too is assumed by him in such a way that any reader of his work might suppose that there was not the slightest reason to suspect that any other theory was possible. No student of Greek history would perhaps assert that the non-Hellenic, non-Indo-European origin of the Ionians was proved ; and there are many besides M. Cavaignac who would reject the idea. But the evidence which suggests the idea cannot be confuted by ignoring it.

[2] ξάνθος in Homer, just like the various epithets applied by ancient authors to the hair of the Celts, must not be assumed as necessarily meaning " golden-haired " or " sandy-haired," which would be the modern interpretation of " fair-haired " as applied to a race. These epithets may have had that meaning in some cases ; but all that they necessarily imply is that the hair was not black. Even dark brown hair would have struck the Greek of the fifth century as light in colour when compared to his own.

[3] France (Gaul) affords one, and probably two, such instances. Save in Aquitania the Iberian tongue does not appear to have survived up to the time of the Roman Conquest ; and, later, Latin so completely supplanted Celtic that hardly any trace of the latter survives in modern French.

[4] Sir Arthur Evans : " Journal of Hellenic Studies," 1912.

assume that this was a black-haired race which handed down its colouring to the later Greeks, a race not akin to the " fair-haired " Achæans. It is improbable that two races not akin spoke the same, or even kindred, languages at so early a period in race development ; and furthermore an " Achæan " people existed in Thessaly even so far back as the neolithic period.[1]

It is plain that this Ionian question has not yet passed beyond the field of conjecture ; but it is obviously one of vast importance in the realm of Greek history, since, if further evidence should confirm the theory of the non-Indo-European origin of this branch of the later Greek race, some of the main sources of Western civilisation and ideas will have to be attributed to a people which had, in so far as is known, no kinship with the Indo-European population of modern Europe ; and much that has been written about the superior intelligence of the Indo-European by self-congratulatory Indo-Europeans will have to be considerably revised.

The Creto-Mycenæan art did not perish with Gnossos, or, later, with Mycenæ. It seems to have been preserved, unbroken, but debased, on the eastern shore of the Ægean ;[2] and perhaps, too, in Greece itself.

[1] See Wace and Thompson, op. cit.
[2] See again Evans, " J. H. S." 1912. Sir Arthur Evans speaks (p. 279) of the connection between Crete and S.W. Asia Minor shown by place-names and similarity of cults; also on p. 285 of the immature representation of the Double Axe found by Mr. Hogarth in the temple treasure at Ephesus. Art is so closely associated with religion in early times that identity of cult almost presupposes identity of art. Mr. Hogarth (" Ionia and the East," p. 9) does not seem to have any belief in any wide extension of Minoan culture to the coast lands of Western Asia Minor, though he admits that it is apparent at Hissarlik (Troy), and at some points in Carian and Rhodian territory. But he also points out in another passage that the archæological exploration of Western Asia Minor, where it has been carried out, has, with the exception of that at Hissarlik, and of his own explorations at Ephesus, stopped at the remains of the historic period. Surely no negative argument of any value can be drawn from such very exiguous premisses.

Identity of culture is often conspicuously shown in identity of burial customs, and especially in the forms of tombs. It is a remarkable fact to which, as far as I am aware, attention has not been drawn, that the tomb of Alyattes as described by Herodotus (i. 92) bears a most remarkable resemblance to the tomb of Æpytus which Pausanias describes (viii. 16 (3)) from autopsy as existing in Arcadia in his day. Speaking of the tomb of Alyattes, Herodotus says : " There is there the tomb of Alyattes the father of Crœsus, of which the base (κρῆπις) is formed of large stones, while the rest of the tomb is a mound of earth." Of the tomb of Æpytus, Pausanias says : " It is a mound of earth of no great size, surrounded in a circle by a base (κρῆπις) of stone." For a similar κρῆπις we must go to the stone circle of upright slabs enclosing the pit graves at Mycenæ. It may be regarded as certain that these graves were not originally exposed to view as they are now ; and the probability is that an earthen mound which

THE SECOND MILLENNIUM BEFORE CHRIST

It may even be that, after centuries of comparative decay, it was rejuvenated when, in the middle of the first millennium, the Greek race acquired such a strength and prosperity as is wont among all peoples of all ages to give birth to some unusually brilliant form of culture.

On the question of the racial origin of the Greeks of the historical period the available evidence does not cast any certain light, though it suggests great and startling possibilities which may perhaps never be realised. It is, however, probable—it might be said that it is almost certain—that the Greeks known to history were not of pure Indo-European origin, but had in their veins a large element of the blood of that Libyan race, a branch of which evolved the Minoan and Mycenæan civilisation. It is again certain that this civilisation did not die when its creators ceased to be the lords of the Ægean region, but lived on in some of its manifestations to inspire, especially in the domain of art, those Hellenic races which poured in successive waves over the Greek peninsula, races virile and energetic, and with an innate capacity for acquiring culture, though the stage which they had reached at the time of their invasions was elementary as compared with that which they found existent in the lands round the Ægean.

Asia Minor

Any attempt to reconstruct the ethnography of Asia Minor in the second millennium B.C. would result in many guesses and few facts.[1] The wealth and attractiveness of many parts of its area have ever drawn to it immigrants from the lands around. Apart from that it is the natural bridge between Europe and Asia, and the natural route for such peoples of the plains of East Europe as have from time to time discovered that the Mediterranean region has a climate more genial than that of the lands north of the Euxine.

At all times in the history of Asia Minor the Halys River,

covered them has weathered away in the course of time. The intent of the κρῆπις was to keep the earth in position. It must be admitted that the existence of the κρῆπις in the three cases is not likely to have been a mere coincidence, but is far more probably due to a method of tomb construction associated with a particular form of culture. The tomb or tombs at Mycenæ are admittedly of the Mycenæan age. Æpytus belonged to a heroic past when the second book of the " Iliad " was compiled (see lines 603-4). In Greek tradition he was represented as the son of Arkas and Pelasgus, showing that he belonged to that Pelasgian race which later Greek tradition regarded as the aboriginal population of Greece. It looks as if certain elements at any rate of the Mycenæan culture had survived in the Lydia of the middle of the first millennium before Christ.

[1] Cf. Hogarth, "Ionia and the East," p. 28.

which divides the peninsula into two more or less equal parts, tended to form a dividing line between peoples whose racial and cultural connections were with the West, and those whose relations both racial and otherwise were rather with the East. In the south-west of the peninsula the Carians and Lycians had been settled from time immemorial. Their racial kinship is unknown; but the inscriptions of Lycia, though no one has as yet succeeded in interpreting them, are in a language which has no affinity to any European tongue. The Carians certainly, and the Lycians probably, acquired some of the civilisation of Minoan Crete; and it may be that both races were connected with the Cretans by ties of kinship. The same may perhaps be said of the Lydians of the middle region of the west shore of Asia Minor. In the later half of the second millennium the Phrygians, an Indo-European race of Thracian stock, invaded the north-west of the peninsula, and founded a kingdom which was destined to last for several centuries, until the rise of the Lydian power brought it to an end. But it is probable that before this time Thracian settlers had found a home to the south of the Propontis, for the narrow waters of the Hellespont and Bosphorus are but slight obstacles to the passage from Europe to Asia. The Mysian and Bithynian migrations seem to have come at the dawn of the historic period; but that people of this race were already settled in North-west Asia Minor before this movement took place seems so probable as to be almost certain.

East of the Halys dwelt that mysterious people the Khatti, or Hittites, who evolved a civilisation of their own, independent alike of Cretan culture and of the civilisation of the Euphrates plain. Confined originally to the region north of the Taurus, and probably at first no more than a loose confederation of kindred clans, the Hittite power became centralised in the fourteenth century before Christ, and rose to a commanding position in the world of the Near East. Northern Syria and part of Upper Mesopotamia were conquered, and Carchemish near the Euphrates became a great Hittite city. Pteria, some miles east of the middle Halys, became a great fortified capital of the north part of the kingdom, and remained a place of note in Asia Minor till the days of Herodotus, long after the Hittite power had fallen, so long indeed that the former existence of that power does not appear to have been known to the Greeks of Herodotus' age. It is probable that the White Syrians of Cappadocia whom that historian mentions were survivors of the old Hittite stock.

Egypt and Mesopotamia

The story of this millennium in the regions of the Euphrates

THE SECOND MILLENNIUM BEFORE CHRIST

and the Nile is one which does not concern greatly the development of affairs in the Mediterranean world ; and the respective histories of the two regions are matters of such magnitude that they demand individual treatment such as cannot be allotted to them in a work which is concerned with the development of history and civilisation in Mediterranean lands. It is only when their influence bears upon the development of western civilisation that such of their story as accounts for the exertion of that influence must be told. In the world of art Egypt both contributed to, and received contributions from, that art which developed in Crete, though in respect to essentials each, independent of the other, developed its art on its own lines. In the Euphrates region the first beginnings of the Assyrian Kingdom date from the latter half of the millennium.

Along the north coast of Africa from Egypt westwards, how far westwards it is impossible to say, extended that Libyan race from which the Minoan of Crete seems to have sprung. Of its history at this time nothing is known, save that when those fugitive peoples from the north-west of the Mediterranean were attacking the shores of Egypt, it assailed the delta from the west. From time immemorial that part of Egypt seems to have been occupied to a certain extent by kinsmen of the invaders.

CARTHAGE

But on this south coast of the Mediterranean the phenomenon most significant for later history was the existence of Phœnician trading stations extending at any rate from the Gulfs of the Greater and Lesser Syrtis to the Pillars of Hercules, and even beyond to the south Spanish shores of the Atlantic. That existence goes back to an antiquity far beyond the earliest records of extant history, and it may well be that the earliest of these settlements were founded before this millennium began. But up to its close they seem to have been directly dependent upon the mother country. It was not till the next millennium that Carthage became first a semi-independent, and later an independent political centre, for these western Phœnician settlements.

PHŒNICIANS

But in the later centuries of the millennium there came an expansion of Phœnician trade on the north coast of the Mediterranean which was of considerable significance in the development of the life of those Greek lands where the process of invasion and settlement by the Hellenic races was going on at the same time. It may be assumed that while the Cretan sea-power controlled the Ægean the Phœnician trader was warned off as a trespasser. But with the fall of the Cretan thalassocracy the Ægean was thrown open to Phœnician trade, inasmuch as there was no concentration of naval power in the region which could have excluded the enterprising Phœnician from its waters. The new invaders and settlers in the Greek peninsula were too a land and not a sea-folk; and, as they had to acquire the art of navigation, they may have welcomed the Phœnician trade which brought to them not merely some of the amenities but some of the necessaries of life, especially in the shape of food in times of scarcity. The tradition of this Phœnician period survived a thousand years later in what was almost certainly an exaggerated form; for it is probable that Herodotus is only reproducing the view current among the Greeks of his own day when he ascribes some of the most important elements in Greek civilisation to Phœnician influence. Modern investigation tends to discount this view. The confused period which followed the fall of the Mycenæan civilisation on the Greek mainland raised an almost impenetrable veil between the life of the land in the first millennium and the civilisation of the millennium which had preceded it. Greek tradition never pierced the veil. It knew indeed of an aboriginal population which was not Hellenic, a tradition embodied in the various references which Herodotus makes to the Pelasgi; but it had probably no idea of, and certainly never realised, the degree of civilisation which this fabled people had attained, a civilisation from which the Hellene had borrowed much which he attributed later to the Phœnicians. But whatever the Greek did or did not owe to the latter, his trade intercourse with that race must have been a first introduction to the splendours of that civilisation which had sprung up behind the eastern shores of the Mediterranean.[1]

But the story of the millennium cannot be brought to a close without reference to the stormy happenings which succeeded the fall of the Cretan power, and preceded the fall of the Mycenæan dominion or dominions in Greece. The evidence of what took place is small in quantity, but it is significant of events which changed the very face of those regions in the eastern Mediterranean which were destined to play the greatest part in subsequent history.

THE FIRST INROAD INTO GREECE

The fall of Gnossos took place about 1500 B.C. What race was responsible for the catastrophe is not known; but it is conjectured that those offshoots of the Cretan race which had introduced its civilisation into the Greek mainland at Mycenæ

[1] For the Phœnicians and Carthage, see Bosworth Smith's "Carthage and the Carthaginians" (Longmans, 1897).

and other centres returned like rebellious children to destroy the mother city of their race. The history of the next century in the Levant shows that the catastrophe was of no ordinary kind ; that the aim of the invaders was not merely to substitute one dynasty for another in Crete, but at least to make things so unpleasant for the population of the Gnossos region that a great part of it at any rate sought new homes, and in so doing caused prolonged disturbances on the shores of the eastern Mediterranean. The invaders can hardly be identified with Achæan invaders of Peloponnese, for, unless that war known as the Trojan War has been post-dated by two centuries, and unless the sagas from which the " Iliad " was compiled were wrong in representing the dominion of Atreus in Mycenæ and Sparta as having been founded only one generation before the Trojan War, it is not until two hundred and fifty years after the fall of Gnossos that the Achæan dominion in Peloponnese was established. The Cretan catastrophe may have been but one phase of a tragedy which seems to have affected not merely Greece, but also Asia Minor, and perhaps Italy, caused by an advance from middle Europe of new races which sought to settle in these peninsulas. This movement of thrust was not of a sweeping character which carried all before it within a short space of time. The turmoil in the Mediterranean recurs at intervals in a total period of three hundred years, which suggests that the northerners advanced in successive waves. In two regions, Cyprus and Palestine, peoples of Cretan culture settled ; but the Cypriote settlement was long anterior to that of the Philistines in Palestine. The former was probably made by fugitive Cretans after the fall of Gnossos, whereas the Philistine settlement was two centuries later, and was made by a people whose culture indeed was Cretan, but whose original home is unknown. These were successful settlements by fugitives from lands where Cretan civilisation had prevailed. But on more than one occasion between 1400 and 1200 B.C. Egyptian records speak of attacks made on the seaboard of that country by the combined fleets of various peoples whose names, as given in the Egyptian lists, show that Danaans (Greeks), Lycians. Etruscans, and even nations of Italy, were among their number, It is not necessary to assume that the Danaans came from Greece itself. It is probable that in the early phases of the movement of the Greek-speaking peoples southward the adventurers had no fixed idea as to where they would seek a final settlement ; and some elements may have sought a home otherwise than in the Greek peninsula. The attacks on Egypt do not appear to have been mere piratical raids in quest of plunder, but to have aimed at permanent settlement in that rich country. The

Egyptians warded off the attacks; but they did not altogether get rid of the disappointed assailants, some of whom settled at suitable points on the neighbouring shores of the Mediterranean, from which they for more than two centuries made themselves a nuisance as pirates.

The Etruscans

The apparent mention in the Egyptian records of Tyrrhenians or Etruscans among the assailants of Egypt during these centuries of confusion suggests that that mysterious people was on the move, thrust forth probably from what had hitherto been its home by one of the migrant races from the north. What that home was is not known. The earliest traces of its settlement in Italy show it to have attained before ever it came thither a civilisation far in advance of anything that prevailed at the time in the Italian peninsula. It is not conceivable therefore that it evolved *ab initio* in its new home that peculiar culture which is associated with its name. Of the original sources of that culture there are only two which can be suggested: the Minoan civilisation of Crete and the Hittite civilisation of Asia Minor. Points of resemblance can always be found between parallel stages in the evolution of the culture of different peoples, because man's development tends to follow main lines which are quite independent of racial contact. But there are divergences of detail which, when very marked, are clear indications that no such contact has taken place. On these latter grounds it is not possible to assume that the Etruscan civilisation was derived from a Minoan source. But comparison with the civilisation of the Hittites brings out certain points of resemblance which are certainly striking, though not perhaps conclusive.[1] With the Etruscans of the historic period the Greeks had little to do. Commercial intercourse was strictly discouraged by a certain rivalry and consequent hostility; but it was after all the Greeks in the distant settlements in the western Mediterranean to whom this rivalry was important. Thus it is probable that any tradition with regard to the Etruscans which prevailed among the Greeks at home was uninfluenced by personal feeling. This tradition represented the Tyrrhenians (Etruscans) as having been originally settled in Lydia,[2] and Thucydides states that a mixed population of Tyrrheno-Pelasgians lived on the Chalcidic peninsula on the north coast of the Ægean in his own day.[3] Lydia in an early Greek tradition may simply mean Anatolia; but it is interesting to find that archæology and tradition are

---

[1] See Hall, "The Ancient History of the Near East," p. 336.
[2] Hdt. i, 94.
[3] Thucy. iv, 109.

THE SECOND MILLENNIUM BEFORE CHRIST

in agreement as to the original home of the Etruscan race. The presence of Tyrrhenians in Chalcidicé, and the fact that the Etruscan settlement was originally in the extreme north of Italy,[1] suggest that the migrant people reached that country through the Balkan peninsula.

It is probable, as has been said, that the movement of thrust from the north was a wide one affecting a large part of the north shore of the Mediterranean; though in Greece alone did any memory of it survive in later tradition.

Original Home of the Invaders of Greece

For several centuries successive waves of invaders swept over the land; and their eventual amalgamation with the pre-existing inhabitants produced that Greek race which was to play so great a part through many long centuries of Mediterranean history. That they all spoke dialects of Greek seems beyond doubt; but the question as to what was the original home or homes of these Greek-speaking races is, except in the case of the Achæan branch of them, uncertain. It is assumed that they were of Illyrian stock, former dwellers in those lands of the Adriatic which lie north of north-west Greece. The historical records of the Illyrian region are dim even in those periods of history when a bright light is shining on the regions which lie east, west, and south of it; but if, as can only be the case, the assumption is founded on a supposed similarity of type and language between the Greeks and Illyrians of the historic period, then certain questions arise. The Illyrian stock survives in the region at the present day, for neither Macedonian, Roman, nor Turk ever succeeded in dispossessing the virile population of this most difficult region, a large portion of the acreage of which is at an angle of at least forty-five degrees with the horizon. The physical type remains; and it presents certain contrasts to the typical physical characteristics of the ancient Greek. But, after all, the Greek physique must have been modified before the historical period by a large admixture of Libyan (Mycenæan) blood. The Illyrian race extended northwards to the Save, and must have formed in Roman times the basis of the population of the provinces of Dalmatia and Upper Mœsia, though Celtic elements had intruded into the northern fringe of the region. If these Illyrians spoke a tongue akin to Greek, then it is somewhat strange that these two provinces came within the Latin-speaking half of the Roman empire. This is a difficulty which is neither wholly inexplicable, nor wholly explicable. Of the original home of these Hellenic wanderers this alone is certain, that it was in a land where iron could

[1] The settlements in the basin of the Padus were lost at a later date.

be obtained either by manufacture or barter; and it is true that in the north part of the Illyrian region, in the modern Bosnia, iron was mined on a considerable scale in Roman times. For the conquest of the Greek peninsula was but one example of what must have occurred many times in unrecorded history, the conquest of the age of bronze by the age of iron. Civilisation, culture, ideas—all yield before superior weapons. History has taught the lesson again and again; but there always have been, and always will be, those who are either ignorant of, or wilfully deaf to, its teachings. The traditions of these successive invaders were in the historical period profuse but confused. Great modern historians of Greece have tried to reconstruct the story; but no two are in agreement as to the facts. As far as south Greece is concerned the first invaders were the Achæans. Men of this race had been settled in Thessaly from time immemorial; but it is impossible to say in the first place whether the invaders were drawn exclusively from that region, or whether they were accompanied by relatives from farther north; and, secondly, it is not certain whether the Achæan movement was due to self-impulse, or whether a wave of invasion from the north drove the Thessalian Achæans southward. Later tradition speaks of two earlier invasions—a Bœotian, and a Thessalian or Thesprotian. If the latter is an historic fact then the displacement of the Achæans from a large part of Thessaly may have been the cause of their invasion of the Mycenæan region. But it seems certain that the race was still represented in southern Thessaly at the time when the Homeric poems were composed; and Achæa Phthiotis was a geographical name in Thessaly so late as the fifth and fourth centuries, and even later.[1]

[1] With regard to what follows I ought perhaps to say that I do not on the evidence feel justified in following the various theories which have been formed with regard to the presentation of life and of events given in the Homeric poems. I am not persuaded that the picture drawn of the life of the Achæan age is really borrowed from that of the Mycenæan period. Such resemblances to the life of the early period may be explained by the very natural hypothesis that the conquerors from the north, people of comparatively rude civilisation, borrowed certain amenities and perhaps institutions from the life of the people whom they had conquered. The palace wherein Menelaus lived at Sparta is almost certainly one of the Mycenæan age. I may assume that most readers will be aware that certain sections of the Homeric poems are of much later date than their context. The sections later in date contain matter which reflects the life of the period at which they were composed, matter from which no deductions can be drawn as to the life of the age at which the ancient parts of the poems came into being. What I have said is of course only applicable to the sections which are of earlier date.

The chronology of the period, if it can be called chronology at all, is dependent on the date of the Trojan War, the starting-point of so much of the chronology of the historic age of Greece. By calculation it works

THE SECOND MILLENNIUM BEFORE CHRIST 23

The overthrow of the Mycenæan dominion in the Peloponnese was certainly the work of a people who were in possession of weapons of iron. The Atreidæ established a dominion which included the whole of Eastern Peloponnese, and may have included the whole of the peninsula. This does not look like the work of a people who were flying for their lives from invaders from the north, people who moreover could match iron against iron. Agamemnon and Menelaus were the sons of Atreus the founder of the dynasty, which, taking the traditional date of the Trojan War as B.C. 1194, presumes that the conquest took place in the second half of the thirteenth century before Christ. Though the conquerors were men of the iron, and the conquered men of the bronze age, the civilisation of the former, especially in relation to artistic development, seems to have been of a much ruder type than that of the people they dispossessed. In decorative art they had not passed beyond geometric design and elementary colouring, and were quite incapable of producing the beautiful freehand decoration and brilliant colours which had distinguished the work of the Minoans and their Mycenæan colonists. That the majority of the conquered remained in Peloponnese may be regarded as certain ; but it is at the same time probable that some fled to other lands ; and perhaps the Minoan Philistines in Palestine may have been one of these fugitive bands.

Of the material objects which the old civilisation had produced the new-comers seem to have made use ; but they seem to have caught nothing of the infection of the civilisation itself. What they borrowed from it they spent as capital ; and when that was exhausted they relapsed once more to the old simple lines of their former life. Had the Achæans imbibed some of the old Mycenæan culture, had their lives been permanently modified by contact with it, it is inconceivable that all trace of a memory of this prehistoric civilisation could have vanished from later Greek traditions. All that the later Greeks knew was that there had been an aboriginal race in Greece whom they called the Pelasgi : that Minos had been a thalassocrat, which in their conception meant little more than a rather superior pirate ; but they knew nothing of that civilisation which lay for three thousand years in a forgotten grave till the explorer of the nineteenth century after Christ unearthed its relics and some of its realities.

ACHÆANS IN PELOPONNESE

How far the Achæan conquest introduced a new social and

out at 1194 B.C. of the Christian Era. I accept the date, not as an historical fact, but because we do not possess any knowledge which would justify us in substituting for it some other date.

political organisation with Greece is not known, because the monuments of the Mycenæan civilisation disclose but certain aspects of the life of those who created them. But it may be safely assumed that the comparatively rude invaders from the north did not renounce their former life and institutions on settling in their new home. How far the Homeric poems give a true description of Achæan civilisation in the period following the conquest of Peloponnese is a question much debated. It has been suggested that some of the sagas from which the poems were compiled go back to the Mycenæan princes and nobles, and that consequently they depict a life and institutions which were not those of the Achæan age. On that hypothesis it must be assumed that, inasmuch as these Mycenæan princes and nobles were speaking a language which was neither Greek nor akin to it, these sagas were not originally in the Greek language. Yet they do not bear the impress of translation.

It is infinitely more probable that the earliest parts of the poems give a picture of life in Greece in the short period which intervened between the fall of the Mycenæan culture and the Dorian invasion; and that the Mycenæan elements which the ingenuity of modern criticism has discerned or professed to discern in the poems are, if their presence be admitted, due to the fact,—in itself by no means improbable,—that the conquerors adopted at any rate certain material elements of the higher civilisation of the conquered. The borrowings of a conqueror from the life of the conquered, whatever they may be, do not in the first instance take the form of political institutions; and the political institutions depicted in Homer are such as by a natural course of political evolution would develop into the institutions of the Greece of the historic period; and, more than that, large elements of them still survived even to the dawn of that period. There is one feature in them which suggests very forcibly that they are to a certain extent the product of a period in which a conquering race is settling down in a conquered land among a subject people against whose possible hostility the conquerors have to guard. The whole land is constituted in a series of military aristocracies, where the chieftains represented the barons of the period of the Norman Conquest, and the people their armed retainers. In Peloponnese chieftains like Agamemnon and Menelaus were probably the overlords of minor chiefs. Even in the old home of the Achæans, in south Thessaly, such institutions prevailed: but there they were due, it may be conjectured, not to the necessity of keeping a conquered race in subjection, but to the danger from those races which were in movement from the north during this very disturbed period. The Achæan barons, whether under some overlord or not, are the chief element in this political constitution. If they have an overlord, their subjection to him is not very marked. This form of the upper ranks of society lasted on for several centuries till the dawn of the historic period, with this modification, that some of these quasi-feudal barons became monarchs ($βασιλεῖς$), while others formed the aristocracy in the states. In the original constitution of this society the under-chiefs formed a council of advice to their superior, advice freely given and freely expressed, but which the " king " might take or not according to his pleasure. The power and constitution of this council, especially the fact that its functions were limited to giving advice without the right of enforcing it, are so similar to that of the Senate in early Rome and in the early Italian states that it may be assumed that it is an institution of far more ancient date than the conquest of Mycenæ, and may go back to a time at which the Greek and Latin branches of the Indo-European race were one. But a parallel and quite independent evolution is, of course, quite possible. Below the nobility came the mass of the people, in Peloponnese and perhaps in some other parts of Greece a privileged among a subject race, in Northern Greece presumably the lowest class. Though, constitutionally speaking, possessing no political power, they must as a people in arms have preserved a certain political influence, to this extent at any rate—that on questions affecting them the king would be anxious to find out their views before he himself came to any final decision. But the most remarkable fact in this political system is that the power of the king in respect to initiative, executive, and administrative functions is final. He is almost as much an absolute monarch as the greatest tyrant of later days.

That there exist in this primitive constitution all the germs of the constitutions of that free Greece of many centuries later is plain. They developed and were modified in the dark period which succeeded the Dorian invasion; but when the light of history dawns upon them they are there still, the King, the Council of Elders, and the Assembly of the people. In the early historical period the powers of all are modified; but each of the three institutions continues to exist as a separate and independent entity with its own individual genealogical descent into that most glorious age of Greek life, the fifth century, and even beyond.

The Indo-European character of these institutions depicted in the Homeric poems is emphasised by the fact that they are not merely similar to, but identical with the institutions of early Rome, institutions which retained their early character for a much longer period than they did in Greece. Rome developed into a so-called democracy ; but even in its most democratic days, there were features in its constitution which are of a most extraordinary character, quite irreconcilable with the democratic idea. And every one of these extraordinary features is found in the political institutions of that life which is depicted in the Homeric poems. The powers of the early kings of Rome, powers inherited to the full by the consuls of the early Republican period, are absolute in these very departments of government in which the power of the Homeric King is absolute. The Roman freeman was almost at their mercy. The council and senate, though consisting of a powerful band of nobles, is merely a council of advice to the magistrate, whether King or Consul. The Senate at Rome in later days usurped some of the powers of other elements in the constitution ; but its strict constitutional position remained the same. It is again strange to find in a democratic government an assembly where there is no freedom of debate. In this the Roman assembly resembles the Homeric Agora. Thus Homeric institutions are essentially Indo-European, that is to say, they are not Mycenæan, they are Greek ; and, as implied in those parts of the Homeric poems which are of earliest date, they are the Achæan institutions of the post-Mycenæan, pre-Dorian period. The poems throw light on other circumstances of the times. Piracy is rife, as it probably had been since the fall of Minoan sea-power.[1] Cattle-raiding was quite a gentlemanly employment ; another sign of the confused lawlessness of this period of transition. On the other hand, family ties and family morality are strong, which is due perhaps to that cult of ancestors which played such a part in the lives of the Greek and Roman peoples far on into the ages of high civilisation. Hospitality to guests and strangers was a duty and a convenience at periods and in lands where the temporary host of to-day might be the temporary guest of to-morrow.

In one respect alone, the position of women, does Homeric life contrast with the life of later Greece. In Homer their position is one of influence in private, and perhaps too in public life. Why their position had declined so greatly in the society of six centuries later is not known.

PROPERTY IN LAND

The idea of private property is so natural an instinct in the human race when applied to that which a man has fashioned with his own hands, or has acquired by bartering some production of his own for that of another, that there is no need to discuss that phase of it here. Property by inheritance is also natural among a people in which the family tie is strong. But the idea of

[1] Hom. Od. iii, 71 ; ix, 252.

property in land is not found in the earliest stages of human civilisation, when man was in the main a flesh-eating animal, and perhaps a nomad as well. No doubt the early pastoral races regarded certain regions of pasture as theirs by right of use ; and this may be the earliest form in which landed property came into existence ; but the right is communal, not personal. Certain passages in the earlier parts of the Homeric poems are said to suggest a communal holding of land at the time. Later passages from the Odyssey clearly indicate that private property in land had come into existence. This may be due to increase in cultivation in times more settled than those of the early period of the conquest ; or perhaps to the conversion of a pastoral people to agriculture. The nobility of the time may also have asserted the right of ownership.

The origin of the idea of property in land is one which has been much debated. In the early Greek and Roman world it has been ascribed to a very small beginning, family proprietorship of the ground wherein the ancestors of the family are buried. That seems a theory both inadequate and fanciful.

It is only among the Teutonic races that the growth of the idea of property in land may be traced, in its first stages in Germany, in its later stages in Saxon England. The change from nomadic life to settlement in a definite region led to cultivation. The land cultivated was at first the property of the community ; but the products of the land did not go into a common store, but were the property of the man or the family who had cultivated the particular allotment in that year. In other words the idea of private property in land began not with the land but with the crops which the land produced. The land remained the property of the community, and the lots were changed annually. In the second stage, among the Teutonic settlers in Britain, the annual allotment has passed away, and the lots have become the permanent holdings of the individual families. The idea of proprietorship has passed from the crop to the land itself ; and the proprietorship is that of the family and not of the community. Yet traces of the old communal right still survive, in that the community can still lay down what lands shall be left fallow in each year ; and, again, uncultivated land remains communal property. Thus the family land is not a family freehold in the full sense of the term ; and the limitation in respect to ownership is narrowed down still further by the fact that the land cannot be sold or left by will. Private ownership and full freehold in England were the creation of post-Conquest times.

At no period in Greek history is the evidence on property

[1] See Fustel de Coulanges, " La Cité Antique."

in land very clear. It is indeed evident that private ownership existed in later times, and may have been the rule. It seems also probable that this was largely individual ownership; but there is reason to suspect that family ownership existed side by side with the latter. Communal ownership or communal rights, especially in relation to pasture, was almost certainly recognised with regard to uncultivated land. It still exists, and probably has existed from time immemorial, in the Balkan peninsula.[1]

All that is known of land-owning in Ancient Greece suggests that, as among Teutonic peoples, the property was originally in the crop, not the land on which it was grown. That other less natural and more arbitrary means of acquiring such proprietary rights would be practised in a community organised, like early Greece, on an aristocratic basis, would almost certainly be the case. But the *concept* of private property in land had in all probability the same origin among the Hellenic as among the Teutonic peoples.

There is reason to believe that the tide of this Achæan invasion[2] did not expend itself in Peloponnese, but that a wave of it flooded Crete. It seems to have reached Peloponnese late in the thirteenth century; and it is significant that in the earlier years of the next century, about 1196 B.C., Egypt, then ruled by Rameses III, was attacked by a mixed horde of tribes, of which two seem to have been of Cretan origin. This points to a displacement of the Cretan population by invaders; and it is most probable that these invaders were an offshoot of that " Achæan " horde which had recently destroyed the Mycenæan power in Peloponnese.

The sceptical school in Ancient History, which flourished greatly some thirty years ago, inspired by a spirit of denial which led them to regard those who accepted any ancient traditions of the Greek world as wanting in critical acumen, was disposed to treat the story of the Trojan War as a myth. Later critics, with a credulity which is founded upon evidence, have come to the conclusion that, though it may not have been fought quite as the Homeric poems depict it to have been, nor for the reasons therein set down, it is a historical fact. The interesting

---

[1] In Modern Greece, or at any rate in Bœotia (I cannot say whether by general law or by local custom), a man who cultivates uncultivated land acquires rights of ownership over the land cultivated which are good against all save the State. Nor can he be dispossessed by the State except for public purposes, such as the making of a road, etc.

[2] Both here and in previous passages I use the term " Achæan " of this invasion, partly for clearness' sake, partly because the people of that race seem to have played the principal part in it. But I must not be understood to imply that no other races of the Hellenic family took part in it.

conjecture has been made that the Greeks were fighting for a free passage of the Hellespont to the corn regions of the Euxine, a passage within striking distance of the lords of Troy.[1] Those who can best realise the economic position in Greek lands will best realise the force of this conjecture.

Dorian Migration

If the traditional chronology be true,—and there is no sure evidence available which would enable the modern world to go behind it,—the Achæan dominion in Peloponnese must have lasted a little more than a century. Then there descended on the land those Dorians whose migration figures so largely in the tradition of later times. They formed the last of those successive waves of migration which changed the whole character of the population of the Greek peninsula. Later tradition, fostered especially by Sparta, represented them as having descended on Peloponnese from that little Dorian plain at the head of the Cephissus valley. Mere considerations of space make that quite impossible. The people who overthrew the Achæan dominion in Peloponnese could never have been packed in so small an area. The Dorian inhabitants of the Cephissus region in the fifth century can have been no more than a small section of the immigrants which had been left behind; but in that century it was convenient for Sparta to represent that little land of a few square miles as the metropolis of the Dorian Greek, since it afforded her a plausible excuse for interfering with the affairs of Greece north of the isthmus, when a better excuse was wanting.

The new-comers seem to have been made of sterner stuff than any of the previous Hellenic invaders of Greece. It is not known why they were able to overcome those Achæans who but a century before had subdued the old civilisation of the Peloponnese, but it is probable that they were possessed of more efficient weapons of iron than their Achæan predecessors. For centuries they posed and were accepted, even by their enemies, as a race apart. They regarded themselves as a chosen people, born to rule others; and for centuries they maintained themselves as a governing and privileged class among the populations which they subdued, populations which in many cases were still in a position of serfdom six centuries after the conquest had taken place. They were still the unacknowledged aristocrats of the Greek world of the fifth century. At the time at which they made the conquest their culture was far inferior to that of the Mycenæan age which had come to an end but a century before, and inferior probably to the Achæan culture which had supplanted it, not perhaps without borrowing elements from it.

[1] See especially Leaf on the Homeric Question.

But if aught of that non-Hellenic culture had survived the Achæan conquest, even those remnants of it must have perished under the Dorian sway. A rugged people is apt to regard as effeminate the culture and life of a race it has subdued; and a civilisation may become too humanitarian relative to the world around and the times in which it is evolved. But this civilisation which perished for the time in Greece was destined to survive on the eastern shores of the Ægean, and to avenge itself by a peaceful conquest on those who had temporarily destroyed it in Greece. In later centuries the self-conceit of the Athenian rendered that people sedulous in spreading the idea that the Dorian, and especially the Dorian of Sparta, was incapable of attaining to those heights of civilisation represented by life at Athens in the fifth century; and till very recent times the modern world, knowing only the life of Sparta in the fifth century, accepted this prejudiced view at its face value. But the excavations at Sparta made some fifteen years ago have shown that the Dorians ruling there, so far from being incapable of that artistic development which formed so large a part in the civilisation of Greece, had up to a certain definite point in their history advanced in this form of culture almost *pari passu* with the other populations of Greece, though it was from them that they had originally borrowed it. There are times in the history of any nation when, if it is to survive, the qualities demanded from it are other than those which promote the advance of civilisation. Sparta recognised this about the sixth century before Christ, and turned to a new and sterner form of life with startling suddenness and deliberation. But this change was unknown to the modern world of twenty years ago; and its discovery has modified very considerably the concept of the great period in Greek history. There is no record nor even a hint of it in the writings of the fifth century, for the good reason that neither Greek authors nor any other Greeks outside Sparta ever pierced the veil of mystery which hid its life from the outside world. The tragic drama of Lacedæmon in the fifth century was acted on a stage behind a curtain which had fallen in the sixth, never to be raised till the great days of Greece had passed away. All memory of the Sparta of the past was lost in the endeavour to guess the truth of the present. Archæology in the twentieth century after Christ has given to the world that which the written history of the Greeks of the fifth century before Christ never knew.

CHAPTER II

THE FIRST TWO CENTURIES OF THE FIRST MILLENNIUM BEFORE CHRIST, 1000–800 B.C.

MANY views may be entertained as to the best way of presenting the story, not of a single nation, but of a series of nations which are working out their own destiny in one and the same period on lines sometimes parallel, sometimes divergent, sometimes convergent. Chronic convergence suggests the chronological method which will be followed in this story of the Mediterranean region, even though the teller of a story on such lines must face the difficulty arising from the fact that the close of a chapter in the history of one race is rarely coincident in time with the close of a chapter in the history of another. Eras in the history of the Mediterranean races do not begin to correspond until they all come under the dominion of Rome. Every historical method has its imperfections ; and all that the adoption of any particular method can do is to reduce those imperfections to their lowest terms. And so in this work the close of a century will be taken as far as possible as the close of a chapter in the parallel histories of the Mediterranean peoples. Geographically speaking the method employed will be in each era to follow the clock from the Pillars of Hercules along the north shore of the inland sea, and back again along its southern shore.

CONDITIONS OF ANCIENT LIFE

It is perhaps impossible for the modern world to realise how the ancient world lived ; and of the men of that world it may be said, as a historian has said of the mediæval English, " they cannot come back to us, and our imagination can but feebly penetrate to them." This might have been said with more emphasis of the inhabitants of the ancient world in the days preceding the Roman Principate, and with but slightly less emphasis of the inhabitants of the Roman Empire in the first two centuries of our era. The difference between the life of the ancient and mediæval and that of the modern world is due mainly to the enormous advance with respect to communication, and especially of land communication, which has been made within the last century by the invention of the railway and the steamboat. Days have been converted into hours. In some most important respects the life of Europe in the seventeenth century approximated more to the life of the centuries before Christ than to that of the Europe of the present day.

It is probable that the vast majority of the population of the ancient world passed the whole of their lives within an area extending but a few miles from their birthplace. To such the world outside was a world of fable and romance of which they knew little save such news as travellers brought them; and, except on the few highways of the world of that day, the traveller must have been a rare visitor. What was the outlook on life possessed in the Greece of the fifth century by a dweller in Thessaly, in the Dorian plain, or in the remote valleys of western Arcadia or Messenia ? It is not possible to realise the extent to which such a confined existence narrowed not merely the knowledge but the intelligence of the majority of the men of antiquity. Their history is unwritten save when they come into the limelight of those great events which attracted the ancient historian; and so not merely the facts, but even the circumstances of their daily life cannot be realised by men whose existence is passed under circumstances fundamentally different from those in which the men of the ancient world spent their days. The difficulties of communication were such that communication was in many instances rare even between close neighbours, how rare is shown by the number of dialects or differences in the use of terms which developed in such a comparatively open land as Saxon England.[1] And if such was the case in England in the first millennium after Christ, what must have been the case in the remote valleys of such a rugged land as Greece in the first millennium before Christ ? No made highways existed in the Mediterranean region of Europe until the Romans began to make roads in Italy; and it was not till the days of Augustus and the early Empire that any made roads existed outside Italy, save the one great route through South Gaul to Spain, and the Egnatian Way which led through the Balkan peninsula to the Eastern empire of Rome. Greece even in the days of her highest prosperity made no roads, if the twelve miles of sacred way from Athens to Eleusis be excepted. She had not the money wherewith to construct such highways, and even imperial Rome could not have borne the expense of making

---

[1] Even the low Berkshire Downs were a sufficient barrier between the dwellers north and south of them for terms common in the Hampshire of Saxon times to be either unknown, or at any rate unused, in Berkshire; and vice versa; and this difference in use of terms survived until the days of railways.

FIRST TWO CENTURIES OF FIRST MILLENNIUM 33

a road system had she not had to hand cheap labour in the form of legionary and other troops whom she could employ on such work in time of peace. It is only the enormous wealth which has poured into Europe from outside in modern times, combined with the invention of the macadamised road, which has made it possible for the modern states of Europe to construct highway systems. In the Mediterranean area and outside Europe the Royal Road to Susa of the days of the Persian dominion may have been in part a made road, but its "royal" character may have been limited to the provision of caravanserais and relays of beasts of burden at intervals in its length.

Land communications in this ancient world consisted of unmade tracks, many of which must have been available only to the wayfarer on foot,[1] some to the traveller on horse-back, and very few possible for wheeled vehicles. The existence of rapid means of communication in modern times makes it hard for the modern to realise what its absence meant to the ancient world. It was one of the causes of the normal smallness of the ancient as compared with the modern state. It was always difficult for a central government to control areas at any distance from its centre inhabited by people who were impatient of its control. Revolts and suchlike disturbances might come to a head or ever the news of their inception could reach the ruling city, and the passage of troops to the region affected must be so slow that such revolts would always be formidable and difficult to deal with. The average Mediterranean state was far too weak to attempt the control of more than a small region; and even in the case of those states which established their empire over others, the centrifugal force soon became effective, and the germs of disintegration are apparent at an early period. The plots in the various tragedies of empire in the ancient world have a marked similarity in this respect until Augustus established effective means of communication in the Roman dominions. The history of the Kingdom of Assyria is an almost monotonous story of cruel struggles to maintain its rule over all parts of its empire which lay outside the area of Assyria proper. Within a century after the founding of the much better organised Persian empire the outlying satraps are all but independent monarchs,

[1] The more rapid means of communication in the Greek world, apart from smoke signalling or shield signalling, which is only recorded on special occasions, and under special circumstances, were by professional runners, as in the case of Philippides, who carried the news of Marathon to Sparta. Had the Greek invented a Morse alphabet and applied it to heliographic signalling, he might have changed the history of the world. He seems to have come as near to it as the Roman road-maker did to macadam.

and have in some cases all but founded family dynasties. The Roman Empire under the Republic is little more than a forced confederation of states, kept together with ever-increasing difficulty. The governors of outlying provinces became ever more independent of the central authority, until the question became not whether they or the central government should control the empire, but which governor should be master of the Roman world. The empire was saved and unified by the great road system which Augustus inaugurated, and his successors carried vigorously to completion.

But the establishment of rapid means of communication in modern times has rid the world of a danger more commonplace, more chronic, and greater than any arising from political disruption, the danger of famine and starvation. It is in this respect that it is most difficult for the modern world to realise the ever-present danger under which its forefathers lived. Failure of crops in a particular district excites little alarm nowadays, unless the failure extend over a very large region, because it is well known that the deficiency can be promptly met by rapid importation of food supplies from elsewhere. The margin of safety in respect to the food supply of the world was less than even the ever-contracting margin of the present day; and the lands where a surplus of supply existed were in point of time more distant from some of the main centres of population than the great food-producing countries of the present day are from Western Europe. In the earlier centuries of the first millennium before Christ the danger of local famine and starvation must have been not merely an ever-present possibility, but an often-present actuality, especially in those poorer regions by which the Mediterranean is largely surrounded. But even in rich regions conditions of weather may bring about failure of crops on a large scale; and, when this does occur, the results are often more terrible owing to the inhabitants being less prepared for such contingencies than the inhabitants of poorer regions where they are of more frequent occurrence.

Even when a supply was available from some other region it would frequently be the case that the famine-stricken population had no means of purchasing it. The daily life of the man of the ancient world was far more precarious than the life of a citizen of to-day, and in no region of the Mediterranean was the danger greater than in Greece. But it is perhaps in English history that this ever-threatening danger of ancient life may be most clearly illustrated. The Black Death in 1349 tends to overshadow in the records of disaster the appalling famine which prevailed in England only thirty years before that time, from 1315 to 1317, a famine due to a series of wet seasons. If this could occur in a land which had at the time a considerably larger area under corn than it has at the present day, and a population but a fraction of what it is now, what might not occur in that Mediterranean region of still earlier times where the population was much larger relative to the cultivable area ? As far as historical record goes it was the Greek who first organised a foreign food supply for his own people ; but the tale of how that was done belongs to the story of Greek colonisation.

But lack of means of communication was not merely one of the main reasons for the smallness of the states of the ancient world, it was also responsible for another feature of their life. The Greek philosophers of the fifth and fourth centuries described the genesis of the state in various terms according as they looked on it from an abstract or a concrete point of view. One of these theories described man as going through a social evolution which aimed at giving him αὐτάρκεια, economic independence. When in the course of that evolution he had attained to the society called the state, he had reached a form of association which would supply all his wants without the necessity of going outside it. Therefore the state was, as it were, the culmination of social life. This is only one of the theories ; but it is one which is perhaps nearer to reality than some of its fellows. To the modern reader the idea may seem fanciful. To the man of the ancient world it was one of the commonplaces of life. Few were the communities which in those days of difficult and consequently expensive communication could afford to import that which they could not produce themselves. Even in small communities production had to cover all the necessaries of life, clothing, food, and implements.[1] The mind of the mass of mankind in those early centuries was absorbed in the struggle for existence. The ordinary man had neither the leisure nor the means to contribute to that growth of ideas in the realms of politics and ethics which created those institutions which Greece and Rome have handed down to the modern world. That was the work of the leisured few who lived in those select centres where wealth accumulated, and still more of that intellectual class which was supported by members of those wealthy families who were ready to hear some new thing, and to pay for so doing. But to the mass of the men of those centuries those ideas were

[1] From the earliest Saxon period up to the end of the seventeenth century, until, that is to say, the time when the making of through roads was undertaken in England, the English village community was what the Greeks would have called αὐτάρκης, economically independent. It had to be. Anything which was brought from a distance in those days of bad communication was a luxury ; and it had not the means of buying the expensive.

Religion

Such are the broad facts of the material life of the Mediterranean world. But man from ages far beyond the dawn of history has always been possessed by a feeling amounting almost to an instinct that there is an unseen world in this life, and an unknown world hereafter. To the ancient dweller on the Mediterranean this feeling was an uncomfortable one, for the one world raised ghosts, and his views on the other were never cheerful, and often pessimistic. It is to man's feelings and beliefs on these questions that the word "religion" has been given. The religions of Egypt and of the Euphrates region do not seem to have affected in any way the religious views of the Indo-European peoples on the north shore of the Mediterranean until the cult of Isis made converts among the heterogeneous population of a Rome which had become cosmopolitan as the centre of a cosmopolitan empire. The study of these religions is a study by itself which has little to do with Mediterranean life. It is strange that the religion of Persia, which was far more spiritual than those of Greece and Rome, did not attract the mind of the Greek. But the long rivalry and hostility between the two races may have deterred the Greek from any inclination to borrow aught from the life of his hereditary foe.

Within very recent years investigation into the religions of Greece and Rome has been made with great minuteness.[1] To the student of religions such investigations are interesting and important; but the less pious student of history, on reading such works, is every now and then tempted to suspect that the modern author is dealing with an esoteric religion, and that the elaborate theology there depicted was unknown or ignored save by the initiated few who were interested in its invention. These minutiæ of religion had little or no traceable influence on the general development of Greek and Roman life. But there are various more elementary superstitions which had.

The religions of Greece and Rome are so similar that it may be assumed that they had a common origin in a far past when the Hellenic and Italian peoples were one. Each was composed of two elements, wholly distinct from one another in intent and origin, which may be conveniently distinguished as Nature Worship and Ancestor Worship respectively. The former had to do with the present, the latter with a special concept of the future life. The former developed into a state religion; the

---

[1] See Dr. Farnell's "Cults of the Greek States," and the late Mr. Warde Fowler's various works on Roman religion.

latter was always the cult of the family or clan. Despite the fact that any attempt to reconstruct the origins and early forms of these two branches of superstition must be largely theoretical, yet it is fairly certain that nature worship originated in man's sense of his powerlessness in face of the forces of nature, and also from the sense of mystery and fear which is called into existence by the more remote recesses of physical nature—a wood, a chasm, or a cave. Man's imagination has always tended to people the voids of the world with fairies, sprites, or hobgoblins; and he sometimes deifies or half deifies these fancies. It was not merely primitive man who regarded the natural world as a realm in which neither law nor order prevailed, a realm in which all was incalculable, as indeed it was to him. Even among the Greek race this conception of nature prevailed till the latter half of the sixth century. Thus man sought to propitiate that which he could not control. The local river with its destructive floods was conceived of as controlled by a wayward river-god, who would be malignant, and send floods to destroy the crops, unless he were propitiated by prayer and sacrifice. Then in a wider sphere of the powers of nature was the rain which the rain-god who controlled it might send in over-abundant quantities to rot the crops, or might withhold and kill them through drought. And so the rain-god had to be propitiated in like fashion. In the immaterial realm of imagination he peopled the mysterious recesses of the world with wood nymphs, fair women with a female uncertainty of temper which might make them very unpleasant unless propitiated in some way. And so with other powers of nature and other creations of the imagination. Further experience added more gods, especially when he heard perhaps that the dwellers in the valley over the hill had got excellent results from the propitiation of some nature power which he himself had overlooked in his sphere of worship. All this may seem very childish; but then the man of the ancient world, owing to the comparative seclusion of his life and the very limited diffusion of anything which can be called knowledge, was a child, and remained so in many respects to the end of the story. The Roman in quite a late period of his cultural development was borrowing from Greece and introducing into his own religious system worships of powers of nature which he himself had overlooked, such as the worship of Æsculapius, the representative of nature's healing power.

The reverence with which the gods were treated seems to have been subject to strange fluctuations. They are dealt with with a somewhat free hand in the Homeric poems, where they are represented as subject to some of the most frail of human frailties. They are objects of fear rather than of reverence.

Yet in later days of the Greek and Roman states they are the gods of the state at whose worship every citizen is bound to attend lest his absence call down their wrath on the whole nation. Perhaps this argues nothing more than the growth of a priestly influence greater than any which prevailed in Homeric times, a growth rendered all the more probable from the fact that in both the Greek and Roman world the established religion was in the hands of members of noble families who made use of it for their own political purposes, and were therefore profoundly interested in promoting and maintaining a reverent popular attitude towards it. Thus religion became associated with politics; and, the relation once established, it became a lasting feature in political life.

The nature worship of Greece and Rome did not assume the beneficence, but rather the malignance of the divine nature. It was in its original conception merely a means of propitiating powers which might work evil to mankind. That was its main, and probably in the first instance, its only use. It had no creed; nor did it enforce any moral code. The moral system of the community was evolved by common sense out of experience; and if the experiences of two nations differed, then a difference in their moral code might be expected. The morals of the Greek are in many respects in sharp contrast to those of the Roman.

A system of religion which was evolved originally from an infinite number of local worships of the various manifestations of the powers of nature never suggested the idea of tolerance or intolerance of the worships of others. If they did not bow down before these powers, well, so much the worse for them; if they did, there was no harm done to anyone else.

That this nature worship had become anthropomorphic long ere history began is shown by the depiction of the gods in Homer. The majority of mankind has always tended to conceive of divinities in human shape; and even the devotees of religions which expressly reject this idea have never been able to grasp the concept of a divine being free from all human attributes in a sort of unhuman spiritual vacuum. Man must think in terms of man. Judged from the irreverence of the tales in Homer it looks as if the upper classes of the then Greek world were passing through a period of primitive scepticism, promoted, it may be, by a desire to break down such political influence as the king exercised by reason of his monopolising the priestly functions. It was another tale later when both the political and priestly functions of the king passed into the hands of the nobility. Then there came a religious revival—in the interests of the nobility; and the common man was given to understand that neglect on his part to attend the worship of the gods was a sin of omission which might bring disaster on his fellow-citizens, and would therefore be duly punished. Thus as a state religion the worship of nature became pure formalism; though long after it had ceased to have any real significance as the religion of the state, it remained a very real element in the life of the rural cultivator, who still sought the protection of prayer against pestilence, flood, and the uncanny shapes with which his imagination peopled the world. It would be foolish to say that his attitude was foolish.

But as a state religion this worship retained its hold on the minds of the Romans for a much longer period than on the minds of the men of the Greek world. It is unnecessary to ascribe the earlier decline of its influence on the Greek to the superior cleverness or sophistication of that race. The main cause was probably political, due to the fact that it had become associated with the political power of that nobility which got control of the state religion: that was quite sufficient to destroy its influence with that Greek democracy whose attitude towards aristocracy was uncompromising, whereas that of the Roman was acquiescent.

But at some very early period in the connection between religion and the state a new idea had developed, the adoption of some special deity as the special patron and protector of the individual state. Thus, though the worship of the gods in general was the religion of the Greek world as a whole, yet the tendency of each state was to select some special deity for special worship. Athené at Athens, Hêra at Argos, and other deities elsewhere play this part. How the idea originated in the Greek world is not known. It may mark the beginning of that tendency which man displays ever more and more as he advances in civilisation to regard the divine power as one, a tendency which was nearing its full development among the educated class of the days of Herodotus. But, even so, the idea of the one patron god is but a faint suggestion of monotheism; and in the case of the Greek it may have been due to an influence coming from the East, where it seems to have dominated the religions of the Semitic races. Jehovah is the patron god of Israel, just as Baal and Ashtaroth are of the Phœnician cities; and so intimately is the idea of protection bound up with their conception of the deity that Israel at times of national calamity, when the protection has seemed to prove inefficient, is only too ready to pervert to the worship of other deities which, tested by recent facts, have proved more effective. But, whatever its origin, this peculiar and, in a sense, unexpected emanation of nature worship became so prevalent in the pagan Mediterranean that it was passed on to Christian times in the form of the adoption of the patron saint by the cities of the later world.

Thus the Greek or Roman of early days was a more or less perfunctory attendant at worship which made no spiritual or moral appeal to him. He was a conformist and no more. But when he went back to his own home he had around him that which might remind him at every hour of his life of a religion which had a wholly different origin to that nature worship which had been adopted and modified almost beyond recognition as a state religion. This was ancestor worship.

Its origin is quite independent of the origin of nature worship; and its development was on different lines. It is difficult to distinguish any point of convergence, still more of contact, between the two, save that of course they have both their share in those characteristics which form the connotation of any mental disposition or outward observance to which the term religion can be applied.

It is just as universal in the Greek and Roman world as nature worship, and is marked by the same uniformity within itself; but, whereas the objects of nature worship were common to all, those of ancestor worship were confined within the bounds of the single family, or at most of the clan. It is probably far older than the dawn of civilisation. It was ages old when history began. That it was developed and elaborated within the historic period is no doubt the case; and it is only from what is known of it at that period that the causes which brought it into being can be surmised.

Family ties in Greece and Rome, and especially in the latter, were of a much more binding character than any which are found in the institutions of modern states. The power exercised by the head of the family was absolute, including in early times that of life and death. Nor did the ancient world recognise any " coming-of-age " at which the children became emancipated from the control of their parents.[1] The stringency of these family institutions goes back probably to a time when the family or clan had to be organised for its own defence against an outside world which recognised no law save that of might, a state of society which demanded that kith and kin should be kept under one controlling hand, that of the head of the family or of the clan. Thus the head of the family represented to the family a sort of earthly providence on which depended the welfare of each member of it both in time of war and peace. He represented too that abstract force, the continuity of family tradition. And so, when he came to die, his kinsmen cherished the hope that

[1] For the constitution of the family, see Fustel de Coulanges, " La Cité Antique."

the protection which he had given them in life would not die with him, but that his spirit would survive to exercise a ghostly guardianship over those whom he had left behind, provided that the body in which the spirit had resided and would continue, as they believed, to reside, was buried very nigh to his earthly home; and provided too that the manes was propitiated by family prayer and sacrifice. This desire to keep the spirits of the departed, and especially of the great departed, in touch with the survivors of the family is a feature common among races more primitive than were the Indo-Europeans of the Mediterranean even at the earliest period of which any knowledge survives. It is just possible that this idea of protection which lies behind ancestor worship suggested the patron god as protector of the state.

But behind ancestor worship lies a larger idea, that belief with regard to the fate of the dead which was most prevalent and most persistent in the pagan world. Unsophisticated man has never been able to accept the idea that the dead perish utterly. The doctrine of annihilation has been at various ages fashionable among intellectuals; [1] but it has never been popular. Wherever it has appeared it has always been a pose. To speak of the idea of a future life as instinctive in man may seem a misuse of terms, and a begging of the question of immortality. Among primitive peoples it seldom takes the form of a belief in the immortality of the soul, inasmuch as the very concept of the soul is for the most part lacking to them. That view of the after-life was evolved at a much later time. In the Homeric age there is a belief in the future life as a thin presentment of the bodily life on earth, a life in a world where men are mere shadows of their former selves, impalpable ghosts without strength —" the strengthless heads of the dead "—who must drink of the blood of victims ere they are able to utter the sounds of human speech. It is all set forth in that unforgettable description of the visit of Odysseus to the under-world. It might perhaps have been anticipated that the almost reverent popularity of the Homeric poems in after-times would have tended to render this view prevalent in the later Greek world ; but, as a fact, there is little or no trace of it in the popular beliefs of later centuries. The mode of burial most customary in Greece for many centuries, combined with the oft-repeated testimony of verses in the Greek Anthology, that treasure-house of the everyday thoughts of the old world, shows that the belief most prevalent with respect to the life after death was that the spirit resided with the body in the grave ; that it lived an unseen life amid the surroundings it had known in its bodily life, and

---

[1] Cf. various verses and epigrams in the Greek Anthology by the Alexandrian author Callimachus.

was still capable of enjoying the good things of this world. It was a pathetic if crude expression of the longing which mankind has felt at all ages to discount the phenomenon of death by rejecting the idea that the loved ones who have died have passed away for ever into a nothingness from which their individuality can never emerge, and by substituting for it a faith not merely in their survival in a world in which those who outlive them will meet them after death, but in their ghostly presence in the scenes they had known in their bodily life on earth.

This conception of the fate of the dead is, as the monuments show, as old as anything which can be called civilisation. It was the prevalent idea among the mass of the Greek people throughout the great period of their history, and on and on through the centuries until Christianity converted them to a more hopeful view. It was more or less natural that this idea of the life of the dead should be accompanied by the belief that the dead could not be happy unless their bodies were buried amid the scenes they had known in life. It was believed that burial away from the old home condemned the spirit of the dead to misery; and hence it was a duty laid upon the survivors to make every effort to carry the body of one who had died far away for burial in the land he had known in life. Cremation, which is found in the fifth century side by side with the practice of burial, was probably resorted to in cases where the body could not be transported to the home land by reason of the distance, or when contamination from the bodies of those who had died of plague was an overwhelming danger to the survivors. That international custom of surrendering the bodies of the dead after battle to the side which had lost the field, a custom so strong that any infringement of it was peculiarly shocking to the Greek mind, originated in this belief. The case of the burial of the Athenian dead on the field of Marathon is noted by Greek authors as exceptional; but it was probably justified by the consideration that it was on that ground they had won exceptional glory; and after all they were Athenians buried on Attic soil. The story of Greek history has been so told in modern times that readers are given the impression that the Athenians of the latter part of the fifth century were intellectual enthusiasts in whom the teachings of philosophy had destroyed all superstition and attachment to the old faith. But a profound belief in this view of the after-life was responsible for that otherwise inexplicable event in the very last years of the fifth century, the execution of the generals after Arginusæ; and it was the popular attachment to the old faith and the old views of life which combined to bring about the condemnation and death of Socrates.

But it is not necessary to seek for the confirmation of this idea in the outstanding incidents of Greek history. Numbers of epitaphs, both actual and literary,[1] in the Greek Anthology, especially such as record the death of those who perished at sea far from their native land, lament their fate as spirits condemned to misery in consequence of their being bound to a body buried away from the familiar scenes of their earthly life.

Though the modern world has of late years sought to reduce the concept of hell to something which its forefathers would not have recognised under that name, yet the ideas of heaven and hell, of places, that is to say, where in an after-life good is rewarded and evil is punished, may be said to be essential features in the spiritual life of the Christian civilisation of the West. The ancient world had not conceived the idea of transferring the due rewards of good and evil to an after-life. There were indeed the Elysian Fields. There was Tartarus. But the Elysian Fields were a land of twilight where the pleasures of life were reduced to insipid forms; and the man of the ancient world preferred to take his pleasures unadulterated. The idea was the creation of poetical, not of popular fancy. Tartarus was a hell for heroes, especially those who defied the gods. The common sinners of this world were not threatened by this aristocratic place of punishment, and left all interest in it for those for whom it was reserved, a class of demi-gods which had died out in an early stage of society.

So the average man of the old world did not conceive of an after-world of reward or punishment for offences committed while in the flesh. He attached at various times many and various fanciful attributes to the after-life; but that was not one of them. He had, on the other hand, a strong and healthy superstition that wrong-doing was punished in this life; and the feeling was so strong that it was a very sound ethical deterrent in respect to offences against some of the most important relations of life. When Herodotus moralises on the action of the Athenians and Spartans in killing the heralds of Darius, he does not speculate on what punishment the wrong-doers may expect in Hades, but as to which of the calamities which subsequently befell those states was sent on them in retribution for their misdeeds. At the end of the first ten years of the Peloponnesian War the Spartans, says Thucydides, had a feeling that their failure was due to their having been the first aggressors in the war, and having broken the oath which they had sworn to observe the Thirty Years' Peace of fifteen years before.

It is impossible to say whether this superstition goes back to the primitive age. It is possible that it was promoted in the first instance at a later time by priests of various sanctuaries

[1] I.e. not on actual tombs, but composed as purely literary efforts.

who showed themselves in this as in other respects anxious to make the relations between states and individuals of that ordered and civilised character which can only be attained by the observance of certain moral ties, such as justice and good faith. Doubtless in the case of the violation of an oath it was expected that the punishment would come from the god in whose name the oath had been sworn. But, even so, the prevalence of the superstition suggests a vague conception of a spiritual power, nemesis, retribution, which is distinct from, and greater than the power of the gods. The Greeks, if not the Romans, were ever trembling on the verge of monotheism ; and mankind, when it has come to some faint conception of a supreme power, naturally associates it with unity rather than multiplicity.

Even as this Mediterranean religion never formulated any idea of heaven, so also it never conceived any definite scheme of a reward for virtue in the after-life. This was perhaps a corollary of the idea that wrong-doing was punished in this world. A ghostly life attached to the body in a grave amid familiar surroundings seems to have been all the happiness which the most prevalent superstition anticipated for the dead. It was not perhaps till a comparatively late age that the living came to regard rest as the greatest gift which the after-life could bestow. Rest is happiness, unrest is misery in the world of the hereafter.

But in all the phases of the views as to the after-life one curious and, in a sense, irrational feature is present, the conception that the unhappiness of the disembodied soul may be due to causes quite outside the control of its possessor during life in this world. Whatever a man may have been in life, the mere fact that his body is buried in some land foreign to him is sufficient to condemn his spirit to unhappiness. So, too, under the other form of belief, burial in a spot where rest seems impossible entails the same misery.[2]

[1] This is the theme of many verses in the Greek Anthology. But, as they belong to a late age, they do not throw any light on the question of the origin or age of this conception.

[2] Cf. among other verses in the Greek Anthology :

  Crushed by the waves upon the crags was I,
   Who still must hear those waves among the dead
  Breaking and brawling on the promontory
   Sleepless ; and sleepless is my weary head.
  For me did strangers bury on the coast
   Within the hateful hearing of the deep ;
  And death which lulleth all can't lull my ghost :
   One sleepless soul among the souls that sleep.
    Archias, first century B.C. (version by Andrew Lang).

  Who buried me when dead where three ways meet,
   Curse him alike unburied and unblest ;
  Since o'er my corpse the tramp of passing feet
   Robs me in death of death's eternal rest.—Julianus.

Still it is not so irrational an idea when associated with a conception of an after-life in which reward and punishment play hardly any part. The explanation may be found in the "tragedy" of life which is so prominent in the plots of the Greek dramatist, where the tragedy is that part of life beyond man's control—the accidental, and where man is conceived as being largely the plaything of chance. Even death did not destroy the power of fate.

Such then was the outline of these ideas, religious and quasi-religious, which played a large part not merely in the early Greek and Roman life, but, in the case of the mass of the Greek race at any rate, continued to exert an incalculable if decreasing influence for centuries after the intellectual minority of it had transferred its allegiance from religion to philosophy. To understand the history of the two great Mediterranean peoples it is necessary to realise so far as possible the circumstances and ideas in which they lived. This is why the attempt to picture them has been made thus early in this book.

The somewhat fitful light which ancient tradition and modern archæology cast upon the happenings of the second millennium before Christ dies away in the first two centuries of the first millennium. Yet the circumstances of an unstoried past may sometimes be realised to a certain extent by reading back from the circumstances of a storied future ; and that is the only process of conjecture which can be applied to the history during this period of those lands and peoples which are of most importance in the later story of the Mediterranean region. The silence of later tradition with regard to the incidents of these two centuries may suggest that in Greece and Italy at any rate there was no incident of such an outstanding nature as to win immortality in the folk-tales of later time. Doubtless the life of the time had its storms, but not like the tempests which had swept the Mediterranean world in the previous period. There were no epoch-making events—if it is permissible to use a term which has been so much misused in recent days.

But the institutions of the various peoples were pursuing their course towards their development in the historic period ; and it is by marking the obviously antique survivals of later times that some impression may be formed of the general nature of the earlier phases of these institutions.

SPAIN

All that is known of the Spanish peninsula between 1000 and 800 B.C. consists of one small item of positive conjecture. On the negative side it may be said that, for reasons which will be stated in connection with Greece, it is improbable that the

Celtic inroad had as yet taken place. There is no reason to suppose that the Phœnician had as yet any dominion in Spain; but he had already founded trading settlements on the south coast in the neighbourhood of the Straits of Gibraltar, of which the most important, Gades, was reputed to date from 1000 B.C. Such were the beginnings of a Punic civilisation in the south of the peninsula which was destined to make the region peculiarly receptive of the Latin civilisation which Rome brought with her many centuries later.

Gaul

Nothing is known of Gaul until the Phocæans founded Massilia in 600 B.C.; and even after that time, until its Mediterranean coast became a matter of interest to Rome, the extant information with regard to it is very meagre. In the time of Herodotus, a century and a half after Massilia's foundation, it is still unknown in Greek geography, for that author, whose knowledge represents in all probability the high-water mark of the geographical knowledge of his day, speaks of Pyrene, obviously the Pyrenees, as a city. Gaul was probably at this age inhabited by Iberian and Ligurian peoples. The date of the Celtic invasion of the country is not known; but it is almost incredible that the people who were exercising a military domination over the original inhabitants in Cæsar's time could have maintained that position for nine hundred years. The invasion of Britain by these Brythonic Celts is reckoned to have taken place about 300 B.C.; and it is quite possible that it was several centuries later than the invasion of Gaul.[1]

Italy

The earliest traditions of Italy do not go back beyond the reputed date of the foundation of Rome, fifty years after this period closes. The Etruscans may have been settled in the north of the peninsula before it begins; they were certainly there before it ended, and were occupying a considerable region north of the Apennines in the basin of the Padus as well as that region south of the range which is their home in historic times. It is possible that their league of cities was under a monarchy at this period; but the real power in the country seems to have been at all times in the hands of feudal barons who lorded it from great fortified castles built on the most inaccessible hills. Whether they had already made a branch settlement in the rich lands of Campania on the Bay of Naples cannot be said. They had introduced into the land a civilisation which was probably

[1] Greek authors seem to imply that the Celts were in Gaul when Massilia was founded in 600 B.C.

of Hittite origin among people which at the time were in a comparatively early stage of cultural development.

The tribes of Latin kin of the middle and south of the peninsula had probably acquired many of the elements of civilisation, but few of its amenities. Perhaps even at this early date the Greek trader was affecting the life of the south shore of the peninsula by introducing among its people ideas and objects belonging to a civilisation more advanced than their own. But, if any conclusion is to be drawn from later days, then the middle and south Italians were pursuing an agricultural life which was very self-centred, neither having nor seeking communication with the outside world, and supplying their own simple wants from their local resources. When these peoples emerge into the dim light of recorded tradition their political institutions are of the same type as is found among the Greeks of the Homeric period, in fact the similarity is so close, that it may be conjectured that their institutions go back to a time before the separation between the Hellenic and Italian branches of the Indo-European race took place. It is probable that each larger centre of population had its king whose powers were in many respects absolute ; a senate of local nobility whose functions were purely advisory ; and an assembly of the people which did little but express by acclamation assent or dissent to such proposals as the king thought well to put before it.

IONIANS IN ASIA

The successive waves of Hellenic immigration into the Greek peninsula seem to have overcrowded a land which, inasmuch as only a little more than one-fifth of its area is capable of cultivation, was ever liable to chronic difficulties in respect to overpopulation. The works of Greek authors are full of traditions relating to movements eastward to the islands of the Ægean, to the shore of Asia, to Crete, and to Cyprus and elsewhere, of bands of emigrants drawn from all parts of Greece. It would be unsafe to put faith in the absolute truth of any one of them ; but, though the details may be untrustworthy, yet the mass of them affords convincing evidence of repeated instances of a general migration from the Greek mainland, especially to the islands and the Asiatic coast. Nor can there be much doubt that that movement was due to the influx of successive invaders who raised the population of the peninsula to numbers which it could not support. The outstanding item in these traditions is the settlement of the Ionians on the coast of Asia, where they founded those cities which were destined to play so great a part in later history. The Greeks of the historic period had but a vague idea of the date of these foundations, but they put it at about 1000 B.C. Whether it was the earlier Achæan invasion of Peloponnese or the later Dorian invasion, or both, which drove them across the sea, it is not possible to say; but the mass of traditions points to the fact that, probably in the tenth century, numerous non-Ionian emigrants from all parts of Greece joined in what were at that time comparatively recent Ionian settlements, to become merged later in name and in blood with their Ionian predecessors. It may be that the Ægean islands had up to that time remained in the hands of a population akin to the Minoan and Mycenæan race; for the Hellenic invaders from the north, a land-faring people, can hardly have taken to the sea immediately on their arrival in the Greek peninsula. Many an unrecorded fight must have taken place when these bands of desperate refugees from the mainland attacked and vanquished the old population of the islands.

It may be that some of these migrations were caused by a desire to escape from that quasi-serfdom which the Dorians imposed on races which they conquered; but tradition represents this movement as having affected parts of Greece in which the Dorian never settled; and the main cause of it must have been the influx of new population into a country where the balance between the food supply and the inhabitants was more often than not on the wrong side.

NAVIGATION

These migrations across the Ægean must have done something to promote knowledge and skill in navigation. The pre-Hellenic population had possessed these things from time immemorial; but the invaders from the north had, no doubt, to be persuaded to take to the water, partly by the example of the survivors of the pre-existing population, partly by those chronic failures in crops to which all parts of the world are subject, but which were peculiarly dangerous in a land where the margin of safety was always finely drawn. Local scarcity drove the cultivator " to take his boat-paddle down from the rafters among the smoke "[1] and to voyage to the nearest region where food could be obtained. The very land compelled its people to sail the sea. The sheltered waters round the coast were formed by nature to be the nursery of unskilful beginners in navigation. The Ægean with its frequent islands was a schoolroom for the young sailor. It is not strange that the Greek became famous for his skill as a seafarer in a world which had a unanimous preference for the land. Indiscriminate admiration and enthusiasm for the Greek has produced in modern literature strange travesties of his life and character, which could only be justified

[1] Hesiod.

on the assumption that the Greek was a liar in depreciation of his own virtues, a form of untruth which can hardly be attributed to him. He has been made to pose as an ancient representative of modern types ranging from the reckless Elizabethan adventurer to the mid-Victorian Liberal. Consideration of the latter claim may be deferred till the story of a much later century has to be told. Still even the wildest literary enthusiast could hardly read a mid-Victorian Liberal into the tenth century before Christ. But if these two centuries mark the rejuvenescence of that art and practice of navigation among the dwellers round the Ægean which the Minoan Cretan had exercised many centuries earlier, it is because the circumstances were such that the men of the Greece of that day had to choose between starvation and navigation; and they preferred the possibility to the certainty of death. It is perhaps impossible to realise all the perils to which the sailor was exposed at all periods in the history of the ancient world, even when in later Roman times the ships which sailed the Mediterranean were larger and better built than they were in the most prosperous days of Greece. The very materials which give strength and seaworthiness to the wooden ships of modern times were either rare or lacking in ancient days. The wood which the Mediterranean shipbuilders had to use was inferior for the purpose, peculiarly ill adapted to exposure to the water for any length of time; too soft to be made into a really compact structure; and too weak for it to be used in making vessels of any large size. If to these disadvantages be added the absence of a compass, and the inability of the vessels of the Greek build and rig to sail into the wind, or even to row against it when blowing with great strength, it is possible to form some conception of the danger which the ancient navigator ran of being lost on the open sea or wrecked on a lee shore. To him Scylla and Charybdis were not phenomena which were confined to the Sicilian Strait. He feared the storm which might come up at any time out of the blue of the Mediterranean; and of the Greek as of other early navigators it may be said that he and they would have avoided the sea routes, had the land routes of the region been possible for not merely his purposes but his necessities. The Odyssey breathes a breath of the spirit of adventure and of the restlessness of the man who has pierced the unknown; but these are but patches of light in an otherwise dark picture. Had the Greek taken a joy in the sea, had he faced it under the inspiration of that spirit of adventure, some traces of these feelings would surely have been found in those verses of the Greek Anthology which throw light on many centuries of Greek life. But there the sea is associated with darkness, disaster, and death; and the best that can be said of it is that it is sometimes calm. Doubtless in later centuries, as Greek trade developed, and the Greek thereby acquired a wealth such as he could never have got from his own land, the hope of gain discounted the peril. But even so that trade was largely concerned with the supply of daily bread; and by that time the Greek sailor knew that the Mediterranean had not on its shores any Eldorado which might inspire a man with a spirit of daring, reckless as to the means provided there was a hope of attaining the end. The Greek would not have listened to the song of the sea as sung by the poet on shore. His view of it was founded on experience, not on illusion.[1]

These two centuries must be the period in which the Greek drove the Phœnician trader out of the Ægean. The extent of Phœnician trade in that sea may have been exaggerated in later Greek tradition, which tended to ascribe to Phœnician influence various elements in Greek life which were inherited more probably from the Minoan and Mycenæan civilisation of the past, a civilisation which later Greece never realised. The Minoan legend survived like a broken fragment of some work of art, a fragment too insignificant to suggest the glory of the whole. Many places in the Ægean were regarded as former centres of Phœnician trade. In how many of these cases the legend is true or fictitious it is impossible to say; but Cythera and Thasos were great centres of its activities. The legendary settlement in Thebes is on the other hand almost certainly fictitious. But it may be assumed that after this great impetus had been given to navigation, and the Ægean had been freed from the commercial invader, Greek trade spread rapidly beyond that sea; and that expansion must have been carried far before these two centuries came to a close. The legend of the Argonauts, which points to Greek navigation having reached the Euxine, may refer to a period earlier than 1000 B.C.; but it is probable that at least after that date the Greek had developed on the north shore of that sea that trade in corn which was to be so important an economic feature in the later Greek world. There was certainly communication with Cyprus, which may have been extended as far as Egypt. Sicily and the West, a land of fable when the saga of the Odyssey came into being, was probably visited by Greek navigators during these centuries. It is even said that the influence of Corinthian trade had reached as far

---

[1] It is necessary at this point, the very beginning of the story of Greek navigation, to make the Greek attitude to that department of life in which he showed such activity quite clear. The widespread nature of this activity, and the all-important part which it played in Greek life, has led authors to read into it an enthusiasm for the sea which the Greek never entertained, unless he is misrepresented in his own literature.

as Carthage by the beginning of the eighth century. To these centuries must also be ascribed the beginnings of that pre-eminence in trade which the Asiatic Greeks enjoyed over those of Europe right down to the sixth century. They must have got a long start of the Greek world at home while the latter was dominated by peoples who had yet to be educated to seafaring life.

EARLY GREEK COMMUNITIES

The social and political life of the Greece of that day, like the rest of the story of the time, can only be conjectured from the vague traditions of some centuries later. The Dorian invaders founded no doubt states of some size where they figured as the privileged ruling class among a population of serfs. Elsewhere in the land the political units were of small area, a town, may be not larger than a modern village, with the territory immediately round it, or in some cases small federal unions of villages. The nature of the country, where the barriers are many and of a character far more formidable to traverse than the hill barriers of other parts of Europe, tended to confine intercourse and, consequently, political units, within very narrow limits. Thucydides says that the Ætolians of his day, who lived in villages, without any town as political centre of the region, afforded a sample of a form of life which had at one time been the rule in Greece. But the invasions must have taught the population generally the lesson that small political units were too weak to face an attack from outside ; and that would give that impulse to synœcism—the combination of the scattered population of a large district into one political unit with one political centre—which led to the formation of the comparatively large political units existent at the beginning of the period of Greek colonisation shortly after 800 B.C.

The clan system was all-prevalent and strong. The heads of the clan, the nobility of the period, had sufficient interest and power to maintain the system for several centuries more. That a kingship, similar in general character and power to that of the Homeric period, survived, in most parts of Greece at any rate, there is no reason to doubt, the king being either the head of the local clan, or, where synœcism had taken place, the head of the most powerful clan in the new combination, while the heads of the less powerful clans became, as it were, a new order of nobility. The disturbed period of settlement which must have followed the great invasions would demand the military organisation of those who would be safe ; and that would promote the maintenance of the kingly office. Under the king a council of nobles would still exercise advisory functions, and the assembly of the people the formality of assent or dissent. It is no doubt the case that in many of the states aristocracies took the place of kingdoms before the end of these two centuries. But these aristocracies are more characteristic of the next period.

Asia Minor

The most important event in the Asia Minor of these centuries was the settlement of the Ionian Greeks on its coast. The Dorian settlement on the Carian coast may have also fallen within the period. Of the date of the Æolian settlement on the north part of the Ægean coast of Asia nothing is known, though the late Greeks seem to have had a general impression that it preceded that of the Ionians.

It is probable that these settlers found on that coast, in Caria and in the Troad certainly, and also it may be in the district between them, peoples with a civilisation which represented that of Minoan Crete. In the world of art they seem to have fallen much below the level attained in Crete and Mycenæ centuries before this time; and it is probable that they were decadent in other respects. But it is likely that this art and civilisation would, even in its decadence, affect the new-comers, many of whom must have had in their veins the blood of that early race of the Greek mainland whose kinship to the Minoan Cretans is presumed, and also of those Cretan settlers who set up centres of culture at Mycenæ and elsewhere. Was the Greek art of later centuries due to a revival of that Cretan art originating in the settlement of these Europeans among Asiatic kinsmen who had maintained the tradition? It is difficult to assume that the freehand art of the great days of Greece was evolved from the geometric art which the Hellenic races brought with them from the north.

The great days of the Hittite kingdom had come to an end before this millennium opened. The attacks of Assyria from the east and of the Phrygians from the west had broken it; but the Hittite population maintained itself in the eastern part of the Anatolian (Asia Minor) peninsula.

In the hinterland of the Greek settlements the Phrygian power was making history rapidly, but not written history, for its story was too old for the Greek tradition of the eastern side of the Ægean, save that the legend of Midas shows that its wealth and splendour impressed the contemporary Greek. It seems to have grown to power and to have attained to large territorial development in these two centuries, reducing the early Lydian kingdom to a vassal state, and later bringing into subjection the Hittite population and all that remained to them of their once great empire. Either in these centuries or in that which followed

FIRST TWO CENTURIES OF FIRST MILLENNIUM 53

it carried its frontier to the Taurus. Yet the Phrygians do not appear to have been a people filled with the lust of conquest, but to have settled down to a diligent life of agriculture in the regions which they conquered. That is perhaps the reason why the Greeks of later times knew little or nothing of the tale of the days of their greatness.

In the Semitic lands beyond the Taurus the kingdom of Assyria was rising to supreme power in the Euphrates region. But it is the circumstances of its death rather than of its life which affected Mediterranean history. That Mesopotamian civilisation which was to have a traceable influence on later Greek life was rather set back than advanced by the barbarous spirit in which the Assyrian interpreted the rights of conquest.

Egypt was passing through a series of vicissitudes which belong to Egyptian rather than Mediterranean history.

In North Africa Carthage was as yet a mere Phœnician colony or trading station. According to one late Roman tradition [1] its foundation dates from a century before that of Rome—about 850 B.C. But another [2] puts it at a much earlier period, fifty years before the fall of Troy, thus setting back its age by 400 years. But when the two centuries now under consideration came to a close it was still a dependency of the home state on the far eastern shore of the Mediterranean.

[1] Justin, xviii, 6, 9.   [2] Appian, Punica, I.

CHAPTER III

THE EIGHTH AND SEVENTH CENTURIES BEFORE CHRIST, 800–600 B.C.

THE shadows which people the darkness before the dawn of history begin to take more definite shape in that great eighth century before Christ which saw the foundation of Rome and the beginnings of that colonising activity which scattered the Greeks and Greek culture over a wide area of the Mediterranean region.

SPAIN AND GAUL

Of Spain and Gaul nothing is known in these centuries. The Celtic inroad into the two countries may have fallen within the period; for Massilia was founded in the last year of the seventh century; and every reference made by Greek authors to the Celts in Gaul seems to assume that they were there from the very beginning of the Phocæan occupation. The Phœnician settlements in Spain seem to have remained much as they were in previous times, if any judgment can be formed from what occurred on the east coast of that country in the sixth century.

ROME, EARLY HISTORY

In Italy everything centres on the foundation of Rome. The written tradition of the early age of its existence has only survived in authors who wrote about the end of the first century before Christ, Livy and Dionysius of Halicarnassos. The similarity of their versions indicates that the tradition of the monarchical period had by that time taken a stereotyped form; which would suggest that they borrowed it from previous writers, as no doubt they did. The tradition itself has often been examined by expert critics in modern times; and, though their conclusions differ in detail, yet it is generally agreed that, stripped of certain obviously mythical matter, it gives a fanciful tale of incident, but a fairly trustworthy picture of those features of the period which were of most importance in the subsequent development of the Roman state.

But for him who would reconstruct the history of that period, especially in relation to those political institutions which were

THE EIGHTH AND SEVENTH CENTURIES

destined to last through many centuries of Rome's existence, the innate conservatism of the Roman people preserved a certain amount of evidence in the archaic elements which they retained in the constitution even to the very end of the Republican period, and in some cases into the period of the Principate.

There is one element in the tradition of early Rome as it appears in the writers of the first century before Christ which must be ruled out as pure fiction, the part alleged to have been played by wandering bands of Greeks in what may be called the prelude to the foundation of Rome itself. This was undoubtedly the work of Greek writers who were anxious to claim that their race had participated in the foundation of that power which dominated the world of their day. Another version of the tradition attributed to Æneas of Troy a large share in the events which preceded and led up to the foundation of the city. Virgil adopted a tale which was at least four hundred years old in his time. But he had an excellent precedent for so doing in that the Roman government had officially accepted it as early as the time of the First Punic War. Other governments besides that of Rome have adopted legends for political convenience.

There can be no doubt that Rome was of native Latin origin. The fact that it was a city state and that its early institutions and their early political development are curiously similar to what existed and occurred in the early Greek world does not support any theory of Greek origin or even Greek influence at this period. The city state in Greece and Italy was the outcome of physical conditions existent in both those countries. The similarity in the early development of political institutions is attributable to the fact that, given two peoples who start from similar political conditions, the early stages of their progress towards popular liberty are more likely than not to resemble one another.

Even those who do not know Italy will have heard of the plain of the Campagna. To call it a plain is to use a term relative to the rugged regions which surround it. It is a country of ridge and furrow; but the ridges are not so high, nor the furrows so deep, as in the lands north, south, and east of it; and so it was a land which afforded pasture where it did not admit of cultivation. It was one of those regions which, owing to its attractions being superior to those of the lands around it, would be much sought for and much fought for by early peoples who had much to gain and little to lose by shifting their dwellings to the richer areas of the world. It may be assumed therefore that the Latins who occupied the plain when history began had been one of the most virile of the Italian peoples, and the continual struggle to maintain possession of what they had got had kept their virility in training. It had also had the political effect of forcing the various communities of the plain into a confederacy with a common religious centre [1] on the Alban Mount.

As to the beginnings of Rome itself, it may have owed its existence to its having been at the lowest point at which the Tiber could be conveniently crossed. Such has been the origin of many a city famous in ancient and modern times. But the tradition that it was founded somewhere about 750 B.C. may relate to a historical fact; and the ascription of its foundation to pre-existing local communities which united in one on the Palatine Hill is at any rate in accord with a tendency common at that age; while certain elements in the institutions of later Rome suggest that they were due to a fusion of communities. But the tradition tells not merely of a fusion of communities but of races, Latin, Etruscan, and Sabine, in the new foundation. That a Sabine element was merged at a very early period with the original Latin settlers is likely; but that Etruscans were mingled with them is most improbable.[2]

The composite character of the early foundation is shown perhaps in the existence of the three original tribes, Ramnes, Tities, and Luceres, survivals probably of the clans which united to form the joint community.

More important divisions of the people were the curiæ, of

[1] The idea of the unity of the state is so strongly combined in the ancient world with the idea of unity of worship that it could not conceive of political unity without religious unity. Even a confederacy must have a common religious centre, as the Latins had in this instance, and like the Pan-Ionian sanctuary which was the religious centre of the somewhat loose confederacy of the Ionian cities on the Asiatic coast. States which had won empire, and wished to unify that which they had acquired, sought always to establish some common form of worship for the whole of their empire. Athens wished to set up the worship of Athene as the cult of her empire. When the policy of unifying the empire of Rome was inaugurated under the early principate, Cæsar worship was set up as a cult common to all the peoples in the dominion of Rome. Neither in the case of Rome nor elsewhere did such a policy imply the suppression of local cults. They were allowed to go on just as before; and their worshippers were in no way interfered with, provided always they conformed to the cult of the unified state. If, like the Jews and Christians, they refused to do this, then the refusal was treated as a political offence, not for convenience' sake, but because it was actually believed to be founded on political disloyalty.

[2] In dealing with the histories of Greece and Rome in these volumes, considerations of space impose on me the necessity of treating incidents of purely temporary effect and importance quite briefly, even if they are touched on at all. The essential subject-matter chosen is those incidents and institutions the occurrence or development of which affected those later political and social systems from which modern civilisation has borrowed so largely.

which there were thirty.[1] These divisions survived as mere political ghosts even to the last days of the Republic; and it is very difficult to say what they were like when in the flesh. Each curia had its own religious ties, a common worship and a chapel. They appear to have been local in the sense that their members were neighbours of one another living in one locality. The attribute of a common worship survived in the last days of the Republic, and the attribute of locality may still have been technically in existence, though it had lost all real significance, inasmuch as the political functions of the curia had become so unimportant that its members did not think it worth while to take part in them. Their real importance is that they are the first form taken by those political groups which are so unique and outstanding a feature of Rome's political institutions. The freemen of the Assembly (comitia) of this early period did not give individual votes as members of the Assembly, but as members of the groups (curiæ) of which the Assembly was formed. Thus the thirty curiæ gave thirty votes, the majority of votes within each curia determining the vote of the curia itself.

This feature of the Roman constitution is not merely of academic interest owing to its peculiar character, but of the utmost importance, as it was largely responsible for the peculiar, and at times paradoxical, nature of the development through which that constitution passed, and had the most marked discernible influence on the history of the Romans as a nation, as well as much influence which is not perceptible by a world which can never realise from written records all the realities of the life of the ancient world. During the four-and-a-half centuries of the Republic drastic reforms were made in the composition of the Assembly: new forms were set up, with new methods of voting. But in all of them the group system was maintained, though in the later forms the groups were centuries and tribes instead of curiæ. The group system favoured the interests of men of high birth and of wealth in respect to the functions of the Assembly—legislation and the election of magistrates—for it is easy to set up machinery such as may control the voting of a group, though very difficult to influence the decisions of an Assembly where the citizens have direct individual votes on the questions brought before them. In the days of this early form of Assembly, the comitia curiata, very little machinery would

[1] Pelham, "Outlines of Roman History," points out the recurrence of the number 3 and multiples of it in the early institutions of Rome, the Senate of 300, the primitive legion of 3,000, the Vestal Virgins, and the Augurs. This was no doubt due to the triple tribal division already mentioned.

be necessary, because the patrician families in each curia could exercise an overwhelming influence. This must have declined in the later Assembly of the Centuries (Comitia Centuriata), to this extent at any rate, that a class of wealthy citizens came to share with the nobility of birth the control of the majority of votes in that form of Assembly. The last established form, the Comitia Tributa, the Assembly of the Tribes, made the exercise of influence of that particular kind impossible ; but the new nobility which had sprung up elaborated a system of bribery which was as effective as it was corrupt. To the possibility and effectiveness of these forms of control is largely due the constitutional paradox that in the last three centuries of the Republic the government is in form a democracy, in fact an oligarchy ; and both the possibility and the effectiveness are attributable to the system of group voting in the Assembly.

In the constitution of this early period the three elements, King, Senate, and Assembly, bear a close resemblance to the constitutions of the Homeric age in Greece ; and it is possible that they go back to a period when the Italian and Greek races were one. But the Roman kings are not like the Homeric kings. The latter were kings *qua* leaders of the war-host ; the former were leaders of the war-host *qua* kings. Roman kingship is kingship in a later stage of development than that of the Homeric age ; and in no respect is this more marked than in its elective character. The curious forms attendant on the choice of a new king survived in republican times in connection with the choice of a new consul ; and though in Cicero's day the process of election was customary in the choice of consuls, it was quite well known that election in the sense of a popular vote as between various candidates for office was not a necessary part of the process, but merely a concession made by the consuls for the year when they presided over the selection of those who should succeed them in office. The consuls had the power of nominating the candidates for office, and, more than that, could reject any nomination made by anyone else. So, if they only nominated two candidates, and refused to accept any other nominations, there would be no election ; and the right of the people would have been limited to the acceptance or rejection by acclamation of the candidates so nominated. There is no question but that this curious archaism of centuries later was derived from the forms observed in the choice of the old Roman kings. This is further shown by the fact that if the consuls of the year died before they could hold the consular elections for the next year, an official called an interrex (" intermediate king ") was appointed to hold the elections, or, strictly speaking, to nominate the consuls for the next year. The very survival of such a title in republican times shows that the whole process was inherited from the days of the kingship.

In old Rome, when the king died, the Senate was responsible for the choice of an interrex whose duty was to nominate the next king. Thus the kingship was not hereditary; though no doubt under ordinary circumstances members of the late king's family stood by far the best chance of being nominated to the succession. The person nominated was presented to the popular Assembly for its acceptance, and that acceptance, if given, was ratified by the Senate. Once appointed the king exercised a most extraordinarily absolute power in many of the departments of government. He was supreme judge in matters both civil and criminal; and from his infliction of even the death penalty there was no appeal. He was the absolute commander of the army. He was in control of the state religion. He was the sole power which could initiate legislation; and the Senate and the assembly could only meet when he chose to call them together, the former to give him advice which he need not take, the latter to accept or to reject by acclamation any legislation which he might propose to it. These powers descended undiminished to the consuls of the republican period; and a popular movement against their arbitrary character in the administration of justice is the first step taken by the Roman people in its struggle for civil liberty.

The tradition of the reigns of the first four kings was elaborated in later times by the addition of purely fictitious matter. Yet there are elements in the story which may be accepted as historical: the very limited area of the territory of Rome, which did not extend for more than a few miles from the city: continual struggles with near Latin neighbours: and an extension of territory in the direction of the sea. Then comes the dynasty of the Tarquins, kings of Etruscan race, of whose doings something like a historical record survived in later days. But these doings belong to the story of the sixth century, though, according to the accepted chronology, this dynasty must have come into power in the seventh.

Greek Colonisation

In the story of the Greek world of these two centuries the interest centres in an extraordinarily active period of colonisation, which begins early in the eighth century and comes to a sudden close at the end of the seventh. It is commonly said to have owed its impulse to the expansion of trade; but there are various striking phenomena connected with it which are hard to reconcile with that theory, and suggest indeed that it transposes cause and effect. If the desire for trade expansion pure and simple was at the bottom of the movement, then it is strange that the Greek of later times did not bring this into prominence in the many references to colonies and colonisation which are found in later Greek authors. They with almost one accord ascribe this movement of colonising activity to political tension within the states. With these later authors, to whom politics were an absorbing interest, and economics an unknown science, such a statement of cause is natural. It was left to Plato [1] to explain a phenomenon which was economic in its origin and political in its results :

" when men who have nothing, and are in want of food, show a disposition to follow their leaders in an attack on the property of the rich—these, who are the natural plague of the state, are sent away by the legislator in a friendly spirit ; and this dismissal of them is euphemistically termed a colony."

But the historians, to return to their evidence, attribute to the land question most of the political movements which led to colonisation. They imply that all productive areas were already occupied, and the landless folk went out to found a colony. The land question suggests that food question which had been, and was destined to be, an ever-existent factor in the economics of the Greek world at home. That the cause of the phenomenon of Greek colonising activity is not merely political is shown by the fact that the political trouble ($\sigma\tau\acute{\alpha}\sigma\iota\varsigma$) was just as rife after the colonising period came to an end as it was during the period of its duration. With the opening of the sixth century the colonising activity of the Greek world dies away suddenly after a century and a half of energy. Yet $\sigma\tau\acute{\alpha}\sigma\iota\varsigma$ is just as marked a feature of Greek political life after that time as it had been while colonisation was still in progress. It has been already said in reference to the story of the previous centuries that the question of food supply was probably the main reason for that great migration of the population of Greece from Europe to the Asiatic coast which succeeded the Dorian migration. Food shortage is an ever-present, and acute phases of it an ever-recurrent, phenomenon in Greek history ; nor can there be much doubt that such an acute phase set in early in the eighth century.

Colonising activity on the part of a state or of a race generally implies that the community has a surplus population. It is only on the strongest compulsion that men leave well-known scenes for unknown dangers in foreign lands ; and the causes which drove the Greek from that home whose light and colour appealed so vividly to him cannot have been otherwise than of a compelling nature. Furthermore, when account is taken of the main trend of Greek colonising activity, the economic nature

[1] "Laws," 735 E, 736 A.

THE EIGHTH AND SEVENTH CENTURIES

of the movement becomes still more apparent. It is in the great corn-producing regions of the then known world that the activity is mainly concentrated, in Sicily, South Italy, and the Euxine. It is, too, towards the close of this period that Egypt is overrun by the Greek trader.[1]

Colonisation tended to do away with its main cause, food shortage. The settlements in Sicily and on the north shore of the Euxine did much to solve the difficulty at home by rendering the acquisition of foreign corn far more easy than it had been before; and the great economic question of Greek life took a new form in which the main problems were the creation and maintenance of circumstances in Greece itself which would enable the Greek to pay for the foreign supply, and the keeping open of those routes which led to the sources of supply, especially the route to the Euxine through the Hellespont and Bosphorus. The Hellene in Greece gradually evolved an economic condition of things under which he was enabled under normal circumstances to purchase abroad that which would make up for the deficiency in his own land. This purchasing power was provided in the case of some states by the promotion of manufactures and the export of manufactured goods, and probably in the case of nearly all by extending the growth of the vine and the olive, the products of which would always find a ready and profitable market in a Mediterranean world where their cultivation was much more limited than at the present day. To these sources of profit must also be added that derived from general trade.

The foundation of the colonies must have resulted in an enormous increase in the sea-borne trade of the Hellenic world, a trade the profits of which would accrue largely to the maritime states of Greece proper, thus placing them in a very favourable position with regard to the purchase of food from abroad. But the non-maritime states could not fail to derive advantage from the fact that food supplies were brought to their very doors. A clue as to their position is afforded by a passage which Thucydides inserts in the reported speech of the Corinthians at Sparta in the spring before the Peloponnesian War.

"The states more inland and out of the highway of communication should understand that if they omit to support the coast powers the result will be to injure the transit of their produce for exportation, and the reception in exchange of their imports from the sea."[2]

Whether these words were actually spoken by the Corinthians is a matter which does not affect their validity as evidence on the economic question. They state a consideration which could

---

[1] See the passage on Egypt later in this chapter.
[2] Thuc. i, 120.

not have occurred a priori to Thucydides or any other writer of the fifth century. They are founded on the experience of the past.

The Greek system of colonisation was marked by a feature which is not found in the colonial enterprises of other races ancient or modern. The typical Greek colony, immediately after it was founded, started on a career of political independence of the mother country in so far as all the essentials of self-administration are concerned. The absence of means of communication rendered it impossible for a mother city to exercise governmental control over a distant colony. This would have meant too the exclusion of the population of the new foundation from the exercise of political rights of which the Greek was jealous even before the days of complete democracy. But it was bound to the mother country by a tie which had great significance among the peoples of the ancient world, the obligation to acknowledge its attachment to the gods of the state from which it originated by the despatch of an annual mission with offerings. The idea of "one god, one state" was so fundamental in the life of the ancients that it is possible perhaps to exaggerate the measure of separation between a colony and its metropolis which seems to be implied in an independent political administration, and to regard the religious tie as a mere rather than as a practical sentiment. The tie of official worship was a strong political bond in ancient life.

Within two areas of the Mediterranean, Sicily and South Italy on the one hand, and the Euxine on the other, were concentrated the majority of the Greek colonies. These together with Egypt were the grain regions of the then world. Egypt, a monarchy of fluctuating power, but always powerful enough to confine Greek enterprise within its borders to certain definite limits, offered the Greek a field for trade but not for colonisation. The great grain region of northern Syria might have had its attractions, had not the drastic policy of the Assyrian Semite made any enterprise there impossible. In the west Mediterranean the determination of the Phœnicians to keep that sea closed to all save their own trade, together with the piratical enterprises of the Etruscans, discouraged attempts at Greek settlement save on the part of those Phocæans who settled at Massilia and in its neighbourhood at a period when the more eligible sites had been taken up by earlier Greek colonies. The Adriatic was to the Greek of these centuries a cul-de-sac which led nowhere save to the amber route across Europe. He colonised Hatria at the mouth of the Padus for the purpose of that trade [1]; but

---

[1] The geographer Kiepert denies that this was a Greek colony. It was certainly an Etruscan town in later days, as he says. But there is a tradition that it was a Greek colony in earlier times.

the colony seems to have died away to nothing at an early period ; and, for the rest, there were no other gains of any importance to be made along the Adriatic shores. It is true that at a much later period, in the third century before Christ, Corcyra pushed forward her colonies along the lands which border the Dalmatian coast ; but that was probably with intent to secure a share of that trade which Roman enterprise had opened along the Savus River with the middle Danubian region and the Dacian Kingdom.

With the age of colonisation begins the first period of Greek history in which the chronological matter is trustworthy. It would be natural for the new foundations to keep a strict record of their annual magistrates ; and from these lists the date of the foundation of the colony could be calculated. Miletus, greatest of the Greek trading cities of the time, was the leader in colonisation. There was a natural tendency for the states most active in colonising enterprise to concentrate their activities in certain regions which, to use the language of modern politics, they regarded as spheres of influence. The sphere of Miletus was the Euxine ; while its trade rival, Megara, concentrated her efforts on the Propontis, the antechamber of the greater sea. Of the Milesian colonies Sinopé and its offshoot Trapezus have their own place in subsequent records ; but of greater importance to the Greek world were those towns on the dreary north coast, of which the Greek trader must have known so much and the Greek historian knew so little. They stood between the Greek world and starvation ; and their inhabitants amassed great wealth as the middlemen between the half-civilised corn-growers of the plains of south Russia and the Greeks at home.[1] It is to archæological research in south Russia rather than to the written records of history that whatever survives of the story of these towns is due, for, important as was the practical part which they played in Greek life, they contributed but little to those sides of it which interested the Greek historian. Their world was to the average Greek a dim inhospitable country with an execrable climate of extremes such as deterred all save the traders who had business with them from visiting their coasts. And thus they lived for centuries, far on into the period of the Roman principate, a life in which long periods of prosperity were chequered by brief periods of adversity, a backwater of Greek life hardly ruffled by the storms which disturbed the main stream. With Cimmerian, with Scyth and with Sarmatian in turn they established friendly relations, not perhaps without some disastrous preliminary misunderstanding with new-comers to the region, which, when it had passed, left them free to develop

[1] For the history of the Greek settlements on the coast of south Russia, see Rostovtzeff, " Iranians and Greeks in South Russia."

from the gold with which their barbarian neighbours entrusted them goldsmith's work the like of which the world has never seen.

Chalcis and Eretria were at the height of their greatness in Greek trade. Of the two the former played the greater part in colonisation. On the three-fingered peninsula of the Macedonian coast of the Ægean it founded a series of cities whose very number makes it difficult to determine their *raison d'être*. The three fingers are not very rich land, indeed Athos is a precipitous waste ; but it was probably the timber and general trade of Macedonia which attracted the settlers.

On the south coast of Italy the Achæan colonies are of peculiar interest because they were not sent out by a state which, so far as is known, was in any way prominent in Greek trade. The district of Achæa, which forms the northern fringe of the Peloponnese, was for the most part extraordinarily poor, for its cultivable area was confined to a narrow strip of low land on the shores of the Gulf of Corinth, the breadth of which is seldom more than a few furlongs, at the foot of the rugged northern ridges of Cyllene and Erymanthus. It was the food question which drove the Achæan abroad. To the south of him the Arcadian on the other side of the great range inhabited a land where it was difficult to win a livelihood from the soil, save in the great central plain which was taken up by the territories of Orchomenos, Mantinea and Tegea. Hence the Arcadians were participators in many a colony sent forth by other states, and had in the past sent out to Cyprus from their own land one of the earliest Greek colonies of which there is any record.

These Achæans of Peloponnese had, it would seem, been refugees from Achæa Phthiotis in Thessaly at the time of one of the successive invasions from the north ; and had, as it is conjectured, been accompanied in their migrations by that tribe called Hellenés which were their neighbours in Homeric times.[1] In the earlier period of this new joint settlement this northern territory of Peloponnese was known as Hellas, and those colonists who founded the cities on the south Italian coast were known as Hellenés rather than Achæans. But as these colonies, especially Sybaris, developed rapidly into some of the greatest and most prosperous towns in the Greek world of that day, the region in which they had been planted came to be known as Great Hellas (Magna Græcia), by comparison with

---

[1] For a full statement of the theory briefly touched on here, see an article by Prof. Bury in the " Journal of Hellenic Studies." It seems to the present writer by far the most probable theory which has been put forward in ancient or modern times as to the way in which the name Hellenés came to be applied to the whole Greek race.

the small and insignificant cities of their motherland. The name itself implies a comparison with a smaller Hellas, which precludes the possibility of any contrast with the whole of the Greek world at home. Owing possibly to the early prominence of these Achæan colonies in Greek trade, the national name of their inhabitants came to be used by the south Italians as a name for all Greeks alike; and from Italy it spread over the whole Greek world.[1] This Achæan colonisation affords evidence that the food supply at home was the cause of settlement abroad. The other Greek states prominent in colonisation are the great commercial states of the period; and so Achæa seems to play an exceptional part in the movement. But it is easy to misinterpret the nature of the exception by regarding the colonising activity of Achæa as due to over-population, and that of the commercial states as due to a desire to widen and solidify their trade connections, for Miletus had certainly trade connections with the Euxine before ever she became a colonising power, and states like Corinth and Chalcis had trade connections with Sicily and the West before ever they planted a colony there. In truth the exceptional feature in the Achæan colonisation is that, though the state was not great in commerce, it carried through its new settlements overseas off its own hand, whereas other non-commercial states of Greece which suffered from over-population contributed to colonies which the commercial states sent out. That was a natural course for them to adopt, for these states had the means in the form of ships, and the experience, in the form of knowledge of the regions outside Greece. But if the list of the commercial states of the Greece of this period be marked, it will be noticed that those regions which had the largest share of fertile territory, such as Thessaly, Bœotia, Ætolia, Elis, Lakonia, and Messenia are conspicuous by their absence from it; and these states play but a small, and in some cases, an untraceable part in the colonising activity of the period. Growth of commerce in a land not merely attracts to it population from outside, but promotes the increase of the indigenous population. It is not strange therefore that the commercial states of Greece should have been peculiarly affected by the question of the support of their population, all the more so as their territories were, if fertile, very small, and in one case, that of Megara, notoriously unproductive.

[1] The origin of Græci, the Roman name for the Greeks, is far more astonishing. The Graii were a small tribe occupying a territory in the Oropus district of Bœotia not much larger than an English parish. They were sharers in the foundation of Kymé on the Gulf of Naples, the first Greek community which the Romans came to know. Hearing the name Graii first there, the Romans came to use it for the whole Greek race, converting it into Græci in order to avoid the hiatus in the Greek name.

Taras, later Tarentum, was exceptional on the south Italian coast, as being a Dorian colony. In the first period of settlement it was outshone by the Achæan colonies, especially Sybaris and Croton; but when they passed away into the darkness of destruction or the twilight of decline, it stood out as far the greatest of the Greek settlements in Italy, and did more than any of them to spread a modified Greek culture in the south of the Italian peninsula, and to influence eventually the growing civilisation of Rome itself. Sybaris had a brief period of splendour, marked by wealth and luxury so great that it added a word to the proverbial vocabulary of even the modern world. This was due to its peculiarly favourable position for trade as being at the east end of an easy and short land passage to the western or Tyrrhenian Sea, affording to that Milesian trade confederacy to which Sybaris belonged a route to western Italy alternative to that through the Sicilian strait which was commanded by towns attached to the rival trade confederacy of Samos.

In Sicily and the toe of Italy the colonies were of more miscellaneous origin. Here the people of Chalcis established a second sphere of influence more important than that on the Macedonian coast. In the short space of twenty years, between 735 B.C. and 715 B.C., they founded four towns, of which two were destined to play a great part in Sicilian history—Naxos, Catané, Leontini, and Zanclé, the later Messana. Of these the last commanded the Sicilian Strait on the west, and its inhabitants persuaded Chalcis to occupy Rhegion on the east side of the strait, and so secure the control of that important sea passage for that Samian trade confederacy of which Chalcis was so important a member. It was there in north-east Sicily that Chalcidian interests prevailed. But probably in the case of all these colonies the settlement, though officially Chalcidian, was composed of settlers drawn also from various states on friendly terms with Chalcis. Naxos, for instance, was named after a Naxian band which joined the Chalcidians in its foundation.

In the south-east of the island Dorian settlements sprang up. Corinth's trade interest in Sicily may have been, probably was, of older date than the foundation of Syracuse in 734. Here she had to drive out previous Chalcidian settlers, just as in the same year, if tradition be true, she drove out Eretrian settlers in order to found a colony of her own in Corcyra, the key position on the route to Sicily. Corinth's position on the isthmus rendered her the natural entrepôt of trade between Sicily, Italy, and the Asiatic mainland; but it was probably her trade partners in the east who carried the goods to her across the Ægean, while she forwarded them westward in her own vessels, and also carried goods from the west to hand over to her Asiatic allies at Corinth. This western trade was the very blood of life to the great commercial city, and fiercely did she resent any serious competition in this her special sphere of trade influence, a resentment which was destined to bring many woes to Greece in the fifth century. Dorian Megara founded Megara Hyblæa on the coast just north of Syracuse. Rhodes founded Gela ; and Syracuse threw out colonial offshoots at Acræ, Casmenæ, and Camarina. Gela threw off later the colony of Acragas which was destined in later Sicilian history to be second only to Syracuse in wealth and importance. On the west coast of Italy Sybaris had established small offshoots at the other end of that easy overland route to the western sea of which she herself commanded the eastern extremity. But further north in the Bay of Naples was a Greek colony Cymé which later tradition reputed to be the oldest Greek colony in the west ; a joint foundation of Chalcis, Eretria and Cymé (in Eubœa) to which the Graii of Oropus contributed a small quota and a name which has become great in history.[1] Further north up the west Italian coast the Greeks could not penetrate by reason of the jealous and piratical power of Etruria.

The great enterprise of the Phocæans in the western Mediterranean belongs really to the seventh century ; but its story may be conveniently included in the history of the great centuries of Greek colonisation. The fact that they chose Massilia, a site designed by nature to be a great trading centre, as their place of settlement, shows that before its foundation in 600 B.C. the Greek trader had become acquainted with this out-of-the-way corner of the Mediterranean, and its possibilities for trade with the hinterland. From Massilia the Phocæans expanded east and west, founding minor settlements along the coast of the Riviera, and pushing westwards beyond the shores of Gaul to the east coast of Spain. But there their success was apparently of brief duration ; for at no long period after the foundation of these factories the Greek venturers on the Spanish shore were expelled by the ever-jealous Phœnicians advancing from the south. Of all the colonial foundations of the Greeks that of the Phocæans of Massilia was destined to attain to the greatest territorial power, and to have the longest life as an independent community. For almost exactly five and a half centuries Massilia was the dominant power in south-east Gaul. By the time when Gaul had become of interest to the Romans it had acquired a dominion extending from the Rhône to the Alps, and stretching for a considerable distance north from the Mediterranean coast. It was an independent and honoured ally of Rome for several centuries, until Julius Cæsar punished

[1] See page. 65, n. 1.

it for its hostility to him in the time of the civil war by depriving it of much of its territory, and rendering it little more than a provincial town of the empire. But for these five and a half centuries it had braved those Celtic storms which on two occasions had well-nigh brought Rome itself to destruction. Various stories of the Phocæans show that they had in their veins that wild blood which often makes men inconvenient to their more pacific contemporaries, but a blessing to the after-generations of their race.

Finally towards the close of the seventh century certain folk from the island of Thera, joined and jostled later by immigrants from southern Peloponnese, settled on the north African coast in a small but fertile patch of that otherwise mitigated desert known as Cyrene. Here they set up a kingdom which dragged out quite a long existence. Here, too, they bred horses, and cultivated that mysterious silphium plant which ardent guessers conjecture to have conferred on ancient the same blessings that castor oil does on modern civilisation. It seems to have been more popular than its supposed modern representative, for the trade was certainly very lucrative.

In the later half of the seventh century the tyrant of Corinth, Cypselus, developed a new idea of colonisation on lines corresponding to those which have prevailed in the modern world. He conceived of a colonial empire of Corinth in which the colonies should not be independent communities of the normal Greek type, but dependencies of the mother country which might serve as trading centres and factories for the promotion of Corinthian trade. With that end in view he subdued Corcyra, which, though a colony of Corinth, had formed a fleet of its own, and was probably competing with the mother country in the western trade ; and his son Periander, who succeeded him in 625, seems to have been responsible for the foundation of a whole series of settlements on the trade route to the west, Chalcis and Molycria on the coast of the Corinthian Gulf, Sollium, Astacus, Anactorium and the island of Leucas on the coast of Acarnania, together with Ambrakia, Epidamnus, and Apollonia farther north. Later Potidæa in the peninsula of Chalcidicé was founded on much the same principle. The commercial expansion of Corinth at this time was no doubt partly responsible for, and eventually promoted by, the decline in the last years of the seventh century of Chalcis and Eretria, those two ancient trading states, a decline which they themselves promoted by engaging in that disastrous Lelantian War which involved so many of the states of the two rival trade confederacies of the day.

After two centuries of vigorous expansion the colonising activity of the Greeks dies a sudden death about the beginning

THE EIGHTH AND SEVENTH CENTURIES 69

of the seventh century, never to be revived in its original form, for the cleruchies and rare colonies of Athens in the fifth century belong to a different phase of political and economic development.

The cessation of this activity, though it seems surprisingly sudden, is comprehensible. Greece had solved half the question of over-population and foreign food supply. The other half had to be solved by different means, by maintaining control of the avenues to the great food regions of the world, and by producing at home in Greece the means whereby the products of these regions could be purchased. And this she succeeded in doing for several centuries.

That colonial expansion was of almost incalculable influence on the mental outlook of the Greek race is beyond question; but its first-hand effects must have been confined at home to the populations of those states which definitely participated in it, and have been but of second-hand influence on the remoter populations of the agricultural states. But Greece ceased to be the world for the Greek. The foundations of his later cosmopolitanism had been laid.

Constitutional Changes in Greece

During these two centuries, while the Greek was so active abroad, great changes were taking place in the political institutions of many of the states in the country. The earliest stages in the struggle for liberty had begun, though the changes which they brought about had but little influence on the liberties of the mass of the people; yet they are steps in the ladder which the Greek had to climb ere he reached full political freedom.

There is a curious similarity between the successive stages by which this freedom was attained not merely in the states of Greece, but also at Rome. The general course is the same everywhere, though the details may differ, and though the process of change may be much more rapid in some states than in others, and though the changes themselves were more violent in Greece than at Rome. But so similar are the courses of political evolution everywhere that it might almost be suspected that men are acting from impulses instinctive in human nature. The early struggles are between the upper classes and monarchy. The struggle is the same, but the result is not quite the same everywhere, though in the majority of cases the nobility comes out victorious, and monarchy is succeeded by an aristocracy, a patrician aristocracy in Greece as well as in Rome. In some of the states of Greece this aristocracy is at first limited to members of the royal house; whilst in others the quasi-feudal nobility, which had existed side by side with the king even in

Homeric days, usurp the prerogatives of the monarchy.[1] But even in Greece, in cases in which the new rulers were members of the royal house, their rule was brief, and the nobility soon won their share in the government. The term "republic" applied to the constitution of Rome which succeeded the kingship tends to disguise the fact that the government of republican Rome was for many years a very close aristocracy.

In Greece Thessaly never progressed beyond this stage so long as it was an independent state; and the Aleuadæ of Larissa, the Scopadæ of Crannon, and the Creondæ of Pharsalus are in the fifth and fourth centuries feudal families playing a part which the nobility in the other states of Greece had ceased to play some centuries before.

The question has often been raised as to whether the ancient monarchies of Greece originated in headship of a clan or leadership in war. The clan system continued to exercise great influence on Greek life for ages after the kingship had been abolished in most of the states, and therefore it is improbable that these monarchies of the early Greek world rested upon it. The early kings of Greece seem to have been kings *qua* leaders in war, especially at the restless period of the invasions from the north. When the effects of this settlement and unsettlement had passed away, the kingship passes away in most parts of Greece, and, though dates are not known, there cannot be much doubt that the majority of the monarchies came to an end either before or just after the two centuries at present under consideration opened. Later history shows that the clan was rather the support of the nobility than of the kingship, the upholder of those families which stood foremost in it; for Cleisthenes in Attica in 509 shows by his deliberate policy of breaking up the clan that he is aiming at the overthrow of an aristocratic family influence such as the legislation of Solon eighty years before

---

[1] The monarchy of the Melanthidæ at Athens was limited to a ten years' presidency in 752. But Athens was probably till the time of Solon somewhat backward among the Greek states in respect to political evolution.

It should be stated that the movement is going on in the Greek cities of Asia at the same time as in those of Europe. At Ephesus, Cymé, and Lesbos aristocracy takes the place of monarchy. In Corinth on the other hand the monarchic rule of the Bacchiadæ is replaced by an aristocracy confined to that family. In Mytilene and Erythræ, the change from monarchy to aristocracy takes the same form. In the Peloponnesian states, Argos, Messenia and Sparta, the monarchy maintained itself till a much later date,—in the case of Sparta practically till the end of that state's existence. But in all these cases it was in a very modified form.

(The subject of Greek Constitutional History is somewhat dry. The best account of it in English is in A. H. Greenidge's "Handbook of Greek Constitutional History," Macmillan, 1896.)

had not broken—an influence which, so long as it existed, made complete democracy impossible.

Of the rule of these aristocracies in the Greek world very little is known except the unanimous tradition of a later democratic age that it was oppressive to the lower classes. The tradition may contain a large element of truth; but, whether true or not, it was one which was certain to prevail in that later age which loathed aristocratic government, and called it oligarchy. Many of these aristocracies were in existence in the earlier period of Greek colonisation; and it is to the discontent of the lower classes with their rule that later ages ascribed the impetus which led to the sending out of colonies. But the emigrants were probably far more the victims of circumstances than of their fellow-men, for, apart from over-population, which neither the aristocrat nor anyone else could remedy within the limited area of the home state, the fact that the extremely restricted area of cultivable land was taken up created a landless class whose condition in an age when the crafts were but partly developed, and professions non-existent, must have been nearly desperate. But colonisation, while tending to cure the disease of the state, infected it with another. It increased the number and accessibility of foreign markets to such an extent that a commercial class far richer than any of the pre-colonising period sprang into existence in the trading states of Greece, a class which began to rival the nobility in wealth, and so came to resent all the more bitterly a political and social inferiority to the old aristocracy of birth.

A form of aristocracy sprang up in many of those colonial settlements of Greece which had been founded, so the democratic tradition of a later age said, by those who had sought refuge from aristocratic oppression. It arose from the procedure followed on the first settlement of a colony on its destined site. The land available for cultivation was divided into allotments ($\varkappa\lambda\tilde{\eta}\varrho οι$) which were distributed among the settlers; and, naturally enough, none remained undistributed. Hence when the population of the colony increased, and above all when circumstances introduced new settlers, a landless class arose in those very communities which had been formed to solve the same difficulty in Greece at home. The descendants of the original allotment-holders became the aristocrats of the colony, and kept jealous hold on its government. The oppressed became the oppressors. It is the old tale of opportunism in human affairs. Every man would rule the world his own way, if he could; and so every man is a would-be monarch, or, failing that, a would-be oligarch, or failing that, a convinced democrat. But these colonial aristocracies came into being far later than those of the older communities of Greece and the Asiatic coast ; and the tale of their overthrow is a tale of two centuries later.

The movement against aristocracy did not originate with the same class in all states alike. In those prominent in trade, of which Corinth was the type, it came from that class of traders which had so increased in numbers and wealth by reason of that trade expansion which colonial enterprise had brought about. In a few states, such as Sicyon, it was a movement of that Ionian population which had been brought into subjection by the Dorian invaders. In others it was a rising of the proletariat against the nobles. But all these classes recognised or came to recognise that revolutions against powerful vested interests cannot be carried through by committees, but must be accomplished under the leadership of some individual who can combine the conflicting interests of the individual revolutionaries into united action. In this early Greek revolution, as in other revolutions, such leaders were apt to find themselves virtual sole rulers of the state, a position which they took measures to stereotype in the form of tyranny or perpetual dictatorship. Hence rose that much abused personage the Greek tyrant. In Rome this stage in the evolution towards political liberty never eventuated ; though the possibility of its so doing was ever in the Roman mind during the period when the Roman proletariat was striving to free itself from the control of a narrow oligarchy.

But though the overthrow of monarchy is the first step in the path to popular liberty, the overthrow of aristocracy is not the second. The second step seems to have been taken while aristocracy was still in existence. It is the struggle of the proletariat for civil liberty. Both in Greece and Rome a certain advance towards such liberty had been made before the fall of aristocracy, and both in Greece and in Rome that fall was largely due to the fact that the people generally came to realise that the civil liberty already won was liable to be abused by the powers in being, and also could never be advanced to a satisfactory stage, unless the mass of the people won a political liberty such as would guarantee the civil liberty already acquired, and make the acquisition of full civil liberty a possibility. Such political liberty could only take the form of democracy. In the history of Rome the process stands out more clearly than in that of Greece. The struggle between the orders, the Patricians and Plebeians, is in its earlier phase a struggle for civil liberty, for the protection of the person of the commoner against the arbitrary power of the aristocratic magistrate. But when that is over, the lower classes find that arbitrary interpretation or evasion of the law is still possible for the patrician magistrate ; and so the second phase of the struggle is for a political liberty which will secure that the rights of civil liberty already acquired shall not be violated ; and that can only be attained if the mass of the people have ultimate control of the government, which means that an aristocracy must be converted into a democracy. With the establishment of a democracy the struggle between the orders comes to an end at Rome. In the case of some of the states of Greece the two phases in the struggle do not stand out so clearly ; but that is probably due to much of the evidence having perished. In Athenian history, however, where the two steps in the evolution came later than in some of the Greek states, the two steps in the process stand out clearly in the records.

The first phase, the struggle for civil liberty, takes the form of an agitation for the publication of law in a written form. The conditions under which early law existed in Greece and Rome are difficult of realisation in a world where knowledge of the law is at any rate accessible to all citizens. In the monarchical state the administration of the law had been in the main in the hands of the king ; though there is faint evidence of a jurisdiction of some sort exercised by the nobility. But neither king nor noble was bound by any code, because there was no code to bind them. Their decisions were given on any principles they chose to adopt, though no doubt a certain tradition of custom sprang up even in this early period. But there is no reason to suppose that the custom became so established as to be binding on the judicial authority of king or noble ; so that their decisions might be of the most arbitrary kind. With the abolition of the kingship, the royal functions passed undiminished into the hands of the magistrates of the aristocracies, and the judicial functions were exercised with the same arbitrariness as before. In criminal matters the common people knew neither the frontiers nor the penalties of crime. They were at the discretion of the judge. In civil jurisdiction, in Rome at any rate, the noble lawyers invented formulæ which they only knew, and which had to be copied verbatim in any legal transaction, such as one recording the sale of land, which was to have validity. This was, it need hardly be said, lucrative to the few holders of the secret, but expensive to the uninitiated mass of the population. Of the various agitations in various Greek states which overthrew this pernicious system little is known ; but they resulted in the publication of codes of law drawn up in many cases by individuals to whom the commission was given. In Rome the result was the publication of the Twelve Tables. These codes contained matters of the most miscellaneous character, religious, moral, and legal ; they were in fact in most instances a kind of recitation of the ancestral customs of the community, rather than a table of laws in the modern sense. The Athenian code is that of Draco, which was promulgated in 621 B.C. Parts of it which can be pieced together from references in later authors show a system of punishment of such severity that Draco's name became a byword with the Athenians of after-time, a probable injustice to him, as he can have done no more than reveal the principles, such as they were, and the practice of the secret criminal law and procedure of the previous period.[1] So the proletariat won, or thought it had won, its civil liberty. But disillusionment was to follow. Detailed facts with regard to the sequel are not known, for they are probably concerned with obscure acts of injustice to obscure individuals, soon forgotten as individual incidents, but bitterly remembered as part of a policy of oppression. The written code could not control the actions of an aristocratic judge whom an aristocratic government would rather sympathise with than punish for violations of a code which it disliked. That taught the people that civil could only be guaranteed by political liberty; and so Greece killed aristocracy, while Rome clipped its wings in drastic fashion by a series of measures which threw open the highest offices of the state to the hitherto unprivileged class. Thus in Greece aristocracy was succeeded by tyranny.

Greek Tyrants

To the Greek of the fifth century the tyrant was anathema. Herodotus, who seems to have had a painful experience of tyrants in his old home at Halicarnassus, does not fail to reproduce the worst that was said of them by his contemporaries. But, when all the evil and all the good they did are weighed against one another in the scale of judgment, the balance is not much, if at all, on the side of the evil. Later democracy owed more to them than it knew, or would have wished to know. They gave to colonisation an energy and direction which it would never have had under the mere impetus of political and economic difficulties. Representing as they did in most of the trading states that mercantile class which they had led in the attack on the old aristocracy, they promoted everything which could benefit the trade of the states. Their tyranny, using the word in the modern sense, was confined to severity against those whose position

[1] Of the Draconian code as given in the Polity of Athens ('Ἀθηναίων Πολιτεία) attributed to Aristotle I may say that I do not believe in it. It makes the code appear milder and more liberal than it is represented as having been by any other ancient authority. Of the general value of the treatise I will speak later in reference to fifth-century history; but this I may say now,—that its evidence is suspect whenever it varies from other ancient authorities in the direction of representing the policy and actions of conservative statesmen at Athens as having been more liberal than popular tradition represented them to have been.

A SELECTION FROM
Messrs. Methuen's New Books
Spring, 1929

A complete list will be sent to any applicant

BIOGRAPHY, MEMOIRS AND HISTORY

GERMAN DIPLOMATIC DOCUMENTS, 1871-1914. Selected and translated from the Documents published by the German Foreign Office, by E. T. S. DUGDALE. With an Introduction by J. W. HEADLAM-MORLEY, C.B.E., Historical Adviser to the Foreign Office. In Four Volumes. Volume II: 'From Bismarck's Fall to 1898'. 25s. net.

A HISTORY OF ENGLAND FROM THE EARLIEST TIMES TO THE BEGINNING OF THE PRESENT CENTURY. By HILAIRE BELLOC. In Five Volumes. Volume IV: 1525-1688. With Maps. 15s. net.

JEWISH LIFE IN MODERN TIMES. By ISRAEL COHEN. With Illustrations. A New and Revised Edition. 10s. 6d. net.

THE DEVELOPMENT OF THE BRITISH EMPIRE SINCE 1783. By PROFESSOR A. P. NEWTON, University of London, King's College, and PROFESSOR J. EWING, Rhodes University College, Grahamstown, South Africa. Illustrated. 5s.

A HISTORY OF THE MODERN CHURCH. By J. W. C. WAND, M.A., Fellow, Dean and Tutor of Oriel College, Oxford. 7s. 6d. net.

THE ANCIENT EXPLORERS. By M. CARY, D.Litt., and E. H. WARMINGTON, M.A., Readers in Ancient History in the University of London. 12s. 6d. net.

LOUIS XVI: The Last Phase. By GERALD A. TATE, Author of 'The Captivity and Trial of Marie Antoinette'. Illustrated. 5s. net.

STUDIES IN THE NAPOLEONIC WARS. By SIR CHARLES W. C. OMAN, K.B.E., M.A., M.P., Chichele Professor of Modern History in the University of Oxford. With Diagrams. 8s. 6d. net.

GENERAL LITERATURE

LETTERS OF TOLSTOY AND HIS COUSIN COUNTESS ALEXANDRA TOLSTOY. Translated and Edited by L. V. ISLAVIN. 7s. 6d. net.

SOME ITALIAN SCENES AND FESTIVALS. By DR. THOMAS ASHBY. Illustrated. 6s. net.

SPAIN: A Companion to Spanish Studies. Edited by E. ALLISON PEERS, M.A., Professor of Spanish in the University of Liverpool. With Maps. 10s. 6d. net.

ENGLISH THOUGHT IN THE NINETEENTH CENTURY. By D. C. SOMERVELL, M.A., Author of 'A Short History of Our Religion'. 6s. net.

PORCELAIN PAGODAS AND PALACES OF JADE: Musings of an Old Collector. By A. E. GRANTHAM, Author of 'Hills of Blue'. Illustrated. 15s. net.

THE DUBLIN OF YESTERDAY. By PAGE L. DICKINSON. 6s. net.

A selection from Messrs. METHUEN'S NEW BOOKS—Spring, 1929

GENERAL LITERATURE—contd.

WILD-FOWLERS AND POACHERS: Fifty Years on the East Coast. By A. H. PATTERSON. Illustrated. 15s. net.

ALL SORTS OF PEOPLE. By GLADYS STOREY. Illustrated. 10s. 6d. net.

THE SILENT CITIES. A Book of British War Graves. By SIDNEY C. HURST. With 958 Illustrations and 32 Maps. 7s. 6d. net.

EAT AND BE HAPPY. By Dr. JOSIAH OLDFIELD, Author of 'Eat and Get Well' and 'Eat and Keep Young'. 3s. 6d. net.

EARLY PRAYERS. By JOHN OXENHAM and RODERIC DUNKERLEY, B.A., B.D., Ph.D. 2s. 6d. net.

THE GAMES OF CHILDREN. By HENRY BETT, M.A. 5s. net.

'THE BRITANNIA' AND HER CONTEMPORARIES. By B. HECKSTALL-SMITH, Part Author of 'The Complete Yachtsman'. Illustrated and with Plans. 10s. 6d. net.

CASTE IN INDIA. By EMILE SENART. Translated from the French by IVY CLEGG. 10s. 6d. net.

ESSAYS

ON GETTING THERE: and Other Essays. By RONALD A. KNOX. 5s. net.

OLD FRIENDS IN FICTION. By ROBERT LYND ('Y.Y.'). 5s. net.

NOW ON VIEW. By IVOR BROWN. 5s. net.

THE MUSICAL GLASSES: and Other Essays. By GERALD GOULD. 5s. net.

PLAYS

TOAD OF TOAD HALL: A Play based on Kenneth Grahame's 'The Wind in the Willows'. By A. A. MILNE. 5s. net.

HUMOUR

MR. PUNCH ON THE LINKS. Edited by 'EVOE' (E. V. Knox). Illustrated. 6s. net.

ILLUSTRATED BOOKS AND BOOKS OF ART

VERMEER THE MAGICAL. By E. V. LUCAS. Illustrated. 5s. net.

MUSULMAN PAINTING. By E. BLOCHET. Translated from the French by CICELY M. BINYON. With an Introduction by SIR E. DENISON ROSS, C.I.E. Illustrated. (*The Connoisseur's Library*) £3 3s. net.

THE ARMOURY OF THE CASTLE OF CHURBURG. By OSWALD GRAF TRAPP. Translated with a Preface by J. G. MANN, B.A., B.Litt., F.S.A. Illustrated. £4 14s. 6d. net.
This edition is limited to 400 copies.
Also an edition on Hand-made Paper, limited to 10 copies at £8 8s. net.
Also an edition in German, limited to 400 copies, in the same size and with the same Plates, 95 Reichs Mark.

WATCHES. By G. H. BAILLIE. Illustrated. (*The Connoisseur's Library*) £3 3s. net.

A selection from Messrs. METHUEN'S NEW BOOKS—Spring, 1929

ILLUSTRATED BOOKS AND BOOKS OF ART—contd.

WATCH AND CLOCK MAKERS. By G. H. BAILLIE. (*The Connoisseur's Library*) £2 2s. net.

JAPANESE GARDENS. By Mrs. BASIL TAYLOUR (Harriet Osgood). Illustrated in colour by WALTER TYNDALE, R.I. New Edition. With a new Preface. £1 5s. net.

SPORT

FISHING WAYS AND WILES. By Major H. E. MORRITT. With an Introduction by LORD HOWARD DE WALDEN. Illustrated. 6s. net.

THE TALE OF A WYE FISHERMAN. By Captain H. A. GILBERT. Illustrated. 6s. net.

TOPOGRAPHY AND TRAVEL

IN SEARCH OF SCOTLAND. By H. V. MORTON. Illustrated. 7s. 6d. net.

THE NORFOLK BROADS. By W. A. DUTT. Fourth Edition. Illustrated. 21s. net.

CATHEDRALS OF FRANCE. By HELEN W. HENDERSON. Illustrated. 7s. 6d. net.

SO YOU'RE GOING TO ITALY! And to Switzerland and the Tyrol! By CLARA E. LAUGHLIN. New and Revised Edition. Illustrated. 10s. 6d. net.

WHERE IT ALL COMES TRUE IN ITALY AND SWITZERLAND. By CLARA E. LAUGHLIN. Illustrated. 7s. 6d. net.

ROME AND HER TREASURES. By Mrs. ARTHUR STRONG and Dr. GILBERT BAGNANI. Illustrated. 7s. 6d. net.

A CANADIAN PANORAMA. By YVONNE FITZROY, Author of 'Courts and Camps in India'. Illustrated. 10s. 6d. net.

TEN THOUSAND MILES THROUGH TWO CONTINENTS. By Mrs. PATRICK NESS. Illustrated. 12s. 6d. net.

THE FRINGE OF THE MOSLEM WORLD. By HARRY A. FRANCK, Author of 'East of Siam' and 'Roving Through Southern China'. Illustrated. 12s. 6d. net.

A WAYFARER IN THE PYRENEES. By E. I. ROBSON. Illustrated by J. R. E. HOWARD. 7s. 6d. net.

THE OLD-WORLD GERMANY OF TO-DAY. By GERALD MAXWELL. Illustrated. 7s. 6d. net.

ONE HUNDRED KILOMETRES ROUND FLORENCE. By M. MANSFIELD. 6s. net.

BRITTANY. By S. BARING-GOULD. Illustrated. Sixth Edition, completely Revised by IVOR DANIEL. (*Little Guides*) 5s. net.

PHILOSOPHY, PSYCHOLOGY AND RELIGION

A MODERN THEORY OF ETHICS. By W. O. STAPLEDON. 8s. 6d. net.

PLATO: Timaeus and Critias. By A. E. TAYLOR, M.A., D.Litt., Litt.D., F.B.A., Professor of Moral Philosophy in the University of Edinburgh, Author of 'Plato, the Man and His Work'. 6s. net.

A selection from Messrs. METHUEN'S NEW BOOKS—Spring, 1929

PHILOSOPHY, PSYCHOLOGY AND RELIGION—contd.

ETHICAL PROBLEMS: An Introduction to Ethics for Hospital Nurses and Social Workers. By BEATRICE EDGELL, D.Litt., Ph.D., University Reader in Psychology at Bedford College, London, Author of 'Mental Life'. 5s. net.

MODERN MATERIALISM AND EMERGENT EVOLUTION. By WILLIAM McDOUGALL, M.B., F.R.S., Professor of Psychology in Harvard College, Formerly President of the Society for Psychical Research and of the Psychiatric Section of the Royal Society of Medicine. 7s. 6d. net.

STUDIES OF SAVAGES AND SEX. By A. E. CRAWLEY. Edited by THEODORE BESTERMAN. 10s. 6d. net.

LECTURES ON ETHICS. By IMMANUEL KANT. With an Introduction by DR. PAUL MENZER. Translated from the German by LOUIS INFIELD, B.A., O.B.E. 10s. 6d. net.

AN INTRODUCTION TO MODERN LOGIC. By L. SUSAN STEBBING, M.A., Reader in Philosophy at Bedford College, London. 10s. 6d. net.

ISLAM: Beliefs and Institutions. By FATHER H. LAMMENS, S.J. Translated from the French by SIR E. DENISON ROSS. 8s. 6d. net.

ARCHAEOLOGY

A SEASON'S WORK AT UR OF THE CHALDEES. By H. R. HALL, M.A., D.Litt., F.B.A., Keeper of Egyptian and Assyrian Antiquities in the British Museum. 15s. net.

GREEK AND ROMAN BRONZES. By WINIFRED LAMB. Illustrated. (*Handbooks of Archaeology*) 25s. net.

A HANDBOOK OF FIELD ARCHAEOLOGY. By R. E. MORTIMER WHEELER, M.C., D.Litt., F.S.A. Illustrated. (*Handbooks of Archaeology*) 12s. 6d. net.

SCIENCE AND TECHNOLOGY

THE TECHNICAL ARTS AND SCIENCES OF THE ANCIENTS. By ALBERT NEUBURGER. Translated by HENRY L. BROSE, M.A., D.Phil. Illustrated. 25s. net.

THE NAPPE THEORY IN THE ALPS. By PROFESSOR FRANZ HERITSCH. Translated from the German by P. H. BOSWELL, O.B.E., D.Sc., Professor of Geology in the University of Liverpool. With Maps and Diagrams. 12s. 6d. net. (*Geological Series*)

METHUEN & CO. LTD. 36 Essex Street, LONDON, W.C.2

and ambition were likely to disturb their rule ; but many a democracy has under like circumstances behaved with much greater cruelty to political opponents. Confiscation was not in the forefront of their political programme ; and those whom they deprived of their property were generally persons who under the circumstances of the time were asking for trouble. Moreover these confiscations were as a rule made in, and devoted to, the public interest. Their exactions in the form of taxation were as a rule moderate. They did, as was natural, acquire wealth greater than that of their contemporaries ; but in many cases they used it for the advancement of literature and art, of which they were patrons as enlightened as any that the democratic world of later days could show. Good, bad, or indifferent as they were morally, they had most of them the sense to know that their interest consisted in promoting the interest of those they ruled ; and a bad man may be a good ruler if he has that saving sense. For the Greek democracy they bridged the great gulf of revolution ; so that the Greek people passed in safety over the abyss which has been so fatal to peoples who have rushed into revolution guided by many minds rather than by one.

Culture

Short as were the reigns of the tyrants of this period, yet their rule and policy must, in combination with colonial enterprise, have produced a remarkable change not merely in the life but in the whole mental outlook of the lower classes of the Greek states. The Greek proletariat of the days of aristocracy lived an obscure and meagre life devoted to a bitter struggle for existence. It emerges in the sixth century as a class which is already on its way to make world history. It has passed through an education. It had long been trained in the school of adversity. But in this period, under the economic influence of the results of colonisation, it enters a school of comparative prosperity where the schoolmasters are the tyrants.

Bards had sung in the halls of the nobles in the age of aristocracy. The tradition of their work which has survived confines itself to a record of their activities in genealogy,[1] a dry and somewhat unpromising field for the poet. But doubtless the tale of his ancestry told in verse was pleasing to the early baron, especially when it was traced back to a god. On the insecure basis of these genealogical epics the early chroniclers of Greece founded their chronology. But the eighth century produced

[1] Cinæthon of Lacedæmon is mentioned as one of them by Pausanias (ii, 3 (7)). But there were many others whose works were used by the early chroniclers.

other epic poets who dealt with chapters from the old legends, and even with heroic stories of their own day.

The seventh century saw the birth of new styles in poetry, the iambic and the lyric, and the earliest exponents of these styles carried them to a perfection which was never excelled in after-ages. Archilochus of Paros, Alcman, who lived at Sparta, together with Sappho and Erinna of Lesbos are names which would add a glory to any century of a nation's life. For many successive ages of later Greek literature they were regarded as some of the brightest stars in the constellation of Greek poetry ;[1] and the modern world has confirmed the verdict by its admiration for the fragments which survive of their work, and by its sense that the loss of the remainder is irreparable in world literature.

But to the historian the most striking feature of this literary age is the contribution which Sparta—to the Athenians of the fifth century the philistine, illiterate Sparta—makes to it. Eumelus, the epic poet, Tyrtæus, Alcman, Thaletus the Cretan, were all either born there or resorted thither as to a place where their work would be appreciated. The fact belongs to the eighth and seventh centuries ; but the explanation to the sixth, in the course of the history of which it will be given.

Of the history of the period little is known except the records of colonisation. Athens, a state of late economic, and consequently of late political development, was rapidly overtaking the other states of Greece in that race whose goal was democracy. The life archonship which had succeeded the monarchy was reduced to a tenure of ten years about 752. In or about 683 the single decennial archon gave place to nine annual archons. Then in 621 came the code of Draco, followed in the next year

---

[1] Cf. Leonidas of Tarentum in the third century before Christ :

> Stop, for this grave Archilochus doth hold,
> The old Iambic poet, whose eternal fame
> Hath reached the lands of sunset and of dawn.
> Loved by the Muse and him in Delos born,
> The very soul of music he became ;
> And to the lyre the tale of love he told.

Cf. also Antipater of Thessalonica in the first century A.D. :

> Judge not of men by monumental stones ;
> This simple tomb contains great Alcman's bones,
> Leader supreme of pure Laconian song,
> Who now in death has joined the glorious throng
> Of Muses nine. But whether Lydian earth
> Or Lacedæmon gave the poet birth,
> Those two fair lands dispute with one another :
> —'Tis a wise poet, sure, who knows his mother.

The same appreciation of Sappho and Erinna is shown by Antipater of Sidon (first century B.C.) in verses in the Greek Anthology.

by the famous attempt of Cylon to establish himself as tyrant.

Argos is still a great power in Peloponnese, threatened indeed by Sparta, but strong enough to defeat her at Hysiæ in 669 and to wrest that much disputed frontier region of Cynuria from her.

But of far more sinister import in Spartan history of this age was her conquest of Messenia in a war which lasted from 743 to 724, a conquest which had to be maintained in a second Messenian war in which the Messenian national hero Aristomenes played a great part. From Pausanias' account of it it might be calculated to have begun in 685 ; but it is almost certain that this date is far too early. Messenia proved a heritage of woe to Sparta ; but that is part of the story of the sixth and following centuries.

ASIA MINOR

Asia Minor issues in these centuries from a period for which the sole sources are brief inscriptions relating to the Hittite dominions and the vaguest of vague Greek tradition into one in which the historian feels on firmer ground of evidence.

LYDIA

The history of Lydia is told by Herodotus in the first book of his history ; and many legends from the story of that kingdom are contained in other later Greek writers, for Lydia had attracted the attention and excited the imagination of the Greek as being the first of those oriental empires of which he came to know— empires the magnitude and splendour of which far exceeded anything which had come within his previous experience.[1]

While during these two centuries the Greek race had been passing through a comparatively peaceful period of construction and expansion Asia had passed through catastrophes of a terrible nature which brought about the fall of the great kingdom which had been dominant within its area for centuries past.

When these centuries open Phrygia is still the chief power in Asia Minor ; and it remained so till early in the seventh century, when the great invasions of the Cimmerians broke its hold on the peninsula and reduced it to comparative insignificance. On its ruins its neighbour Lydia rose to greatness. The Lydian succeeded to a large part of the heritage of his former masters.

Of the early history of this state the Greek had little to tell save the names of shadowy dynasties, legendary history adorned by folk-tales which had doubtless been for centuries past part of the current fiction of the bazaars of western Asia. Some of them were not always told of the Lydian kings ; but popular

[1] *See next page.*

78 A HISTORY OF THE GREEK AND ROMAN WORLD

fancy had a tendency to connect such stories with the founders of dynasties, and so Gyges the Lydian did not escape this tribute to his greatness.[1]

With Gyges, however, begins something like a historical era in the story of Lydia, for it was in his time that the first blow of

---

[1] For the convenience of those who may read the sketch of oriental history contained in this chapter the following scheme of dates, actual and approximate, may be useful for reference.

Assyria.	Media.	Persia.	Babylonia.	Lydia and Asia Minor.	Egypt.
	715. Deioces reigning. He and his people made captive by Assyria. 713. Assyrian campaign in Media.			Late in the eighth cent. dynasty of Heracleidæ.	715 ? Sabaco dies. Sethon succeeds.
708. Sargon in relation with the Greeks of Cyprus 705. Sennacherib king.				692. Line of Mermnadæ begins with Gyges. 690–680. Cimmerians overthrow Phrygia.	
668. Assurbanipal.				667. Cimmerian invasion. Lydian embassy to Assyria.	663–2. Assyrian invasion of Egypt and end of Ethiopian dynasty. 660. Psammetichus king. (Saïte dynasty.)
	655. Phraortes.			652. Ardys.	652. Psammetichus expels the Assyrian garrison.
647. Assurbanipal destroys Elam. 645. Defeat of Cimmerians by Assyrians at Mt. Taurus.	645–35. Media united under one king. 633. Assurbanipal invades Media. Death of Phraortes. Cyaxares king. 632–630 ? Scythian invasion.				
625. Death of Assurbanipal.			625. Nabopolassar sent to Babylon as viceroy.		632. Dorian settlement in Cyrene.
				620. Ardys seizes Priene. 615 ? Sadyattes. 610. Alyattes.	611. Necho II.
613. Babylonia and Media make war on Assyria. 612. End of Assyrian empire.					

the Cimmerian invasion fell on western Asia Minor, and by the destruction of the Phrygian power paved the way for the rise of Lydia to greatness. Not that Lydia escaped disaster; but in her case it was not fatal. It was over-run, and its capital Sardes, all save the citadel, was taken; but this inroad into Lydia seems to have been no more than a devastating raid.

The Cimmerians

Within the last few years the world has learnt more than it ever knew before of the Cimmerian people.[1] It was not merely a tribe of wild raiders from a wholly barbarous race; but a nation which had brought to the plains of south Russia a civilisation which was by no means in its infancy. It appeared in Russia about the second half of the eighth century as the first wave of a series of invasions by peoples who had attained to the Iron Age, and established a dominion over part of an aboriginal population which had developed the civilisation of the Copper and Bronze Age. It settled in the neighbourhood of the Sea of Azov and the Straits of Kertch, the Cimmerian Bosphorus of ancient geography, and mingled with the peoples which it had conquered. There it set up a kingdom with which the Greeks of Miletus established such friendly relations that it was possible for them to plant colonies on the Cimmerian coast, and to establish a corn trade from which they profited, and an import trade of Greek manufactures which the Cimmerians appreciated. The Scythian invasion of Russia must have followed hard on the heels of the Cimmerians, so that the latter found it necessary to consolidate their hold on the territory they had won by forming in alliance with the Greek settlers a stable kingdom known to later history as that of the Cimmerian Bosphorus. The Scythians settled in the Kuban region east of the Azov and north of the Caucasus; and it is possible that it was Cimmerians who had been extruded by them from some neighbouring region who made that raid on Asia Minor which kept that peninsula in ferment for a considerable number of years. Greek tradition implies that the Scyths were responsible for the Cimmerian movement. But from Assyrian records it is known that in the latter half of the eighth century these two races, apparently in combination, had made repeated attacks on Assyria from the north. These remained without result; and another possible explanation of the Cimmerian attack on Asia Minor is that it was made by Cimmerians who had failed in one of these attacks on Assyria. As to its date there is some doubt as to whether it took place early or late in the second half of the seventh century. But it opened what must have been a long period of agony for the Asia Minor penin-

[1] See Rostovtzeff, op. cit.

sula, for not until 645 or even later was the horde almost wiped out by the Assyrians in an attempt to pass southwards through the Taurus range. The remnant settled permanently in a part of Cappadocia which was always thereafter called Gimir by the Armenians. Apart from that fact history knows them no more, though it has much that is interesting to tell of their kinsmen who remained north of the Euxine.

Early in the invasion the Cimmerians had overwhelmed Phrygia and destroyed for ever the greatness of that monarchy. To that without doubt is due the rise of Lydia under Gyges, that Lydia which had hitherto been but a vassal kingdom of the great Phrygian state. But Lydia's time of suffering came; and in 667, as is known from the Assyrian monuments, she appealed in vain to Assyria for help against the Cimmerians. The appeal is not strange, for Lydia appears to have had a considerable trade with the Euphrates region.

It was Gyges who began the attacks on those Greek cities which held the natural outlets of the Lydian trade westwards. Yet Miletus helped him in his defence against the Cimmerians; and it was perhaps in return for that that he allowed the Milesians to found the colonies on the Hellespont and Propontis, Abydos, Lampsacus, and Cyzicus. They would also bar the way for any Thracians who might try to move southwards to aid their Cimmerian kinsmen, for the latter seem to have been of Thracian stock. Disappointed of Assyrian help Gyges turned to Egypt, with results which had more influence on that country than on his own. In 652 he perished in a grand attack made on Lydia by the Cimmerians in conjunction with the Lycians and other races of western Asia Minor. Then came the turn of the Greek cities of the coast. With the exception of Magnesia on the Mæander, which was destroyed, they seem to have been successful in resisting the attack; and not very long afterwards the Cimmerians turned east to meet their fate in the Taurus at the hands of Assyria.

Freed from the Cimmerian Lydia rose to greatness; but little is known of its history in the last part of the seventh century, save a somewhat wearisome series of attacks on the Greek cities of the coast, most of which appear to have led to no permanent result.

Assyria

Meanwhile beyond the Taurus was being acted a drama which was destined to end in the last years of the seventh century in one of the greatest catastrophes the world has ever known. The Assyrian empire was at the height of its power in these two centuries up to within a few years of the fall of Nineveh. But its history hardly touches Mediterranean civilisation. It is difficult to say whether the Semite in an imperial position showed more cruelty or more incapacity; but Asia was a chamber of horrors during the centuries of his rule. Surrounding peoples were conquered; but the yoke laid upon them was so cruel that they preferred to face death and torture rather than submit to it; and so Assyrian history as told on Assyrian monuments is one long recital of conquests, revolts, and reconquests. The Semitic Assyrian's interpretation of empire was the right to bleed white the territories and peoples which he brought under his control. There is no trace of any attempt to organise any enlightened system of imperial government, or to win over the conquered peoples to peaceful submission by a rational system of administration. To the contemporary Greek the land beyond the Taurus and behind the Syrian coast was all but a *terra incognita* while this empire lasted, a land of blood and peril from which he shrank. His ignorance of it is shown by the lack of knowledge displayed by Herodotus, probably the best informed Greek of his century, who cannot distinguish between Assyrian and Babylonian, and calls the latter by the name of the former. The only Greeks who are known to have had relations—it can hardly be called contact—with that empire are the Greeks of Cyprus, who, after spending what were probably some very happy and profitable years in piratical raids on the Cilician and Syrian coasts, discovered suddenly that they were up against a great and awful power which claimed dominion over their victims, and was likely, unless appeased, to take a terrible vengeance. So, as the Assyrian monuments tell, they abandoned their evil ways and made a submission recorded on a monument which still survives, a pillar of black marble with Sargon's head thereon, which was set up at Cition in 708.[1] The submission meant probably a payment of tribute and no more, for Assyria had no real power on the sea.

But the fall of Assyria was not without consequences which were destined to modify the whole of Greek history; and to understand the origin of those consequences it is necessary to understand the circumstances of the fall.

In 647 Assyria had for the first time attacked Elam, the region east of the Lower Euphrates in the south-west of modern Persia, and at the time when the attack fell the cradle of that Persian dynasty whose empire was destined eventually to supplant that of Assyria in west Asia. The attack was at first unsuccessful; but in the end Susa, the capital, was taken. Assyria was however exhausted by continual warfare, though

---

[1] It was discovered at Larnaca in Cyprus in recent times.

at this moment, only forty years before she fell, she appeared to be at the height of her power.

Then suddenly the records fail. There is some sudden catastrophe such as is not uncommon in oriental empires.

Even in the later period of her greatness Assyria had used the Scythians as allies against Armenia, and probably too against the Medes, who dwelt in the north part of the plateau of modern Persia. In the latter half of the seventh century the Median kingdom, a vassal state of Assyria, had revolted, and Assyria seems to have called in the aid of the Scyths against it. The latter defeated the Medes who had been attacking Nineveh itself in a siege which is referred to by the prophet Nahum.[1]

" Woe to the blood-stained city : it is full of lies and robbery, and the prey departeth not. The noise of a whip, and the noise of the rattling of the wheels, and of the prancing horses, and of the jumping chariots. The horseman lifteth up the bright sword and the glittering spear ; and there is a multitude of the slain, and a great number of carcases ; and there is no end of their corpses ; they stumble upon the corpses."

The events of this terrible time in Asia, which passed almost unnoticed, because almost unknown by the Greeks, were followed with a fierce delight by those inhabitants of Palestine who had suffered much, and feared more, from the Assyrians. But they were not fated to pass unscathed through the catastrophes of the following years.

Having defeated the Medes, the Scythians turned against their Assyrian allies, and, though Nineveh did not fall forthwith, yet for some twenty or more years these northern raiders devastated the Euphrates region and Syria, and penetrated even into Palestine. It must have been a period of hideous confusion. The Jews felt naught but joy at these attacks on Assyria :

" The strong among the mighty shall speak to him out of the midst of hell, with them that help him." . . . " Asshur is there and all his company ; his graves are about him ; all of them slain, fallen by the sword."[2]

Such was the funeral hymn which the Hebrew poet composed on the death of his ancient enemy.

But these rejoicings over a fallen foe were turned to panic when the terrible warriors of the north appeared in Palestine, from the walls of whose fenced cities the scared inhabitants watched the wild horsemen of the steppe over-running and devastating their land.[3] It is all described by Jeremiah in that

[1] iii, 2–7.

[2] Ezekiel xxxii, 26. This is part of that great passage in which Ezekiel sums up the history of the fall of the great oriental kingdoms of his day.

[3] For a description of the Scythian invasion in Palestine, see Jeremiah i, iv, v, vi. Cf. also Zephaniah i, 2–7, and 15–18.

passage [1] which is so well known because it is so magnificent :

"Wherefore a lion out of the forest shall slay them, and the wolf of the evening shall spoil them ; a leopard shall watch over their cities ; everyone that goeth forth thence shall be torn to pieces."

And again of the Scythians themselves : [2]

"So I will bring a nation upon you from afar, O house of Israel, saith the Lord ; it is a mighty nation : it is an ancient nation, a nation whose language thou knowest not, neither understandest what they say. Their quiver is an open sepulchre. They are all mighty men.' [3]

The Scythians, the terrible horsemen of an apocalypse of a new world in the east, did not destroy the Assyrian empire ; but those twenty years of raiding in its area so enfeebled it that it fell an easy prey to some old neighbours and vassals who were only too anxious to pay in one bloody reckoning the debt of centuries of blood. The Scythians seem to have gone back northwards. Many of them, however, never returned to south Russia, but settled in Pontus, Cappadocia, and Armenia, where the record of their name survived in later times.[4]

It was a combined force of Medes and Babylonians who destroyed Nineveh so utterly that never again did the Assyrian play any part in the history of the Euphrates region. The final catastrophe must have been awful and picturesque. But the Greeks knew naught of it save the fact ; and the Babylonian monuments do not deal in picturesque detail. The probable date of the fall of Nineveh is 612.

The Medes

With its fall the Medes appear for the first time on that stage of Mediterranean history on which they were fated to play so great a part. They were an Iranian race, a branch of that Indo-European family of peoples to which the Persians and the Scythians also belonged. Their home was the mountainous west part of the plateau of Iran between the Caspian and the Zagrus range. As the ultimate founders of the great Persian empire they as a people excited the curiosity of the Greeks ; and Herodotus has preserved various tales, of a more or less romantic nature,

---

[1] v, 6.   [2] vi, 15.

[3] I have always felt that Æschylus, had he been a Jew, would have written just as these prophet poets of Palestine wrote. I have even been obsessed by the unorthodox idea that some of the writers of the last centuries covered by the books of the Old Testament were not inferior to Æschylus as tragic poets.

[4] In Armenia in classical times were two districts, Sacatene, the country of the Sacæ, and Scythene, the country of the Scyths. In physiognomy and cult the peoples of this region show a close resemblance to the people of the Scythian district of Russia.

of the early history of their dynasty. Still, despite their romantic character, it is possible from them and from references in the Assyrian monuments to form some general idea of the history of the race prior to the fall of Nineveh.

There is evidence of a very dim period in which they were a loose confederacy of tribes which were united in the form of a kingdom apparently in the last years of the eighth century, under a ruler whom the Greeks knew as Deioces.[1] He does not however appear to have been the independent monarch of the Median tradition which Herodotus followed, but to have been a vassal of Assyria. The history of Media in the first half of the seventh century is, so far as it is known, a history of revolts from Assyria, and reconquests by that power. But in the second half of that century the Median kingdom seems to have won its independence, temporarily at any rate, under Phraortes, who perished in an attack on Nineveh about 633. But he had previously conquered Persia, that land which was destined henceforth to be lastingly associated with the Median name. It is with the dynasty rather than the people of this region that the early story of the rise of Persia is concerned. The power was in the hands of the Achæmenids, a family whose founder seems to have been chief of the Persian tribe of the Pasargadæ. When the Assyrians attacked Elam in 647 the Achæmenids seem to have got the east part of it, Anshan, as their share of the spoil, for it is a king of Anshan, Teïspes son of Achæmenes, who appears in the Behistun inscription of Darius; and it was this king of Anshan whom Phraortes made tributary. Phraortes was succeeded by Cyaxares, whose name appears as Hurakshatara in the Behistun inscription. Twice he attacked Nineveh. On the first occasion the siege had to be raised owing to the inroad of the Scyths, against whom he turned and by whom he was defeated. But years later, when the Scyths had retired from the Euphrates region, he and Nabopolassar of Babylon were the destroyers of the remnant of the Assyrian kingdom; and it is they who share the spoil. Babylon got Babylonia and Syria; while the Median kingdom included probably the whole of the west and south-west of modern Persia, the upper basin of the Tigris and Euphrates, and that Armenia (Urartu) which had been a dependency of Assyria. The rest of his reign and all that he did belongs to the story of the sixth century.

EGYPT

It was in these two centuries that the relations between the

[1] He is probably the Dayaukka of the Assyrian monuments. The territory round Ecbatana, the Median capital, is called by the Assyrians Bit-Dayaukka, "House of Dayaukka," which suggests that he played the part of the founder of some sort of dominion in that region.

Greeks and Egypt became far more intimate than they ever had been in the past, a fact no doubt greatly attributable to the growth of Greek trade under the influence of colonisation, and also to Egypt's importance to the Greek as a granary at a time when he was seeking to solve the food question at home. Late in the eighth century Egypt was under the rule of a line of Ethiopian kings whose real home was on the middle Nile. Egypt was attacked by Assyria in 701 when Tirhakah was king. The bone of contention was Syria, where Egypt was trying to revive her ancient sphere of influence. But Egypt resisted the attack successfully.[1] In 663–2 however the Assyrians marched on Egypt, put an end to the Ethiopian dynasty, and garrisoned the country with Assyrian troops. It is in connection with these Assyrian garrisons that the Greeks first appear in Egypt.

The story of this time as given by Herodotus is utterly confused by the fact that he never came to understand that there was a brief period in which Assyria held Egypt under military control, though he is dimly conscious that there was a sort of interregnum between the fall of the Ethiopian and the beginning of the Saïte dynasty. What seems to have been the case is that Assyria administered Egypt through Egyptian governors of twelve regions; and of these governors Psammetichus, the founder of the Saïte dynasty, was one. It was he who brought the Assyrian rule in Egypt to an end; and Herodotus has got a curious, but, so far as it goes, true tale of the means by which this was accomplished.[2] He says that the oracle of Leto at Buto had told Psammetichus that " he should obtain vengeance when brazen men rose up out of the sea; and Ionians and Carians afterwards landed in Egypt in brazen armour, when Psammetichus allied with them and dethroned the eleven kings." Certain passages in the Assyrian monuments of this time show that Gyges of Lydia had been doing something which the Assyrian kings disliked, and would certainly have resulted in unpleasantness for him had he not lived so far away " near the crossing of the sea." Gyges had, as has been related, applied to Assyria for help against the Cimmerians, a request which had been refused; and that seems to have turned his attention to Egypt, where he might square accounts with Assyria by helping to raise trouble there; for he could hardly expect the as yet comparatively humble Psammetichus to give efficient aid against the Cimmerian invaders. It was doubtless Gyges who sent the brazen men from out of the sea, and so got into bad odour at

[1] This incident is described in the Old Testament (2 Kings xviii, xix) and also in Herodotus (ii, 141). It is very interesting to compare the two accounts. The kingdom of Judah had taken the side of Egypt.
[2] ii, 152.

Nineveh. But it is not to be assumed that these Ionians and Carians were Gyges' own troops and subjects. The part he probably played was that of agent for Psammetichus in hiring mercenaries from lands whose domestic economy bred soldiers of fortune.

In 652 the Assyrian garrisons were expelled, and Psammetichus became the first king of the Saïte dynasty. His Ionian and Carian mercenaries he settled near the Pelusiac mouth of the Nile with intent that they should act as a garrison for the defence of Egypt towards the isthmus of Suez. Herodotus further says that Egyptian youths were sent to these Greeks to be taught the Greek language, and that they were the ancestors of the later interpreters. If this is true, it suggests that Psammetichus contemplated a strong trade connection with the Greeks. But what is certain is that these Greeks maintained close relations with their own land; and consequently the history of Egypt from this time onwards becomes well known to the Greeks. It was not merely as a garrison that these soldiers were useful to Psammetichus. It was on them that he supported his power, a policy which caused such discontent in the old Egyptian army that, if a tale told by Herodotus be true, it deserted almost en masse to the native kingdom of those Ethiopians who had been ejected by the Assyrians from the rule of Egypt.

It must have been the philhellenic policy of Psammetichus which encouraged the Milesians to found the " Milesian Fort " on the Bolbitine mouth of the Nile. Psammetichus died about 611; but his philhellenic policy did not die with him; and in the next century Egypt was well on the way to becoming as hellenised as was possible in a land where change merely ruffled the surface of a calm immemorial life.

CARTHAGE

Of Carthage it may be said that when these centuries closed it was on the point of taking up a position independent of control but not of influence from its motherland on the east shores of the Mediterranean. It was probably the activity of the Sicilian and Massiliot Greek early in the next century which made it necessary for Phœnician interests to be championed by a power within immediate striking distance of the aggressors.

CHAPTER IV

THE SIXTH CENTURY, 600–500 B.C.

IN the sixth century the story of the Mediterranean region is beginning to emerge from the dimness of tradition into the half-light of partially recorded history. It is in the Greek world that the history is most important, for it is the century in which its two greatest states underwent certain profound changes which were not merely to affect but to mould the whole of their subsequent history. In that same world, too, there was fated to spring up a school of thought which modified all the ideas of the Greek with regard to the visible universe, and a new cult which must have affected his ideas with regard to the world invisible.

SPAIN

In Spain, so far as is known, things remained much the same as in the previous century, save that the Carthaginians resented and resisted the gradual extension of Massilia's trade factories on the east coast, and drove out the settlers after the settlements had lasted but a short time.[1]

GAUL

In Gaul Massilia was probably organising trade communications with the interior, and making some beginning in the acquisition of that territory which eventually extended from the Rhône to the Alps.

ROME

In Italy the youthful state of Rome was passing through a period of semi-eclipse. Roman tradition of a later age attempted to camouflage the true history of the time by an account in which the true and the misleading were mingled together; still one thing it could not disguise, the fact that Rome was governed during the last period of the monarchy by kings of an Etruscan race. But Rome is represented as having become all of a sudden a considerable state with large territory in Latium and southern Etruria; and then, when the last of the line of

[1] Their life seems to have been brief. Herodotus had evidently never heard of them.

kings is expelled, and the republic is established, she resumes once more the guise of a small community struggling with hostile neighbours. There can be little doubt that that which appears in the Roman tradition of this period as a dominion of Rome is really the dominion of those Etruscan kings who ruled her.

The Etruscan race was at the time at the height of its power. In the Padus basin that had not as yet been shaken by the Celts. It ruled Etruria and Umbria ; had penetrated south of the Tiber, and held the rich region of Campania, that much-sought and much-fought-for land near the Bay of Naples. Its feudal lords were ever seeking new lands where, from fortified centres, they might establish and hold sway over subject populations. And in this period the infant state of Rome, lying between the upper and nether millstones of Etruscan power north and south of the Tiber, seems to have been crushed into submission to the Tarquins,[1] Etruscan lords of south Etruria.

But though this period in early Roman history may have been one of political humiliation such as later tradition would gladly disguise, it is probable that the foreign rule contributed within a century more towards the general development of the Roman state, than that state, had it been left to itself, could have accomplished in a much longer time. The Etruscan was a builder on a scale of magnificence such as the other populations of the peninsula had never conceived ; and the city of Rome, a collection of squalid buildings when the Etruscans took it over, was adorned by them with structures comparable to those of the great imperial period. The Etruscan relations with the outside world brought the little self-centred community to a knowledge of a life far larger, and of a civilisation far greater, than its own. In constitutional matters of course the rule of foreign kings interrupted such development as had taken place in the previous period ; and, when the last of these kings was expelled, the authors of the new republic had to take up the story more or less at the time where it had left off more than a century before. But the fact that they were able to do so suggests that the early institutions had not been wholly abrogated under the foreign rule ; and the little which is known of the history of the period shows that such was the case. It was natural that the elective character of the old monarchy could not be applied to the kingship of foreign despots ; but in other respects the former political institutions, the Senate and the popular Assembly, seem to have continued their functions, though, may be, in a modified form. As far as the mass of the people was concerned this foreign rule was beneficial, not, it may be assumed,

[1] Etruscan " Tarchon," probably not a proper name, but meaning " lord."

from any liberal tendencies on the part of the rulers, impulses to which feudal lords are not prone, but because it suited their policy to play off the people against the native Roman nobility, from whom they had most to fear. The Roman proletariat never forgot the position which it acquired under the Tarquins; and so under the early Republic it resents the attempt of the nobility to push it back into its former political obscurity. The influence of the old patrician families in the Senate was weakened by the addition to their numbers of a hundred families from the Latin states subject to the Tarquins, families known in after-time as the " gentes minores." Though at first a modifying element in the constitution, they identified themselves under the early Republic with the rigid conservatism of those patricians into whose ranks they had entered.

But by far the most important reform of the period was that of the army, carried out by Servius Tullius. Under the old system each of the three tribes had contributed 1,000 infantry to the legion, and 100 to the cavalry. The much-enlarged territory of the kingdom demanded a larger force, and Tarquinius Priscus, the predecessor of Servius, had contemplated the creation of three new tribes. That proposal met with so much opposition that he confined himself to doubling the numbers of the army without increasing the number of the tribes. But the reforms of Servius Tullius went much further, and had a far-reaching effect on the future political as well as the future military history of the state. The full significance of the change can only be understood if two principles which had the greatest force in the politics of the Mediterranean states in Italy and Greece be recognised. The first is older than history—that it was the duty of every man who had a property stake in the state to serve it in war. The second develops in the historical period—that it is the right of those who serve the state in war to have an adequate voice in its government. Servius Tullius had no reason to enunciate in practice the first principle, for it had existed from time immemorial; and, as to the second, he was to be the unconscious founder of it in the Roman state. His motive was a motive of the moment, to break down the class system and the system of curiæ, in both of which forms of association the old nobility had a commanding influence. He killed two birds, military inefficiency and the power of the old nobility, with one stone in the system which he devised. It set up a new grouping of citizens into classes and centuries, the former being graduated on property qualifications according to the wealth of the individual as a landowner.[1] Applied to the

---

[1] This feature in the Servian organisation seems to me to dispose of that idea which is put forward in some histories of Rome that that

military organisation of the state the principle led to the better armament of the soldiers. Ancient states were too poor to provide weapons for their army at the public expense. Each citizen had to provide his own; and the Tullian system laid down that the richer the citizen the more effective should be the panoply with which he should provide himself; and, further, as a corollary, that the best armed, that is to say, the richest citizens, should fight in the front ranks of the legions, and the ranks behind them should be graduated according to classes. So, though it was destined to confer benefit on wealth, it also laid on it corresponding expenses and duties. By this means two legions of 4,200 men each were raised. But there is a distinction in their ranks which becomes of great importance later. Of the five classes formed, the first three were rich enough to provide themselves with the arms of a heavy-armed soldier, but, of course, on a graduated scale. The fourth and fifth served as light-armed. Of the 4,200 men in the legion 3,000 were heavy-armed, and these formed the real fighting element in the service, since for reasons which need not be considered here, the cavalry, which was drawn from the very richest class of the citizens, and the light-armed at the other end of the scale, were never very effective elements in Roman warfare. Thus the really effective element was drawn from what was equivalent to a middle class in the state; and in the later days of the Roman Republic, when the government had come to fear the proletariat, it was very persistent in retaining a property qualification for service in the heavy-armed force, the legionary troops of later times, lest the danger from the proletariat should be increased by its acquiring military efficiency. The history of the last half-century of the Republic was to prove that this fear of the Roman government was not without foundation. But long ere that time came this Servian organisation had been used as the basis of popular movements, and manipulated as a means of anti-popular repression.

Of the fall of the last Tarquin there were many traditions in later times, of which the only trustworthy one is that he fell, and a Republic was established at the reputed date 509.

GREECE

The history of Greece in the sixth century centres in those two states which were to play the greatest part in the history of the race when at the zenith of its power and brilliance.

city owed its prominence largely to the convenience of its position for purposes of trade in Italy. More than that, my own view is that the Roman was essentially an agriculturist right up to the time when he first acquired possessions outside Italy. If I am right in my recollection this view was expressed by Professor Rostovtzeff in some lectures he delivered in Oxford some years ago.

THE SIXTH CENTURY, 600–500 B.C.

When the century opens Athens is a state backward in development when compared with most of its neighbours, and of small account among the powers of Greece. It had played no part in the great colonising expansion of the two previous centuries; had little trade, and that purely local; and, generally speaking, had contributed nothing to the growth of Greek civilisation. Geographically Attica was a backwater of Greek life lying off the main lines of communication. Its soil was poor, and even its plains were less fertile than the other alluvial plains of Greece. The invaders of previous centuries had passed it by for lands of greater fertility, and so its population was traditionally autochthonous, a surviving remnant of the aboriginal race of Greece. Such was the tradition, and it is probable that it contained a large element of truth. It was still living the life of old Greece and of the various contemporary agricultural states; a self-centred life which aimed above all at being self-supporting, since the population was far too poor to purchase abroad such supplies as they could not produce at home. For the mass of the population it must have been a life of permanent poverty and chronic distress; and just when this century opens distress had reached a peculiarly critical stage, due to over-population.[1] That was a trouble ever besetting the states of Greece. It was accompanied by another, the existence of a distressed class whose nature and origin has been such a fascinating mystery to scholars that they have tended in their works to treat it as the main cause of the trouble, and to thrust into the background the far graver question of over-population. To understand the agricultural question in Greece it is necessary to realise that its cultivated land falls into two categories, the alluvial plains on the one hand, and the lower slopes of the hills ($\dot{v}\pi\omega\varrho\dot{\epsilon}\eta$) on the other, of which the plains are usually very fertile, while the hill slope is only capable of producing certain crops satisfactorily. But of the three plains of Attica, the Thriasian, in the neighbourhood of Eleusis, is mostly barren; that of Athens only partly fertile; and that of Marathon very fertile wherever it is not marshy. So the country generally was not one which could carry other than a thin population. Its inhabitants at the time were divided into three classes; the Diacrii, or men of the upland, who were made up probably of the goatherds of the hills,[2] and the cultivators of the hill-slopes; the Pediæis

---

[1] The best account of the Solonian age is in Plutarch's "Solon." What Plutarch's sources of information were it is impossible to say; but they were much superior to those which he used in writing some of his "lives."

[2] Some authors have spoken as if shepherds are common in Attica. Of course there are sheep there; but the grass, owing to the dryness of the climate, is small in quantity, and consequently sheep-rearing is by no means so common as in some other parts of Greece.

or men of the plain, comparatively rich landowners; and the Parali, or men of the coast, who would be at this time mainly fishermen, with a certain number of people engaged in a local trade in the Saronic Gulf and its neighbourhood.

It was among the Diacrii that the trouble arose relative to a class of cultivators called Hektêmori. All that this name really discloses is that the fraction one-sixth applied to them in some way; and the most common and most rational explanation of this is that they were tenants who paid one-sixth of the produce of their land by way of rent to their landlords. Thirty years after Solon's time the Diacrii reappear as the discontented class which raised Pisistratus to the tyranny; and, as his remedies for their distress were of an agricultural character, it is practically certain that the Hektêmori belonged to this class, and, in that case, they must have been cultivators of the hill-slopes.[1] Of their connection with the land-holders of the plain it is only possible to conjecture that the latter had had rights, perhaps of pasture, over this land, and thus, when the Diacrii brought it into cultivation, they demanded one-sixth of the produce as rent. In the pre-Solonian age it was necessary for the cultivator to grow grain for food as there was no import from abroad; and the financial difficulties of the Hektêmori were probably due to an attempt to grow corn on land unsuited for it.[2] The result was debt to their landlords with that form of slavery into which the bankrupt debtor of that age fell as a sequel.

Solon's agricultural reforms were not of a surprising character. There was no scheme of land confiscation. He abolished slavery for debt; and he seems to have wiped out existing debts by his $\sigma\epsilon\iota\sigma\acute{a}\chi\theta\epsilon\iota a$, or "throwing off of burdens." The events of thirty years later show that his reforms did not do away with the ills of the small cultivators.

It is in respect to the trade question in Attica that his greatness was shown. Plutarch's account of it is fortunately given in the language of the financially inexpert.

---

[1] Professor Bury in his Greek History speaks of them as labourers whose wage was a sixth part of the produce of the land they cultivated. If so, the cause of their distress is not easy to understand, because the plain, when cultivable, is very fertile. Again their successors in the next age are undoubtedly the small cultivators whose cause Pisistratus took up; that is to say, they belong to the Diacrii, which would hardly have been the case had they resided with the land-owners of the plain. Furthermore large land confiscation was not part of Pisistratus' programme till after the battle of Pallêné, in the last years of his reign; and up to that time he was dealing with circumstances of land in the possession of its owners *before* his time.

[2] The modern Greek does not grow corn on the hill-slopes. When cultivated they are devoted to the vine and olive.

"Seeing that the city was becoming filled with people who were continually resorting to Attica from all parts for security's sake, and that the major part of the land was unproductive and poor, and that the sea traders were not accustomed to import commodities among people who had nothing to give in return, he diverted the attention of the people towards manufactures (crafts), and made a law that it should not be incumbent on a son to support his father unless the latter had taught him some craft." . . . "Solon, by adapting the laws to circumstances rather than circumstances to the law, and because he saw that the nature of the land afforded a meagre competence to those who worked it, and was not equal to the support of an idle and unemployed population, gave a dignity to manufactures, and ordered the Council of Areopagus to superintend the sources of the supply of necessities, and to punish the idle."

In these simple words are recorded an economic change which was to modify the whole later history of Athens. The policy of providing for the purchase of foreign food supply by the export of manufactured goods is a commonplace in modern times; but it was a very remarkable conception for a statesman of the beginning of the sixth century. There were great statesmen in the ancient world after Solon; but until Augustus reorganised the Roman world there was never so great an economist as he, if a man's capacity be tested by wide foresight. His change of currency from the heavy Æginetan standard to the light Euboic was doubtless due to the fact that an import trade in corn could best be established through trading states which at the time used the Euboic system. During the sixth century, by a process about which the meagre records of the time are silent, Athens is, by reason of this legislation, becoming a great manufacturing and trading state; for, though the Pisistratid policy did not aim at the promotion of trade, Attica emerges at the end of the century as one of the great mercantile states of Greece, having entered it as a purely agricultural state. In respect to the prosperity of the population the advance was fated to cut both ways; but the balance of gain and loss was much on the side of the former. For the moment Solon provided against the scarcity by forbidding the export of corn.[1]

The new constitution promulgated by Solon in 594 was only slightly less important than his economic measures. It is probable that in the short quarter of a century which had elapsed since Draco's constitution [2] was promulgated the Athenian

[1] It might be supposed that in view of the deficiency, the corn grown in Attica would always be consumed on the spot; but experience in modern famines has shown that holders of food in famine districts are but too apt to export to other districts which can pay for it rather than to dispose of it to a starving population which cannot.

[2] In reference to what I am about to relate I would say that I have no belief in the truth of the account of Draco's constitution given in the 'Ἀθηναίων Πολιτεία. Valuable as is the light which that work throws on history, it is discrepant with other authorities; and the great discrep-

people had discovered that which the Romans and others discovered in their climb to freedom, that the civil liberty of the lower classes cannot be satisfactorily guaranteed save by the possession of political liberty.

After-time hailed the constitution of Solon as the foundation of Athenian democracy ; and there is no real reason to suppose that after-time was mistaken. It was a leap rather than a step towards popular liberty. The people were divided into four property classes with a graduated system of taxation whereby the higher class paid a higher assessment on its property than did the one below it.[1] Only the highest class was eligible for the highest office, the archonship. Lower magistracies were open to the second and third classes. The lowest class were simply members of the Assembly (ἐκκλησία). But the real power of the new democracy lay in the law courts, where any citizen might sit in judgment on a magistrate who was accused of abuse of his office. Both in Greece and Rome the first phase of the fight for popular liberty is an attack on the wide arbitrary powers which the magistracy had inherited from the kingship.

Solon also established a Council of 401 members, the chief business of which was to prepare business for the discussion of the Assembly. Its main intent was no doubt to ensure the proper transaction of business in a somewhat unwieldy body ; but, as controlling the programme for discussion, it had a certain initiative in legislation, and it also prevented the Assembly from falling under the control of the magistrates.

The ancient council of the Areopagus continued to exist as the guardian of established custom ; and as such it may have exercised a power of negativing legislation which ran counter to it. But its former aristocratic composition was done away with

ancies are all of one kind. Whenever it has to deal with the outstanding " conservative " figures in past Athenian politics, Draco, Aristides, Thucydides the son of Melêsias, etc., it invariably depicts them as having been infinitely more " liberal " than the democratic tradition of the fifth and fourth centuries represented them as having been. My impression is that its sources for a great deal of Attic history were of a very restricted period and of a very restricted kind, namely political pamphlets issued by the reactionaries of the revolution of the Four Hundred in 411 with a view to persuading the ultra-democrats of the time that conservative policy in the past had not been so black as it was painted, and to inducing them thereby to support the measures which the reactionary revolutionists proposed. Nor do I believe the treatise to be the work of the writer of the " Politics," i.e. of Aristotle. It may have been the work of one of his pupils who found what he thought he wanted in a limited field of past political literature. But if Aristotle did make use of the work, it was with extreme discretion.

[1] To accept the assumption of the 'Αθηναίων Πολιτεία that these classes existed in Draco's time is to go against all the evidence of other authors. Draco's code was, so far as we know, legal rather than political.

THE SIXTH CENTURY, 600–500 B.C.

by the admission to it every year of the nine archons which the people had elected for the previous year.

The introduction of the system of the lot into the selection of magistrates is due to Solon. The nine archons of the year were selected by lot from forty previously elected candidates. Enthusiastic modern apologists for this principle of choice have ascribed it to a certain reverence for the will of Heaven. That is as it may be. But if so, religious feeling was singularly happy in promoting democratic interests.

In the thirty odd years which follow the legislation of Solon there is a dim tradition of political confusion. The trouble, as in his time, was agricultural distress, but in a different form. That is plain from the sequel. It results in the discontented raising Pisistratus to the tyranny. He was a man of noble family who as commander of the Athenian army had, somewhere about 570, won for Athens the island of Salamis and the Megarian port of Nisæa. Of the vicissitudes of his tenure of office it is not necessary to tell the dreary tale.[1] The importance of the man is due to what he did when in office. Even in democratic Athens of the next century, when tyrant was a loathed name, the period of his rule was spoken of as a golden age. He departed from the usual practice of tyrants by allowing the Solonian constitution to continue in working; but he provided for a due control of it by keeping the magistracies in his own family. This may have helped to mitigate his after-reputation. But his great work, a work which had lasting and beneficent results in Athenian history, was done on behalf of that class, the Diacrii, which had raised him to the tyranny.

The hill-slopes of Greece, ill adapted to the growth of any form of grain, are excellent for the cultivation of the vine and the olive. He persuaded the cultivators to give up their hopeless attempt to get subsistence by growing corn on this land, and he provided them with the means of converting the land into olive gardens and vineyards. No amount of persuasion would have been any use had not these poverty-stricken cultivators been lent the capital necessary for the starting of such plantations, for the olive does not become a paying crop for

---

[1] The chief dates in the Pisistratid period are:

561–60. Pisistratus tyrant.
556–5. Pisistratus driven from the tyranny.
550–49. Pisistratus restored to the tyranny.
550–49 ? Pisistratus driven out a second time.
540–39. Pisistratus restored to the tyranny.
536. Battle of Pallêné.
528–7. Death of Pisistratus. Hippias becomes tyrant.
510. Expulsion of Hippias.

some years after planting, and the vine takes time to mature.[1] He provided the means by making money advances to the cultivators. The effect of this change was far-reaching in Attic life. Its immediate effect was to supply Attica with a means of purchasing foreign food over and above any resources supplied by trade and manufactures, for the olive and the vine were cultivated at that day in areas much more restricted than at the present time. The produce of one acre of hill-side under the olive or vine would buy far more foreign corn than ever that acre would grow. It improved the economic position of the cultivator of the hill-side to such an extent that this class, which is the discontented, the ultra-democratic, section of the early sixth century, becomes a contented rural population in the fifth, quite satisfied with its position except when the brief raid of the Persians and the more prolonged devastation of the Peloponnesian War bring ruin to its lands. It has changed its place in the scale of political parties even by the end of the Pisistratid dominion, and has become a middle party of moderate democratic opinion inclining to conservatism. And so it remains during the fifth century.

Side by side with this agricultural development there must have been going on a silent trade development. Pisistratus did not encourage it : that is expressly stated in the ancient evidence. But whether he liked it or not, he, like other Athenian statesmen after him, had to take measures to secure the food supply of Attica from outside, all the more so as his agricultural policy must have decreased the home supply of grain to a certain extent. He recaptured Sigeum on the Hellespont, which had been in Athenian hands before his time, but had been lost. It is probable, too, that he encouraged Miltiades, the grandfather of the Miltiades of Marathon, to accept the tyranny of the Thracian Chersonese (Gallipoli peninsula) on the north shore of the Hellespont. These two acquisitions secured the most important part of the passage to the Euxine corn region in south Russia,[2] and it is practically certain that that was the whole intent of them. There is no general trade policy behind them. Also this policy of looking eastward for her corn supply is inherited by those moderate democrats of the fifth century who are the direct political descendants of the supporters of Pisistratus,

[1] I cannot on the question of space cite the evidence in support of what is here said. It will be found in my book " Thucydides and the History of his Age," p. 69 ff.

[2] I cannot understand why some modern historians of Greece represent these measures as the beginning of a policy of empire on the part of Athens. Pisistratus would certainly not have promoted such a policy ; but, more than that, empire for Athens must have been at the time beyond the realm of dreams. Athens never dreamt of empire till she had got it.

THE SIXTH CENTURY, 600–500 B.C.

whereas it is to Sicily and the West that the face of the ultra-democrat is ever turned.

In the world of art and letters Pisistratus contributed greatly to the artistic and intellectual development of Athenian life. Under his hands Athens was adorned with buildings far more splendid than any she had hitherto known; and a recension and compilation of the text of Homer, with slight distortions and additions for contemporary political purposes, was made at his instigation.

For eighteen years after his father's death Hippias son of Pisistratus ruled in Athens, and was then expelled by the Spartans at the instigation of that famous Alcmæonid family which had been leaders of the Parali during this century, and was destined to lead ultra-democracy in the century following. Up to a certain time the Pisistratids had been on friendly terms with Sparta; but when in 521 Hippias entered into relations with Argos he committed a crime which Sparta was sure to punish when occasion offered. But, even so, Sparta expected, as the sequel shows, that Athens could revert to the old aristocratic and oligarchic government of pre-Solonian times, which was the last idea the Alcmæonids had in their minds, though they did not disclose that to Sparta. After Hippias' expulsion there ensued some years of confused party fighting in which Sparta played a somewhat feeble and ignominious part. But the story of that falls in with the story of politics at Athens in the first decade of the next century. A constitution was promulgated by Cleisthenes in 507, the first definite constitutional settlement made after the expulsion of Hippias.

Constitution of Cleisthenes

The chief feature of the Cleisthenic legislation was the measure which established the artificial tribes in place of the four Ionic tribes of Attica in which the bond of clan relationship, with its corollary, the influence of great families, and the consolidating tie of locality, were obstacles to the establishment of true democratic government. It was the family influence at which his blow was really aimed; for its strength had been shown in those struggles with aristocrats, headed by Isagoras, which had taken place since the expulsion of Hippias. This was successful, for family influence founded on the old tribal relationship is not apparent in the politics of the next century. But he also tried to break up the old parties of the plain, the hill, and the coast by putting demes (village communities) from each of them in the same tribe. It is true that the names Pediaci, Diacrii and Parali pass out of Athenian politics after this time; but the local basis of division between the oligarchic, middle, and extreme democratic parties of the fifth century is practically the same.[1]

As compared with the constitution of Solon the most important modification was the extension of the power of the Council (Boulé). It was increased in numbers to 500, 50 from each tribe. It controlled the action of the magistrates, who had to make reports to it, and to receive orders from it. It had large financial powers and considerable control of foreign affairs. It still, but perhaps never emphatically, controlled the programme of business to be brought before the Assembly (Ecclesia). Cases of the impeachment of magistrates came, in the first instance at any rate, before it. It was indeed the most powerful body in the constitution, more powerful than the magistrates, more powerful than the Ecclesia. The general tendency of democratic development in the fifth century is for the Assembly to encroach on the prerogatives of the Council, a process which is practically complete in the fourth.

Sparta

The history of Sparta in this century is a subject on which, in consequence of recent discoveries on the site of that town,[2] it is necessary to exercise considerable reserve, for, though what has been found has proved conclusively that the view previously held as to the social life and development of the state in early days was wrong, it has not provided material for more than a conjectural reconstruction of the facts.

The constitutional changes which had in previous centuries marked the history of most of the other Greek states had passed lightly over Sparta. The monarchy survived in that peculiar dual form which originated probably in the combination of two communities in one state. It had its Senate or Council and its Assembly like other Greek states; and to a certain extent there had been a democratising of the constitution in the form of limitations set upon the royal powers by the establishment of the ephorate. Thus its history had always been in a sense unique among the histories of the Greek states. But from at any rate the later part of the sixth century onwards it appears as a community under a military system so stern that two of the strongest features of ordinary human affairs, family life and individual life, are repressed almost out of existence. Save that it is not

[1] Some writers of Greek history claim that Cleisthenes was successful in this also; but it will be shown from the party history of the fifth century that the clash of economic interests between these classes had, in a modified practical form, an influence on politics similar to that which they had in the sixth century.

[2] Made during the excavations conducted by the British School at Athens in the early years of the present century.

celibate, it is a community resembling one of the Orders of Knights which the crusading period of the Middle Ages brought into existence. It stands like an island high and dry in the great stream of literary, artistic, and philosophical development which swept over Greece in the fifth century. The Greek of that age seeing, or thinking he saw, what Sparta then was, deduced from the terrible rigidity of its life the conclusion that that life had always been the same for centuries past. In point of fact the Greek of the fifth century knew very little more of contemporary Sparta than is known by the modern world. The aristocratically minded of other Greek states regarded it as a land which bred gentlemen, while their own bred cads; and the democrat pictured it as a home of an unintelligent, unenlightened collection of Philistines.[1]

But the modern world has been wont to accept the picture of Spartan life as drawn by the democrats of other states, and to assume that it was not merely true of the Sparta of the time at which it was drawn, but of Sparta ever since Sparta was Sparta. That is now proved to have been wrong. Up to some date, probably in the sixth century, the development of the life of the land in art and literature was at least equal to that of other Greek states. Then suddenly all changes; and the Spartan population emerges from the change as a people whose sole interest is military efficiency without its usual accompaniment of imperial ambitions.[2] In such a life there was no room for the advance of a culture in art and literature. The latter dies forthwith; and the former fades away.

Greece and Greek authors in the fifth century attributed the Spartan system of life then prevailing to Lycurgus, the famed lawgiver, who was believed to have flourished centuries before that time. It seems quite certain now that Lycurgus was not the author or creator of this system, and was of much more recent date than fifth-century Greece supposed. If he was connected with any change in Spartan institutions, it is possible that it was with a movement which raised the power of the nobility at the expense of that of the kings about 700 B.C., a movement of which there are obscure traces in the tradition relating to Sparta.[3]

[1] A strange picture of Lacedæmon is drawn in Pater's " Plato and Platonism." As a picture of the actual life of Sparta it is unhistorical; but it is probably near the truth as a picture of the ideal of Sparta cherished by enthusiastic but uninformed philo-Laconians in other Greek states.

[2] In much of what I have written and shall write of Sparta before this change took place I follow the late Mr. Dickins's article in the " Journal of Hellenic Studies " of 1912. With regard to Sparta after the change, I cannot accept his theories.

[3] The colonisation of Tarentum was probably due to the migration of some citizens of the state whom this movement had displaced.

But the great change in Spartan life must have come at earliest not less than a century after that time. It was almost certainly caused by the results of the Second Messenian War, which ended about 620 in the complete subjection of Messenia to Spartan rule, and the addition of its population to that serf class of the Helots of which Sparta was already ruling large numbers in Laconia. Sparta had indeed won the Messenian plain, a very fertile land, the addition of which to her territory must have been very beneficial to the private interests of those of her citizens who received allotments in it. But there was another side to the picture,—and a very black one. The population of Lacedæmonian territory can be calculated to have consisted at this time of approximately 30,000 Spartiates, about the same number of Periœci,—a subject race, but not in serfdom,—and at least 250,000 Helots, of whom probably more than half belonged to the newly conquered region. It was not long before the Spartans realised the ever-present danger to which a ruling class in such a minority was exposed among a fierce serf population probably nine or ten times as numerous as themselves; and it may be that some unrecorded incident which occurred after the Second Messenian War forced her to realise the situation. 550 B.C. has been suggested as the date of the change. The date seems too late; for, had it occurred at that time, the Greek world of the fifth century must have known of it. The historians of that age could hardly have been so ignorant of it as to suppose that the life of Sparta as they knew it had been the life of Sparta from time immemorial. The early years of the sixth century are the latest date which is probable,—it might almost be said possible; and that, too, brings the transformation near to the date of that which was almost certainly its cause, the Second Messenian War.[1] Up to this time the Spartan had lived the average life of the Greek world, a life which took itself not too seriously, a life joyous in such joys as it could afford, a life made happier for the leisured class,—and at Sparta the Spartans with their bands of serfs all belonged to that class,—by an interest in that world of art and literature which was expanding so rapidly in the seventh century. And suddenly all is changed; and for this life is substituted one more stern, and perhaps more dreary, than any which any other race has ever adopted with premeditation, one of the training-school and the drill-yard

---

[1] Mr. Dickins thought that the war with Tegea, which seems to have taken place between 560 and 550, was the immediate preliminary of the change at Sparta. But he put a peculiar interpretation on that war. Read in the light of many similar after-events, it seems to have been no more than an attempt on the part of Sparta to warn off neighbouring states from tampering with the Helots.

almost from the cradle to the grave, in which most of the ordinary desires and ambitions of humanity are sternly repressed. Intercourse with the outer world, which the Spartan had in the past been as free to enjoy as any other Greek, was now cut off by regulations which excluded all strangers from presence in the land ; and, as far as the outer world is concerned, a blackness of darkness of mystery so descends on Lacedæmon that the Greek of the fifth century never knew its life, nor understood its policy. And yet for centuries the Spartan supported this existence, such was the danger in which he lived. He had a wolf by the throat ; and he dare not relax his grasp. Many Spartans of the next two centuries must have lived without knowing any other form of life : but the few who did become acquainted with the outside world showed a marked reluctance to return to life as lived at Sparta.[1] But there was some element in Spartan training which the contemporary world never knew, and the modern world has never discovered. Mere military communism could not have produced some of the ablest Greeks of that age, and such, viewed dispassionately, were some of the Spartans of the fifth century.

In the closing years of the century that strange and puzzling figure, the Spartan King Cleomenes, appears on the stage. But his exploits are more closely connected with the history of the fifth century than with that of the sixth.

Of the other prominent states of Greece in this century the records are very defective. Corinth, as is shown by what has been found in Sicily, was continuing to carry on a vigorous trade with the West ; but these discoveries also show that as the century goes on Athens is competing more and more with her, with results which were to have a baneful influence on the history of the fifth century. Sicyon is playing the part she always played, that of port for the interior trade of the Peloponnese. Argos is anxious for the maintenance of her ancient prominence among the Peloponnesian states, which was seriously threatened by the increased military strength of Sparta.

---

[1] Mr. Dickins seems to have been in agreement with the view I expressed in the chapter on Spartan Policy in " Thucydides and the History of his Age " that the adoption of this system of life was due to fear of the Helots. Of course that view is supported by various references in Greek authors. But I go further than this and say that the policy of Sparta in the fifth century, which has seemed both to ancient and modern writers so unenterprising and vacillating, was really due to the ever-present danger in which the Spartan lived. Mr. Dickins thought it was due to political rivalry between the kings and the magistracy of the Ephorate. Apart from the fact that it leaves certain features of Spartan policy unexplained, the theory seems utterly inadequate to account for a phenomenon so striking.

Western Greeks

The Greek colonies of Sicily and the West were passing through a period of calm as compared with their stormy history in the next century. Cymé in Italy was at the height of its prosperity. The Etruscans were in its immediate neighbourhood in Campania, but were as yet in an inferior position in that region. In Sicily the old native population was entering on the first stage of Hellenism; but also, by intermarriage with the Greeks, was beginning that process of de-Hellenisation which eventually made the Sicilian a Greek of a special type. The Greek cities themselves were rapidly rising to wealth and prosperity on some of the richest soils in the Mediterranean. Acragas (Agrigentum) was developing those olive lands the produce of which she exported to Carthage, thereby winning great wealth. In Italy Sybaris and Croton stood out among the Greek cities of the day as second to none in prosperity. They and their neighbour Locri had stretched their territory across the toe of Italy to the Tyrrhenian Sea; and to the transit trade across the route which they commanded their wealth was largely due. But Sybaris perished in 510 at the hands of her neighbour Croton, a tragedy which made all the more impression on the minds of the Greeks because it befell a community whose luxury they had envied and deplored. But luxury and tragedy were not the only elements in the life of the Italiot Greek of this century. Comedy also contributed to it. The Greek played many parts in life, and tried to play more: but, if there was one for which he was eminently unfitted, it was that of the ascetic. He tried as many experiments in politics as modern America has tried in religion; but never did he try a stranger one than was tried at Croton and some of the neighbouring cities in the late years of this century. The philosopher Pythagoras had come to Croton from the Ionian East, bringing with him much genuine learning, and various fanciful theories of life, one of which inculcated the desirability of living in an ascetic brotherhood. Eccentricity can always make a temporary convert of the would-be eccentric; and Pythagoras was able to found such brotherhoods in Croton and its neighbouring towns; and not only that, but these brotherhoods got hold for a space of the government of their cities. It must have been a bitter time for those outside their select circles who wished to live the free and somewhat joyous life of the average Greek; and the bitterness would not be diminished by the fact that the local oligarchs, a class which in later times of Greek history sought to divert intellectual and social movements to their own ends, got control of these brotherhoods. Even Greek enthusiasm for novelty could not stand the experiment; and it was soon brought to an end, but not until it had

THE SIXTH CENTURY, 600–500 B.C.

illustrated the principle of brotherhood by destroying Sybaris.

The history of Asia Minor at this period is so intimately bound up with that of the Euphrates region that it would be inconvenient to deal with them separately.

MEDES AND PERSIANS

The fate of the Assyrian kingdom in the last years of the seventh century had left the Median and Babylonian monarchies joint heirs of her former dominions. The first half of the sixth century is a period of interregnum between the Assyrian and Persian empires. Of the rest of the reign of Cyaxares, the Median king who had taken part in the destruction of Nineveh, neither the Persian inscriptions nor Herodotus have anything to tell us except that the latter records a war and an unfought fight with the Lydians on the Halys in 585.[1] But it is plain that in the twenty years which intervened between the fall of Assyria and this battle Cyaxares had reduced the mountain regions of Armenia and Eastern Asia Minor, districts inhabited by races and fragments of races.[2]

Cyaxares died in 584 and was succeeded by Astyages, in whose reign Cyrus conquered Media. Of the other events of his reign nothing is known, though he plays a part in the fantastic legends which gathered round the person of Cyrus. Cyrus is the Kurush of the inscriptions who succeeded his father as king of Anshan[3] about 559, judging from the references in the Babylonian records. He revolted against Astyages and overthrew the kingdom of the Medes in 550.

The fact that Nabonidus of Babylon regarded the change with comparative indifference as a mere domestic matter, and the close relationship of Mede and Persian in later history, suggest that Cyrus was, as the legends imply, connected with the Median royal family, and that the Medes therefore regarded the change of dynasty with more or less equanimity.

---

[1] Hdt. i, 74.

[2] Herodotus mentions incidentally the surrender of Scythians to Cyaxares. These, though Herodotus does not know it, would be those Scythians who had settled in eastern Asia Minor after the great raid on Asia. What the war was about Herodotus does not say; but it lasted five years, and then was brought to a close by a peace in which the Babylonian king and the ruler of Cilicia played the part of arbitrators, a peace which was hastened by an eclipse of the sun which deterred the combatants from fighting a battle already set. This eclipse had been calculated and foretold by Thales the Milesian. It is calculated that eclipses of the sun visible in north Asia Minor occurred in 610 and 585. The present eclipse belongs to the later date. This date is the keystone to the comparative chronology of the Greek and the Christian eras.

[3] For Anshan, see p. 84.

Lydia

At the beginning of this century Alyattes is ruling in the Lydian kingdom. He it was who warred with the Medes for five years. But the greater part of his reign was taken up with attacks on the Greek cities on the coast, and especially on the greatest of them, Miletus, then under the tyranny of Thrasybulus. His attacks were more determined and more effective than those of his predecessors; but the permanent results were small. Colophon was captured, and Smyrna destroyed, while a treaty was made with Ephesus, a city which is more than suspected of having played the blackleg in the wars between its fellow Greek cities and Lydia. However partial may have been his success against the Greek cities, it is known from sources other than Herodotus that he added, between 584 and 566, the Troad, Mysia, Bithynia, and Caria to his dominions. He died in 561, and was succeeded by the famous Crœsus.

The personality of the last Lydian king attracted to an extraordinary degree the attention of the Greeks of his own and after time. To them he was a dazzling figure at the head of a great empire, the nearest and the first they had known of those oriental kingdoms which impressed the Greeks by their size and magnificence as compared with the small, poor states of their own homeland. His predecessors had adopted the policy of courting the European Greek through the oracle at Delphi while attacking the liberties of the Greeks of Asia; and this policy Crœsus not merely adopted but emphasised. It is calculated that during the short fifteen years of his reign he gave to Delphi gifts which, reckoned in modern money, would have a value of more than a million pounds sterling. Furthermore, by means of splendid presents he cultivated friendly relations with prominent families in various states, such as the Alcmæonidæ at Athens, and, generally speaking, posed as an ardent philhellene. His philhellenism may have been genuine or not; but he was certainly successful in persuading the Greeks of Europe that he was not merely an admirer but a splendid friend.

He carried the conquests of Lydia as far as the Halys river; and he was the first of Lydian kings to bring into subjection those Greek cities of the coast the control of which was so necessary to a Lydia which was playing the part of middleman in the trade between east and west. But when once he had conquered the Asiatic Greek cities he adopted a most conciliatory attitude towards them, respecting their local institutions, and seeking to win over the priestly caste by offerings to the temple of the Branchidæ but little inferior to those he had made to Delphi.

Having settled the affairs of the western border of his kingdom Crœsus turned his attention eastwards, where the proceedings of Cyrus were beginning to alarm not merely him but Babylon and Egypt also. With these powers he formed a secret anti-Persian alliance; but the secret, if Diodorus is to be believed, was disclosed to Cyrus by an Ephesian. He had also formed an alliance with Sparta, so Herodotus says: but it was not destined to have any effect in the coming war, for no Spartan contingent was ever sent across the Ægean. That Cyrus got some inkling of the alliance seems certain; otherwise it is most improbable that he would have dealt with the distant Lydia before he had settled accounts with Babylon. He was over the Taurus before Crœsus expected him, and the Lydian defence had to be organised in a hurry. The tale is not a long one. There was a battle; a Lydian retirement on Sardis; a siege and capture of that place; and the death of Crœsus, probably by suicide.

Thus the Lydian kingdom fell in a moment, as it were, never to rise again: and it fell, not in the decadence of age, but at the very height of its young and vigorous life. To the Greeks the spectacle was bewildering, so bewildering indeed that they were never able to give a rational account of how it came to pass.

But their feeling did not begin and end with bewilderment. They were intensely shocked at the part which Delphi, the Greek shrine which Crœsus had enriched, the Greek community to which his philhellenism had been most conspicuously shown, had played in leading him to his doom by sending an ambiguous oracle saying "that if he warred with the Persians he would overthrow a mighty empire." Despite the pious faith with which Herodotus regards the utterances of the Delphic oracle, he is unable to conceal the terrible shock which this apparent deception caused to Hellenic sentiment all the world over. To the Greek of Europe it appeared as though the oracle had betrayed its best friend, and his also.

After the fall of Sardis Cyrus was called away to the eastern borders of his dominions where the Bactrians and Sacæ were giving trouble. Lydia rose, and mercenaries from the Greek cities took part in the rising. It was put down by an army which Cyrus despatched under the command of one of his lieutenants; and from that time forward the Lydians sank into an apathy of defeat from which even the great Ionian revolt of half a century later failed to rouse them.

Then came the turn of the Greek cities, in the tragedy of whose life the leading motive is disunion. They were brought one by one under Persian sway; and, after Caria and Lycia had been subdued, the whole of Asia Minor was in the hands of the conqueror.

Of the states of Ionia only the island state of Samos survived. About 533 a certain Polycrates made himself master of the island. He was a man of much ability and energy and few scruples. Piracy, trade, engineering, and territorial acquisition were all included in the field of his manifold activities. In his brief day Samos enjoyed a prosperity such as she had never known before, a prosperity due probably to its being the only independent Greek trading community on the Asiatic coast. Samos might have remained for long a solitary outpost of Greek independence had not Polycrates allowed himself to be trapped by the satrap of Sardes, who put him to death. Not long after his death Samos fell into Persian hands in 516.

Persia

In the east Cyrus extended the borders of the Persian empire to the very frontiers of India. In 538 he captured Babylon, and overthrew the new Babylonian kingdom. He died in 529.

His tomb may be seen at the present day. " I am Cyrus, the king, the Achæmenian," is the only part of his epitaph which survives. It would be too little for a lesser man. It is sufficient for him now that he has been twenty-five centuries dead.

Cyrus was succeeded by Cambyses, who in his short reign, —he died in 522,—added Egypt [1] and Libya as far as the Greater Syrtis to the Persian dominions. There were some troubles with his brother Smerdis about the succession, accidents such as are apt to happen in the best regulated polygamist families.

The new orientalism with which the Greek was brought into contact by the conquest of Lydia was of a character different to that which had preceded it in western Asia. The Medes and Persians belonged to the Iranian branch of the Indo-European family of nations. Though an oriental in his domestic life, the Persian contrasted in politics and religion with those races which had hitherto ruled in Asia in that he had an ideal of empire which did not confine itself to the extraction of merciless tribute from the subject races, and a religious ideal far above the gross conceptions of deity which had prevailed among the Semitic peoples. He seems to have accepted the institutions of the nations he conquered, subject always to a reasonable tribute and a general conforming to the interests of the empire as represented by the Persian governor and his officials. In religion he was a monotheist with a creed far more spiritual than any to which either Greek or Roman ever subscribed at the most enlightened periods of their history, a creed which recognised

[1] See " History of Egypt," p. 110.

an absolute Good which would only triumph in an after-life.
In ordinary morality he was at least the equal of, and perhaps superior to, the Greek. Such, briefly, was the nature of that Perso-Medic race to which the Ionian Greeks of Asia succumbed not long after the fall of Sardis in 546.

Asiatic Greeks

Thus within the space of this one century the Greeks of Asia had passed successively under two masters. They were fortunate in one respect, that neither master was hard or exacting. It is probable that the only change made in their life was that they had to pay tribute. Under Persia, but not under Lydia, they had in the case of war to furnish contingents. For the rest their ordinary life must have gone on much as before. It is true that though their governments maintained a local independence of a more or less municipal form, yet they must have been greatly modified in working by the policy which Cyrus adopted of setting up a native tyrant in each Greek city whose interest it was to act as agent to Persia. But tyrant or no tyrant, the intellectual brilliancy of the Ionian cities of this age could not have flourished under any form of rule which cast a dark shadow on the liberty of individual life. The yoke of Lydia and of Persia was easier to bear than that of Athens in the next century. The importance of Ionian thought and learning during this period is twofold: it is responsible for the first beginnings of Greek philosophy, and it gave the Greek a wholly new conception of the world of nature. As a general system it was a curious combination of science and guesses at truth, of which it is only too probable that the science originated in Babylonia, and the guesses in Asia Minor. It is impossible to believe that the scientific element in this strange amalgam of truth and conjecture, which utterly revolutionised some of the most fundamental ideas hitherto prevailing in the Greek world, was evolved in a few years from the unaided inner consciousness of the Greek. The general history of the century suggests the possibility that the impetus to this movement originated in a knowledge that the Greek for the first time acquired of that science which had been carried to such a high pitch of development by the world-old civilisation of Mesopotamia. During the rule of Assyria the state of Asia must have been such as to deter any foreigner from entering the region south of Taurus. The traveller was much more likely to share the death than the life of the native population. But when Assyria came to an end, and the comparatively civilised rule of Media and Babylon, and later, of Persia, was established, Greeks seem to have flocked to the Euphrates region. Large numbers are known to have served as mercenaries in Babylonia. It is certain that the trader and the traveller went thither also, and brought home with them some of that learning and science relating to natural phenomena which the Babylonians had developed for centuries past. Much that was brought back would be no more than vague ideas; but that some real scientific knowledge came with the ideas is shown by the reference to Thales the Milesian and his calculations of the eclipse which interrupted hostilities between the Medes and Lydians on the Halys. Many of the theories put forward by the Ionian philosophers, guesses though they are, are guesses founded on some knowledge of which they had heard, but which they had never grasped. In other cases their views look like philosophical inductions from physical facts which have come to their knowledge. It is not so much their individual theories as their general effect on the Greek mind which is important in Greek history. The world of nature appeared in a new guise. To the Greek before this time $φύσις$ (nature) had connoted a physical world without law or order, a universe of chance and change. Ionian philosophy not merely modified but reversed this view; to the Greek of the next century $φύσις$ connotes a world governed by laws some of which man had discovered, and others which he might discover as time went on. Emanating from this is the idea of a divine power governing the world, something impalpable which the Greek never tried to define, but which he sometimes designated, as Herodotus does, as the divinity ($τὸ\ θειόν$). Therefore when the philosophers laid down in the fifth century the dictum that the state existed $φύσει$ "by nature," they meant "by the divine ordering of nature," thus giving it a quasi-sanctity of which some of their successors, to the great indignation of Plato, tried to rob it by alleging that it existed $νόμῳ$, "by convention." But this conversion of ideas brought about in the Greek mind of the sixth century was the greatest single step which it ever made towards intellectual civilisation.

This period saw also the beginning of Greek geography in the writings of Ionian writers, who first compiled route books for commercial purposes, and later, with the aid of increased knowledge, provided by the opening up of Asia to travel, schemes of general geography illustrated by actual maps. The latter were dominated by an idea of symmetry suggested probably by the new idea of nature as a world of law.

An unrealised future can rarely be the subject of useful conjecture; but the position in Lydia towards the close of Crœsus' reign was such that, had the kingdom survived, the hellenisation of Asia Minor might have been anticipated by 250 years.

EGYPT

In Egypt the same process was going on. In both the process was brought to a sudden end by a Persian conquest. The Persian slew the offspring of a civilisation which was eventually to slay his own. In 611 Necho II. had succeeded Psammetichus as king of Egypt. He took advantage of the disorders accompanying the fall of the Assyrian empire by making an attempt to reassert Egypt's dominion over Syria. But in 605 the Babylonians inflicted a terrible defeat on him at Carchemish on the Euphrates.[1]

So Babylon got Syria; and Necho became so nervous at the nearness of the Babylonian frontier that he enlisted a number of Greek mercenaries. More will be heard of these in the next reign.[2]

A remarkable incident of his reign was the circumnavigation of Africa by certain Phœnicians in his pay. Herodotus does not believe the tale, and cites triumphantly in disproof the one fact which proves its genuineness, that at one stage in their voyage " they had the sun on their right," which means that they entered the Southern Hemisphere.[3]

Necho died in 594 and was succeeded by Psammetichus II. In his reign a deputation from Elis in Peloponnese was in Egypt. Herodotus says that it came to discuss the Olympic Games with the king, a subject in which he can hardly be expected to have had a profound interest. It is more probable that it was arranging for a supply of corn. He made an expedition against Æthiopia, which is mainly of interest because certain of his Greek mercenaries anticipated a practice common to modern civilisation by cutting their names on one of the colossi of Rameses II at Abu-Simbel. It is significant that the Greeks who did this were Ionians and Rhodians, men from the richest part of the Greek world.

In 589 Apries succeeded to the throne. Further meddling in Syria led to the Jewish captivity in 588. His reign ended in a native rising in 569 against the employment of Greek mercenaries, and a battle at Momemphis in which the Greeks were overpowered by numbers. Apries perished also, and was succeeded by Amasis who had led the rising. His reign is of the greatest importance in the story of Greek relations with Egypt.

Considering the part he had played in the destruction of

---

[1] For his invasion of Syria see Herodotus, ii, 158–9. Cf. in O.T., 2 Chron. xxxv, 20–22, and 25. Jeremiah, who is pro-Babylonian, and anti-Egyptian, has much to say of the subject. For his attack on the Philistines see Jeremiah xlvii.

[2] The number of Greek mercenaries serving at this time in Babylonia and Egypt is somewhat eloquent testimony to the chronic over-population of Greek lands to which reference has been already made.

[3] Hdt. iv, 42.

the Greek mercenaries it might have been expected that his reign would be marked by an anti-hellenic policy of Egypt for the Egyptians. But he showed himself markedly philhellene. The probable explanation is that as a usurper of the throne he found it necessary to have at hand some support against any feeling which might arise among the Egyptians about one who was not of royal race sitting on the throne of the Pharaohs. Herodotus [1] says that he showed great kindness to the Greeks, and gave them Naucratis as a residence; but stipulated that no Greek imports should be landed elsewhere in Egypt. Naucratis was a unique Greek community to which all the chief trading states of the Asiatic Greeks contributed; but only one European state, Ægina, is mentioned in connection with it. It was not a colony, for Egypt would not have allowed such a settlement on her soil; but it seems to have had municipal autonomy, and its inhabitants were allowed the free exercise of their religion. The philhellenism of Amasis was shown more markedly in the contributions he made to Greek temples, to the rebuilding of the temple at Delphi, and, in the form of gifts, to that of Hera at Samos, a tribute to his friendship with Polycrates. His friendly policy brought the Greeks in large numbers to Egypt, where they settled not merely at Naucratis but all over the country;[2] and the earlier Greek settlements near the Pelusiac mouth of the Nile were transported to Memphis and its environs.

Amasis was well on the way to anticipate the Ptolemies by turning Egypt into a Helleno-Egyptian kingdom, a policy naturally unpopular among the native Egyptians, which gave rise to the depreciatory stories circulated about him, some of which Herodotus has preserved. His was a long reign troubled towards the end of it by apprehensions with regard to the ambitions of Cyrus, apprehensions only too well justified by the conquest of Egypt by Cambyses, and its passing under Persian rule.

In Libya the Cyrenaic Greeks had had chequered relations with Egypt. It had attacked them, and failed to conquer them. With Amasis, however, they were on friendly terms; he is said, in fact, to have married a Cyrenaic Greek. But his fate and their fate were the same, to fall under the rule of Persia in the reign of Cambyses.

CARTHAGE

The severance of the direct dependence which Carthage had had on its Phœnician metropolis must have fallen within

[1] ii, 178–9.
[2] Hdt. iii, 26 mentions Samians who penetrated even to the Great Oasis.

this century. It seems to have been brought about by an amicable understanding, for the relations with the mother country remain friendly, so much so that Carthage in 480 is ready to oblige the Persian rulers of Phœnicia by attacking the Sicilian Greeks, and so creating a diversion favourable to the Persian attack on Greece itself. The foundation of Massilia had alarmed and annoyed Carthage ; and it is probable that it led eventually to an understanding between her and the Etruscans with intent to render things as unpleasant as possible for the Greek settler or trader on the western sea. Accordingly Carthage pushed her settlements northwards along the east coast of Spain, and destroyed the infant trading factories which Massilia had founded there. The Phocæans were baulked too in an attempt to colonise in Corsica. The Phœnician trading settlements west of the narrows of Sicily seem to have passed under Carthaginian control, among others those towns, Lilybæum, Motye, and Panormus, which were destined to bring much trouble on Carthaginian, Greek, and Roman.

CHAPTER V

THE FIRST HALF OF THE FIFTH CENTURY, 500-450 B.C.

ANY general characterization of the story of the fifth century before the story is told would be for those who have some knowledge of it superfluous, for those who have none incomprehensible. The tale may be left to suggest its own moral.

SPAIN

In Spain, now that Phœnician interests were represented and directed at a centre whence a nearer view of them could be obtained, it is probable that their development proceeded with some rapidity; and the first real penetration of the south of the Peninsula by Punic civilisation may date from this age.

MASSILIA

In Gaul Massilia was reinforced by certain fierce Phocæan intransigeants who, after the collapse of the Ionian revolt in 493, refused to submit once more to Persian rule.

ROME

In Italy Rome was living out half a century of life under its new Republic. Later tradition ascribed the expulsion of the Tarquins and the establishment of the Republic to the year 509.

In the history of other countries, when the reader approaches a change from a monarchy to a Republic, he is prepared for a story of a great political upheaval bringing about drastic constitutional change. But the revolution at Rome was not a popular rising against a native government, but the overthrow of an alien monarchy; and that is perhaps the reason why the constitutional change was reduced to the lowest terms of any such change in history.

For the single king were substituted two consuls who inherited undiminished the arbitrary power of the kings. For the rest everything went on as before in the sense that there was no other formal change. The duality of the new supreme magistracy implied a certain check on arbitrary power; for though

THE FIRST HALF OF THE FIFTH CENTURY

there was not at this time, nor ever was at Rome, any idea of the joint responsibility of the magistrates for public policy, and each consul of the year could choose and carry out his own policy without consulting his colleague, yet there was this check upon his action, that his colleague could negative it by his veto. It is not known that this power went back to the beginning of the Republic; but it is almost certain that it did. Furthermore the annual character of their office as compared with the life tenure of the previous kings tended to mitigate the very large arbitrary powers which they had inherited from the kingship.

For more than two centuries after the foundation of the Republic the constitutional history of Rome is concerned with the struggle between the patrician and the plebeian orders. The patrician nobility of Rome was not a class due to conquest like the Dorian nobility in Greece, nor did it represent the original body of the population. There is no tradition of a conquest or of a time when the Plebs did not form part of the body of citizens. As Rome was formed from small communities which had amalgamated, so the patrician nobility was formed of those families which had been originally the leading families of those communities.[1]

The Roman constitution, though modified in many respects during the four and a half centuries of the Republic, is always a constitutional paradox. From the very beginning of the Republic it is in form a democracy, in fact an oligarchy; and so it remained till the time of Julius Cæsar. At the very outset of the Republic the plebeian was constitutionally just as much and as fully a citizen as the patrician. In the Assembly his vote was as good as that of the patrician. He was eligible for membership of the Senate, and for election [sic] to the magistracy. His position was politically much superior to that of the lower classes in the early states of Greece. Yet in point of fact his power as a voter in the Assembly was curtailed, and his eligibility for the Senate or for office was practically a dead letter. The Assembly of the Curiæ (Comitia Curiata) of the early monarchy still existed; but it had been shorn of its legislative and elective functions. These had been transferred to a new form of assembly, the Assembly of the Centuries (Comitia Centuriata) which came into existence as the result of the army reforms of Servius Tullius, and, like the army then created, was graduated into classes of different property qualifications. The number of centuries, each

[1] For instance, of the great Roman families of later days the Juli came originally from Bovillæ, and the Claudii were not originally Roman. Other families whose origin outside Rome is shown by their ancient cognomina are the Furii Medullini, the Sulpicii Camerini, etc.

of which contributed one vote, was 193,[1] of which 98, a majority of the whole number, were composed of eighteen centuries of the Knights, and eighty of the first class, that is to say of the citizens of the highest property qualification. The vast majority of the plebeians would be in the lower property classes.[2]

Thus, as each century, however many members it contained, had only one vote as a group, the centuries of the Knights and of the first property class could outvote the centuries in which most of the plebeians were included. As to the choice of the consuls, this Assembly is commonly spoken of as electing them. That is a most misleading term to apply to the process. The mode of choice of the consuls at Rome was a very curious feature in that curious constitution. In strict constitutional form the process was nothing more than that which had been followed in the choice of the early kings of Rome before the time of the Tarquins, save that, inasmuch as the previous chief magistrate, the consul, was usually alive, there was no need to appoint an interrex, except in the very rare case of both consuls having died before they had nominated their successors.[3] The process was carried through in four steps : the existing consuls nominated their successors ; the Assembly of the Centuries by vote accepted or rejected the nominees ; if the Assembly accepted them, the Senate ratified or refused to ratify the choice ; the Assembly of the Curiæ (Comitia Curiata) conferred on them their " imperium," which gave them the right of exercising the powers of their office. This was the only political function retained by this primitive form of the Assembly after the creation of the Assembly of the Centuries.

Such was the original form of this peculiar method of magisterial selection ; and right on to the end of the Republic it continued to exist in theory, and, in some respects, in practice. It arises as a corollary from this that the existing consuls might, if they so pleased, nominate only two candidates for the two consulships of the next year, in which case there would be no election by the people ; and the power of the Assembly would be restricted to the acceptance or rejection of the persons nominated. But, as a fact, very early in the Republic, the existing consuls must have become accustomed to nominate more than two candidates, so that the people in the Assembly might exercise

---

[1] The number may not have been so large in the early days of the Republic.

[2] The name " century " must not be taken to imply strictly a number of 100 men and no more. Probably from the very earliest times the centuries of the lower classes, at any rate in the Comitia Centuriata, consisted of several hundred persons.

[3] For the mode of choice of a new king, see p. 549.

a choice, that is to say, elect two candidates out of a larger number. But even in Cicero's day the existing consuls might have restricted their nominations to two persons, though it is certain that, had they done so, there would have been a tremendous outcry. It may have been the case that from the very beginning the mere right of nomination was not confined to the consuls. It may have been exercisable by private individuals; but from a practical point of view this was of very little significance, since the consuls had the right of rejecting any nomination, and could thus limit the nominees to their own list. When later the prætorship was established as a magistracy of the second rank, the same method of choice seems to have been applied to this office also.

A recognition of these dry constitutional details is necessary for the understanding of that peculiar phenomenon in Roman constitutional history, namely that the constitution, though democratic in general form, was aristocratic in detail, and consequently in fact.

Constitutionally the plebeian was just as eligible for the consulship or for any other magistracy as the patrician; yet until 367 no plebeian ever held one of them. The method of exclusion was quite simple. The patrician consuls of the first days of the Republic neither nominated, nor would accept the nomination of, any plebeian. But why did not the Assembly of the Centuries by persistent rejection of patrician nominees force the consuls to nominate at least one plebeian? It has already been pointed out that the Assembly was so constituted as to favour the aristocratic vote. Under the earliest Republic there can have been few plebeians in the centuries of the first class, and none in the Equites. As time went on, and the number of rich plebeians increased, the influence of the Plebs was more felt; and eventually the legislation of 367, which opened the magistracy in actual fact to the Plebs, was the result.

But there is one more fact which must be recognised for the right understanding of Roman constitutional history, and that is the enormous power of the magistracy. It had had its counterpart in Greece in the days succeeding the abolition of the kingship, for example in Athens in the days before Solon, or, at any rate, before Draco. But in Rome it continued in theory, and to a large extent in practice, to the end of the Republic. The sole power to initiate legislation, the administration of justice in matters civil and criminal, the executive, or power of putting into operation the laws, and the whole administration of the state—all these things were absolutely in their hands. They were in fact autocrats during their year of office. Certain of these powers were reduced in some cases in later days;

but to the end of the Republic the majority of them were attributes of magisterial authority at Rome.

The fight for freedom at Rome is not a fight for a democratic paper constitution—that existed from the beginning of the Republic—but for a democratic reality. The reality, when it came, was stillborn.

The first stage in the fight is the battle for civil liberty against the arbitrary judicial power of the magistrates, who decided criminal cases on an unwritten, unknown code—if code there was—and from whose sentence there was no appeal. Later tradition put the passing of the Law of Appeal (Lex de Provocatione) in the very first years of the Republic. That is as it may be. But its effect was that from all magisterial sentences involving the life or civil status of a citizen, the prisoner could appeal to the Comitia. This had the effect of making the magistrate little more than a judge in the first instance, and of setting up this Assembly as a protective, if cumbersome, criminal court. The law itself is said to have been a concession on the part of the consuls to those plebeian land-holders who formed the mass of the legionary heavy infantry. But subsequent experience showed that consuls might disregard it; and thus the Roman learned the fact that civil can only be assured by political liberty.

It is significant that in the fight for liberty the Roman wins his rights *qua* soldier and not *qua* civilian.

It was a military revolt which brought about the next reform, the establishment of the Tribunate of the Plebs, an office neither originally nor at any later time a magistracy of the Roman people.[1] It was to have a fantastic constitutional development in future history; but, as first established, its sole function was to protect the plebeian against the arbitrary power of the magistrate. It was indeed a buttress of the Law of Appeal. It was said to have been established in 494.

Reform seems to have proceeded rapidly, for in 471, so it is said, the tribunes were given the right to convene and address meetings of the Plebs (concilia plebis) and to put resolutions to them. They had probably done so before; but now the practice was legalised. The concession was more important than it might appear, for the right of calling and addressing a public meeting at Rome was at all times confined strictly to those in actual office. The Roman had throughout a profound distrust of irresponsible political chattering; and adhered to the sound principle that those who propound policies should have the responsibility of carrying them out in practice. So

---

[1] Appian calls it " an opposition to the magistracy, rather than a magistracy."

the right of addressing the people was confined to the magistrates and the tribunes of the Plebs. By 449 the number of tribunes had been raised to ten, at which it remained thereafter.

The next stage in the struggle was for a written code of law. After ten years of strife a commission of the patricians (decemviri) promulgated about the year 450 the Twelve Tables, a curious medley of the usage and law of the past; but important as guaranteeing that every man might know the law under which he should be judged.

Under the rule of the Tarquins Rome had been part of a peaceful Etruscan dominion. After their fall her territory was reduced to the lands between the Tiber and the Siris, and she found the task of self-defence a much harder one than before. She and her Latin neighbours in the plain of Latium suffered from the attacks of the neighbouring hill tribes; and so they concluded in 494 a confederacy for self-defence, which the Hernici, a hill tribe, joined in 486; but up to 449 Rome and her allies suffered many grievous things from raids of the hostile mountaineers.

Greece

The history of Greece in the first half of the fifth century is, owing to the hostility of Persia, inseparable from that of Asia Minor and the Euphrates region; but the story of affairs in Greece itself is not comprehensible unless a clear view is first obtained of two factors in the situation, the parties in Athens and their political aims, and the foreign policy of Sparta.

Parties at Athens

Parties in Attica when Pisistratus first obtained the tyranny were three in number, corresponding to the existent classes, of which the Pediaci were the oligarchs, the Parali the middle, and the Diacrii the ultra-democratic party. During Pisistratus' time the economic betterment of the condition of the Diacrii had brought into being a prosperous rural population, which ceased consequently to be the ultra-democrats of pre-Pisistratid times, and emerged in the time of Cleisthenes, from 510 onwards, as a party of moderate views, a middle party of conservative democratic tendencies. It is the Parali of former days, the former men of the coast, and now the craftsmen and sailors of Athens and Piræus, who have become the extremists, probably under the stress of poverty brought about by unemployment due to the competition of a slave labour which the new com-

[1] See page 73.

mercial capitalist, who had sprung up by reason of the Solonian legislation, was able to employ.[1]

Ancient historians are apt to distinguish but two parties at Athens in the fifth century, which they call by the contrasting names of Aristocrats and Democrats. As a fact the three parties of the sixth century lived on through the fifth with the same fundamental political differences as had existed between them as of old, though the names Pediaci, Diacrii, and Parali disappear because the political and economic questions which divided those classes in the sixth century, the questions with which these names are especially associated, have changed in character in the fifth. Instead of them appear an oligarchic or aristocratic party, a middle or moderate democratic party, and an ultra-democratic party. In practical politics the oligarchs, being few in number, and being aware that they could not under the one-man-one-vote principle of democracy carry any policy of their own, voted with the moderates as being by far the less objectionable of their two opponents. Thus the Greek historians came to treat what was really a coalition of two parties as a single party, and for the sake of convenience included in the name of aristocrats that middle party which was quite ready to accept aristocratic support, but not by any means willing to adopt aristocratic ideas or policy. It is only when the situation of the time renders only one policy possible for aristocrats and moderates alike that it accepts the leadership of aristocrats, of a Miltiades or a Cimon.

In home affairs the ideal of the aristocrats was an oligarchy of the ancestral type; whereas the moderates desired a democracy with a franchise based on the hoplite census. Both parties alike would have wished to make agriculture the main economic interest of the state; their policy, in other words, was to retain the old character of Attica as a self-centred community without any outside interests such as would entail large obligations abroad.

The fight with the ultra-democrats for the maintenance of this policy came to a head between 490 and 480; and, though it ended in the defeat of the coalition conservative party, yet that party shows itself throughout the latter half of the century in the opposition which the coalition makes to the policy of empire. It was the tragedy of an inevitable course of events that this anti-imperialist party should become responsible for a course of action which made empire an almost unavoidable necessity.

[1] I have not noticed that any Greek History so far published has recognised this change in parties in the sixth century. I have described it in my "Thucydides and the History of his Age," published in 1911. It is the clue to Athenian party history in the fifth century. Unless it is recognised, that party history becomes a maze of puzzles and inconsistencies.

THE FIRST HALF OF THE FIFTH CENTURY

Of the ultra-democrats it need hardly be said that their policy was a full democracy with a manhood franchise. It is difficult to say what policy they put up against that of the conservatives [1] between 490 and 480. It was probably a trade policy in some special form; and it was certainly one which would have laid on Athens responsibilities outside Attica. Later when in 462 this extremist party became predominant in politics, finding an empire existent in fact though not in name, it accepted it as a welcome legacy from its opponents. As far as general policy in Greece during the century is concerned, the oligarchs show themselves quite ready to accept a Spartan hegemony as the price of an oligarchic constitution at Athens; the moderates are quite willing to accept a dual hegemony of Sparta and Athens in the Greek world at home; the ultra-democrats aim first at the hegemony, and later at an empire of Athens over all the Greek world.

Even in respect to domicile the parties of the fifth century resembled closely those of the sixth. The aristocrats were the rich land-owners of the plain. The moderates were mainly composed of the small rural cultivators, now a prosperous class; while the urban population of Athens and Piræus was mainly ultra-democratic. The proximity of the latter to the meeting-place of the Assembly gave them a preponderance in politics quite out of proportion to their numbers, which were perhaps inferior to those of the moderate democrats. The tendency of the policy of the city state to be at the mercy of the urban population, too often the least desirable element in the community, was one of the fatal weaknesses of that ancient institution.

POLICY OF SPARTA

The policy of Sparta in the fifth century was dictated by that position of the Spartiate population with reference to the Helots which had come to a head early in the previous century. Some contemporary and later writers had a general idea that such was the case; but neither they nor the mass of the Greek world had any real knowledge of the internal affairs of Sparta, so important was it for that state to conceal the facts of the case from the rest of Greece by rigidly excluding strangers from its borders. Hence ancient writers could do no more than give the story of such incidents in Spartan history as fell outside the bounds of Sparta itself, without any knowledge of the motives which had prompted the Spartan government to act in this or that way on any special occasion. Thus the incidents seem as if they had

[1] I shall in future speak of the coalition between aristocrat and moderate in Athenian politics, at all times when it is in effective existence, as the conservative party.

taken place in a world where the law of cause and effect did not rule, and the guesses at motive are either wrong or inadequate.

It is fairly plain that in Sparta itself the policy of the state was ruled during this century by a party formed of a majority of the population which was convinced of the necessity of conserving the available forces of the state for the maintenance of the position with regard to the Helots, and was consequently opposed to any policy which might involve Sparta in obligations which would necessitate the employment abroad of any large Spartiate force for any protracted period. This party may for convenience sake be denominated the National Party. On the other hand it is also certain that there was a minority which disliked the cast-iron system of life at home; which was unconvinced, or refused to be convinced, of the absolute necessity of protection against the Helots; and which every now and then, under the leadership of some prominent individual, got the half, though not the whole, of its way, in some act of policy. That accounts for the otherwise inexplicable cases in which some particular policy fails for a cause which does not appear in the records in history, but is obviously to be sought in Sparta itself. This may be illustrated by Sparta's attitude during the century towards the oligarchical party at Athens. Both parties at Sparta would have preferred Athens to be under an oligarchy. Both parties knew that no oligarchy at Athens, even if set up, could maintain its existence without persistent Spartan support. This would have meant the frequent if not permanent presence of a Spartan military force in Attica, a policy which the National party would not accept for a moment. The Imperialists supported it, because an oligarchical Athens would have been in practice a dependency of Sparta; and on some occasions, by means which are not now known, they were able to give military assistance to the Athenian oligarchs. But it always fails, either because the force is too small, or because dissension breaks out among the invaders.

It was the Nationalist party which guided Spartan policy during the century with a consistency in strong contrast to the obvious inconsistencies of Spartan history as told, but not explained, by the historians. Sparta's military strength was kept at home as far as possible; and a stern, even cruel, policy of repression was observed towards the Helots. In Peloponnese Sparta provided against the possibility of some neighbour tampering with the Helots by maintaining a control of the peninsular states through a Peloponnesian league in which she was supreme. Megara came into it; so did Corinth; both from fear of Athens. Corinth was important as having a navy; but was inconvenient as having interests wider than non-commercial Sparta wished to support. Argos stood out in inflexible jealousy of that power

… which had usurped her leadership in Peloponnese. Sparta was strong enough to have forced her into the league had she wanted to do so; but she wanted to sleep undisturbed, and Argos would have been a restless bedfellow.

Greece north of the isthmus was, according to the Nationalist policy, too far off for direct political action; and Sparta's interest in it was only aroused when disturbance there meant disturbance in the Peloponnese. Here Sparta's policy was diplomatic. The Bœotian confederacy was played off against Attica with a view to maintain a balance of power: and friendship with Delphi was carefully maintained so that its influence might be used in Sparta's interests.

Wars with Persia

The history of the first twenty years of the century, so far as it is known, centres on the enterprise of Persia against Greece, while that of the second twenty years is concerned largely with the enterprise of Greece against Persia. In the last ten years of the half-century the interest centres in the first Peloponnesian War.

After the death of Cambyses in 522 a pretender who put himself forward as Smerdis, brother of the late king, ruled for a time, till a conspiracy of the Persian nobility overthrew him; and Darius, who was probably related to the Achæmenid family, seized the throne. He must have been one of the ablest men in ancient history. But the satraps of the provinces seem to have refused to recognise him; and thus it befell that he had to reconquer the empire, a task which took him several years. He then set himself to carry out an organisation of his dominions which, whatever its defects, was conceived in a much more enlightened spirit than had been shown by any of the previous empires of the East. If he made one error, it was perhaps in liberality, in that he left to the conquered peoples too much of their native institutions. This tended to differentiate the satrapies to such an extent that in later years, in weaker hands than his, the empire tended to develop into a loose mass of subkingdoms in which the satraps exercised an hereditary, quasi-monarchical, and almost independent rule. Such a state of things was indeed guarded against in the original organisation; but no amount of organisation could prevent the decay of an empire the rulers of which became more and more the products of the life of the harem.

It is difficult to guess what instigated Darius to carry his rule into Europe. It may have been a certain nervousness as to the behaviour of the Asiatic Greeks so long as their brethren across the Ægean were free from Persian rule. But this seems too small a cause for so large an effect. The true motive of the design has not survived in record, and cannot now be conjectured.

A preliminary of the advance in Europe was that Scythian expedition which has been rendered famous and fabulous by the way in which Herodotus tells the story of it. Its date is uncertain; but it must fall between 513 and 508 B.C. Its object was not conquest, as it would seem, for the possession of the northern shores of the Euxine would have been a source of weakness rather than of strength to Persia. It is probable that movements in south Russia indicated or suggested another Scythian raid into Asia like that of a century before, and that Darius wished to forestall anything of the kind by giving the Scythians a home lesson. The close kinship of race between the Scythian and Persian would make it easy for him to get information as to what was taking place in Scythia. The lesson seems to have been learnt, for the future troubles of Persia did not come from there.

Part of Herodotus' story is the celebrated tale of the proposal of Miltiades to the other tyrants of Ionia to break the Danube (Ister) bridge, and thus leave the Persian army stranded in south Russia. It came to nothing; but it is significant of a feeling which was to show itself in action a few years later in the outbreak of the Ionian revolt.

On his way back from the Danube Darius detached Megabazus with an army to conquer Thrace. He certainly subdued the coast district as far as the all-important passage of the Strymon in the neighbourhood of the later Amphipolis. A little later Otanes, successor to Megabazus, took Byzantium and Chalcedon on the Bosphorus, and reduced the islands of Lemnos and Imbros. There can be little doubt that the campaign in Thrace was planned with the intention of securing that narrow well-marked route along the north coast of the Ægean which led to Greece, and that, had not other events intervened, the invasion of Greece would have taken place in the first decade of the fifth century. Had it done so, the result must have been very different from that of the invasion of 480–79; for a Greece which had not taken the measure of the military boot of Persia at Marathon would have been terrified into submission by the awe-inspiring magnitude of the great empire. Even in 480 it was found difficult to organise resistance. The Ionian revolt was the first salvation of Greece.

Ionian Revolt

The tale of the revolt as told by Herodotus gives both in general and in detail a very misleading picture of what really happened, and conveys a wrong impression of its importance in Greek history. Herodotus had some grudge against the

Ionians, arising possibly from personal experience of political troubles in his early life at Halicarnassus, which caused him to present their character and their exploits in the most unfavourable light. Judged by the light of facts the revolt was an almost audacious venture very bravely carried out.

The prime-mover was Aristagoras, who had succeeded his relative Histiæus, whom Darius had interned at Susa, in the tyranny of Miletus. There seem to have been others in the Ionian cities who were in the plot from the beginning.[1] Herodotus also tells a tale that Histiæus sent from Susa a message advising a revolt tattooed on the head of a slave, and that Aristagoras acted as haircutter at the end of the journey.

To ensure success the Ionian fleet must be mobilised to make joint action possible ; and as this could not be done by the Ionians without giving the design away at its commencement, Aristagoras artfully proposed to Artaphernes, satrap of Sardes, an attack on Naxos, a place peculiarly attractive because that island had become the heir of Samos as an entrepôt of Ægean trade, and had acquired wealth thereby. Artaphernes accepted the plan, and mobilised the Ionian fleet in 499 B.C. The attack on Naxos failed, and, so says Herodotus, Aristagoras was, as adviser of the venture, in a very awkward position. It is more probable that he was exactly in the position in which he had wished to find himself. A meeting of the conspirators was held immediately after the return from Naxos, and the revolt was decided upon, Hecatæus, the celebrated geographer, who advised against it, being in a minority of one. The first measure of the conspirators was the deposition of all tyrants, both those on the fleet and those in their respective cities—a natural measure as they had been Persian agents.

Aristagoras then went off to Greece to seek help. The tale of his visit to Cleomenes King of Sparta became no doubt famous in Greece. The most interesting items in it are that Aristagoras brought with him a map of the world engraved on a bronze tablet ; and that he emphasised the superiority of the Greek heavy-armed infantry men over anything Persia could put in the field, thus stating a truth which it took Greece another hundred years to learn. Cleomenes was probably an imperialist : but his imperialism was confined to Greece. And so the request for help was refused. From Athens, however, was obtained an aid of twenty ships. " These ships were a source of woes to the Greeks and to the barbarians," says Herodotus, who regarded the revolt as the great mistake of the century.

Its tale as told by Herodotus is dull and uninteresting, and

[1] See Hdt. v. 36, which shows that there were other conspirators already in existence.

extraordinarily indefinite in its chronology ; so that the dates which follow must be accepted with reserve.

In the spring of 498 ships from Athens and Eretria arrived on the coast. Whether they took part in a naval victory which the Ionians won over the Phœnician fleet on the Pamphylian coast is not known : but later, in the summer, an attack was made on Sardes, and Artaphernes, who had had to throw up the siege of Miletus, was besieged in the citadel. But the Greeks had to fall back from Sardes, and on their retreat were defeated, not very badly as it would seem, at Ephesus. In the autumn the Athenian fleet returned home, withdrawn probably by the philo-Medic ultra-democrats of the time.

In the spring of 497 the Ionian fleet brought about the revolt of the Hellespont region, and with the summer both Caria and Cyprus revolted from Persia ; but in the winter Cyprus was again reduced. In 496 Persia put forward a great effort, and there was fierce fighting in the Hellespont district and in Caria, in which latter region the Persians suffered in the autumn a great defeat at Pedasus. Late in the year Aristagoras died at Myrcinus ; and very shortly after his death his exiled relative Histiæus arrived at Sardes from Susa, having got his release by persuading Darius that he could settle the revolt and, if Herodotus is to be believed, could do many things besides. But as Artaphernes, who probably knew more about him than Darius did, proved inconveniently inquisitive and suspicious, Histiæus thought it best to get beyond his reach and go over to his fellow-Greeks. However the Milesians would not have him ; the Chians would not trust him ; and the Lesbians got rid of him by providing him with a capital of eight ships wherewith to set up a private pirate enterprise at Byzantium. This in the autumn of 495. During that year Persia was pouring reinforcements into western Asia Minor, and Miletus, the centre of the revolt, was attacked in the spring of 494. Then came the disastrous naval defeat of the Ionians in the battle of Ladé. Despite the fact that some of the cities are represented by a suspiciously small number of ships, the pan-Ionian fleet numbered 353 vessels, so that the battle must have been on a scale only equalled in Greek history by that of Salamis. Herodotus has tales of bravery and cowardice to tell of the battle ; but as contributions to truth they are suspect. Miletus fell shortly afterwards ; and with its fall the revolt collapsed. Persia spent the earlier part of 493 in sweeping up the mess in Ionia.

In the tragedy of the contest between Persian and Greek the modern world is wont to look on the Persian as the villain of the plot, a view which may be justified by the fact that the Persian sought to rob the Greek of his political liberty. But

THE FIRST HALF OF THE FIFTH CENTURY 125

the Persian was a very civilised villain. If the proposed action of the Athenian democracy towards the revolted Mytilenians during the Peloponnesian War be compared with the policy which the Persian adopted to the cities of Ionia after the revolt, the brutality of the Athenian comes into strong contrast with the extraordinarily humane treatment of the revolted subjects of Persia. This too was the behaviour of a people who had lived in a world where every hideous form of cruelty to a recalcitrant subject had from time immemorial been regarded as justifiable. Even the most prejudiced Greek author was unable to rake up a grave charge of cruelty or even of severity against the Persian on this occasion. There was not even a restoration of tyrants to act as Persian agents. Popular governments were set up in the cities, and a financial survey of their resources was made with a view to equable taxation. They were moreover compelled to set up machinery for the peaceful settlement of inter-state disputes.

CLEOMENES

Before continuing the tale of relations between Persian and Greek, the story of Cleomenes of Sparta must be told as an interlude in this particular act of the world's history. He is one of the most puzzling personages with which the historian of Greece has to deal. He was one of the most prominent and one of the most disturbing characters of his day. When not engaged in troubles which he himself had made he sought relaxation in participating in others for which other people were responsible —that is at any rate the impression conveyed by the somewhat inadequate annals of his stormy life.[1]

He seems to have come to the throne in 520. The importance of the story of his reign in Greek history arises from the light which is thrown on the relations between the nationalist and imperialist parties at Sparta, and the effects of the clash of their policies on the external enterprises of that kingdom. His accession had been disputed by his half-brother Dorieus, who, worsted in the conflict, sought a home abroad, first in Cyrene, and later in Sicily, where he subsequently perished in conflict with the Carthaginians.

About 519, Platæa, which then and ever disliked the hegemony of Thebes in Bœotia, applied to Sparta for protection. As this would have probably involved military interference, Sparta refused, but suggested Athens as patron; and Athens took over the responsibility. The nationalists in Sparta thus

---

[1] The dates hereafter given for events in the life of Cleomenes are approximate. For discussion of this problem, see J. Wells, "Journal of Hellenic Studies," 1905.

killed two birds with one stone : they avoided incurring direct liabilities north of the isthmus, and they induced Athens to undertake a trust which would certainly tend towards unfriendly relations with Thebes, promoting that balance of power which was the nationalist ideal in Northern Greece. Athens was indeed still under Peisistratid rule ; but the Peisistratid relations with Sparta, formerly friendly, had been much modified by a flirtation between Hippias and Argos about 521. This it was without doubt which induced the Spartans to help the Alcmæonidæ in the expulsion of Hippias in 510. That particular piece of policy somewhat missed fire when Athens showed a strong disposition to establish a democracy. Still the nationalists would have preferred a democracy to an obligarchy which could not stand on its own legs and would be dependent on continuous Spartan support. But when Isagoras at Athens tried to set up an oligarchy Cleomenes managed on two occasions to intervene in his favour. A unanimous Sparta could have had her own way in the Athens of that time ; but on the first occasion, probably owing to nationalist opposition, the force was too small to effect anything permanent ; and on the second, in 507, though Cleomenes seems to have had more of his own way, the fundamentally divided policies of the time brought about a quarrel between the two kings, and the invasion came to naught, save that it involved an irreparable disaster to Chalcis, which, with Thebes, had been in alliance with Sparta in the matter.

Subsequent events were to show that Cleomenes was becoming more and more influential at Sparta, and ever more dangerous to the nationalists and their policy. He did indeed refuse the request of Aristagoras in 499 ; but then, as has been already said, his imperialism was confined to the Greek mainland.

The imperfect records of the time streak its history with light and darkness ; and the next appearance of Cleomenes is about 494, when Argos seems to have been giving some trouble, sentimental or real, to Sparta. So the Spartans invaded that state under Cleomenes' command, and won a victory at Sepeia which practically wiped out the Argive army, putting Argos out of action in Greek politics at home for many years to come. The next incident was in connection with one of those wars between Athens and Ægina, the story of which is so confused in Herodotus that it is difficult to assign any dates to them. The hostility was due to Ægina's jealousy of the growing trade of Athens. One of these wars falls in the middle of the nineties of the century. But the danger to Athens became great just before the time of Marathon when the determination of Persia to punish Athens and Eretria for their share in the Ionian revolt became known, and Ægina, so it is said, conceived the idea of helping to crush her rival by assisting Persia. The anti-Persian party at Athens [1] appealed to Sparta for help, and, as that party was the conservative party which Cleomenes had tried to help some fifteen years before, that king took hostages from Ægina and deposited them at Athens. For some reason or other the king Demaratus, who was probably leader of the national party, disapproved of this policy, and the quarrel was so severe that Cleomenes got up a charge of illegitimacy against him, a charge peculiarly difficult to meet owing to the unusual domestic life at Sparta. Demaratus having been deposed took refuge at the Persian Court, that home of rest for the disgruntled Greek politician of the fifth century. But Cleomenes' intrigue in the matter got noised abroad, so that he too had to fly to a moral climate less severe than that of Laconia. He went first to Thessaly, and then came back to Arcadia, where he probably spent his time, as Pausanias did after him, in tampering with the Helots across the Spartan border, a course of action best calculated to annoy and alarm that national party which had opposed and probably deposed him. Later he went mad, and was brought home to the care of his friends only to die by his own hand. Thus perished a Greek who would probably, for good or evil, have made a greater name for himself, had he not been a Spartan.

Expedition of 492

Not a year had passed since the suppression of the Ionian revolt when the Persian general Mardonius was despatched in 492 into Europe with Greece as his objective. The size of the expedition is indicated by the fact that a large fleet accompanied the army, probably for commissariat purposes, a plan which Cambyses had adopted in his invasion of Cyrene. Herodotus is doubtless right in surmising that the intention was to make large conquests in Greece,[2] though Athens and Eretria were the declared objective. But the expedition never got beyond Macedonia, owing, says Herodotus, to a great disaster to the fleet off the promontory of Mount Athos and a defeat by the Brygi. It may be safely presumed that the naval disaster and the loss of commissariat transports made it impossible for the army to advance further; and so it had to return to Asia.

Marathon

Two years later the attempt to invade Greece was repeated on a smaller scale inasmuch as the design was limited to the

[1] See later, p. 129.   [2] Hdt. vi, 43, 44.

reduction and punishment of Athens and Eretria. This is the famous Marathon expedition.

The story of the campaign as told by Herodotus is full of manifest discrepancies due to his having not known, or not believed, certain true elements in the tradition of it as preserved in his day some forty years later. He wrote when Athens was under the Periclean democracy; and the democrats of the middle of the fifth century had every reason to disguise or deny the truth with regard to what had happened in the year 490. The key to the story is in the political history of Athens between the expulsion of Hippias and Marathon, a story which has come down in a fragmentary form indeed, but in one in which it is possible to trace the main line of events.

Parties at Athens 510–490 B.C.

The struggle between Cleisthenes and Isagoras from 510 to 507 shows that the numerical balance of the two great parties at Athens was very fine, that the moderates with their oligarchic supporters under Isagoras were at least as strong as the ultra-democrats whom Cleisthenes led. To speak of a party being " in power " at Athens at any given time would be a misleading use of terms, for one party might be predominant at one meeting of the Assembly, and at the next the other might have a majority. It all depended on the numbers of the rural population who put in an appearance at any given meeting. In this twenty years there are policies and reversals of policies which show that the predominance was continually shifting from one side to the other.

The intervention of Sparta in 507 had indeed been futile; but it had scared the ultra-democrats inasmuch as it showed that Sparta was prepared to support the conservative party at Athens. They felt evidently that the new democratic constitution could not be safe unless they as a party gained some outside support to counterbalance that which Sparta was ready to give to their opponents. So in one of the years between 507 and 499 they despatched an embassy to Artaphernes, the satrap of Sardes, asking for an alliance. He demanded that the embassy should give earth and water, which the embassy did, evidently not understanding that Persia would take this as a token of Athens' submission. From this time forward they regarded themselves as having an alliance with Persia, whereas Persia regarded Athens as a subject. But the embassy " was blamed " on its return, says Herodotus, which means that, while it was away, the conservative party had again become for the time predominant. At some date not long after this, Hippias having failed to get restored to Athens by the help of

Sparta, went to Artaphernes, who, thinking that he would be a useful Persian agent in the land of the new Persian subject, took up his cause, and demanded from Athens his restoration as tyrant. It is necessary to realise what would be the attitude of the Athenian political parties to this demand. The moderate rural party owed its prosperity to Pisistratus, and was perfectly well aware of the fact. But in the first place Pisistratus was one thing and Hippias was another, and secondly a demand made by a foreign power which was supporting their political enemies was not likely to find favour with either the moderate or the oligarchical element among the conservatives. Nor can there be much question that the extreme democrats disliked the idea of the restoration of the tyranny which they themselves had overthrown; but as a refusal to accept the demand would have meant the end of the supposed alliance, and as that would have meant the possible establishment of an anti-democratic form of government with the aid of Sparta, it had to swallow the tyrannical pill. The conservatives must have been predominant too when Aristagoras came to Athens in 499, and when in 498 aid was sent to the Ionian rebels, for the ultra-democrats would not have adopted a policy calculated to exasperate their supposed ally Persia. But a few months later the democrats manage to get the aid withdrawn. The acceptance of Hippias by the party is indicated further by the election of Hipparchus, a member of the Pisistratid family, as archon in 497.

For the next four years nothing is known of internal affairs at Athens. The silence may be due to a war with Ægina. But in 493 events developed rapidly, and in a way ominous for ultra-democracy. The democrats managed to get Themistocles elected to the archonship, and to fine Phrynichus for that play, " The Capture of Miletus," which had been directed against their policy in withdrawing aid from the Ionian rebels. With that their success ended. Miltiades returned from his tyranny in the Thracian Chersonese, a fugitive from that Persian vengeance which he had done all he could to deserve; and with him the conservatives acquired a leader of prestige and capacity such as they had wanted. The ultra-democrats prosecuted him for tyranny, and his acquittal shows the strength of the voting power of the rural population when it was attracted to Athens by business of great importance. It is probable that the next three years before Marathon were a very anxious time for the ultra-democrats. Conservatism was in the ascendancy, and it must have seemed as if the only question was the date at which some reactionary reform of the constitution would be attempted, action which may have been deferred by the trouble with Ægina. This no doubt strengthened the tie between the ultra-democrats and Persia, and led to that agreement by which they undertook in case of a Persian invasion of Attica to take action in the Persian interest. They were guilty of a medism which had not in the day of Marathon that evil connotation created for it by battles as yet unfought and events as yet to come.

Space would not permit of a long discussion of the difficulties raised by Herodotus' account of Marathon; but the majority of them vanish when the position of the ultra-democrats at the time is realised, and the truth of the tale of Alcmæonid medism, which Herodotus so weakly denies, becomes evident.

The results of Mardonius' expedition of 492 had been the conquest of Macedonia and the reconquest of southern Thrace.

CAMPAIGN OF MARATHON

The disaster at Athos did not cause Darius to give up his scheme for the conquest of Greece, though it modified the means to be taken to that end. He determined that he must first get a footing on Greek soil before he attempted to carry out the larger design; and Athens, if subdued, would afford him a base of operations against the other states, and, incidentally, Athens and Eretria might be punished for the part they had taken in the Ionian revolt. Later tradition was enthusiastic in exaggerating the magnitude of the expedition of 490.[1] Herodotus never states the numbers of the Persians, maybe from a profound distrust of the numbers reported in the tradition of his own day; but he does say that the number of ships on which the army was transported across the Ægean was 600, and that suggests a force numbering at most 60,000 men, and possibly not more than 40,000. The commanders were Datis and Artaphernes, the son of the great satrap at Sardes. During the passage of the Ægean Naxos was attacked and damaged, and a landing made at Delos, where the Persians treated the sanctuary with respect. Then Carystus in south Eubœa was attacked, after which came the turn of Eretria, which resisted bravely till treachery did its work. The population was removed to exile on the lower Euphrates.

From Eretria the Persian armament crossed the Euripus and landed on the small plain of Marathon in the extreme northeast of Attica about twenty-four miles from Athens. The intention was to draw the Athenian army from Athens, and so give the philo-Medic ultra-democrats in the city the opportunity for seizing the capital, and for making preparations to admit the Persians. The completion of their preparations was to be

---

[1] In this account of Marathon I am limited to a statement of conclusions from the evidence. The discussion of the evidence will be found in my book "The Great Persian War."

signalled to the Persians, who would then leave a containing force to hold the Athenian army at Marathon, while the rest of them went round by sea to occupy Athens.

Meanwhile the Athenian commanders at Athens were in a difficulty. They could count on the hoplites, who would be drawn mainly from that conservative rural population which had opposed the extremists for the last twenty years; but they knew well that the ultra-democrats had relations with the invader and were quite ready to betray Athens to him. Thus they dare not at first withdraw the army from the capital. But it is plain that there came some reversal or mitigation of the situation, probably due to the news of what had happened at Eretria, information which was well calculated to disillusion the ultra-democrats as to the real intentions of Persia, and to show them that what they had regarded as an alliance was not looked on in that light by the Persian government. At any rate, the Athenian generals found it safe to march the army to Marathon, where the Persians, who had been waiting for a signal from the ultra-democrats, had not moved. A hurried message had been despatched to Sparta for aid; and, later, after the battle, a moderate Spartan force did arrive to give the oligarchs that strictly limited assistance which the nationalist party was ready at all times to give them.

At Marathon the position for some days was stalemate. Miltiades, now one of the ten generals or commanders of the tribal regiments, had persuaded the polemarch or commander-in-chief, Callimachus, and the council of war [1] to defer any attack on the Persians until the latter showed signs of moving. The position of the Athenians at the precinct of Heracles among the hills above the plain was too strong for the Persians to be able to attack it with any hope of success; and so the Athenians could bide their time and wait for the coming of the Spartans. On the other hand it was all-important for the Persians to anticipate that arrival; and so, after waiting in vain for the signal, they determined to act. On a certain morning the Athenians found a Persian force drawn up in order of battle at the south end of the plain, while the rest of the army was embarking in the fleet. This was the moment which Miltiades had anticipated; and so the Athenian army descended the valley of Aulon (the Funnel) to the attack. Greek hoplite armies were always drawn

[1] Herodotus did not understand the system of command in the Athenian army in 490. In 487 a change in the system took place; and Herodotus mixes up the old system with that which prevailed in his own day. Callimachus as polemarch was the genuine commander-in-chief, and had the command in battle. General questions of strategy were decided by a council of war composed of the polemarch and the ten generals who commanded the regiments of the tribes.

up for battle with peculiarly strong wings. This feature of Greek military practice was purposely exaggerated in the Athenian army at Marathon, and in the battle which ensued, though the thin Athenian centre was driven in, the wings drove back the Persians opposed to them, and then fell on the flanks of the Persian centre, which seems to have been practically wiped out.

The promptness with which the victory had been won enabled the Athenians to get back to Athens before the Persian force which had been sent round by sea could land at Phalerum. The Persians attempted nothing; and the curtain falls on the tragedy of Marathon.

Two thousand Spartans arrived shortly after the battle, and a contingent of Platæans actually took part in the fight, over whom a large amount of sentiment has been wasted by authors who seem to forget that, if Athens were not saved from Persia, Platæa would not be safe from Thebes. Also after the battle had been won the Alcmæonidæ gave the Persians the long-expected signal, a strange tribute both of welcome and farewell. Apparently they had refused to share the disillusionment of their party.

Marathon is not perhaps one of the decisive battles of the world, though its results were of great importance in that it gave Athens a reputation which was to lead to empire in a near future which as yet no man could have foreseen. It also showed that the Greek hoplite had no equal among the soldiers of the then world of the East, a lesson which, as has been already said, the Greek took a hundred years to learn.

PARTY HISTORY 490–450

The history of Greek politics generally from 490 to 480 is almost a blank. The position of the conservatives at Athens was greatly strengthened; and Aristides, who had no doubt been the real leader of the moderate section during the events of 490, was elected archon in 489. But in some way which is not really known Miltiades wrecked the position by a failure in an attack on Paros, of which Herodotus gives an account so confusing that any conjecture as to the real story is impossible.

It is quite certain that during this decade the party struggle of the previous twenty years was continued with great vivacity on both sides, and that the questions involved were of the most crucial and far-reaching influence on the future development of the state. Of the nature of two of them there is suggestive though not complete evidence. To the nature of the third the situation before and after Marathon points distinctly. In practical politics the three questions and their solutions were largely interdependent.

In the previous three-quarters of a century Athens had developed enormously both as an agricultural and a commercial state; and as the agriculturists tended towards moderate conservatism, while the craftsmen and sailors of the commercial world were mostly extreme democrats, there was a clash of political as well as economic interests between the classes. Thus the question whether Athens was to remain a self-centred agricultural state of the old Greek type, or to expand as a commercial state with the external political obligations thereby entailed, was the question of the time. Further, the problem of unemployment was certainly becoming a pressing one; and lastly the extreme democrats, having lost the support of Persia, were looking for some means of counteracting the support which Sparta seemed inclined to give to the conservatives. On the Spartan question they were more apprehensive than they need have been; but then no one knew the secret workings of Spartan policy.

The conservatives must have held the upper hand for a short period after the fall of Miltiades, for a law of ostracism, passed in the official year 488–7 with a view to allaying acute political dissension by exiling for a time one of the chief dissenters, was put in operation against Megacles the Alcmæonid the same year. But in the next year 487–6 a law introducing the application of the lot to the election of archons must have been the work of the democrats. It was impossible to entrust the command of the army to a polemarch elected by lot, and so it was put in commission to the body of the ten generals (stratêgi), a body the powers of which so increased during the century that its functions came to include the management of the details of foreign affairs.

But the measure which brought all the questions of the hour to a head was Themistocles' proposal, made in 484–3, to use the largely increased revenues from the mines of Laurium for the purpose of adding 200 vessels to the Athenian fleet, an addition which would make it by far the largest in the Greek world. If this was done, it would be all over with the conservative ideal of keeping Athens an agricultural state; and the proposal raised a fierce controversy which resulted in the victory of the democrats and the ostracism of Aristides.

The motives of this measure are hardly less important than its results in later history. Herodotus, who draws much of his history of Themistocles from sources hostile to that statesman, says that a contemporary war with Ægina was that which weighed with him in making the proposal, and does not credit him with that foresight implied in the motive attributed to him by Plutarch, the anticipation of a repetition of the attack from Persia. In so far as he was actuated by military considerations, the story of Plutarch is the more probable. But it was a commonplace charge against him in later literature that by this measure he gave the " seafaring mob " the control of the state. Modern historians of Greece have mentioned the change without explaining it, as if it ought to be just as clear to a reader of the nineteenth and twentieth century as it was to a reader of the fifth century before Christ ; and the modern reader is left wondering what was its political significance to democrats all of whom already possessed the vote in a very democratic constitution. Its real significance was that whereas in the past the military power of the state had been with the army of conservative hoplites, it now passed to democrats who, withdrawn in large numbers from the reach of the hoplites by service in the fleet, could with that fleet block the corn routes and starve the remaining population of Attica into surrender should it attempt to overthrow the democratic constitution. Its significance in this respect was shown in the revolution of the Four Hundred in 411. Conservatism was very dominant after 480 ; but it never attempted to tamper with the constitution. Themistocles had given that democracy which had been disillusioned in 490 a support at home more effective than the Persian support which it had lost. Another effect of the increased fleet would be the employment of large numbers of unemployed as sailors on board it, a policy which every government of Athens right up to the close of the century had to adopt on as large a scale as the circumstances of the moment permitted.

A consideration which neither Themistocles nor any other Athenian statesman of the time could ignore was the securing of the route to the foreign sources of corn supply, for which the great fleet would be a satisfactory guarantee. That the encouragement of general commerce was part of his scheme is shown by his making it easy for resident aliens to settle in the country, men no doubt who had large tradition and experience of commerce in the older trading states.[1]

PERSIAN WAR OF 480

While these things were going on in Greece the Persian was meditating and preparing a grand attack on that country.

[1] There is reason to believe that the resident alien (metic) was throughout the future history in Athens a very influential person in Athenian trade, and that the native Athenian did not show particular aptitude for the business. The number of metics who appear as suitors in the law cases with which the private speeches of the orators of the late fifth and of the fourth century are concerned is very large when compared with that of the native Athenian litigants. It may be suspected that the metic came to play in Athens the part which Jewish and German firms were playing in British trade before 1914.

Darius seems to have begun his preparations almost immediately after the failure at Marathon ; but they were interrupted and diverted from their purpose by a great revolt in Egypt which broke out in 486 or 485, and took two years to suppress. Before its suppression Darius died. He was one of the most remarkable and most enlightened organisers of empire that the ancient world saw, and must have been one of the greatest men it produced.

His successor Xerxes was probably an abler man than the picture drawn of him by Greek authors would suggest, for their judgment applied but one test to his capacity, his failure in the great attack on Greece. After the suppression of the Egyptian rising he continued the collection and organisation of the means for carrying out the design of his predecessor. It is probable that since Marathon news of what was happening in the Persian dominions but rarely reached Europe, and then only in a vague form, so that the stir of preparation throughout the empire was known to few, and rightly interpreted by fewer still, in Greece. It is clear from the evidence of Herodotus that even when it became known, and even when the Greeks generally recognised that the object of attack was in Greece itself, many clung to the idea that it was no more than a repetition of the Marathonian campaign aiming at the punishment of Athens. Even when the Persian heralds were sent to the Greek states demanding earth and water, the unconvinced remained unconvinced, for the same measure had been taken as a preliminary to the attack of 490.

And now for the first time the Greek states illustrated that repugnance to union for joint action which was to be in the end fatal to the liberties of a race passionately devoted to liberty. Man cannot help being an individualist because he cannot help being an individual; and on the marked individualism of the Greek was based his passion for liberty, and his conception of it. The greatest intellectual figure in Greek history laid down that "man is by nature a social being" ; but he also postulated the limitation of the largest social unit, the state, to an area of very small size. The Greek would have liked to live in a world where a man could do as he liked without interference from or with his neighbours. This implies that his individualism, though very strong, was not as a rule of that brutal type which will pursue self-interest without any regard for the rights of others. But even primitive man came to recognise that he must in his own interest combine with others for self-defence above all, and, having done so, discovered that such an association brought amenities to life. And so the Greek had in the past climbed the ladder of society from the family to the clan with its village community, and from the clan to the state. But he was supremely conscious of the fact that association in a community carries with it the sacrifice of certain individual interests to those of the community, and that the larger the community the larger the sacrifice. He was determined that the sacrifice should be reduced to its lowest terms; in other words he considered that the balance between loss and gain was achieved when a man was a member of a society, the state, which offered him in return for the sacrifice of self-interest reasonable security against aggression from outside, and a reasonable supply of the necessaries and amenities of life. The marked physical features of his own country emphasised, and in a sense imposed on him, that conception of the limits of political association; and a life lived for centuries under the conditions of a city state, whose existence was not as yet threatened by the growth of any great aggressive world power in its immediate neighbourhood, so habituated him to that form of life and this conception of it that by the time of the opening of the fifth century he was unable to shake off this habit of mind, and adapt himself to the conditions of a world whose whole aspect was changed by the rise of aggressive world-powers like Persia and Macedon. The sentimental tie of race, customs, and religion was very strong, as every reader of Herodotus must recognise; but the whole spirit of the Greek world, educated by long use and tradition, was hostile to the political realisation of this sentimental unity. The political unit of the federation or confederation, as being a larger unit than the state, demanded a sacrifice of individual interest which the Greek would not make if he could help; and if, urged by fear or compulsion, he made it, he made it with the determination that the sacrifice should be as brief as possible. Hence the political unity of Greece was almost beyond realisation, and confederations of states formed for some particular purpose had within them from the beginning a centrifugal force which, unless checked by the superior force of a controlling state, must bring about their early dissolution, and that too very often before the purpose for which they were formed was attained.

The antipathy of the Greek to leagues or confederations was illustrated on various notable occasions in this century: in the difficulty in forming a combination to resist this attack in 480; in the dissolution of this league as soon as the danger in Greece was over; in the difficulty which Athens found in keeping together the league of Ægean states formed against the Persian in 477, even at a time when the safety of these states was by no means secured. Again even Sparta's Peloponnesian League, though cemented by the fear of Athenian aggression, fell to pieces after 421, never to be revived again in the same form.

In the fourth century the failure to combine against Macedon illustrated even more forcibly the same tendency.

Apart from the general disposition to avoid membership of a league, there is no doubt that some of the Greek states believed the coming expedition was aimed against Athens alone, and that if they gave earth and water they might escape the storm. Even Delphi, that centre of information to which the Greeks had been wont to resort for news from the outside world, believed that Athens was the sole object of the expedition, and advised the Athenians to fly to the ends of the earth; and it was to Athens alone that such advice was given. To the Cretans and Argives she counselled non-intervention.[1] Delphi's view was that if the Athenians could be induced to leave Greece, the expedition might never come, and that in any case the mischief might be confined to Attica if only the other Greek states would not interfere. But even "slow-witted" Sparta had made up her mind as to the real nature of the danger; and it was doubtless through her influence at Delphi, which was always great, that the priestly authorities there recanted, and even urged Athens to resistance. The rest of the states went various ways —some no doubt because they shared the error of Delphi with regard to the real intent of the expedition; some out of mere consideration of what they conceived to be their personal interest; others, the so-called patriotic states, because they believed that the liberties of all Greek states alike were in peril. In Thessaly the baronial families, led by the Aleuadæ of Larissa, medised, while the lower, half-serf class was ready to fight the Persians if the other Greeks would help them to protect Thessaly. Bœotia was divided in mind, if Plutarch is to be believed, though Herodotus states that it medised from the beginning, a statement which it is hard to reconcile with the story of the Thebans at Thermopylæ. Argos stood out of the defence on the excuse that after the disaster at Sepeia in 494 she had nothing to put in the field; but events later in the century suggest that she medised, and that not passively, but with intent to hamper the defence. That Sparta took one side in the matter was quite sufficient to make Argos take the other, regardless of whether her action was justifiable on any other ground. The rest of the states of the mainland chose the patriotic part, not in all cases with enthusiasm, but under compulsion coming from Sparta. Outside Greece proper the Cretans on the advice of Delphi, so they said, refused all aid. Corcyra adopted a half-hearted policy, waiting obviously to see how the cat would jump. Gelo

---

[1] Various authorities on Greek history have assumed that Delphi medised. I do not take this view for reasons fully stated in my book "The Great Persian War," pp. 232 ff.

of Syracuse, who had at his disposal a combined military and naval force greater than that of any other Greek state, was no doubt well aware that he was going to have his hands full at home, for he must have known by the time the Greek invitation reached him that the Carthaginians were by an arrangement with Persia organising an attack on the Greek states of Sicily which was to synchronise with the Persian attack on Greece. Herodotus' long account of the negotiations with him is rather picturesque than trustworthy.

The great Persian army collected at Sardes late in 481; and Xerxes spent the winter there. In the spring of 480 it began its march, first to the Hellespont, and then along the north coast of the Ægean to Therma in Macedonia.[1] Two great engineering operations, the bridging of the Hellespont [2] and the canal across the neck of the Athos peninsula, show that the art of engineering had been carried to a high pitch of development in the East.

The Greek league of defence had by now been formed, and the question arose as to the strategy which should be followed in resisting the attack. The main determinant was the nature of the Persian advance, a dual advance by land and sea, in which the fleet played both the part of a commissariat and that of an attacking force. The numbers of the invading army as given in Herodotus are hopelessly exaggerated, as no doubt they were in the tradition of the Greece of his day; but a reasoned modern calculation estimates the number of infantry as 300,000, together with a considerable force of cavalry.[3]

But that is indeed a large army, far larger than any which could be fed on the very limited food resources of Greece. The consequence was that, as the Greeks were evidently aware, the fleet *must* for commissariat purposes remain in touch with the army, otherwise the latter would starve; and consequently the Greek strategy was founded on the consideration that if the advance of *either* branch of the invading force could be stayed at a certain geographical point, the other branch could not advance to any distance beyond it. In deciding whether they would concentrate their main efforts on stopping the advance of the army or of the fleet, the Greeks were doubtless influenced by two considerations, the nature of the line of advance by land as compared with that by sea, and their past experience in battles with the Persian on the two elements. Both considerations

---

[1] Herodotus' account of this route leaves no reasonable doubt that he had traversed it himself.
[2] The rapid current of the strait and its width, from half to three-quarters of a mile, render this feat one which a modern engineer would not lightly undertake.
[3] Macan, Hdt. vii, viii, ix. Vol II, p. 160.

THE FIRST HALF OF THE FIFTH CENTURY

would lead to the same conclusion, since the passage to Greece from the north is for military purposes restricted to a line which offers no alternative save in its passage through Thessaly, and entails the traversing of narrow defiles at three points in its course, the Vale of Tempe in north Thessaly, Thermopylæ in Malis, and the narrow strip of land in Bœotia between the foot of Helicon and the western shore of Lake Copais, whereas the only narrow sea passage was that through the Euripus at Chalcis, which the Persian fleet could turn by passing outside Eubœa. Past experiences, too, drawn from Marathon and Ladé, were all in favour of a land defence; and moreover the Greeks were well aware that the Persian fleet outnumbered their own, and contained a very large element from Phœnicia, the home of the most reputed sailors of the day.

But the question was complicated by the attitude of Sparta and the Peloponnesians. Sparta was nervous about denuding Laconia of troops owing to the danger it would run from the hostile Argos and the still more hostile Helot, so she did not want to despatch a force north of the Isthmus; and the Peloponnesian states were equally reluctant on more general grounds of self-interest to do anything of the kind. After all Athens was the only state north of the Isthmus on whose assistance implicit trust could be placed, for the loyalty of the rest to the patriotic cause was at the best shaky. But Athens had no mind to leave her land to the mercy of the invader; and the other Greeks could not contemplate for a moment the withdrawal of the great Athenian contingent from the Greek fleet. So Athens got her own way; and the Peloponnesian consented reluctantly to the policy of defending the north. The Vale of Tempe was chosen at the request of the Thessalian commons as the place for the first stand; but, though a considerable force was sent there, including Athenians under the command of Themistocles, it was discovered that there were so many various ways of turning the passage through Tempe that the chance of defending it against superior numbers was unlikely. And so the expedition retired from Thessaly, and the Thessalian commons, being deserted, medised like their masters.

THERMOPYLÆ

It is probable that this led to a renewal of the Isthmus controversy; but the northern policy, backed by Athens, again prevailed, and it was determined to defend the Pass of Thermopylæ.

This was not a pass between mountains on either side, but one between the precipitous north slope of the Œta range, and the south shore of the Malian Gulf. The sea in those days approached very close to the mountain foot in three places in the course of four and a half miles ; and, where the sea did not come in, its place was taken by impassable marsh. Of the three narrows the Middle Gate, as it was called, was peculiarly defensible, because there the sea came literally to within a yard or two of the foot of the cliff ; and just where the narrows terminated, the track climbed a mound or bastion about two hundred feet high projecting from the cliff face. Here, if anywhere, an army could stop the advance of one of far superior numbers. It is true that the position might be turned by a path over the mountain ; but that was so difficult that a very small force might provide for its defence. The main point, however, was that the Persian army *must* go through Thermopylæ to get southwards. There was no other way by which any large force could advance.

Here then it was decided to make a second stand ; and, as the decision seems to have been belated, there was no time to lose. The force which actually went to Thermopylæ was 300 Spartans under their king Leonidas, 2,120 Arcadians from various towns, 400 Corinthians, 200 Phliasians, 80 Mycenæans, 700 Thespians, 400 Thebans, 1,000 Phocians, and the whole force of the Opuntian Locrians. Thus, excluding the unknown number of the Locrians, and adding the light-armed which would be present with the Spartan force, the number of defenders was 7,300.

On his arrival Leonidas explained to the Locrians that his force was only the vanguard, as it were, of a large army. But the larger army never came. The reluctance of the Peloponnesians had shown itself in action. They disliked the design, as they wanted to reserve their men for the defence of the Isthmus, which they were fortifying with feverish haste. So they sent but a small percentage of their available troops, hoping no doubt that the Bœotians and Phocians would contribute largely. At any rate the army could retreat if the pass was forced.

A necessary adjunct to the defence was the blocking of the northern Euripus with the Greek fleet in order to prevent the Persians from landing troops behind the defenders of Thermopylæ ; and to this necessity must have been due the absence of an Athenian contingent from the army there, for the Athenian hoplites would have to be present as fighters on board that large Athenian fleet at Artemisium in the north Euripus, since in Greek naval warfare of that time boarding tactics were mainly employed. The defenders made the summit of the mound at the Middle Gate their chief line of defence. For four days after arriving before it the Persians put off the attack, expecting a Greek retreat. Then for two days a fierce but resultless attack was made on

THE FIRST HALF OF THE FIFTH CENTURY 141

the Greek position. After that the Persians were at a loss what to do, until Epialtes, a native Malian, offered to lead a body of men along that path of the Anopæa by which the position at the Middle Gate could be turned. That evening a Persian band started along the path, and about the early morning took by surprise the Phocians who were guarding it, passing them by without their offering any resistance. This must have been announced to Leonidas a few hours later. On hearing this he detached a part of his troops, ordering them to go home, *so they said*, but probably with instructions to defend the path into the pass behind the mound. That they did not attempt to do. Doubtless he hoped with the remaining troops to be able to defend the Middle Gate, provided that those which he despatched could stop the Persian band on the path of the Anopæa. The courage of Leonidas was not the insensate courage of a self-sacrifice which involves the lives of others, but that calmer courage which will face great risks to attain great ends. The last fight must have been already engaged ere they heard that those who had been sent to stop the Persian in the path of the Anopæa had made no effort to fulfil their task. After that they fought with the courage of despair. The Spartans died round the dead body of Leonidas, and with him died the Thespians. The Thebans surrendered, so Herodotus says.

The story of the last fight as told by him is told with the simple eloquence of one who knows that he is telling the greatest story of his time, and is intensely conscious of the grandeur of it.[1]

Coming down the hill-side from the south, passing across the summit of the mound, and running down the steep north slope of it to what was then the sea, are even at the present day the foundations of that Phocian wall which Herodotus mentions, with a gap where the gateway in it stood formerly, just as he describes,[2] so that one who visits Thermopylæ to-day may stand on the very ground on which Leonidas stood, and realise the scene of that old fight with a vividness not afforded by any other site on other famous battle-fields of history.

SALAMIS

While these things had been going on at Thermopylæ, the Greek fleet which had its base at Artemisium on the north Euripus had been defending the passage of the strait against the Persian fleet. There had been several battles, and, though Herodotus half-disguises the fact, it is fairly clear that the fighting had not been favourable to the Greeks, though the Persians had not succeeded in forcing the straits. But the Persian had not

[1] Hdt. vii, 223. [2] Hdt. vii, 176.

come off unscathed, for a squadron of two hundred vessels which had been sent outside Eubœa to block the south end of the Euripus was wrecked in the Hollows of Eubœa, that series of bays on the shore of the island south of Chalcis. But the news of the disaster at Thermopylæ made the presence of the Greek fleet in the Euripus no longer necessary, and so it retired southwards through the strait, and finally took up its anchorage in the Strait of Salamis off the Attic coast. The Athenians had expected to find that an army had been sent to Bœotia to defend the narrow passage between Lake Copais and Mount Helicon. Needless to say the Peloponnesians had shown by cutting down their contingent at Thermopylæ to a minimum that they were not going to engage in any enterprise of the kind. The strategic position of the Greeks at this moment was as bad as it well could be. North of the Isthmus there was no land force in existence, for the Athenian hoplites were aboard the fleet. The fleet in the Strait of Salamis could be no aid to the Isthmus line of defence, which was nearly thirty miles away; and a battle in the open Saronic Gulf off the Isthmus against the greatly superior numbers of the Persian fleet would almost certainly have ended in disaster. Moreover there was no reason why the Persian fleet should not ignore the Greek fleet in the straits and sail on to the Isthmus to land troops behind the defence.[1] The Greek fleet went to Salamis to review the situation. It stayed there to help in the removal to safety of the Attic population. Some were sent to Trœzen, but others to the island of Salamis. The latter measure made it necessary for the Athenian fleet to remain in the strait to protect the refugees.

Meanwhile the Persian fleet arrived at Phalêrum Bay on the coast of Attica, only about four miles from the eastern entrance of Salamis strait. The Persian army entered Attica, and proceeded to lay waste the country. In its march south a detachment of it had tried unsuccessfully to raid Delphi—a strange venture if Delphi had medised.[2]

If a vague and inconsistent tale in Herodotus be true, a few Athenians had occupied the Acropolis of Athens, where they

---

[1] Some modern writers on Greek history have depicted the taking up of a position in the Strait of Salamis as a great strategical move on the part of the Greeks. The answer to such a theory is in the story of what happened at Salamis. If the Persian fleet had been bound in any way to attack the Greek fleet in the straits before moving on to the Isthmus, why did Themistocles show such anxiety to tempt the Persians to attack the Greeks? *He* seems to have thought that the Persians were under no such strategic necessity; and for my part I prefer to trust his view of the situation, rather than that of modern writers on the history of the time.

[2] See notes on Delphi, p. 137.

put up a vain defence against the Persian attack. But Herodotus' account leaves it quite uncertain whether the defence was a serious military operation, or whether it was carried out merely by certain of the population who had not been in time to escape to Salamis.

The channel between that island and the mainland begins on the east just off the mouth of the harbour of Piræus. It runs first north for about a mile and a half, having in the middle of it the island of Psyttalea, and on its west side the long narrow peninsula of Cynosura. Between Psyttalea and the Attic mainland it is about seven furlongs, and between Psyttalea and Cynosura from five to six furlongs broad. The channel then turns at right angles due west for about three and a half miles, being under a mile broad in this part, with a fairway of about three-quarters of a mile. It was in this eastern channel that the battle was fought. The channel then turns once more at right angles due north past the island of St. George, and, after two miles, enters the Bay of Eleusis, which is really a wide part of the channel itself. In the bay it turns west; and then enters a channel running south-west to a very narrow shallow western entrance off the coast of the Megarid. The total length of the channel is about twenty miles.

While the above events were taking place in Attica the position of the Greek fleet was one of uncertainty and alarm. It consisted of 366 ships, of which 180 were Athenian manned by Athenians, and 20 Athenian manned by Chalcidians. Of the rest of the fleet 20 were Megarean, and 30 Æginetan, so that 250, or more than two-thirds of the whole number, belonged to states which would be keenly interested in opposing any movement from Salamis towards the Isthmus, as in that case their lands and their people would be at the mercy of the Persians. On the other hand the Peloponnesian contingents from Corinth, Sicyon, Sparta, Epidaurus, Trœzen, and Hermione would be naturally anxious with regard to the defence of the Isthmus, and well aware that the position at Salamis would not in any way contribute to it. And so there arose fierce debates during the days of waiting as to whether the fleet should remain in the strait or should move southwards. The commander of the whole fleet was, as at Artemisium, Eurybiades, the Spartan admiral; and, holding that position, his voice must have been of great influence in the council of the admirals, a fact which is thrust into the background in the surviving versions of the story of the battle, all of which are drawn from Athenian sources, and in all of which the personality of Themistocles overshadows those of the other commanders present. In a sense the picture is true, for the critical question was not so much whether the

Greeks should remain in the strait as whether the Persians could be induced to attack them there instead of passing onward to aid their own troops in an attack on the defences of the Isthmus; and on both these questions the advocacy or action of Themistocles was decisive. But Eurybiades must have contributed largely to the decision to remain in the strait. Herodotus describes Adeimantus the Corinthian as the most bitter opponent of Themistocles' views; and, though the story has been regarded as a malicious invention of later times, there is much reason to believe that it is true.[1] In the pages of Herodotus Themistocles plays the double part of the hero and the villain of the piece, according as the historian is drawing on sources which were politically favourable or unfavourable to him thirty years later. Thucydides, an author of no enthusiasms and of peculiarly cold judgment, speaks of his ability in terms such as he never uses of the other characters which appear on the stage of his history in a passage which is probably the truest picture ever drawn by any author of that which the world calls genius. "Themistocles was a man who displayed genius in the most unmistakable way, and in this respect calls for admiration in a special and unparalleled manner."[2] His speech at the critical meeting of the admirals is reported at length by Herodotus;[3] and, though the language may be the work of the historian, the matter of it was almost certainly preserved in a true form in the tradition of later years. The main point which he argues is the necessity of fighting in narrow waters against a fleet which in manœuvring power is superior to that of the Greeks. He winds up with the threat that if the Athenians find themselves deserted at Salamis, they will desert the Greek cause altogether and retire to Siris in Italy.

Despite the bitterness of the debate it is almost certain that the Peloponnesian Greeks could not have seriously contemplated retirement from Salamis unless they could persuade the Athenians to accompany them. That would have been to adopt a plan which was certain to end in disaster instead of one which offered some chance of success, faint though it must have seemed to them at the time.[4]

The next events are crowded into the latter part of the day preceding the battle, and the morning of the battle itself.

Themistocles had prevailed on the Greeks to remain in the

[1] For the attitude of Corinth to Athens at this time, see p. 163.
[2] Thuc. i, 138. The whole passage is worth quoting; but, as I have no space wherein to do so, I can only recommend it to the reader.
[3] Hdt. viii, 59.
[4] In the following account of the battle I have been led by considerations which are fully explained in my account of Salamis in "The Great Persian War," pp. 344 ff.

THE FIRST HALF OF THE FIFTH CENTURY 145

strait for the time being at any rate; but the more difficult part of his task remained, to induce the Persians to attack the Greeks in those narrow waters. With this intent, either late in the afternoon or early in the evening before the battle, he sent a message of pretended treachery to Xerxes to the effect that the counsels of the Greeks were divided, and their fleet consequently in confusion, so that everything offered the prospect of an easy victory for the Persians in case they attacked forthwith. Xerxes fell into the trap; and so during the night the main Persian fleet took up its position across the east end of the strait south of the island of Psyttaleia in a line running east and west, while the Egyptian squadron was despatched to block the western strait between Salamis and the Megarid, a much narrower channel with a very narrow fairway down the middle of it. The Greeks seem to have been at the time well inside the eastern strait near the modern town of Salamis. Even now the Peloponnesians were agitating for a retreat; but Aristides, who had evidently had his ostracism revoked, arrived by ship from Ægina and reported the blocking of the western strait, so that retreat was out of the question; and the Greeks prepared to fight.

On the morning of the battle the Persians began their advance into the eastern strait in two broad columns through the channels on either side of Psyttaleia; but in wheeling round to the left to get round the bend in the strait the two columns seem to have got in one another's way, and confusion ensued which resulted in the Persian front being in échelon with the right wing pushed forward. The Greek movement eastwards to meet them must have begun very shortly after that of the Persians into the strait, and the fleets must have met somewhere north of the extreme point of Cynosura. Of personal incidents in the battle Herodotus has much to tell: of the manœuvres nothing. The Greeks employed the boarding tactics customary with them at that day, while the narrowness of the strait and the crush of vessels prevented the more experienced elements in the Persian fleet from employing those manœuvring tactics in which they were probably far superior to the Greeks of the year 480.

Salamis is one of the biggest naval fights in history, and the scene when from 800 to 900 vessels met in those narrow waters must have been terrific beyond description. It is possible too that a similar scene, on a much smaller scale, was being enacted in the western strait between the Corinthian and Egyptian squadrons of the two fleets; but that part of the story is camouflaged in Herodotus by a malicious and obviously untrue Athenian tradition of Corinthian treachery.

In the great fight in the eastern strait, at any rate, the victory was with the Greeks; but they were so stunned or so exhausted that they hardly realised the victory which was theirs, or, if they did, were not in a position to follow it up.

Viewed in the light of knowledge after the event, Salamis is the decisive battle of the war; yet the events of the next year were to show that serious dangers threatened the Greeks after Salamis was won. The Persian fleet made its way back to the Asiatic coast, while Xerxes himself went back by land, taking troops with him, but leaving Mardonius with probably a large part of the original land army to " complete " the reduction of Greece. Herodotus reports this army of Mardonius to have consisted of 300,000 men. A more conservative estimate would put it at not more than 200,000.

After Salamis southern Greece was safe: but so long as Mardonius remained in the land Greece north of the Isthmus was in peril lest he succeed in establishing a new Persian frontier at the south frontier of Bœotia, or even at the Isthmus. There could be no rest for the Greeks so long as this possibility threatened them. Mardonius retired for the winter to Thessaly, a land far richer in food supplies than the rest of Greece. But doubtless the commissariat vessels of the Persian fleet left with him the bulk of the provisions they had on board.

On finding the Persian fleet had fled, the Greeks from Salamis sailed as far as Andros to get further news of it. Arrived there, they debated the question of going to the Hellespont to break down the bridge, but decided against this course of action. Both in reference to this debate and its sequel Herodotus has various tales to tell to the discredit of Themistocles, tales which may be dismissed as the inventions of opponents of his politics. The substantial element in the tradition is that Themistocles did use the fleet for the purpose of exacting contributions towards the cost of the war from certain islands and towns of the Cyclades. When the fleet returned to Salamis the Greeks were under the impression that the whole Persian army intended to retreat to Asia, and it was only later that they discovered that Mardonius had remained behind, and that it would be necessary to prepare for another campaign.

It is a striking illustration of the very mixed sources from which Herodotus drew the history of this time that he, after relating a whole series of calumnies against Themistocles, tells the story of his having been hailed by the Greeks generally as the man who had deserved best of his country, and of his having been received at Sparta with an honour such as had never been accorded to any foreigner. It might have been expected that Athens would have appreciated the honour paid to its commander; but, so far from that having been the case, there seems to have been a political attack made on him after his return;[1] and it is most significant that, despite his conspicuous success in the previous year, he holds no command either by land or sea in 479.

THEMISTOCLES

It is strange to realise how small is the record of the life of Themistocles which has come down to the modern world. It consists of a few outstanding incidents connected with the critical phases of a critical period, and no more. Plutarch's biography of him is not the most successful of that author's works; and, if Plutarch, who was a genuine researcher into any evidence existing in his day, was unable to say more than he has said, it is not surprising that the modern world finds the story of his life fragmentary. In Themistocles' day the literary world had not as yet invented biography.

But it is clear in a general sense that Themistocles, though a thorough-going democrat, was not the type of man whose leadership democracy will accept save at a dangerous crisis. Democracy will always allow mediocrity to lead it into difficulties, and may then appeal to genius to get it out of them. If a genius is available, all may be well. If not, then, if the circumstances be critical, another democracy has committed constructive suicide. There is no trace or even hint in the records that survive that Themistocles had ever a large permanent body of political supporters, though there is abundant evidence that he had a large permanent body of political opponents. Those whom he might have served, and did serve in crises, would not under normal political conditions place their trust in one whose mind was far quicker and more accurate in its working than the mind of the average man. The political career of a man of political genius is apt to be a personal tragedy; just as that of the mediocre man in high position is apt to be a national one. With Themistocles the tragic finale seems to have begun in the winter of 480–79. It is indeed possible that the passing of the control of Athenian affairs at this time into the hands of Aristides was part of a political agreement entered into when that statesman was recalled for the events of 480; but it is much more probable that it was due to a mistaken feeling among the democrats that the danger was past, and that they need no longer support the dangerously able man who had saved them from it.

In the spring of 479 the Persian fleet was at Samos, gathered there with intent, as it would seem, to prevent a Greek naval attack on the Asiatic coast. A Greek fleet of 110 ships under the Spartan king Leotychides gathered at Ægina, the Athenian

[1] Hdt. viii, 125.

contingent being commanded by Xanthippus. Urged by certain Ionian refugees the fleet advanced as far as Delos; but, as it did not go beyond that point, the naval position was for the moment stalemate.

Platæa

Meanwhile Mardonius was taking action by seeking to detach Athens from the patriotic side by diplomacy and alluring promises. This roused Sparta to send an embassy to Athens. It was unnecessary. Athens refused to listen to Mardonius' envoy, and announced her refusal to the Spartan envoys in a speech of highly decorated sentiment ending with the practical suggestion that Sparta should send help, a thing which Sparta was not very anxious to do, as the sequel proved.

Mardonius now moved south into Bœotia, and with a view to creating an impression invaded Attica again, the population of which had been removed a second time to Salamis, for the expected Spartan aid had not come.

The attitude of Sparta at this time would be incomprehensible did it not illustrate in a striking way that very genuine fear which Sparta felt of sending any very large force outside her own borders. So Athens sent an embassy to Sparta which plainly hinted that, if Sparta did not move, Athens would—in an unpatriotic direction. Sparta's army was ready, for it was despatched with rather dramatic secrecy, that is, unknown to the Athenian ambassadors, while the latter were still at Sparta. Sparta's plan had been founded on the hope that, if Attica were once more overrun, the Athenians would consent to take part in the defence of the wall at the Isthmus, for, now that there seemed no fear of a naval attack, any threat of the withdrawal of the Athenian fleet would no longer arouse any overwhelming emotion at Sparta. But when Athens threatened desertion, the matter appeared in a different light, and Sparta was compelled to fall in with the Athenian plan of a defence north of the Isthmus.

The Spartan army which was despatched was of a type unusual with Sparta, for it included 5,000 Periœci and 35,000 Helots, as well as 5,000 Spartans. The Helots were doubtless hostages for the good behaviour of their friends while the Spartan army was out of the country. The army made its way first to the Isthmus, where it was joined by those contingents of the Peloponnesian states which were not already engaged on the construction of the defensive wall. From the Isthmus the whole army moved forward to Eleusis in Attica, where the Athenian army from Salamis joined it.

It is probable that news of this movement had decided Mardonius to retreat from Athens. His army was not in the position of the Persian army in the previous year, which had had no lines of communication to trouble about, as it had the fleet as its moving base of supplies. So it was necessary for him to fall back. But he sent first a cavalry raid into the Megarid, probably to find out what the Greeks were doing. He himself retreated to Bœotia by the pass of Decelea. With these movements the campaign of Platæa may be said to have opened.

It was not the mere fear of what Athens might do if deserted which moved the Peloponnesians to venture their armies north of the Isthmus. If they did not go to meet the invader a new Persian frontier might be established on the north border of Attica or even at the Isthmus, a possibility they could not contemplate.

Attica and the Megarid are divided from Bœotia by a continuous chain of mountains stretching from the head of the Corinthian Gulf to the Euripus, the Cithæron-Parnes range, of which the highest summits are 4,500 feet high, and the lower ridges from 2,500 to 3,000 feet. It is traversed by five passes which in order from east to west are : the Pass of Deceleia, on the Athens-Tanagra route ; the Pass of Panacton, a lofty passage on the direct route from Athens to Thebes ; the Pass of Dryoscephalæ, or the " Oakheads," on the Athens-Eleusis-Thebes route ; a pass about one and a half miles west of the last on a route from Athens to Platæa which branches from the last route just south of the range ; a pass one mile west of the last on the direct route from Megara to Platæa ; a pass or rather passage round the westernmost end of the range, right above the Gulf of Corinth. Of these the Dryoscephalæ, the Athens-Platæa, and the Megara-Platæa passes debouch on the field of battle.

The Greek army entered Bœotia through the Dryoscephalæ Pass, and took up a position on the mountain side just north of it, though the centre was in a valley which runs northward from the pass.

Mardonius had taken Thebes, some eight miles away from the pass, as his base of operations. He now moved south towards the Asopus, which is quite a small stream about three miles from where the Greeks had taken position, and, after pitching his camp south of the river, attacked the Greek centre in the valley with his cavalry. This was the first occasion on record of the Greeks having fought with Persian cavalry ; and their success in resisting this attack seems to have given them confidence—perhaps over-confidence—with regard to the fighting qualities of the Persian horsemen. They determined therefore to move into the open country away from the mountain side to the summit of a ridge which rises a few hundred feet above the level of the Asopus to the south of that river, and is separated from the lower slopes of Cithæron, which lie south of it, by a somewhat deep depression. In this depression are two springs, of which the more easterly bore the name of Gargaphia. To this ridge then the Greeks moved with intent, as it would seem, to take the offensive against the Persians. Apparently the attack was to be of the nature of a surprise, for it would seem from Herodotus' somewhat vague and unskilful account of what took place, that they moved during the night into the depression, where they would be out of sight of the Persian camp, took up their formation there, and then ascended to the top of the ridge. But on gaining the summit they found that the Persians had got wind of the movement, and had also shifted their position westwards further up the Asopus, where they stood just north of that river between the Greeks and Thebes, which was some six miles away.[1] Thus any plan of a surprise attack was foiled, and the Greeks remained for days inactive on the summit of the ridge. Reinforcements had come to them since they entered Bœotia; and at this time their numbers must have reached their highest point, which may be calculated from the figures which Herodotus gives and implies to have amounted to 108,200 men, of whom only 38,700 were hoplites. The rest were light-armed, a type of force never very effective in the Greek armies of that time. The largest hoplite contingents were those of Sparta (10,000), Corinth (5,000), Sicyon (3,000), and Athens (8,000).[2] Pausanias, a Spartan, was commander-in-chief, and Aristides was in command of the Athenian contingent.

This second position of the Greeks had two disadvantages. The water supply of the army was dependent mainly, if not entirely, on the spring of Gargaphia: and the army was exposed to the attacks of the Persian cavalry far more than it had been in the first position. Furthermore it left the mouths of the passes, which were from one and a half to two miles in the Greek rear, exposed to Persian cavalry raids. On the eighth day after the taking up of the position a Greek provision train was captured at the mouth of the Dryoscephalæ Pass. For the next two days there was skirmishing on the Asopus; but on the eleventh day the Persian cavalry crossed the river, and not merely harassed the Greek army with javelins and arrows, but cut off their access to the Gargaphia spring. The same thing happened on the next day. The position of the Greek army was critical, almost

[1] The detailed topography and discussion of the battle will be found in my book "The Great Persian War."

[2] Some calculations which I made some years ago with regard to the population of the various Greek states, based on the numbers put by them into the field on this and other occasions, tended to confirm the numbers given on this occasion by Herodotus. I think he must have had access to a first- or second-hand copy of an official list.

desperate; and it was absolutely necessary to fall back. It was determined, therefore, says Herodotus, to retreat to the "Island," a piece of land of which he gives a description so accurate that it can be easily identified with a hump on one of the ridges running north from Cithæron between two of the sources of the Oëroë, a small river which runs into the Corinthian Gulf.

The tale of what happened is very confused in Herodotus' account; but it may be suspected that there was a good deal of confusion, and perhaps of panic, in the Greek army. It is certain that Spartans on the right of their line did not move towards the "Island." They moved south-east towards the exit of the Dryoscephalæ Pass, probably with intent to clear the mouth of the pass before joining the other Greeks. The Greek centre moved towards the Island; but, as the move must have been made in the dark, they seem to have missed their way, and arrived near the town of Platæa, three-quarters of a mile west of the Island. The Athenians on the Greek left started late, making for the Island, which as a fact they never reached, for they were attacked by the medised Bœotians in the hollow beneath the ridge. Nor did the Spartans reach their destination. They too had been delayed by the refusal of one of their captains to retreat, and they were caught by the Persians, who, on noticing at dawn that the Greeks had deserted the ridge, had advanced to the attack. The fight took place near a temple of Eleusinian Demeter, which would locate it about half-way between the summit of the ridge and the modern village of Kriekouki. Both the Athenians and Spartans were victorious, the latter so decisively that the Persians' retreat to their camp became a rout, and the camp was taken. The Greek centre seems to have moved to the support of the fighters. Part of it which had gone to the aid of the Athenians was badly cut up by the Theban cavalry.

But the Greek victory was decisive, though, if ever a victory was pulled out of the fire at the last moment, it was that of the Greeks at Platæa. They were a beaten army when they retreated from the ridge; and, had Mardonius left them alone, it is only too possible that they might have percolated through the passes of Cithæron and left the Persians in possession of Bœotia. Mardonius made the mistake of matching comparatively light-armed Persians against the Greek hoplite, with the result that he learnt a lesson which the Persian never forgot. Man for man the Persian was no doubt as good and as brave a fighter as the Greek; but here, as so often in history, it was arms, not the man, that won the day.

The fate of the after-world was at stake in that fight beneath the shadow of the temple of Eleusinian Demeter.

A tithe of the spoils was dedicated to Delphi. Near the great altar there was set up a golden triped upon a lofty stand of three entwined snakes, on which were engraved the names of the Greek states which had sent contingents to Platæa. The snake pillar was removed to Constantinople by Constantine; and, amid all the vicissitudes of the history of that great city, it has survived, a mutilated fragment saved from the wreck of the great monuments of Greek story.

After the battle the leaders of Theban medism were surrendered and executed at Corinth. Of the retreat of the Persian army Herodotus has nothing to say; but it must have streamed back to Asia in a miserable and ever-diminishing train.

Mycale

While these things were going on in Bœotia the Greek fleet under Leotychides had carried the war to the Asiatic coast, for it was known that Ionia was ready for revolt. To Samos, the headquarters of the Persian fleet, the Greeks first made their way; and, on the Persians withdrawing to the coast of the mainland, followed them to Mycalé, where a considerable Persian army had been assembled. The ships of the Persian fleet were drawn up on land, and protected by a stockade. For this the Greek naval force was not prepared; and it was only after considerable hesitation that the Greeks determined to risk a battle on land. It ended in a complete victory, in the later phases of which the Ionian Greeks serving with the Persian army turned upon their masters.

"Thus," says Herodotus, " Ionia revolted a second time from the Persians."

The Western Greeks

The Greek cities of the West had been passing through those stages of political development common to the Greek world. Two centuries of settlement had converted the original settlers into a landed aristocracy who owned all the land and governed the state, excluding all new-comers from the land and the rising commercial class from the government. It was as champions of the latter that tyrants were established in the chief towns of Sicily in the latter part of the sixth century.

Carthage

On the other side of the Mediterranean Carthage had been developing rapidly as a great and wealthy commercial aristocracy which had large interests throughout the western sea and possessed settlements in western Sicily which made her covet the whole of that fertile island. So when at the instigation of

THE FIRST HALF OF THE FIFTH CENTURY

Persia the Phœnicians proposed to Carthage that she should attack the Siciliot Greek cities simultaneously with the Persian attack on Greece in 480, Carthage welcomed the opportunity of assailing them when no aid could come from Greece, and collected a large and very miscellaneous mercenary force from North Africa, Spain, and even Gaul.

It was fortunate for Sicily that the most powerful city, Syracuse, was at the time under the control of Gelo, a very capable and somewhat drastic tyrant, for he had energy, capacity, and influence sufficient to get the cities, laying aside those jealousies which under any form of government other than tyranny they cherished as their birthright, to combine for the common defence.

After landing at Panormus in western Sicily the Carthaginians under Hamilcar marched along the coast to Himera with the intent to take it. Thero, tyrant of Acragas, was in the neighbourhood with a force insufficient for an attack on the Carthaginian besiegers; so he sent an urgent message to Gelo at Syracuse to come up with all speed. Gelo started to the rescue with a force said to have amounted to 50,000 infantry and 5,000 cavalry.

Having intercepted a message to the effect that cavalry was coming up from Selinus to assist the Carthaginians, he sent his own cavalry by night to the Carthaginian camp, into which they were admitted under the impression that they were the Selinuntian horsemen. Here they killed Hamilcar and set fire to the Carthaginian ships in the naval camp, while Gelo assaulted and took the camp of the Carthaginian land force. Then ensued a murder grim and great.

As a pure example of the military art, Himera did more credit to the victors than did Platæa. While it was won by reason of a well-devised plan, Platæa was won in spite of an ill-devised one.

Had Gelo followed up his victory by an attack on Carthage itself, there is little doubt that he might have changed the history of the ancient world; for Carthage had staked all on the success in Sicily, and had lost. She succeeded however in patching up a peace on very degrading terms, and Gelo contented himself with using the war indemnity for the striking of some of the most beautiful coins which were ever produced by those Greek moneyers who carried that art to such perfection. At any rate he gave Sicily peace from Carthage for seventy years.

ATHENS, 478–462

There has already been occasion to say that it would be very misleading for any author who was dealing with the political history of Greek democracies, and especially of the democracy of Athens, to speak of any party as being "in power" at any particular period. In the democracies of city states the policy of the moment depended on the vote of the moment; and at Athens that depended largely on whether the conservative rural population attended a particular meeting of the Assembly in such numbers as to outvote the extremists of Athens and Piræus. Thus a truer expression of the facts of the case may be arrived at by using the word "predominance."

The most striking feature in the party history of Athens in the thirty years which follow the close of the Persian War in Greece is that till 462 the conservatives were predominant, whereas from that date onwards the extremists controlled the general policy of the state. The beginnings of this change may be traced as far back as 466, the date of the battle of the Eurymedon. Up to that time the successes attained in the naval war against Persia on the Asiatic coast had been moderate, and did not in any way guarantee the security of the Ægean from Persian attack. More was accomplished in that one day on the Eurymedon than in all the previous twelve years of warfare.

Till then the allied fleet in commission, of which the Athenian fleet formed a large and ever-increasing part, had to be maintained on a great scale; and the consequence was that the "seafaring mob," the extremists of Athens and Piræus, was employed in such numbers abroad that its party could not control the vote in the Assembly. The nature of the warfare did not call away for service any large number of the hoplites; so that conservative element and its leaders were able to have much their own way in directing the policy of the state.

But after the Eurymedon there was no need to keep so large a fleet in commission, and many of the crews came back to Athens, who, finding themselves unemployed, proceeded to attack the existing directors of the policy of the state, and eventually to modify that policy to such an extent as to make the change amount almost to a revolution. After that it is the ultra-democrats who control the affairs of Athens almost continuously till the very last years of the century.

Such is the general position underlying Athenian politics in this period.

After Platæa Athens took in hand the reconstitution of her devastated city and land. Difficulties immediately arose with Sparta on the question of the rebuilding of the walls of Athens. Sparta's general policy could not contemplate the establishment of a powerful state north of the Isthmus, and so she sought on a manifestly improbable pretext to prevent the refortification of the city. Themistocles tricked her by diplomatic mis-state-

THE FIRST HALF OF THE FIFTH CENTURY

ments until the wall was an accomplished fact. Sparta resented the treachery, and Athens the interference; but both hid their feelings for the time. Nevertheless these things were the beginning of enmity between Sparta and Athens.

Outside Greece the patriotic league of states was practically committed to the liberation of the Ionian Greeks, and, incidentally, of the islands of the Ægean. It was a committal of which most of them would have been very glad to be rid. So Pausanias, the victor of Platæa, took command of the allied fleet, which was at first no doubt a heterogeneous collection of ships from continental Greece, the islands, and the Asiatic coast. But the continental contingents, with the exception of those of Athens and Sparta, soon slipped away; and when, later, Sparta retired, a new anti-Persian league came into existence the membership of which was, with the exception of Athens, wholly different from that of the league of 480.

Under Pausanias' command Cyprus, a dangerous base for a Persian attack on the Ægean, was conquered; and then Byzantium, all-important on the Greek route to the Euxine corn district, was captured. Here certain strange developments took place. Pausanias, as victor of Platæa and conqueror of Cyprus and Byzantium the most prominent Greek of the moment, was not minded to go back to parochial obscurity in Laconia; and so, seeing that this fate must in the ordinary course of things await him, he determined that the course of things should not be ordinary. He accordingly intrigued with Persia; and, his overtures being well received, was candid enough to acknowledge the grace of Persian favour by outward and visible signs. He was recalled to Sparta, tried for treason, and acquitted—why or how it is difficult to say. In his place the Spartans sent out a certain Dorcis to command the fleet; but the allies had by this time given the command to Athens, and so Dorcis went home, and the Spartans withdrew from the league, not perhaps to the regret of the national party.

In 477 the anti-Persian league was organised by Aristides; and, as Delos was taken as the sacred and political centre of it, it came to be called the Delian League. That island too was chosen as the treasury and meeting-place of the council of the league. This might suggest an equality of partnership such as seems never to have actually existed among the members. The two main provisions of the arrangement made by Aristides concerned the league army and the league navy respectively. To the army every state was under an obligation to contribute, though probably from the very first levies were seldom if ever called for from the smaller states, places not larger in many cases than a moderate-sized modern village. With respect to the navy it was provided that any state which liked might in lieu of contributing ships and crews subscribe to the league funds an amount fixed by Aristides, a course which an ever-increasing number of states preferred to that of personal service. This contribution was called the φόρος, or tribute. It was nominally a contribution to the funds of the league as a whole, but, as it was all paid over to the state which supplied vessels in place of the contributor, and as Athens and no other state supplied the vessels, this tribute went from the very first to Athens and to Athens alone ; and, if a rather doubtful passage in Thucydides be rightly interpreted, the treasurers who received and paid out this money were from the first Athenian citizens. This it was that gave Athens that position in the league which she converted into empire. To Aristides and to the Athenian statesmen who succeeded him this addition to the income of the Athenian state was a godsend inasmuch as it enabled the Athenian government to give employment and support to that unemployed class to which there are several emphatic references in the somewhat meagre historical records of the age.

In politics Aristides, a moderate democrat, seems to have directed the policy of the now predominant conservative party, while Cimon, son of the Miltiades of Marathon, who belonged to the aristocratic section of the coalition, commanded the fleet. If the surviving records of the conquests made by the league be complete, then the gains made in the first eleven years of its existence were not very striking. Eion on the Strymon was captured about 476. Probably many smaller places in other parts were brought into the league by Cimon. Later he captured Scyrus, that island nest of pirates in the north Ægean. Carystus in south Eubœa, which had not joined the league, was forcibly compelled to do so on the principle that all Ægean states were benefited from the league's work, and therefore all must contribute to it. In 467 came the revolt of Naxos and its suppression, of which more anon ; and in 466 came the land and sea fight on the Eurymedon, a victory so great that it dispelled for a generation at least all fear of Persian interference in the Ægean. Some of the allies thought that it had dispelled it for ever.

In the internal affairs of Athens in these years Themistocles is a mysterious figure. Aristides, though he had been bitterly opposed to the creation of the great fleet, was quite prepared to use it now that it was in existence. He could not in fact adopt any other policy, for the route to the Euxine and the corn region had to be freed from Persian control, and, again, service in the fleet was solving, for the time being at any rate, that very troublesome problem of unemployment. The reconciliation between Aristides and Themistocles seems to have lasted till 478 at any rate, when they co-operated in the matter of the refortification of Athens; and it may have endured longer than that. But it is evident that in consequence of some bitter quarrel which arose later Themistocles was ostracised. The extant authors give vague generalities, which could hardly have entailed an appeal to ostracism, as the cause of it. What the real nature of the dispute was is not therefore known; but the circumstances of the time suggest that it was connected with that question of foreign policy which was so critically important to Athens, namely whether she should look west to Sicily or east to the Euxine for her corn supply. Throughout the latter half of the sixth and the whole of the fifth century the policy of the ultra-democrats is to look westwards, and of the moderates to look eastwards, in this matter. Only a few years later than this Pericles adopted a marked form of the western policy. The first few years of the new league must have made it quite clear that Aristides and his friends were, like their former benefactor Pisistratus, looking east, for their attention is concentrated on the war with Persia. There is of course in the tradition of the life of Themistocles a very persistent allegation that he had doubtful, if not traitorous, relations with Persia on various occasions; and though the black colouring given to the allegations may be the work of malicious political opponents, yet the relations themselves may have existed to a certain extent, a faint heritage from that Marathonian time when Themistocles' own party was in alliance with the Mede. Thus he may not have wished the war with Persia to be pushed too far.

But, apart from this possible negative side of his policy, there is almost convincing evidence of a positive policy of securing the connections of Athens with the western corn region of Sicily.[1] It may be therefore that the political trouble which brought about his ostracism was the eternal controversy between the conservatives and the extreme democrats as to whether Athens should extend her interests westwards or eastwards. The date of the ostracism is uncertain. It was probably about 474.[2]

[1] He named his daughters Sybaris and Italia, a peculiar form of nomenclature to which Greek statesmen who wished to show or win political interest abroad were addicted. Cimon named his son Lacedæmonius. Themistocles had special relations with Corcyra and Acarnania, both on the western route. The reference in Herodotus to his threat at Salamis to transfer the Athenians to Siris in Italy is significant. Tradition also ascribed to him relations with Syracuse.

[2] Some authorities put it later. But I cannot square the later date with that war in Peloponnese of which Themistocles was almost certainly the promoter.

War in Peloponnese

After leaving Athens he went to Argos; and, so Thucydides says, visited other places in Peloponnese. If there was no causal connection between these journeys of his and the serious attack made at this time by Argos and Arcadia, except Mantinea, on the Spartan domination in Peloponnese, then the coincidence of the two phenomena is one of the most remarkable accidents in history. The hostility of Themistocles towards Sparta ever since the close of the Persian War in Europe is most marked. It may be that he thought that Sparta had shown a very dangerous hand when she objected to the building of the fortifications of Athens. But there can be little doubt that he engineered that combination against Sparta which suffered defeat in two battles at Tegea and Dipæa.[1]

Finding Themistocles a very uncomfortable and dangerous lodger in their neighbourhood, the Spartans thought it well to try to get him removed thence by his home authorities, and so charged him at Athens with participation in the Persian intrigues of Pausanias. Whatever his views on Persia may have been, it is not likely that he was a participator in Pausanias' somewhat wild doings. But it is very probable indeed that he had collaborated with that discredited Spartan in an attempt to stir up the Helots, the policy which Sparta most feared on the part of her enemies. That it was which touched the Spartans; but, knowing that such a charge would excite little emotion at Athens, whereas philo-medism would be regarded as a capital crime, they associated him in their representations with this item in their indictment against their recalcitrant fellow-countryman. Pausanias' guilt with regard to the Helots was discovered; and he was starved to death in a temple in which he had taken sanctuary. As for the Athenians, they sent to fetch Themistocles back to Athens; but he, having no desire to be fetched, fled first to north-west Greece, whence he eventually made his way across Macedonia and the Ægean to Asia. He went up to the court of Susa, and, winning the favour of Artaxerxes, received the lordship and revenues of Lampsacus, Myus, and Magnesia on the Mæander, which he retained till his death at a date unknown.

The Athenian Empire

There are certain tragedies in the history of the world for

[1] It is peculiarly illustrative of the records of this period that we should not know anything of this obviously important war were it not for a chance reference in Herodotus (ix, 35).

Alcibiades' policy in Peloponnese, which came to an abrupt conclusion at Mantinea in 418, was almost certainly a deliberate copy of the policy promoted by Themistocles on this occasion.

which the deliberate and purposed action of individuals, political parties, or nations is manifestly responsible. But the tragedy of history appears in its truest form when human action leads to circumstances and catastrophes which the agents could not have desired at any time, and could not have foreseen until they had progressed so far along a path of policy that for them there was no turning. That was the situation which developed in the beginnings of the conversion of the Delian League into an Athenian Empire. The political party which controlled affairs in the years in which the first steps towards empire were taken was that conservative party which neither then nor at any other time was imperialist in feeling. Yet it may be said to have handed over an empire ready made to that imperialist ultra-democracy to which the control of Athenian policy passed.

The league suffered, probably at a very early stage, from that centrifugal tendency which always prevailed in leagues of Greek states. Naxos showed by her revolt in 467, made at a time when the western but not the eastern Ægean was fairly secure, that she was quite ready to desert those who had won her security before theirs had been attained. Athens as head of the league treated her with perhaps needless severity in suppressing the revolt; but there can be little doubt that there were many states which were ready to follow Naxos' example if they thought they could do so safely and successfully. Thucydides, by no means a friend of empire, says that there were many cases in which states omitted to fulfil their league obligations, either by failure to furnish contingents when called upon, or to pay tribute; and that Athens as head of the league had to enforce these obligations, and so became unpopular with her own allies. The interests of discipline are seldom appreciated by the disciplined. Meanwhile a sullen hostility had taken the place of the more or less friendly relations between Athens and Sparta in the years 480 and 479; and it may be safely assumed that Corinth was not doing anything to diminish it.[1] But the crisis came after the Eurymedon in 466, that battle which seemed to have done the work of the league once and for all. It was natural that the now unwilling allies should think that the time had come for the dissolution of the league: that the danger from Persia was over, and that, with the ceasing of the *raison d'être* of its existence, the league should cease to exist. Subsequent history was to show that the great Athenian fleet kept the Persian out of the Ægean and beyond the power of interfering with Greek affairs. With its disappearance at the end of the century Persia again became formidable to the Greek states.

But Athens, unpopular by reason of her very patriotism,

---

[1] For Corinth, see p. 163.

hated as a taskmaster in a task which now was done, dare not dissolve a league whose members would with the aid of Sparta exact retribution from her for those severities which she had inflicted on the individual states in the interest of the whole body of them.[1] In the years succeeding 466 Athens must have employed much constraint to keep the league together. And that constraint spelt empire. What would have been the solution of the matter had the conservatives remained in control cannot be said. The ultra-democrats saw that it meant empire, and gladly accepted it as such, for it solved many home problems in which they were profoundly interested.

Of the constitutional development of Athens during the dominance of the moderates nothing is known—possibly because there was none. The Aristotelian treatise attributes to Aristides a very democratic measure of which he is not likely to have been the author.

Aristides seems to have died about 469 whilst engaged on an expedition to the Pontus, made probably with a view to making good the relations between Athens and the ruler of the kingdom of the Cimmerian Bosphorus. Cimon, a good general but an inferior statesman, succeeded to the leadership of the conservative party.

After the Eurymedon in 466 things developed with rapidity, as many of the democrats who had been serving on the fleet were now in Athens and could vote in the Assembly. Of the various causes which brought about the overthrow of the conservative control, the most efficient was probably certain relations with Sparta.

SPARTA

The history of that state between 479 and 466 is a dreary one. The unexpected growth of Athenian power in and through the league was very disquieting. She tried to recoup herself in Thessaly; but King Leotychides made a failure there. Then came the attack from Argos and Arcadia; and, though that was defeated, yet in 468 Argos destroyed Mycenæ, a protégé of Sparta. But the blackness of Sparta's outlook culminated

---

[1] The defence and justification of the action of Athens in these years is best stated in the speech which Thucydides puts into the mouth of the Athenian embassy at the congress at Sparta in the period just preceding the outbreak of the Peloponnesian War (Thuc. i, 73 ff.) No one who can appreciate the possibilities of the case would allege that the words were actually spoken by the Athenian ambassadors. But as a historical document the speech is of greater value if it is, what it probably is, Thucydides' own résumé of the arguments used in justification of the Athenian empire in the Athens of his own day.

in 464 with an earthquake which destroyed large numbers of Spartiates and led to a serious rising of the Helots which utterly upset a plan Sparta had formed to assist those islanders of Thasos who had revolted from Athens.

This revolt took place in 464. In nature it was different from that of Naxos three years before, because it was brought about by some commercial dispute as to the ownership of the gold mines on the mainland opposite Thasos, to which Athens laid some claim. This looks as if it was caused by the policy of the ultra-democrats. The revolt was suppressed.

Sparta's danger from the Helots, who had made Mount Ithomé in Messenia the centre of their insurrection, caused the aristocratic party in Athens such anxiety that Cimon, with more zeal than discretion, persuaded the Athenians to listen to an appeal for help which had come for Sparta, and to send a force to aid in the siege of Ithomé. The subsequent history of this expedition suggests very strongly that this appeal came from only one of the two parties in Sparta, and that the other did not like it. Be that as it may, when the aid did not meet with immediate success, and Ithomé remained untaken, some one repented of having made a request which disclosed the real situation to a foreign state, for Sparta's policy had been to keep the rest of Greece in the dark as to her real position with regard to her serf population. So the Athenian soldiers, who, when on the spot, were likely to be inconvenient witnesses of fact, were sent away with more promptness than politeness. It was doubtless this error of policy on the part of Cimon which led to his ostracism.

ULTRA-DEMOCRATS AT ATHENS

Meanwhile the ultra-democrats had been preparing their road to political predominance by attacks on the members and the powers of the Areopagus, that ancient council which, by its services in 480, and in consequence, no doubt, of the predominance of the conservatives in the next fourteen years, had regained much influence, the exact nature of which is not disclosed by the authorities. The general result of all that had occurred at Athens since the Eurymedon was that in 462 the ultra-democrats got the upper hand in Athenian politics under the leadership of Ephialtes. He died very soon after this, and the leadership passed to Pericles.

PERICLES

For more than thirty years Pericles was destined to exercise a much-disputed but almost unbroken control over Athenian policy. Of his capacity as a statesman many opinions have been expressed. To some he seemed, and has seemed, no more than a clever demagogue; while others have regarded him as one of the greatest and most enlightened statesmen of the ancient world, a view founded mainly on the admiration expressed for him by Thucydides. Plutarch discloses facts which make so enthusiastic a judgment hardly tenable. Judged by his acts he seems to have been a very able opportunist, using that term in a more sympathetic sense than that in which it is commonly employed, for he was faced during his political life with problems which only a political genius in control of a world-power could have solved, but which even the greatest statesman, working with limited resources, could only have met, as Pericles met them, by such expedients as were available at the time. It is true that his opportunism is a feature of his later rather than of his earlier policy, for his political life may be divided into two much contrasted periods, of which the first lasts till the disaster in Egypt in 454, and the second from that time till the day of his death. In the earlier period he seeks to solve the difficulties of Athens by a most pronounced imperialist policy. In the later, taught by failure, his imperialism is of a more limited character. As to the difficulties he had to meet, and the ways in which he tried to meet them, it will be well to speak of them when the constructive side of the second phase of his policy is inaugurated after the Thirty Years' Peace of 446.

The circumstances which supervened in the years which immediately followed the change of political predominance in 462 may have suggested to Pericles that the opportunity had arrived for a venture of amazing boldness relative to the resources of Athens and its empire, an attempt to get control of all the three great corn regions of the Mediterranean. That would have meant an economic control of the whole Greek world which could have been easily converted into political domination—a Hellenic empire of Athens with Egypt included in it. Athens already controlled the supply from the Pontus by her control of the route thence. If she could only get a similar hold of the route from the West, the Corinthian Gulf, and bring Egypt under her control, the other Greek states would simply have to beg their bread from her.

The first step was taken before circumstances suggested the conception of so large a design. Naupactus, a harbour on the north side of the Corinthian Gulf, was seized from the Ozolian Locrians; and, at some date not long after its acquisition, Helot refugees from Ithomé were planted there.

War, 459–446

In 459 came the great temptation: Egypt was in revolt against Persia, and Persia, which was not the Persia of fifty years

THE FIRST HALF OF THE FIFTH CENTURY

before, was finding great difficulty in suppressing it.[1] Inarus, the king of the rebels, applied to Athens for help ; and Athens sent a fleet of 200 ships to his assistance. It may be regarded as quite certain that Athens did not do this for unselfish motives ; nor had Pericles any general anti-Persian policy. There was a prospect of getting hold of Egypt, and the circumstances in Greece were favourable, for Sparta was either still engaged in the siege of Ithomé,[2] or was so exhausted by the Helot revolt and the earthquake that she was not likely to move.

The campaigning in Egypt went on till 454, when the great Athenian expedition was destroyed by the Persians, only a few survivors of it reaching Cyrene. This disaster was destined to change wholly the policy of Pericles.

But during these years Athens was engaged in a great struggle in Greece which arose out of a frontier dispute between Corinth and Megara. Athens took up the cause of Megara, which state seems without more ado to have joined the Delian League. At any rate the Megarid was now at the disposal of Athens ; and a more valuable acquisition for the control of affairs in Greece she could not possibly have made. It commanded the passage of the Isthmus, a passage peculiarly difficult owing to the difficulty of the passes over Mount Geranea ; and it afforded through its port of Pêgæ direct access to the Corinthian Gulf. Sparta and Peloponnese generally were cut off from land communication with north Greece ; and Athens for the first time got convenient and direct access to the great passage through the gulf to Sicily and the West.

ATHENS AND CORINTH

It is now necessary to say something of those relations between Athens and Corinth which were destined to have such sinister significance in the tragedies of fifth-century history.

Up to the time of the formation of the great Athenian fleet in the years just preceding 480 their relations had been friendly,

---

[1] It is not possible to determine on the literary evidence alone whether the determination to send an expedition to Egypt or the trouble with Corinth about Megara came first ; but I am inclined to think that Athens would have hesitated to undertake so large an expedition had she had the war with Corinth on her hands.

[2] For my own part I believe that the siege of Ithomé was over by this time. I cannot understand why Steup in his edition of Classen's Thucydides substituted δεκάτῳ for τετάρτῳ, in the text of i, 103. This would imply that the siege of Ithomé went on till 455. But the settlement of the Messenians took place almost certainly at the end of the siege ; and that settlement seems to have been in existence in 459. Again, it is most unlikely that Sparta would have undertaken the large expedition to north Greece in 457 which ended in the Battle of Tanagra had the siege not been brought to conclusion.

not because Athens was not competing with Corinth for Sicilian trade, for archæological discovery in Sicily shows that her trade with that island developed from practically zero at the beginning of the sixth century to a considerable volume at its close, nor yet because oligarchical Corinth had any disinterested love for democratic Athens, but because at the beginning of the fifth century she regarded Ægina as a much more inconvenient trade competitor. The coinage system of Sicily and the West shows how serious the Æginetan competition was then, and had been in the past. Corcyra employed the Æginetan standard of currency, and so did half—the Chalcidian half—of the cities of Sicily. Therefore Ægina was the enemy, not Athens; and moreover in those wars with Ægina in the first twenty years of the fifth century Athens had been doing her best to cripple her, and had thus been doing Corinth's work. And so Corinth was ready to back Athens, as she did when the Spartans invaded Attica about 507 by protesting against the interference, and again about 498 by lending Athens ships for a war with Ægina. But all this friendly feeling was turned to bitter hostility when Athens suddenly leapt into the position of by far the greatest naval power in the Greek world. Herodotus' various stories of bitter Corinthian hostility to Athens even when they were allies against the Persian in 480 may be exaggerated; but they are true in essence. And so it is not strange that Athens took up the cause of Megara in 459.

In the war which followed Athens' energy and operations were concentrated on getting command of the Saronic, and especially of the Corinthian Gulf; and by the time the war died down in 453 she was in control of Ægina, the Megarid, Bœotia, Achaia, Naupactus, Zacynthus, and Cephallênia, and had made determined attempts to capture Sicyon and Œniadæ: she had, in fact, an almost complete control of the Greek end of the corn route from the West.

Nothing could show more clearly the depression both physical and mental which prevailed at Sparta during these years than the apparent apathy with which she looked on at events which might have changed for ever the destiny of herself and of the Greek world. Only once, in 457, did she move, and then on the pretext of protecting the Dorians of north Greece against Phocian aggression. That this was a mere pretext is shown by the size of the force she employed, 11,500 hoplites from Peloponnese, of whom 1,500 were Spartans. Her real object was to re-establish a strong control of Bœotia by Thebes, as a set-off against Athenian power north of the Isthmus, and perhaps to break the Athenian hold on the Megarid. The expedition crossed the gulf on its outward way; and, shirking any direct attack on the Megarid

THE FIRST HALF OF THE FIFTH CENTURY 165

on its way home, made a feint towards Athens which brought the Athenians to meet it at Tanagra.[1] A victory there secured for the Peloponnesians a passage of the Megarid; but it had been so hardly won that no attempt was made to hold the Megarian territory.

But the disaster in Egypt undid all that success which Athens had attained nearer home. Yet she came very very near to realising the dream of a pan-Hellenic empire.

Meanwhile early in the war she had carried out certain works which were fated to modify the art of war and the history of the Greek race.

On getting hold of the Megarid in 459 she had connected Megara with its port Nisæa, about two miles away, by Long Walls. The next year she did the same with Athens and Piræus.[2] It is probable that it was at the instigation of Pericles that the work was carried out; and he lived to show its effectiveness thirty years later.

With the disaster in Egypt in 454 comes that change in the policy of Pericles to which reference has been made. A depressed Sparta and a disillusioned Athens made a five years' truce in 451; and so Argos, which had in recent years had an alliance with Athens, thought it well to secure herself against Sparta and her allies by a Thirty Years' Peace.

Though in this last decade of the first half of the century Pericles had made a beginning with that organisation of the Delian League which was to bind the states to Athens by bonds which destroyed all semblance of equality of membership, and in internal politics had passed measures which were designed to meet the pressing needs and demands of a formidable mass of unemployed, yet the major part of this organisation and remedial legislation must belong to the period when peace gave him the leisure for solving those problems of peace which were for the Athenian statesmen of the time more difficult than the domestic problems of a period of war.

But Pericles infused into the Athenian democracy a spirit of imperialism which he could repress but not exorcise. Wild dreams of conquest in Sicily and Carthage were dreamed by the Athenians of this period, so Plutarch says. The dream was to be repeated forty years later, and the awakening was to be yet more terrible than on the occasion of its first occurrence.

[1] A tale of collusion with the oligarchs at Athens may or may not be true.
[2] The fortification of Piræus is ascribed by one ancient author to the archonship of Themistocles in 493. That is almost certainly wrong. It was probably included in the scheme of the refortification of Athens in 478. But there is not any reason to suppose that Themistocles conceived even in 478 the idea of Long Walls.

Sicily

After the battle of Himera strange things had taken place in Sicily. Tyranny had won great glory; and never can it have seemed to be more firmly established. Yet within twenty years it has disappeared from the island.

The victorious Gelo died about 478, and, after certain disorders, was succeeded by Hiero, whose court became a literary centre more splendid than the world had ever known.[1] But though the lot of the literary genius was a pleasant one at Hiero's court, the population of his dominions had a restless time, being shuffled like cards, and shifted from one home to another at the tyrant's will. The policy may have been politically or even economically sound; but it was not calculated to win the affection of those on whom the experiment was tried; and this may have been the cause of the popular movement which overthrew tyranny in the next decade. In 474 Hiero's fleet defeated the Etruscans, those bitter opponents of Greek expansion in the West, at Cymé. Hiero died in 466, and his younger brother Thrasybulus succeeded to the tyranny. In 465 the Syracusans rose and set up a democracy. By 460 Sicily had become a land of democracies. For more than fifty years these lived a quarrelsome life of mutual bickerings, jealousies, and wars, with Syracuse as protagonist in the miserable drama, that Syracusan democracy which was ever desirous to deprive others of that freedom which it had won for itself. Amid these sordid surroundings of disunion and dissension was born the art of rhetoric.

[1] Æschylus and Pindar spent several years at his court. Simonides spent there the last years of a long life. Bacchylides was there also, and the philosopher Xenophanes.

CHAPTER VI

THE SECOND HALF OF THE FIFTH CENTURY.
450-400 B.C.

SPAIN AND GAUL

OF Spain and Gaul in this second half of the fifth century nothing is known. Carthage was doubtless consolidating and extending her possessions, and above all exploiting the mines of the greatest mining region of the ancient world. In Gaul Massilia may have compensated herself for withdrawal from the east coast of Spain before the advance of Carthage by extending her influence along the coast between the Rhône and the Alps and into its hinterland.

ETRURIA

In Italy this half-century was marked by circumstances which favoured the ultimate growth of Rome. So long as the Etruscan power was at its height she had been hemmed in by it, being far too weak to attempt to contest its superiority. All that she could win was her independence of its control. But Etruria was now in a state of decline to which Hiero by his victory at Cymé, the Celts by an advance from the north, and the Samnites by their advance from the south, were all contributing. In 423 the latter captured Capua, and the Etruscan dominion in Campania came to an end. Though the Samnite advance threatened Rome in a way, yet it relieved her of immediate pressure from those neighbouring hill tribes whose raids had been a sore trouble to her, for the Volsci and Æqui were weakened by Samnite attacks, and the Sabines were now attracted southwards by the successes of their relatives in Campania and elsewhere.

ROME: STRUGGLE OF THE ORDERS

Meanwhile the struggle between the orders was being carried on with its usual vehemence. The plebeians made some advances on the road to liberty; but it is noticeable that some of the legislation of these years aims rather at securing and consolidating the advance already made. It was becoming more and more evident that the mere passing of laws in the interests of the commons could not guarantee them liberty against the enormous arbitrary power of the patrician magistrate; and in this half-century the leaders of the Plebs must have been becoming more and more conscious that civil liberty could only be assured by political liberty, which, translated into practical politics at Rome, meant that the Plebs must win its way into the ranks of the higher magistracy. It is in this half-century that the conviction leads to action.

In 449 were passed the Valerio-Horatian Laws, one of the most important milestones on the road to freedom. They deal with various questions. The law of appeal was reaffirmed, a significant illustration of the difference between liberty in theory and in practice. One of the laws also dealt with resolutions (plebiscita) passed in that Assembly of the Plebs which the tribunes could summon and address. Livy obviously exaggerates the terms of the law, making them more drastic than they really were; but it is probable that henceforth any such resolution as had been ratified by the Senate was made binding not merely on the Plebs but on the Roman people as a whole. Thus was given to the Plebeian Assembly a power which was to have enormous influence both for good and evil on the subsequent history of the Republic. The sanctity of the person of a tribune, hitherto guaranteed by the oath of the Plebs, was now established by law; and it was further laid down that there should not under any circumstances be an interruption in the succession of tribunes.

The legislative power thus acquired was used in 445 to make legal mixed marriages between patricians and plebeians, a hard blow to that social exclusiveness which had been a strong buttress to patrician power.

In the same year an attempt was made to throw open the consulship to plebeians. The patricians dare not make an out-and-out resistance to the proposed law; but they managed to bring about a compromise by the creation of a new office, that of tribune with consular powers, open to plebeians as well as patricians, a concession which satisfied the plebeians for the moment, as it gave them access to the real if not to the titular power; and in about two years out of every three in the next three-quarters of a century they managed to get consular tribunes elected instead of consuls.

Also in this period they won admission to the lowest of the regular magistracies, the quæstorship, an office which up to 447 had been filled by nomination by the consuls. Henceforth the quæstors were elected by the Assembly of the Tribes, if the ancient authorities are to be trusted on this point. Anyhow the result was that in 421 a plebeian was for the first time in the office of quæstor.

In 435 the censorship was established, an office which was from the first of an aristocratic character, and so remained to the end of the Republic. Its department of power was carved out of the many powers of the consuls, the most important political function allotted to it being the revision of the list of the Senate every five years by the appointment of new members, and the removal of old ones who had lost their moral or financial status. The establishment of the office was the work of the patricians, who, in view of the evident fact that the consulship must soon succumb to the plebeian assaults, were anxious to restrict its powers before the plebeians got hold of it.

The mention of the Assembly of the Tribes (Comitia Tributa) raises the question as to the origin and form of that particular mode of assembly. Just as the Assembly of the Centuries (Comitia Centuriata) had been established even before the days of the Republic as a form of assembly more democratic than the ancient Assembly of the Curies (Comitia Curiata), so at some unknown date in the history of the Republic the Assembly of the Tribes was established on still more democratic lines, in that it did not involve that preponderance of the voting power of the richer over the poorer classes which was the marked feature of the Comitia Centuriata. The system of group voting is indeed maintained in it; but the groups are not centuries but tribes, each of which was formed of citizens residing in the same locality, men not having any necessary close relationship, though residence in the same region may have implied in the early days of the Republic a large existence of such a tie between them. The Assembly of the Plebs (Concilium Plebis) was organised on the same basis of grouping; and, as it came to be also an absolute legislative authority, Roman historians of the days of the Empire tended to confuse it and its activities with those of the Assembly of the Tribes.[1]

ATHENS

Shortly after the disaster in Egypt in 454 the war in Greece died away to nothing, both sides being weary and worn out. The great dual effort of Athens in Egypt and the Corinthian Gulf represents Pericles' policy of universal empire; but from 454 onwards he confines himself to the consolidation of the existing dominion of Athens, a policy the necessity for which was forced on him by the greatness of the disaster in Egypt, and emphasised by the disasters which preceded the Thirty Years' Peace of 446.

[1] Some modern authorities have denied the existence of the Comitia Tributa. The evidence against that view is well stated in Greenidge, " Roman Public Life," Appendix I, p. 445.

Both in Attica itself and the Empire that policy must have been forced in some form or other on any statesman who tried to direct the fortunes of Athens in the fifth century, no matter the party to which he belonged.

Solon and Pisistratus had between them solved the question of the means of purchasing food from abroad. Themistocles by the creation of the great fleet had provided the means by which that supply might be assured. Aristides and Cimon by using the fleet for the purpose of freeing the passage to the Euxine from Persian control had actually assured it. It was a great thing for Athens that this most pressing problem had been solved; but another problem hardly less dangerous and less pressing remained, that of unemployment, combined perhaps with over-population.[1]

UNEMPLOYMENT

It is probable that unemployment had begun to weigh upon Athens so early as the last quarter of the sixth century, and that the evil was rife among those ultra-democrats who had overthrown Hippias. The growth of Athenian trade in that century had brought into being the commercial capitalist; and at all times in the ancient world the tendency was to invest capital in slaves whether for the working of crafts or for the cultivation of large estates, so much so that periods of prosperity in the life of an ancient nation are almost invariably periods of economic difficulty for the lower classes. By the time of Themistocles the pressure seems to have become a danger, for, though the policy of the great fleet was due to various causes not connected with the question, yet subsequent ultra-democratic policy points to its having been one of them.

But behind the policy of reducing unemployment by service on the fleet was the further question as to how the expense of the upkeep of such a fleet could be met, for, though the produce of the mines at Laurium was sufficient to create the ships, yet there is no reason to suppose that it could have met the cost of keeping them in commission. Having no better plan available at the time, Themistocles seems to have conceived the idea of supporting it by revenues from a trade enlarged by the introduction into Athens of skilled foreign traders in the position of

[1] I cannot in the space at my disposal deal with all the contemporary evidence as to the seriousness of the unemployment problem in Athens at this time. Those who can obtain the loan of the book,—it is out of print,—" Thucydides and the History of his Age " will find the evidence set forth there on pp. 176 ff. For those who cannot get hold of it I may cite such passages as Pseudo-Xen., "De Rep. Athen." i, 15: (Arist.) 'Αθ. Πολ, 24, 25: Plut. "Peric." ii, 12.

THE SECOND HALF OF THE FIFTH CENTURY

resident aliens (metics). Whether the plan might have succeeded it is impossible to say, because circumstances supervened which prevented its ever being put on trial; but trade that is overtaxed has a tendency to take wings and fly away.

In the period from 478 to 466 the difficulty was met by the necessary employment of very large numbers on the great fleet then in commission, so that it never became one which Aristides and the conservatives had really to face; and that fact did not pass unnoticed by one ancient author, who speaks of this period as one in which Aristides met the question of unemployment in this way. But when after the Eurymedon in 466 the necessity for the maintenance of the great fleet in commission ceased to exist, then the problem became more serious than it had ever been before, for the great increase in the trade of Athens after 479, testified to by various Greek authors, meant increased capital and the increased employment of slaves. Moreover the captures made during the war brought an ever-increasing number of them into the Greek market. There follow four years of seething political confusion which end in ultra-democracy under Ephialtes and Pericles getting the upper-hand in 462.

But the years of warfare against Persia in and about the Ægean had given the Athenian sailor the idea, in most respects a true one, that he was the saviour and protector of the liberties of the Greek race, and that it was certainly to his interest and to that of the Greek world generally that he should continue to play this part—at a suitable salary. The position of a destroying angel on a limited income had no attractions for him. The mental step from such an idea to that of empire is a short one; and from that of empire to still wider empire is shorter still. The position of the Athenian democrat in the later half of the fifth century is strangely combined of compulsion and inclination. But he was a man who was determined to wring from others those gifts of life which his own home circumstances denied him; and to do this, if he could, in a lordly way, either as the master of the Greek world, or, failing that, as the controller of an empire. Empire solved the question of the moment and made a great future possible. He appears, not in the writings of those contemporaries who knew him, but in works of modern imagination, as a species of literary dilettante who took an intelligent delight in the plays of Æschylus, Sophocles, and Euripides, works which appeal but little to any save a highly educated modern audience. It is perhaps irreverent to suggest that if a free picture-show had been established in Athens the attendance at the classical drama might have fallen off. He welcomed the works of the great tragedians and of Aristophanes and other comedians because, fortunate in his limitations, their compositions were the only forms of the drama open to him; and mankind will seek on any stage the luxury of laughter and of tears. But it was not a race of literary dilettanti which fought the long struggle of the Peloponnesian War, and, when crippled by a disaster at Syracuse, greater relatively than any single disaster which has befallen any state in history, when hampered rather than supported by a mass of disloyal allies, not merely defied but would have beaten off the attacks of the other Greeks had not they been supported by Persia. In that last fierce fight he had his back to the wall; and he fought like a man. That will be understood and conceded by all to whom the story of those last years of the century is known. But what is not always recognised is that the Athenian democrat had had his back against the wall the whole century through, face to face with evil circumstances for which no one could be held responsible, circumstances the outcome of a perverse economic development such as will recur in various forms at different times in human affairs. If this made the Athenians hard in their dealings with their fellow-men, then it may perhaps be urged in their defence, to paraphrase what Thucydides says of war, that " necessity, by making it difficult for men to win their daily bread, is a stern schoolmaster, and reduces men's passions to the level of their circumstances." The courage which the Athenians showed in seeking a solution for the troubles which beset them was accompanied by other qualities less admirable. They proved themselves hard masters of those they ruled, exploiting them to an extent which could not be justified on the plea of necessity.[1] In that funeral oration which Thucydides puts into the mouth of Pericles the claim to empire is supported by the plea of superior culture. The Athenian is represented as the apostle of a higher civilisation in the Greek world. Other states and other races have sought to disguise aggression under the cloak of missionary enterprise, having decided that they could govern the world better than the world could govern itself. Nor does the arrogance of the claim imply necessarily that it is untrue. The question is as to the amount of self-interest that lies behind it, and the translation of self-interest into practice. The Funeral Oration may represent no more than the Thucydidean conception of the Periclean ideal. But it was almost certainly founded on at least the tenour of speeches which Pericles made, and as such is no more than a camouflage of brutal facts, an expression of the

[1] Our whole view of the morale of Athenian rule has been immensely modified by the facts with regard to the coinage of the Asiatic Greek cities under Athenian rule brought out by Professor Percy Gardner in his " History of Ancient Coinage." Mr. Head's " Historia Nummorum " was misleading on that subject.

divine right of a culture which the speaker asserts to be superior to that of the subject states. Every imperial or would-be imperial state that the world has seen has put forward similar ideas as a forethought or afterthought of empire.

Such were the men whose destinies Pericles had to guide, and for whose necessities he had to provide, during the thirty years of his control of Athenian policy; and it may be imagined that he found them a hard team to drive along the road of prudence, all the more so as he their leader had set them an example of almost unbounded ambition, of which he came to repent but they never did until there was no place left for repentance. That is why in the second phase of his statesmanship, in the later phase of his directorate of Athenian policy, he was faced by an opposition coming from a formidable extremist section of the once united party he had led. And yet all his life through he is seeking to find a solution of the problem presented by the economic conditions; and it is mainly to that end that his policy both at home and abroad is directed. Though his home policy was only rendered possible by the existence of the empire, yet it is sufficiently distinct from his imperial policy for it to be possible to treat it as a separate department of his life's work. But, as it is conditioned by the existence of the empire, it may be well to deal first with his policy towards Athens' quondam allies.

IMPERIAL POLICY OF PERICLES

The democrats in 462 took over from the conservatives what was an empire in all but name. Those most unintentional imperialists had created an empire because they dare not uncreate a league. The democrats accepted the gift in full.

Strategically speaking the various states of the Delian League had always been at the mercy of Athens whenever she wished to bring pressure upon them. They were either islands or coast towns exposed in case of revolt to attack by an Athenian fleet whose strength was overwhelming as compared with their own feeble navies, or as compared with the navies of the other states of the Greek mainland. Athens could isolate any revolt; or, if several states revolted together, could take them in detail, while preventing any help reaching them from sympathisers in Greece itself. The only assistance they could get would be from a diversion created by an invasion of Attica; and Pericles provided against the effectiveness of that more effectively than perhaps he, and certainly more effectively than anyone else, supposed, when in 458 he built the Long Walls from Athens to the sea at Piræus. After that was done the strategic strength of the Athenian Empire was such as has rarely been equalled in the case of any similar state. The changed attitude of the Athenian government under its new democratic controllers towards the members of the league was shown in the war which broke out in 459. Hitherto the league resources in men and ships had been used only for league purposes. The Egyptian expedition might have been represented as undertaken on their behalf inasmuch as it was an attack on a Persian dependency; but any argument that the operations in the Corinthian Gulf were in conformity with the design for which the league had been constituted would have been very far-fetched; and the allies cannot have cherished any illusions on this point. The very fact that Athens used league resources in this war made it quite clear that the Delian League had become an Athenian Empire. The transfer of the treasury from Delos to Athens in 454 is far less significant, for, as has been already said, the tribute paid into this treasury had gone to Athens from the very first, so that the change had at most a sentimental significance; and, moreover, it was made on the proposal of Samos from fear lest, after the disaster in Egypt, the Persian fleet might once more appear in the Ægean. The organisation of the empire was the gradual work of years, an accumulation of items of policy of different dates all having as their object the securing of the forced loyalty of the various states. Probably little was done before the disaster in Egypt, for the wars of the previous five years had solved for the moment the economic difficulty with regard to the unemployed proletariat, since it served for pay in the great fleet then in commission. The real difficulty was to come when the situation had to be solved, not on the lines of war, but on those of peace.

But whether on lines of peace or war, the solution was absolutely dependent on the tribute which came in from the now subject states; for it was that which rendered it possible to keep the great fleet in commission, and formed, too, the basis of the economic policy of Pericles when the war died away. The Athenian democrat came to regard himself as absolutely dependent on that tribute. A new theory was created to justify its use, namely, that it was paid to Athens as guarantor of the peace of the Ægean; and that, if she managed to maintain that peace at an expenditure which did not absorb the tribute income, then the balance saved was her own to do with as she liked. Hence in his later years Pericles used it for the beautifying of Athens with intent to employ the unemployed, and for various other objects designed to the same end.

It must be recognised, however, that the tribute levied was not a heavy burden on the individual states; it was, in fact, a somewhat cheap price to pay for safety against Persia. But the allies did not look at it in that way, for they supposed the danger from Persia to have passed away for ever and ever, while in any case they resented the appropriation of the surplus by Athens instead of the assessment being reduced in time of peace. As regards Persia, they were mistaken; for the events of the last decade of the fifth century were to suggest, and those of the first decade of the fourth century were to prove, that Persia could again become formidable to a divided Greece when the great Athenian navy had vanished from the seas.

But in many other respects the hand of Athens lay heavy on her subjects. Even the tribute was assessed by her, though there is no reason to suppose that she abused a right she had probably arrogated from the now effete council of the old league. Constitutions were dictated to various subject states,—to how many is not known,—a more or less necessary measure in a political world where the oligarch hated his democratic fellow-citizen far more than he did the oligarch of even a hostile state. Still, in some of the states Athens tolerated oligarchies, for, though they might be hostile to Athens both as a democracy and as a ruling power, yet the small numbers of those responsible for the government made them more easy to control in respect to Athenian interests. The fragmentary inscriptions which survive show the constitutions imposed on some of the subject states to have been democratic in form but oligarchic in character. In form they appear to be copies of the constitution of Athens itself; but in fact they are very different. The Council ($\beta o u \lambda \acute{\eta}$) which controlled the business brought before the Assembly of the people is in these constitutions a body with far greater powers than those of the Council at Athens, for it is put in a position to control the policy of the state. It was not freely elected, for an Athenian officer was present at the selection of nominees, and could exclude from the list anyone who was suspected of disloyalty to Athens, so that it consisted of a personnel packed in the Athenian interest. An Assembly of all the citizens of one of the subject states would almost certainly contain a large anti-Athenian majority, so unpopular was the rule of Athens. So the government, in name a democracy, was really a philo-Athenian minority banded together under the form of a democratic Council.

But Athens had to protect the philo-Athenian minorities in the subject cities in another way also. A philo-Athenian brought before the popular court of his own state on any charge could hardly escape condemnation by the anti-Athenian majority. And so Athens withdrew all cases involving the death penalty or the loss of civil rights to her own courts. To her subjects this seemed high-handed dealing; but in point of fact it made for justice. Cases involving charges of disloyalty to the empire were naturally tried at Athens. But undoubtedly one of the most unpopular features of Athenian control was the presence of Athenian officials, either overseers or commanders of garrisons, in the allied states, with what were evidently very large powers of control over the local government. Athenian garrisons were not likely to be popular in the cities in which they were planted, all the more so as they were probably sent only to those of known or suspected disloyalty.

Such are the main features of the organisation of the empire, an organisation plainly designed to bind it hand and foot to Athenian rule.

Trade of the Empire

But while all these things are compatible with a reasonable interpretation of imperial rule, and, though they imply a good deal of interference with political liberty, do not suggest any tyrannous restrictions on the ordinary business of life and such-like matters, yet outside the written records of the time the evidence of the coinage of the Asiatic Greek cities under Athenian rule implies that there was a darker side to the picture: that Athens deliberately manipulated the trade of the empire in her own interests and against those of her Asiatic subjects, those cities which had in the past held the foremost place in Greek commerce. It is not merely that she had got the corn trade of the Euxine into her power to such an extent that she distributed the grain from that area not merely to the cities of her own empire, but to some of the states of continental Greece in quantities determined by her. Byzantium was the distributing centre, where officials resided who had charge of the distribution. But the commerce of the empire generally was brought under a control, which may have amounted to a tyranny, by forcing the subject states to adopt Attic coinage, weights, and measures, and to cease from issuing silver coinage of their own. It is only the three remaining free allies who are not thus restricted; and even their coinage may be interfered with in case of revolt. It is of course possible that the policy merely aimed at the consolidation of the empire by unification of the coinage and metric systems; but the fact that this policy is used as a punishment for revolt suggests that it curtailed not merely the freedom but the profits of the trade of subject cities, and transferred some of the latter to Athens.

Thus, as far as the empire was concerned, the financial difficulties of the economic situation at home were met by the income derived from the tribute, and by a continuation of Themistocles' policy of promoting and extending Athenian trade.

THE SECOND HALF OF THE FIFTH CENTURY 177

The disaster in Egypt in 454 had an almost immediate effect on home politics and home policy. Its most important result was undoubtedly that change, to which allusion has been already made, which it brought about in the policy of Pericles. The change begins from that time; but, as a state of war continued till the Peace of 446, it is more noticeable after that year. The failure of the great plan seems to have shaken the democratic control of affairs, for Cimon was recalled from banishment, and was commanding the Athenian fleet in an attack on the Persian position in Cyprus during the last year of his life,—a war policy which suggests that the conservatives held the upper hand at the moment. Just after his death a great victory was won at Cyprus both by land and sea; and this was effective in bringing about the Peace of Callias in 449, with which the long war with Persia came to an end. The conservative revival at Athens,—if there had been one—had been brief.

The successful revolts of Megara and Bœotia in 447, together with other minor losses incurred by the Thirty Years' Peace, complete the ruin of Pericles' great design.

Peace Policy of Pericles

But the war had been merely smouldering for five years before it was extinguished by the Peace,[1] and, as usual, the economic difficulties which the period of feverish war activity between 459 and 454 had temporarily solved came home to Athens to roost. Feverish activity in active warfare gave place to feverish activity in home legislation with a view to alleviating a situation which could not be cured. It was plain that the unemployed population must be artificially supported out of the income from the empire; and, with a view to limiting the obligations of the state, a law was passed in 451 limiting the citizenship to those born from Athenians on both sides. The date of the law is significant. It is that of the Five Years' Truce with Sparta. In the next year settlers were despatched to Andros. The policy of sending out citizens to settle abroad is carried out with great vigour during the rule of Pericles, so much so that it may be calculated that 15,000 citizens, a very large proportion relative to the citizen population of Athens, went out to such settlements during his lifetime; and the practice was continued after his death. The settlements were not usually colonies, but rather bodies of Athenian citizens (cleruchs) who received allotments of land in regions outside Attica, very often

---

[1] An actual truce for five years had been made by Athens and Sparta in 451. See p. 165.

in the territories of disloyal subject states which had to pay for their disloyalty.[1]

The terms of the Thirty Years' Peace of 446 involved the surrender by Athens of all that she had won in the war since 459. She had failed in her attempt to get more; so for the future she must confine herself to the attempt to keep what she had got. On that point Pericles had made up his mind; and his subsequent policy is an outward and visible sign of his acceptance of the position. He cultivates friendly relations with other Greek states, and even soothes the feelings of the implacable Corinth, who, when Sparta and other Peloponnesian states suggest interference in the revolt of Samos against Athens in 440, protests against such action, laying down the principle that each state should be allowed " to discipline its own allies." Corinth had not so much to fear from an Athens which had no longer direct access to the western trade route through the Gulf of Corinth; and it is even probable that she had come to some agreement with Athens with regard to the pooling of that western trade.

Perhaps the most marked sign of Pericles' complete change of policy with regard to the West is the interest he showed after 439 in the Pontus; for "Westward Ho!" had ever been the cry of that ultra-democratic party which he led, and it was the West which he had sought in the recent struggle with Corinth and her allies. And now of a sudden all is changed, and for a brief period the ultra-democrats turn their eyes eastward, and seek by a naval display in the Euxine to consolidate Athenian interests on the shore of that sea! Furthermore, in 443, Athens had shown her new mildness of disposition when, in founding the colony of Thurii, in Italy, on the western trade route, she had made it so Pan-hellenic that the non-Athenian soon got the upper hand of the Athenian element. This was a very different Athens from that which a few years before had been straining every nerve to get that trade route under her own absolute control. It was not the fault of Pericles, nor of any other individual, nor of any state, that this period of goodwill was fated to last but ten short years.

At some date not long after 446 the law limiting the citizenship was put into strict operation in relation to the distribution of a gift of corn made by Psammetichus, king of Egypt, with the result that more than a quarter of the claimants were struck off the list of citizens.

[1] In the eight years from 450 to 443 settlements of allotment holders (cleruchies) were sent out to Andros (*circ.* 450), Naxos (*circ.* 447), the Thracian Chersonese (*circ.* 447), Lemnos (*circ.* 447), Imbros (*circ.* 447), Colophon (*circ.* 446), Hestiæa (*circ.* 446), Chalcis and Eretria (*circ.* 445); and colonies to Brea (*circ.* 446) and Thurii (443).

THE SECOND HALF OF THE FIFTH CENTURY

Pericles' new policy was a confession of the failure of the old. Ultimately it had the effect of estranging from him the wild men among the extreme democrats, and of bringing over to his side some at least of the moderates. But it took both sides some time to recognise the change, so that not long after the Peace, probably in 443, the conservatives, now led by the moderate democrat Thucydides, the son of Melêsias, made a grand attack on him, based, it would seem, on the unfair treatment of the quondam allies. It failed ; and Thucydides was ostracised. Doubtless the subject states were seething with a discontent which, unfortunately for them, could not, for strategic reasons which have been explained, find expression in general revolt. But in 440 Samos, the most powerful of the three independent allies of Athens, and owner of a fleet of 50 triremes, revolted. The trouble began about Priene, a town on the coast of the mainland, which Samos had claimed as her possession, but Athens had handed over to Milêtus. When Samos retaliated by attacking Milêtus, Athens intervened and overthrew the Samian aristocratic government, whereupon some members of it got help from Pissuthnes, satrap of Sardes, and recaptured the island. The flame of revolt spread along the Carian coast, the cities of which went over to Persia ; but, more important than all, Byzantium, the key to the corn trade, threw off its allegiance, and various other cities on the Thracian coast followed suit. Sparta, where the unbounded ambition of Athens as shown in the recent war seems to have convinced even the nationalists that a passive policy towards her was no longer possible, and by whom the change in Pericles' policy was not as yet recognised, thought of intervention ; but, when Corinth, her most important ally, protested, she gave up the idea. After a fierce struggle the revolted towns were reduced in 439.

It was in the decade following 446 that Pericles began and carried out his scheme for the embellishment of Athens, knowing well the psychological impression which the possession of a magnificent capital makes on the minds both of rulers and of ruled. And so within the space of a few years arose some of the most beautiful buildings that the world has ever seen. Nor was it merely an incidental fact that their construction gave employment to that mass of unemployed which the cessation of warfare had thrown on the hands of the Athenian government. That was an essential feature of the scheme.

SOCIAL LIFE UNDER PERICLES

But though these buildings even in their ruin are some of the most glorious monuments of western civilisation, yet they are not the greatest contribution which Pericles made thereto.

Like some of the tyrants of the past, he gathered round him an intellectual coterie of men with new ideas which, when developed in later days, were to influence and mould the whole social and political life of the Mediterranean world. Up to that time the great intellectual movements among the Greek race had originated with the Greeks of Asia Minor and of the West. Athens had not till then been an intellectual centre, though she had produced, and was producing, great dramatists whose work the Athenian masses appreciated, partly because they had no other drama to appreciate, partly because thus far the dramatists had dealt with ancient customary themes closely associated with that old life and belief to which even that bold political experimenter, the Athenian democrat, was strongly and, as he thought, virtuously attached. Æschylus and Sophocles had not violated the traditions and superstitions of the past. The political innovations of Athenian democracy had not been the outcome of idealism, but had been forced upon it by the hard necessities of life. In all save politics,—in the ordinary affairs of life, that is to say—it was wedded to ancestral social and religious ideas to such an extent that it was ready to prosecute and kill those whose teachings tended to upset them. But the young ideas of the fifth century which it so bitterly resented became middle-aged in the fourth, and old thereafter, and so gradually made their way into the customary life of the average Athenian and the average Greek, mingled strangely with those old superstitions which died so hard that they never died so long as the Greek remained the exponent of his own mode of life. To regard the audiences which appear in the Dialogues of Plato as in any way representative of the average Greek or of the average Athenian is to set up an ideal which comes at every turn into conflict with the known facts of Greek history and with the possibilities of human nature as represented by the Greek or by any race which has existed in the world. The intellectual life of which Athens became the centre and remained the centre for centuries was lived by the intellectual few, and supported by a well-to-do leisured class drawn not merely from Athens itself, but from all over the Greek world. To its teachings the average contemporary man was indifferent, provided they did not corrupt the youth, as those of Socrates were said to have done. It is true that the teachings which were novel and ignored at one age might in some practical form or other make their way into the life of the next, and become regarded as part of immemorial custom. But even so, they only modified, they did not transform, the life of the average Greek, who remained to the end of the chapter the devotee of meticulous, superstitious, and customary usage. Intellectual achievements were in Greece as elsewhere attained by the intellectual few. They were bolder than those of other races of the time, because they were the work of men who had renounced superstition, and sought in a religion of humanity a clue to the problems of life which the divinity would not vouchsafe and natural religion did not afford.

In the intellectual life of Greece the last half of the fifth century was a period of activity the like of which not even Greece was ever to see again, for the teachers of the new learning were in many cases the creators of the ideas they taught, and not merely the critics and reformers of the dicta of predecessors. It was the age of the Sophists, a body of men some of whom Plato, because he differed from their views, treated with so much contempt that their very name has become a byword in modern language. It is those of them who were teachers of politics whom Plato attacked, only a fraction, though a very important fraction, of the whole number; but neither they nor their fellow-teachers did aught to justify the disrepute which has become attached to the name by which they were called. They were certainly not charlatans, nor were they casuists save to those to whom the art of reasoning was as yet unknown; and, on the other hand, they diffused throughout such of the Greek world as cared to listen to them the highest forms of the knowledge of the day. With the mass of the people they were unpopular, partly because their teaching was only available for those who could afford to pay for it; but, in some cases, because it attacked the old traditions and superstitions of the past. Two main currents of thought met in the Athens of that day, that natural philosophy of the Ionian school dating from the latter half of the sixth century, and a new philosophy which originated in the Sicilian West. The latter had had a curious development. To its first form the name of philosophy can hardly be given. The sudden rise of democracy in the Sicily of the sixties of this century had shown men that power lay with the best speaker, especially in communities where, as in the Sicilian cities, the local aristocracy had either perished or been degraded at the hands of the tyrants. Then clever heads began to see that there were certain tricks in speaking, in the art of persuasion, which were peculiarly effective with the vulgar mind; and they elaborated out of them a system to which was given the name of rhetoric. The study became popular inasmuch as it opened the way to power to others besides those possessed of the natural gift of eloquence. But elaboration of form led to consideration of subject-matter; and hence politics, the subject-matter of public oratory, was systematised and became a subject of instruction. But as the nature and morals of the individual affected those of the mass, and vice versa, the study of politics gave rise to the study of ethics. It is remarkable, though not perhaps unaccountable, that the study and practice of rhetoric did not come into vogue at Athens in the time of Pericles. It was not till the visit of Gorgias in 427, on an embassy from Leontini in Sicily, that Athenian politicians came to appreciate the art, an appreciation which was immediate and enthusiastic. It must have been, however, about this time that the sophistic teachers of politics, face to face with that, to them, extraordinary political phenomenon the Athenian empire, came to revise their original dicta as to the origin of the state. It was flattering to the newborn democracies of Sicily to hear that the state as a society existed " by the divine ordering of nature " ($\varphi\acute{v}\sigma\varepsilon\iota$), an expression which the new Sicilian philosophy borrowed from that of Ionia. But, confronted with the phenomenon of the Athenian Empire, which at this time presented all the unity of a single state, they were in a difficulty, for to say that such a state existed by the divine ordering of nature would have been to preach a doctrine which would have shocked the fundamental Greek idea of liberty; and to say such a thing in any state in Greece save Athens would have been equivalent to suicide. Yet here was a state which was an exception to the rule—and the very thing which every department of the philosophy of that day was striving after was to find rules without exceptions. So the old rule had to be discarded; and a new doctrine was put forward to the effect that the state existed " by convention " ($\nu\acute{o}\mu\varphi$), meaning thereby that by nature the right of the strongest was always the best, but that in civilised human society the strong made conventional concessions to the weak. Thus they exasperated Plato in the next century, and started a controversy upon which no agreement has been reached after more than two thousand years of intermittent wrangling.

The most famous sophist of the day, Anaxagoras, was among the intellectual friends of Pericles. Various were the subjects with which he dealt; but as he dealt with certain questions in a way which shocked the conservative superstition of the mass of the people, he had to fly from Athens. The fate of Gorgias was different, because he was not called upon to deal with such highly controversial subjects; and it was the form, and not the matter, of what he said which took the Athenian world by storm. Pericles had died but two years before, and since his death no one had arisen whose claims to the political leadership of Athens were incontestable. Hitherto eloquence had been looked on as a natural gift possessed by the fortunate, but unattainable by those who did not possess it. But now something that was, if not eloquence,

THE SECOND HALF OF THE FIFTH CENTURY

at any rate a very effective mode of public speaking, might be acquired by learning and practising some quite simple rules.

RHETORIC AND THE GREEK LANGUAGE

Political leadership was now within the reach of any student who cared to give his attention to rhetoric. Pleading in the law courts, a part which many had to play in that somewhat litigious community, lost many of its terrors to a man who was instructed in this most effective art. To the Athenian of education it was a wonderful discovery which offered possibilities undreamt of in the past;—and he can never have dreamed of the revolution which his zeal in pursuit of it was to bring about in the Greek language. Lysias was at his prime when Gorgias came to Athens; yet before he died he became the greatest exponent of the new eloquence. Still he may have learnt something of it in his old home at Thurii. Others like Antiphon made a great name therein before the century closed. But it was not merely the tricks of rhetoric, antithesis, and so forth, that had attracted attention to the eloquence of Gorgias. He spoke a richer Greek than Athens had ever heard before, a Greek with a width of vocabulary and expression such as the Athenian had never conceived. Greek was, and remained right up to the end of the classical period, a language of simple vocabulary, though adapted in form to shades of expression far finer than those which are possible in the other languages which have played their part in the history of the western world. Even Aristotle had to create a vocabulary out of phrases. For all kinds of ends, good, bad, and indifferent, the Athenian set to work on this new Greek with such zeal that in the last quarter of the fifth century he evolved that pure style of the early fourth century which rendered Greek so perfect a medium of expression. And while the politician and the pleader were evolving by mutual intercourse the spoken and written eloquence which made the fourth century famous, one man, the greatest writer and the greatest thinker of his age, Thucydides, who experienced but the first three years of this intellectual movement in Athens, just enough to appreciate its immense possibilities, was after 424 cut off by twenty years of exile from those who by a companionship and rivalry in labour brought that style to perfection. He had to work out his own style in the new Greek, cut off as he was from those who brought it to such rapid development. The Greek of the speeches and of certain reflective passages in his narrative is the summit of his attainment, and it is the language of a great man struggling single-handed with a material which he finds hard to manipulate, language grand in its ruggedness, but admittedly unlike any Greek that any other Greek author ever wrote.

The Athens of the last quarter of the fifth century was a strange society composed of a limited class which had, when not on service, both the means and the inclination to discuss and pursue every abstract question that the wit of man could raise : of another, also small, which was developing the new Greek for practical use in politics and the law courts, and meanwhile unconsciously creating a new literary prose : of rural dwellers who yearned only for a peace which would restore them to that prosperity which they had won from the land : and of a proletariat which was prepared to conquer the world or to defy it in order to gain a greater empire than it had got, or to retain that empire which it had won.

The prosecution of Anaxagoras, the friend of Pericles, may have been incited by persons politically opposed to him ; but his condemnation was due to outraged popular superstition. Other charges which aimed at weakening the position of the great statesman were brought also against his unofficial wife Aspasia, and against his friend the great sculptor Phidias. From what political party they proceeded the records of the time do not clearly indicate ; but it is plain that in the decade following 446 some of the ultra-democrats who had been solid in support of him before that time had come to recognise that his new view of Athenian imperialism was not theirs, and had gone into opposition as an out-and-out imperialist section who disapproved of what they regarded as a milk-and-water foreign policy. It is probable that from them proceeded the attacks on his two friends. But Pericles must certainly have been supported at this time by a majority of the Athenian voters, so that it would seem as if some of the moderates, won over by his policy of goodwill towards the Greek states outside the empire, had come over to his side. Moreover, the strange course which politics at Athens took in the controversies which preceded the outbreak of the great Peloponnesian War can only be accounted for by lines of division between political sections other than those which commonly divided the aristocrats, moderates, and extreme democrats during the rest of the century.

CAUSES OF THE PELOPONNESIAN WAR

The ten years of peace may be said to have come to an end with certain events which took place in 436. They were like a cloud no bigger than a man's hand on the far northwestern horizon of Greece, a region in which Corcyra had for a century past played a lonely part, living her own life without interference with or by other Greek states, an all-important station on the great route to the West, yet unimportant so long as she afforded the other Greek states, especially Corinth and Athens, a free passage along it—which she was glad enough to do provided they did not interfere with her lucrative western trade. Also she had at this time the second largest navy in the Greek world, which did much to guarantee her against interference on any frivolous pretext. Up the Adriatic coast, north of Corcyra, Epidamnus, a colony of hers, was being harassed by certain aristocrats whom its democrats had expelled; and so the latter applied to Corinth, as the mother-city of their founder, Corcyra, for assistance. Between Corcyra and Corinth there had existed a bitter enmity dating from the time when the Corinthian tyrants had reduced Corcyra from the position of colony to that of dependency. Corinth now took up the cause of Epidamnus, which was unfortunate, though perhaps Greek sentiment would have felt that the ultimate metropolis of that colony was bound, if called upon, to aid it. The Corinthians sent out new colonists of their own, an act against which Corcyra protested, though she offered to submit the affair to arbitration. This proposal Corinth answered by sending 75 ships and 2,000 hoplites to attack Corcyra, an expedition which the Corcyrans defeated badly at the mouth of the Ambraciot Gulf. Meanwhile Epidamnus surrendered; and Corcyra spent the next few months in making matters very unpleasant for the various Corinthian settlements on the Acarnanian coast. This in 435. Corinth, having no mind to sit still under these proceedings, spent two years in preparing an overwhelming attack, a threat which so alarmed Corcyra that she appealed to Athens for help, while Corinth by a simultaneous embassy put her case before the Athenians.

To understand what followed it is necessary to realise the position of Athens in the matter.

There was every reason to apprehend that Corinth, who was being aided by several smaller states in her neighbourhood, would crush Corcyra and make it a dependency. If she succeeded in so doing, she, being thereby in absolute command of the route to Sicily, would be in a position to go back on any agreement she had made with Athens with regard to the use of it. This was a possibility which Athens could not face, not merely on the general question of trade, which, though very important to her, was less critical than the prospect of being cut off from the western corn supply should anything occur to block the narrow and precarious route to the Euxine through the Hellespont and the Bosphorus. Persia was on one side of that route; and Byzantium had been recently in revolt. Yet Athens did not wish to break the Peace; and so she compromised by forming a purely defensive alliance with Corcyra. And now it was Corinth's turn to fear lest Athens should get such a control of Corcyra as to block the Corinthian trade with the West, the main source of that state's prosperity—and probably, what is more, of *her* corn supply. The situation was one of the tragedies of history in that a most dangerous and critical state of circumstances had arisen such as was like to lead to untold trouble and misery—to a war which both sides would have avoided, and for which neither could be said to be deliberately responsible. After this events developed with terrible rapidity.

In the autumn of 433 the Corinthian expedition sailed, and a great but indecisive battle was fought at Sybota in which a small squadron of Athenian ships took a deferred and unwilling part. But the Corinthians dare not renew the attack. Athens had now to face the open hostility of Corinth. She had in her empire a Corinthian colony, Potidæa, on the Chalcidian peninsula, on which, in distrust of its loyalty, she made demands which were refused. It was supported by Perdiccas, king of Macedon, a shifty potentate, whose policy, as shown later, was kaleidoscopic opportunism. The Athenians attacked the place, and won a battle there in 432 in which certain Corinthian and Peloponnesian forces took part. War between Athens and Corinth was now engaged, and the sole remaining question was as to the number of other states which would be drawn into it. Pericles had made up his mind that matters had gone beyond possible reconciliation, and that, as war must come, it would be well to bring things to a head as soon as possible, since a period of uncertain peace, during which Athens' ill-wishers might tamper with her discontented subjects, would be more dangerous than a state of open war in which the Athenian fleet would cut off all such communications, and hostages in the form of contingents would secure the loyalty of the allies. And so in 432 he issued the Megarian Decree. The decree itself excluded Megara from all ports and markets of the Athenian Empire. To Megara it was a disaster : to other states it was a threat. Megara does not seem to have retained that prominence which she had formerly had in Greek trade ; but she had continued to carry on an important manufacture of textile fabrics which brought her wealth, and raised her population to numbers which so small and so peculiarly unfertile a state could not support save on food supplies got from abroad. Athens controlled the Euxine grain trade at Byzantium, from which place she distributed the corn to various states both in and outside her empire, of which Megara was almost certainly one. Thucydides puts into the mouth of the Corinthians a statement which hints that there were other states outside the Athenian Empire in a similar position of dependency. To Megara the decree meant something like starvation. Pericles had evidently made up his mind that the war would begin whenever Sparta came in : that she would eventually come in : and that she should be forced to come in soon by this outrage on her ally. There was also the possibility that Megara would have to give in, in which case the control of her territory would give Athens both a control of the Isthmus, and such direct access to the Corinthian Gulf as would be most valuable in a war with the Peloponnesian League.[1]

Corinth was by this time moving heaven and earth to get the Spartans to take up the cause of herself and Megara; but she found it very difficult to get that power to stir. Archidamus, who had long been king, was against interference, partly because he represented that national party which was opposed to the incurring of obligations abroad, partly because he distrusted the effectiveness of Sparta's resources against those of Athens. But it soon became evident that, if Sparta did not move, that Peloponnesian League which was the foundation of the policy of the national party would break up ; and so Sparta took the lead of a war confederacy which included all the Peloponnesian states except Argos, and also Bœotia, Corinth, Megara, and Ambracia. On the side of Athens were the cities of her empire, Corcyra, and also Acarnania, save Œniadæ,—a very important exception.

It is not possible to speak with certainty as to the attitude of parties at Athens towards the war, because neither Thucydides nor any later author gives any detailed information on the subject. The aristocrats would certainly be against war ; but they were a small minority. The ultra-democrats would certainly be for it. Of the moderates it can only be said that, inasmuch as they sacrificed their lands and came into Athens at Pericles' bidding, he must have convinced them of its necessity or inevitability. But when it came to the question as to how the war should be conducted, there was a fundamental difference between parties. The ultra-democrats wanted a vigorous aggressive strategy, whereas the moderates dreamt of wearing down the Peloponnesians by passive resistance, and thus avoiding that mutual exasperation which might prolong the war to an

---

[1] In speaking of the causes of the war, Thucydides was influenced by his view of thé whole twenty-seven years of warfare from 431 to 404 as one war. That view was not taken by his contemporaries, nor by any known fourth-century author. They all speak of three wars : (1) the Ten Years' (or Archidamian) War, from 431 to 421 ; (2) the Sicilian War, from 415 to 413 ; (3) the Ionian War, from 413 to 404. Thus, when Thucydides speaks of the hostility of Sparta to Athens as the *verissima causa* of the war, he is thinking of a cause which ran like a thread through the whole twenty-seven years of warfare. When he denies that the affair of Epidamnus was the true cause of the war, he is again referring to the whole war. He would not have denied that it was the cause of the Ten Years' War. He ignores the Megarian Decree as a cause.

indefinite extent. The strategy which Pericles was influential enough to impose on the state was a practical application of the view of the moderates ; but it was adopted for military, not for the political reasons for which they supported it.

Pericles knew, what everybody knew at the time, that the attack on Athens, and especially on Attica, would be conducted on the immemorial lines of Greek warfare, and that, as for war by sea, there was no navy or combination of navies in the Greek world at home which could face the fleet of the empire, partly owing to its overwhelming size, partly owing to the high state of training to which its personnel had been brought, training which made it capable of executing manœuvres most effective against a less skilled enemy, and of a nature which the unskilled could not employ without disaster to themselves. In Greek naval warfare, as in the naval warfare of other ages before the invention of armour-plated vessels and guns of long range, naval tactics went through certain cycles of development which are apt to recur within quite a short period according to the skill of the people who employ them. The three forms are : boarding tactics, those employed by the Greeks at Salamis, and by all the Greek fleets save the Athenian at the opening of the Peloponnesian War ; manœuvring tactics, aiming at cutting through the enemy's line and charging the weak parts of his vessels, a plan which could only be resorted to by fleets with highly trained crews such as the Athenian at the opening of this war ; end-on ramming with a ship with peculiarly strong prows, a plan adopted by the Syracusans in the last naval fight in the Great Harbour at Syracuse.

The superiority of the Athenian fleet was tacitly admitted by its opponents in the Ten Years' War. Corinth contested its supremacy in the Corinthian Gulf, where it was only represented by a small squadron, and made a failure. Once only did the Peloponnesian fleet venture so far as the Asiatic coast, and then only to run away again so soon as the Athenian fleet was rumoured to be in the neighbourhood. Athens' position at sea was incontestable ; and both sides knew it from the beginning.

PLANS FOR THE LAND WAR

On land the position was not so one-sided. The Peloponnesians could put in the field a far larger army than Athens and her allies ; and both their strategy and that of Pericles were determined by this fact. The plans of both sides were of a very simple character. The Peloponnesians, with the exception of Archidamus, were convinced that, if they invaded Attica, one of two things must happen, either the Athenian army must meet them in battle, in which case it would be badly defeated ; or, if it refused battle, an unimpeded devastation of Attic territory would soon bring Athens to terms. They were not to be persuaded that a design which had always succeeded in Greek warfare would not be successful now. They did not realise, what Archidamus suspected, that Pericles had introduced into warfare a factor which was destined to upset all the preconceived ideas of the past, and to revolutionise the art of war as practised in the Greek world.

The Greek Art of War

Greek warfare in the fifth century as it appears in the pages of contemporary writers is one of the paradoxical phenomena of history. The sole effective element in a Greek army of this and previous time was, and had been, the heavy-armed soldier, the hoplite ; and he was only effective on those plains which formed but a fifth of the area of Greece. The Greek light-armed forces (ψιλοί) played hardly any part in deciding a battle, and very little part at all in fighting of any kind. They were little more than baggage carriers—an Army Service Corps. Yet, if a hoplite force did get on that rugged ground which forms four-fifths of the area of Greece, it could be effectively attacked by Greek light-armed troops, because it could not maintain that close order which was an essential feature of its mode of fighting, just as it was, though in not quite so strict a sense, that of the Roman legion up to the time of Marius. But, as a fact, in warfare in Greece a hoplite force which invaded an enemy's country could always compel the enemy to meet it on the plain, because otherwise it could devastate that plain and those lower slopes of the hills which were the only cultivable ground, destroying crops and, what was far more serious, olive trees and vines, and thereby reducing the population to a position in which they would have no food supply for the next year, and no means of purchasing a supply from abroad. There were plenty of strong places about the land where the assailed might have taken refuge beyond the reach of any hoplite force ; but, though such an acropolis was necessary for the storing of movable property and as a refuge for non-combatants, the fighting force of the state could not shut itself up in it and look on while the crops and fruit trees were being destroyed. It had to attempt to save the cultivated lands by fighting on those lands, that is to say, on the plain, the only ground on which a hoplite force could act. Greek armies were notoriously incompetent in the attack on walled fortifications of any kind, because they were never, owing to the conditions above outlined, called on to practise the art.

At the time of the opening of the Peloponnesian War this

method of warfare had become stereotyped in Greece; and as in military affairs changes are only apt to be made when suggested by practical experience, and such practical experience of the new conditions of war was as yet lacking to the Peloponnesian Greeks, they assumed, in spite of the doubt expressed by Archidamus, that the methods of the past would be effective in the present.

The strategy of the Peloponnesians at the beginning of the war consisted solely in the design of the invasion and devastation of Attica. That, as they thought, would bring Athens to her knees. The Corinthians cherished the private design of forcing the passage of the Corinthian Gulf by destroying the Athenian squadron at Naupactus.[1]

To meet the Peloponnesian strategy Pericles had, and knew, or at least suspected, that he had, a trump card up his sleeve in the shape of the linked fortress of Athens-Piræus, which enclosed an area sufficient to receive all the population of Attica, and, owing to the incapacity of the Greeks in attacks on walled fortifications, was, if not impregnable, at any rate not likely to be assaulted by soldiers who, apart from inexperience in such operations, were accustomed to fight in close order, and averse to fighting under any other conditions. Also, and above all, with the Athenian fleet in command of the sea, food could be imported freely, and Athens could never be scared or starved into submission, nor her army forced to give battle to a superior Peloponnesian army by that devastation which was the immemorial plan of Greek warfare.

That was at the bottom of the strategy of Pericles, the success of which was to be shown by the Ten Years' War.

The hotheads amongst the ultra-democrats disliked it; nor can it have been popular with the conservative rural population, as it involved the sacrifice of those cultivated lands on which they had spent a century of successful labour. Yet Pericles carried the plan through,—how, the contemporary authors never fully explain. He also discouraged in the most emphatic way any scheme of conquest during the war, having in his mind the ambitions of that extreme democratic wing which had gone into opposition to his policy of recent years.

---

[1] The Corinthian speech inserted by Thucydides in his account of the Second Congress at Sparta (i, 118 (2)—125 (1)) is a passage which Thucydides inserted in his history many years after the context was written. It sketches designs which were never operative till the time of the Ionian War; and it was inserted by the author when, after the Sicilian Expedition and the beginning of the Ionian War, he came to regard the whole twenty-seven years of warfare as one. (See my "Thucydides and the History of his Age," p. 445.)

THE SECOND HALF OF THE FIFTH CENTURY

THE TEN YEARS' WAR [1]

The story of the Ten Years' War from 431 to 421 as told by Thucydides is for the most part a catalogue of incidents relieved every now and then by a detailed description of exciting events, such as the siege of Platæa and the operations about Pylos. The modern reader has to evolve the strategy of either side by induction from the facts.

The war was fought in seven regions: Attica, Megara and Bœotia, the Corinthian Gulf and north-west Greece, Peloponnese, Sicily, Macedonia and Chalcidicé, and lastly the Asiatic coast.

In Attica the population was concentrated within the walls of Athens and Piræus at such time as the Peloponnesian army was in the country, save that small garrisons were left in small fortified places such as Œnoë, Phylé, and Panactum. The Peloponnesians invaded Attica five times in the ten years, in 431, 430, 428, 427, and 425. In 429 the plague, and in 426 numerous earthquakes, caused the invasion to be omitted; and after 425 the Athenians had the Spartan prisoners from Sphacteria as hostages against invasion. The damage done was undoubtedly great; but it did not force on a pitched battle, and never seemed to be in the least likely to bring about an early decision of the war. So the whole Peloponnesian plan of attack went to pieces. "There had been a time," says Thucydides, "when they fancied that, if they only devastated Attica, they would crush the power of Athens in a few years." [2]

The frequency and importance of the operations in the Megarid were due to the fact that it commanded the Isthmus in two senses, both the land passage from north to south, and the passage from the Saronic Gulf on the east to the Corinthian Gulf on the west. If Athens could get hold of it she could cut the communications between the Peloponnesians and Bœotia, for the passes of Mount Geranea were difficult and defensible; and she would also have through the port of Pêgæ direct communication with the Corinthian Gulf.

So long as Bœotia remained in the war Athens was, as it were, nipped by pincers; and it is not strange that she tried to knock Bœotia out. It was by Thebes that the first move in the war was made before actual hostilities had begun between Athens and the Peloponnesians. She attacked Platæa, which was all-important to her, as it commanded the only passes through Mt. Cithæron by which she might communicate with the Pelopon-

---

[1] I can only deal with the most important features of it here. Its details are considered much more fully in my book, "Thucydides and the History of his Age," pp. 333 ff.

[2] Thuc. v, 14.

nesians without passing through Attic territory.[1] The attack failed; but two years later the Peloponnesians showed the importance they attached to the possession of the town by first besieging and then blockading it till it capitulated. It seems strange that Athens did not make any attempt to relieve a place which was important to her for practical as well as sentimental reasons; but in the years during which the siege lasted she was adhering more or less strictly to the strategy laid down by Pericles.

Megara, cut off from the Pontus corn supply, must have been in very evil plight during the war.[2] Athens did all she could to get possession of her territory. The port of Nisæa was blockaded by ships stationed at the west end of Salamis. But in 429 Brasidas the Spartan, that daring and most attractive character who was to make so great a name in the war, scared the Athenians badly by attempting a raid on Piræus from the Megarid through Salamis. In the later years of the war in this region Demosthenes plays a great part. He was a soldier of genius who introduced into the Athenian strategy of the last five or six years of the war various designs which, had they been carried out successfully, would have ruined the enemy's plans and given Athens a decisive victory. In so far as they failed, the failure was in the means, not the end. He seems to have been connected politically with those extreme democrats who had never liked the passive strategy of Pericles, and wanted to attack Sparta and her friends by pronouncedly active operations; and it was on designs of this nature that Demosthenes set himself to work. He developed four main plans: to prevent the Peloponnesians from using a land passage towards Sicily through Acarnania and north-western Greece; to force Megara to come over to Athens; to blockade the Peloponnese by establishing round it a ring of fortified posts; to attack Bœotia from both sides and force her out of the Peloponnesian alliance.

In this last region his first scheme was an attack on Bœotia from the north. He tried in 426 to get through Ætolia with a hoplite force, only to learn how useless and helpless such a force was in a rugged country,—a lesson he never forgot. So that plan broke down at its inception. Two years later, in 424, he tried the same plan, but from the head of the Corinthian Gulf this time, while the main Athenian army invaded Bœotia from the south-east. But owing to some mistiming the attacks were not simultaneous; and furthermore, the Bœotians refused to divide their forces, and put their whole strength against the army coming from the south-east. In a great battle at Delium,

---

[1] For the passes of Cithæron, see p. 148.
[2] Cf. the starving Megarean of Aristophanes.

remarkable in military history from the fact that the Bœotians introduced that unusually deep-ranked phalanx which was to win Leuctra in the next century, the Bœotians defeated the Athenian army. In the same year a great attack on the Megarid had failed because Brasidas had hurried up troops over the passes of Geranea and saved Megara from falling into Athenian hands.

In the region of the Corinthian Gulf and north-west Greece the whole situation was determined by the necessity under which the Peloponnesians lay of keeping up that line of communication with the corn region of Sicily which was hampered by the Athenian squadron at Naupactus and blocked, as a sea passage at any rate, by the hostility of Corcyra. It was designed to turn Corcyra by opening up a well-marked land route through Acarnania and Epirus. The Acarnanians, naturally enough, disliked the idea, and Amphilochian Argos, close to the east shore of the Ambraciot Gulf, liked it no better; and so, so long as the Peloponnesians persisted in their attempts to open up this route, both posed as allies of Athens. Œniadæ was the only Acarnanian town which took the Peloponnesian side, hoping, doubtless, to derive much profit as the port at the south end of the route. Consequently in the early years of the war it received much unwelcome attention from the Athenian commanders; and in 424 it was forced by the other Acarnanians to fall into line with them.

Athens could not afford to keep a large fleet on this side of Greece; and therefore the Peloponnesians, represented by Corinth, showed an activity which they carefully avoided on the side of the Ægean. A big Athenian fleet was temporarily off the coast in 431 engaged in an attack on some of the Corinthian trading stations on the Acarnanian shore. But, when it went home, an Athenian squadron was sent in 430 to Naupactus under the famous Phormio. In this year began the trouble in the north-west in the form of an abortive attack which the people of Ambracia, a Corinthian colony, made on Amphilochian Argos. Next year the Peloponnesians sent a considerable force under one Cnêmus, which, uniting with certain barbarian allies, attacked Acarnania, only to be defeated by the Acarnanians at Stratus. In the same year a Peloponnesian fleet, mainly Corinthian, tried conclusions with Phormio, a great seaman in command of a squadron the crews of which had been trained to a perfection such as had never been attained, and never was attained, in any other Greek navy. Phormio defeated them; and when later, with numbers which appeared overwhelming, they attacked him once more, he snatched another victory,—this time out of the fire. The account which Thucydides gives of these actions is one of the most graphic pictures of warfare which any historian has ever drawn ; and it brings out that fact which is so important relative to the later history of the war, that the superiority of the Athenian navy at this time rested not merely on the number of the vessels but on the superlative skill of the crews. Alas for Athens when those crews perished at Syracuse ! She could build new ships, but never again could she build up such crews as manned her fleet at the beginning of the Peloponnesian War.

Corcyra turned out a broken reed as far as the war was concerned. The Corcyrean aristocrats and democrats preferred fighting one another to fighting anyone else ; and some very confused and bloody proceedings took place, which conferred no advantage on those who took part in them, but benefited posterity in that they inspired Thucydides to write certain reflections on political disorder which the after-world has ever admired, but never digested.

In 426 that fire-eater Demosthenes appears on the western scene of the war with a large fleet. But before he had accomplished anything with it he was enticed away by that plan of attack in Bœotia, the history of which ends in its preface in Ætolia. He lost one reputation to make another. The Peloponnesians had sent a very considerable expedition to attack Naupactus by land. That place was saved by the Acarnanians. So the expedition moved north to attack Amphilochian Argos in conjunction with the Ambraciots. Demosthenes, accompanied by a very few Athenians, hurried after them, and, taking over the command of the Amphilochian and Acarnanian force, defeated the Peloponnesians at Olpæ, a little isolated hill on the east coast of the Ambraciot Gulf. Immediately afterwards he wiped out the Ambraciots at Idomene, a few miles farther north. They were brilliant victories which brought to an abrupt and permanent conclusion all Peloponnesian enterprises in those parts. From the story of the war in this region may be drawn a judgment such as Thucydides would never express,—that the Acarnanians were some of the best fighters of their day. While fighting their own battles they had fought the battle of Athens in the north-west. But they were not minded to fight it in other regions of the world ; and so concluded with their neighbours the Ambraciots an agreement which secured the peace of that part of Greece.

At Corcyra, in 425, Eurymedon the Athenian admiral forced the aristocrats to surrender. He was tricked into handing them over to the democrats, who murdered them ; and thus he became the instrument under providence of restoring peace to that distressed land.

The Athenian strategy round Peloponnese was greatly

modified about the middle of the ten years of the war by the adoption of a scheme which was born in the fertile brain of Demosthenes. During the earlier years the operations there had been confined to coast raids by the Athenian fleet, which seem to have been merely intended to give the rural population of Attica some spiritual compensation for the devastation of their own lands, in order to render them less impatient of the Periclean strategy. By 426 Demosthenes, having wound up the skein of war in the north-west by his victories at Olpæ and Idomene, now conceived a great scheme for the blockade of Peloponnese by the establishment round it of permanent fortified posts. His operations in the north-west must have made communication between Peloponnese and Sicily difficult; but, as the vessels of those days were, owing to the soft nature of the wood of which they were constructed, incapable of keeping at sea for any lengthened period, a blockade of the Peloponnese with fleets having their bases at Piræus and Naupactus could never be effective, whereas it might be from bases established at short intervals round the Peloponnesian coast. Thus in 425 he proposed to occupy Pylos. He was not official general for that year; but, though his scheme was officially regarded as somewhat mad, he was allowed to use an Athenian fleet which was passing Pylos as a means of landing troops on that promontory, and, for the rest, left to fend for himself. This he did with such unexpected success that the official command began to take the affair seriously, and sent him substantial aid, first in the form of a fleet, and later of troops under the command of the demagogue Cleon, who was probably a political friend of his. This resulted in the permanent occupation of Pylos and the capture of some very valuable Spartan prisoners on the neighbouring island of Sphacteria. As this success converted the Athenians to his scheme, they seized in the same year Methana, a small peninsula on the south coast of the Saronic Gulf, and in 424 took and occupied Cythêra, thus, as Thucydides more than hints, blocking the sea route between Peloponnese and Egypt.[1] So Peloponnese was practically cut off from every foreign source of food supply by Athenian stations all round it, from which not only the Athenian fleet, but also privateers, could prey on trading vessels which tried to run the blockade.[2] It was a great design; and it might have decided the war had not Athens been unnecessarily scared by events which happened elsewhere.

The operations of Athens in Sicily during this war, and, to a certain extent, the great expedition of later years, can only

[1] Thuc. iv, 53.
[2] For implied reference to this blockade, see Thuc. vi, 90. and vii, 17.

be understood by reference to that which had been going on in the island for some thirty years past.

Syracuse and Sicily

The division and weakness of those Sicilian democracies which had succeeded the tyrannies had encouraged the native population, the Sicels, under the leadership of a certain Ducetius, to throw off the Greek yoke. Having settled accounts with Ducetius, the Sicilian Greeks proceeded after their usual fashion to settle accounts with one another in a way which Athens could not ignore. Athens had during the war of 459 and the following years tried to get control of the route to Sicily; and, when this turned out a failure, had sought to secure her interests there by treaties made about 454 with certain Sicilian cities. She had undoubtedly large general trade interests in the island, quite apart from the question of the corn supply, with regard to which her position has been explained in reference to the troubles between Corinth and Corcyra.[1] Also during the Ten Years' War she was desirous of stopping the export of corn thence to the Peloponnese.

But in a political sense she neither was at this time, nor had been in the past, aggressive in Sicily. It was Syracuse which had played that part in the Sicilian drama. That town had for some fifteen years before the Peloponnesian War enjoyed a position of superiority among the Siciliot cities by reason of wealth, her population, her admirable situation, and her central geographical position among them. She had shown a wish to translate superiority into predominance. Syracusan democracy was not content to play a smaller part in Sicilian politics than Syracusan tyranny had played earlier in the century. The Sicel war had deferred the ambitions of all the Siciliot cities alike; but when that came to an end Syracuse and Acragas developed a rivalry for the hegemony of the Greek part of the island. The defeat of Acragas about 445 left Syracuse in a commanding position. From that time till the great Athenian expedition there is a see-saw of politics in Sicily. Whenever Syracuse supposes Athens to have her hands full elsewhere she starts a policy of encroachment upon the independence of her neighbours. But the moment Athens shows, or threatens to show, herself ready to interfere in Sicily, she seeks to alarm into combination against alleged Athenian aggression those very cities whose liberties she had been intending to attack. Such proceedings Athens could not regard with indifference, for Syracuse was not merely a colony of Corinth, but devoted to Corinthian interests; and thus its supremacy would have been a death-

---

[1] See p. 185.

blow to Athenian trade with the island. The foundation of Thurii in 443 suggested to Syracuse that the Greek states generally had still an inconvenient interest in the west. But when Samos revolted in 440, and Athens' hands were full, Syracuse prepared to renew the policy which she had had to drop when the Thirty Years' Peace had set Athens' hands free. She nearly doubled her army and navy. Before she could act the revolt of Samos was suppressed, whereon she relapsed into prudent inactivity. The Epidamnus trouble brought Athens into close relations with Corcyra, half-way to Sicily. Syracuse had to keep quiet.

But Syracuse had by this time made it quite clear to Athens that if Athens got into difficulties at home she would move in Sicily ; and so in 433, when it became clear that war in Greece was probable, if not inevitable, Athens made treaties with Rhêgium and Leontini. It was certainly no part of Pericles' design to assume the aggressive in that quarter while engaged in war in Greece ; and all that was aimed at was a maintenance of the *status quo* in Sicily while the hands of Athens were full at home. When the war at home began the Peloponnesians cherished hopes of large assistance from Sicily, ill-founded hopes, for it was not the habit of Syracuse to sacrifice her own opportunities to serve the purposes of her friends ; and at this particular juncture she wanted all her resources for her own purposes at home. The war in Greece had not lasted long before she, with the aid of the other Dorian cities, except Camarina, attacked Leontini, which was allied with the other Chalcidian cities, and also with Camarina and Rhêgium. This brought about the Athenian expedition of 427.[1]

The actual operations in Sicily are individually unimportant. The number of ships sent by Athens was small, only twenty altogether. It is true that a reinforcement of forty ships was subsequently despatched under Eurymedon and Sophocles to help the original expedition in a task which was proving too big for it. Fighting, sometimes desultory, sometimes more active, went on from 427 till 425, the main object of both sides being the control of the Sicilian Strait. No decisive success was attained by either side ; and in 424 Syracuse adopted a policy normal with her under such circumstances. She got together a general congress of the Sicilian cities at Gela, and by frightening them with the bogey of Athenian intervention induced them to patch up a peace on the basis of the *status quo*, a peace to which the Athenian generals assented, since it brought about the very state of things for which Athens had been striving.

[1] The tale of Athenian intervention in Sicily is told in Thuc. ii, 7 ; iii, 86, 88, 90, 99, 103, 115–16 ; iv, 1, 24–5, 58–65 ; v, 4.

But when the fleet returned home the hot-headed ultra-democrats, who disliked such a half-hearted war policy, got the generals fined for their alleged incapacity.

No sooner had the Athenian fleet left Sicily than Syracuse was at her old games again, and another war began. But by this time the Ten Years' War was dying away into nothingness, and so Athens contented herself with sending an embassy to protest against these proceedings. When in the next year, 421, the Peace of Nicias brought the war in Greece to an end, Syracuse, as usual, dropped her aggressive policy like a hot coal. In the school of Hellas of that day Syracuse plays the part of the big boy who bullies the smaller boys when the head master is busy elsewhere.

The war in Macedonia and Chalcidicé, "the parts Thraceward," is most remarkable for the long and costly siege of Potidæa, and, later, for the expedition of Brasidas, with lighter interludes provided by the proceedings of that chameleon Perdiccas, king of Macedon, a singularly active and singularly ineffective participant in that which took place. In importance the great venture of Brasidas overshadows all else that occurred in this region.

In 424 he got together a somewhat scratch army of 700 Helots armed as hoplites, together with hoplite volunteers from Peloponnese, inasmuch as the Spartan government would not entrust him with any regular force for what it probably regarded as a wild-cat scheme. But Brasidas was just the wild cat to carry out a scheme of the kind. He made an adventurous and rapid march through those Thessalians whose friendship and hostility were at the time a matter of uncertainty to friends and foes alike ; and, after capturing certain towns in Chalcidicé, he took Amphipolis in 424. This was the great strategic point of the region. The Strymon river, after rising in the rugged southern outliers of the Rhodopé range, expands into a series of marshy lakes which bar the passage from west to east. But just before reaching the sea it breaks through a coast ridge where the firm land on either side of the river makes a passage possible. On the eastern bank of the stream, half-way up a hill rising from the river, stood Amphipolis. Brasidas in possession of Amphipolis was in possession of the key to the route to the Hellespont ; and the Athenians knew well that if they lost the Hellespont they lost the war, and probably the empire, for an enemy in occupation of that region could cut off the corn supply from the Euxine. The Spartan authorities, who now began to think that there was more in Brasidas' plan than they had supposed, despatched reinforcements to him ; but Perdiccas, if he did not like an Athenian neighbour, disliked still more the idea of a Spartan one, and so got the Thessalians to bar the passage of the Peloponnesian force. Without additional troops Brasidas could not push on through Thrace to the Hellespont.

But the alarm of Athens was great, sufficiently great to make her conclude in 423 an armistice of one year which might perhaps have led to permanent peace had not Brasidas flatly refused to observe it. So when it was over and the war began again the Athenians despatched a large force under Cleon to Amphipolis, where it was badly defeated by Brasidas just outside the town. In the battle fell Cleon, a cheap loss to Athens unless he is much misrepresented by Thucydides, and also Brasidas, to whose character the term " beautiful " might be applied had not that word in such a connection become debased by too promiscuous use in modern times.[1] The state which produced in one century a Leonidas and a Brasidas cannot have been the Sparta of Greek democratic tradition.

On the Asiatic coast during this war a state of comparative calm prevailed for the very good reason that the Peloponnesian fleet dare not cross the Ægean to disturb it. Only once, when Mytilene revolted in 428, did their fleet venture to pay what was little more than a week-end visit of sympathy to the rebels, only to execute a quick and unobtrusive retirement when the Athenian fleet appeared in the neighbourhood.

The failure to recapture Amphipolis so dispirited the Athenians that in the year 421 they concluded the Peace called the Peace of Nicias, the name of the general who presided over the negotiations. The danger from Amphipolis was sensible, but not so great as the Athenians imagined. Two attempts, the one above mentioned, and a later one, to get reinforcements through to Brasidas, had failed. But the weariness of a war of ten years had reduced them to a state in which they could not realise the situation ; and so they accepted a peace which, had all its terms been fulfilled, would have re-established for Athens the *status quo*.

The adversaries of Athens had much more real cause for despair, a despair which they showed in the five years which succeeded the Peace. The mere narrative of fact in the fifth book of Thucydides' history leads to the same conclusions which must be drawn from the events of the war itself. Athens' enemies were absolutely broken in spirit, not because they had suffered any individual disaster of great magnitude in the course of the

---

[1] I think that it is almost certain that after Thucydides' exile in 424 he went to his property near Amphipolis, and there met Brasidas, for he knows so much of those incidents of the war in which Brasidas played a part. Another suspected friend of the historian is Demosthenes, the Athenian general. Wherever Demosthenes played a part, e.g. at Olpæ and Pylos, Thucydides is able to give a full narrative of events.

war, but because the war itself had clearly demonstrated to them that the imperial city, which represented in theory and in practice all that the Greeks most loathed, was ultimately invulnerable against such resources of attack as they had at their disposal. On the side of the offensive the blockade of the Peloponnese, incomplete as it may have been, must have set them thinking furiously. And for both sides the war had illustrated that which the Ionian War was to prove, the extreme precariousness of the position of states which are dependent on others for a part at any rate of the food supply of their population.

But the main reason for the depression of the enemies of Athens was that the old methods of Greek warfare had broken down. Devastation had failed to accomplish its immemorial object. The old world of Greece was dissolving like a dream because the simple strategy of that warfare which had maintained its fabric had been proved to be hopelessly antiquated.

The position of Athens was infinitely stronger than it appeared on the face of the treaty.

Politics at Athens during the Ten Years' War

In the home politics of Athens during the war the war overshadows everything else. But as far as party predominance is concerned, the frequent presence of the rural population in Athens, due partly to their being concentrated there in the spring and early summer of the year when raids might be expected, partly to their being attracted to meetings of the Assembly by the critical nature of the questions to be decided, prevented the ultra-democrats from having all their own way in determining the policy of the state. In so far as a judgment can be formed from the politics of those who were elected generals after Pericles' death in 429, there was thereafter a see-saw in party predominance, dependent mainly on whether the aggressive strategy of the ultra-democrats was or had been recently successful. The prosecution and condemnation of Pericles in 430 was a momentary victory for those ultra-democrats who disapproved of his unenterprising war policy; but a reaction soon came, and from that time till the last years of the war, when the conservatives had become a definite peace party and were able to carry through the peace, the ultra-democrats can only get their way intermittently.

The finance of the war caused considerable anxiety. The money which Pericles had accumulated in the days of peace was soon exhausted; so that in 428 a property-tax (Εἰσφορά) had to be imposed on the citizens, followed three years later by a raising of the tribute some sixty per cent.

The confused history of the five years which intervene between

THE SECOND HALF OF THE FIFTH CENTURY

the Peace of Nicias and the Sicilian Expedition is representative of the confusion of mind which prevailed at the time among the states of Greece. There is an almost bewildering series of permutations and combinations of alliances due mainly to the intense dissatisfaction with which Corinth and Thebes regarded the terms conceded to Athens, and also to the failure of Sparta, and a resulting refusal on the part of Athens, to fulfil the terms laid down by the treaty. Sparta's great Peloponnesian League had broken up, never again to be reconstituted in its original form or with its original strength.

ALCIBIADES

There appears, too, on the scene a new actor, who was destined to make and unmake history. The tales of the frivolity, unconventionality, extravagance, and irreverence of the youth and early manhood of Alcibiades tend to distort his real personality to the minds of those who forget that capacity is not always associated with an unblemished reputation. Thucydides, who cannot be suspected of any sympathy with the party with which Alcibiades associated himself, nor with the designs for which he was responsible, supplies a corrective to any judgment of his capacity which may be distorted by moral considerations. Speaking of him in reference to the supreme crisis in the affairs of the Athenian Empire, he says:

" Alarmed at the greatness of his licence in his own life and habits, and of the ambition which he showed in all things soever that he undertook, the mass of the people set him down as a pretender to the tyranny, and became his enemies; and although publicly his conduct of the war was as good as could be desired, individually his habits gave offence to every one, and caused them to commit affairs to other hands, and thus before long to ruin the city."

This may read as a grudging witness to the greatness of the man; but it is all the more emphatic as testimony to his ability because it is forced from one whose judgment of capacity is unrivalled among historians. Whatever his faults, Alcibiades is one of the great men of history.

That ambition was a marked feature of his character is unquestionable; in fact, his life is a series of chapters of ambitions. Before the Peace of Nicias he is seeking to get the lead of the conservative party held at the time by the somewhat commonplace Nicias. The war-weariness of the people made it probable that that party would be in the ascendant for some years to come. But Sparta would not negotiate the Peace through him; and Nicias was the safe man who is loved by caution and by a not too pronounced conservatism. After 421, bitterly anti-Spartan, Alcibiades makes a bid for the leadership of ultra-democracy, which he eventually gains at the expense of the somewhat incompetent Hyperbolus, on whom had fallen the office, if not the mantle, of Cleon. As such he carries the design of the Sicilian Expedition, hoping in case of its success to become the presiding genius of a Panhellenic empire. Next he is at Sparta, seeking by his advice to win for that state the first place in Hellas, and for himself the first place in that state. When he finds that Sparta will not lend itself to his ambitions, he schemes for his return to the Athenian service; and, when he has accomplished that, wins such success for Athens in the war that he has some prospect of playing the part of a Pericles in a restored Athenian Empire. But the people distrust him, just as they had distrusted Themistocles; and so, once more in exile, he goes to the Persian dominions with intent to make Persia the arbiter of the fate of Greece, and himself the instrument by which the Greeks shall be controlled. And there he and his ambitions died.

Self-seeking he certainly was; but it is equally certain that he was a man of most unusual capacity.

POLICY IN PELOPONNESE

His rise to influence in the ultra-democratic party was rapid; for he was fortunate in that the failure of Sparta to carry out her obligations under the Peace had discredited that conservative party which had negotiated it, and had resulted in the ultra-democrats gaining the control of affairs. He was probably the instigator of the alliance between Athens and Argos in 420; and he certainly was the contriver of a great scheme to overthrow the Spartan power in Peloponnese, a scheme similar to, and probably suggested by, the combination against Sparta which Themistocles had engineered in Peloponnese some fifty years before.[1] The ball opened in 419, when Argos attacked Epidaurus with a view to opening direct communication with Athens across the Argolid peninsula. But the design came to a head in 418, when the generals who controlled the military policy at Athens were of the conservative party; so that when Argos, Mantinea, and Elis made their great effort, Athens merely sent a contingent which represented the minimum of her treaty obligations with the allies. And yet in the great battle at Mantinea in that year, even according to the testimony of Thucydides, who gives the Spartan account of it, Sparta won a narrow, though a great, victory,—in other words, she only just escaped defeat. Had Alcibiades been general at the time, Athens would have been represented by a much larger force; and, unless the story of the actual battle is much distorted, victory would in that case have gone to the side of the allies. It is Thucydides,

[1] See p. 158.

THE SECOND HALF OF THE FIFTH CENTURY

too, who puts into the mouth of Alcibiades the words : " I compelled the Lacedæmonians to stake their all on the issue of a single day at Mantinea."[1] Alcibiades' design came near to antedating the ruin of Sparta by half a century ; and its failure was not due to him but to the fact that, when the crisis came, the direction of affairs was not in his hands, nor in those of his political sympathisers. Sparta made no attempt to follow up the victory. Having taken up the sword reluctantly, she willingly laid it down. It is all characteristic of her attitude in these years when she is living under the shadow of that disillusionment which the Ten Years' War had brought to her. No amount of provocation on the part of Athens could persuade her to renew her attack on that ambitious state ; and indeed, until Alcibiades himself a year or two later told her the truth, she did not know the full extent of its ambitions, nor realise the danger with which Athens threatened the whole Greek world.

In 417 the long tragedy of the last thirty years of the century is relieved by a comic incident. Hyperbolus, who had been leader of the ultra-democrats, finding himself more or less ousted from the position by Alcibiades, conceived that the time had come for a political trial of strength between his commonplace self and that embodiment of qualities the very brilliance of which was repulsive to all who shared his own commonplaceness. He carried through a measure involving an appeal to ostracism. Alcibiades promptly joined forces with Nicias, the leader of the conservatives, with the result that Hyperbolus himself was ostracised to the amused scandal of the Athenians, who were thereby convinced that ostracism was a weapon which was apt to cut the hand of him who wielded it, and so never employed it again. Had Nicias been less stupid, he would never have saved a formidable, and ruined a feeble, opponent.

Melos

In 416 the Athenians sent a considerable expedition to attack the island of Mêlos. It had a Dorian population with a natural attachment to Sparta, of which it was originally a colony ; for which reason it had never come into the Delian League. It had been neutral during the Ten Years' War, but, despite its neutrality, Athens had made an abortive attack on it. From that time it had been hostile ; but what form its hostility had taken is not disclosed. The attack of 416 would be historically unimportant had not the inhuman severity of the Athenians in putting the inhabitants to death when they refused voluntary surrender disclosed that extraordinary temper which prevailed among the Athenian democracy in this last

[1] vi. 17.

part of the century, a temper which had been shown in 427 with regard to the punishment of the Mytilenian rebels. Thucydides brings it into purposed relief in the speech of Cleon on the former, and in the Melian Dialogue on the latter of these two occasions, passages which show the sense in which the Funeral Oration of Pericles is to be taken. He does not draw any moral therefrom: that is not his way. But he is consciously illustrating how a people which seeks to claim dominion over others on the plea of inflicting on them a form of culture superior, or alleged to be superior, to their own, may develop a brutal tyranny of conduct.

The Sicilian Expedition

In the same year, 416, occurred events which led to the great expedition to Sicily. Egesta appealed to Athens for help against Selinus and Syracuse. The latter was once more stirring up trouble in Sicily under the mistaken impression that after ten years of warfare Athens would be unwilling to take up arms. So far from that being the case, Alcibiades, glad of the excuse for intervention, found ample support from those ultra-democrats who were ever dreaming of a Panhellenic empire. The conquest of Sicily was only to be preliminary to the conquest of Italy, and to a later attack on the free states of Greece at home with the added resources of Sicilian and Italian conquest,—as Alcibiades explained at a later date to the astonished Spartans. It was a most ambitious plan. But the question is whether it was wise to undertake it at this particular time, and whether it could have succeeded in Sicily. That above all which must have encouraged the ultra-democrats to support it were those events of the previous five years which had shown in the most unmistakable way that no amount of irritation short of a direct attack on Peloponnese would induce Sparta to take up arms, and a consequent realisation of the truth that Athens had been far more successful in the Ten Years' War than she had at first supposed. Sparta's dislike of foreign expeditions had been shown quite clearly by past experience; so that it might be regarded as certain that she would not display active sympathy with a distant Sicily,—she who had just recently shut her eyes to the treatment of her relatives in Mêlos. Nor would Corinthian interests in Sicily appeal to her now that Corinth had gone her own way and renounced the Peloponnesian League. It is even probable that Sparta welcomed at the time an Athenian design which would keep that all too energetic state busy away from Greece at home. She had no inkling of the ulterior designs of Athens until Alcibiades disclosed them later. If Sparta did not move, the other Greek states were not likely to do so, or, if they did, could not do anything very formidable. In view,

THE SECOND HALF OF THE FIFTH CENTURY

therefore, of the situation at home, the Sicilian Expedition was not a hare-brained venture, but a well-devised scheme which did not involve the taking of any unreasonable risk. The situation in Sicily was also favourable. Apart from the disintegration of the common interests of the Greeks there caused by the rivalries of the various democratic states, the aggressive policy of Syracuse had set the Sicilian world by the ears, and she was not, if attacked, likely to enlist in defence of her own liberty states whose liberties she had repeatedly attacked in the last fifty years. The wisdom of the Sicilian Expedition must be judged before, not after, the event, in the light of the situation which existed when it was first undertaken. Nicias, leader of the conservatives, protested against the plan, but in vain, for even the hoplites, so Thucydides says, were attracted by a design " which offered the prospect of pay for the present, and an inexhaustible source of pay for the future." The invasions of Attica in the previous war had undoubtedly impoverished that rural class, from which the hoplites were largely drawn, and had " reduced their disposition to the level of their circumstances," so that the quondam opponents of empire were now seeking relief from an income which empire alone could bring.

The tale of what happened at Syracuse as told by Thucydides is one of the most vivid narratives in history, manifestly the work of one who knew intimately the ground on which fighting took place. The improbable suggestion has been made that he was in the town during the siege,—improbable, because it is not in the least likely that he would have run the risk of capture by the Athenians, almost certain death to him. It is after the siege that he visited the place ; and it is evident that he talked with the Athenian prisoners, for his information as to contemporary events in Athens ceases at the date of the departure thence of the last reinforcements sent to Sicily.[1]

THE MUTILATION OF THE HERMÆ

The preparations for the expedition were being made when a mysterious event, the mutilation of the Hermæ, took place at Athens. Apart from the fact that such an act was sure to offend popular superstition, Hermes was regarded as the patron deity of democracy, wherefore the outrage was regarded as an insult and attack on the Athenian democracy. No one knew at the time who were the authors of the outrage, and no clue was ever obtained later as to their identity ; but Alcibiades' youthful reputation for profanity was bad, and

[1] It is impossible in a history of this size to give a description of all that occurred at Syracuse. It is the result of that expedition, rather than the expedition itself, which is important in history.

there were plenty of people who were opposed to him and his plans, so that it was not difficult to fasten suspicion on him. It is probable that members of the oligarchic section of the conservative party knew all about it, and that the intent of the outrage was to excite popular superstition against the expedition while, incidentally, involving the promoter and chief leader of it in a serious charge such as would detain him at Athens. But if that was their intent, they had to modify their plans in two respects : to give up, in despair no doubt of a conviction, the prosecution of Alcibiades before his enthusiastic supporters on the fleet had sailed ; to alter the indictment to a charge of profanation of the Mysteries, a charge of old standing which Alcibiades probably could not deny. The whole circumstances of the case, and the particular fact that the original charge was dropped, render it most improbable that Alcibiades had anything to do with a matter peculiarly calculated to upset his great design. So his enemies deferred the prosecution and altered the charge. But the plot led eventually to his recall.

So Alcibiades went off with the expedition, having as his colleagues Lamachus and Nicias, of whom the former was somewhat of a fire-eater, if Aristophanes' caricature of him be true to life, and the latter the very embodiment of hesitating caution. What proved to be the critical moment of the whole expedition supervened very shortly after it reached Sicily. The question was debated between the generals whether they should without delay make a direct attack on Syracuse, or whether they should start operations by bringing definitely to their side various other of the Sicilian cities. Lamachus was all in favour of the former plan, whereas Alcibiades favoured the latter ; and the cautious, vacillating Nicias fell in naturally with the less venturesome design of Alcibiades. The event was to show that Lamachus was right. Syracuse, with that democratic stupidity which ever prefers to place implicit trust in its own ignorance, and is ever anxious to ignore the plainest warnings of danger, having refused to lend any ear to the reports which had reached Sicily as to the size and intent of the expedition, had therefore made no preparations worthy of the name to meet the Athenian attack, and was at the moment when the Athenians arrived in such a condition that she must have succumbed to the first assault. Had Syracuse fallen, there was no other city state in the island which could have made more than a mere show of resistance to the expedition. Alcibiades made the mistake of his life when he opposed Lamachus' design, a mistake which was to be fatal to himself and to Athens. But more than the fate of Alcibiades and of Athens was at stake at that conference of the generals. At that conference those three Athenian citizens were unconsciously deciding the fate of the civilised world. Had Athens captured Syracuse, she would have conquered Sicily. Had she conquered Sicily, it is almost certain that with its added resources she could have conquered the Hellenic world; and there would have been a Hellenic Empire in the eastern Mediterranean ruled by a Greek race into which the realisation of imperial power would have breathed a spirit very different from that which animated the invertebrate and obsequious humanitarian into which the later Greek developed. As for Rome, she might never have been given the chance of contesting the empire of the Mediterranean with a Hellenic race which had learned to know the advantages of political union.

RECALL OF ALCIBIADES

Thus the Athenians began to fritter away valuable time in minor operations, while the Syracusans put forward a feverish energy in making preparations for resistance. These things had barely begun when Alcibiades was recalled to stand his trial at Athens. Knowing that, with all his friends in Sicily, he would almost certainly be condemned, he gave his escort the slip at Thurii, and made his way to Sparta, where he did various things which had a capital effect on the result of the war.

ALCIBIADES AT SPARTA

There now comes that incident or period in his life which has caused modern opinion, under a mistaken idea of the ethics of Greek patriotism, to regard Alcibiades as one of the greatest traitors in history, in that he not only fled to his country's enemies, but gave them advice which led eventually to the ruin of Athens. To the Greek patriotism did not connote that which it does to the world of to-day. In his scale of ethics the concept nearest to the modern idea was racial, exemplified by the feeling that Greek should support Greek if it came to a question between Greek and barbarian; and even that feeling was often rendered inoperative by individualistic considerations. But it had a certain effect on the attitude of the Greek of one state towards the Greek of another, in that patriotism had no racial frontier within the Greek world. The difference between the Greek and the modern view is really due to the fact that the party divisions in the politics of a Greek state implied in an economic sense far more than such party divisions do at the present day. The precarious economic condition of the Greek world made the question whether the constitution of the state should be oligarchic or democratic, conservative or liberal, a question which affected the daily life of each citizen to a far greater extent than the life of the modern citizen is affected by the existence at any particular time of a conservative or progressive government in his country. Democracy was run economically in the interest of the poorer against that of the richer classes ; and the reverse was the case where the constitution was oligarchic. This had the effect of creating a stronger tie between oligarchs in different states, and democrats in different states, than between the oligarchs and democrats of the same state, to such an extent that no one expected an oligarch to be loyal to his own state if its constitution were democratic, nor a democrat in an oligarchical state to be loyal to the state as such.

Thucydides puts into the mouth of Alcibiades a speech which he is represented as having made on his arrival at Sparta. It is probably no more than Thucydides' own idea of the kind of defence that a Greek of his day would put up under such circumstances, a typical rather than a personal argument. There is no shamefaced apology for treason, simply because Alcibiades' conduct would not have struck any Greek as treasonable. What he is concerned to prove to the Spartans is that he is no longer a democrat ; that he has washed his hands of a democracy in which he has never believed,—probably one of the truest things that Alcibiades could have been represented as saying,—and that, therefore, Sparta need not be afraid of taking his advice. And, what is most significant of the moral attitude of the Greek to such conduct, the Spartans took his advice.[1] Persuaded by him, they adopted two most important measures : they occupied and fortified Decelea in Attica on the hills north of the plain of Athens ; and they sent a competent general, Gylippus, to Syracuse.[2]

The Athenian Disaster at Syracuse

To Gylippus the salvation of Syracuse and the ruin of the Athenian Expedition were largely due. After a siege of two years it became plain to the Athenians that, as they could not take Syracuse, their only course was to go home.

[1] It became a commonplace with Greek historians to say that Sparta favoured oligarchy whereas Athens favoured democracy in the Greek world. It is, of course, true. But Sparta's support of oligarchy was not on theoretical grounds, but for the practical reason that, for a state like her, which wished to control other Greek states with as little direct interference as possible, a government of the few was infinitely more easy to deal with than one of the many. It is easier to establish satisfactory relations with hundreds than with thousands. Athens herself had recognised the same thing when she inflicted constitutions only nominally democratic on her subject allies.

[2] The list of competent Spartans in the fifth century is remarkable : Cleomenes at Sepeia ; Leonidas at Thermopylæ ; Eurybiades at Salamis ; Pausanias at Platæa and in Cyprus ; Leotychides at Mycalé ; Archidamus ; Brasidas ; Gylippus ; Lysander in the Ionian War.

THE SECOND HALF OF THE FIFTH CENTURY 209

The vacillating Nicias was now in command; but he had at his side Demosthenes, the hero of the Ten Years' War. The latter had persuaded Nicias of the necessity of a retreat; but an eclipse of the sun on August 27, 413, upset the superstitious piety of the commander-in-chief, and caused him to delay the departure. In the period of waiting the Athenians were defeated in a naval battle in the harbour. Then the Syracusans blocked the exit of the great bay, and the Athenians were again defeated in an attempt to force it. After that, having burnt their remaining ships, their army attempted a retreat westwards to the mountains. But the road was blocked; and, as they could not force the passage, they had to surrender. It is probable that hardly a single man of the expedition, either soldier or sailor, ever returned to Athens. History has known greater disasters; but never one so complete, nor so terrible, relative to the man-power and the other resources of the state upon which it fell.[1] Of the heavy-armed of the native Athenian army the numbers serving in Sicily do not seem to have been very large. Only 1,500 men went with the original expedition, while it is certain that only a small proportion of the hoplites who accompanied Demosthenes were native Athenians. Athens seems to have drawn mainly on the subject states for her land army in this expedition. But the crews of the Athenian vessels must have been almost entirely Athenian;[2] and it was the loss of them which was eventually fatal to Athens. The ships she could replace; the land army was indeed impaired, but only to a certain extent; but those crews which it had taken half a century to train in peace and war could not be replaced in the brief period of hurried preparation for the Ionian War, so that the navy of Athens could never again resort to those daring and effective naval tactics which it had employed during the Ten Years' War. Apart from the question of quality, the mere loss in naval ratings, which must have amounted to some 24,000 men, was one which a state

---

[1] The numbers reported to have been despatched to Syracuse by Athens and the various states of her empire are:—
    415. Original Expedition :
        60 triremes (12,000 men).
        34 other galleys.
        5,100 hoplites, of whom 1,500 were of the regular Athenian hoplite force; 700 were Athenians of the lowest property class (thêtes) armed as hoplites; 2,150 of the allies; 750 Argives and Mantineans.
    414. Either 10 or 20 ships under Eurymedon (2,000 or 4,000 men).
    413. 73 ships (not all Athenian) (14,600 men).
        5,000 hoplites of the Athenians and their allies.

[2] The reference to mercenaries on board the Athenian fleet in the Second Corinthian Speech in the first book of Thucydides is to the time of the Ionian War.

with at most a very few hundred thousand inhabitants could not replace at short notice : and so for the rest of the war the crews of the Athenian vessels are to a certain extent mercenaries.

Decelea

Decelea had been occupied by a Spartan force in March, 413, with the result that Attic territory had been from that time onward systematically devastated, and the land route from Eubœa to Athens, along which the Athenians had hitherto brought the Pontus corn, probably because privateers rendered the passage round Sunium unsafe for unconvoyed trading vessels, had been blocked. But now the attack on Athens and her empire was about to be carried out on a larger scale and with a vigour such as the Spartans and Peloponnesians had never shown until Alcibiades disclosed to them the far-reaching ambition of the designs of Athens. They had made up their minds that the Greek world would never be rid of peril so long as the empire existed. Hence the persistence they showed amid the varied fortune of the desperate fighting which marked the nine long years of the Ionian War.

The Ionian War

The scene and strategy of this war are in contrast to those of the war between 431 and 421. If an imaginary line be drawn down the middle of the Ægean from north to south, it will divide the two areas of warfare, for it is to the west of that line that nearly all the fighting of the Ten Years' War took place, while the area of operations in the Ionian War lies almost entirely to the east of it. This change of scene is due to the destruction of the Athenian fleet at Syracuse, which rendered it possible for the Peloponnesian fleet to face the Athenian on the Asiatic coast on terms such as had not existed in the previous war. But the story of the Ionian War would have been very different had not Persia intervened with financial aid such as made it possible for the Peloponnesians to support a large fleet, and to repair the many severe losses in ships which they sustained during the war. Land warfare with a citizen army which, owing to the nature of warfare in Greece, could always force, or be forced into, a decisive engagement within a short time from the beginning of hostilities, involved a brief campaign and little expense. But with naval warfare it was different. The expense of building ships in any numbers was more than the average Greek state could face ; and, when the fleet was created, there was no means by which an enemy's fleet could be forced into an engagement, so that it might be necessary to keep the sea for months before any decisive result was arrived

THE SECOND HALF OF THE FIFTH CENTURY

at. The sailors were not, like the hoplites of the army, men who could meet their own expenses; and altogether it was far beyond the resources of an average Greek state to support the expense of keeping a fleet at sea for any prolonged period. Had not Persia acted as paymaster, the Peloponnesian naval effort in the Ionian War must have died away to nothing long before Athens was beaten or even humiliated. And a naval effort was absolutely necessary if any decision was to be reached. The Ten Years' War had proved only too conclusively that Athens could not be crushed by a land attack. The occupation of Decelea, severe as were the losses which it inflicted on Attica, could never decide the war, as Agis, their king, who commanded there, told the Spartans after a comparatively brief experience of its effects. The Hellespont region was the heart of the Athenian Empire at which the mortal blow could be struck, and at which it was struck by Lysander at the final battle of Ægospotami. Athens and Brasidas had known this during the Ten Years' War; but the Ionian War had not gone far on its course before every one knew it. There was only one way by which the Hellespont could be seized and held; and that was by sea.

Alcibiades had found that Sparta was quite willing to take advice, but unwilling to pay for it; in other words, that Lacedæmon was not a country in which personal ambitions could be satisfied. Certain alleged scandalous relations with the wife of the absent Agis made the place too hot to hold him; so by 411 he had fled to Tissaphernes. But before going he had managed to do Sparta a bad turn. Both Pharnabazus, satrap of Dascyleum, and Tissaphernes, satrap of Sardes, had made overtures of alliance to the Peloponnesians; and Agis at Decelea was all in favour of accepting the offer of the former, as his satrapy bordered that fatal Hellespont region. But by the time these offers came in Alcibiades had made up his mind that, since Sparta and her interests offered no career to him, his ambitions could only be satisfied in case he could manœuvre a return to Athens; so, being naturally undesirous to ruin the state on which his latest conceived hopes were now based, he persuaded the Spartans to make terms with Tissaphernes rather than with Pharnabazus, knowing well that the loss of the Hellespont would be fatal to the Athenian Empire, whereas losses on that Ionian coast which bordered the satrapy of Sardes would only cripple it. Thus in 412 Sparta accepted Tissaphernes' offer. In that year revolt spread like wildfire along the Ionian coast.

PERSIA

The rivalry of policy between Tissaphernes and Pharnabazus shows the degree of independence to which the satraps of the outlying provinces of the Persian Empire had attained. To the Greek Persia still presented the appearance of mighty power. The weight was there; but the energy necessary to move it had died away in an eastern harem. Still, Persia had money; and that was what the Peloponnesians wanted.

So when Alcibiades joined Tissaphernes in 411, his break with Sparta was complete. He proceeded accordingly to undo as far as possible the alliance he had forwarded between Tissaphernes and the Peloponnesians by pointing out to him that his present policy could only end in the establishment of a Spartan instead of an Athenian dominion on the Ionian coast, an idea which struck Tissaphernes as having something in it, so that he much abated his energy in supporting the Peloponnesians.

But Alcibiades' designs were never of a purely negative order. About that time, therefore, he opened communications with the captains of the Athenian fleet at Samos, some of whom were oligarchs, and probably all of whom were anxious to get rid of a democracy which had been responsible for the Sicilian disaster. To such men the terms of Alcibiades' offer were designedly attractive. He offered to get Tissaphernes to transfer his financial support to the Athenians if they would consent to adopt an oligarchical form of government. Of course, it was understood that Alcibiades was to be restored to Athens as agent of Tissaphernes. Of the oligarchs at Samos only Phrynichus suspected that there was more than met the eye in the proposal which Alcibiades had made; and so he refused to have anything to do with it and him. Peisander and others, however, took it so seriously that they proceeded to lay the foundations of that strange incident in Athenian history known as the Revolution of the Four Hundred.

The Revolution of the Four Hundred

The foundations of the road to change had been laid already. A Commission of Ten had been appointed some time before to manage the affairs of the state. It seems to have been composed of moderate democrats, and to have had such large powers, especially in the matter of finance, that it must have usurped to a great extent the functions of the democratic Council ($\beta o v \lambda \eta$). But, though its establishment shows the changed feeling of the Athenian people, and a distrust of a democracy whose ambition had led to the disaster in Sicily, the old constitution had still continued to exist. Alcibiades' proposal offered a so much wider vista of reform according to conservative ideas that Peisander, ignoring the distrust and opposition of Phrynichus, went off from Samos to Athens to carry things through.

The tale of the revolution is variously told by Thucydides

THE SECOND HALF OF THE FIFTH CENTURY 213

and the Aristotelian treatise (Ἀθηναίων Πολιτεία), and has been variously treated by modern historians of Greece; but the main outlines of the story seem clear.

It was not a revolution in its inception, so long as the proposals of Alcibiades were accepted at their face value. But when it was discovered that he had promised that which he could not perform, and when, despite of that, the conservatives, especially the oligarchic element among them, determined to carry the movement through, then their proceedings became revolutionary in character. On his arrival at Athens, while still the hollowness of Alcibiades' offer remained undiscovered, Peisander managed to persuade the Assembly to vote for what he represented as a temporary oligarchy. He also took various measures elsewhere in support of the movement. But it soon became clear that Alcibiades had promised more than he could perform; that his influence with Tissaphernes was not what he had represented it to be; and so he dropped out of the picture for the time being. Alcibiades being out, Phrynichus came in to carry on the movement.

To understand the further course of it, it is necessary to realise the general political position at the time. In Athens itself circumstances were favourable to the revolutionaries, because so large a number of the extreme democrats were on the fleet at Samos that the voting power of that party was a considerably reduced, and it would be easier, therefore, to give constitutional air to the proceedings by getting the Assembly to pass such changes as might be proposed, especially if a moderate amount of terrorism was employed. It was absolutely necessary for the revolutionaries to give a constitutional appearance to their actions, for, though their hoplite supporters might have swept Attica clean of all opposition, and although a moderate amount of violence might have been concealed from the crews at Samos, any open revolutionary action of a high-handed character would alarm that fleet which could starve revolutionaries and hoplites alike by cutting off the corn supply. So the promoters of the movement acted throughout with one eye on Athens and the other on the fleet at Samos.

Their first proceedings were venturesome. Certain ultra-democratic leaders at Athens were removed by assassination, no one knowing the authors of the murders. That the political clubs into which the oligarchic section of the conservatives was organised were responsible was probably suspected at the time and need not be doubted now.

On paper the programme of the revolutionaries was moderate. They professed to aim merely at the establishment of what they called an "ancestral constitution" (πάτριος πολιτεία), the main features of which were that the franchise should be confined to those of the hoplite census and that pay for all save war service should be abolished. In this profession the moderate section of the conservatives were quite genuine; but the oligarchs were not, as was shown by their subsequent proceedings.

The clue to the further course of events is that the oligarchs, while pretending to fall in with the moderate programme and to be ready to act with their moderate allies, were determined so to direct the course of affairs that they might at a certain point in their development get control and establish an out-and-out oligarchy the maintenance of which was to be guaranteed by the support of that Sparta with which Athens was engaged in bitter war,—a plan typical of that Greek patriotism which ever preferred a pet constitution to a beloved fatherland.

After carrying various preliminary measures through meetings of the Assembly, they arranged for a meeting of that body at which their *coup-d'état* should be carried out, a meeting held outside the walls on the plea that the hoplites must be ready to face any surprise attack from the Spartans at Decelea, an excuse which served their purpose, since their hoplite supporters would appear in arms, and thus be able to crush any opposition. The thing was carefully staged in such a way that the presidents (ephors) of the oligarchical clubs controlled the proceedings, and, as no would-be suicide was present, it was decided without opposition that a commission should be appointed to draw up a constitution, and that the control of the state *ad interim* should be in the hands of a Council ($\beta ουλή$) of four hundred members. Inasmuch as the oligarchs controlled the meeting, they had no difficulty in packing this Council with their own supporters, no one caring to take the risk of nominating anyone in opposition to them. So far they had completely hoodwinked Theramenes, the leader of their moderate allies, a man who could, according to circumstances, be stupidly honest or astutely dishonest. But once in control of the Council they threw off the mask by making it quite clear that they intended to convert their *ad interim* body of four hundred into a permanent institution, and by applying to Agis at Decelea for Spartan support. Agis refused. The national party at Sparta was not going to give permanent military support to any Athenian constitution. With that the oligarchic plot broke down.

What followed is a mystery on which no contemporary author throws any real light. For a period, presumably a short one, Athens lived under a moderate constitution, of which Thucydides says that it was the best she enjoyed in his time; but he never says when, why, or how it came to an end.

IONIAN WAR (*continued*)

Up to the end of 412 the operations of the Peloponnesians in the war had been practically confined to the Ionian coast. But owing to the bad relations, sedulously promoted by Alcibiades, which then supervened between them and Tissaphernes, they turned to Pharnabazus, and in 411 proceeded to attack the Hellespont region. The peril for Athens became great when Byzantium revolted, and still greater when Eubœa followed suit. Other towns in the Propontis broke away, especially the important Cyzicus. Athens did something to restore the situation by naval victories at Cynossema and Abydos; but it was still very grave for her when the year closed.

And then of a sudden all is changed! Alcibiades is back with the Athenian fleet directing its operations with an ability the like of which no other commander, not even Lysander, displayed during the twenty-seven years of the war. Why he came back is known. How he got back is a mystery. Tissaphernes, furious that his acceptance of Alcibiades' advice had thrown the Peloponnesians into the arms of Pharnabazus, was quite ready to make Alcibiades reap what he had sown, a prospect which the latter evaded at the first opportunity. But why those Athenian democrats on the fleet took back that recent advocate of oligarchy cannot be explained except by the aptitude which that clever political sinner displayed on various occasions in his life for finding some place for repentance.

Either late in 411 or early in 410, Mindarus with a superior Peloponnesian fleet drove the Athenians out of the Hellespont: but was defeated later by Alcibiades in a great naval battle at Cyzicus in March, 410. This changed the situation so much that Sparta was ready to make peace on the basis of the existing state of things, terms which the ultra-democrats would not accept, as they involved the sacrifice of most important parts of the empire. In 409 the situation was not much changed, so that Pharnabazus was ready to make peace with Athens. The recovery of Byzantium by Alcibiades was the most important event in the year.

At last, in 408, Alcibiades went back to Athens for the first time for nearly seven years. Xenophon's account of his reception at Piræus shows that his great successes in the war had by no means killed political opposition; and, as it would seem from what occurred subsequently, the opposition was mainly ultra-democratic. The distrust of him is not strange. In the previous fourteen years of his life he had been at different times a friend of conservatism, of ultra-democracy, of Sparta, of Persia, of oligarchy; and his old love, ultra-democracy, might well look askance at a lover with so stratified a record. He was suspected, too, of keeping a new love, tyranny, in the background.

It is in this same year 408 that there appeared on the scene of war two men, Cyrus and Lysander, whose collaboration was fated to bring it to a conclusion. A Spartan embassy had pointed out to the government at Susa that Tissaphernes and Pharnabazus were much more eager to oppose one another's interests than to promote those of Persia ; and so Cyrus, a member of the royal house, was sent to combine under one hand the Persian resources in the west. He was the subsequent hero of that great venture, the anabasis, the plan of which was almost certainly formed in his mind during the next few years, suggested by his observation of the superiority of the Greek hoplite to anything which Persia could put into the field, and the consequent possibility of winning the Persian throne with the aid of a hoplite force. That made him anxious to cultivate friendly relations with any Greeks he could : and the Peloponnesians were at hand.

Lysander is a sinister figure alike in Athenian and Spartan history, the man who was destined to ruin the greatness of the two greatest states of Greece. In that cautious ability which works slowly and surely towards great ends he was the equal of any Greek that ever lived ; and, if his actions do not display the brilliant capacity of Alcibiades, that may be due to a conviction that the long way to great ends is safer and more certain than the short. This was the man who in 408 came out to command the Peloponnesian fleet on the Asiatic coast. Had he been pitted against Alcibiades in the last years of the Peloponnesian War, a very exciting page would have been added to history. With Cyrus a ready and willing paymaster, Lysander was a formidable enemy to Athens.

But the struggle between the two great men was not to come off ; for the Athenians, who distrusted Alcibiades, seized on a defeat at Notium, inflicted on a lieutenant of his who had disobeyed orders, as an excuse for depriving him of his command : —" and so brought ruin on the state," says Thucydides.

Conon succeeded him as commander of the Athenian fleet on the Asiatic side. His proceedings show that he was at this time a bad admiral but a first-rate pirate.

Lysander was meanwhile consolidating the Peloponnesian position on the coast by establishing oligarchies in the cities, each with a Spartan governor in charge. Neither this policy, which entailed the residence of Spartans away from home, nor the close attachment to Persia, was popular with the national party at Sparta ; in fact, it is at this time that that struggle between the nationalists and the imperialists, which was to be of capital importance in Spartan history, begins. There had, as has been seen, been outbreaks of imperialism in Sparta earlier in the century ; but since the ruin of Pausanias the nationalists had had it much their own way. But now both the circumstances of the time and the man of the time, Lysander, were on the imperialist side. The national party was really anxious to come to terms with Athens, as it was becoming alarmed at the necessity of continuing a war which kept so many Spartans away from home.

By Spartan law the command of the fleet was strictly annual ; so Lysander was superseded in 407 by Callicratidas, a nationalist, whose views, being known to Cyrus, caused his enthusiasm to cool down. Persian money supplies began to fall off. In accordance with the wishes of his party Callicratidas sought to bring the war to an end by a decisive victory ; wherefore he collected a very large fleet on the Asiatic coast. As Conon was pursuing his usual piratical policy of raiding that coast with a scattered and inferior fleet, his peril was great. But Athens made a great effort to save him, and in July, 406, a new Athenian fleet of 110 ships put to sea. And when the decisive moment came Callicratidas had unwisely detached a part of his fleet to besiege Mytilene, so that in the great battle at Arginusæ which then took place his ships were inferior in number to those of the enemy. Victory went to the Athenians in a sea-fight in which the number of ships engaged was larger than in any other naval battle between Greeks. But the tactics employed show how greatly Athenian naval skill had fallen off since the days of Phormio twenty years before.

Sparta once more offered peace on the terms of the existing *status quo*, which would have meant to Athens the permanent renunciation of Euboea and of nearly all her continental possessions on the Asiatic coast. As after Cyzicus, Athens refused the terms. In view of the desperate resolution of the Athenian democrats to maintain the empire, the refusal is not surprising ; but Athens celebrated the victory in a fashion unparalleled in history, and, on the face of it, inexplicable except on the assumption of national lunacy. Such at any rate must be the impression created on the mind of the modern reader who regards the average Athenian of that age as one who had exchanged the superstitions of religion for the fancies of philosophy. The victorious generals were prosecuted on the charge of having left the living and the dead to their fate in the water-logged vessels after the battle. They alleged that a storm had prevented any attempt at rescue ; but the Athenian jury which tried them, convinced that they had thereby condemned the spirits of their fellow-countrymen to eternal unhappiness by failing to bring back their bodies for burial amid the scenes they had known in life, pronounced the death penalty on them; and all who did not escape were executed, save Theramenes, who played the dastardly part of a lying informer against his colleagues. The victory was a catastrophe rather than a success, all the more so as it brought Lysander back as practical director, though not as titular commander, Peloponnesian affairs on the Asiatic coast. He resumed his old policy of establishing oligarchical clubs, and of keeping on friendly terms of financial dependence on Cyrus. However cautious his strategy might be, he was convinced that only in the Hellespont region could the war be brought to a decisive conclusion; so thither he now turned. The Athenian fleet followed him, and in the strait itself in the autumn of 405 was fought the great battle of Ægospotami, where the incompetence of the Athenian commanders led to the defeat and destruction of their fleet. Alcibiades, who was in the neighbourhood at the time, warned them of their folly, but in vain. He tried at the last moment to save that Athens which he might have saved had he been allowed to do so.

The fact that the battle took place in the autumn, just at the time when the previous year's supply of corn from the Pontus would be running low, and the new supply not in, brought about the collapse of Athens, for, though there was a show of further resistance, it was impossible in face of impending starvation; and Athens was left to the mercy of her lifelong foes. Sparta's allies would have seen her blotted out from the face of the earth; but that would not have suited the policy of Sparta, for it would have left Bœotia in too commanding a position north of the Isthmus; and Bœotia had shown quite clearly of late years that she was not disposed to submit to the dictation of Sparta, with whom her sole tie had been a common fear and hatred of Athens. So Sparta determined to settle matters with Athens her own way. Unfortunately for both states the nationalists and imperialists at Sparta were not of one mind as to what that way should be. Lysander by his great success had strengthened the imperialist party; and his policy of placing Spartan governors in the states of the Asiatic coast had won adherents of men who were not minded to return to private effacement at Sparta from posts in which they had tasted the joys of rule and of personal aggrandisement. Lysander's plan was to set up a philo-Laconian oligarchy in Athens after the pattern of those in the Asiatic cities, the very policy which the national party had always opposed throughout the century under the fear that it would entail something like the permanent employment of a Spartan force outside Lacedæmonian territory. The nationalists seem to have thought that an Athenian democracy without an empire would not be dangerous to Sparta or to anyone else save Athens; but to have regarded that solution as impossible in view of recent disaster, and so to have favoured a moderate democracy on the basis of the hoplite census.

Tyranny of the Thirty

In Athens meanwhile much political confusion existed. Since the ultra-democrats had reacquired control after the collapse of the Revolution of the Four Hundred, they had directed the state policy under the leadership of Cleophon. It may be guessed that Cleophon was the mover in deposing from command that Alcibiades who had aforetime ousted Hyperbolus from the leadership of the ultra-democratic party, preferring, like the professional politician that he was, to mismanage affairs himself rather than allow them to be managed by Alcibiades or anyone else. He had carried the war to a bitter end; and refused all overtures of peace, knowing well that his power was dependent on success, that is to say, on the complete restoration of the empire. And now peace had come, and the empire was completely lost.

So when a political reorganisation became necessary, the first step of the would-be organisers was to get Cleophon out of the way. He was condemned and executed.

On the surface the general tendency of the time was towards a compromise in the form of that " ancestral constitution " or moderate democracy such as that at which the moderate conservatives of 411 had aimed. But, as in that year, there was much going on beneath the surface; and again the oligarchs were the underground workers. Their design was the same as on the previous occasion: to pretend to assent to the plan of the moderate conservatives, that is to say, to the establishment of a democracy based on the hoplite census, and so to arrange the course of events that some body so small that they might get control of it might be appointed as an *ad interim* government and, with the aid of Sparta, be converted into a permanent form of oligarchical government. Theramenes, the leader of the moderates, was probably put off his guard by the consideration that the oligarchs were not likely to repeat a trick which had failed on the previous occasion.

Lysander came from Samos to overawe the meeting of the Assembly at which the first step was to be taken. This did not alarm Theramenes, who had some tie of friendship or acquaintance with him. But doubtless Lysander had arranged matters with the oligarchs behind Theramenes' back. All that was done at the meeting was to appoint a Commission of Thirty to draw up a constitution, a commission ten of which seem to have been nominated by Theramenes, while the oligarchs secured the other twenty places. It was soon seen that the Thirty had no intention of hurrying with the task of drawing up a constitution. They appointed, indeed, a Council, and also magistrates,—naturally enough persons who were either of their own way of thinking, or who could be terrorised. After that began a programme of executions. The first to suffer were the informers (sycophants) of the old democratic régime, who got no more than they deserved. Then the Thirty asked for a Spartan garrison, which was sent, and, secured by this support, proceeded to execute political opponents. Theramenes began to see that his supposed political allies were no more honest than they need be, and so tried to force their hand by insisting on the enlargement of the government, whereon the oligarchs proceeded to choose 3,000 men, a measure they discounted by disarming the rest of the citizens. Then they went on to execute personal enemies and wealthy dwellers in Attica. Theramenes protested against this with no other result than that Critias, the leader of the oligarchs, accused him before the Council, and he was condemned and executed. Thus he died more nobly than he had lived.

The excesses of the Thirty had scared many citizens into flight to the neighbouring states; of whom a certain number, led by Thrasybulus, returned to Attica and seized Phylé, a fort on the direct route to Thebes, where they defeated a Spartan detachment sent to expel them. Then they made their way to Piræus, where they fought a successful battle with the oligarchs, in which Critias was killed. This was practically the end of the episode of the Tyranny of the Thirty, though the matter dragged on for some time longer.

It is needless to say that this democratic success was by no means pleasing to Lysander, who hastened too late to the support of the oligarchs. But the national party at Sparta was not going to let him have his own way in the matter. They despatched a force under Pausanias which settled affairs at Athens by allowing the re-establishment of the democratic constitution.

No event in the internal history of Greece seems to have shocked the Greek world more than the cruelties perpetrated by the Thirty. They were an outrage on the humanitarianism of what was by far the most humane race in the ancient world.

SICILY

Gelo had taught Carthage such a lesson at Himera in 480 that, much as she coveted the fertile island of Sicily, she did not till the last years of the century attempt to take advantage of the quarrelling and disunion which prevailed among the Greek democracies. Opportunity for intervention was offered to Carthage in 409 when the Greek city of Segesta asked for help against Selinus. The expedition which she despatched was of a magnitude which betrayed the design,—no mere plan of assistance to Segesta, but one of the conquest of the whole of Sicily. The Carthaginian commander, Hannibal, after taking Selinus, an unready democracy with unready democratic allies, moved on to attack Himera. And now among the Sicilian cities a supineness due to the lack of the most elementary foresight gave place to flurried alarm. The small Syracusan squadron which Hermocrates, the leader of the Syracusan democracy during the Athenian siege, had taken to help the Peloponnesians in the Ægean was recalled. A fleet was got together which rescued half the population of Himera; but the remainder, with their city, perished miserably at the hands of the Carthaginians. So Himera of 480 was avenged by Himera of 409. But there Hannibal stopped, not feeling able, apparently, to do more now that Sicily was aroused.

Hermocrates had before his return been officially banished from Syracuse by one of those intrigues which were easily engineered in a Greek democracy against any citizen of unusual capacity. Finding on his return that Syracuse would not receive him, he went off on a bold filibustering expedition against the recent Carthaginian acquisitions on the north coast with such success that there were many in Syracuse who wanted to have him back, and not a few in Carthage who wished to square accounts with him and the Greeks of Sicily for the damage he had done. He tried a return to Syracuse; but the attempt cost him his life.

In 406 Carthage came again with a still larger expedition, with Acragas, the wealthy town of south Sicily, as the first object of attack. A large Greek army from Syracuse and other towns which tried to relieve it met with some temporary success. But after an eight months' siege Acragas fell. There was dissatisfaction at Syracuse,—dissatisfaction with the generals who were alleged to have betrayed Acragas by their incompetence, —dissatisfaction, too, with a form of constitution which favoured incompetence. Dionysius, a former partisan of Hermocrates, took advantage of the situation to gain the tyranny of Syracuse by successive steps and pose as the champion of Greek liberty in Sicily. His first essay in this new part was unsuccessful, for he failed to relieve Gela when it was attacked by the Carthaginians, and was either bribed or driven to make in 405 a treaty with Carthage which left that state mistress of all save eastern Sicily. How Dionysius repaired the perilous situation thus created is part of the story of the fourth century.

CHAPTER VII

THE FOURTH CENTURY, 400-300 B.C.

SPAIN AND GAUL

THE story of Spain and Gaul during this century is almost a blank. In Spain Carthage was doubtless consolidating her interests in a country which was throughout the history of the Mediterranean the land on which that world in general was most dependent for its supply of metals, and Carthage in particular for some of its best troops. The large employment of Spaniards in the Carthaginian wars in Sicily during the last years of the fifth century shows the extent of the control which Carthage exercised at that time in the Spanish peninsula.

In Gaul Massilia was living a life as yet undisturbed by the rivalries of the two powers which in the next century were to struggle for the mastery of the western Mediterranean world.

ROME

During this century the story of Italy becomes what it was to remain for a thousand years, the story of Rome; for it is in this century that Rome all but carried through her conquest of the peninsula.

Within the state of Rome itself the struggle between patrician and plebeian came nigh to its close, so that when the century ends the constitution has all the outward appearance of a complete democracy. Later history was to prove that the democracy was apparent rather than real, a democracy of form rather than of fact, and that the imperialist sentiment she showed in the conquest of Italy was to die away so soon as that end was attained; for its shores were the well-defined limits of Rome's imperialism under the Republic, and her wide acquisitions of territory in the third and second centuries were forced on her by circumstances, not made from lust of conquest. But Rome's history, both internal and external, under the Republic is one colossal political paradox.

The past history of the state had shown the plebeians that their civil liberty could not be secure until they had won their way to complete political liberty, which meant, when translated into fact, into free access to the higher magistracies, above all to the consulship.

To the quæstorship they had already attained. In the later years of the fifth century the election of quæstors by the Assembly of the Tribes was substituted for nomination by the consuls, with the result that in 421 a plebeian was for the first time elected to the office. That was something; but it was very little, since the office was one the holder of which was little more than the servant of the consul.[1] But now in the fourth century the efforts of the plebeians were centred on attainment to the consulship. The attack on the patrician monopoly of that office had been begun in the latter part of the fifth century, but had been staved off by the patrician device of tribunes with consular powers, an expedient which proved so inconvenient to those who designed it that they spent the next three quarters of a century in persistent but only partially successful efforts to prevent such appointments.

During the first quarter of the century Rome's attention was so much absorbed in the prosecution of war that there was a period of truce in the internal political struggle. But in 377 the Licinian laws, named after their chief proposer, C. Licinius Stolo, were introduced. They were a very miscellaneous collection of enactments, the most important of which was that one consul at least should be a plebeian, and that the priestly college which had charge of the Sibylline books should consist of ten members instead of two, of which ten five should be plebeians. The obstructive powers of the official religious authorities at Rome were such that there could be no guarantee for the freedom of popular legislation unless the plebeians could win their way to membership of the powerful and exclusive priestly body. It was round these two items of the Licinian proposals that the struggle was continued for ten long years. But in 367 the laws were carried.

Another of these laws, which limited the area of public land which any individual could occupy, and the number of cattle which he could pasture on it, was destined to remain a dead letter for more than two centuries, and then to bring about something of the nature of a revolution.[2]

Being defeated with regard to the consulship, the patricians

---

[1] The name "quæstor" implies that the office was originally judicial. At some date, it is not known when, the quæstors became financial officers who simply carried out such financial work as the consuls delegated to them.

[2] I think it will be best for clearness' sake to deal with the history of the agrarian question in one piece in relation to the Gracchan legislation of the second century B.C.

managed in 366 to deprive that office of some of its functions by the setting up of a prætor to take over from the consuls the administration of civil law.[1] It was apparently arranged that the prætor should be a patrician; but the arrangement broke down within thirty years, for in 337 the first plebeian was elected to the prætorship; in fact, when once the plebeians had won their way to the consulship, the other offices fell open to them almost as a matter of course, so that in 356 the dictatorship, and in 350 the censorship, are for the first time held by plebeians. Moreover, in the last year of the century, in 300 B.C., a Lex Ogulnia threw open to them the great priestly colleges. In a democratic sense there remained but little to do.

The story of the wars by which Rome during this century all but completed the conquest of the Italian peninsula is a somewhat wearisome catalogue of defeats repaired and successes won, events the importance of which resides mainly in the spirit with which she undertook the wars in which they occurred, and the determination with which she carried them through. These are factors which have their influence on the whole subsequent history of the Roman people.

The student of history is apt to assume that imperialism is a sentiment almost innate in any people which attains to imperial power. History shows, however, that the sentiment may be of slow growth, or be due to a sudden inspiration; that it may arise from the compulsion of circumstances or from the attraction of favourable opportunities; that it may be due to a desire for gain, or to a desire for security; to prudence, or to ambition. In a certain sense the Roman people of the age of the Republic was never imperially minded; in another it became so.

The Romans began life as an essentially agricultural race, a race of hard-working tillers of the soil whose only wish was to be left in peace to do that life-work which they really loved. But such peace was not to be theirs. In early days the wild hill tribes round the Campagna and the Etruscans on the north had sought to reap what the Roman had sown. To the former Rome had in the last century made those raids more dangerous than profitable; and the latter were now well on the road to decline. But in the present century new dangers arose from the Celts who had settled in the rich lands of the north Italian plain, and in the south from those Sabellian tribes, especially the Samnites, who, descending from the hills of middle Italy, had subdued a large part of the south of the peninsula, and were show-

---

[1] The consuls, properly styled, were really prætors (prætores consules), and, after the establishment of this additional prætor, prætores maximi. But, after the establishment of this third prætor, they came to be called simply "consules."

ing that they were prepared to make themselves masters of Italy south of the Apennines. It is not surprising that the Roman farmer made up his mind in these years that security in the middle of the peninsula could only be ensured by dominion over the rest of it. Hitherto he had never shown himself unprovokedly aggressive ; and even now, in these years in which he was to found an Italian empire, it is from the other side that the aggression comes. The great storm did not break immediately. Etruria had to be dealt with, for, though the Celtic invasion had in the last years of the fifth century deprived it of its rich lands in the valley of the Padus, though the Sicilian Greeks had broken its power by sea, and the Samnites had in 423 robbed it of its rich southern possessions in Campania, yet its frontier, and above all its frontier town of Veii, were within a few miles of Rome, so that raids on Roman territory could be made only too easily. Therefore, in 396, after a long struggle, Rome captured Veii. But hardly had that been accomplished when in 391 a great Celtic storm came from the north. Rome nearly perished. She was defeated in the great battle on the Allia in 390, and the city itself was sacked, though the acropolis was defended for seven months. And then, just when it was about to capitulate, the Celtic army retreated northward, probably called home to the Padus by an attack of the Veneti on their territory. Rome's recovery was so rapid that she was able to repel attacks which the Etruscans made on her fancied weakness, and not merely that, but by 353 she had secured herself further against Etruria by the conquest of the whole of the southern part of it.

Rome's dealings with this territory are typical of her treatment of conquered regions in Italy. There was no enslavement of the conquered. The communities were left with their local liberty under the tutelage of Rome, and civil liberty was left to the population against all authority save that of a Roman magistrate, against whose action their rights were few and difficult to maintain. But that authority was not exercised at this time in a spirit of plunder. It is severe, but, for the age, very enlightened. The most serious loss which the conquered suffered was the confiscation of some of their landed property to the Roman state ; and compulsory service in the Roman army must have been at times a heavy burden. It became a very heavy one two centuries later. Colonies of Romans or Latins were also established in newly acquired territory,—not colonies of the Greek type, but military garrisons which should maintain the rule of Rome.

Meanwhile Rome had been having trouble with her old enemies the neighbouring hill tribes ; but that she soon settled.

Far more serious was the trouble which broke out between

her and her own allies in the Latin confederacy. The alliance had been an equal one; but there is reason to suspect that as Rome increased in power during the early years of this century, she showed less and less inclination to recognise this equality, and began to assume the position of master rather than of equal. This led to twenty-five years of trouble and war, out of which Rome issued as master to such an extent that she was able to revise her relations with the Latin allies, and to reduce them to the position of subjects rather than equals.

The second half of the century is the period of the wars with those Samnites of south Italy who were showing every disposition to contest with Rome the leadership in the peninsula. The wild Samnites of the hills of the south had attacked those relatives of theirs who in 423 had conquered the rich Campanian land, and had become tame by reason of the acquisition of wealth and of Greek civilisation. The latter appealed to Rome, who took their part, glad perhaps to precipitate a struggle which was sure to come. The Samnite peril was so real that even the recently subdued Latins did not dare to impede Rome while engaged with that dangerous race. But when about 341 Rome finished the war and acquired Campania, the Latins, freed from fear of Samnite invasion, rose as one man, only to be promptly crushed. Rome had already done away with the confederacy between herself and the Latin towns. She now dissolved the league which existed between the towns themselves. Some were forced to accept Roman citizenship; others were given what was henceforth known as the Latin franchise, each being bound to Rome by a separate treaty. Roman citizenship became in later days the most valuable right which an ordinary dweller on the Mediterranean could acquire; but in the case of the citizens of these Latin towns its forced conferment meant the sacrifice of the citizenship of a community in which they had been paramount for that of one in which they formed a feeble minority.

Recent defeat by Rome and dangers threatening from Epirus kept the Samnites quiet while Rome was settling accounts with the Latins. But the danger from Epirus died away, and the Samnites seized on the first excuse for quarrel to renew the struggle for supremacy. Unluckily for them, their kinsmen in middle Italy proved lukewarm in the war, and the Lucanians and Apulians, who had more reason than anyone to fear Samnite ambition, sided with Rome. But Rome was heavily defeated in 321 at the Caudine Forks; and in 318 a truce was patched up, after Rome had repaired disaster by inflicting several severe defeats on her foe. The Samnites soon renewed the attack; but, after some early successes, they were deprived by the loss of Nola of their last Campanian stronghold. In 310 Etruria rose against Rome, and the Samnites tried to form a junction with them through the mountainous region in mid-Italy; but this plan the Romans frustrated. Then the Romans invaded Samnium itself, and, though the Samnites were not decisively defeated, they were glad enough in 304 to renew the old treaty with Rome.

The period of this warfare affords an admirable example of the very able policy which Rome pursued in the consolidation of the conquests she had made. The planting of colonies held the conquered regions down in a military sense; but that method of securing newly acquired territory might have occurred to a less able people than the Romans. It was her policy in granting the civil rights of Roman citizenship to selected town communities which was most effective in binding the regions to her, and this in two ways, in that it gave the grantees a personal interest in the Roman state, and also fixed a gulf of jealousy, and to a certain extent of hostility, between them and less privileged communities in their region. It is a very striking policy in an age in which the rights of citizenship were very jealously guarded in all states whose position in the world was somewhat better than those of their contemporaries. But it is not to be ascribed, as it has sometimes been, to the liberality or liberalism of the Roman character. The main object was to increase the number of those whose property qualified them for service in the Roman legion. The other objects have been already mentioned.

It is in this century that the outside world began to recognise that there was springing up in Italy a state of more than Italian importance,—a state which must sooner or later play a part in Mediterranean affairs. The Romans themselves had not the slightest wish to play such a part; but contemporary Carthage and Sparta both regarded her as likely to do so, and Carthage sought by embassy to propitiate this new entrant into select state society.

Greece

To those on whom certain aspects of the history of Greece in the fifth century exercise a fascination the story of the fourth century is bitter reading. It is the tale of one of the greatest failures known to history. Those who have not merely read but thought out the history of the Greek people in the fifth century will realise that that vivid life which made that age most glorious in the history of western civilisation was lived by a few who regarded the realities of the present as mere stepping-stones to those of the future, and were therefore apt to look on that which was going on around them in the practical world as phenomena only interesting as forming a basis of induction for the solution of the fundamental problems presented by human life. It was not till the fourth century that the genius of the age came to realise that it could not adopt an attitude of detachment towards the doings of the contemporary world unless it was prepared to sit still and see the world on which the structure of its wisdom was founded fall in ruins. A splendid literature and a splendid art are luxuries which can only be attained by a people whose political position is strong in the world of its time; for, when the political decay sets in, that very genius which has devoted itself to piercing the veil of the abstract is distracted by the contemplation of practical failure, and is tempted to seek for remedies for the circumstances of the practical world, and to try to solve problems for the solution of which it is but imperfectly adapted.

The splendid legacy which the fifth century bequeathed to the world of after-time was the work of the few, of a very few, not of the many, for genius is a rare gift in any race. And the creations of the fifth century in the realms of literature, art, and thought were not the products of mere talent or ability, but of the rarer gift. Talent and ability may give a man the capacity to develop on right lines that which the originality of genius has created; but they do not in themselves imply originality. The men who in the fifth century created the drama of tragedy, the men who founded the science of history, the men who evolved the ideas of a social system beyond realisation in a world of imperfections, were not mere elaborators of the ideas of predecessors, for their attainments in these departments of intellectual life so far exceeded anything that had preceded them that they cannot be said to have had any predecessors. The rapidity of the intellectual development of the century may be appreciated by those to whom the characteristics of the histories of Herodotus and Thucydides are known. The father of history is the creator of a new type of literature written in a style the attractiveness of which has been acknowledged by all ages capable of appreciating literary greatness. Gifted with an infinite curiosity of mind which led him to travel widely through the world of his time,— even if not quite so widely as he himself implies,—he laid the foundation for that study of humanity on a wide scale which should preface the work of the historian. He is the Odysseus of history He forms from his facts large conceptions of the laws which govern human life, and a vague but strong idea of a divinity (τὸ θεῖον) which is over and above the multiplicity of the national gods, a being whom he conceives of at one time as punishing in this world such wrongs as men have committed, at another as jealous of human good fortune, so that it ever mingles evil with the good, disaster with success. Whether the Greek world of his day had the same conception of divinity is not known. The rest of the Herodotean theory is an attempt to rationalise that great conception of Greek thought, the dualism of life, the idea that the life of man consists of two parts, one due to the exercise of his own free will, and so of his own making, the other the tragedy of life, those happenings over which he has no control. This concept has lived on ever since the Greek created it ; and, though to a sophisticated age Herodotus' attempt to rationalise it may seem childlike, yet ages subsequent to him have again and again sought to explain or explain away that phenomenon of the tragedy of life by the aid of a finite intellect or of an infinite faith.

But though Herodotus lived on for many years into the life of Thucydides, and though the latter knew his work and may even have heard the author recite it, yet between the conceptions of history formed by the two historians there is a great gulf fixed. As compared with the work of Herodotus, that of Thucydides makes a long step towards the writing of scientific history. Were this attributable merely to a difference of nature in the two writers, it would be a matter for the consideration of the literary rather than the general history of the fifth century. But the difference is due to the astounding rapidity of intellectual development in the middle years of the century, a development which Herodotus, who only lived to see its beginnings in his own Greek world, was too old to appreciate, and Thucydides too young to ignore. Thucydides' greatness is not due so much to the teachings of the sophists, as to the results of their teaching on him. They did not inspire him with matter but with form, a conception of the writing of history in such a way that the reader might be led gently by the recital and explanation of facts to a political philosophy which should hold good for all time. He knew that men dislike being taught by any process more direct than that of suggestion ; and therefore, while implying a moral in almost every sentence of those parts of his work to which he devoted the most careful composition, he strictly avoided the language of moralisation. He does not say that " it is important to recognise " this or that. He makes each point so clear that every thoughtful reader must recognise it. It was left to the next age to make political philosophy a special and separate department of history ; and therefore with him the philosophy and the narrative of fact are mingled, and that above all in the speeches which are so notable a part of his work.

Of the larger number of them it may be said that they neither can be, nor were ever intended to pose as, verbatim reports of the words of the men into whose mouths they are put. They serve various purposes; but their main intent is to give in an indirect form the philosophy of history as conceived both by the historian himself and by the political world of his day. If, as is clear, he devoted most care to their composition, and to that of the reflective passages on the tendencies of contemporary politics, then perhaps there are some who might reasonably assume that Thucydides aimed far more at being a political philosopher than a historian.

All this is in strange contrast to Herodotus' conception of history; and the contrast implies an enormous advance in ideas, and this, too, in the short space of thirty years.

And those despised sophists who influenced Thucydides created those ideas which the next century was to dissect, analyse, twist, and formulate in a literature which has had permanent formative influence on western civilisation.

But this active intellectual world of the latter half of the fifth century was but a small, a very small, part of the Hellenic world of the time. It was mainly centred in Athens; though some who shared in it were not native Athenians, but men of wealth and leisure from other states of Greece.

While they were drinking in with avidity the teachings of the sophists, the rest of the Greek world was going its own old way, watching jealously over constitutions which secured their own interests in a land whose resources were not sufficient to go round unless distributed by political means. The Greek democrat was becoming more and more accustomed to live on the taxation of the rich, and ever more accustomed to regard that as a natural mode of existence. He was becoming ever more impatient of any check upon his powers of legislating in his own interest, of any limitation of his capacity to despoil the wealthy, even if the limitation proceeded from institutions which his own democratic predecessors had set up. Thus at Athens, and probably in other democracies where a counterpart of the Council ($\beta o \upsilon \lambda \acute{\eta}$) existed, the democratic Assemblies were shaking off the limitations which such a body could impose on their choice of business, and were coming to dictate to it the subjects which they would like to discuss. It may be easily imagined that if such was the attitude of the general body of citizens to an institution of their own devising, their attitude towards the magistracy showed still greater jealousy of the exercise of magisterial power. The magistrate had always been regarded as responsible for his own mistakes, and had often been severely punished for those he had made; but in the fourth century he may almost be said to have been robbed even of the power of making mistakes, so much had the initiative in politics passed into the hands of private unofficial members of the Assembly. Nevertheless, he was but too apt to be held responsible for the mistakes of others by a populace which had but a short memory for the origin of those policies which were forced on a magistrate by irresponsible mob orators. The magistracy in a Greek democracy had always been a dangerous office : it was becoming more dangerous and an absolutely thankless one. The fate of the strategia at Athens is perhaps typical of the fate of the responsible magistracies of other states. Till towards the close of the fifth century it maintained its power and prestige, and was held with rare exceptions by men of such a social standing as would give them an experience both hereditary and personal of the management of public affairs, and a knowledge of that outside world with which the state had to deal. This ensured a continuity of foreign policy which saved the Greek world from that anarchy into which a world of any age must fall when the foreign policies of the states composing it are mutable and discontinuous. But in the last quarter of the fifth century a new element of low social standing makes its way into the strategia, an element ever apt to exaggerate in public office a power which it has never had the opportunity of wielding in private life. Many of these beggars on horseback rode to the devil, as they have done in other ages ; and in the Greek world as elsewhere they were able to take the state with them to the same destination. But the attitude of these ultra-demagogues to office was cautious and uncertain. It was one thing to advocate before the Assembly a policy, however hazardous and foolish, without any responsibility for its carrying out ; but it was quite another thing when magisterial responsibility rendered the advocate the executor of a policy the failure of which might involve ruin or even death to its proposer. When it became clear that the man out of office had more influence with the people than the man who wielded magisterial powers which were suspected and disliked by a democracy whose one policy was to secure the immediate satisfaction of its whims, and that both power and safety were secured by him who was wise enough to resist the attractions of office, he avoided its responsibilities so far as he could without giving away the fact that his abstention from candidature was due to a wish to avoid the consequences of such policy as he advocated.

Thus discontinuity of policy became one of the most marked features in the interstate relations of Greece, so that no state could count on the friendship of a neighbour whose policy might be reversed by a chance vote in the Assembly. A general attitude of mutual distrust, such as might be translated into hostility on the slightest provocation, prevailed throughout the Greek world ; and that people which longed for a period of peace after the disasters of the Peloponnesian War so arranged its internal affairs that an enduring peace was the least probable result of the external relations thereby brought into being.

It is not merely in the long history of western civilisation but from world-history that men may discern the general truth that states whose foreign relations are bad or unsettled are exposed to grave peril, and the more specific truth that unsatisfactory relations between states are as often as not due to ungrounded suspicions arising from mutual ignorance and consequent mutual prejudice. It is only the select few in the population of one state who have the power, the means, and the understanding to arrive at any true knowledge of the spirit which animates the people of another state. "Comprendre c'est pardonner" is a platitude which is true of nations as well as of individuals. To the mass of one people the mass of another must remain a spiritual enigma. Their mutual interpretations of one another's intentions are mere guesses at truth such as ever tend to put the worst construction on acts of wholly innocent intent. Hence when the foreign policy of a people is decided directly or indirectly by a popular vote influenced by persons uneducated in that knowledge which leads to a sympathetic understanding of the aspirations of others, the result is a war which might have been avoided had affairs been directed by educated experience. Vox populi vox dei! But the god is too often the god of war.

It was not merely in interstate relations that disunion was rampant in the Greek world of that century. In Athens certainly, and probably in other contemporary Greek democracies, the democrat had demanded the right to live, and, to his credit be it said, had in Athens, at any rate, shown an eagerness to work for his living in the guise of protector of the Greek world against foreign aggression. The demand was justifiable. This eagerness showed that the victims of the bad economic conditions of the fifth century formed a proletariat which did not regard the dole of idleness as a satisfactory means of subsistence. But that spirit had died in the Peloponnesian War with those whom it had animated, and for it was substituted in the fourth century the passive determination to use the democratic vote to force from the rich the means of supporting the poor in an idleness due in the first instance to circumstances, but to an ever-increasing extent to inclination. It was not so with all the Greek states. In Arcadia the system could not work because the means to work it were lacking in that poverty-stricken land. And so the Arcadian went forth as a soldier of fortune either in those mercenary armies which were springing up in the Greek states, or in any reckless adventure that offered employment and possible plunder.

THE FOURTH CENTURY, 400–300 B.C.

Art of War

In the last years of the Peloponnesian War an element had been introduced into Greek warfare which was to effect a marked change in the spirit of Greek citizenship. The peltast was the product of Thrace, a land both too rich and too rugged for the effective employment of undiluted heavy-armed infantry. In respect to defensive panoply the peltast was not so heavily armed as to be hampered in movement on bad ground; in offensive weapons he was as well armed as the Greek hoplite. But the main difference between the two types of infantry was that whereas the hoplite was only effective when massed in close-packed phalanxes, or at any rate in close-set ranks, the peltast, owing to his superior mobility, could fight in open order. Hence the training for the two types of force differed considerably; for, whereas that of the hoplite aimed solely at the preservation of the ranks in close order, and the formation did not call for any expertness in individual weapon tactics, the peltast had to be trained, as all troops designed for formation in open order must be, in weapon tactics and the other accomplishments of an individual fighter, a training to which a much longer time had to be devoted than that given to the drill of the hoplite. The contrast between the two types of force is almost exactly paralleled by that between the Roman armies of the days before and after the time of Marius, and to a large extent by that between the English army before and after the South African War of 1900. In the Greek experience it was a case of moderate defensive armour and mobility against heavy defensive armour and comparative immobility; and the experience of the later years of the Peloponnesian War had shown the superiority of the former in certain kinds of fighting. Hence the Greek states of the fourth century had to revise their military experience. The complicated system of drill necessary for the peltast training required so long a period of preparation that it became quite impossible to meet the demands made by it on the old system of army organisation where the soldier had been merely a citizen called out for service in a brief campaign, and for brief intervals of training in time of peace. The ordinary civilian occupation of a citizen would not permit of his being withdrawn from it for prolonged periods of training; and the only way of meeting the difficulty was to recognise the fact that soldiering must become a livelihood in itself to the man who engaged in it, in other words, that the amateur citizen must be replaced by the professional mercenary. The same necessity was laid on Rome when in the time of Marius the complicated gladiatorial system of weapon tactics was introduced into the Roman army. The psychological effect of this necessary change on the citizen population generally was bad in both cases, in that one of the most salutary responsibilities of citizenship was no longer laid on the citizens,—salutary in the sense that every man will give more earnest consideration to political questions for the decision of which he may have to answer with his life.

This revolution in military affairs consummated, especially at Athens, that decline of magisterial authority which had been brought about by the changing spirit of the times. Despite a certain loss of power and prestige, the strategia had remained, at Athens, and probably in other places, the most influential of the magistracies, for the archonship had been democratised almost out of practical existence. But now it became impossible that an amateur general (stratêgos) should command a professional army; and so the strategia came to be held by professional soldiers who played but an indirect and subordinate part in politics. Thus independent magisterial power almost ceased in Greek democracies, and the magistrates became the very humble servants of the Assembly, little more than recorders and executors of its decisions.

No one save the Athenian democrats mourned the death of the Athenian Empire. The Greeks generally, self-centred in what they had come to regard as a watertight compartment of the contemporary world, merely looked on its disappearance as a blessed relief from a power which had destroyed the individual liberties of some, and threatened those of all. It never occurred to them that there were non-Hellenic powers who might cherish like ambitions. Great as was the genius of some of the minds of Greece in various departments of life, it must be admitted that the mass of the Greek world was singularly dull in its appreciation of the larger practical problems of the day, and singularly blind to the manifest trend of events by which their own fate would be decided one way or the other. It is true that among the Greeks of the world outside Greece there came an awakening to the fact that the democratic form of government was not such as to ensure effective resistance in foreign aggression; that liberty could only be maintained by a certain sacrifice of liberty; that the concentration of power in the hand of a despot might be necessary for security against attack from outside. Hence Mausolus in Caria and Evagoras in Cyprus play their part for a time. But small dynasties and dynasts were engulfed in the flood of the Macedonian conquest. In Sicily, on the other hand, the tyrants of Syracuse saved the island from conquest by Carthage.

It is one of the tragedies of history that the Greeks, who, whatever their defects, had conceived of a manner of social life which would have made the world a better place in which to live, did not combine early in the century for the preservation and advancement of Hellenic civilisation at the expense of that orientalism which was once more threatening the Greek world. Knowledge after the event makes it possible to see that the Greeks of the early years of this century exaggerated greatly the danger from that Persia which had, though they did not know it, declined in virility and power since the days of Salamis. As far as the Greeks of that day knew, they were by their lack of unity imperilling all that life meant to them ; and yet they would not combine. On any reasonable calculation of the factors present in the world of the first quarter of the fourth century there can be no doubt that there did not exist east of the Adriatic anything which could have resisted a combined army of the Greeks. The Greek hoplite and peltast were by far the most effective troops of the eastern world of that day ; and Persia, well on her way to become the sick man of the East, must have been an easy prey to a Panhellenic attack. Cavalry could have been raised in Asia Minor ; and the Thessalian horsemen were efficient on ground suited to them. But so wedded was the Greek to the idea of a fully independent isolated state, that he was ready to risk the independence of the Greek states as a whole rather than sacrifice that state particularism which had ever been the foremost article of his political creed. He refused to make the sacrifice when Persia threatened in the first half of the century, and refused again when in its second half he was threatened by the far more formidable Macedonian kingdom. And so he succumbed.

The gloom of the years of this century is reflected in the political writings of the day. The political thought of Plato and Aristotle was dominated and confined by the circumstances around them as they wrote.

POLITICAL PHILOSOPHY

The sophistic teachers of political philosophy in the fifth century had handed down to the fourth various dicta as to the nature and origin of the state which their more famous successors, especially Plato, subjected to a severe criticism. Plato is obsessed with the darkness of the political outlook of his time, which, after the manner of philosophers, who are apt to imagine that the views of their predecessors which have influenced them, either by attraction or repulsion, have had a like influence on their non-philosophical contemporaries, he ascribes to the baneful false doctrine preached by some of his predecessors, above all to that amended doctrine concerning the state, that it exists, not by the divine ordering of nature (φύσει), but by convention (νόμῳ), with the further, to him, pernicious teaching that, if it is a question of "natural" law, then the right of the strongest is always the best. It is true that the Greek had learnt this; but he had not learnt it from the sophists or any other philosophers, but by the hard fact that in any democratic state the party with the largest number of votes could inflict its will on all others. That it was working to the ruin of the Greek democracies has been already said. Plato set himself to reform the evil state of things, and embodied his views in the treatise known as "The Republic." Any modern reader of this work would, unless he had a fairly intimate knowledge of Greek history, class it as a literary production with More's "Utopia" or Butler's "Erehwon," as a purely fanciful sketch of a polity which the author put forward merely as an effort of imagination, without ever conceiving any hope, much less expectation, that any body of men would attempt to imitate or realise it. But this was not the idea of Plato. "The Republic" was a political pamphlet *in excelsis* put forward with a view to inducing the author's contemporaries to adopt in practical life the state system there described. To a reader brought up in the environment of the modern world it might seem absolute lunacy to suppose that the constitutional fabric there constructed could be given a moment's consideration as a scheme for adoption in practice, and he might also think that the lunacy lay not with Plato but with him who credited that great thinker with such an absurd phantasy. Yet there can be little doubt that, though Plato put much of "The Republic" into the form of a theoretical discussion of politics, the actual fabric of the state which he builds upon the constructive conclusions which have been arrived at in the course of the discussion is intended to be the picture of a polity which the Greek of his day might adopt in practical life. Had Plato intended to evolve a constitution out of his own inner consciousness, he would not have reverted to the practical life of the past Greek world for the material wherewith to build up his ideal. As a political philosopher he was a pioneer in literature though not in thought, for he was the first to deal on a large scale with political philosophy as a special branch of history, of which a man might treat without writing the history of his own or of any other time. So his constructive method is simple, resembling that of those early legislators who are said, when commissioned to draw up a code for their own country, to have visited foreign lands, and to have selected all that was best from their laws for insertion in their own compilation. Plato is in "The Republic" far more of a would-be lawgiver than of a would-be philosopher. But, though his method was simple, his conclusions were bold. The Greek had been a bold experimenter in politics; but Plato was the boldest of all. The Spartan social system is one of the strangest in the history of the world. But almost all its most abnormal features are borrowed by Plato for his new fabric of the state. The Pythagorean asceticism made demands on human nature which even the Greek world could not meet; and yet Plato borrows from it one of the most important features of his ideal of social life. On the question of family life he is a revolutionary. He regarded the natural ties of family affinity as an obstacle to the attainment of the highest form of social life, and therefore advocated their reduction to all but a vanishing point. And yet in all these seeming extravagances he is advocating nothing save what had actually formed part of the lives of certain Greek communities in the past. Only in one of the features of his social constitution does he depart from the paths of the past experience of the Greek race. The position of women varied in various Greek states from an effacement from public life at Athens to comparative emancipation at Sparta. Perhaps Plato, having, like other Greeks, a somewhat vague and idealistic view of the real life at Lacedæmon, exaggerated the position of women there, and supposed them to be more emancipated than they really were. But neither at Sparta nor anywhere else in the Greek world had it been seriously proposed that women should fight in warfare. Greek decorative art in sculpture and pottery shows that the Amazonian tradition, which may have originated in the actual facts of an Asiatic past, had taken a great hold on the Greek imagination; so that Plato may have felt that in inserting this un-Greek feature into the structure of a proposed Hellenic state he was merely developing an idea which had already to a certain extent taken root in the Greek mind.

Far and wide as the Greek had travelled on the path of political experiment, he was too much of an individualist to give large acceptance to any communistic view of life. He had tried the Pythagorean experiment and had found both it and himself wanting. He had always regarded what he believed to be the communism of Spartan life with a feeling which was never higher than detached admiration, and was more inclined to fall to repulsion from a system which obstructed the free development of the individual. The dictum that "man is by nature a social being" who can only develop the best part of him by association with others was a philosophical theory which the Greek might accept in itself, though he would have rejected outright any corollary of it which sought to make communism the logical aim of society. It was Greek individualism that Plato was attacking so fiercely, that disposition of the individual to take from life all that he could secure without excessive risk and without due regard for the share of others in life's gifts, that $\pi\lambda\varepsilon o\nu\varepsilon\xi\acute{\iota}\alpha$, seeking to get more than your share of good things, at which, be it said to their credit, all the philosophers railed. It was those wicked sophists of the fifth century, so Plato thought, who had created this evil frame of mind in the Greek world by preaching the doctrine that by nature might is right, a doctrine which as a fact they had never preached, but had regarded themselves as forced to accept by a contemplation of the facts of life in the latter half of the fifth century, especially that great fact, the Athenian Empire. As has been already said, the sophistic doctrine had very little to do with the political attitude of the Greek of the fourth century. That was the outcome, partly of economic circumstances, partly of the attempt to manage the affairs of the Greek world at the dictation of that mass of humanity whose knowledge does not extend beyond the horizon of their limited experience. Greece was playing the tragedy of honest or dishonest ignorance, that tragedy of democratic control which so soon arrives at the second act, catastrophe.

How far Plato was disappointed at the failure of the Greek world of his time to appreciate his proposals cannot be said. In the "Laws," the work of the later years of his life, he recurs to them, or to some of them, in a modified form ; but he must long ere that time have been disillusioned of any illusions he ever cherished. Democracy and its inseparable companion, state particularism, to which the modern world has given the name "self-determination," were obstinately pursuing the path to destruction and "seeking with courage the kingdom of the dead," while certain astute potentates up there in Macedonia were sitting on the fence ready to descend and give the last shove when the path drew near to the edge of the cliff of catastrophe.

Where Plato had failed Aristotle tried to succeed. When it is realised that the greatest intellect of his own, and one of the greatest intellects of all time, a man who knew as much as ever man knew of all that was most worth knowing in the world of his day, wrote a treatise on that subject most attractive to the Greek mind, politics, and, in so doing, strictly confined the scope of his inquiry within the framework of the city state, the conclusion must be drawn that such an author writing in such a way must have had a very definite and limited object in that which he wrote. The modern world with a certain self-conceit has at times assumed that the great man set himself to write a general theoretical treatise on politics with a prophetic eye fixed on its own enlightened self. When it is considered that the mind of Aristotle was of a magnitude which impelled him to deal exhaustively with many branches of knowledge, and of a capacity which enabled him not merely to do so with such accuracy as was possible in the then state of knowledge, but also to advance that knowledge by original inquiry and original thought, is it conceivable that he who knew, as no other Greek of his time knew, the world-state of

Macedon, for he had been tutor to its creator, should have left the political problem presented by it untouched in any treatise which aimed at giving the world a comprehensive view of political theory ? In the " Politics " he is thinking for the Greek world of his own day, a world constituted on a particular social and political system. It is in the " Ethics" that he is thinking for all time ; for he is there dealing with that which everywhere and at all times must be true so long as human nature remains the same.

Like Plato in " The Republic," so Aristotle in the " Politics," aims at being a practical teacher of politics to his contemporaries. He saw that Plato had put forward a would-be practical ideal too ethereal for even the Greek ; and so, in the political doctrine which Aristotle preaches, he is content to descend to the commonplace realities of everyday political life. He, like Plato, would show his fellow-Greeks a practical way of dealing with their political affairs such as would heal the political ills from which Greece was suffering. Yet in one sense he admitted Macedon as a factor into his design. He is very Greek in some ways ; but he is very un-Greek in his view of that which is essential in the life of the city state. The average Greek regarded complete political liberty, meaning thereby the absolute independence of the state, as essential to its life. Aristotle, on the other hand, seems to think that the city state could do the best by its citizens so long as its local autonomy and local life were allowed it : that it could develop this life better if freed from the cares of foreign relations and secured from outside interference by the protection of a greater state powerful enough to ward off all possible aggression, and enlightened enough to leave it its local liberty. It is true that this view cannot be traced back beyond the time when Greece was already under the control of Macedon ; and he may therefore be suspected of trying to make the best of the situation and of persuading the Greeks to do so. But it is also quite possible that he recognised that state particularism, though it did maintain that limitation in the size of the state which he himself advocated, was not a realisable political system in a world in which the divided weak are natural victims for the undivided strong. So he advocated among his contemporaries the reform of what seemed to him a good system which had fallen on evil days, while admitting that the system itself could not stand unsupported in a very imperfect world.

But no considerations of the general trend of political thought in this century would be complete without a statement of the views of the reputedly commonplace Isocrates. It is not easy to see how anyone who knows the history of the fifth and fourth centuries can so depreciate the ability of the one man who saw clearly the perils to which the Greek world of that day was exposed, and had the courage to advocate a most unpopular but effective solution of them.

Isocrates lived a very long life of ninety odd years, which included the period during which the supposed peril from Persia, and, later, the far more real peril from Macedon, were hanging like dark clouds over the Greek world. Men knew the perils: they even exaggerated them; but nothing would induce them to form that political union which might have averted them. So long as Persia was the threatening power, the question seemed to be a revival of that which the early fifth century had to face, whether Hellenism or Orientalism should prevail in the eastern Mediterranean. When the Macedonian peril arose it seemed to be whether Hellenism or semi-barbarism should be the lot of south-eastern Europe, for no one perhaps could have foreseen that the Philhellenic tendencies of the Macedonian rulers in social life would be translated into a political Philhellenism. And so through all his life Isocrates raised the cry of political union in the Greek world. He even had the temerity to cite the example of Greece in the days of the Athenian Empire as the position at which the Greek world of the fourth century should aim. But it was no use. Nothing could cure the individualistic Greek of his mania for state particularism; and the Greek democracies, true to type, refused to realise the peril until it could not be avoided or repelled.

Sparta

The true story of the opening years of this century will probably never be disclosed, for the clue to it is missing, the contemporary events in that Sparta which had now succeeded to the leadership which Athens had lost. Something momentous was going on the true story of which even the contemporary world never knew. It is not that what happened is not known: the mystery is as to how it came about, a question on which the evidence is so deficient that only a conjecture can be formed as to the causes of one of the most critical changes in Greek history.

Till the very last years of the fifth century the national party had managed to maintain in a general sense that foreign policy of Sparta which reduced its foreign obligations to their lowest terms. It had maintained this policy during that century despite the ambitions of prominent imperialists such as Cleomenes and Pausanias. But during the Ionian War, the last phase of the Peloponnesian War, even the nationalists had recognised that the policy of political seclusion must be temporarily laid aside, to be resumed, no doubt, when the war was over, and the danger from Athens past and gone. It was about this resumption that the trouble arose.

When the war came to an end the Greek world regarded Lysander as the man who had won the war, and paid him honours of a very embarrassing character. A dead deified Spartan like Brasidas was one thing : a live deified Spartan like Lysander was another. Sparta had no objection to heroes and gods in the spiritual world ; but in the world of the flesh she disliked them. The nationalists too, apart from deification and such-like extravagances, had very practical reasons for distrusting Lysander. There has already been occasion to say that he is a sinister figure in the history of his time ; but how far this was due to circumstances and how far to the nature of the man is not certain, for one who has made enemies on all sides, who has won the dislike of those who dislike each other, cannot expect or be expected to go down to posterity with a blameless reputation. And that was what Lysander had done. He had set up oligarchies under Spartan superintendence in the states which had come over to the Peloponnesians in the war ; and after the war he showed that this was his idea of a panacea for the ills of Greece. Every democrat in the Greek world loathed him. But the nationalists at Sparta probably loathed him most of all, for his policy meant for Sparta imperialism on a scale such as neither Cleomenes nor Pausanias could have ever dreamed of, a Lacedæmonian empire with Lysander as its uncrowned emperor. The opposition to him at Sparta was intense. King Pausanias was put up to upset his plans in Attica, and succeeded in so doing. In the end the personal victory over Lysander was all but complete, and he retired into an active background ; but his works did not follow him. He had left Sparta a legacy the acceptance or rejection of which alike involved danger. She had through Lysander divorced Athens from her empire, and made the children wards of that chancery of Greece of which she was now the head. And very troublesome ex-wards were those states likely to prove if she renounced her guardianship, for then they might seek some other private guardian whose position might threaten her own. The situation was further complicated by the fact that numbers of Spartans had tasted the delights of rule and of freedom from the restrictions of the domestic discipline of Sparta. They were not going to revert to the old life if they could help it.

But the fall of that age-old policy of Sparta which had steered the state through a century and a half of danger, and had on the whole maintained her position abroad despite the mortal weakness of the position at home, was largely due to most extraordinary economic circumstances which had supervened in Lacedæmon itself. The fundamental idea of Spartan nationalism had been the maintenance of the security of the Spartiate minority against the Helot majority ; and, naturally, it had been supported by the large majority of the Spartiate population. The Spartiates are represented as living a common life to which each contributed out of the proceeds of that land which the Helots cultivated for them. For some reason which is not known, and at which it is not possible to make a probable guess, the majority of the Spartiate population had got into such financial difficulty that they were unable to pay their contributions, and had fallen into a political position ($\upsilon\pi o\mu\varepsilon i o\nu\varepsilon\varsigma$) inferior to those who were still able to do so. Financially speaking, there was no hope for them at home ; and therefore the prospect of service abroad in a Spartan empire was attractive to them. Not being able to realise their ambition owing to the bitter opposition which the nationalists were still able to offer to imperialism, they resorted to that dangerous old plan of the disgruntled Spartan imperialist, conspiracy with the Helots, with the uncertain prospect of founding a new Lacedæmonian state on the basis of the freedom of the whole population, and the certain prospect of the massacre of a part at least of the Spartiate minority. The plan on this occasion was engineered by a certain Cinadon, who, convinced that art was long, found life was short, for his prolonged preparations to bring the plot to the utmost perfection led to its disclosure and his arrest and execution. But this was the last success of the nationalists in their resistance to their opponents. There were now too many Spartiates inside and outside Sparta who were interested in the imperialist policy ; and, apart from that, the circumstances of the Greek world of the time were such as would in any case have made it difficult to resume the confined nationalist policy of the fifth century. And so Sparta drifted into an imperialism which was to ruin her within thirty years.

Persia

The cessation of the war had thrown out of employment numbers of men who had served either as citizens or as mercenaries in the armies of the last ten years of it. That surplus population of Athens which had hitherto lived on the empire was also in such an economic position that it was ready to seek anywhere for a living which it could not make at home. Revolutions in various states had driven forth refugees who were ready to hand for any adventure. And just at this time the adventure offered itself. Darius the Second of Persia had been succeeded by his eldest son, Artaxerxes. His younger son, Cyrus, who had been overlord of western Asia Minor during the Ionian War, had throughout cherished the design of getting the throne for himself with the aid of those Greek hoplites whose military efficiency he

THE FOURTH CENTURY, 400–300 B.C.

estimated more accurately than did the Greeks themselves. He had cultivated Lysander with a view to support from Sparta; but, as Lysander was now under a cloud, he employed another Spartan, Clearchus, to recruit troops for him. Sparta would not give him open support, probably because she had too much else on her hands; but backed him secretly. There were, however, plenty of would-be soldiers of fortune in the Greek world; and so in the spring of 401 Cyrus started from west Asia Minor on his venture with 100,000 Asiatics and 13,000 Greek mercenaries. Xenophon, who played a heroic part in the undertaking, has told the famous tale of the expedition in that "Anabasis" which, despite the too recurrent parasang, is a fine story of the finest adventure in which the Greek race ever engaged. He tells how they marched deep into Asia; how at Cunaxa, just outside the walls of Babylon, they fought with a huge army of Asiatics: how the Greek hoplite force went clean through the Asiatic infantry on one wing, and so far out on the other side that they failed to get back in time to rescue the defeated centre of their army; how Cyrus was slain, and his Asiatic troops fled; how the Greeks defeated further assaults with a light heart, and were so conscious that no one could stand against them that they offered the Persian crown to a certain Ariæus, who declined it. The Persians, only too anxious to get rid of these ironclad immortals, conceded a safe retreat; but Tissaphernes treacherously trapped and slew the Greek generals. And then the rest, undismayed, began a march of eight months, first along the plains of the Tigris, and then through the pathless Armenian mountains which have been the terror of armies of all ages. Only those who know that terrible region can appreciate the greatness of the exploit of these Greeks. The story ought to end with the dramatic scene at Trapezus, where they came in sight of the sea; but it goes on to tell how after their return their fellow-Greeks, whose very admiration of their exploit made them fear the men who had performed it, kept them on one excuse or another near Byzantium, where they found casual employment with Seuthis, a Thracian prince, till a further venture against Persia called them to Asia Minor.

Of the story of the early years of this century down to the Peace of Antalcidas in 386, it may be said that it is one of confused fighting in which many played a part, but none of them an honourable one.

Sparta

The most significant feature of the time is the intense but ill-directed energy of Sparta. It is plain that the national party had been swept off its legs by the rush of circumstances both internal and external ; and that the imperialists were carrying out a policy for the initiation of which Lysander was responsible, which might have been successful under his direction, but could not possibly be so under the planless opportunism of those who now controlled affairs. It is also evident that the many ventures in which Sparta was involved in these years could not possibly have been carried out or even contemplated on the basis of the old Spartiate army. Peloponnesian allies, some willing, some unwilling, were employed in these undertakings ; but large drafts from the Helot population of Laconia and Messenia were drawn upon ; and the old caution which the national party had shown in allowing Helots to serve as hoplites was thrown to the winds. This would in itself imply a great social and political change in the internal circumstances of the Spartan state.

SOCRATES

In Greece, devastated by long warfare, troubles sprang up like weeds in a derelict field. Every one wanted to pay off old scores on old enemies and new scores on one-time friends. In 399 Sparta devastated Elis in return for the events of 418. In the same year Athens condemned Socrates for the events of 403 and of many other years. He had made men think out that which they had no wish to think out. Unfortunately some of his pupils, especially Critias, had done some thinking for themselves, and had put into practice logical conclusions which Socrates never contemplated and the Athenians abhorred. "Only the wise should rule," said Socrates. The wealthy young men who had had the means and leisure to attend the teachings of him and of other sophists identified themselves with the wise, and proceeded to rule as the Thirty Tyrants. The Athenians, too, essentially conservative and superstitious in the affairs of everyday life, resented a teaching which could easily be perverted into an attack on religion, and which supplied their sons with an embarrassing fluency of argument in domestic differences. The Athenians have been condemned for condemning Socrates, a condemnation founded on the assumption that they had just as good an opportunity of appreciating the real character of the man and his teaching as later ages who can realise these things from the pictures drawn in idealised form in the Platonic Dialogues or in a manner perhaps more true to life in Xenophon's "Memorabilia." The popular Athenian impression of him was of a man who wished to undermine the age-old customs and beliefs of their own most superstitious society, and who had by his supposed political teaching brought on Athens the cruel experience of the Tyranny of the Thirty. It is certain that Socrates

THE FOURTH CENTURY, 400-300 B.C.

never intended any political significance to be attached to anything he ever said ; but that was equally certain to be the intention which the Athenians would ascribe to the doctrine which produced a Critias. They were ignorant and mistaken ; but their mistake was just such a one as the ignorant of all ages would be likely to make.

Affairs in Greece

Wars! Wars! Wars! Nothing but wars! Some little, some bigger ; but all of them ruinous to the states which made them. Sparta fighting with Persia about the fate of the Greek cities of Asia, and Agesilaus sent thither with a scratch but effective army in which the men of Cunaxa were but too glad to serve. There was plenty of fuel for the fire in the shape of mercenaries. Even the Athenian surplus population sought a living as soldiers of fortune. Not that Athens was commercially ruined. So far from that being the case, she, while the rest of the Greek states were cutting one another's throats, was building again a commerce which made Athenian coinage known to people far away in Asia whom the Greeks had never seen. But a new commercial state, Rhodes, destined in later times to become the greatest of Greek trading cities, was springing into being. Over Thebes a change was coming which bore fruit not many years later. The control of the government was in the hands of an intellectual aristocracy of considerable ability, which meant that its policy was directed with more knowledge and foresight than that shown by the second-rate leaders of the democratic states. The policy of the national party in Sparta had always been to cultivate friendly relations with Corinth and Thebes, so as to play them off if necessary against Athens. But the nationalists had sought to avoid direct interference north of the Isthmus, whereas the imperialists were ready to interfere anywhere, and anxious to humiliate Corinth and Thebes. This led the latter to get together an anti-Spartan league, the funds being supplied by money which Persia was passing into Greece for the same purpose. The Spartans attacked Bœotia in 395 ; but after Lysander had been slain in an abortive attack on Haliartos, a second Spartan army which had come up retired again without offering battle. This led to the recall of Agesilaus from Asia, where he had been seeking to form a considerable land empire, a plan in which he had attained some success, and might have attained more, could he only have persuaded his friends at home to steer clear of troubles in Europe and concentrate their energies on the Asiatic venture. Now came the question as to how he was to get home. Meanwhile the anti-Spartan league, which Athens had joined reluctantly, and Corinth willingly, got together a large force to attack Peloponnese ; but at Nemea, just south of the Isthmus, the Spartans defeated them in 394, a victory which led to no decisive result. For the next few years the struggle was centred on the possession of the Isthmus. Later in 394 Agesilaus broke through southwards by a great victory at Coronea ; but he could not force the Isthmus, and so had to take ship over the Corinthian Gulf. Meanwhile the Spartan fleet on the Asiatic coast had been defeated by Conon, the old semi-piratical Athenian admiral who now commanded the Persian fleet ; and with the loss of the fleet the Greek towns fell to Persia.

It is not necessary for the general purposes of history to follow the details of the weary war which dragged on till 387. It was a war of varying fortune in which the one man who really distinguished himself was Iphicrates, the Athenian leader of peltasts, who showed the Greek world what it had long suspected, that that type of force had nearly revolutionised Greek warfare. The system of long walls, moreover, which Athens had employed so successfully in the Peloponnesian War, was now being adopted elsewhere in Greece ; and those which Corinth had built to Lechæum proved a formidable obstacle to Sparta's attempt to get command of the Isthmus. Athens, too, aided by Persian gold, rebuilt hers about this time.

Meanwhile Sparta, with a view to detaching Persia from the hostile league in Greece, had begun overtures in 392, on the basis that Persia might have the Greek cities of Asia if she would support the principle that all states in Greece itself should be mutually independent. Both sides of the bargain suited Persia well enough : she got back her old supremacy on the Ægean coast, and it would be a weak and divided Greece which would face her on the other side of that sea. To Sparta the agreement meant that the political union between Corinth and Argos would be broken, and the control of Thebes over the other Bœotian cities would be brought to an end, the two most formidable political elements in opposition to her. So Antalcidas, a Spartan admiral, went up to Susa and brought back with him that celebrated scrap of paper the Peace of Antalcidas, " the Peace which the king sent down," wherein Artaxerxes addressed the Greeks after the manner of a schoolmaster and told them to cease quarrelling and leave one another alone ; which they did—for the time being.

But peaces, whether sent down by kings or others, could not cure the ills of the Greece of that day. Nationalism at Sparta had had a steadying influence, not always recognised, on the Greek world of the fifth century, whereas Spartan imperialism was now turning the Greek world upside down. Sparta was the big boy in the dormitory of the school of Hellas who would not let the little boys sleep.

For the moment the Peace had weakened those states in Greece, Thebes and Corinth, which Sparta most feared. It might have been expected that even Sparta would seek rest from the all but continuous turmoil of more than forty years of war. Not so. In 385 she is attacking Mantinea, and in 384 Phlius. Neither of these states had a clean record it is true. In both of them a democratic government had adopted a policy of confiscation with respect to the property of political opponents, and had furthermore clearly indicated an opposition to Spartan interests. Their weakness could not face the strength of Sparta; and so they had to rearrange their affairs according to Spartan ideas of what was best for them and for herself.

Meanwhile in that out-of-the-way corner of the world, Chalcidice, certain things were taking place which were to affect greatly the fortunes of the whole Greek world. The Greek cities of that region, though they had gladly thrown off the dominion of Athens years before, came to recognise that, deprived of Athens' protection, they were exposed to danger from the wild Thracians on the one side, and the half-tamed Macedonians on the other. Olynthus, the leading city in those parts, had accordingly got together a league of towns which conceded one another mutual rights such as were rarely interchanged between Greek states, and, to complete the union, were demanding that Apollonia and Acanthus should enter it. This the latter, with the Greek spirit of isolation, refused to do, and, when threatened, appealed to the states of Greece. The latter were alarmed at the prospect of a league of Greek cities in a region which had behind it, in Macedonia and Thrace, potential supplies of men and metal such as were not at the disposal of any state in Greece. So the Greek states passed on the appeal of Acanthus and Apollonia to Sparta, who accepted the commission of settling matters, and made great preparations for carrying it out.

All might have gone according to plan had not a Spartan commander, Phœbidas, on his march Thracewards through Bœotia in 383 with an army, seized the opportunity of getting hold of the Cadmea, the citadel of Thebes, with the aid of local treachery. It was an unjustifiable proceeding in time of peace. The Greek world was inexpressibly shocked, for to it certain conventions which make the society of individuals and of states possible were no mere utilitarian ideas, but were sacred principles sanctioned by a divine power which would punish their infringement. It is significant proof of the moral decay which had set in in Sparta under the influence of restless imperialism that she sought to justify the act by a casuistry which would not have deceived the most stupid honesty. Even the philo-Laconian Xenophon[1] condemns her. But Sparta refused to give up the Cadmea; so Phœbidas had to stop in Thebes whilst Teleutias led an army against Olynthus. Teleutias died in 381; but Agesilaus, who succeeded him, reduced Olynthus to surrender in 379.

The seizure of the Cadmea brought matters between Thebes and Sparta to a crisis. The question was how far the rest of Bœotia would back up Thebes.

Division of sentiment in Bœotia did not merely rest on that difference of interest which made union between other Greek states so difficult. There can be no doubt that the population of the country was far from homogeneous in origin: ancient Minyans in the north-west about Orchomenos; Thracians in the south-west; and perhaps an Attic fringe on the southern frontier; populations which had inherited from their forefathers different traditions of life. There had been a sort of confederacy between the cities, with the exception of Thespiæ and Platæa, which had no mind to fall under the control of Thebes. But Thebes wanted a confederacy in which she should be superior; and that set the other cities against a union of any kind. The Bœotians were not the stupid race which they appear to be in Attic tradition, otherwise they could not have produced in literature and in practical life the men they did; and just at this time there came to the front in Thebes one, Epaminondas, whose character and capacity were acknowledged by the Greek world generally, and another, Pelopidas, whose practical talent as a soldier adapted him for the carrying out of Epaminondas' designs.

In December, 379, Pelopidas recovered the Cadmea by stratagem. So far Athens was sitting on the fence, disinclined to break the Peace with Sparta; but in 378 Sphodrias the Spartan suddenly invaded Attica with the intent of seizing Peiræus. It was not that the Athenians had provoked such action; it was that, since the seizure of the Cadmea, Spartan officers conceived that any filibustering expedition at the expense of any state would meet with approval at Sparta. Sparta was becoming an unbearable nuisance to all the states of Greece; so Athens determined to forward a great project of confederation which she had already conceived.

ATHENS

She had taken as little part as she could in the wars of the last twenty years, intent on restoring her economic position while

[1] I do not wish to imply any disparagement of Xenophon as an historian in applying the term " philo-Laconian " to him. The nature of his history will be considered later.

Sparta and the other states of Greece were ruining their own. Already two years before this time she had made unobtrusive treaties with states in Thrace, in the islands, and in Asia Minor, thus forming the nucleus of what might with luck become an Athenian league; and now that Sparta's hands were full with Thebes, she was prepared to come into the open. The mere fact that, after the experiences of the Delian League of the fifth century, the Greek states should have consented to join a league in which Athens was to play a leading part, shows how bitter was the feeling, how utter was the discomfort, which the proceedings of Sparta had caused. Athens was indeed a political danger, but Sparta was a plague to the other states of Greece. So in 377, just a century after Aristides had organised the Delian League, a large number of the Greek states formed a new league on conditions which were carefully drawn up in such a way as to guard against the abuses of the old one. It was a two-sided league between Athens on the one part and the rest of the allies on the other, on the terms that neither side could do anything without the consent of the other. To the allies it was an anti-Spartan league; to Athens it was a possible foundation for the reconstruction of her supremacy in Greece. The chief islands east and west of Greece joined it, as well as the peoples of the wild north-west; in fact, it included nearly all the states not exposed to a Spartan attack by land. But Sparta answered by tightening the bonds of her league, which included all Peloponnese save Argos, the Phocians and Locrians, and in the far north the cities of the recently suppressed Olynthian confederacy. Thebes was associated with Athens, but on far more independent terms than the other allies. Then came more confused and resultless fighting: a Spartan campaign in Bœotia; a victory of the Athenians under Chabrias at Naxos over the Peloponnesian fleet; and so on, and so on, until in 371 an attempt was made to arrange a Peace, accompanied by a further attempt to entrap Thebes into a verbal admission of the independence of Bœotia. But in vain was the snare set before the bird, for Thebes, with whom the policy of hegemony (leadership) in Bœotia was at this time paramount, refused to sign. The refusal meant a break between her and Athens, for Athens began to suspect that Thebes wished to bring the rest of Bœotia under her control with a view to substituting a hegemony of her own in Greece for that which Sparta had exercised to the extreme discomfort of the general Greek world. The main policy of the three leading states of this day was combination of any two against any one of the three which seemed at the moment to have a favourable chance of winning the hegemony of Greece. Athens had less to fear from the distant Sparta than from her next-door neighbour, Thebes.

Leuctra

As for Sparta, she welcomed a cause of quarrel with Thebes, especially on the speciously justifiable ground that Thebes would not leave the other Bœotian communities free in accordance with the Peace of Antalcidas. What she really feared was that Thebes might get the whole strength of Bœotia at her disposal. So Cleombrotus, who was at the moment with a Spartan army in Phocis, was ordered to chastise Thebes. He first moved to Creusis, a little port of Bœotia at the head of the Corinthian Gulf. The road thence to Thebes passes at about its half distance across the upmost valley of the Asopus River, which is here an insignificant brook not more than a yard wide. On either side of the valley rise featureless grey ridges a few hundred feet high. It is a dreary treeless region of grey rock on the ridges and brown earth in the valley, though Helicon a few miles distant forms a magnificent background for the otherwise depressing scenery of the great battlefield. On his march towards Thebes Cleombrotus found his way barred at this little river valley by the Theban army. The main dispositions in the battle are discernible at the present day because there projects from the low ridge on the north side of the valley an earthen platform on which the Thebans set up a permanent trophy of their victory. The tactics of Epaminondas were a novelty in Greek warfare. Theban generals had fifty years before conceived the idea of making a hoplite phalanx of unusual depth so as to give it the advantage of superior weight in the shock of the charge, a manœuvre which they had employed with great effect at Delion in the Ten Years' War. But the battle-line had taken a stereotyped form, in which the best troops on each side were posted on the right wing, the unshielded side, with a view to rolling up the enemy's line, from left to right. Also the advance of an army in battle was wont to be carried out in one line, for the Greek hoplite had a wholesome dread of any exposure of flank such as would be involved in any échelon movement in which one column went forward in advance of its neighbour. From both of these seemingly axiomatic principles of the warfare of the time Epaminondas departed. He placed his best troops, the Sacred Band, on his left wing, opposite to the best, that is the Spartan, troops of the enemy, and he pushed forward this wing to the attack whilst marking time on his right. The rest of the story of the battle may be told briefly. The deep phalanx of the Sacred Band defeated the shallower phalanx of the Spartans, and then rolled up the army of Cleombrotus from its right to its left.

Leuctra was the nemesis of that Spartan imperialism which had made upon the state those very demands and had accepted those very risks which the nationalist party had always realised to be beyond what the resources of the state could afford. The nationalists had consistently refused to adopt in the fifth century that policy which brought about Sparta's ruin in the fourth; for, though Sparta struggled on for some years, yet Leuctra sounded the death-knell of her greatness.

Anyone who reads for the first time the distressing story of Greece in the fourth century will, when he arrives at such epochs as those presented by the Peace of Antalcidas and the battle of Leuctra, read on with the hope that the period of petty, wearying discord may come to an end and be succeeded by a chapter of history from which the tragic futility of the past has disappeared. But the story goes from bad to worse, so that if the events of the thirty years before the battle of Leuctra present a despicable picture of political folly, those of the period after the battle present a picture more hopeless, more gloomy, and, if possible, more contemptible. The wearisome story of purposeless death and destruction need not be told at length. The only permanent impression which it has on history is the conviction it leaves on the mind of the reader that the Greek was a political failure. The best minds of his race created social ideals which the stronger races of western civilisation adopted and put into practice at the instigation of their greater men. But in the Greek world the ideas of its best men were killed by a practical political system wherein the material greed of humanity had the fullest scope. The Greek of the fourth century is the man with the muck-rake of secular history.

It might have been expected that after Leuctra Thebes under Epaminondas would have introduced a higher ideal into the politics of the time. It would have been an easy task, had there not been other Thebans of influence besides Epaminondas. But the pitiful story goes on just the same as before. It shall be told briefly.

Factions in cities are slaying opponents whenever opportunity offers. Arcadia makes a praiseworthy but futile attempt at closer federation, and founds, to signalise the occasion, a new city called Megalopolis, which she peoples with various reluctant inhabitants who wonder how they are to live; and some, finding they cannot, drift away elsewhere and leave their new homes to the lizard and the owl.[1] Within a few years this Arcadian union, founded to defy Sparta, is split into a philo-Laconian north and an anti-Laconian south.

In the next year, 369, the Thebans invade Peloponnese, penetrating into Laconia up to the very walls of Sparta. Finding they cannot take the city, they pass into Messenia, which they liberate for ever from the Spartan yoke and found the new city

[1] ἐρημία μεγάλη 'στιν ἡ μεγάλη πόλις.

of Messene on the site of that Ithome which had been the Helot refuge in the rebellion of 464.[1] Dionysius of Syracuse is now meddling in Greek politics, backing the Spartan interest. But he soon dies.

Jason of Pheræ, the capable ruler of Thessaly, seeing the Greek states wholly interested in one another's business, decided that he might conquer Persia while their backs were turned, and collected a great army for that purpose. But he wasted time over preliminary endeavours to create a good impression, and some young men thought to use it usefully by murdering him. Then ensued weakness and confusion in Thessaly, which Thebes, misled by some evil genius, sent Pelopidas to put to rights. The latter on his second visit north increased the embarrassments of Thebes by interfering in the affairs of Macedon.

But before going to Thessaly, Pelopidas, with certain other delegates from Athens, Arcadia, and Elis, took a trip to Susa, where they seem to have read to the Great King essays on the evil state of affairs in Greece. He told them to go back and tell their friends and enemies to be good boys in future. More he did not do; for he was incapable of doing it. Persia, like others who have been mighty in their youth, had put on much inert flesh in its old age. Unfortunately, at a congress at Thebes in 366, the Greek states refused to be good; and things went on as before.

In the Athenian League meanwhile Athens was developing a tendency to play the same part she had played in the Delian League. The sending of kleruchies, (colonies of allotment-holders,) to Samos and the Thracian Chersonese in 365 was contrary to the express terms on which the league had been constituted.

The one hope for the salvation of Greece had been Thebes, not Thebes in itself, but Thebes under the guidance of Epaminondas. His fellow-worker, Pelopidas, fell in battle against Alex-

---

[1] The city was on one of the twin peaks of Ithome, about 2,000 feet above the plain. A very striking feature of it is the magnificence of the masonry of which the walls and gates are constructed. The fourth-century masonry of Greece is very remarkable. Magnificent examples of it are to be seen at places which cannot have had many hundred inhabitants, such as Eleutheræ at the south end of the Dryoscephalæ Pass, Ægosthena in the Megarid on the Gulf of Corinth, and Limnæa, now Kervasseras, the small Acarnanian town at the south-east angle of the Ambraciot Gulf. Even assuming, as we must, that a great deal of volunteer labour was expended on them, yet the cost must have been enormous relative to the resources of these little places; and the fact that they invested so much in defensive masonry is eloquent testimony to the troublous nature of the times.

It is also remarkable that even little places like Ægosthena and Limnæa, close to, but not on the sea, build long walls ($\sigma\varkappa\acute{\varepsilon}\lambda\eta$) to the shore. The invention of Pericles had revolutionised Greek warfare; and by the fourth century the Greeks recognised the fact.

THE FOURTH CENTURY, 400-300 B.C.

ander of Pheræ at Kynoskephalæ in Thessaly in 363. The loss thereby sustained is doubtful, for it is not known how far he was personally responsible for the disastrous interference of Thebes in the affairs of Thessaly and Macedonia. But in 362 Epaminondas and the Thebans were called south once more to Peloponnese by the ever-recurrent disorders there. With a great army, including the full force of Thebes and large contingents from Argos, Messenia, and southern Arcadia, he all but took Sparta ; and then retired to the Arcadian plain, where he defeated the Spartans and their allies in a great battle at Mantinea. But he himself fell in the battle. Never was the greatness of a state more due to one of its citizens than that of Thebes to Epaminondas. With his death died Thebes' greatness.

With the battle of Mantinea Xenophon's general history, the "Hellenika," comes to an end. It has been customary for those who have an imperfect knowledge of its contents to decry it as a biassed and untrustworthy work.[1] It is neither.

Xenophon was a country gentleman who had developed literary ambitions. Like many a country gentleman of other times, he had spent his youth and early middle age as a soldier ; and his service had been exceptionally miscellaneous. He could write graphically of that which he had seen ; and of the stirring events of his age he had seen as much as, perhaps more than, any man of his time. As a writer his perseverance was not equal to his aspirations. He could write an excellent monograph like the "Anabasis" or the "Memorabilia" ; but when it came to a general history on the contemplated scale of the "Hellenica" his perseverance failed him, so that this work of his is a very desultory production the composition of which was spread over something like forty years. He tried to write history and succeeded in writing memoirs, for throughout the "Hellenika," wherever personal experience fails him, it is plain that research into facts has been either omitted or perfunctory. This, too, accounts for the lack of proportion in his work, the tendency to deal with the less important at great length and to dismiss the more important in a few words. If in his narrative he does injustice to any man or state, it is of far too indiscriminate a character to be called bias, and is probably of a quite unintentional nature due to lack of diligence. He was a philo-Laconian,—but so was every gentleman of his day,—and this may have led him to sympathise with acts of Sparta where sympathy was hardly due. But there is no proved distortion of fact in favour of

---

[1] The best criticism of it is contained in Breitenbach's introduction to his edition of the "Hellenika," one of the most scholarly contributions ever made to ancient history.

Sparta ; and he is at times severe in his judgment of the morality of the doings of that state, and of its political errors.

The historical sins of the " Hellenica " are rather of omission than commission.

MACEDON

For the next quarter of a century the interest centres on the personal career of that able and crafty man, Philip of Macedon. The Greek states continue to wage futile wars on one another, the only importance of which is that they render the otherwise probable inevitable. To a reader with an exaggerated appetite for facts they may be interesting ; but he must seek their record elsewhere.

Macedonia was a country with which the Greeks were glad to trade, and its princes were people whose aid they were glad to get in competitive enterprises up Chalcidice way. Otherwise they were wont to look on the Macedonians with that indifference with which they regarded the semi-barbarians of the Epirus coast, the Molossi and others. The political state of the country resembled somewhat that of Thessaly, a land where feudal barons from their strongholds ruled over an agricultural population. Under such political circumstances the members of certain baronial families are wont to establish a supremacy over their noble neighbours, and to adopt the power, if not the style, of princes : and this is what had happened in Macedonia. These princely families had, as might be expected, developed a strong mutual rivalry ; but some of them had, less expectedly, conceived an ardent desire to pose as ornaments of Greek civilisation, and with that intent had sought vainly to impress the politely incredulous Greek with claims to descent from old kingly families of the Greece of a long-past age. But it is evident that the aspiration to Greek civilisation was sincere, even if its interpretation was peculiar. Racial kinship, and a language so closely akin to Greek as to be practically a dialect of it, facilitated the fulfilment of these ambitions.

In 359 there ascended the throne of Macedon a certain Philip. There can be little doubt that his predecessors had watched the developments of the last forty years in Greece with peculiar interest, inasmuch as they suggested the possibility of the conquest of its divided states by some great unified power. But divisions at home had made it impossible to take advantage of divisions abroad.

Philip's early career had been exciting and variegated. His family had originally been princes of the Orestæ, with a capital at Edessa, later moved to Pydna, near the Thessalian border. Of his predecessors the most able was Archelaos, who reigned in

THE FOURTH CENTURY, 400-300 B.C.

the last years of the fifth century. During his reign the Macedonian army was organised and roads were made. He had moved the capital to Pella; but Dion was his fortified nucleus. The law of succession in the Macedonian royal family was simple. Each possible claimant to the throne sought to murder all competitors; and the survivor succeeded. What with dynastic murders and Illyrian invasions, Macedonia passed through a stormy period for forty years after the death of Archelaos, and, when Thebes intervened, Philip, who was the third son of his father, was taken there as a hostage, to remain there for several years acquiring a lurid but instructive experience from which he was far too clever to fail to profit. After a few more complications, a few more murders, and an Illyrian invasion had cleared the air, Philip became king in 359. He was no barbarian veneered over with Greek culture, but a very able man who had a clear view as to the aims of his policy, and infinite patience and some unscrupulousness in carrying it out. He had determined from the first to make his kingdom great at the expense of his Illyrian, Thracian, and Greek neighbours; so his first task was to reorganise the army. In doing so he made one of those apparently insignificant modifications in the weapons of war which have on various occasions changed the history of the world. Knowing that the Greek hoplite was the most effective soldier in the world as known to him, he created the Macedonian phalanx with spears so lengthened that when it met a Greek hoplite phalanx in a charge the spears of its six front ranks came into action before the enemy came into contact with its first line of men.

He first secured himself by defeating the Pæonians and Illyrians. He then turned his attention to the coast, where a fringe of Greek cities hemmed in the kingdom, cities in which Athens had a special interest as members of her league. The first trouble arose over the much-contested Amphipolis, at that day the one door between the west and the east of the Balkan peninsula. Athens coveted it, and regarded it as her own; but, not being able to recover it herself, made a highly questionable arrangement with Philip that he should capture Amphipolis, and then exchange it with Athens for Pydna, which seems to have asserted its independence of the Macedonian kingdom during the recent distressful period of trouble, and to have joined the Athenian League. Philip settled matters his own way in 357 by capturing both cities and keeping them. So Athens, disgusted at the failure of her disreputable proposal, made war on Philip. Meanwhile the Athenian League was falling to pieces. Her allies on the southwest coast of Asia Minor revolted, and Byzantium did the same.

From 357 to 346 a desultory war went on between Philip and Athens, in which Philip gradually gained, and Athens gradually lost, ground. Its leisurely character made it possible for Philip to engage in other minor enterprises. In 356 he acquired Crenides, thereafter to be known as Philippi, and its all-important gold and timber region. By 353 he had advanced eastwards and captured Abdêra. The contest between two more or less equal powers, one of which is directed by a man of great ability, and the other by the varying vote of a democracy ever ready to act on the advice of the most persuasive speaker whose estimate of the circumstances of the moment is made with one eye fixed on the plans of the adversary abroad and the other on that which is likely to be popular with the ignorant masses at home, can only end in one way. The very greatness of Demosthenes and Æschines, the rivals for the direction of Athenian policy in these years, as orators affords one of the most striking of the many proofs that history provides that the gift of oratory is not associated with the highest practical capacity. Political oratory in the Athenian democracy of this age was at best the cry of half-knowledge appealing to the decisions of ignorance.

In the meanwhile events in Greece gave Philip an excuse for interfering in its affairs. The restless Thebans had taken the side of Delphi in a premeditated revival of its chronic claim to independence of Phocis. Furthermore, Thebes had sought to sanctify her desire for personal vengeance by reviving the Amphictyonic League, which was an anachronistic absurdity at the time, but admirably adapted to support the corrupt interests of the powerful. Thessaly joined her in the matter; and the two together were quite able to control the votes of the minor states of the league. Athens and Sparta took the side of Phocis, but gave very moderate practical assistance. Then arose one of those internecine wars which the Greeks euphemistically termed "sacred." The Phocians, aided by mercenaries hired with the treasure of Delphi, put up such a fight, and made things so uncomfortable for the Thessalians, that the latter appealed to Philip in 353, who, not being troubled with scruples as to the merits of the case or any other moral question, gladly joined in, and drove the Phocians out of Thessaly. He would have advanced south of Thermopylæ had not an Athenian fleet made the passage of the Middle Gate too risky.[1] But Philip retained permanent possession of south-eastern Thessaly.

In was about this time, in 352, that Demosthenes came to the front in Athenian politics. Of the many things he said much might be written. The record of what he did may be more brief.

In Greek home affairs he advocated consistently the weakening

[1] Even nearly a century later ships could get sufficiently near to the narrows of the Middle Gate to attack the flank of any army which tried to force the land passage there,—only a few yards broad.

of the power of Sparta and of Thebes. In view of Philip's position in Thessaly the policy was inconceivably foolish. The one great need of the time was a Greece united to resist the now probable aggression of Macedon. His first diplomatic success was so to alienate the feelings of Sparta by opposing her interference in Megalopolis that she left Athens in the lurch in later difficulties with Macedon.

The acquaintance which Philip now acquired with Greek politics seems to have suggested to his mind the idea that the dependence on Persia which the torn and worn Greek world showed might be converted into dependence on Macedon and turned against Persia itself. He began to dream of himself as a leader of a national war against Persia. The first step in that direction would be the subjugation of Thrace. But Olynthus had proved false to its alliance with him ; and so against it he first turned. This aroused the Athenians, and Demosthenes in particular, who advocated various ineffective ways of opposing Philip. By 348 Philip had captured Olynthus and some of the Greek towns of Chalcidice, most of which he destroyed. Athens was furious, impotent, and alarmed. So in 346 she had to conclude a peace with Philip involving a humiliating acceptance of the *status quo*. All question of Phocis had been excluded from the treaty, for Philip had determined to appear as the *deus ex machinâ* to bring the Sacred War, which still dragged on, to a close. That he had no difficulty in doing ; but his real aim was to be admitted a member of the Amphictyonic League, and thus gain an official peace footing in Greece.

In Athens there was an acute division of feeling as to the policy to be pursued towards Philip. Demosthenes was for out-and-out opposition to him, while Æschines favoured friendly relations. The party struggle was disfigured as usual by the prosecution of opponents on any charges which could be trumped up.

Athens' fear was for the Hellespont, which was threatened by Philip's advance in Thrace. Meanwhile Philip, who had no one to waste his time in talking, had practically annexed Thessaly, made advances in Eubœa, and was threatening north-west Greece. In 342 he overran Thrace as far as the shores of the Euxine. Demosthenes replied with the Third Philippic, in which he made an extremely foolish understatement of Philip's military ability. Philip must have wished that there were a few more like Demosthenes among his enemies, for an enemy who did not take him seriously was just the kind of enemy he wanted at this stage of his career. Demosthenes now went on a lecturing tour through Thrace, Illyria, Thessaly, and the Peloponnese, giving character sketches of Philip to people who had by this time formed a more accurate if not more flattering estimate of it. At Byzantium alone he attained some practical success, in diverting that town from alliance with Philip. He also applied to the Persian king to help the Athenian state with money. That the king would not do; but he adopted the more effective plan of helping certain Athenians, including Demosthenes himself, with money, a modification to which the recipients made no objection.

In 340 Philip marched to the attack of Byzantium and its allies, a move which brought to an end the indecision of Athens, and war ensued. Byzantium was saved by the talent of the veteran Athenian commander Phocion. Disappointed here, Philip spent several months in an attack on the Scythians owing, so the story ran, to an insult inflicted by the Scythian king, an insult which had probably taken a form which tradition does not mention, one of those chronic raids into the Balkan Peninsula which that people repeated at frequent intervals for the next four centuries; for it is significant that, although Philip defeated the Scythians, he did not pass north of the Danube.

The end was now drawing near. Every intriguer in Greece was making use of the revived Amphictyonic Council for his purposes, thus playing into the hands of Philip, who had acquired a controlling interest in it.

On this occasion the trouble arose out of a petty charge made by Æschines against the people of Amphissa to the effect that they had cultivated a sacred field belonging to Delphi. The Council decided against Amphissa; but no Greek state seemed to be very anxious to carry out the execution. Athens might have undertaken the job, but on the advice of the energetic but short-sighted Demosthenes she refused to do so. And so after some desultory fighting Philip was called in in 339 as general of the league.

He promptly passed south, slipping unopposed through the gates of Thermopylæ to Elateia in Phocis. He had at last got through the famous pass; and great was the alarm at Athens when the news reached there. Both he and Athens made a bid for the support of Thebes. Athens, by agreeing to recognise the claim of Thebes to supremacy in Bœotia, won that state to her side, and the two then prepared to meet Philip. The Peloponnese, with the exception of Achaia, held aloof; but most of the states of middle Greece sent assistance, so that an effective army of 30,000 men was raised. On the available evidence it is difficult to understand why Philip did not move on Bœotia before this force was collected; but not till the late summer of 338 did he meet the allies at Chæronea with 30,000 infantry and 2,000 cavalry; and there the two armies, about equally matched in numbers, fought for the liberty or dominion of Greece. The Athenians on the left defeated Philip; but on the right wing the

Thebans were cut to pieces by Alexander, and the whole Greek army took to flight. In this Senlac of Greek liberty the Greeks fought with a determination which did honour to their race. Its decadence was not due to its men, but to its institutions.

The story of the first half of the fourth century is all the more pitiful in that it has to be told of a people which, though it had carried the arts of peace to a height never before attained, had never succumbed to that inertia which is apt to result from the enjoyment of them, but was ready to risk its life in any venture, and to fight fiercely for that political licence which it looked upon as political liberty. Had its energies been directed by the best men of its race instead of by the windbags who won their way to the control of democracies, it might have done great things in the then world, not merely to its own advantage, but to that of mankind in general.

It is easy for a writer of the story of the age to draw morals which are written large on the history of the time ; but nevertheless the tale on this part of the fourth century presents difficulties which the available evidence does not solve.

The Greeks of this century went through a period of sixty years of almost continuous warfare, and yet in the very last years of that period were able to raise large armies and large fleets. To the Greeks of the fifth century such an experience would have been impossible, for the mere reason that, ere it was half-way through, they would have been in such a state of financial impotence that they could not have continued a war. Who could have conceived of the Phocis of the fifth century supporting for years a band of 8,000 mercenaries ? It is true that she had the temple treasure at Delphi to draw upon ; but even so the fact is amazing, and in a sense inexplicable.

In spite of the continuous troubles of the time, Greece must have been making by way of trade a larger income than she had made in the previous century ; yet the evidence that such was the case can hardly be said to exist, for the vicissitudes of warfare absorb the attention of those who contribute to the story of the time. Every state was employing mercenary forces, some to a large, some to a much less extent ; and these were drawn largely from regions like Arcadia, where poverty drove men to seek their fortunes abroad, or from the more backward states, such as Ætolia and Acarnania, where the primitive fighting instinct of human nature had not been tamed by civilisation. In the non-commercial states, especially in Peloponnese, whole districts must have been reduced almost to desolation by the repeated devastation of war : in fact, whatever the profits from trade, the country itself was on the way to that ruin which was to be consummated by the destruction of Corinth in the second century before Christ.

After Chæronea Philip's way was open. He had only to clear up the political mess, and, for the rest, to organise the future of Greece according to his own will.

To Thebes he was severe. It was reduced to the position of a local community in Bœotia, with a Macedonian garrison to ensure its good behaviour as good behaviour was then understood in Greece, for it did not exclude the slaughter of many political opponents by exiles who had returned on the Macedonian occupation.

Athens received terms which surprised her. There was to be no more Athenian League, though she kept, *inter alia*, Samos; and she was to be Philip's obedient ally. Otherwise things were to go on as before. If the respect of this alleged barbarian king for an intellectual civilisation was not genuine, he showed it in a very curious way by the most considerate treatment of his old and most bitter enemy.

The rest of his settlement of Greek affairs may be summarised briefly. He garrisoned Chalcis and Corinth, the strategic keys of Greece. In Peloponnese Arcadia, Messenia, and Elis joined him, preferring a friend outside their kin to enemies within it. After devastating Laconia, he cut the dominion of Sparta down to the lower Eurotas valley.

On the Greeks generally he imposed a league such as would make internecine quarrels a crime which Macedonia would promptly punish; but the league was also to serve what was to him its most important function, as a weapon of war against Persia.

He was not destined to live to carry out the great design of his life. In 336 he was assassinated in consequence of a family dispute. His son Alexander succeeded him without the opposition usual on such occasions, and fully expected on this particular one.

The modern world knows Philip's character mainly from the evidence of those who distrusted and disliked him. How far the picture is true to life it is impossible to say; but he was certainly no saint. He was also without any question one of the ablest men who have played a great part in world history. The exploits of his son are so impressive in their magnitude that the work of Philip seems but preliminary to them, so that men forget that the work of the son would have been the work of the father had that father lived. It may also be questioned whether the overthrow of an empire which was ready to fall in ruins was a greater exploit than the creation within the short space of twenty-three years, out of the weak principality to which he succeeded, of that Macedonian kingdom which Philip left behind him

Western Greeks

During this distressful sixty years of the history of the Greeks at home those in the west had been so much taken up with their own troubles that they had had but little time to rejoice or to sorrow over the fate of their fellow-countrymen, and had only interfered spasmodically with their affairs. Dionysius of Syracuse was proving a hard taskmaster whom it was safer to obey than to oppose. He had no ambitions east of the Ionian Sea. He wanted to bring the whole of Sicily and the Greeks of Italy under his control. He was not going to remain on the mere defensive against Carthage, but was determined to drive the Carthaginians to the African coast, and so rid the Greeks of the nuisance and danger of their neighbourhood. He disposed of military and naval forces far larger than ever a Greek state had possessed, and of the lives of his subjects with a freedom such as the most drastic tyrant of previous time might have envied, but dare not have imitated. He spent a large part of his life attacking and attacked by Carthage, with intervals in which he tried to gain control over the Greek cities of Italy. In neither field of operations was he completely successful, for the Carthaginians held on firmly to west Sicily; and in Italy his success did not extend beyond the cities of the toe of the peninsula. In the Greek world at home he interfered on a small scale on various occasions with results which, owing to the hopeless disintegration of Greece, were much greater than the means employed to attain them; but he never seems to have entertained any design to acquire a footing east of the Adriatic. Over the Greek cities of Sicily he ruled with a sway unbroken and unquestioned, a fact which, when the restless nature of those communities is remembered, is a singular tribute to his capacity and ruthlessness of method. The Sicilian Greeks had badly wanted a master, and they had got one against whose proceedings it was unsafe to rebel or even to protest. His mercenaries came first, his subjects second, in all his considerations. But he not only saved Sicily from Carthage, but also he taught the Sicilian Greek that unified control under the hand of a tyrant was the only means of securing him from slavery to the Semitic foe.

In the later and more peaceful years of his life, when he could easily keep what he had got, and had ceased to desire to get more, he fell a prey to literary ambitions of the highest type. Many men of great practical ability at all ages of the world have supposed that the poetic gift was one of their endowments: have, in fact, been unable to understand how it could fail to be. He took to writing verses on which he asked for the criticism of the literary men whom he had collected at his court. Their candour did not cool his ardour, and, so bad were the verses, imprisonment did not cool their candour.

Among the literary men who came to Syracuse was Plato. Thrice he came, and thrice he went away. Dionysius as a philosopher king had a philosophy of government which was not Plato's.

In 367 the old tyrant died after a reign of thirty-eight years. He had not been a good man, but he had been a competent ruler ; and in times such as those in which he lived the competent bad was a greater blessing than the incompetent good.

His son Dionysius was at first more interested in geometry than government, so that the fashionable amusement of his court was the drawing of circles, rectangles, and such-like figures, on that shore whose adaptability for the purpose was to be the undoing of a later and greater geometrician.[1] Satiated with geometry, Dionysius took to lighter amusements, of which government was not one. So other people conceived the idea of trying their hand at it. The result was various complications which brought about the exile of one of the experimenters, Dion, a member of the royal family, who went to Greece, where he lived the life of a respected country gentleman. Thence he was tempted by friends to undertake a filibustering expedition against the dominions of the incompetent Dionysius. As the tyranny seemed open to competition, other competitors arose, among them a certain Heracleides. Brief tyrannies and prompt murders succeeded one another. It is a pitiful story. In 346 Dionysius resumed the tyranny by the logical method of residues, there being no one else left to assume or resume it. The Carthaginians, who had been watching events in Sicily, chose this time for a great attack. *Faute de mieux*, the Syracusans appealed to Corinth, their mother-city, for help ; but Corinth had its hands full at home, and so could only send Timoleon, a man of sixty-five years of age, to command the defence. This did not sound very promising. Timoleon, however, proved himself a commander of great ability. He was the greatest Greek of his age. He first ejected the incompetent Dionysius, who spent the rest of his life at Corinth, where he found his true vocation, that of a street-jester with a mordant wit.

Timoleon conducted a campaign against the Carthaginians with what were at first inferior resources. But by his ability he was able to evolve order out of disorder, and so to deal with the Carthaginians that they were glad to make a treaty whereby they made a slight gain of territory and the Sicilians the great gain of peace. After that, by one of those wholesale shufflings of population which had now become so customary in Sicily that the Sicilians must have come to regard them as part of the natural

[1] Archimedes.

order of things, he regulated Sicilian affairs on what might have been a permanently sound footing had not later comers interfered with his work. He died in 336, the same year as Philip of Macedon.

The Italian possessions of Syracuse had gone lost some years before, in 356, when the Bruttians, the native mixed race of the toe of Italy, had imposed their sway on the Greek cities which Syracuse had included in her dominion. The Hellenic rule in Italy was on the decline,—on its way to succumb to those native races it had partially dispossessed. Tarentum alone maintained a real importance, and an unreal appearance of strength. On the west coast the greater part of Greek Campania fell into the hands of the Romans between 343 and 326.

A mere narrative of facts can never give a complete picture of the history of a nation, even if it be accompanied by such explanations of them as occur to one to whom the series is known and can be envisaged as a whole. The historian who is contemporary with the period which he describes is apt to take for granted that his readers will be acquainted with those commonplaces of the life of the age which do not show themselves on the surface of those events which are likely to attract the interest of the reader. The Greek historians and moralists of the fifth and fourth centuries wrote for that Greek world which was all the world to them. It is not therefore strange that they should omit all mention of those ideas and facts which made up the everyday spiritual and physical life of the men for whom they wrote. Yet these men were making the history of their time, and making it, as men will always make it, on the foundation of the ideas and facts associated with their individual lives. This element in the history of any age is always important, and nearly always obscure, because it is usually ignored by those contemporaries who alone can really interpret the spirit of their age.

The modern world has borrowed, consciously or unconsciously, so many ideas from the Greek that it is apt to fail to realise how greatly the Greek outlook on life differed from its own.

The history of the facts of the fourth century is inexplicable in many respects without some knowledge of the fundamental ideas which produced them, ideas with which the historians, for reasons already given, do not deal.

The Ethics of Aristotle

From one work of the century, however, the "Nicomachæan Ethics" of Aristotle, can a glimpse be obtained of the outlook on life taken by the individual Greek; but even there it is difficult to draw the line between current views and the personal ideas of the author.

Aristotle wrote the "Politics" for the Greek world, and the Greek world only; but in the case of the "Ethics" it is almost certain that he intended it to be what Thucydides intended his history to be, a "possession for ever,"—and for the same reason, that that with which he deals would be true "so long as human nature remains the same." It is not of limited application like his other great work, though it resembles it in one respect,—that it is, with the possible exception of the pure idealism of the latter half of the last book, written not as a theoretical treatise on the life of the individual, but as a practical guide for the direction of that life. But, though resembling the history of Thucydides in general intent, it contrasts in spirit with the work of the historian in that whereas Thucydides' moral view is un-Greek, the work of Aristotle is intensely Greek in its treatment of ethical problems. It is that feature of it which makes it impossible to pass it over without mention in the history of the fourth century, because it is the one work which explains clearly those elements in the Greek view of life which are most in contrast with that held at the present day; and for the understanding of Greek history it is necessary to understand the Greek.

The actual tendency of the "Ethics" can only be appreciated by one who reads the book. It is one of those great works of the world which leaves on the reader's mind impressions which will abide with him through life; impressions, moreover, not concerned with the minor, but with the fundamental elements of moral existence. There is, indeed, much in it which is hard to understand; but it also contains perfectly clear and comprehensible statements of the principles underlying that which is best in human life, and the means by which the individual may attain to them in practice. Thus far the modern reader will find himself in sympathy with a work which formulates his vague and floating ideas of how the best life may be lived. But there are also elements in it which will not accord with modern ideas of what is best, or, at any rate, most appropriate, in human conduct; and it is those elements which disclose that part of the view of life as a whole wherein the ideas of the Greeks differed from those of the man of the present day.

Long before the time of Aristotle men of the Greek world had formed a vague conception of a divinity (τὸ θεῖον), higher and more spiritual than the gods of the national religion, a being who punished the crimes and to a certain extent decided the fate of man. But this idea was dim and impalpable, so that it never took a form so distinct as to imply a standard of spiritual perfection to which the actions of man might be referred. Aristotle shared with the Greeks of previous time this vague conception of divinity; and though in the tenth book of the "Ethics" he shows in his discourse on perfect happiness that he regards that happiness as divine, and thereby presupposes that to divinity the idea of perfection is attached, yet it never occurs to him to refer human action to a divine standard, and to estimate the value of any grade of attainment in moral virtue by reference to the perfect virtue of the deity of which men of the Greek race had conceived.

Recent Greek philosophy had so far concentrated itself on the attempt to explain everything by logical rule, imagining that perfection might be found by investigating, considering, and formulating the impressions conveyed to the human mind by the senses. It seems to have dreamt in a vague sort of way of the possibility of a revelation of the divinity, and to have yearned after some such thing; but, until such a revelation came, it was convinced that man must be the measure of all things. It is in this respect that the outlook of Aristotle on the problems of life clashes in some cases with the ideas of the present day. With him human virtue or excellence is referred to a human standard, the standard taken by the moral philosophy of his time. It was the only realisable standard, so he thought; and he would no doubt have admitted that it was an imperfect standard, just as he admits that the realisable happiness of his earlier books of the "Ethics" is a lower thing than the perfect happiness which he sketches in the tenth book. But he was not setting himself to idealise life, but to show men how they could attain to the best possible life in a practical world.

Under the Christian dispensation the modern world has become accustomed to refer its estimate of moral value to a divine standard, and to exaggerate the reference by estimating the best of which man is capable as valueless in reference to the standard of perfection,—a logical view, but one not very valuable in any working estimate of moral values. Nevertheless, the exaggeration of the application to the divine standard has produced in modern times one virtue which the Greek and Aristotle never knew, and would have regarded not as a virtue but as a defect, humility, which implies that he who possesses it is conscious of his own worthlessness in reference to a standard of divine perfection. Nor would modesty have appealed to the Greek mind as a virtue, since it implies that a man deliberately gives a false impression of some form or forms of excellence which he might rightly claim for himself, an attitude of mind which may be ultimately referred to the assumption of the modern world that a man is not the best judge of himself and his worth. Modesty aims at the avoidance of conceit; but the Greek world would have said that the virtue in this case is, like other virtues, a mean between these extremes, that $\sigma\omega\varphi\varrho\sigma\sigma\acute{\upsilon}\nu\eta$, sense of your own measure in reference to the world around, which is the very key-note of all Greek moral philosophy. Aristotle and the Greek educated world believed that a man could hit this all-important mean. The modern world doubts it ; and is therefore morally biassed towards the less objectionable of the two extremes.

Closely associated with the human standard of Greek ethics as interpreted by Aristotle is the belief in the necessity of externalisation. The term needs explanation.

It did not require the acuteness of the Greek mind to recognise that a man's inner nature, or, as the Greek would have said, his soul, is something which he can to almost any extent conceal or disguise. It can only be made manifest to others by manner, acts, or speech. One of the bases of the ethics of Aristotle is that a man's conduct and conversation should be such as to give a true impression of the soul that is in him : that it is wrong for a man to claim either by word or deed that which is not a part of his real nature, a principle which would be admitted by modern ethics. But to Aristotle it is also a fault if a man conceals or underestimates by word or deed the worth that is in him ; and there the Greek view represented by Aristotle jars on the modern sense. To the modern world this view of life seems to draw on human nature a cheque which it cannot possibly meet. But, then, the philosophical Greek believed in possibilities in human nature infinitely greater than those which would be attributed to it by a world influenced by the Christian doctrine of its natural worthlessness.

Strange as the idea may seem to the modern man, it was in a sense the logical outcome of a philosophy of life which, starting with the major premiss that man is by nature a social being, deduced therefrom the necessity that the members of a society should have a true understanding of one another's nature, each recognising the true value of his neighbour's, and claiming a like recognition for himself. Such a society was realisable if men could attain to that highest and most comprehensive of all virtues, σωφροσύνη, for that implied that no man would claim more or less than his due because he had a true sense of his measure in relation to the world in which he lived.

Thus if some of the virtues catalogued and described in the "Ethics" offend modern taste in certain details, it is because the Greek hoped from human nature more than the modern world expects.

Aristotle was no dreamer. He had none of the mysticism of Plato. Plato represents the Greek genius approaching the logical form which it attains in the writings of Aristotle. Yet a certain mysticism is inseparable from ethics, since no discussion of an ethical system can evade that ever-present but inexplicable factor, the tragedy of life, that element in human fate which is not of man's own making. Aristotle, being a Greek, was not a fatalist. He did not regard man as the mere plaything of fortune, but as capable of making his life better or worse, which means, as he emphatically says, happier or less happy. In what are perhaps the most striking chapters of the "Ethics," those in which he shows that character is formed through habits, and that habits are formed through acts, an argument the truth of which is apparent to anyone who reviews his own life, he demonstrates that a man's character, inasmuch as his acts are voluntary, is of his own making, and then passes on to the argument that, as virtue of character is productive of happiness, there is a side of happiness which is attainable by the will to do good, to act righteously.

He recognises, however, that that element in life which the Greeks called tragedy may bring misfortunes which must impair happiness; and this leads to a consideration which is one of the most remarkable of all those which are stated in the "Ethics," that, though misfortunes must impair the happiness of the good, yet the good will never become ἄθλιος, a term impossible to translate by a single word, but implying a state of utter misery, the misery of one who sorrows without hope.

It is strange to find that a man whose recognition of a divine nature was vague, and certainly did not include any belief in a divinity to which man could appeal for spiritual support, should have arrived at a conclusion which embodies one of the most important articles of the faith or the convictions of those who, whether Christian or not, believe in a God who does temper the wind of misfortune for those who in act and word appeal to him.

How far Aristotle represents the spirit of the educated world of his age it is not possible to say,—save this, that his treatment of ethics is in respect to form built upon a Greek foundation. In respect to matter it is probably his own, representing a standard hardly attainable in those days of political confusion and decadence. But the basis of form and standard underlying the Nicomachean Ethics is a part of the history of the fourth century on which but little light is thrown by other contemporary writers.[1]

The ancient world had accepted slavery as part of the natural order of things; and such a view was in itself natural to a world in which slavery had from time immemorial existed as an institution. But it is evident that the humanitarian Greek had qualms of conscience as to the justice of the system, doubts which he sought to dispel by laying down a dividing line between those races, especially his own, which had attained to civilisation and culture, and those which still lived in a state of uncultured bar-

[1] For those who do not read Greek the best English translation of the "Ethics" is that by Peters (Kegan, Paul & Co., 1886).

barism. The barbarian was "by nature a slave" was the dictum by which he sought to lull to sleep those questionings as to the justice of the institution. To his credit be it said that he had shown towards slaves a humanity which other races did not display to those whose lives they had bought in the open market.

It was in the age of Aristotle that the question of the justification of slavery as an institution was first raised in literature. Aristotle himself had accepted the system, and had argued that it was part of the natural order of things. But, though the question of its justifiability, when first raised, attracted but little attention, and though the condemnation of the system had at first no traceable influence on social life, yet the question, once raised, had a vitality which could not be killed by the starvation of unrecognition, and, though it never led to the abolition of the institution, it did eventually lead to the alleviation of its severities.

Alexander of Macedon

Alexander the Great was like a son who succeeds to a great business which his father created, and proceeds to enlarge its area of operations far beyond its bounds in his father's time. Under such circumstances there must always be a certain amount of doubt as to the quotas of ability contributed to its making by father and son respectively. Nor is it always safe to accept the estimate of the past, even if it be unanimous, on the character and gifts of a man who has played a great part in the world, a caution peculiarly necessary with regard to the prominent men of ancient history because the estimate of them is formed on what is generally very limited first-hand evidence, much or even the whole of which may be biassed for or against the person concerned. Once the tradition created, the future world accepts it as a fact, having no inclination to look more deeply into the matter. In the present instance Alexander had what the modern world calls a good press, and Philip a bad one.

This caution is not to be regarded as a warning that the judgment which will be here passed on Alexander will be less enthusiastic than such judgments are wont to be. That judgment, whatever it may be, must be founded on consideration of what he did; so, until his doings have been related, it must be reserved. Enthusiasm anterior to the consideration of evidence is apt to dazzle the eye of the mind.

In Philip were combined two qualities which are not always associated in the same person, wisdom as a father with capacity as a man. The ability and immorality of the personnel of the Macedonian court were both remarkable. Philip thought that Alexander might develop his ability under the tuition of Aristotle, and that the moral influence of the great philosopher would be better than that of the sirens of Macedonian court life. So Alexander and his tutor were relegated to the retirement of the little country town of Mieza. Never in the history of the world were such a tutor and such a pupil associated together : a man and a lad who were in their respective worlds of intellect and action destined to influence the whole history of after-time. Tradition relates that Alexander was attractive both in appearance and disposition ; nor is there any reason to doubt that such was the case, though the tendency of the ancient world in respect to statues and other presentments of its masters resembles that of the modern photographer.

Succession to newly created conglomerate kingdoms like Macedonia seldom ran smoothly in those days. Its new subjects, Greek, Illyrian, and Thracian, were all ready to take advantage of the opportunity to throw off the yoke afforded by the accession of a youthful ruler. In the Macedonian royal family charity began at home in the form of the merciful murder of all who might have been foolish enough to compete for the throne with the new occupant of it. This precaution Alexander took,—a very shocking but very necessary measure if he was to live to do his life's work. Having thus purified his domestic hearth he proceeded to show the subject population that he was a chip of that hard old block, his father. At Athens Demosthenes had persuaded the Athenians to do honour to the assassin of that Philip who had treated their state with a forbearance almost without parallel in the stern records of ancient history. He had more recently persuaded the Athenians to complete their fortifications with a view to revolt. The latter operation was enlivened by a dispute between him and Æschines on a proposal which had been made to bestow on Demosthenes a crown in recognition of his services to the state. It was on this occasion that he recited the oration " On the Crown," thus dedicating the greatest monument of his eloquence to a futile personal squabble. Alexander marched into Greece just to show the Athenians and others what might happen to them if they were naughty. He left it at that. He did not punish the Athenians, hoping that they had by now discovered that it was stupid to be silly at the bidding of Demosthenes.

It was the turn of the Thracians next. In 335 he carried out a brilliant campaign even to beyond the Danube which brought that people and various other peoples to a sense of the kind of man with whom they had to deal. On his way home, too, he gave the Illyrians a taste of his quality.

Meanwhile Persia had started a ferment in Greece. Some Macedonian generals had crossed over into Asia. That was bad enough ; but it would be much worse if Alexander came himself ;

so, in order to keep him in Europe, Darius, incited by Greeks at his court, sent money to Athens and elsewhere, some of which got through to Thebes, where certain patriots killed two Macedonian officers and shut up the Macedonian garrison in the Cadmea. The rest of Greece sent congratulations but no help. All of a sudden Alexander, whom rumour had killed, appeared on Lake Copaïs. Thebes was taken by assault and was, save its temples and the house of Pindar, wiped off the face of the earth, those of its inhabitants who were not killed being sold into slavery, —a stern sentence, but that of those Bœotian communities to which he had left the decision of its fate. For the rest Athens made such excuses as she could, evading the demand for the surrender of Demosthenes without making the sacrifices which that politician suggested that she should make in his defence. Alexander accepted the excuses, knowing well that the storms which this fourth-century Æolus could let out of his windbag were mere storms in a teacup, or its Macedonian equivalent, compared with what he would have to face in Asia.

The Persia which he proposed to attack extended from the Ægean to India, and from the Aral Sea to the Nile cataracts. It was greatly decadent from the Persia of a century and a half before. Circumstances rather than good management held it together. Revolts were but spasmodic because the revolted could get no help from neighbours of different race. Even revolt had no special attractions for that political fatalism of the East which accepts despotic rule as a necessary evil. The Achæmenid did not trouble anyone so long as tribute and taxes were paid ; and, after all, any other ruler would have demanded these as a minimum,—and perhaps more,—so what was to be gained by throwing off the Achæmenid yoke ?

Though the government had declined in capacity owing to the enervating effect which education in a harem had on the Persian kings, yet the Persians themselves still maintained those genuine virtues which were directly inculcated in a religion with which, unlike those of Greece and Rome, a moral creed was intimately associated. To the Persian virtue was not a human but a spiritual quality ; not founded on convention, but an essential part of that religious creed which ruled his life. Thus, on the whole, the Persians were the most clean-living people of their time, a characteristic of all races which have longest resisted social and political decay. Thus it was that, though conquered by the superior mechanical devices of Macedon and the Greeks, those parts of the old Persian empire where the Persian dwelt were the first to throw off the Macedonian yoke, and never developed that obsequious humanism to which the Hellenism of Asia Minor sank.

The Persian kings had come to rely largely on mercenaries for the maintenance of their power. Thousands of those Greeks whom the economic conditions and political troubles of their own homeland had driven out to seek their fortunes in some other world were now in the Persian service. There is reason too to believe that in the earlier half of this century many Greeks had settled down to civilian life in the cities of the interior of Asia Minor, a land at last thrown open to them by the Persian policy of playing off Greek against Greek. The semi-independent principality of Caria was half Hellenic.

In 334 Alexander began his great venture with 30,000 infantry and 5,000 cavalry, of whom about half were Macedonians, and the rest Thracians, Illyrians, and Greeks. The army was of a modified and improved Greek type. The longer spear of the heavy infantry made it more effective than the ordinary hoplite phalanx. Peltasts had been known to Macedon ere they were known to Greece, a type of soldier which would be required on bad ground, or against the mobile infantry of Asia. The land in which the army was to be used was not one of limited resources and limited areas where the enemy could be forced to fight a pitched battle by the mere threat of devastation. There was sure to be a certain amount of guerrilla warfare as well as set battles; in fact the Persians would, if well commanded, avoid the latter save where it was a case of resisting the Macedonian advance in some critical strategic position. The cavalry force was an addition to the old Greek type of army, in which cavalry had never played more than a very subordinate part. But Platæa, and probably other unrecorded Greek experiences, had shown how a Greek hoplite force might be reduced to impotence by the excellent Asiatic light horse; and Carrhæ was to show that a similar type of European infantry might even be brought to destruction. Therefore it was necessary to have an effective force of cavalry. But Alexander used the cavalry in a novel way. In a Greek army the first real shock of battle was delivered by the hoplite force. But he gave his cavalry armour so that it might be used for the first shock. His idea was probably that a flexible mobile force of Asiatic infantry, if driven in by the shock of a hoplite charge, could easily avoid heavy loss by yielding or withdrawing, a measure which would not be successful against cavalry.

On the river Granicus in north-west Asia Minor the first battle took place. The Persian army consisted of 20,000 Persian horse, and a like number of infantry, chiefly Greek mercenaries. It was badly mismanaged, so that the cavalry was defeated or ever the infantry came into action. The latter were cut to pieces. It was not that the Greek mercenary soldier was the worse fighter; it was simply that the Greek phalanx could not face the Macedonian, where six lines of spear-heads projected in front of the first rank.

Alexander then marched down the coast of Asia Minor. It was necessary to secure his rear and line of communications before advancing deeper into Asia. Miletus put up a feeble defence. Halicarnassus offered a stubborn resistance in a siege chiefly remarkable for the employment of regular battering-rams by the Macedonians, a type of attack which they certainly had not learnt from the Greeks of Greece proper, who were hopelessly inexpert in siege operations, though the Sicilian tyrants, taught probably by their Carthaginian experiences, had become expert in the art. But it was probably from Asia that Alexander borrowed this device; and after all thousands of Greeks and probably some Macedonians had been serving in the Persian army for many years past.

After this he marched through Phrygia into Cilicia, where news reached him that Darius was coming up with a great army to meet him. The land at that north-east corner of the Mediterranean is the gate of Asia. The gate is a double one, the Cilician Gates through the Taurus range from the plateau of Asia Minor into Cilicia, and the Syrian Gates through the Amanus chain on the passage from Cilicia to the Euphrates region. For a large army there is practically no alternative for the traverse of this narrow and intricate passage. It was for the passage of the Amanus chain that the battle of Issus was fought late in 333. Darius had got together one of those huge unwieldy oriental armies only a fraction of which was really effective, the effective element in the present case consisting of 30,000 Greek and 60,000 barbarian mercenaries. The battle was won by the piercing of the Persian centre, and the consequent flight of the left wing. The loss of the Persians was enormous, if tradition be trustworthy, while that of the Macedonians was very small. Darius fled not with, but in front of, the rest.

Alexander now marched south into Phœnicia. Tyre proved a very formidable obstacle to his intended advance on Egypt, for the city, being on an island, was very difficult to assail, and the Persian fleet was as yet in command of the sea, so much so that it was at that very moment doing very much what it liked in the Ægean. From the side towards the land Alexander attacked the place by a mole, while he got together so large a fleet from the other Phœnician cities, from Cyprus, and from Rhodes, that the Tyrian fleet dare not try conclusions with it. With these ships he attacked the town from the side towards the open sea. In August 332 the city was taken by assault. It is satisfactory to read that the abominable cruelty of the Semites towards prisoners captured from the besiegers was punished by a drastic

THE FOURTH CENTURY, 400-300 B.C.

massacre and the selling of 30,000 of the inhabitants into slavery.

Alexander now marched south on Egypt. But he was detained on his way by the necessity of besieging Gaza, which proved a peculiarly difficult operation owing to the great height of the city walls. Egypt surrendered without attempting resistance. His chief work there was to lay out the site of the new city of Alexandria. Having settled the administration of Egypt, he passed north again through Syria on his way to attack the Euphrates region. At Gaugamela near Nineveh on the Tigris Darius awaited him with a huge army drawn from the eastern part of his empire. Its numbers, probably exaggerated, are said to have amounted to more than a million men. The defeat of this unwieldy mob did not prove a hard task; and with its defeat the organised defence of Persia collapsed.

Thence he marched south; and, after receiving the submission of Babylon, reached Susa, where he found a large treasure of silver. From there he marched north-east towards the plateau of Iran, the modern Persia, forcing his passage through the difficult paths of the Zagros chain. At Persepolis he captured treasure twice as large as that taken at Susa.

It is probable that the amount of precious metal taken at Susa and Persepolis was never really known, and that the sums stated by the historians are merely the invention of traditional gossip. But the treasure had been accumulated year by year by a dynasty which for a century past had had a mania for the accumulation of money and bullion. The mere fact that it was sufficient to convert the old silver standard of eastern Greek trade into a gold one is in itself sufficient evidence of its enormous value.

Policy and Administration

What was at any rate the preliminary policy of Alexander in his organisation of his newly won empire had been already shown in his dealings with the peoples and regions he had conquered up to this period in his campaign. So far from interfering with local religions he showed the greatest consideration for them, being himself quite prepared to bow down in the house of Rimmon or of any other god without prejudice to his adherence to the gods of his nation. This attitude towards the religions of his new Semitic and Egyptian subjects was doubtless due to more than one cause, of which policy may have been one. But the modern world has so modernised the character of Alexander that it tends to forget that he was a man of that ancient world which knew neither proselytism nor intolerance in religion, which regarded it as part of the natural order of things that men of different races should worship different gods, and above all tended to take the view that the power of the gods was territorial, so that if a man passed from one state to another he passed into the realm of new local deities whom it would be well to propitiate on entrance into their domain.[1] "Sua cuique religio est, nostra nobis," said the Roman; but it was also true of nearly all the races of the ancient Mediterranean world.

In secular matters his policy had been to set in charge of the regions conquered a military and a financial official, each of whom was independent of the other, an arrangement which was to the benefit of the conquered, and safeguarded the interests of the supreme ruler.

In the spring of 330 Alexander was in Media, whence he started towards the south shore of the Caspian in pursuit of Darius who had taken refuge with the governor of Bactria. Alexander overtook him, but captured only his body, for he had been murdered by his escort. The body he sent for royal burial at Persepolis, thus for the first time indicating his as yet undisclosed intention of posing as heir rather than conqueror of the Achæmenids. This policy was to have corollaries which were to be very unpopular with his Macedonians, who regarded the Persian empire as the spoil of the conquerors.

After a visit to Hyrcania on the shores of the Caspian he marched east through the modern Meshed to Aria, now northern Afghanistan. He then passed into the modern Seistan. Early in 329 he was in Turkestan, having crossed the Hindoo-Koosh in winter. He then subdued Bactria. In this central Asian region the king remained till the summer of 327. He then marched through Afghanistan to India with an army of 135,000 men. On the Hydaspes, the modern Jhelum, he fought a great battle with Porus, the king of that part of India, in which his veteran army had to face the novel attack of elephants. But the army which Alexander led seems to have been capable of adapting itself to any circumstances which nature or human ingenuity could contrive. He defeated Porus; but he treated the vanquished king so well that he became a loyal ally. He had more fighting in the Punjaub; but did not penetrate further east than the Sutlej, for his soldiers would go no further. After passing down to the mouth of the Indus he performed a wonderful march along that desert shore of the Indian Ocean which stretches from that river's mouth to the outer entrance of the Persian Gulf. He kept touch with his fleet as far as possible, but even so he lost three-quarters of the men on that terrible journey, the nature of which he cannot have foreseen when he embarked on it. He reached Pasargadæ to find

---

[1] The $\delta\iota\alpha\beta\alpha\tau\acute{\eta}\varrho\iota\alpha$, or sacrifices made by the Spartans on the Laconian frontier when contemplating a foreign expedition, were probably carried out with a view to ascertaining the attitude towards the expedition of the gods of the territory which they proposed to invade.

that troubles had arisen in the new empire during his absence in the east.

It is difficult to realise the marvellous character of the exploits performed by Alexander and his army in those years of campaigning. They had passed through some of the most difficult regions of the known world. They had defeated great armies; captured cities which had been, not unreasonably, regarded as impregnable, and fought minor battles without number against those northern peoples of the Persian Empire whose wild courage and independent character that power had never tamed. But more marvellous than all is that which does not come out in the picturesque stories of Arrian and other authors, the organisation which made it possible for the great army to traverse not merely the wide stretches of almost desert plain in north Persia and the region of the Oxus, but above all to cross the Hindoo Koosh and the mountains of Afghanistan. The experience of English armies in those regions affords eloquent testimony to the real greatness of such a military feat. Military history cannot present any parallel to it.

Alexander soon settled the troubles at the centre of the empire. But now he developed a policy which startled and annoyed his Macedonian followers. He himself had already married Roxana, a wild and ruthless beauty from Central Asia. He now added the daughters of Darius and Ochus to his domestic circle. More than that, he made his generals and others of his chief men, to the number of eighty, marry Persian wives. Ten thousand of his Macedonians had already done so, so that in this respect at any rate they had no case against their superiors. But when it came to introducing Asiatics wholesale into the army, discontent broke forth among those Macedonian warriors whose idea was that they alone should exploit that empire they had won. Alexander, like many more ordinary men, was coming to find the friends of youth inconvenient in middle age. It is also difficult for a man to pose successfully as a god before those who have known him as a boy. The Macedonian soldiers, men of a race whose wild warriors had never regarded themselves as the mere tools of those who commanded them, did not regard the conquest of Asia as the work of one man, Alexander, but as that of the Macedonian army; and they were not, if they could help it, going to have that army diluted with inferior stuff. Alexander allayed the discontent for the time being by conceding his Macedonian followers certain outward signs of a social superiority of which he had certainly intended to deprive them. But Macedonia, though it might supply an army for the conquest of West Asia, could not supply the numbers necessary for the occupation of the immense region which had been won. So on the question of the enlistment of Asiatics Alexander had to remain firm.

There had been troubles in Europe meanwhile. Antipater, whom he had left there as regent, had been obliged to teach Sparta a lesson which cost King Agis his life. But he had quarrelled not only with Sparta but also with Olympias, Alexander's mother, a lady with whom it would have been very difficult for anyone who had relations with her not to quarrel, unless her character is much misrepresented in history. So Craterus took Antipater's place as regent in Europe.

Alexander next visited Babylon, where he was met by envoys from all the races of the Mediterranean, even from Carthage, Italy, and the far-distant Spain.

Greek affairs became troublesome again. Alexander had demanded that the Greeks should recognise him as a god. To that the Greeks raised no objection. One god more or less was a matter of indifference to them,—and there were inexpensive forms of sacrifice. But it was quite another form of sacrifice which was demanded of them when Alexander ordered them to receive back twenty thousand exiles whose property had been confiscated in accordance with democratic ideas of justice, and would have to be returned to its owners on their restoration. The Greeks were shocked at such a violation of the principle established by their democracies that a majority might rob a minority by legal means of their own devising, and determined on passive if not active resistance. Athens subsequently evaded the sacrifice by special petition.

About this time Athens was the scene of a financial scandal.

Harpalus, Alexander's treasurer, whose record for dishonesty had in the past been grandiose, bolted with a sum equivalent to more than a million pounds, which he invested in ships and men with intent to make himself a general nuisance in Greece. Bribery was a necessary part of any political plan which was to succeed in that country, and some of his money got to Athens, where it disappeared in a mysterious way. Some inquisitive persons insisted on solving the mystery; whereon Demosthenes, who, like many other prominent men of his day, had passed his life in an atmosphere of suspected dishonesty, was convicted of having embezzled part of it, and had to leave Athens hurriedly.

ORGANISATION

It now remains to consider the system on which Alexander organised the great empire he had won. The only uniformity was in the central administration and its representatives in the provinces. There were two chief administrators, civil and military respectively, over the general affairs of the empire, while in each province there were three officials independent of each other who had charge respectively of the military, the financial, and the general civil administration. But in most of the provinces the last of these must have been little more than a superintendent of a local administration carried on by native officials, sometimes by kings, in accordance with the particular customs of the country; for Alexander was careful to interfere as little as possible with the local system of government to which the nations of his empire were accustomed. Any attempt to impose uniformity on a great and heterogeneous empire such as his would have meant trouble, and perhaps disaster, for him who attempted it. Generally speaking he followed the example of Persia in his liberal treatment of the conquered peoples; and it is probable that he did so deliberately. He departed from the Persian system in one important respect in that he did not put one official in supreme charge of a province.

The most marked feature of Alexander's policy was the founding of cities in various parts of the empire. He is said to have founded seventy, some of which were on the sites of pre-existing towns. The policy served two ends, the military occupation of the country, and the spreading of civilisation through the less civilised regions of the kingdom. The new element in these cities was not by any means entirely Greek, but probably in all of them there was a certain percentage of Hellenes or of hellenised Macedonians; moreover the number of Greeks who settled in the pre-existing cities of Asia Minor must have been enormous. The result was the spreading of hellenic civilisation, or at any rate of elements of it, throughout the whole of Asia from the Ægean to the Indus, though in the eastern part of the empire the influence was exercised on the arts rather than on the manners of life. But Asia Minor became to a great extent hellenised. The educated classes among these Asiatic Greeks maintained for centuries the strongest attachment to the hellenic mode of life and to the country from which it had sprung, so that even in a remote hellenic society in Gadara on the Sea of Galilee Meleager the love-poet bewails his misfortune in having been born outside the confines of Hellas. But the lower uneducated classes of this hellenic diaspora, sprung from ancestors influenced by all kinds of superstitious fancies, became soon infected with the somewhat cheap and vulgar mysticism of the cults of those peoples among whom they settled.

Under the stress of economic poverty the Greek of the fourth century had been driven to a life of adventure in many lands, and if by so doing he had lost something of the Greek that was in him, yet he had all the spirit and independence of the fighting man who is aware of his superiority to those less efficient in the military art. But this spirit had been somewhat broken by the proved superiority of the Macedonian. The life of comparative wealth which he lived in Asia under Alexander and his successors revived in him those instincts of humanity which had made him, and were to make him, a pattern of civilised life in a world which had been brought up from time immemorial amid the discomforts of hardness and cruelty. The easy life in Asia recalled to him that humane spirit which had been sadly dulled and diminished by the ever growing spirit of cruelty engendered by the continual wars and revolutions of the fourth century. He had lost his faith in law which had degenerated into the mere expression of the will of a majority anxious to plunder those who had proved themselves more efficient in the occupations of daily life. Under the rule of Alexander and the Seleucids the Greeks of Asia, even if organised as a local democracy, could no longer abuse the power of a majority, since in that case the central authority would step in to prevent it.

This raises the question as to the effect which this large Greek settlement in Asia had on the life of the western part of that continent. Rhapsodists have sung of the contrast between the free and independent Greek and the poor-spirited native of western Asia accustomed to bow down before autocratic rule, and have dwelt on the blessings which were conferred on the indigenous population by association with men who had developed the art of self-government. They seem to forget that in the fourth century the Greek had shown singular incapacity for self-government : that self-government as understood by him had reduced the Greek world to a state of misery which the Asiatic had never known since the days of the Assyrian Empire, then long forgotten. Many of the Greeks were absolutely sick of attempts to govern themselves, and were as ready as the most passive Asiatic to live under the control of a reasonably paternal despotism. The subsequent history of the Greek in Asia and of the peoples with whom he was associated shows that whatever influence he had on them, it did not take the form of a spirit of revolt against the " debasing " rule of autocracy. It was in social life that his influence was felt. He taught the world in which he lived that a humane world was a happier world for all, even for the strong, than a world in which cruelty was the law of life. It was a lesson which the Near East of the succeeding centuries learned all too well, for it was exaggerated into a humanity which shrank from resistance to wrong.

But the Greek also taught the world a lesson which it has by turns learnt and unlearnt ever since, that beauty is a real factor in life's happiness.

POLICY

Judgments on the aims of the policy of Alexander and on the qualities of the man himself must vary because he never disclosed in words what those aims were, and the known facts are capable of diverse interpretation. His most marked characteristic was a bravery amounting to recklessness. If the man who again and again led the way in the most desperate fighting either in battle or in the capture of walled cities, the man who when he had reached the Punjaub wanted to risk all in further adventure into the unknown, and this too at a time when he had laid the whole of Asia from India to the Levant at his feet, was one who had planned a great scheme for the setting up of an ordered and enlightened government in west Asia, it can only be said that he is the greatest human paradox in history, quite unlike any constructive genius which world politics have ever produced. If he wished to hellenise the East he went a very strange way about it,—he who in the last years of his short life became himself orientalised. All that can be said of him with assurance is that he was a marvellous military genius, perhaps, relative to his time, the greatest that ever lived ; and that by dint of that genius he won a great empire which he proceeded to organise very much on the lines followed by the dynasty he had overthrown. He thought to stabilise it by the old plan of seeking to create an equilibrium between the two main elements in the population, the Europeans who had won the empire for him, and the Asiatics whom he had conquered.

He died on the twenty-eighth day of the month Daisios, 323, at the age of thirty-two years.

CHAPTER VIII

THE THIRD CENTURY, 300–200 B.C.[1]

ROME

IN Rome when the century opens the long struggle between patrician and plebeian is drawing to its close. The plebeians had won access to the consulship and the lower magistracies, —nay, more than that, for whereas they were assured by law of the possession of one of the consulships of each year, their patrician opponents had no such legal privilege. One consul *must* be plebeian, and both might be ; whereas only one consul could be patrician, and neither might be. But there was one circumstance connected with the Roman magistracy which rendered the very democratic appearance of this recent constitutional change a false one. Office in Rome did not carry any salary with it, nor even any allowance for the inevitable expenses of office work in connection with administration. The Roman magistrate, whether consul or another, did not on entering office find a permanent body of government officials who were *au fait* with the details of administration, or any body of clerks who were accustomed to deal with the routine business of magisterial work. Some ancient states could not have afforded, and no republican state would have trusted, such officials, because their very permanency would have tended to give them the opportunity of encroaching on the powers of an annually changing magistracy, and might have led to attainment of the tyranny by some permanent official of peculiar capacity and ambition. Thus neither in the Greek nor Roman states was there any real counterpart of the public offices of the states of modern times. In Greek states like Athens a considerable part of the routine business of government was taken off the hands of the magistrates by the committees (prytanies) of the Council (βούλη) ; but at Rome there was no democratic council of that type, and no body, whether popular or otherwise, to which this routine work could be delegated. When in later days the Senate encroached largely on the functions of the magistrates it was with respect to questions of policy in legislation and other affairs that the

[1] *See facing page.*

THE THIRD CENTURY, 300–200 B.C.

Some dates of the period of the successors of Alexander.

Macedon.	Seleucid Km.	Egypt.	Greece, Epirus. etc.
318. Death of Antipater Cassander king.		Ptolemy I.	
	311. Seleucus I.		
	301. Annexation of N. Syria.		
297. Death of Cassander.			
293. Demetrius Poliorcetes seizes the kingdom.			
287. Lysimachus of Thrace and Pyrrhus of Epirus seize Macedon.			287. Pyrrhus of Epirus. (See Macedon.)
	286. Demetrius Poliorcetes takes refuge with Seleucus.		
285. Lysimachus rules Macedonia, Thrace, and Asia Minor.		285. Ptolemy II. (Philadelphus).	
281. Lysimachus slain in battle with Seleucus. Ptolemy Ceraunus seizes the kingdom.	281. Seleucus assassinated by Ptolemy Ceraunus. Antiochus I king.		281. Pyrrhus begins war in Italy.
280. Ptolemy perishes in battle with the Celts.			275. Celts settle in Galatia.
276. Antigonus Gonatas king.			274. Pyrrhus returns from Italy.
			272. Pyrrhus killed at Argos.
272. (See Epirus.)			Antigonus seizes Epirus.
	262. Death of Antiochus I. Antiochus II. succeeds.		251. Aratus seizes Sicyon for the Achaean League.
			250. Foundation of the Parthian monarchy.
		247. Death of Ptolemy Philadelphus. Ptolemy III. king.	
246. Antiochus II. murdered. Seleucus II. king.			
		245. Great attack on the Seleucid kingdom.	
			243. Aratus brings Corinth into Achaean League.
239. Death of Antigonus Gonatas. Demetrius king.			
			233. End of the kingdom of Epirus.
230. Death of Demetrius. Antigonus Doson king.			228. First Roman embassy to Greece.
	227. Death of Seleucus II. Seleucus III. king.		227. Cleomenes revolutionises Sparta. Earthquake at Rhodes.
	223. Death of Seleucus III. Antiochus III. king.		
		222. Death of Ptolemy III. Ptolemy Philopator king.	222. Battle of Sellasia.
221. Death of Antigonus Doson. Philip king.			
	217. (See Egypt.)	217. Egyptians defeat Antiochus at Raphia.	
215. Philip makes treaty with Hannibal.			
			214. Death of Aratus.

19

encroachment took place. Such an august assembly was not in the least likely to relieve the magistrates of the dull minutiæ of routine.

The consequence of this was that a consul or other magistrate on entering on his magistracy was obliged to constitute his household of freedmen and slaves as a temporary office for the transaction of public business. All this was expensive; and so only men of wealth could hold at any rate the higher magistracies; wherefore the plebeians who held the consulship were not men of the poorer classes, nor were the magistracies in any real sense democratic offices. So long as there was a question between patrician and plebeian, the plebeian consuls upheld no doubt the rights of their order; in fact it is almost certain that the rich plebeians, who were jealous of the political and social position of the patrician nobility, were the backbone of the reform movement. As its champions they were simply agitators for the grant of rights which they themselves would not possess unless they were wrung from the patricians for the whole body of plebeians. Democracy *qua* democracy can have had no attractions for them, —in fact within a comparatively few years of the throwing open of the consulship to their class, a new nobility, one of office rather than of birth, the nobiles, began to make its appearance, composed of those families members of which had held the higher magistracies, and containing at least as many plebeians as patricians. It becomes more and more exclusive as time goes on, till by the end of the third century it was very difficult for a "new man" (novus homo), that is to say one not belonging to the nobiles, to attain to the consulship.[1]

The plebeian had long recognised that his civil rights could not be secure until he had won complete political rights. With his attainment to the highest magistracy, the consulship, he would appear to have gained all that he desired or required. Even membership of the Senate was now open to him, for it had always been the practice at the quinquennial selection of new members of that body for the censors to give a preference to those who had served in the higher magistracies in the previous four years. In the Assembly (comitia) his vote was, nominally at any rate, as good as anyone else's.

Of the three forms of comitia, Curiata, Centuriata, and Tributa, there has already been occasion to speak. By this time the only political function retained by the first of these was the formal grant of the right of exercising magisterial power (imperium) to the higher magistrates on entering office. The other two forms

[1] Even in Cicero's day there was not much opposition to the attainment even of the prætorship by a "novus homo." It was the consulship which was jealously guarded.

of comitia were the legislative and elective bodies. It is quite evident from what occurred at the beginning of this century that the plebeians were dissatisfied with their position as members of these Assemblies. In the case of the Comitia Centuriata the cause of the dissatisfaction is not far to seek, for the eighteen centuries of the Equites (knights), nearly all of whom were the sons of senators, and most of whom would at this time be the sons of patricians, together with the eighty centuries of the first property class, each of which must have been small, and at this time largely composed of members of patrician families, disposed of ninety-eight out of the one hundred and ninety-three votes given in this Assembly under the group system. In the case of the Comitia Tributa, where the group was the local tribe, the cause of dissatisfaction is not so obvious. It is not known when this form of assembly was first instituted, nor is anything really known of its early history, save that it is probable that it was before it rather than before the Comitia Centuriata that most of the proposed legislation was introduced. But its later history suggests that even in it the group system lent itself to a process of magisterial manipulation by which any new voters whose political tendencies were suspect could be distributed among a small number of tribes, so that their vote could have but a small influence on the total vote of the tribes forming the body. It did not matter how large the number of the new citizens might be. If they were all put into eight tribes they only affected a minority of the votes given. The distribution was absolutely in the hands of the censor when holding his quinquennial office. In entering the names of new voters on the list (album) of citizens he could on his absolute discretion put them in any tribe or tribes he wished.

Perhaps there was some such manipulation when this form of comitia was first constituted; but it cannot have amounted to much owing to the fact that each tribe was at that time composed of persons dwelling in a certain locality. What is much more probable is that this very distribution by locality favoured the influence of the patricians in that large numbers of their clients would be dwelling in the same region as themselves, and they would be thus able to influence the vote of their tribe.

Side by side with the comitia there existed the " Gathering of the Plebs " (Concilium Plebis), which discussed matters of interest to the Plebs and passed resolutions (plebiscita) thereon. Such resolutions had no doubt been always binding on the Plebs; but they had never had the force of law (lex). In this body, though the voting was by tribes, the patrician influence could not be directly exerted, for the patricians did not belong to it.

The movement for the strengthening of the power of the Concilium Plebis had begun in the previous century with a law [1] passed in 339 which practically freed that body from senatorial control. Up to that time all the legislation, whether by the comitia (leges) or by the Concilium Plebis (plebiscita), only became valid when it had been ratified by the Senate, a constitutional rule which also, so it is said, applied to elections by those bodies.[2] By this law (Lex Publilia), however, it was laid down that the formal consent of the Senate (auctoritas patrum) to legislation should be given beforehand, a rule extended later by another law to elections. This reduced the consent of the Senate to a mere formality.[3]

The importance of the change is due to the peculiar nature of the power which the Senate [4] had exercised with regard to ratification of laws or elections. Technically speaking the Senate could not refuse to ratify a law on the ground that its provisions were bad or undesirable, or an election on the ground that the person elected was unsuitable. The refusal could only be on the ground that the proper religious forms had not been observed at the time of the passing of the law or of the holding of the election. The power was one which was obviously open to abuse. It would be easy to allege informality with regard to some law or election, when the real ground for refusal to ratify was dislike of the law or of the elected. But it is obvious also that it is impossible to allege informality in the conduct of proceedings which have not as yet been conducted; and so the ratification of laws and elections beforehand by the " patres " constituted little more than a farce.

But it was the great Lex Hortensia of 287 which brought to a close the struggle between the orders. In form it is one of the most ultra-democratic documents in ancient history. It laid down that the resolutions of the Plebs passed in the Con-

[1] Lex Publilia.
[2] I make this statement on the authority of a well-known writer on Roman history. But I confess that there has always been in my mind a doubt as to whether the election of plebeian officers by the Concilium Plebis came under senatorial ratification. The thing is improbable; but there is so much of the improbable in the ascertained facts of Roman history that the possibility of such a control having been exercised cannot be ruled out on the mere score of its improbability.
[3] In various Roman histories the statement is made without any explanation, and the reader is left wondering why the Senate's consent should have become a mere form under this arrangement that the consent should be given before voting took place on the law.
[4] As a fact the senators when acting in such a matter are not strictly speaking acting as senators but as " patres," i.e. as the heads of those patrician families to whom was entrusted the supervision of the observance of ancient religious forms.

cilium Plebis should have the force of laws (leges), that is to say
should be binding on the whole people (populus).

Never, so far as is known, had Greek democracy in its wildest
moments set up a legislative body from which the highest class
of citizens in the state was excluded. It had always relied on
the majority vote. But then the Greek world had never adopted
the principle of group voting; and that form of voting had at
Rome lent itself to official manipulation by which majorities
could be smothered.

As far as the written constitution was concerned, that is to
say that part of the constitution based on statute law, there was
nothing more to be done. In form, at any rate, the constitution
was as democratic as it well could be.

Anyone acquainted with the constitutional history of other
races, who was reading the history of Rome for the first time,
would naturally, when he came to this point in the story, anticipate two things in the further development of the working of
the Roman constitution—that the special extraneous plebeian
element would either disappear in course of time or at any rate
would lose its significance, and that the future constitutional
history of Rome would be that of a people ruling itself on democratic lines. Neither of these anticipations would be fulfilled.
There are many striking paradoxes in the constitutional history
of Rome.

The plebeian organisation, with the tribunes, plebeian ædiles,
and concilium, went on just as before as far as form was concerned; and the Concilium Plebis became in fact the most important legislative body in the constitution, because the tribunes
became the most energetic legislators, and they, not being
magistrates of the Roman people (populus), could not introduce
legislation before the comitia, but only before the Concilium
Plebis. Conversely a consul or prætor could not introduce a law
before the Concilium Plebis, but only before the Assembly of the
People (comitia). Thus two parallel systems of legislation,
mutually exclusive, existed in Rome from this time onwards—
a very extraordinary feature in the Roman or any other constitution. The tribunate of the Plebs remains the same in form,
but comes by degrees to play a part in politics very different
from that for which it had been originally designed, the protection
of plebeian interests.

The failure of that ultra-democratic constitution, the statutory
form of which was consummated by the Lex Hortensia of 287,
to develop on practical democratic lines, was due to more than
one cause. The curious way in which the Roman preserved
the old while adopting the new might well suggest that there
was in his disposition a deep-seated and innate regard for the

past founded on something more than mere sentiment.[1] He set up successively two new forms of Assembly, the Comitia Centuriata and the Comitia Tributa. But the establishment of the Comitia Centuriata does not involve the abolition of the old Comitia Curiata, nor does that of the Comitia Tributa bring about the disappearance of the Comitia Centuriata. The old forms all retain a larger or a smaller part of their old functions. The tendency displayed is conservative, but it is not due to mere conservatism, still less to antiquarianism. The curious retention in form, though not in fact, of the ratifying powers of the Senate is another instance of that tendency; and in it perhaps may be sought the clue to the origin of the tendency itself.

Roman life, both public and private, was largely dominated by a spiritual element which the Roman called " mos majorum," a term which may be literally translated " ancestral custom," with the usual misleading results of literal translation. For it did not imply a mere respect for old-fashioned ways and ideas resulting in adherence to them. It is true that when Rome became great the Roman, conscious of that greatness, sought to adhere to those modes and morals of life on which he believed his success to have been founded. That contributed undoubtedly to the preservation of the mos majorum in ages in which the superstition attached to it was much weakened; but the idea itself originated long before Rome became great, and had probably more influence before than after the days of her greatness. Its influence on politics was largely due to the fact that political forms and religious forms were so intimately associated in the Roman constitution as to be inseparable. Every political institution at Rome, if it went back to a time beyond the memory of man, was of an origin in which the sacred played as great a part as the secular; or, if established within the historical period, had been established by a law in the passing of which strict religious formulæ had been observed. Thus in the minds of the people the various elements in the constitution had a religious as well as a secular sanction; and that is perhaps the reason why the Roman, when setting up new forms, as in the case of the comitia, retained the old with certain modifications. It would have been impious to abolish utterly institutions which had been founded with the approval of the gods. Thus in politics the mos majorum had a religious sanctity attached to it, which made it a strong support for conservatism, and prevented iconoclastic tendencies from developing in Roman democracy. It was a wide term to which a wide appeal could be made on questions

[1] As a colonial pupil once expressed it: " When the Greek set up a new constitution he scrapped the old machinery: when the Roman did so he patched it up."

affecting traditional morality, the observance of religious formulæ, and the maintenance of the auspices.

It has been often said that the Roman constitution was, like the British, a constitution of custom : that this made it flexible : that its flexibility made it durable. The dictum is usually emphasised by comparison with Greek democratic constitutions.

The Greek, especially the Greek democrat, regarded constitutional questions from a point of view different to that of the Roman. Living in a land where the economic conditions were much less favourable than in Italy, the form of constitution under which he lived was no mere question of a little more or a little less liberty for the lower classes, it was very often a question of the provision of that daily bread which with an ever-growing population could not in many states be won by the ordinary processes of a working life. A democratic constitution meant to him a redistribution of wealth in some form or other, either by redistribution of land, or by pay for state services and other less common methods. That being so, his one constitutional idea in founding a democracy was to make the constitution so rigidly democratic that alteration in any other sense might become impossible. Therefore the constitution was reduced to writing so that there could be no argument as to what the constitutional law was on this or that point ; and any alteration of the law was guarded against by penalties imposed on those who proposed constitutional changes, and by elaborate investigations of the terms of any new law which had commended itself to the people in the Assembly. The Assembly at Athens could not make, it could only recommend laws.

Not until a recommended law had been passed by a committee (νομόθεται) appointed *ad hoc* to consider whether its provisions were in any way a violation of the constitution, that is to say, in any way undemocratic, did it become a law of the state. The Greek democrat was as a democrat the most rigid conservative known to history. He would have no compromise with change unless it was to more complete democracy. His constitutions were of so cast-iron a nature that they could only be changed by a revolution—could break, not bend. As to constitutional tradition he rejected it, except in so far as it was democratic. In Greece the bonds between religion and politics had probably never been so strong as they were at Rome ; and they had been much weakened by the determination to have democracy at all costs, that which made the democrat impatient of any obstacle such as the machinery of religion worked by the upper classes would have presented to its attainment. He was infinitely superstitious, but his superstitions had mainly to do with his private life.

Moreover in many of the democratic states of Greece ultra-democracy could not be maintained by the mere power of the vote. In Athens, and certainly in many other states, the ultra-democrats were little if at all superior in numbers to those of moderate views whose democratic ideals stopped short at a franchise confined to persons with property sufficient for the supply of the hoplite panoply—a hoplite franchise. Without the strict paper safeguards of the constitution drastic changes might have been made by a temporary preponderance of the moderate vote in the Assembly ; and the ultra-democrat was determined to provide against accidents of that kind. All that is known of the numerical balance of parties in Greek states tends to falsify the idea of preponderant ultra-democratic majorities in many of the states. The predominance of the ultra-democrats was chiefly due to the fact that they were largely recruited from that urban population which was on the spot for meetings of the Assembly, whereas the moderates were largely composed of the small cultivators of the country districts. Modern writers are apt to class these moderates as democrats without qualification, meaning really that they were not olig-archs. Ancient writers, who found third parties a nuisance in writing political history, class them as oligarchs or aristocrats, meaning thereby that they were not ultra-democrats.

The Greek ultra-democrat was conservative of the present : the average Roman was conservative of the past.

There is no question that in respect to legislation the Roman constitution was infinitely more flexible than that of Athens and those of many other democratic Greek states. It had never entered the head of the Roman either to draw up a comprehensive code of constitutional law, or to safeguard the existing constitution by forms and penalties deterrent of change. In Rome a law passed by the comitia, or a plebiscitum passed by the Concilium Plebis after 287, was final. It became forthwith part of the law of the land. It might deal with some quite minor question, or it might imply a great modification of the constitution, like the Lex Hortensia of 287. The only undemocratic feature of such legislation was that the introduction of the law rested solely with the magistrates, to whom alone the initiative belonged.

But it is somewhat hard to discern where those authorities on Roman history who emphasise the general flexibility of Rome's constitution find any large practical foundation for such a view. That it was not so rigid as the written constitution of a Greek democracy is obviously the case ; and it is equally obvious that Polybius' comments on its flexibility are coloured by a comparison with those Greek constitutions which he knew so well.

The idea seems to be founded on the assumption that a customary practice of the constitution was accepted by the Romans as equivalent to constitutional law—that it became part of that mos majorum which the Roman did undoubtedly regard as having some such equivalence. But did the mos majorum, except in the arguments of those who were interested in the extension of its connotation, ever really include the customary practices which sprang up after 287—practices which the senatorial nobility of a century and a half later were desirous of perpetuating ? The growth of those practices, which converted Rome once more into a practical oligarchy, was due partly to the nature of the Roman people, partly to the circumstances of the time during which they sprang up.

As far as constitutional development without change of formal constitution is concerned, it is just as marked in Greece as in Rome, though it operates in reverse directions : in Greece towards an increase, in Rome towards a decrease in democratical practice. If in Rome there is after 287 constitutional practice ever tending towards a senatorial oligarchy working through the Senate, so in Athens the Assembly is ever becoming more powerful, ever more and more shaking itself free of magisterial power and the control of the Council ($\beta o \upsilon \lambda \eta$) ; yet in neither case is there any infraction of the constitution. Each constitution is flexible enough to adapt itself to the change.

The Roman Proletariat

The mass of the citizens of Rome was very different in nature to that of a Greek state. The average Roman of the days before Rome acquired an extra-Italian empire was devoted to the land he cultivated and to the life on it. Throughout the history of Rome his interest is centred in his personal work in life. All that he demands of the government is that it shall be equal and fair in the administration of justice, and efficient in its protection of the land and citizens of Rome against foreign aggression ; and, for the rest, shall leave him as much as possible alone to carry out his life's work.

He had fought persistently during the two centuries of the struggle between the orders for civil liberty in the first instance, and later for that political liberty by which alone the enjoyment of civil liberty could be guaranteed. The legislation of 287 had completed the edifice of his ambition ; and from that time till the close of the Republic he is careless as to who governs him, provided he is governed with justice and efficiency ; but, if there is a failure in either of these respects he is quite prepared to play an active and emphatic part in politics. As far as justice is concerned the last two hundred and fifty years of the Republic are singularly free from any attempt at official oppression of the unoffending citizen. The illegal severities of the later part of the period are the work of revolutionaries in time of revolution, not of any legally constituted republican government. But in the last century of the Republic there were instances in which the masses of the Roman people showed a momentary and unwonted interest in politics, all of which are attributable to easily traceable inefficiency in the government of the day of a nature to affect the interests of the general mass of the citizens.

Save on these occasions the Roman commoner had but a languid interest in politics. He had no political theories, because he knew none. He knew that the form of the government at Rome afforded him reasonable protection in his private life; and that is all that he wanted to know about it. He would probably have been mystified had anyone told him that he lived under a democracy, a term which would have had no meaning to his eminently practical mind. He had no politics in the sense of attachment to any particular form of government. All that he knew, or wished to know, was that the form under which he lived provided him with what he desired; and when any proposal of law was put before him he did not consider whether it was democratic or undemocratic, whether it was progressive or reactionary, for not merely such terms, but the very ideas conveyed by them, would have had no meaning for him. He regarded any proposal of law from the point of view of his own interest, and voted for or against it on that ground only. The magistrate who proposed a law might be an enthusiastic democrat, some Roman of the senatorial class who had either imbibed progressive principles from Greek literature, or was posing as a friend of the people for the purposes of political advancement; but the average Roman citizen looked at the law, not at its proposer, and voted for or against it, or abstained from voting at all, according as he judged it to affect his own interests. He was quite ready to be guided and governed by men who had the means and the time to engage in public life, even though they were people who would not have asked him to dinner, for his own real wish was to avoid any distraction from the work of his daily life.[1] Whether in the agriculture of pre-empire days, or in the trade of the days of the empire, the Roman was a keen, level-headed worker.

So long as modern historians of Rome talk of " parties " in

---

[1] I am speaking of the Roman citizen before the population of Rome itself became corrupted in the later part of the second century B.C. partly by bad economic conditions, partly by association with the foreign, especially Greek, element which flocked to Rome as the centre of the empire.

Roman politics its history will be an enigma to any thoughtful student of it. In modern times a political party connotes a large body of individuals who are adherents of certain political tenets. The Roman masses had no political tenets in the ordinary sense of the term, and therefore they did not belong to any political party. There were no parties at Rome in the modern sense. Yet, especially in telling the story of the last century of the Republic, historians use language which would convey the impression that the progressive and rather revolutionary politicians of the day had a large permanent following among the lower classes of the Roman citizens. As a fact they had none. Any success they attained,—and it was little and momentary,— was due to the inefficiency of the official government of the day, not to popular support of any principles they professed. The use of the term " populares " as a name for the so-called reformers of the last age of the Republic evokes an idea of a radical party with a large following among the lower classes. In point of fact the " populares " were a small coterie within the Senate itself which saw that the ruling majority in the Senate was showing inefficiency in government, and took the only practical means they could take to remedy affairs—a direct appeal to the people. So long as they proposed measures to remedy palpable inefficiency the people supported them ; but even then no reliance could be placed on that support unless the cause and effect of the proposal were so clear that the masses could understand them.

The general position in the last two and a half centuries of the Republic is then that the Roman did not care by whom he was governed so long as he was governed justly and efficiently ; and that is why in the century and a half which followed the passing of the Lex Hortensia the government, though remaining a democracy in form, became in fact an oligarchy. The process of change within this period was slow, and for the most part silent. How it worked, and what brought it about, will be best left for consideration in dealing with the first violent reaction against it under the leadership of Tiberius Gracchus in 133.

ITALY

The events of the latter half of the fourth century had reversed the position of things in middle and southern Italy. Rome rather than Samnium was the threatening fact. But even now Rome would have left the Samnites alone had they shown an unaggressive disposition. In 298, however, they began to harass their neighbours the Lucanians, who were allies of Rome. It was a mistake on their part, for they were hedged round with enemies, Rome on the north, Lucania on the south, and Apulia on the east, all of whom regarded their ambition with suspicion, and had good reason for so doing. So now Rome invaded Samnium, laid waste the country, and took various strongholds. As in the previous war Samnium turned for help to those races of the north who were still free, the northern Etruscans and the Umbrians. The Etruscans had been restive in the last years of the previous century. An unprovoked attack which they had made on Roman territory had not only been defeated, but Rome had invaded northern Etruria ; and the Romans on their return march southwards had defeated the Etruscans in a great battle on the Vadimonian Lake.

But this had happened fourteen years before ; and now, when the Samnites appeared on the Etruscan border with an army, all free Etruria, some Umbrians, and above all a large number of Celts from beyond the Apennines joined them. The Romans had so genuine a fear of the Celts that they raised the largest force they could collect, four Roman legions and a still larger number of Italian allies, to meet the danger. The campaign, a brief one, ended in the desperate battle of Sentinum in 295, in which Rome won a complete but costly victory. The Celts present in the battle were wiped out. Etruria paid a war indemnity ; and the Samnites were left to fight by themselves, which they did with such desperation that when, four years later, in 290, their resistance ceased and Rome forced them into an alliance, it was one on equal terms.

Except for further trouble with the Celts in 284, which resulted in their defeat and the acquisition of the territory of the Celtic Senones, Rome spent the next nine years in consolidating, by the usual method of founding colonies at important strategic points, the lands which she had won. Venusia protected Apulia and Lucania. The Sabine territory was annexed in 290 ; and colonies were established at Hadria and Castrum on the Adriatic coast. A colony at Sena held down the newly acquired territory of the Senones.

But the close of the Samnite War had left the southern tribes of Italy, who had acquired so much of Greek civilisation as to make them desire its material products, free to raid the Greek towns of the south coast, proceedings in which not merely the Samnites but Rome's old allies the Lucanians joined. The towns appealed to Rome, offering in return for protection to recognise her suzerainty. Rome gave the protection, and garrisoned the towns. Tarentum, however, the most powerful of them, though an official ally of Rome since 301, did not like the idea of her suzerainty ; and when Rome, contrary to the existing treaty, sent a squadron thither, the Tarentines practically destroyed it.

This brought about a crisis and the intervention of a man

who taught Rome a lesson she would have been glad to be in a position to forget, that Italy would not be left alone to arrange its affairs its own way either under the control of Rome or of any other Italian state. The Tarentines found that Pyrrhus, king of Epirus, was not merely ready but anxious to help them.

Political Ambitions of Rome

It is very difficult to estimate the political aspirations of Rome at this time, except the negative fact that she had no ambition whatever to make acquisitions beyond the shores of Italy. But it seems on the whole probable that a policy of bringing the whole of the peninsula under her control had taken definite form. Yet even that policy had been forced upon her. Of the various forms which imperialism has taken in history that of Rome was of the slowest and most reluctant growth. It did not result, like the empire of Alexander or that of Napoleon, from the ambition of one man backed by the ready assent of a nation, leading to the formation of an empire quick to come and quick to go. It was not like the Athenian imperialism which was the child of opportunity and necessity, where foreign acquisition solved economic difficulties at home. It resembles the British Empire only in that slowness of growth which seems a necessary condition of any lasting dominion. But it was not due to the expansion of trade interests, nor to the discovery which a trading race may make that there are parts of the world where a man may earn his living better than he can in an already crowded home. It was an empire forced upon a people whose ideal was to be left at peace to do that life's work which it loved, to cultivate the Campagna, and let the rest of mankind go its own way. The ideal seemed possible in that early world of near horizons. But human nature is not so constituted as to be indifferent to the superior prosperity of a neighbour, even if it be due to the personal exertions of him who prospers, still more if it is supposed to be due to any advantage derived from the nature of his territory. Thus in the early age of Rome's existence the raiders from the hills had sought to rob the Roman in the plain. Etruscan feudal lords had coveted a revenue derived from such a hardworking population. In self-protection Rome had been driven to acquire by long years of warfare such additional territory as might protect the nucleus of her possessions. Then, when that seemed to be accomplished, the Celts had become a danger to the Italian peoples, and the Samnites had developed the ambition of bringing the whole peninsula under their control. So the Roman was borne along by the blast of circumstances to bring under his control the lands of others whom he would gladly have left to themselves if they would only have left him to himself. Doubtless before this century opened he had conceived the necessity of bringing the whole of the peninsula under his dominion. But at the shores of the sea his ambition was stayed, not by the sea, but by his own inclination. And now Pyrrhus was going to prove that even the sea could not render Italy safe.

Pyrrhus of Epirus

Pyrrhus was a gentleman adventurer on a large scale, who in the scramble for kingdoms which followed the death of Alexander the Great had carved out for himself a realm in Epirus, the wild home of a wild people. He had conceived the idea of a Hellenic Empire of the West correspondent to that which Alexander had won in the East. Carthage was to be included in it. Rome does not appear to have come into his original calculations either one way or the other until the affair at Tarentum showed him that Rome was prepared to encroach on the empire of his desires. He came over to Italy with a great army, thinking to have to deal with a semi-barbarian race which, in the view of those who did not know it, there would be no difficulty in defeating. The war which followed was a bloody one. In 280 he defeated the Romans on the Liris, a defeat largely due to the Romans not knowing how to deal with the elephants of the Epirote army. The Greek cities then joined him; and so did those Italians of the south who had good reason to fear and hate Rome. And, when he might have brought the war in Italy to a victorious conclusion, he turned aside to the accomplishment of his great scheme, a Hellenic Empire in the West. In Italy the Greek cities were all he wanted. But Rome would not assent to any foreign power, whether Epirote or otherwise, establishing a footing in Italy; and maintained this attitude in spite of a second great defeat at Asculum in 278. Impatient at the postponement of his plan Pyrrhus, leaving garrisons in the Greek cities of Italy, crossed to Sicily, where he drove the Carthaginians to the west end of the island. The Greeks, ever the friends of those who were strong enough to succeed and the enemies of those who were weak enough to fail, helped him with enthusiasm until the tide turned against him at Lilybæum. So in 276 Pyrrhus, having disgusted the Sicilian Greeks by failure, went back to Italy, where he found the Italians more righteously disgusted by his desertion. In the next year the Roman consul, M. Curius Dentatus, defeated him at Beneventum; and he retired across the Adriatic a very disappointed man. Between 275 and 269 Rome crushed all further resistance in the south of Italy, and in the succeeding years established her position there and in middle Italy by founding colonies of which the best known are Beneventum and Ariminum. Rome now ruled Italy from the northern Apennines to the Sicilian Strait.

Organisation of Conquered Regions

The extraordinary duration of the Roman Empire was due far more to certain features of its organisation than to the military prowess of the Roman people. No state organisation of the present day bears any resemblance to that which Rome now established in Italy, nor yet to the modified form of it which was applied to the provinces which she won later. Many serious defects in practice are observable in the working of the design in the following centuries; but the design itself was admirably calculated to secure the interests of the supreme power without interfering unduly with the liberties of the inhabitants of the subordinated communities. The Roman government never conceived the idea of making the body of citizens into a military caste governing tribute-paying subjects with no rights of their own; partly, no doubt, because the Roman citizens had no taste for such a life, partly because the number of citizens was too small to hold in subjection an Italy inhabited by a population whose disabilities, if uniform, would have bound them together in opposition to Rome. There was further the fact that the conquest of Italy had been spread over a long period and had been very gradual, so that a policy of dealing with subject communities had grown up, one dictated originally by circumstances, but developing into a more or less systematised form with the growth of experience.

While Rome was as yet a little city state struggling for existence, and gradually extending her borders in that struggle, she had been glad to become a member of the Latin League on equal terms with the other towns of that confederacy. Those who dwelt within the small regions brought under her sway became Roman citizens, and in the League all citizens of the confederate towns were on an equality.

But when the Latin League was broken up, and Rome became the president, and not merely a member of Latin Italy, a new policy was adopted whereby some of the Latin towns received Roman citizenship, while others were accorded inferior, henceforth called Latin, rights.

In order to understand the Roman system of administration in Italy it is necessary to realise that the ancient world was constituted politically on lines very different to those which prevail in modern times. It consisted at this time and for many centuries later of two forms of political units, the city and the tribe. Italy at this age is typical of the rest of the world which subsequently came under the rule of Rome. In the richer districts cities had sprung up each surrounded with its own territory, and each, strictly speaking, an independent state, though long before this time cities inhabited by people of the same race had found it advisable to form confederacies or leagues for mutual protection. Thus when Rome is dealing with Samnium she is not dealing with a unified state, but with a series of political units inhabited by Samnites and united in a league.

In the poorer mountain districts of middle Italy Rome had to deal with tribes which had never been in an economic position to found city states. Their cultivation and pasture was too limited or too sparse for the concentration of any considerable population at one point. Here the tribe, not the city, was the unit.

Rome's policy both at this time, and later when she acquired a provincial empire overseas, was to accept the city as a unit wherever it existed, but to refuse to recognise any form of league or confederacy of cities. Thus in the settlement of Italy which took place after the conquest Rome did not have any agreement with Samnium, Lucania, and so forth, but a separate agreement with each city of those regions by which that city was accorded certain rights as an ally (socius) of the Roman people. In middle Italy where the tribes were small, and there were no city states, she recognised the tribe as a unit, and made an agreement with it. In her later overseas empire the republican government of Rome recognised only the city unit; and, where the city state did not previously exist, as in Spain, carved such states out of the tribal territories. The attainment to dominion in Italy, though unsought in the sense that it was no part of Rome's original ambition, had been facilitated by the fears and jealousies of the other Italian peoples; and its maintenance was largely due to the central position of Rome, which enabled her to strike quickly and decisively at any danger-point before any combination of enemies could become dangerous. But it was the mutual fear which the Italian populations felt for one another which most favoured Rome, for it was to Rome that the timid turned for help when a neighbour proved threatening. Lucanians and Apulians fear the Samnites and turn to Rome. The Greek cities fear the Lucanians and Samnites and turn to Rome. Rome can always pose as the friend of the oppressed and profit thereby. When Italy came under her dominion it was to her interest to maintain this division. But she did not do it thereafter by playing off Lucanian against Samnite, or Greek cities against the Lucanians, for politically speaking there were no more Samnites, Lucanians, Greeks; but there were dozens of cities, Samnite, Lucanian, Greek, and so forth, it matters not which, bound to Rome each by its own treaty granting it its own rights in relation to Rome. Nor would Rome have recognised any argument that because such and such a Samnite town community had received certain rights under its treaty with Rome, this or that other Samnite town should receive the same. She had in former days differentiated the rights granted to the towns of the Latin League when that league was dissolved simply because she wanted to differentiate between those which had behaved badly and those which had behaved fairly well. Experience had shown that this policy did not merely fulfil its original object, to encourage fidelity to Roman interests, but also created a division of interest between those with greater and those with lesser rights such as rendered combination against Rome difficult. The division of interests by differentiation of rights became a settled policy of Rome to which she may be said to have adhered till the end of the second century A.D., though it had lost much of its significance before that time came.

In the present settlement of Italy all the many communities with which Rome made treaty arrangements were styled " allies " (socii) of the Roman people. But the allies were in two grades, the Latin allies, and the rest. Latin rights were originally granted to many of the towns of the Latin League at the time when the league was broken up. They were almost equivalent to the rights of the full Roman citizen, except that the Latin had no vote in the Roman Assembly. But things had changed greatly since these rights were first granted. Circumstances had made it advisable to incorporate the inhabitants of the towns to which they were originally given in the body of Roman citizens. Practically the only towns in Italy now possessed of these rights were the so-called Latin colonies which had been founded for the purpose of holding down conquered territories, and had been peopled by Romans. These communities had the right of local government within their own territory, but in all external relations were under the control of Rome. Their citizens were not Roman citizens because they had not got the vote ; and a Roman citizen who transferred his domicile to one of these towns lost his Roman citizenship and acquired Latin rights, though, vice versa, a citizen of one of these Latin towns who migrated to Rome became *ipso facto* eligible for Roman citizenship, provided he left behind him sons and property in his former home.

With regard to the non-Latin socii Rome's policy was to sunder as far as possible all ties between them, making their dependence on Rome their one external bond. Thus in most cases no rights of trade or intermarriage were allowed between inhabitants of different communities, since such relations would be sure to create between them ties which might have resulted in a combination of sentiment dangerous to Rome. Also, whereas the rights of the Latin towns were the same in all cases, the rights granted to the non-Latin or ordinary socii varied, there being no common or stereotyped form of grant running through all the many treaties which Rome made with these communities, except that each community was free in respect to the local government of its own town and district, or, in mid-Italy, in respect to its own tribal territory. The differentiation of rights was determined on one of two grounds, former services or hostility to Rome, and civilisation; but with respect to the former it is necessary, in view of what took place in Italy after the Second Punic War, to emphasise the fact that at this time no community in Italy, however bad its relations with Rome might have been in the past, was deprived of its local autonomy, or compelled to receive a Roman officer as superintendent of its affairs; and with respect to the latter, the two extremes of civilisation in Italy, at this time represented by the Greek cities on the one hand and the comparatively backward communities of Bruttium on the other, were distinguished by the former being the most favoured, and the latter the least favoured with respect to the rights conceded to them. In between the two extremes were communities with various gradations of local privileges, graded for the most part on the test of civilisation.

The principle of grading the rights of subject communities by the test of civilisation is one of the most marked and most admirable features of the Roman system of government both during the Republic and during the Principate. It is true that in the latest ages of the Republic the policy became obscured by the jealousy with which the grant of citizenship came to be guarded; but under the Principate it may be said to be the most striking and dominant feature in the general internal policy of the Empire.

The use of either the term federation or confederacy with regard to the political position thus established in Italy is not really justifiable because no state stood on terms of equality with Rome, and no direct bond of union existed between the states. They were merely individual allies of a Rome which determined at her own discretion their mutual relations to one another, and controlled absolutely their relations with the world outside Italy.

But Roman power and control did not rest merely on her political relations with the other states. She herself was by far the strongest state in the peninsula, for her own territory amounted to about one-third of its area, extending down the west coast from Caere to the Bay of Naples, and thence inland to the line of the Apennines, and, in places, beyond that. Apart from this she held outlying regions such as the land of the Senones on the north-east, and various other patches of territory confiscated from their former owners and settled by Roman citizens.

The communities outside Rome inhabited by Roman citizens were not all of the same type. The Roman colonies, that is to say the military foundations, and the non-Roman towns to which citizenship had been granted (municipia civium Romanorum) had the full franchise. Other non-Roman towns had received Roman citizenship without the right of voting in the comitia (civitates sine suffragio). Lower on the scale of importance came settlements of citizens too small to be given municipal constitutions, the " fora " and " conciliabula civium Romanorum."

The Roman town communities enjoyed, like those of the allies, full rights of local administration under constitutions having a certain similarity to that of Rome, but determined and capable of modification by the central government. Non-Roman towns which had been given Roman rights were naturally unacquainted with Roman law ; so præfects were sent from Rome to superintend and administer justice in these outlying communities of Roman citizens. Præfects of a different kind were placed in charge of those districts in which the settlements of Roman citizens were too small to form municipalities.[1]

The military force at the disposal of Rome was very large, for all the allies had to furnish to the Roman army contingents commanded by native officers but under the orders of the Roman general.

THE ROMAN ARMY

The Roman army as originally constituted was of the type customary in the city state, a force in which every able-

[1] I append for clearness' sake a list of the grades of communities of Italy with the chief elements in their political constitutions :

(1) Coloniæ Civium Romanorum : full Roman citizenship : local autonomy : inhabitants were Roman citizens at the time they were founded.

(2) Municipia Civium Romanorum : towns to whose population, not originally Roman, the full franchise had been granted : local autonomy ; but justice administered by a præfect sent from Rome.

(3) Fora or Conciliabula Civium Romanorum : villages in rural districts inhabited by Roman citizens : full franchise : some local autonomy ; but a præfect sent from Rome at the head of the administration.

(4) Municipia sine Suffragio : towns to the population of which the citizenship of Rome had been given without the right of voting : local autonomy, but præfect from Rome for judicial purposes.

(5) Coloniæ Latinæ : had Latin rights, which implied full civil liberty : inhabitants could get the Roman citizenship by transferring their domicile to Rome.

(6) Civitates Sociorum : local autonomy in varying degrees.

bodied citizen who had reached manhood was liable for service. The pay was small, little more than equivalent to an allowance. So long as warfare was confined to the brief campaigns by which differences with other small states could be settled, the system was possible, inasmuch as the citizen was not withdrawn from his civilian business in life for such a period as to impair his personal interests. But the larger scale on which Rome had of late years waged war had necessitated the retention of citizens in the ranks for more than one campaign, so that it had been necessary to make the pay for service more substantial.[1] In tactics the close order of the old phalanx had been given up, probably because it was not adapted to warfare in the mountain districts of Italy, and a more open order had been introduced which necessitated more prolonged military training. The general tendency of these modifications had been to weaken the identity between the soldier and the citizen; but it was left to the army reforms of Marius, more than a century and a half later, to destroy it, with fatal results to the Republic.

THE PROCONSULSHIP

The prolonged nature of the campaigning brought into being a new method of dealing with the consulship. It was obviously most undesirable to withdraw a consul from the command of an army if his annual tenure of office came to an end in the middle of a campaign; and so resort was had to the device of prolonging his command (prorogatio imperii) and of conceiving him as acting on behalf of the consuls of the year (pro consule). This device, first employed in 327, became quite common after that date. Applied later to the commands of governors in the provinces, it was the origin of that proconsular power which proved in the end too strong for the central republican government at Rome, and made the foundation of the Principate not merely possible but almost inevitable.

With the conquest of Italy Rome had attained to the limits of those imperial ambitions which circumstances had forced upon her. But the enterprise of Pyrrhus had shown her that Italy had to be defended against other people who had imperial ambitions of a less involuntary character. Had the Roman dominion in Italy been without a rival in the western Mediterranean it might have gone on for at least several centuries as a

[1] Some modern authorities assume that the system of payment for service was introduced at this time. It seems to me, however, that the ancient evidence implies that the system was much older than this, though possibly it may have been up to this time little more than an allowance for expenses.

self-centred empire with no desire to interfere with others, and too strong for others to wish to interfere with it.

AGRICULTURE AND TRADE

In many histories of Rome that state is represented as a power which had developed even before this time trade interests which must, had they existed, have spread westwards, since the west side of the Apennines is the fertile region of the peninsula, while the east coast is not merely deficient in harbours, but faces the blank wall of the Dinaric Alps on the opposite side of the Adriatic.[1] The tendency has been to read back the keenness which the Roman showed in trade after the development of the empire, and especially after the acquisition of the eastern provinces, into that period at which Rome's dominions were confined to Italy. It is doubtful whether,—it might almost be said that it is improbable that,—Italy itself had much to export, or any large means of purchasing imports. The decline of the Greek towns with the exception of Tarentum was doubtless partly due to political causes ; but had they continued to play the same relative part in the trade and manufactures of the Mediterranean as in former days they must have maintained their wealth if not their political vigour. To the Greek world Italy had been important as a source of the supply of corn. But for more than half a century the supplies of Egypt had, owing to the Macedonian conquest, been far more available to the Greek than when that land had been under Persian rule ; and, apart from that, the immense scale of the Greek emigration to Asia Minor and other parts of Alexander's empire must have largely reduced the population of Greece and its dependence on foreign supplies. Within the same period another factor had come into the trade world, the effect of which must have been great though not now traceable in any detail,—the practical establishment of a gold standard in the lands east of the Adriatic owing to the enormous accumulations of that precious metal discovered at Susa and Persepolis, and let loose on a world which had up to that time known a silver standard only. The Greek cities of Italy, which had not the gold wherewith to meet the change of standard, must have been placed at a great disadvantage with their fellow-countrymen in the East who now belonged to a region where gold had largely superseded silver as the basis of finance.

Among the native Italian peoples trade in the ordinary sense

[1] This view was contested by Professor Rostovtzeff in lectures delivered at Oxford some years ago. I had formed the same view before hearing his lectures ; but they dissipated any vestige of doubt I may have retained on the question.

of the term had never flourished hitherto, because the average Italian farmer had but little surplus stock to sell when he had lived off the produce of his land. The idea that a century after this time he was hard hit by the import of foreign corn from Sicily and elsewhere is an exploded one. His bad economical position in that age and his threatened disappearance were due to the devastations of the Second Punic War and the encroachment of the capitalist. And about this time, in the sixties of the third century before Christ, the whole of Italy must have been feeling acutely the effects of the long wars in which Rome had won her dominion over the peninsula. But the Italian as well as the Roman ideal of life was to make a living off the land by growing what was needed for food and clothing; and, for the rest, if there were a surplus, spending it on cheap articles which added somewhat to the comfort of life. After all this is exactly the self-centred, self-sufficing form of life which satisfied the English cultivator for nearly a thousand years.

ROME AND CARTHAGE

The great struggle between Rome and Carthage was not due to the clash of trade interests in the western Mediterranean, for, as far as Rome was concerned, there were no such interests to clash, which is shown by the fact that the relations between the two powers had been quite friendly up to the time when a certain event took place which had nothing to do with trade. Had no such thing occurred there was no reason why Rome and Carthage should not for centuries have gone their own ways side by side in the Mediterranean world.

Rome's settlement of Italy can hardly have been complete when in 265 certain Campanian mercenaries who had seized Messana, finding themselves hard pressed by Hiero of Syracuse, the champion of Greek interests in Sicily, appealed for aid to Carthage. Rome's absolute indifference to anything outside Italy which could not affect affairs in Italy itself is shown by the fact that she had never displayed any disposition to covet the rich lands which Hiero ruled. She treated Syracuse as a weak, harmless neighbour, a useful buffer state between her and the possessions of Carthage in west Sicily. Carthage also ruled Sardinia; and, had the interests of Rome and Carthage clashed before this time, Rome might have regarded with uneasiness a position which gave Carthage two convenient bases for a naval attack on Italy. But interests had not clashed; and so far Carthage had shown every disposition to let the Italians fight out their own internal destiny. Nevertheless Carthage in western Sicily was one thing; and the prospect of Carthage in eastern Sicily, separated from Italy at the Sicilian Strait by only two miles of sea, was another. Pyrrhus had made Rome nervous with regard to possible interference in Italy from outside ; and, though Carthage, when she unfortunately accepted the request for aid sent by those mercenaries at Messana, and thus involved herself in a war with Hiero, may have had no ambition other than her ancient desire to get complete control of the island, yet, apart from the fact that Rome could not regard with indifference the presence of a great naval power within two miles of the Italian coast, the action of Carthage in taking up war with Hiero, an ally though not a dependant of Rome, was certain to be interpreted at Rome as a direct threat to her position in Italy.

When the Carthaginians threw a garrison into Messana Rome in 264 sent an army across the straits and drove the Carthaginian garrison out. Hiero, evidently thinking that Rome was going to keep Messana for herself, suddenly sided with Carthage ; but he got a rap over the knuckles which made him see the error of his ways, and in the next year 263 became, what he was to remain, the faithful ally of Rome.

Thus was lighted one of the greatest conflagrations in history.

Carthage, the great power with which Rome now for the first time came into conflict, had begun life centuries before as a trading settlement of the Phœnicians, a small town whose territory comprised little more than the sites of its houses, a community existing on sufferance at the will of the surrounding native population. It grew and grew as time went on ; and at some date not determinable became independent of its mother city in Phœnicia. It is plain from her co-operation in the attack of Persia on the Greek world in 480 that, if at that time independent, she was anxious to promote the interests of the mother-country by compliance with the desires of its Persian masters. The conquest of Tyre by Alexander the Great drove many Tyrians to the old colony, so that from that time forward Carthage was the centre of the Phœnician branch of the Semitic race.

But several centuries before this time political expansion had been more or less forced on her by the advance westward of those Greek trade rivals who showed every intention of encroaching on that sphere of trade influence in the western Mediterranean which Carthage and the cities of Phœnicia regarded as their own, so that perhaps the assistance given to Persia in 480 may be attributed to motives less altruistic than those above suggested. By the time of the beginning of the third century B.C. Carthage had gradually extended her dominions to include all Africa now known as Tripoli, Tunis, Algeria, and Morocco, the west part of Sicily, the whole of Sardinia and Corsica, together with numerous settlements on the south and east coasts of Spain, and, in what is now Andalusia, considerable territory in the hinterland. In military power the state was formidable, having at its command supplies of men from among the warlike races of north Africa and Spain. On the sea there was no state or combination of states which could vie with it.

But the Phœnician Semite, like the Assyrian Semite before him, had but one idea of the government of an empire, the reduction of the subject peoples either actually or virtually to the position of slaves, forced either to labour for their masters or to purchase a partial liberty by heavy tribute. Carthage showed none of the consideration which Rome had shown to the people she brought under her sway ; and hence she could not, when disaster came, tide it over, as did Rome, by the attachment of her allies, for her subjects had more to gain by her failure than by her success. This was one of the main causes of her defeat in the Second Punic War.

The constitution was of a curious kind, composed of oligarchies within oligarchies, of which the smallest central body held the greatest power. The two chiefs of the state, the suffetes, were little more than figure-heads. There was a Senate, an elected body ; than a smaller body which exercised the administrative powers of the state ; then a still smaller body composed of a very few members who were the real controllers of the state, for with them rested a judicial power which made them masters of even the most exalted officials.

Enlightened moralists of liberal views have in modern times ascribed the ultimate failure of Carthage against Rome to a fate which is supposed to decree that a race with free institutions shall triumph over one with institutions less free. Fate does not always act in that way. In an international struggle a bad constitution well worked is apt to triumph over a good one badly worked ; and, if the results of the Punic Wars are to be ascribed in any way to the respective political circumstances of the two antagonists, they are due to the comparative cleanness of government in Rome at this time relative to the corruption and jealousy which prevailed in government circles at Carthage. The leading men of the Italian state had been brought up under an age-old tradition which forbade the exaltation of the individual, for Rome was till the last century of the Republic remarkable for her repression of individualism in public life ; while in the African state leading families and leading men were ever engaged in a jealous rivalry for the highest place and the greatest power. Hence the national hero of the hour had ever more enemies than friends among his fellow-countrymen, so that a national failure was preferred to the personal success of a rival. That was why Hannibal was never properly supported in Italy. That was

THE THIRD CENTURY, 300-200 B.C.

why the Second Punic War was really a war between Rome and the great Carthaginian family of Barca rather than between Rome and Carthage.

FIRST PUNIC WAR

At the beginning of the First Punic War Rome was faced by the difficulty of fighting a power of great naval strength which could only be assailed by sea. The sea was an element on which the Roman had no experience because he had not sought any. But he now had subjects, the Greek cities of Italy, and an ally, Syracuse, all of whom were from several centuries of past experience skilled in the construction and management of ships, so that he had plenty of naval architects and builders at his disposal and could no doubt raise crews both from the Greek cities of Italy and Sicily, and from the native fisher population of the Italian coast. The practical commonsense of the Roman taught him that such a personnel hurriedly got together could not vie in skill with Carthaginian crews which had had years of training, and inherited a long experience in the manœuvring of fighting vessels ; so he determined to place his trust in boarding tactics, and to let the enemy do his best or worst in the manœuvres of ramming and so forth. He is credited with having invented the " corvus," a gangway slung at the side of a vessel which could be let down on to the deck of an enemy's ship, and would hold that ship by spikes which pierced the deck of the vessel on which it descended. Without such a device boarding tactics would have been hardly practicable against a fleet with superior manœuvring powers whose ships could inflict fatal damage without exposing themselves to assault by the marines of the vessel they attacked. But with the aid of the corvus the Roman legionaries on the fleet could capture by assault vessels which, relying on manœuvring power, would have their complement of marines reduced with a view to lightening them for the purpose of rapid evolutions.[1]

Many were the variations of success and failure which Rome experienced in this, one of the fiercest wars she ever fought, the failures being due to inferior experience or bad judgment, the successes to a fierce pertinacity which won through at the last moment. Both sides suffered terrible losses in men and material,

---

[1] Much has been written in praise of the Roman for having created a fleet in so brief an emergency. In view of the fact that he had at his disposal some of the best advice and practical skill in naval matters available in the world of that day, this praise has always seemed to me to be rather overdone. He is far more to be praised for the capacity which he showed in devising the one means by which he could use the fleet in such a way as to counterbalance the superiority of the enemy's experience.

for disaster, when it did come to either, came in a wholesale form. As far as land fighting was concerned the war was fought out in Sicily and Africa, while the battles by sea took place off various parts of the Sicilian shore. In 262 Rome captured Agrigentum. In 261 she built her first fleet of 100 quinqueremes and 20 triremes, with which in the next year she defeated the Carthaginians off Mylæ.

Then came four years of indecisive warfare, whereof the Romans became so wearied that in 256 they attacked the Carthaginians at home in Africa, an attack which might have brought the war and Carthage to an end, had not the Romans made the grievous error of withdrawing one of the consuls and half the army before success was completely attained, leaving the other, the famous Regulus, to complete what seemed an easy task. By a supreme and seemingly final effort Carthage destroyed Regulus' army as an army ; and the escape of the few survivors on board a rescuing Roman fleet was marked by a still greater disaster, the loss in a storm of 284 out of the 364 vessels.

In 254 the Romans captured Panormus in Sicily ; but the fleet which captured the place was totally destroyed in a storm the next year. It looks as if the scratch crews of Rome were not equal to the difficult task of managing big vessels in bad weather. In 249 the Roman fleet was badly defeated off Drepana. In the next few years the Romans were trying to force the Carthaginians out of Sicily, and Hamilcar Barca was retaliating by ravaging the Italian coasts with his fleet. Things were looking very black for Rome. She had lost not merely a fleet but a navy ; and there was no public money wherewith to build another. But the private contributions of citizens overcame the financial difficulty, and in 242 a fleet of 200 great ships started to dispute with Carthage the command of the sea. With it Catulus won the great victory of the Ægates Islands off Sicily, and Carthaginian resistance suddenly collapsed. Carthage agreed to surrender those Sicilian possessions to which she had clung for centuries and to pay a large war indemnity.

Thus ended the first round of the fight between Rome and Carthage. Neither side had received a knock-out blow, so that it was certain that there would be a second round. Rome was thoroughly alarmed for the safety of Italy, and Carthage thoroughly dissatisfied with the results of the naval warfare and the loss of territory on which she set special value. Thus both went to work to repair defects of inexperience, and to take other measures of precaution in view of the renewal of the struggle.

The war had shown Rome that Italy could not be safe so long as Carthage had naval bases in convenient striking distance of its coast in Sardinia and in Corsica. Of Sicily she had acquired the

Carthaginian portion by the treaty at the end of the war in 241 ; and three years later, in 238, on pretext of an invitation from the islands themselves, she annexed Sardinia and Corsica despite the wrath of Carthage expressed in the language of one who is at the moment too timid, because too unprepared, to act.

Thus Rome between 241 and 238 embarked on the acquisition of an overseas empire which she had no desire to acquire and no wish to govern, an attitude which the government of Rome maintained to the end of the Republic, despite the fact that the mass of the Roman people, after the acquisition of the eastern provinces in the next century, became, from personal experience of the gains which the individual Roman citizen might draw from the provincial empire, materially if not sentimentally imperialist. But there were no profits either for the government or for the individual to be got from those luckless islands Corsica and Sardinia ; and western Sicily was not likely to pay for itself so long as it had to be garrisoned against Carthage.

As to the government of the new territories all that is known is that in the first instance one of the prætors or quæstors was put in charge of Sicily ; and in 238 two new prætors were created to rule Sicily on the one hand and Corsica and Sardinia on the other as their " provinciæ " (departments of administration). Thus the term " provincia " came to acquire a territorial significance. Whether there was any further organisation of the government is not known. If there was, it may be regarded as certain that, in accordance with the later and invariable policy of Rome, it was organised on the basis of the existing native institutions. The Roman government of the Republic did not want to govern absolutely or directly areas which it would rather not have governed at all.

Roman Imperialism

Those who read the long-drawn tale of Roman warfare without looking to the causes of the wars which Rome waged almost continuously for more than three centuries are apt to rush to the conclusion that the Romans were an aggressive race which, having carried the art of war to a high efficiency, determined to use its skill to its own advantage by subduing every people and every land within its reach from which some gain might be drawn. Until Cæsar mainly from motives of private ambition and interest undertook the conquest of Gaul, Rome never waged a single war save on provocation from outside which neither Rome nor any other state which was ready to fight for its existing interests could overlook. Under the Republic she never tried to camouflage the greed for rule by fictitious grievances : she had no reason for so doing, for she had no such greed.

The "Roman peace," which became a watchword for Rome herself, and a byword to all those who disturbed it, was a genuine expression of the feeling of a people which desired above all to live at peace. If the hill tribes of middle Italy would have left her alone in the Campagna; if the Samnites had not threatened her position in middle Italy; if Carthage, and, later, Macedon, had not threatened her position in the whole peninsula; if the Seleucid kingdom had not interfered with her interests in the Balkan peninsula and Greece, Rome would never have advanced step by step to the conquest of the Mediterranean region. The dangerous laxity of the ties which bound her empire together under the Republic, the incompleteness of her conquests, the vagueness of her frontiers—it might almost be said the non-existence of them—the imperfectness of the organisation of territories brought under her rule, and above all the reluctance the government of the Republic showed to bring new lands under the rule of Rome, preferring to leave them, if possible, in the position of client states—all of these things are irreconcilable with the true imperialistic spirit, and are rather the characteristics of those who grudge the trouble of managing property which they have not desired to acquire.

The events of the year 225 illustrate in a very remarkable way how Rome might be forced to do that which she would certainly have done long before had the imperialist spirit been in her. She had carried her conquest of Italy to the Apennines years before this time. North of them lay the basin of the Padus, a region richer than all the rest of Italy put together, the very land to attract a race of born cultivators like the Romans had they desired to better their position at the expense of others. They were however quite ready to live on terms of peace with those Celts who inhabited it, and to leave them in enjoyment of their fertile home. But that volatile, restless race has ever preferred the discomforts of violence to the comforts of peace; and so in 225 the Celtic tribes of the Boii and the Insubres descended from their rich lands in the north to raid the poorer regions of peninsular Italy. This showed Rome that there could be no peace for her or her possessions so long as these Celts were left to raid at their will. By 222 she had brought them into submission as subjects, not allies, and secured their land by colonies at Placentia, Cremona, and Mutina, and by carrying the Via Flaminia as far north as Ariminum.

ROME AND GREECE

From across the Adriatic Illyrian pirates had been troubling the Italian coast, and Rome had to send an expedition to suppress them, of which the chief importance is that it brought Rome

The Second Punic War

In the twenty odd years which had elapsed since the close of the First Punic War Carthage, in accordance with a policy devised by a man of an extraordinarily able family, that of Barca, had sought not merely to compensate herself for the losses in Sicily, Corsica, and Sardinia by acquisitions in Spain, but also to provide thereby a base of operations for an attack by land on the position of Rome in Italy. On the sea the Carthaginians had had all their calculations upset by the unexpected efficiency Rome had developed in naval affairs. Thus any attempt to invade Italy by sea would have involved enormous risk of disaster.

What the position of Carthage was in Spain at the time that the First Punic War ended it is, in the absence of records, impossible to say; but probably that part of the peninsula now known as Andalusia had been included in her dominions for a long time past. In this twenty years Hamilcar Barca, his kinsman Hasdrubal, and his son Hannibal had carried the Carthaginian dominion up the east coast as far as the Ebro (Iberus). Rome had watched these proceedings with interest and anxiety. In 226 she had claimed Spain north of the Ebro as her own sphere of influence, and had stipulated that Saguntum should be left as an independent buffer state between the territorial interests of Rome and the territorial possessions of Carthage.

But Hannibal had not any intention of allowing an arrangement which had been forced on Carthage to interfere with his plans. He could not advance on Italy and leave Saguntum, which was rendered friendly to Rome by danger from Carthage, on his line of communications.[1] So in 219 he attacked and took that town. This meant war; and Hannibal knew it and desired it. Yet even now Rome never imagined that Carthage, though represented by Hannibal, would attempt the apparently impos-

---

[1] That is the reason usually given for Hannibal's attack. My own impression is that he was prepared, when once he had entered Italy, to cut his connection with Spain, and to rely for supplies on Italy itself, especially on the Celtic region of the north where, in view of its recent conquest by Rome, he could rely on sympathy and support. If Rome fell to a direct attack, then his end was accomplished. If it did not, he could in south Italy look for supplies of men and material from Carthage, for even if the Roman fleet maintained a command of the sea, yet no fleet of that age could keep the sea in such a way as to prevent blockade running all along the stretch of the south and south-east coasts of Italy.

sible task of invading Italy from the north; and so she prepared to fight Hannibal in Spain and to attack Carthage in Africa. This mistake gave Hannibal time to act. He left New Carthage early in 218, and was already at the Rhône when Scipio with the Roman army destined for Spain reached Massilia. A hurried attempt of the Romans to bar his passage of the great river failed, so that Hannibal arrived in north Italy by crossing the Alps under Mont Genèvre,[1] without having met with any opposition worth speaking of. The army with which Hannibal entered Italy consisted of only 26,000 men, which seems a ridiculously small force wherewith to attack a state which had at its disposal a potential force nearly thirty times as large as this. He was evidently under the impression that the allies of Rome would welcome deliverance from Rome's dominion, so that, if he obtained some preliminary success, they would join him in large numbers. But the yoke of Rome had not been heavy; and her domination in the peninsula had given Italy a peace and happiness too recent in origin for the distressful period of internecine quarrels which had preceded it to have passed from the memory of men. During the many years of the presence of Hannibal's army in Italy Rome's allies in the north and middle of the peninsula remained faithful to her, and even in the south those who eventually sided with Hannibal only did so because Rome could not protect them, so that their choice lay between death and destruction on the one hand, and submission to the Carthaginian on the other. Had Rome's policy in Italy been one begotten of domineering imperialism, her Italian empire must have perished within a century of its foundation.

Rome's miscalculation of the strategy which would be followed in the war rendered her unprepared to meet Hannibal north of the Apennines with aught but hasty preparations. Defeated in an engagement on the Ticinus, she tried in a battle

[1] I have simply adopted, on grounds which I have not room to state what seems to me to be the most probable theory as to the place at which Hannibal crossed the Alps. It is the one most supported by the ancient evidence. It is also on purely topographical grounds the route he would be likely to take. The coast route he would avoid as it would involve the passage through Massiliot territory. The native Gauls further inland were likely to be more friendly to one who was on his way to attack the power which had recently subjugated their kinsmen in the Padus basin. Also it is certain that Hannibal would adopt a frequented route, and, if possible, the most easy and the most direct. That the Mont Genèvre route was convenient is shown by its use by Pompeius on his march to Spain in 77 B.C. It was sufficiently far north to avoid Massiliot territory; and was infinitely more direct than the passes of the Great and Little St. Bernard. Besides, had he used either of them, he would have entered Italy through the lands of the Salassi, and not through those of the Taurini, as he is expressly said to have done.

on the Trebbia to save the all-important position at Placentia,[1] and there suffered a severe defeat.[2]

From the Trebbia the natural route southwards is by Ariminum (Rimini). But Hannibal took the unexpected course of striking south across the Apennines into the basin of the Arnus (Arno). He had been reinforced by Celtic contingents, for his success had dissolved any hesitation which the Celtic tribes had felt about following their own inclination to take sides against Rome. The horrors of the passage of the Apennines and marshes as described by Roman authors may be discounted by the tendency ever shown by the vanquished to seek comfort in the imaginary sufferings of the victor.

In April 217 Hannibal reached Lake Trasimene pursued by the Roman army under Flaminius, for whom he there set a trap into which that rash commander walked, to the utter destruction of himself and his army.[3]

From Trasimene Hannibal marched to northern Apulia, to the neighbourhood of the modern Foggia, a region which offered him three advantages, horses for his Numidian cavalry, the possibility of communication with Carthage, and the further possibility of the revolt of the southern Italians against Rome. The results of the rashness of Flaminius had been such that Rome had entrusted the command of her army to the cautious Fabius, who annoyed and harassed Hannibal by keeping to the higher ground and refusing to give battle in the plain, while making it ever more difficult for him to gather supplies from the country owing to his bands of foragers being cut off in their raiding expeditions, But the Romans got tired of this waiting game which seemed to lead to no definite results. So in 216 they despatched a large

---

[1] Placentia (Piacenza) was the greatest strategic position in Italy. It was the lowest point on the Padus where the river could be conveniently crossed, for, apart from the great size and violent current of the stream itself, its banks from Placentia to the sea were and are bordered by extensive marshes. From Placentia westwards the Apennines, in this part a somewhat formidable range, protect the peninsula from the north, and at Placentia itself approach within a few miles of the Padus.

[2] I have examined the Trebbia region. It may be due to dullness of perception on my part; but I cannot understand the arguments of those critics who allege serious discrepancies between the accounts of Polybius and Livy. If, as seems to me to be certainly the case, the battle was fought a few miles east of the river, and a few miles S.S.W. of Piacenza, then the accounts of both authors are comprehensible and reconcilable.

[3] There has been much controversy as to whether the battle was fought on the north or on the east side of the lake. My own impression is that it took place in the wide valley running north from the lake on the west side of the modern village of Tuoro. Various scholars have argued for the eastern site.

force under the consuls Æmilius Paulus and Terentius Varro to crush the army of Hannibal. They made the attempt at Cannæ in 216 with the result that their army was annihilated.

The immediate effects of Cannæ were appalling to Rome, and discreditable to the Carthaginian government. Every one, excepting the infatuated opponents of the Barca family at Carthage, was ready to help Hannibal; but, before looking forward, it is necessary to look backward in order to understand why Roman troops should have experienced three such defeats as the Trebbia, Trasimene, and Cannæ.

Roman and Carthaginian Troops

With the exception of the campaign against Pyrrhus, and the fighting with the Celts in which Rome had suffered great defeats by the Epirote army and the disaster on the Allia, the Roman army had been matched against Italians whose mode of warfare was not unlike its own. In Rome's early warfare in Italy she had relied on the serried ranks of the phalanx, in which the soldiers never learned the art of individual fighting. More recently she had adopted a somewhat more open order, in which the mass units were smaller, and individual initiative in weapon tactics was more demanded. But even in the Roman army after the new model the amount of individual initiative was small; and in the now smaller unit of the maniple the maintenance of close order was still regarded as of paramount importance, a fashion in tactics which did not encourage individual skill in the use of weapons, though it tended to render the individual soldier something more than a mere component of a large mass. But the experience of warfare of all ages has shown that an army which has been trained in such a way that the men composing it can if occasion arise use their weapons with skill in single combat is, unless its armament is markedly inferior to that of its adversary, an infinitely better fighting machine than the army composed of soldiers trained to look for defence in the maintenance of close order with the men to the right and the left of them. Hannibal led an army drawn from those fighting races of the West whose very barbarism had accustomed them to live with weapons in their hands; who were not accustomed to turn the sword into the ploughshare or vice versa, or to be called on to face the perils of war only when their fellow-countrymen were called on to do the same. The close formation which the Romans favoured was all very well when things went well; but, if once the ranks were pierced, the soldiers accustomed to fight in it were all but helpless against troops trained by experience or by art in the devices and tricks of single combat. For an army trained to close formation defeat spelt disaster. It broke because it could not bend. If the history of Roman warfare during the days of the Republic up to the time of Marius be surveyed, one of the most striking features of it is that with a Roman army defeat almost invariably meant disaster. The Second Punic War taught a lesson which the Romans never learned till a hundred years later, that the Roman military machine was at this time unfitted to cope with warfare as practised by the fierce races of the western Mediterranean region, the Gaul, the Spaniard, and the Numidian. Even under their own barbarian leaders they were terribly formidable. Under a Hannibal they were deadly opponents. It was the fact that the Romans came victorious out of the Second Punic War which blinded them to the lessons which the war had taught. For the next half-century Rome was engaged against eastern enemies of races of inferior virility whose whole military tradition was founded on the close order of the Greek phalanx, a formation to which the tactics of the Roman legion were superior. But in the latter half of the second century before Christ further experience against the races of the West taught Roman soldiers of experience like Marius and Rutilius Rufus that drastic military reforms were necessary, and an ever-growing experience of disaster forced the Roman government into a reluctant and silent acquiescence in the reforms.

THE WAR AFTER CANNÆ

South Italy with the exception of the Latin colonies and Greek towns came over to Hannibal after Cannæ. Philip of Macedon made an alliance with him in 215 which was to have serious consequences in future in that it impressed on Rome the lesson which the invasion of Pyrrhus had taught her, that Italy's safety might be threatened from the Balkan Peninsula. In 214 Syracuse, no longer ruled by Hiero, revolted; and in 212 the Greek cities of Italy were lost to Rome. But that grim persistence of character which had been formed during several centuries of struggle in Italy now showed itself in Rome's refusal, despite the apparently desperate nature of the situation, to make any disadvantageous compromise. But the most determined persistence would not have mended the situation had not those who managed affairs at Rome shown a remarkable capacity in dealing with it. By 212 Rome must have known that counsels at Carthage were disastrously divided: that there were leading men there who would have welcomed more the failure than the success of Hannibal in Italy because they feared more the possible domination of the Barca family at Carthage than any disaster which might overtake what was to a great extent a private venture of that family in Italy. At Carthage the influence of the Barcas had declined since the war began ; and its opponents were not in any way minded to restore it by helping Hannibal to final success. So he was left in the air as it were in South Italy, where the position became one of stalemate, a general invincible against the resources which Rome had at her disposal, and a Rome invincible against the resources of the general.

Philip of Macedon found that designs on Italy meant trouble nearer home. Rome forced him to give up the siege of the allied city of Apollonia ; and the friendly relations established between Rome and Greece at the time of the recent chastisement of the Illyrian pirates led the states of that country in 211 to welcome an excuse for harassing that state which had attacked their independence a century before. So Macedon passed out of the picture as far as the war in Italy was concerned.

In 212 Syracuse was recaptured. Meanwhile Hannibal's resources were weakening ; for he could do nothing, and the government at home would do nothing, to repair the ravages of inexorable time. Rome began to take the offensive in the form of an attempt to recover Capua and Campania. Hannibal tried to relieve the town, but found himself too weak for the task, so sought to create a diversion and impression by marching silently up to the very walls of Rome. The diversion did not come about ; and any impression that was made was made on his own mind,—a disspiriting one. He realised that he could not capture Rome.

So Capua fell to Rome in 211 ; and Hannibal, now deprived of his main source of supplies, the rich Campanian plain, was compelled to retire to the south. Then another period of stalemate supervened until in 208 Rome got from Massilia the alarming news that Hasdrubal, the brother of Hannibal, though defeated by a Roman army in Spain, was on his way to help Hannibal in Italy. Every one at Rome knew that Hasdrubal must at all costs be prevented from joining Hannibal ; so great was the rejoicing when the consul Claudius defeated and slew him on the river Metaurus in 207. After that Italy was safe, though for four years more Hannibal maintained his position in Bruttium.

The recent years of warfare from 211 to 206 had been made remarkable by the successes of the young Publius Scipio in Spain. It is probable that, in the then state of affairs in Italy, Carthage but little expected an attack in that quarter, apart from the fact that the Barca family had made Spain a sort of base, for their family influence would not tend to make their obstinate political opponents peculiarly solicitous for its welfare. By 206 Scipio had driven the Carthaginians clean out of the peninsula ; and, as Sicily was now secure, nothing remained but to finish the war as speedily and decisively as possible, for Hannibal in

Bruttium was impotent outside the small area of territory which he held. Scipio thought he could be ignored, an opinion which eventually prevailed, though some authorities did not agree with it. So in 206 Scipio was given the province of Sicily with the express intention that he should use it as a base of operations against the African dominions of Carthage. In 204 he crossed to Africa. Twice in 203 he defeated the Carthaginians; but they would not give way till in 202 he defeated Hannibal, who had been recalled from Italy, at Zama. The Carthaginian army at Zama must have been of a very different quality to the armies which Hannibal had hitherto led. Save for the remnants of his veteran force which had crossed over from Italy with him, there can have been few if any of those Spanish or Numidian troops which had been such a splendid element in the armies of Carthage, for Spain had been lost, and Numidia under the leadership of its prince Massinissa had gone over to the Roman side when Scipio landed in Africa.

The Peace left Carthage her personal possessions in Africa, and no more, for Numidia became a Roman sphere of influence. Rome took over the burden of governing Spain as a province, and a sore burden it proved at times during the Republic, though it was one of the most flourishing provinces under the Empire. But the exploits of Hannibal and Hasdrubal had shown that it could be used as a base of attack on Italy; so Rome dare not leave it as a land open to the possible revival of Carthaginian influence. If ever a country lost a war by internal dissension, it was Carthage in this war. Had Hannibal been supported just before or just after Cannæ, he must have broken down the resistance of Rome in Italy. That such support could have been sent is shown by his withdrawal from Italy in the last years of the war. But the discussion of the might-have-beens of history is unprofitable, and the conclusions are inevitably unconvincing. Still the prevalence of a great Semitic state in the western Mediterranean must have greatly modified the subsequent history of western Europe.

Of Hannibal it is unnecessary to speak at length. On solid and unassailable grounds he has been judged to have been one of the greatest military geniuses in history. His very exploits show that, as a strategist, as a tactician, and as a trainer of men, he has only been rivalled by Alexander the Great, Julius Cæsar, and Napoleon.[1]

[1] It is difficult to compare with them the great man whom the present world has learned to know, Marshal Foch, for the conditions under which they waged war were so different. But perhaps the considered judgment of the future will confirm the opinion which some hold now, that that great living soldier is worthy of a place with them in that temple of fame where the gods are not mere idols.

Hellenic Civilisation in Italy

It is in this century that Hellenic civilisation began to exert a marked influence on that ruder Italian civilisation which had hitherto prevailed in Rome and middle Italy, though the southern peoples of the peninsula had known, appreciated, and used the material products of Greek culture for centuries past, and had been at any rate superficially infected with some of its spiritual elements by contact and commerce with the Greek trading cities on the Italian coast. But up to 300 B.C. Rome and middle Italy had merely touched the fringe of the second-hand Greek culture of the south Italian peoples. Rome had indeed at an early period borrowed gods from Greek religion, such an interchange of deities being easy and natural between peoples whose official worship represented ultimately the worship of the forces of nature. Greek pottery had made its way to Rome in quite early times; but, till the opening of this century, Rome had not borrowed or acquired from the Greeks anything either material or moral, save an alphabet, which was of a nature to modify Roman life. Nor is it probable that even the Romans of the higher social and official ranks had found it necessary to acquire a knowledge of the Greek language until the events of this century brought Rome into contact with the Greeks at home, and into diplomatic relations with the kingdoms of the successors of Alexander. Thus a knowledge of Greek, the lingua franca of the diplomacy of the East, became almost a necessity to Romans who contemplated an official career, with results on the life of society at Rome which extended far beyond the field of international intercourse.

The Roman in Trade

The contact with the Greek trading cities of south Italy, combined with the contemporary expansion of the Roman dominions, brought about a change in the life of a large section of the Roman middle class which was to have a great effect on the future social development of the state; but, as the effects of this change from an agricultural to a commercial life do not make their appearance on the surface of things till well on in the next, the second, century, the details of it may be left till the story of that century is told. For the present it will be sufficient to say that in 269 B.C. Rome adopted a currency system from the Greeks, the previous system of exchange by cumbrous copper coinage having been far too clumsy for it to be supposed that users of it were interested in anything more than a restricted local trade.

But when once direct connection was established between

THE THIRD CENTURY, 300–200 B.C.

the Romans and the Greek world at home the influence of the Hellenistic culture spread rapidly through the upper ranks of Roman society. It tended both for good and evil in Roman life. It introduced the Roman to intellectual and material luxuries which he used in a somewhat clumsy fashion tending ever towards the extravagance of novelty and inexperience, and towards an appreciation of the less desirable elements in the newly acquired culture. Opposition to individualism, in the form of deliberate repression of the prominence of individuals, had been almost as marked a feature of Roman as of Spartan life. But the Hellenism which Rome now learnt to know was intensely individualistic, calculated to promote the growth of individual ambition in those who came under its influence. Though it was not till the last century of the Republic that this influence began to have a practical effect on public life, yet even in the later years of this third century the prominence of those who do great service to the state is in marked contrast to the almost ungrateful obscurity into which the benefactors of the early age of the Republic were thrust.

In religion the educated Greek, or rather the educated Hellenistic world, had long lost all faith, save that it mingled with various philosophical creeds elements derived from the base local superstitions of those eastern peoples with whom the Greek had mingled. In Rome, under official priestly influence, the official religion was making ever-increasing demands on the time and patience of its official adherents, provoking a spirit which yearned for emancipation from the boredom of conforming to the ritual of a cult whose unrealities, well known to that higher society of Rome which had an official knowledge of them, were quite sufficient to destroy any belief in its spiritual reality. The Hellenistic atheism soon made converts among the Roman nobility, who came to look on religion as little more than a useful aid in the political control of the uneducated masses. The conservative element in politics made spasmodic efforts to stem and throw back the tide of atheism; but the nature of the official religion was too hollow and unspiritual to reconvert minds half educated on bad literature.

Knowledge of the language led to knowledge of the literature of Greece. It was naturally the decadent Hellenistic literature of the age which first attracted the attention of the Roman, and of it, *faute de mieux*, he showed a ready appreciation. It would be unreasonable to expect more from a people to whom literature was a novelty. Greek comedy and tragedy were introduced at Rome in the form of translations or plagiarisations of Greek originals; but tragedy was not appreciated by the Roman mind, and the comedy was not copied from that of the best age. It may be said parenthetically that such political comedies as those of Aristophanes would never have been allowed by the authorities at Rome. Roman consuls and prætors did not appreciate the humour of being caricatured on the stage.

Among the upper classes the philosophical literature, among the lower classes the dramatic literature of the Hellenistic world, had a debasing influence on that moral severity which, whatever its defects, had played the greatest part in forming and preserving the best elements of the Roman character. With a longer experience Roman taste in literature improves, so that the later Greek literary influence did to a certain extent undo the evil which the earlier had done. But the modification of the Roman character under the influence of Greek literature and intercourse with the Greek goes on, tending in some respects to better things, in some to worse, but always towards such a transformation of the ideas which had governed Roman life that they become a mere tradition which affects only the lives of the best Romans of the later days of the Republic and of the period of the Empire.

THE EAST

The close of the fourth century before Christ left the eastern world in a process of settlement which seemed to be drawing nigh its end. The successors of Alexander had by twenty years of fighting reduced their rivalries to something like a stereotyped form, which meant that they had reached a position where there appeared more prospect of loss than gain from further attempts at mutual spoliation.

Macedonia itself had been held against all comers by Antipater, one of Philip's contemporaries, who had passed it on safely to his son Cassander. Ptolemy, the most far-sighted of Alexander's marshals, had established himself in Egypt immediately after Alexander's death; and his dynasty was destined to outlast all the other Macedonian kingdoms by several generations. The vast domains of Alexander in Asia had changed hands over and over again; but after 311, when Seleucus rode from Egypt to Babylon with a mere handful of horsemen to conquer the East—and succeeded!—that intrepid adventurer, who alone of Alexander's officers had not repudiated his Persian wife, a fact to which he owed his popularity in the Oriental regions, made himself master of the whole area between Euphrates and Indus. He did not attempt to re-occupy the Punjaub, contenting himself instead with making a treaty of peace and alliance with the great Sandracottos (Chandragupta), a native Indian king who, fired by the example of Alexander, had mastered all the Ganges and Indus plains, and was glad to buy off Seleucus' invasion by the surrender of a herd of five

THE THIRD CENTURY, 300–200 B.C.

hundred elephants, the ultimate source of supply of all the elephants used by the Macedonian kings, including Pyrrhus, in their third-century wars. After defeating in 301 Antigonus the One-eyed, his chief rival in Asia, Seleucus annexed north Syria; and what was left of Antigonus' power remained in the hands of his son Demetrius Poliorcetes, called "the Besieger" because of his failure, in the years immediately preceding Ipsus, to take the great commercial city of Rhodes. The Rhodians thereafter adopted a permanent policy of neutrality, and their city was extremely useful, as a financial centre, to all the kings of the Greek East, as well as to the greatly expanded world of commerce and industry. Demetrius after 301 maintained his magnificent navy at full strength—he is perhaps the first instance in history of a purely maritime great power, that is to say one with no territorial basis whatever; for his land possessions consisted of little more than a large number of coast cities from Corinth to Sidon.

An almost perfect balance of power appeared now to be the result of the struggles of the successors of Alexander. The Greek and Oriental world was divided between five great rulers, all called kings, for in 306, beginning with Antigonus and Demetrius, they had by common consent relinquished the now meaningless title of satrap, and were, as Alexander had been, accorded divine honours by their Greek subjects.

There seemed to be no special reason why one should preponderate over the rest.

None of them could afford to be behind the others in professing respect for the autonomy of the city states. Athens adopted, for a short time successfully, the Rhodian policy of neutrality, and resolved to be content with a purely cultural hegemony of the Greek world. In the years after Alexander's death Athens in the "Lamian War" had made a gallant attempt to win her independence. Demetrius of Phaleron had, under Cassander, ruled Athens for a number of years, establishing a practical constitution based upon the political teaching of his master Aristotle; but he was driven out and had now gone to Egypt, where he acted as philosophical adviser to King Ptolemy, who organised, probably under his direction, the famous Museum at Alexandria as a great research centre in which Aristotelian science entered on a period of development. The world seemed about to enter upon a new age of enlightened government and economic prosperity.

Seleucus organised his extensive empire in two parts, with one capital at Antioch on the Orontes, where he himself resided, and another at the city of Seleucia on the Tigris, in which he installed his son as viceroy. So much for the work of peace. But death intervened to disturb the apparent calm.

In 297 Cassander of Macedonia died, and, as usual in Macedonian princely houses on such occasions, much murder and family fighting ensued, of which the firebrand Demetrius, anxious for employment befitting a prince, took advantage to seize, first the dominion of Greece, and in 293 the throne of Macedonia. To the rest of Alexander's successors Demetrius had been a nuisance as a free-lance operating round the coast of Asia Minor; but to have one of such restless ambition as king of Macedonia was more than they could stand. So Seleucus seized Demetrius' principality of Cilicia; Ptolemy seized Cyprus; and they deputed Lysimachus of Thrace and Pyrrhus of Epirus to drive Demetrius out of Macedonia, which they did, thereafter dividing the kingdom between them. Demetrius, after a dash into Asia Minor, where Agathocles son of Lysimachus and starvation pressed him, appealed to the charity of Seleucus in the winter of 286-5. After Seleucus had hesitated, and finally refused, and after much guerrilla warfare in Cilicia and north Syria, Demetrius fell into his hands and was placed in safe custody.

In the same year 285 Lysimachus evicted Pyrrhus from his newly won possessions in Macedonia, and conquered Thessaly.

At intervals in this confused fighting it is necessary for the understanding of the position of the moment to strike a balance of the losses and the gains of the various rivals for empire.

At the end of 285 Lysimachus ruled Macedonia, Thrace, and the whole of Asia Minor as far as the Taurus range. Seleucus ruled the whole of the rest of the Asiatic possessions of Alexander. Ptolemy reigned in Egypt.

The dreary story of murder and troubles continues.

Ptolemy abdicated in favour of his second son, to be later known as Ptolemy Philadelphus. His eldest son, Ptolemy Ceraunus, who must have been one of the most artistic scoundrels of an astute and somewhat scoundrelly age, fled to the court of Lysimachus, where he played the part of a third-century Iago, poisoning the mind of that king against his son Agathocles to such an extent that the father had the son assassinated. When the truth came out Ptolemy fled to the Court of Seleucus, that home for the lost dogs of rival dynasties. The assassination of Agathocles caused such discontent in the realm of Lysimachus that Seleucus thought he saw his way to the full heritage of Alexander's empire; so he overran Asia Minor, and in a great battle Lysimachus was slain. But Seleucus' long day was nigh its close. Having crossed over to Europe, he was assassinated on his way through Thrace by the unspeakable Ptolemy Ceraunus in the year 281.

His son Antiochus succeeded to a kingdom the western part of which his father had but recently won, and Ptolemy Ceraunus

THE THIRD CENTURY, 300–200 B.C.

seemed like to win, for the army of Seleucus in Thrace had come over to him.

The murder of Seleucus following the death of Lysimachus brought inevitable confusion into the European remnants of Alexander's empire. The Illyrians had long before asserted their independence of Macedonia. Epirus under Pyrrhus had also broken away; and that enterprising monarch had added Acarnania to his dominions. But his realm, though extensive, being poor, he wished to add richer regions to it. Hence his subsequent enterprise in Italy and Sicily.[1] In Greece Antigonus son of Demetrius, called Gonatas, maintained the possessions which that fierce father of his had won, ruling most of the country directly, and other regions as client states. Athens enjoyed a nominal independence. Sparta maintained her independence by force of arms, despite defeat. Her old spirit was not as yet dead. Messenia also remained free.

Ptolemy the Unspeakable, alias Ceraunus, had been hailed king of Thrace and Macedonia by that most mercenary of mercenary armies which had come over to him after his murder of Seleucus. He found his title disputed, first by Antiochus, who wanted to avenge his father, secondly by Pyrrhus on grounds of general ambition, and thirdly by Antigonus son of Lysimachus. He turned for help to his brother Ptolemy Philadelphus in Egypt, but found it for the moment in the rivalries of his opponents. Antiochus could not get into Europe, and so made peace; Antigonus got a rap over the knuckles and retired to Greece; Pyrrhus became absorbed in dreams of conquest in the West. The unspeakable one sought to strengthen his position by further peculiarly foul and treacherous murders.

The Celts

It was just at this time that the Celts broke into eastern Europe and Asia. The troublous state of Macedonia enticed them from their homes on the middle Save and the Danube. Apparently this was not the first raid they had made on the Balkan peninsula, but it was by far the most serious. In the spring of 280 they defeated Ptolemy Ceraunus, who perished after the battle, thus ending a life of a vileness remarkable even among the lives of that peculiarly brutal age. In 279 a second swarm of Celts came to join their friends. These passed southwards into Greece. The Greeks put up a strong resistance at Thermopylæ; but the Celts seem to have turned the pass by the path of the Anopæa, for they made their way south to Delphi, whose treasures were the main object of their raid. But there

[1] See p. 294.

they failed. They fell back, an ever-wasting company, in a long retreat to that home on the Danube which few of them ever reached. But another band, of whom it will be necessary to speak later, made their way into Asia.

The Struggle for Macedonia

The death of Ptolemy resulted in disorder which had now become chronic in Macedonia. There were many who wanted the throne; but no one whom the Macedonians particularly wanted. Antiochus the Seleucid and Antigonus Gonatas were the most serious competitors. But the former, finding that he could do nothing effective, retired in favour of the latter. Antigonus, after defeating in a great battle near the Propontis the Celts who had overrun Thrace, gradually wore down his opponents, and in 276 became king of a much-reduced Macedonia which no longer included Thrace or the Illyrian region. Fortunately for him, Pyrrhus of Epirus was at this time occupied with the carrying out of his great design in Italy and the West. But peace from this quarter came to an end when Pyrrhus, disillusioned with regard to his great western scheme, returned in 274 with his army to Epirus, and forthwith sought compensation in Macedonia. Having overrun that country except its coast towns, in 273 he invaded Greece. The Greeks, who disliked Macedonian rule in general, and the rule of Antigonus in particular, welcomed him as a deliverer. Even Sparta was prepared to remain neutral, had not Pyrrhus incautiously interfered with her affairs. She beat off Pyrrhus' first attack. The Spartan spirit was not dead. But the end of Pyrrhus' stormy life was near. He fell shortly afterwards in an attempt to storm Argos town, and with his death freed Antigonus of his most dangerous enemy.

Though Pyrrhus was cursed with that restless ambition which prevailed like a disease among the prominent men of the age succeeding that of Alexander, his character was not stained with the deceit and cruelty which are the outstanding features of the men who were his contemporaries. He had a nobility which is singularly lacking in them. He was a true friend and a generous enemy in a world where friendship was seldom more than the specious cloak of treachery, and enmity was regarded as justifying the most hideous vengeance on a defeated and captured foe. His faults, and especially that restless ambition which added to the confusion of a world which longed for peace, were the outcome of the circumstances of an age in which a man could only resist the ambitions of others by pursuing his own, a world too which was flooded with soldiers of fortune ready to serve anyone who would pay, regardless of the cause for which they fought. The Seleucid family was the storm-centre. If it could only have got over the habit of yearning for that which did not belong to it the world of that time might have gone much better. Its members had a perverse ambition to be the sole heirs of Alexander. The Ptolemies on the other hand sat still in Egypt, quite content with a land which afforded all the comforts of life. If anything like Cyprus, important for the supply of ship timber, might be picked up cheaply, they picked it up; and the less respectable and more restless of their family they sent to seek their fortune abroad.

The death of Pyrrhus brought to an end the greatness of the Epirote kingdom. Macedonia and Epirus fell to Antigonus, and Acarnania became independent.

The task of Antiochus son of Seleucus was not an easy one. Nominally his realm stretched as far as India; but the allegiance of the satrapies beyond the Zagros chain was always doubtful, and in some cases non-existent. That is perhaps one reason why he was anxious to compensate the losses eastwards by gains in the west near the home of the Macedonian race. In Asia Minor after the death of Lysimachus, the tendency was for the land to split up into principalities, of which that which was to attain the greatest fame in the future was the realm of Mithradates in north Cappadocia and Pontus. Another such principality was that of Pergamum. Bithynia also had local independence. The whole political situation in Asia Minor was in the melting-pot; and no one knew what was to come. What were the relations of Antiochus to the various locally independent communities is uncertain. Some of them seem to have been his client states and others to have refused any form of submission to him. Even in Thrace Antiochus had possessions, at any rate in some of the coast districts.

The Celts

Affairs in Asia were further complicated about this time by the appearance of the Celts on the Asiatic side of the Bosphorus. They played havoc in the west part of the peninsula of Asia Minor for a time, and then formed permanent settlements in northern Phrygia, in a district to be known thereafter as Galatia. This took place about 275. In life and constitution Galatia remained genuinely Celtic until it fell under the dominion of Rome.[1] With the Celts in Galatia such hold as Antiochus had over the western part of Asia Minor was greatly weakened. He seems to have eventually accepted the general position,

[1] Like their compatriots in Gaul and southern Britain they settled in the land as a race of warriors ruling and exploiting the previous inhabitants of the country.

though he attacked them fiercely about 270, and won a victory which reopened the route to his possessions in west Asia Minor. Any attempt to reduce that region would have been both costly and risky. Still he held most of the Ægean coast towns, with the exception of those in the principality of Pergamum and in a small district on the mainland belonging to Rhodes. He also held Phrygia, Lycaonia, Lycia, Pamphylia, and the greater part of Caria.

The Ptolemies had been showing an unusual interest in Ægean trade, and had acquired certain coast towns of Caria as well as the island of Chios. But the Gallic invasion gave pause to further enterprise on their part.

But throughout Asia Minor local independence was the rule, so that the land must have been a perfect museum of constitutions of various form, democracies, aristocracies, principalities, and local hierarchies under the rule of the priestly caste of one of the many forms of worship which had centres in the country.

RHODES

Rhodes was a remarkable state, the Venice of the age, with a small territory but a very powerful and efficient navy which made the Diadochi cautious in any aggressive action against her. Since Rhodes, being essentially a trading state, was peaceably disposed, excuses for attacking her would have had to be invented. The state was ruled by an aristocracy which was the most enlightened government of the age, keen to adopt every improvement in the art of war, and so liberal-minded in the arts of peace as to provide for the poorer population a system of relief from poverty such as no state of that time had ever dreamt of establishing, and no state of previous time had ever established in so liberal and effective a form.

Antiochus carried out a great agrarian or colonisation scheme in Asia Minor and north Syria, settling Greeks and Macedonians in various towns old and new, with intent that they should act as *points d'appui* for his rule, and should reduce to an ordered life of peace those soldiers of fortune who had become a drug on the war market, begetters and begotten of the wars of the last fifty years. Even beyond the Zagros, where his authority faded ever more and more the further east it went, he sought to secure his power by similar foundations and settlements. Persia proper, for some reason unknown, was excepted from this policy. His nominal possessions in India were practically independent under the rule of Sandracottos, who had extended his dominion right across the north of the peninsula to the mouth of the Ganges. Antiochus, recognising the inevitable, maintained friendly relations with the rulers of this broken fragment of his empire.

His father Seleucus had before his death subdivided the great satrapies of the middle empire into smaller governorships in order to avoid the concentration of a large power in the hands of one governor. East of the Zagros, for some unknown reason, no such change was made. But all these satrapies included minor divisions: municipal areas in the more civilised regions, self-governing under the supervision of the satrap; principalities in the areas where tribal institutions prevailed, of which the princes were often the clients rather than the subjects of the central power. The system indeed bears a strong resemblance to that in the Roman provinces under the Republic.[1]

Of the finances of the state but little is really known. It is however certain that in the rural districts a tithe system prevailed, while in urban communities a poll tax was levied from which the Greek and Macedonian settlers were exempt. This tithe system was destined to be an evil heritage to Rome when she acquired west Asia Minor.

The military system of the empire was centred, as might be expected, on the Macedonian population, all of whom were subject to the levy. That also applied, but in a less important sense, to the rest of the population, with the curious exception of the Greek town communities, which were exempted from compulsory service, though a Greek might offer himself as a mercenary if he would. Antioch on the Orontes was the capital of the empire; but Seleucia on the Tigris, with its immediate neighbour Ctesiphon, and Sardes in Lydia were, as it were, secondary capitals.

EGYPT

In Egypt Ptolemy II, called later Philadelphus, had succeeded to the throne in 285. The earlier years of his reign were supported by his abdicated father, and threatened by his disappointed brother, Ptolemy Ceraunus, of whose vile life the story has been already told in brief. The death of Ceraunus, happy for all save himself, left Philadelphus with a free hand. The Ptolemy family having been purified by the murders customary in Macedonian princely races, Ptolemy himself proceeded to redress the balance by marrying his sister Arsinoë, widow of two former husbands, Lysimachus of Thrace and another, who had been released from Arsinoë by a merciful death. To the Greeks the marriage was a scandal: to the Egyptians an act of political propriety.

Ptolemy's dominions included Cyprus, southern Lycia, and some scattered possessions off and on the coast of south-west Asia Minor. He was also patron of a confederacy which included most of the Greek islands of the Ægean,—an office not purely honorary, since he exacted tribute from the islanders. From the Ptolemys the contemporary world could get nothing for nothing, and very little for little.

In Egypt the power of the kings was complete. There were not, as in the Seleucid kingdom, communities which managed their own local affairs by local government. The king's officers administered the country directly. Alexandria and Naucratis possessed but a show of local administration, and the native Egyptian towns probably none at all. The Ptolemies found themselves heirs of a world-old civilisation and system of administration to which the only modification which they applied was a stricter organisation of the existing institutions. That essentially Greek town, Alexandria, became the capital under Ptolemy the Second. Founded by Alexander, it was within a century of its foundation the greatest centre of trade and of learning in the contemporary world. Ptolemy did all that he could to make it what it became, the centre of Greek culture. From every quarter of the Greek world he attracted all who were greatest in literature, science, and art, and this not merely, like the Greek tyrants of old, from motives of self-aggrandisement and the love of splendour, but because he had a real personal interest in the studies pursued by the educated world of his day.

The settlement of Greeks and Macedonians in the rest of Egypt was on a large scale; but it was made up to a great extent of the discharged soldiers of the large army which it was necessary for the government to maintain, not so much against revolt on the part of the comparatively passive native population, as against the ambition of the Seleucids.

Jews in Egypt

Among other immigrants into Egypt at this time was a large body of Jews who settled chiefly in Alexandria, imbibing there ideas which had a great influence on the intellectual and spiritual development of a race whose interest had in the past been for the most part confined to the question of conformity or nonconformity to the national religion.

Meanwhile the native Egyptian population went on living that changeless life which makes the centuries of Greek, Roman, Arab, or Turkish dominion seem ephemeral.

King Worship

A very curious and remarkable phase of superstition develops during this age in the Asiatic dominions of the successors of Alexander, the deification not merely of dead kings but also of living monarchs and of prominent members of royal families.

It is not a practice which can have been in any way encouraged under Persian rule,[1] for the religion of that race excluded all idea of the possible divinity of the human being. Whether the non-Persian element in the empire had come to regard the Great King as a divine providence is another question; but, whether it had or not, the setting up of temples or the establishment of worship in his honour would have been wholly inconsistent with the spirit of the Persian religion. In Egypt the people were accustomed to some form of deification of their rulers; and the growth of such a cult was easy and in a sense natural in that kingdom; but its existence in the Seleucid dominions is difficult to explain, especially among the Greek population. With them the only spiritual foundation on which it could have been built was the hero worship of the classical age.[2] It is also possible that the Greek of this time, whatever may have been the case among his decadent descendants of a century or two later, regarded it merely as a politic sign of obedience to the ruling power. The practice now established becomes of great significance in the first century of Rome under the Empire.

Trade and Finance of Egypt

Egypt had always been of importance in the world of Mediterranean trade; but under Ptolemy Philadelphus she opened up with the East, and especially with that India which the campaigns of Alexander had brought to the notice of the Mediterranean peoples, a trade which was to introduce to Europe many hitherto unknown products of that distant world.

Ptolemy's revenue system in Egypt was an elaboration of the somewhat elaborate system which already existed in the country. It was of extraordinary minuteness of detail; but aimed at one thing only, the increase of the government income. Taxfarming was a part of the system; and, though the farmer was strictly supervised, yet he made the position of the peasant cultivator a hard one. In the dependencies of Egypt—Libya, Cyprus, and southern Syria—the revenue system was but a slightly modified form of that prevailing in Egypt itself.

In foreign affairs Ptolemy Philadelphus tended to depart from that policy of non-interference which his father had fol-

[1] The worship of the "dæmon," divine spirit, of Persian kings is quite a different thing. It seems to have been the worship of the spiritual power which directed their actions, perhaps conceived of as dwelling in them, but certainly not a worship of the kings themselves.
[2] Brasidas was allotted some form of worship at Amphipolis after his death there. It is also reported that Lysander was accorded divine honours in the Asiatic Greek cities at the end of the Peloponnesian War. This was certainly an extension of the idea lying behind hero worship.

lowed. His ambitions, above all in the Ægean, caused bad blood between him and the Macedonian and Seleucid kings, so much so that the Ptolemy rather than the Seleucid family becomes the disturbing element in eastern Mediterranean politics. Macedon and the Seleucids found it necessary to combine against Egyptian aggression.

SYRIA

Syria, especially southern Syria, was the bone of contention between the Seleucids and the Ptolemys; and several wars, of which little record has survived, took place, in which the tide of conquest ebbed and flowed in somewhat bewildering fashion. Then there comes a long war and much fighting round the Ægean, in which everybody joins on one side or the other, including Antigonus Gonatas of Macedon, who takes the side of Antiochus, and issues from the war stronger than when he entered it. So long did the war drag on its weary length that Antiochus I left it as a heritage to his son Antiochus II. He himself died in 262 at the age of sixty-four. It was not till 250 that peace was made.

But for some reason not known the war, though it had not ended unfavourably for the Seleucids, had shaken the kingdom. The Ionian towns on the Ægean had been conceded independence; so also had certain Phœnician cities. Mithradates of Pontus forswore his allegiance; and nothing happened when south Cappadocia declared its independence. But more important than this was the falling away of the great satrapies of Parthia and Bactria. Ptolemy had meanwhile gained in the war. It is true that Cyrene had broken away. But it had been recovered; and now his rule extended far north into Syria, while in Asia Minor Lycia, Caria, and the Cyclades were his.

Ptolemy Philadelphus died in 247. He had never tried to be a great general; he had only tried to be a prudent man—and he had succeeded. His Ægean enterprises were the weak point in his policy; but it may be the case that they merely aimed at diverting the Seleucids from enterprises in Syria such as might have been dangerous to Egypt. To the world of learning and culture his services were inestimable. He was succeeded by his son Ptolemy III.

In 246 Antiochus II was poisoned by his wife Laodicé, and Seleucus II reigned in his stead. But the murder of Antiochus' Egyptian wife Berenicé by Laodicé brought upon the land a storm in the shape of an invasion from Egypt. Ptolemy III overran the whole of northern Syria and Cilicia in this campaign. He then crossed the Euphrates and invaded Babylonia. The result was that practically the whole of the kingdom of the

Seleucids east of Taurus submitted to him. Even west of Taurus the kingdom suffered serious losses. The coast districts in Asia Minor and all the possessions in Thrace were lost. Antigonus Gonatas did not at all like to have the ambitious Egyptian as so near a neighbour; so he came into the war. His Greek possessions were of precarious loyalty; but between 245 and 243 a naval victory off Andros, which he won over Ptolemy's fleet, not merely stayed but set back the tide of Egyptian success; and his general resistance to Egypt in the Ægean kept Ptolemy so busy in those parts that Seleucus had a breathing space wherein to restore his fortunes further eastwards.

Ptolemy by a surprise attack had gained successes which he could not consolidate. Cilicia, northern Syria, and the Ionian towns came back to Seleucus. Consequently the eastern satrapies renewed their allegiance. Then followed a good deal of fighting for the possession of northern Syria, in which both sides suffered. Seleucus tried even to invade Egypt, with disastrous results for himself; and in 240 a peace was patched up. But even so the much-harassed world of the Near East was not to enjoy peace. There ensued a civil war in the Seleucid kingdom between Seleucus and his brother Antiochus, a war fomented by their fond mother Laodicé, whose affections were fickle and disastrous. Antiochus' strength lay in Asia Minor, where many of the independent states joined him. But his greatest strength lay in the Galatian mercenaries, that race which since its settlement in Asia Minor had shown a willingness, or even eagerness, to play the part of spoon in any devil's cauldron that anyone might wish to stir. Antiochus found the handle of the spoon too hot to hold. And so for some time Asia was harassed and harried by the Gauls.

A relief from the long tale of misguided greed, bloodshed, and cruelty is afforded by the heroic resistance which the small principality of Attalus of Pergamum put up to all the attacks of Antiochus and the Celts. Both assailants suffered well-deserved defeats. In 228 Antiochus, who had roamed through western Asia in a fruitless search for help, was murdered in Thrace by a band of Gauls.

Through the murder of Antiochus Seleucus recovered an undisputed but not undiminished rule of his dominions. In the embarrassments of the civil struggle he had had to purchase assistance by many concessions made to principalities and communities both in and outside his realm, so that the actual power of the Seleucid kings was from this time forward less absolute and direct than aforetime. The attachment of the provinces beyond the Zagros became merely nominal or ceased altogether. Bactria and Sogdiana legitimatised a position of practical independence by renunciation of obedience; and others of the north-eastern provinces followed suit. Parthia, too, declared its absolute independence under native rulers, the forerunners of those kings who were to be an exaggerated terror to Rome in later days. Seleucus started forth to reduce the north-eastern satrapies to obedience; but a rising in Syria recalled him. It was started by one of those royal ladies whose influence and actions in this period might serve as a warning to those who regard women as a steadying influence in politics. Seleucus came back and killed her. But he was never able to take further measures against the revolted provinces of the north-east ere death overtook him in 227.

Egypt's ventures in the Ægean and its neighbourhood were an unfortunate exception to a policy which was in general marked by enlightenment and common sense. That, at any rate, *seems* to be a fair judgment of it. But for a century after the death of Alexander the world of the East was ever threatened by any dynast who found himself in such a position of power as to hold out a prospect of his becoming full heir to the great conqueror. Even Ptolemy III had not resisted the temptation. In other respects he showed himself a true heir to the policy of his father, a wise and, for the times, humane ruler. To his enlightened patronage of culture and letters the modern world owes in all probability more than, in the absence of direct evidence, it can appreciate.

Meanwhile Attalus of Pergamum had turned against his former ally, Seleucus, tempted by the prospect of conquering Asia Minor. Seleucus crossed the Taurus with an army to attack him, but was murdered by the troops he could not pay. This happened in 223.

The army decided that a full-grown man must succeed him, and so chose his brother, Antiochus III.

The war against Attalus had to be carried through. It ended in that monarch being driven back within the narrow limits of his hereditary dominion.

Greece

The history of the Greek world during this century is one of local events, chiefly petty quarrels, which have left no trace on world history. Only the major results of these squabbles are of any importance; and even of them only those need be recorded which account for the condition of Greece at the time at which it came into contact with Rome.

The Greece of this day enjoyed a past reputation which stood it in good stead amid the storms of the time. The Greeks and Macedonians abroad, who regarded themselves as the apostles

THE THIRD CENTURY, 300-200 B.C.

of Greek culture, treated with respect that land from which that culture had sprung, ignoring and pardoning the petty policies of its petty states as harmless expressions of the irritability of learning. The learning was decadent; but it did not seem so to a greatly decadent world. Kings courted a people whose praise they peculiarly appreciated. The avidity with which they studied and patronised Greek learning was only equalled by that with which they pursued their personal ambitions. The experience of the fourth and third centuries would suggest that it had not come to bring peace to the world but a sword. It certainly had no humanising influence on those dynastic devotees of it whose record of murder and cruelty has seldom if ever been surpassed in the most barbarous periods known to history. The one blessing which it conferred on the world of the time was that it tempered the wind of destruction for the shorn sheep of Greece, so that the Greeks had the exclusive privilege of inflicting on one another the evils which other more innocent races suffered in worse form from foreign foes. In the Greek sanctuaries the most popular king of the moment, whether a Ptolemy, an Antiochus, or an Antigonus, doubled the part of god and devotee. The moral and intellectual standard of the Greek world of the day is shown by the zeal with which it deified and worshipped the Macedonian generals and their descendants. In fact, Greek learning and culture was at this time that hollow sham which will fascinate the half-educated of all ages, whether Macedonian or otherwise. Not that it did not produce here and there men whose talent was great for the sifting of that which the genius of former ages had produced; but they were few, and their work, with the exception of that of Zeno and Epicurus,[1] was at best a second-hand treatment of that which others had done, a formulating of the technical side of language and literature.

But by far the most striking feature of the time was the utter failure of this Greek humanism to humanise its most zealous and most powerful devotees.

Hellenistic Culture

If the term speculation can be applied to philosophies springing from the imaginings of men of very various moral character, then it can be applied to the philosophy of this period. The best of it has survived in literature if not in thought; and glimpses can be got of the worst by antagonistic references to it in the works of those who condemned it. But this bad philosophy was a living influence in a world which attributed divinity to the holder of power, however exercised, since amid the multitude of views put forward by decadent persons of wit there could always

[1] See pp. 343-4.

be found some which would justify any action, however abominable. Still, if the rulers of the then world of the Near East did not always put into practice the lessons they had learnt from Greece, their zeal for Hellenic culture was effective in impressing it on large areas of the realms they ruled, with results which were sometimes beneficial to the regions so affected. It is indeed too often the case that when a new culture is impressed upon or adopted by a people to whom it is strange, they are apt to acquire the bad as well as the good element in it; in fact, the bad may prove the more attractive of the two.

The glamour of all that is Greek tends to create an exaggerated impression of the effect which Greek culture had on the Asiatic. Even in Asia Minor Orientalism lived on side by side with Hellenism; and in the rest of Asia, though the material side of Hellenism had its effect in modifying the material arts of life, the Greek spirit never supplanted those customs and ideas which ages of Oriental culture had implanted in the Asiatic mind. East of the Taurus Hellenism was represented by mere islands in a vast sea of Orientalism which was ever wearing them away. Even in Asia Minor the Hellenic culture was soon infected with the mysticism and superstition of the native races.

Economically speaking, Greece was in some respects in a better, in others in a worse, condition than in the fourth century. Trade was perhaps staving off the ruin of a land wasted by almost continuous war. The large settlements abroad had brought relief to former over-population. Educational culture, which had aforetime tended to concentrate in Athens, was now, for good or evil, widespread through all the states. But that pestilent political disunion continued to exist. The most terrible tribulation and disaster in the past had never cured the Greek of that folly. Party conflicts within the states themselves were just as rife as ever. Part of the land had fallen to the Macedonian power, while the islands belonged to Egypt; and Macedonian and Egyptian parties in each city of the mainland added fuel to the political disruption of the time.

The Achæan and Ætolian Leagues

In the early years of the century was formed that Achæan League which was to play a great part in the near future of Hellas. After many years of struggle for life, it acquired a more settled existence by its alliance with Pyrrhus of Epirus in 273.

North of the Gulf of Corinth an Ætolian League was at the same time in process of formation. It was distinctly anti-Macedonian, which was quite enough to make Pyrrhus of Epirus and Lysimachus of Thrace its friends. Its patriotic action in resisting the Gallic invasion increased its prestige and power so much that Antigonus of Macedonia thought well to seek its alliance.

Its constitution was unusual, in fact unparalleled, in the Greek world up to that time. The communities which joined it became Ætolians. The Phocians, Malians, and others abjured their old nationality for the new one. But its town communities had all of them equal rights, since the acceptance of Ætolian nationality did not imply subjection to the Ætolians proper. Also the towns retained independence in local matters. The chief power in the league rested with a stratêgos (general). But the most remarkable feature in its constitution was the Council, for the composition of which the principle of representation was for the first time recognised, each town sending representatives to its meetings. The Greeks of the more advanced states would never have assented to such an arrangement.

Piracy and robbery on a large scale were the favourite occupation of the members of the league; so it was well to keep on friendly terms with them. Also they were the champions of Greek freedom.

MACEDONIA

Of the history of the Macedonian kingdom during the reign of Antigonus Gonatas few details are known, save such as concern themselves with his wars with the Ptolemys in Greece and the Ægean. He had a hard life which was one long struggle to maintain his kingdom against Celts and Illyrians on the north, against the kingdom of Epirus on the west, and for the regaining of those possessions which had been lost in Greece. He, like his contemporaries, was a friend of Greek learning; but his life, unlike theirs, was not stained by acts of barbarity which gave the lie to any claim to the possession of the Greek spirit of humanity.

GREECE

It was after Pyrrhus' death that a large part of Peloponnese and middle Greece returned to its allegiance to Macedon, not without much ejectment or murder of enemies belonging to the anti-Macedonian party. Sparta was the centre of anti-Macedonian resistance, and Egypt was ready to back her. Under Sparta's leadership an anti-Macedonian league was formed in Peloponnese, including Elis, Achaia, and the chief cities of Arcadia. Megara and Athens joined later. Of the war which ensued with Antigonus little is known. There was a siege of Athens, and a battle at Corinth in 265, and after that Alexander of Epirus joined the enemies of Antigonus. He wished to win back the possessions which his father Pyrrhus had won from Macedonia, and he had lost. It proved an unfortunate venture for him. His defeat left Antigonus free to resume the siege of Athens, which fell into his hands about 261. Then followed the battle of Cos, which relieved Antigonus of all immediate fear from Egypt. As for Athens, she remained for a long time a nominally free state bound to the Macedonian interest. The Peloponnesian members of the league played but a feeble part in the war. The war ended probably in 260.

The little Achæan League acquired an important accession in the adherence of Sicyon, which Aratus, one of its banished citizens, had freed from the hand of a tyrant. Both Aratus and the league were destined to play a prominent part in the history of the latest period of Greek freedom.

In 246 troubles again arose in Greece. Alexander, son of Craterus the brother of Antigonus, who had succeeded his father as regent of Macedonian Greece, declared his independence, and was supported by the Achæan League, the Ætolian League taking the side of Antigonus. In the end Antigonus came out victorious; and Alexander died a death which may have been natural, but probably was not. But Antigonus' success was brief. Aratus, now stratêgos of the Achæan League, was the hero of the next few years. By a sudden bold surprise he seized Corinth, a success which led to the accession of Megara, Trœzên, and Epidaurus to the league. But the Ætolian League was jealous of its rival, and so there ensued a war in Peloponnese in which it established in Arcadia an influence to counteract that of the Achæan League in the north of the peninsula.

The tale of party conflicts, party murders, and internecine wars goes on without cessation. He who would admire the Greek character must shut his eyes to the pitiable state of Greece in the fourth and third centuries, a state due solely to the utter political incapacity of a race which regarded nothing short of licence as liberty; which regarded power as giving the holder the right to plunder at his will, and looked on the murder of political opponents as the only method of dealing with political opposition. Unbridled democracy in Greece had meant the rule of the ignorant and corrupt. Its opponents had been driven to retaliations such as are the outcome of exasperation. The result was two centuries of misery to which no country at any other period of European history can afford a parallel. Should anyone regard this judgment as too pessimistic, let him read the dreary tale of war, murder, and spoliation which forms nine-tenths of the story of Greece in these centuries, and then try to realise what it all meant to the people who lived through it all.

THE THIRD CENTURY, 300–200 B.C.

In 239 Antigonus Gonatas died, and was succeeded by his son Demetrius. From this point the story of the kingdoms and other states east of the Adriatic shall be told with a brevity which alone can make it readable, those incidents alone being related which did have some influence on the history of later and greater centuries.

Not long after Alexander's death the royal rule in Epirus came to an end in the year 233, and the land sank into an obscurity from which it has never emerged.

The real interest in the Greek history of this time centres in that of the Achæan and Ætolian Leagues. The friendship between the former and Macedon turned to enmity and a war which led to a rapprochement and alliance brought about by the diplomacy of Aratus between the two hitherto rival leagues. He took the opportunity of trying to detach from Macedon its possessions in Peloponnese. With Megalopolis he succeeded; but attempts in Argos resulted in one of those defeats which became so usual that they called forth the epigram that Greece was sown with the monuments of victories won over Aratus.

The most remarkable feature of the next few years was the sudden rise of a great piratical power in northern Illyria, whose attacks on the Greek towns of the Adriatic and the coasts of Italy led to the intervention of Rome and its consequent suppression.[1]

Demetrius of Macedon died in 230, and, after an interval of disorder, was succeeded by Antigonus, nicknamed Dôson, an able man who soon put things to rights. About that time Athens revolted from Macedon. Her example was followed by Hermioné and Argos, which thereafter joined in 229 the Achæan League. Phlius joined later. The ambition of Aratus was that the league should include the whole of Peloponnese, and be thus independent of Macedon and of help from Egypt.

The constitution of the Achæan resembled in most respects that of the Ætolian League. All citizens in the league had equal rights in all the cities; in other words, there was a citizenship of the league as such. Its strength promised the attainment of that peace which Peloponnese both needed and desired. But it differed from the rival league in that its sovereign body was not a Council to which the states sent representatives, but an Assembly of which every citizen in the league was member. So doggedly did the more civilised states of Greece cling to the principle that every citizen should participate personally in the government. But, though all might vote, yet their votes did not directly affect the decision of the Assembly. The question was decided by the votes of the states, so that the vote of the individual was only

[1] See p. 308.

contributory to the vote of his state. The stratêgos, the chief annual magistrate, had very large administrative powers, especially in the conduct of war. There was also a Council of Ten, elected by the states and sitting permanently, which conducted much routine business. The towns of the league were allowed to maintain such constitutions as they preferred, tyranny alone being excluded. Inasmuch as there was no pay for attendance at the Assembly, and the distance to be travelled was great in many cases, the management of the league affairs tended to be in the hands of the citizens of property; so that, though democratic in form, the government was aristocratic or timocratic in fact. In fighting power the league was much inferior to its rival, partly because its population was more civilised and less virile, partly because its people had long lived under the protection of Macedonian garrisons.

Sparta's power, with a population wasted by continual warfare, had greatly declined, though the old spirit and discipline still remained. She had maintained her position chiefly by the support of Egypt. But she had not escaped those internal political troubles which were the curse of Greece. She had viewed the growth of the Achæan League with considerable mistrust, suspecting the aggressive tendencies of Aratus, who, knowing Sparta's mistrust, mistrusted her,—with the usual result, a war, in which fortune wavered. Sparta was weak; but its king, Cleomenes, was one of the most capable generals of the time. Checked and hampered in his policy at every turn by the overweening power of the ephors, he carried out a great revolution, slaying the existing holders of the office, and abolishing the office itself. But this was not all. A drastic redistribution of land was made, the few large estate owners being obliged to surrender the major part of their property for allotment to poorer citizens and metics (resident aliens). This reform gave him a force of 4,000 hoplites, which he armed with the long Macedonian spear. All this took place in 227.

Supported with money by Ptolemy III, Cleomenes carried on the war in such fashion that the Achæans were reduced to despair. At this juncture Aratus made an appeal to Antigonus Dôson, for the dispute had come to a question of personal rivalry between Cleomenes and Aratus for the control of Peloponnese.

About this time Antigonus was carrying on an anti-Roman policy on the Illyrian coast, seeking to destroy Roman influence there and substitute his own. As the Second Punic War was threatening, Rome had for the time being to ignore his policy.

Meanwhile Cleomenes had overrun nearly all the lands of the Achæan League. The position was so desperate that the league was obliged to seek from Antigonus such assistance as might counterbalance the moral if not active support which Ptolemy was giving to Cleomenes. In 224 Antigonus marched south with a large army. The result of certain manœuvres rather than fighting was that Cleomenes had to fall back on Laconia, and Antigonus was made leader of a miscellaneous league of Greek states. The policy of Macedonia towards the Greeks was from this time forward a return to that of Philip and Alexander, whereby the states were nominally allies with complete local independence, but in all external relations with one another and the outside world under the control of Macedon. The intermediate principle of ruling through tyrants in the Macedonian interest Antigonus renounced,—probably as impracticable.

But Cleomenes was not done with yet. In the spring of 222, when a large part of the Macedonian army had gone home, he broke out, and committed havoc in Megalopolis and Argos. In the summer Antigonus, having collected an imposing force, marched on Laconia, whereon Cleomenes took up his position at Sellasia on the great route to Laconia from the north. All might have gone well with the Spartans had not Ptolemy come previously to an arrangement with Antigonus by which, in return for concessions not mentioned in the story, he withdrew his aid from Cleomenes. So the latter had to stake his all at Sellasia; and he lost it in that great fight. He fled to Egypt, where the now repentant Ptolemy received him kindly, even liberally.

The immediate result of Sellasia was that Antigonus, having marched into Sparta, proceeded to revoke the constitution which Cleomenes had set up; to expel the new landowners; and to restore both the old constitution and the property of those who had been despoiled under the recent redistribution of land. He destroyed the new conditions of Spartan life; but he could not destroy the old spirit of the race. The state itself became part of the miscellaneous league.

Antigonus was called home almost immediately by an Illyrian invasion. He defeated the invaders. But the strain of war after war had been too much for him, and in 221 he died, leaving behind him a reputation rare indeed at that time. Capacity and bravery were not rare qualities in that age. Righteousness and humanity were. He possessed all of them.

THE NEAR EAST

At Antigonus' death the position of the three great kingdoms was normal, if anything can be called normal in that age of change. Macedonia had recovered its supremacy, though not its direct rule, in Greece. The Seleucids were in possession of the only parts of their kingdom which they had really ruled in the past, from Media to the Taurus, with large patches in Asia Minor. Egypt held southern Syria and Libya, and was supreme in the Ægean. Of the rest of the world Thrace was a confused collection of warring tribes, and in Asia Minor there were various principalities and free towns, of which the Pergamene principality of the Attalids was perhaps the most important, though those of Prusias in Bithynia and of Mithradates in Cappadocia were of quite considerable extent. In Greece the Ætolian League was fiercely independent, while its Achæan neighbour was much under the control of Macedon. Rhodes was, however, the richest and the most powerful of the free Greek states.

The mention of Rhodes recalls an incident which indicates that the times were becoming less barbarous and unsettled than they had been in the century of competitive ambitions which followed the death of Alexander. When somewhere about 227 Rhodes suffered terrible damage from an earthquake, the Macedonian, Seleucid, Egyptian, and Syracusan rulers vied with one another in sending gifts of great value to relieve the necessities of the suffering state.

It so happened that the death of Antigonus in 221 nearly coincided with those of Seleucus III in 223 and of Ptolemy III in 222. This was unfortunate, because dangerous in a world so constituted as that of the third century. In Egypt the successor was a weakling and a fool. In the other two kingdoms the new kings, though young, were energetic and capable. From this time the greatness of Egypt declines under the rule of Ptolemy Philopator.

The incapacity and feebleness of the new Ptolemy tempted Antiochus III to try to recover what the Seleucids had lost to Egypt in Syria. But before anything could be done Media and Persia revolted. The revolt of Media became serious when the rebel satrap Molon crossed the Tigris and occupied Babylonia. But in a battle east of that river his army was totally defeated and the revolt suppressed.

Antiochus then turned against the Egyptian possessions in Syria. For a long time all went so well that he reached the borders of the Sinaitic desert. Here he was met by a great Egyptian army which had been secretly collected, and was defeated in 217 at Raphia in a battle which was one of the greatest of its time. Fortunately for him Ptolemy was so anxious to get rid of the war that he got off with the loss of what he had won in Syria.

Meanwhile a certain Achæus, in command of a large army which he had hired after the fashion in which armies could be raised at that time, was in practical possession of the Seleucid dominions in Asia Minor, where he was making himself a nuisance to everybody in general, and to the Pergamene kingdom in particular. So when in 216 Antiochus had his hands free to take action against him, the minor powers of Asia left Achæus to resist as best he could. The affair ended in a prolonged siege of Sardes, which Antiochus did not capture till 214. Thus he recovered his possessions west of Taurus.

The next years of his reign were occupied with a campaign to recover the far eastern provinces, in the course of which he marched through Media and Parthia as far as Bactria in the Oxus basin, a military exploit, as far as that age is concerned, only second to that of Alexander the Great. From there he marched to the modern Afghanistan. All these lands he brought back to at least temporary allegiance to the Seleucid power. It was not till 205 that he got back to Seleucia on the Tigris.

Meanwhile under the weak rule of Ptolemy Philopator things in Egypt were going badly. A great native rising, caused mainly by burdensome taxation, became so formidable that even the hereditary foes of Egypt, the Seleucid kingdom and Macedon, had to send assistance to save the kingdom for its Macedonian king. The one general principle which each king recognised was that a Macedonian, if possible himself, should rule in the heritage of Alexander. So the rising was suppressed, with the usual aftermath of wholesale executions.

It was on the whole fortunate for Ptolemy that the excellence of the system of government established by Ptolemy Philadelphus and the capacity of officials who, whatever their personal character, were trained administrators, made it possible for the machinery of government to run smoothly in spite of the neglect of a ruler who was indifferent to all save his personal pleasures. So the kingdom did not fall to pieces, but maintained its possessions, and in outward appearance its former strength.

Greece

In the Greek world at home the death of Antigonus brought confusion. All the enemies of Macedonia thought that the accession of the young king offered a favourable opportunity for breaking loose from Macedonian control. The Ætolians, who had always, like poor but warlike races of the period, been inclined to piracy and brigandage, now took these up as regular professions, plundering all and sundry by sea and land. This caused a general outbreak of war.

The Achæan League, members of which had suffered from these depredations, stirred itself, partly because the grievances were serious, partly because Aratus hoped to get Philip the young king of Macedon on its side, and, in case of success, to get the whole of Peloponnese into the league by forcing the few cities and states which now sided with Ætolia to give up that connection. The relations between Macedonia and the Ætolian League had been so bad for a long time past that the Achæans found no difficulty in persuading Philip to take their side. Sparta, which some years before had been forced into alliance with Macedonia, a tie which she ever disliked, renounced the connection and declared war on the Achæan League, following this up immediately by an invasion of neighbouring territories in 219.

Divisions, troubles, and hostilities, the normal conditions of life in Crete, brought that island into the war, as rival cities and rivals in the cities appealed to either side for help. The struggle in the island went so much in favour of the friends of Macedon that Philip's influence extended through the whole of it.

As for the Achæan League, the opening of hostilities found it utterly unprepared for war. It had no mercenary soldiers in its employ, a type of force on which the citizens of the civilised states of Greece had become so accustomed to rely that they showed considerable reluctance for personal service.

But Philip's action was energetic. In one campaigning season he attacked the Ætolian possessions in southern Acarnania; and in the next, that of the year 219, he worked havoc among the Ætolian allies in northern Peloponnese. In 218, after failing to capture Cephallenia, he made a surprise attack on Ætolia in the absence of the Ætolian main army. Meanwhile the Achæan League was giving a miserable display of military inefficiency and helplessness which continued till when, in 217, Aratus, who was now getting on in years, became once more stratêgos.

On news of the Roman defeat at Trasimene the plans of Philip took a new turn, which was to have fatal influence on the relations between Rome and Macedon. Illyrians, relying on Roman friendship, had shown themselves only too ready to take advantage of Macedon's embarrassments by invading her territory. Philip thought to rid himself of the nuisance by attacking them while their friend Rome was engaged in a death-struggle in Italy itself. This made him so anxious for peace elsewhere that he proposed terms to the Ætolians to which the latter agreed.

He began his campaign in Illyria in the summer of 217. But after Cannæ, when it seemed safe to take sides definitely against Rome, he opened relations with Hannibal, thus demonstrating to Rome the fact that Italy was threatened with danger from the east as well as from the west, that which Rome did not forget, as Macedon was destined to discover later. Another discovery the Macedonians made more promptly was that Rome was not, despite her almost desperate embarrassments, going to let her control of the Illyrian coast lapse by default; for, whatever might be the case on land, the Roman power by sea was unimpaired. Philip's Achæan allies had no liking for such enterprises, above all Aratus, who ever feared that a strong Macedonia might mean a subject Hellas. From this time onward Philip's popularity in Greece declined.

In 214 Aratus died. His had been a strange career in which fortune and misfortune, prudence and audacity, and many other contraries of life, had been mingled. As a statesman he had, by a certain wise opportunism necessitated by the weakness of his resources, raised the Achæan League from an insignificant union of cities to a considerable force in the Greek world, and this despite the fact that as a general he had shown more boldness than capacity in command of a league army composed largely of men who would have preferred to have been represented by mercenaries. Some of his contemporaries laughed at him; but it would have been well for the world of his day had some of the laughers possessed a tithe of the good qualities which he possessed. He was an honest man in a world which regarded, and had reason for regarding, honesty as the worst policy.

Philip gained success in Illyria which caused the Romans some anxiety. Fearing lest he might join Hannibal in Italy, and not being able to spare troops to act against him, Rome by means of the Ætolians raised troubles in Greece which brought his Illyrian enterprise to an abrupt conclusion, and dissolved for ever the dream of an invasion of Italy. In 212 hostilities were opened with an Ætolian attack on Acarnania, supported more or less by a Roman fleet. In a short time nearly all Greece was ablaze. Attalus of Pergamum took part in the war on the side of the Romans and Ætolians, thus founding a friendship of long duration between his state and Rome. Of the details of the war itself it is not necessary to speak. For the first five years Philip maintained himself with difficulty owing to his being unable to face the enemy by sea, the Macedonian fleet having been allowed to decay by reason of the neglect of his predecessors. But his task became easier when in 208 the threatened invasion of Italy by Hasdrubal from Spain made it necessary for Rome to withdraw from the war in Greece for a space of two years. In 207 the neutral states of the Hellenistic world did their utmost to bring about a peace; but Rome, now freed from fear of Hasdrubal, encouraged the Ætolians to resist, and so negotiations fell through.

Just at this time there came to the front in the Achæan League a man who was to make his mark on the history of the age, the subsequently famous Philopœmen. He was now over forty; but in his earliest years, at the great battle of Sellasia and elsewhere, he had shown military capacity such as to win high praise from Antigonus Dôson. Convinced of the bad state of the Achæan army, he introduced a more effective method of training which converted it from one of the most ineffective into one of the best armies of the Greek states of the time. It had also been hampered by using the short spear and imperfect shield of the Greek hoplite in fighting with troops armed after the Macedonian fashion. With his newly modelled army he marched against the Spartans, who, thinking that they had an Achæan army of the old type to face, marched joyfully to meet him near Mantinea. There they discovered their mistake, and were defeated with a loss of 4,000 dead. The Ætolians, finding themselves in a bad way, having applied to Rome for help which was not sent, since Rome was busy in Spain, made peace with Philip and the Achæan League in 206. After peace was made quite a considerable force of Romans appeared in Illyria. Yet they could effect nothing owing to their numbers being much inferior to those of Philip's army. But both Philip and Rome had other designs on hand, and so peace was made in 205, neither side gaining or losing much.

The story of the Hellenic and Hellenistic world in this century is a striking commentary on the doctrine which has been so often preached in modern times, that the advance of civilisation and knowledge tends to peace and goodwill among men. It is a doctrine to which every one would gladly give credence, to which many have given credence in the past, and will in the future; but it is one which is refuted by the whole history of the human race. The disorder, cruelty, and misery of this third century before Christ cannot be set down as the natural outcome of a period of settlement after the death of Alexander, unless it be assumed that the most civilised races of their time could not be expected to reorganise the world on a peace basis in so short a period as a century and a quarter. It was not a world on its defence against the attacks of barbarism, in the agonies of a murdered civilisation. Civilisation was doing its utmost to commit suicide; and would have succeeded had not the Roman barbarians stepped in in the next century to force on the superior civilisation a peace which it had never allowed itself to enjoy.

In respect to humane education it was, relatively to the time, as widely educated as any age of which history has to tell; but the most striking result of that education was an exaggerated individualism which incited the dynasts to eternal discontent with what they had got, however great it might be, and with the eternal desire to get more at the expense of others: which in the democracies of Greece led to the clash of interests between states which sought mutual gain by mutual robbery, and between individuals who were ever ready to murder political

THE THIRD CENTURY, 300-200 B.C.

opponents with a view to acquire their power and property. Nor were such occurrences exceptional; they recur in the history of almost every year of this century and a quarter, and in the case of Greece itself had been the most prominent features in its history for two hundred years past. Greek political and social ideas had flattered the conceit of humanity. The demand for free thought and free speech had made it possible for the half-educated charlatan and for the imaginative criminal to air ideas which, accepted by the ignorant, gave the former the notoriety for which he longed, and the latter the opportunity for which he sought. In postulating the godhead of man the Greeks destroyed all belief in a god, while in illustrating it they destroyed all belief in morality. The result was a world where misery was terrible, and most terrible in that land from which those ideas had sprung. History teaches that the idea of a god who rewards that which is good and punishes that which is evil is a factor necessary in any well-constituted society; and the history of periods when men have tried to dissuade themselves of such a belief suggests that the idea is a reality. It may be that with the Greek the fault lay in the fact that he had built an intellectual edifice on the inferior spiritual foundation of a religion which in so far as it was public was purely formal, in so far as it was private was meticulously superstitious.

But the very material and spiritual confusion of the time led some of the greater minds of the age to seek some system of moral life which might alleviate, if not cure, the ills from which humanity was suffering, and to formulate those ideas in a philosophical creed which might be a guide to a better life,—a thread which a man might follow through the maze of uncertainties to which the obscurities of a debased speculation had led.

It was about the beginning of this century that Zeno, the founder of the Stoic philosophy, began to preach those philosophical doctrines which were to guide the lives of some of the best men who flourished in the succeeding centuries. His teaching implies an intellectual and moral revolt against the world of his day, against the mental and physical lawlessness of his time, and the misery it had brought and was bringing on the world. That teaching developed after his death, elaborated by those who taught it into a kind of pagan Puritanism. Yet in its original form it was not of that severe and somewhat narrow morality into which it developed when systematised by later teachers, but laid down a line of conduct to which every good man might conform without feeling that he had by so doing narrowed the reasonable scope of life. " Man is happy and virtuous in proportion to the degree in which, under the guidance and enlightenment of reason and knowledge, he conforms or accommodates himself, first to the law of his own nature ; secondly, to the law of society ; thirdly, to the law of Providence,"—such is the summary of the basis of that which Zeno originally taught.[1] This is at any rate certain, that his whole teaching is a reaction against the popular doctrines of his day and the evils they had brought upon the world. It is also certain that the doctrine implies, and was always meant to imply, an almighty reason, a divine spirit or god ruling the universe.

Contemporary with Zeno was Epicurus, the founder of that Epicurean system which lived for centuries side by side with Stoicism, and came to share with it almost the whole realm of thought and educated morals. It is impossible to state its doctrines briefly.

Epicureanism has come to connote a sensual life of pleasure, a connotation which distorts the original doctrine. Zeno insisted on the cult of the soul, whereas Epicurus inculcated the cult of the body, and the satisfaction of bodily desires and bodily pleasures, *but* according to reason and virtue. The modern popular idea of Epicureanism is really applicable to those Hedonistic teachings which were so much in accord with the base instincts of this age of the third century, inculcating the pursuit of pleasure and the satisfaction of personal desires regardless of the feelings and rights of others as the real end of life. Some Jew of Alexandria described it and its effects in the second and third chapters of the Book of Wisdom, a true picture of the life of the century as well as of the teaching of the Hedonists.

Philosophy could confirm, but it could not cure, the ills of the age. It was left to the Roman sword to do that.

[1] Ferrier, " Lectures on Early Greek Philosophy," p. 423.

CHAPTER IX

THE SECOND CENTURY, 200-100 B.C.

PROVINCIAL ADMINISTRATION

ROME issued from the Second Punic War with the uncontested supremacy of the western Mediterranean, with a new region, Spain, on her hands, the size of which necessitated its division into two provinces, Hither and Further Spain, each with its own governor. For these offices she created two new prætors, just as she had done for the government of Sicily and Sardinia with Corsica shortly after the close of the First Punic War. To the Sicilian province had been added the dominions of Hiero. This was the last case in which Rome increased the number of the regular magistrates with a view to providing for the government of provinces. For the government of provinces acquired after this time she provided by the expedient of prolonging magisterial powers (prorogatio imperii)[1] beyond the term of one year, and sending out those to whom this extension was granted to govern provinces as deputies of the magistrates at home,—as proconsuls and proprætors. The general organisation of these early acquired provinces takes the form which becomes stereotyped under the Republic, and is retained with but slight modifications under the Empire. To the modern world the term " province " connotes the idea of a region where a local government exercises control over inhabitants all of whom have the same rights, or, when these rights are in any way differentiated, the differentiation is between classes, not communities. The constitution of a Roman province was of a very different nature.

It was a political unit in only one real sense, in that it was governed by one governor ; in fact, the term " province " as applied to it implied no more than that it was the " department of administration " of the magistrate who governed it. It was not a region in which one system of law prevailed, because it was not a region in which all the inhabitants had equal rights. The Roman citizen domiciled within the province may be left out of account, because the Roman citizen was the Roman citizen in all provinces alike. But the position with regard to the provincial

[1] See p. 300.

may be perhaps put most clearly by saying that a Sicilian provincial had no rights as an inhabitant of the province of Sicily, but only as a member of the urban community in Sicily to which he belonged, and the rights he got as member of that community might be very different from those possessed by a Sicilian of some other community. The provincial's rights were communal, not provincial. The central government at Rome had no relations with the province *qua* province, but different and independent relations with the different urban communities in the province, each set of relations, that is to say, the rights granted to each community, being settled by a separate agreement with Rome. Each province was a bundle or aggregate of urban communities which had no rights *en masse*, which had no relations *en masse* with Rome, but had only this in common, that they were under the rule or superintendence of one Roman governor, and paid as a rule in direct taxation a lump sum to which each community contributed its quota, a quota arranged with the other communities in the province, with the certainty of the governor's intervention in case of a failure to agree. On the setting up of a province the Senate at Rome drew up a Lex Provinciæ, which scheduled the rights of the individual communities. Every square yard of land in the province belonged to one or another of these communities, so that the rights of every provincial were determined by the rights of the community in which he was domiciled.

The establishment of urban communities in the provinces of Spain must have presented some difficulty in the first instance. Along the coast town communities had been established by Carthage; but in the interior the selection or establishment of such communities must have required careful arrangement. In the settlement of Italy Rome had recognised the tribal unit in the middle of the peninsula. That policy was not adopted in Spain, probably because the tribal unit was too large; and in any case Rome had every interest in breaking up the tribal connection.

Thus in a general sense the provincial organisation resembled that which had been applied to Italy, with this practical difference, that the rights which had been granted to the Italian communities were as a rule superior to those granted in the provinces. But the principle of separating the interests of communities by granting them varieties of rights, which had done so much for the disintegration of opposition to Rome in Italy, was adhered to in the arrangements made in the new provinces.

The system of organisation was not a bad one from the point of view of either the government or the governed. The serious evils which are subsequently apparent in its working were of a practical kind, due to circumstances which had not as yet come into being.

Constitutional Changes

During the period of the First and Second Punic Wars there was coming over the Roman constitution a silent change which has been foreshadowed in that which has been already said with regard to the developments which followed the Lex Hortensia of 287. By the end of the Second Punic War it had come to this—that a professedly democratic constitution was being worked by a narrow and capable oligarchy. For clearness' sake it will be well to consider the details of this change in connection with those events of the year 133 which raised the whole question of its validity as an established feature of the constitution.

For the first half of the present century the interests and activities of Rome were almost entirely concerned with the eastern world. Of her western provinces Sicily is happy in having no history. The Greek cities acquiesced in an inevitable which was more tolerable than the inevitable which had preceded it. To them the change was merely a change of masters, a Rome dominating the whole of the island instead of a Syracusan tyrant in the east and a Carthaginian government in the west. Otherwise their life went on much the same as before, for Rome had even accepted the Hieronian taxation system by tithes as part of the organisation of the province, perpetuating also that strict supervision of the tax-farmer and his operations which had been characteristic of the working of the system in Sicily to the immense advantage of the cultivator, who was thus protected against arbitrary exactions.

Spanish history during the century was on the other hand somewhat stormy. This was due to the fictitious nature of the conquest. Rome claimed the whole of the peninsula; but, as a fact, when she took it over from Carthage her rule cannot have extended far inland from the east coast, though it may have included all that is now known as Andalusia. The conquest of the interior plateau had to be carried out; that of Lusitania (Portugal) was never really completed under the Republic, and that of the north-west stood over till the days of Augustus. It was probably the incompleteness of the conquest as well as the intractable character of the Celto-Iberian inhabitants which made it necessary for Rome to keep a large garrison there during the whole of the century. The south part of the country, which had learnt something of Punic culture, acquired Latin civilisation rapidly.

Italy

In Italy Rome had to settle accounts with those who had taken part with Hannibal. The Gauls of the north lost whatever independence had been left them after the conquest of thirty years before. In the south Rome was terribly severe with those allies of hers who had found in submission to Hannibal that security which Rome could not give them. Large tracts of land in Apulia, Lucania, and Bruttium were confiscated and handed over to Roman settlers or occupiers, while large numbers of communities lost every semblance of local autonomy, their inhabitants being deprived even of civil rights. Both town and individual passed under the arbitrary rule of a magistrate sent from Rome. It was the bad position of these southern peoples which gave strength to that agitation for the Roman franchise which broke out in Italy in the last thirty years of this century.

Complications east of the Adriatic were not of Rome's seeking. Her connections with the kingdoms of the successors of Alexander had been confined to treaty relations with Egypt, whence she got corn, certainly during the Second Punic War, and probably before that time, in consequence of the devastation of Italy by long-continued warfare.

The Roman and Trade

With the acquisition of Spain, Rome had come into possession of the greatest metalliferous region of the ancient world. That was certain sooner or later to bring her into prominence as a trading state and to set up an important connection between her and the great markets of the eastern Mediterranean.

One of the most striking phenomena in the history of the Roman people is its conversion from an agricultural race to a nation of traders of great keenness and great capacity, with an area of operations as wide as the civilised world of the time. The diligence which the Roman had always shown in whatever he undertook and his enormous capacity for work were sure to seek an outlet wherever gain was to be found; so that it is not strange that when in the first instance contact with the Greek showed him the gains from trade and the methods of making them, and, when in the second, he acquired a dominant and privileged position in lands outside Italy which gave him immense advantages in his trading relations with the populations of the new provinces, an ever-increasing number of the race forsook agriculture for commerce. Of the beginnings of this change nothing is known, though the fact of it is quite apparent. This, however, is certain, that it originated at the time when Rome came into close contact with the Greek cities of Italy. The acquisition of

Campania may be taken as the probable starting-point, in that it brought Rome into close relation with the Greek cities of the region of the Bay of Naples, and it brought into her possession the richest region in peninsular Italy, a land which must at all times have produced more than its population could consume. Till Rome acquired this region it is difficult to see how the Roman could have developed any trading activity worth speaking of, for such activity implies that the race exercising it has either surplus food or some widely appreciated product to export, or is advantageously situated for a transit trade by sea between regions on either side of it. No one would allege that Rome had at any time such a position with regard to the sea; and the statements commonly made with regard to Rome's central position in Italy and its advantages for the land trade of the peninsula are due to a failure to realise how very small the volume of such trade must be in a land with hardly any made roads, hardly any stretches of navigable river, and no great variety of products such as would encourage the transfer, still less meet the expenses of transferring goods from one region to another. The interior trade of Italy between the Italian peoples was probably limited to the pots and pans and cheap luxuries which the packman could carry about the country on pack-horses.

The first definite indication of the growth of a trading class in Rome is a Lex Claudia of 218, which practically excluded senators from engaging in overseas trade. A few years later a rich trading class in Rome is able to help the government with a loan for the prosecution of the Punic War. This shows that that class of wealthy traders outside the senatorial ranks which came to form the most important element in the Equestrian Order of post-Gracchan times was already in being. But of still greater importance were the small traders who migrated to the provinces to prosecute there all sorts of trade on a small scale, from that of a pedlar upwards, for, once initiated into trade methods, and once possessed of a field for their exercise in the provinces, the Roman became one of the keenest and most effective traders in the ancient world. The path to empire which the Roman had hitherto followed reluctantly, was now the path to gain, and for the rest of the duration of the Republic there is a paradox of sentiment in Rome, the government being averse to the acquisition of new territory, while the individual Roman is determined that Rome shall keep possession of what she has got, and wishes, no doubt, that she should acquire more. The system of client states provided a sort of compromise between these differing sentiments and policies; for within their area the Roman trader was probably not in a less privileged position than he was in actual provinces.

THE BALKAN PENINSULA

In the Balkan Peninsula Philip of Macedon had shown that he required watching. Rome had checked him during the recent war by allying herself with the Greek states, an alliance which kept his hands full at the time, but was likely to involve Rome in the local disputes of that part of the world: in fact, the Second Punic War was hardly over when such an occasion arose owing to Philip having attacked Athens. Illyrian piracy and Macedonian ambition especially, as shown in the desire to take advantage of Rome's embarrassments in Italy at the time of the Hannibalic invasion, had forced Rome to interfere in trans-Adriatic politics. So, as in human life one thing leads to another, the trouble with Macedon had led to Rome making with Greek states engagements which she could not break without a dangerous loss of prestige on the far side of the Adriatic. At the same time, the last century of the history of the Balkan Peninsula was not such as to hold out hopes of lasting peace even to the most persistent optimist.

As a fact, Greece went on its own old way, expiating the quarrels of silly children with bloodshed and ruin. The signatures to the last treaty [1] were hardly dry ere war began again between Lacedæmon and the Achæan League. The popularity of Nabis, the then king of Sparta, a ruler who tortured his richer subjects in order to extract money from them, gives a fair idea of the moral condition of the Greek world of the time. Philopœmen, the able leader of the Achæan League, had no difficulty in dealing with Lacedæmon with his new model army. His policy was to rid the league of dependence on Macedon and Philip. But in 200 he went to Crete, leaving the league in the lurch. Meanwhile Philip had since the peace been busy in making enemies all around him.

In Egypt the death of Ptolemy IV (Philopator) had led to disorders. To those restless souls Philip and Antiochus the disorder in Egypt was an irresistible temptation. By agreement they made a simultaneous attack on the Egyptian possessions. Antiochus attacked Syria and annexed it after a battle with the Egyptian army near the sources of the Jordan.

Meanwhile Philip sought to overrun the Ægean. From Egypt, from Rhodes, and from Attalus of Pergamum went appeals to Rome. But ere Rome intervened Rhodes and Attalus inflicted a terrible defeat on the great Macedonian fleet near Chios. Philip soon recovered, and began an attack on the Egyptian possessions in the south-east Ægean, some of which he took, only to lose most of them in the following winter.

[1] See p. 342.

Philip's conduct in these years is that of a pestilential lunatic. He had already gone far in folly; but his sins might not have been visited on his head had he not gone further. The appeals of Egypt and Rhodes to Rome, based on a sentimental friendship due to amicable trade relations, were not likely to move to action a power which had just passed through a Second Punic War, and did not include sentiment among strong political ties. But when Philip proceeded to violate the territory of Athens on the basis of a fictitious quarrel, Rome was obliged in her own interest to take notice of an outrage on an actual ally. Of the war which followed between Rome and Macedon it is not necessary to give details which are merely variants of the dreary tale of battle and bloodshed which has now extended through two hundred and more years of Greek history. The Romans landed in Epirus. Philip appealed on all sides for help in a war against western barbarism to peoples who were not favourably impressed with the form of civilisation which Philip represented. Antiochus was busy on his own selfish ends in Syria. The other states looked the other way. And so Philip had to face alone the storm which he alone had raised. In 198 the consul Flamininus defeated him on the Aous, and in the next year crushed his further resistance in a great battle at Cynoscephalæ. Then came a peace by which the Macedonian kingdom was cut down to narrow limits and robbed of all its external possessions. It became practically a client state whose foreign affairs were under Roman tutelage.

The sequel to the treaty, the proclamation of the freedom of Greece, was in a sense more important than the suppression of Macedonia. Sentimental Hellenists have ascribed it to a respect for that intellectual and literary eminence of the Greeks of which, as a fact, even the most select circles at Rome must at this time have had but little knowledge. The act is only a particular example of Rome's general official policy, which was opposed to the accumulation of responsibilities overseas. Roman commerce would have the same advantages in a practically as in an actually dependent Greece.

Pyrrhus of Epirus and Philip of Macedon had demonstrated clearly to Rome the necessity of preventing or suppressing the growth of any power in Macedon or Greece which might be strong enough to disturb the peace of Italy. With that infatuation for aggression which weighs like a curse on the successors of Alexander, Antiochus regarded the defeat of Macedon and the weakness of Egypt as a favourable opportunity for seizing the Egyptian possessions round the Ægean, which he proceeded to attack in 197, the year after he had completed the conquest of Syria. Till 192 Rome resolutely shut her eyes to his doings. But when in that year he crossed over into Greece she could no longer remain inactive, all the more so as the Ætolian League had entered into alliance with him. It had been bad enough to have Philip as a near neighbour on the other side of the Adriatic, but to have Antiochus, whose power Rome greatly overestimated and consequently feared, as a neighbour, was unthinkable. Yet so reluctant was she for further venture beyond the Adriatic that, had Antiochus acted with energy in 192, he might have had time to create for himself a very strong position in the Greek peninsula. In 191 a large Roman army under Glabrio arrived and so defeated Antiochus in a great battle at Thermopylæ [1] that he withdrew hurriedly to Asia. The Roman fleet was already on the Asiatic coast, where it had crushed the fleet of Antiochus. In 190 the army under the new consul Scipio followed it thither, and inflicted on Antiochus a great defeat at Magnesia. Destiny, not choice, had led the Romans now for the first time into Asia.

This was a rough awakening for one whose dreams had included the conquest of Rome, an enterprise which the great Hannibal, who had taken refuge with Antiochus, had suggested.

In the settlement which followed the battle of Magnesia Rome carefully avoided the policy of annexation. But she pushed back the Seleucid frontier to the Halys and the Taurus, making all kingdoms, principalities, and cities west of that boundary allies of the Roman people. In previous negotiations with Antiochus some years before this time the Romans had told his ambassadors that they were convinced that if they were to maintain their position in Greece, they must have a foothold in Asia. Thus inevitably were the Romans led on to empire in the East. But it is probable that, even so, the Romans would not have gone to Asia had not Antiochus come to Europe.

Both now and right on to the end of the Republic, nay, even under the early Empire, Rome preferred to have a belt of client states between her own dominions and the " nationes externæ," whether civilised or not, to having possible foes in direct contact with lands under her direct rule. As part of the present arrangement Rome increased the territories of Pergamum and Rhodes with a view to making these states strong enough to be effective representatives of the interests of Rome in the peninsula. It was in 189 that this settlement was made.

The Macedonian spear (sarissa) had made the Macedonian the master of the eastern world. Of the same world the mastery was to pass to the Roman sword, that Spanish weapon which the Romans had adopted from their experience of war in Spain.

---

[1] The mysterious wall, the remains of which run for many furlongs up the mountain-side between the Middle and East Gates of the pass, was very possibly constructed by Antiochus on this occasion.

The art of war had, moreover, been developing towards formations of ever-increasing mobility. In eastern warfare the close-set phalanx still played a great part; and the more mobile peltast had since the fifth century also played a great part there. But the Romans had evolved a legionary formation in which soldiers as heavy-armed as the Greek and Macedonian infantry were disposed in smaller and more flexible units than the phalanx, a device which rendered the Roman soldier armed with the Spanish sword a fighter superior to, and more practised than, any troops which the Hellenistic East possessed. That superiority is very marked in the wars of the first half of this century in the East. Later Rome was to learn the lesson which the Hannibalic war would have taught her, had she not been victorious,—that she would have to increase the mobility of her formation and the individual fighting capacity of her men if she was to face successfully those bands of efficient individual combatants which she met in the armies of the wild tribes of the West, whose methods were less conventional and more vigorous than those of a civilised East with a long tradition of armament and tactics such as were effective enough against the Asiatic peoples.

GREECE

Anyone who did not know the childish perversity shown by the Greek race for two centuries past might expect that the freedom of its states under a Roman protectorate would have been welcomed as a happy relief from centuries of misery. Macedon under its ever-restless rulers had been a disturbing factor; but much of the evil had been caused by the hopeless inefficiency of a race which had assumed that the world could be run on democratic principles aiming professedly at the brotherhood of man, but producing actually a state of things in which each individual resented either openly or sullenly any subordination to his supposed equals, and every state was ready to undertake any aggression which might increase the prosperity of its individual citizens.

There were several reasons for the restless policy which prevailed in Greece. The country had been wasted by two centuries of wellnigh continuous warfare, especially in recent years when the armies afoot in the land had been of unusual size. The settlement made by Rome in the internal affairs of the states had leaned towards the establishment of oligarchies, which meant the return of many exiles whose property had to be restored to them, and the banishment of those citizens who had in the last few years been prominent in opposition to Rome. Economic ruin, political discontent, and exile created a numerous class of malcontents who had nothing to gain from the peace which Rome had forced on the Greek states, and therefore regarded any possible change as being probably a change for the better.

The exploits of Antiochus gave the Greeks something else to think about for the next few years; but when Rome had settled with him in 189 the Greeks began to think about one another, which, according to the established fashion of three centuries past, meant war.

MACEDON

In the recent war against Antiochus in Greece, Philip of Macedon had taken the side of Rome, partly, no doubt, because it was dangerous for him to do anything else, partly because, if Antiochus won the war in Greece, he was likely to stay there, whereas the Romans had hitherto shown a desire to leave Greece and the lands east of the Adriatic to look after their own internal affairs. But the peace which Rome had concluded with Antiochus in 189 had not been favourable to Philip's interests, and he felt that he had been hardly treated, all the more so as the king of Pergamum, whom he hated, had received accessions of territory, whereas the arrangements made by the treaty had hemmed in Macedonia to such an extent as to make expansion impossible. So he spent the last ten years of his life till his death in 179 in building up and increasing the resources of his kingdom, and in promoting hostility to Rome among the states of Greece. It is quite evident that he intended, had he lived, to try conclusions once more with Rome.

He left his plans as a deadly heritage to his son Perseus. The son continued his father's policy. The Romans, quite aware of his proceedings and their aim, declared war on Macedon. It was a brief war, though at its outset the courage and enterprise of Perseus won successes over some incompetent Roman commanders. He had tried to enlist Antiochus Epiphanes in his designs; but the Seleucids, having burnt their fingers in the prosecution of their own enterprises, had no mind to burn them again in prosecuting those of others. The great Roman victory at Pydna in 168 not merely brought the war to an abrupt close, but was the death-blow of that Macedonian kingdom which had changed the face of the whole world of the East.

GREECE

Meanwhile the Greek states had resumed that life of petty ferment which was ancestral with them, fomented by the intrigues which Macedon had been carrying on among them for twenty years past. In the cities and leagues pro-Roman and anti-Roman factions quarrelled, assassinated, and carried on generally in that fashion which had for a century and a half past caused annoyance to others and ruin to themselves. So, when it came to a settlement of Macedonia, it came also to a settlement of Greece.

MACEDON

Once more in the settlement Rome showed her dislike to the direct responsibilities of empire. Nothing was annexed. No new province was constituted. Macedonia was divided into four separate states, dependent on Rome, paying tribute, disarmed, but with a local republican autonomy. The system must break down; but in her desire to avoid imperial responsibilities, Rome made trial of it. It lasted almost exactly twenty years. It produced what it was almost sure to produce, a pretender to the revival of the Macedonian monarchy; and when, in 146, he was suppressed, Rome was obliged to constitute Macedonia as a province. Even then the reluctance of the government of the Republic was shown in the vagueness of the Macedonian boundary. The province had no boundary towards the north, and never had until the time of the Empire. The Roman dominion in Macedonia melted away gradually into the sea of barbarism which lay to the north of it, so that no one could have said where Roman territory ended and the barbarian world began.

In Greece, from Rome's point of view, the trouble in the last few years had arisen from the growth of anti-Roman parties in the various states.[1] In the previous twenty years Rome's policy towards the Greek states, in so far as it had been active, had consisted in the accommodation of interstate quarrels, and a determination to repress any state which sought to acquire a power much superior to that of its neighbours. The Achæans, though publicly friendly to Rome, had shown a disposition to aggrandise their league, and so a thousand of their chief citizens, including the historian Polybius, were shipped off to Italy. The same treatment was meted out to prominent opponents of Rome in various states. Some territorial readjustments were made; but none of any real importance.

It might have been expected that by this time the Greeks would have learnt that their best policy was to live their lives under the protection of a great power which could and would protect them, but was quite ready to leave each state to manage its own affairs. But they had forgotten nothing and learnt

---

[1] I have not given in detail an account of the maze of quarrels and disputes which arose in Greece during this period. They have no real influence on the history of any year save that in which they took place. Their foolishness was such that the murders which accompany them add dignity to the story.

nothing. They were afflicted with that lack of common sense which is so often the accompaniment of cleverness devoid of ability.

Settlement of Greece

The Achæan League, unwarned by what had happened, tried in 148 to extend its power by forcing Sparta to come in. In vain Rome threatened. The league went to war with her. In two years it was utterly broken, and Rome in her exasperation destroyed in 146 Corinth, Thebes, and Chalcis, three of the great strategic positions in the peninsula. Greece was dismembered. All leagues were broken up, while aristocracies in the Roman interest were established in all states, and a tribute imposed. In name the Greeks remained free, and indeed the land was not made a province; but it was placed under the general superintendence of the governor of the recently established province of Macedonia.

Thus ended the liberty of a race to which for more than two and a half centuries liberty had been a curse.

Commercialism in Rome

But the destruction of Corinth by Mummius had not been merely due to a desire to destroy a centre of Greek resistance. It is about this time that Rome's foreign policy degenerates from self-interested liberality to self-interested greed. The old desire to be left at peace to live an agricultural life in Italy, that which had made Rome averse to direct rule abroad save where no other alternative was possible, was being supplanted by new ideas which were the outcome of that commercialism which had been growing ever stronger for a century past. Not merely was a powerful capitalist class springing up in Rome itself, but thousands of the lower middle class had deserted agriculture in Italy for trade in the provinces. Whatever the Greeks of that age were politically, they were commercially very serious competitors to Roman traders who sought to operate in the wealthy lands of the East. From about 150 B.C. onwards there is in Rome a silent conflict between a senatorial government whose members are excluded by law from any open participation in trade, and are consequently investing capital in land in Italy, and a large and influential body of citizens outside the government whose monetary interests are purely commercial, and centred mainly in the provinces and allied states. The government remains at least cautious about the direct acquisition of territory, and probably opposed to it. But in the middle of this century Rome's whole policy with regard to the empire begins to take a vicious turn, which, when complete towards the end of the century, converts a rule which had been reasonable and, so far as is known, honest, into one of scandalous dishonesty and oppression. The attitude of government circles towards the provinces and provincial rule becomes complicated by various considerations. Rome itself is becoming bigger, richer, more luxurious; and life in it, especially public life and the holding of office, is becoming more and more expensive; in fact, a public career at Rome is calculated to reduce all but the richest men to bankruptcy before they arrive at the prætorship. So the politician seeks to restore his finances by accumulating money during his tenure of a provincial governorship. If that had been all, the question would have been simple; and every man of every class in Rome would have become an ardent imperialist, for the tax-farmers, bankers, and business men great and small are all drawing large profits, some legitimate, some not so, from the provinces. But despite its personal embarrassments and the moral corruption arising from them, the governing class, with centuries of experience and tradition behind it, is well aware that imperial expansion must prove a positive danger to Rome unless it can be accompanied by a paralleled expansion of her armed forces, a policy which would be faced by various difficulties: that of enlarging an army of the type of that of Rome to the necessary size; that of converting any large part of it into a standing force without making changes in its composition to which the government was absolutely opposed; that of paying and supporting the army when so enlarged. On the last point it was quite certain that the provinces, exploited by the official on the one hand and the trader on the other, could not stand the taxation necessary for so large a purpose. The provinces brought in an income sufficient for the government at Rome to be able to free the Roman citizen in 167 from direct taxation; but even when the provincial empire under the Republic reached its largest extent the public income from the provinces was never large. Some cost more than they brought in, some less; but the balance on the right side was never great, and was ever liable to vanish if an expensive war was on hand. Under the Republic it was to the Roman individual rather than to the Roman state that the profits from the provincial empire went, so much so that it may be said that under the Republic the provinces were run in the interest of the individual citizen, whereas under the Empire they were run in the interest of the state.

It was the growth of the spirit of commercialism which in the middle of this second century before Christ began to corrupt Roman dealings, not merely with her subjects, but with states allied to her. The Roman trader was awaking to the fact that the East offered a field for exploitation far richer than any which could be found in the West. The trading element, both great and small, was becoming so powerful a body in the state that no government dare ignore its interests as expressed in its wishes, and above all the Roman government of that day, which knew well that its power rested on a very disputable constitutional basis. In the East the Roman trader found himself up against serious competition, especially from Corinth and Rhodes, and perhaps also from the kingdom of Pergamum. It is evident that he was determined to get rid of this by political means. The government, not daring on the one hand to disappoint the wishes of the traders, and on the other anxious to avoid direct annexation, adopted one of those policies of political hedging which, implying a conflict and accommodation of the interests of two parties, almost invariably leads to injustice being done to a third. So when in 167 Rome settled the affairs of Macedonia, she made a resettlement of affairs in Asia and the Ægean to the extreme disadvantage of her very faithful allies Rhodes and Pergamum. The cynicism of the transaction indicates clearly the moral decay which commercialism had introduced into Rome. On various allegations, most of them probably false, Rhodes was deprived of her possessions on the mainland in Lycia and Caria, while Delos was set up as a free port to compete with Rhodian trade, which it did so effectively as to ruin Rhodian commercial prosperity. Moreover the state was deposed from the position of free ally to that of dependant of Rome. The enemies of Pergamum, especially the Galatians and Prusias of Bithynia, were encouraged to attack it; and its dependency Pamphylia was declared independent.

In Asia Minor, too, about this time the protectorate of Rome was pushed forward east of the Halys by alliances with the kings of Pontus and Cappadocia. There is no real justification for Rome's policy to Rhodes and Pergamum. They were sacrificed to the weakness of a home government not strong enough to be honest. But Nemesis came. Rome, by weakening the two powers which alone were strong enough to keep the peace for her in her Asiatic protectorate, had sown the wind, to reap in the next century the whirlwind of the Mithradatic War. Trouble soon broke out; and for the next thirty years the Roman government was so occupied with affairs at home and in the West that she, to the immense loss of her prestige, left the East to travel its own rough way of disorder.

EGYPT

But Rome had become, in spite of herself, the arbiter of the East, so that in 163 she interfered in the affairs of Egypt, restoring Ptolemy Philometor to that throne of which he had been deprived by his brother Euergetes. The latter was compensated with Cyprus. In the same year, the Seleucid throne falling vacant by the death of Antiochus Epiphanes, Rome sent Octavius to act as guardian to the young Antiochus.

Having thus settled, as she thought, affairs in the East, Rome left them to ferment for thirty years.

Spain

While these things were going on in the East certain events were happening in Spain which, though they might seem to be of but momentary importance, were to lead to other events destined to have a capital influence on the history of the last fifty years of the Roman Republic. Rome had acquired from Carthage at the end of the Second Punic War in name the Spanish peninsula, in fact, the southernmost part of it and a fringe of territory of uncertain depth along the east coast. For the first twenty-five years, therefore, after she acquired it, she was much occupied in extending her rule towards and over the central plateau. By about 179 this work had been to a certain extent accomplished, though the conquest of Lusitania was incomplete, and that of the north-west, the modern Galicia and Cantabria, had not been really attempted. Then followed thirty years of comparative peace in Spain. But in 149 there came a rising under a certain Viriathus which it took the Romans sixteen years to put down by the capture of Numantia in 133. The events of those sixteen years included various Roman defeats which popular report ascribed, with at least some truth, to the incapacity of the Roman commanders, but thinking men attributed to the decadence of the Roman army. The latter came nearer the truth. There *was* a certain decadence ; but the real fact, as the events of the last years of the century were to prove, was that the Roman army as then constituted was not fitted to face the methods and tactics of the fighting races of the West.

Africa

Despite the hard terms inflicted on her at the close of the Second Punic War, and despite the encouragement by Rome of Numidian attacks on Carthaginian territory, Carthage had, owing to her excellent system of agriculture, and her advantageous commercial position, recovered greatly from the disasters of fifty years before. This recovery was watched by Rome with much the same jealousy and apprehension as that felt by Germany at the recovery of France after the war of 1870. Government circles in Rome came to look on Carthage as once more constituting a political danger, while commercial circles were annoyed at the competition of Carthage in trade. Thus Rome was on the watch for a cause of quarrel, which she found, or professed to find, in the resistance of Carthage to certain Numidian raids on her territory. And so in 149 began the Third Punic War. Even certain prominent Romans, such as Scipio Nasica, regarded Rome's declaration of war as wholly unjustifiable. Even against the now sorely weakened Carthage, a mere shadow of its former self, military success was so slow as to emphasise the lessons which the war in Spain was teaching ; but in 146 Carthage was taken and utterly destroyed, a sacrifice to that commercialism which was undermining the morale of the Roman people.

But the Roman people was becoming convinced that the successes in Spain and Africa had been so hard won as to point to dangers which imperilled the existence of the empire ; so that, when Tiberius Gracchus took measures to remedy the defects, he found support from that mass of the Roman people which, though indifferent as a rule to politics, was keenly interested in the preservation of an empire which brought them large personal gains ; and, though ready to live under an efficient government whatever its form, was quite as ready to attack an inefficient one.

The Growth of the Power of the Senate

During the period of the great wars, which had by the time of Tiberius Gracchus lasted nearly one hundred and fifty years, a change, always gradual, and for the most part silent, had come over the Roman government, a change which, though not due to any modification of the written constitution, had brought about such modifications in its working as to convert it from a democracy into a narrow oligarchy. The causes of this change lay partly in the almost complete indifference with which the mass of the people regarded the form of government under which they lived, provided that it was just and efficient in its rule. They knew that the constitution established in the course of the struggle between the Orders afforded them ample means for protection, if protection became necessary, and ample opportunities for changing the personnel of the government if that became desirable.

The other main cause which brought about the great though gradual change was the disorganisation of the normal life of the community due to a state of war which passed through periods of a very critical character when ordinary constitutional processes were not adapted to meet situations which called for the employment of unusual powers or for action of unusual promptitude.

A contributory cause was the springing up during this period of a new and most important department of government, that of the provinces, for which no provision was made in the constitution as it stood in 287, so that it fell to that element in the government of the state which happened at the moment to be most influential.

The magnitude of the change which came over Rome in this century and a half can only be realised by recalling the constitutional position existent immediately after the passing of the Lex Hortensia in 287.

Of the three powers in the constitution, the magistrates, the Senate, and the Assembly in its various forms, the first possessed the sole right of initiative in legislation, had sole administration of the state, and was sole executive in putting the law into operation. The Senate had been robbed of all its powers strictly so called. The power of ratifying, or refusing to ratify, laws had been practically nullified; and its sole function was that of a council of advice to the magistrates,—advice which the magistrate need not seek if he did not want to seek it, and need not take even if he had sought it. Its constitutional position was apparently hopelessly weak, though in practice its prestige as a body, and the experience of its members, gave it a certain influence which no magistrate could with safety ignore. The Assembly possessed the sole right of legislation and election; but its democratic character and powers were largely discounted by the fact that free speech was not permitted at Rome, the magistrates only having the right to address any form of meeting of the citizens. Nor did it possess any even indirect means of exercising an initiative in legislation.

Yet at the end of this period of a century and a half the Senate, a body whose strict constitutional position was so weak as to be almost nil, emerges as the controlling element in the constitution, a position not attained by any legislation, but by a gradual, silent, practical change in the way in which the constitution worked. It acquired its new power chiefly at the expense of the magistrates, who were gradually reduced to obedience to its wishes, and so placed at its disposal the very wide powers attached to magisterial office. The magistrates became the instruments of senatorial government. The Senate did not usurp any of the magistrates' powers; it merely used the magistrates themselves as instruments for their exercise. With respect to the Assembly, on the other hand, there was a certain usurpation of powers, some of which came to be regarded as legitimate even by the opponents of the Senate, or at least were never seriously contested by them; others which were claimed by the Senate, but never conceded by its opponents.

The legislation of the half-century before 287 had, as has

been said, shorn the Senate of its one real power, that of the ratification of law; but after 287, even had not the great period of war supervened, it is probable that a permanent body such as it was would have gradually acquired influence over the annual magistrates, especially as they, if not already members of the Senate, would have the prospect of becoming so very shortly after holding office, and would therefore be anxious to win popularity with it by showing deference to its advice. Moreover, the number of magistrates had been gradually increased until from 197 onwards [1] there were eight magistrates possessed of full power (imperium), a state of things which must lead to a certain conflict of authority which could only be regulated by some central authority such as the Senate. The practice of giving individual magistrates " provinciæ," departments of office, had grown up before this time; but by a custom established during this period the Senate determined at the beginning of the year what department should be filled by each individual elected to the prætorship for that year.

The circumstances of a critical period of warfare made it still more to the interest of the magistrate to consult the Senate and take its advice. The Roman magistrates had in this period to incur responsibilities proportionate to the extraordinarily large powers which they wielded: to take decisions on which the very fate of the state might depend. Having at their elbow, as it were, a body of experienced men who were there to give them advice, what more natural than that they should ask their advice, and by taking it shift from their own shoulders the responsibility for momentous decisions? The very prolonged period of the warfare, and the frequency with which reference was made to the Senate, led to the practice becoming a habit, the habit a custom, and the custom coming to be regarded as a constitutional obligation on the magistrate, not merely in matters of critical moment, but with regard to every act of importance which a magistrate proposed to do. It was in legislation that this now imperative custom was most significant, for no magistrate, save some political crank, ever dreamt of introducing a bill before the Comitia without the leave and approval of the Senate. Thus the Senate acquired a probouleutic power, that

[1] The gradual increase in the number of magistrates had taken place as follows under the Republic:—
    Original.—Two Prætores (consules) or later prætores maximi.
        364.—Prætor urbanus, for civil jurisdiction among citizens.
        242.—Prætor peregrinus, for civil jurisdiction in cases in which aliens were concerned.
        227.—Two prætors for the government of Sicily and Sardinia.
        197.—Two prætors for the government of Hither and Further Spain.

is to say, a power of determining what proposals of law should or should not be laid before the Assembly of the Roman people. It was *de facto* a more effective form of authority than that old power of ratification which the Senate had lost by the legislation of the fourth century.[1] Nor was this custom confined to the regular magistrates, the consuls and prætors, but was regarded as equally binding on the tribunes of the Plebs. The growth of it was, too, very rapid; for even so early as 232 the action of the tribune Flaminius in proposing a bill contrary to the wishes of the Senate was regarded as shocking by all persons of respectability. The same view was taken of the action of the prætor Thalna in 167, when he submitted the question of war with Rhodes to the people without consulting the Senate.

The tribunes, essentially representatives of the people, were probably forced into line in this matter by the Senate's artfulness. The veto of a tribune could stop any proposal made either by a fellow-tribune or by a regular magistrate, a power which, as the Senate saw, cut both ways. It was not difficult for it to secure by bribery or other means the election of some devotee of its own as one of the ten tribunes of any given year; and few must have been the years in which the Senate failed to have a tribune at its command who could be put up to veto any proposal, legislative or otherwise, which had not been previously approved by the Senate. Thus it had a very strong negative control of legislation such as made defiance of its wishes somewhat futile. In point of fact the tie between the Senate and the Tribunate seems to have been very close, so that before the time of Tiberius Gracchus the tribunes had been admitted to a seat in the Senate, and the holding of the office had come to be regarded as giving ex-holders a sort of prescriptive right to be chosen as members of that body.

The record of the year of Cannæ, 216, shows that by that time the censor in choosing new members of the Senate was expected to select first of all those ex-magistrates who were not as yet members of it. Thus the power originally possessed by the consuls, and later by the censors, of free selection of those who should be members of the body, became gradually restricted till towards the end of the period, even before the time of Gracchus, the field of choice had become almost wholly limited to ex-magistrates, so much so, indeed, that a field of choice can hardly be said to have existed. Furthermore, in some way which is not now known, the power of expelling members from the Senate, which the censors had formerly exercised at their discretion, was limited, in practice at any rate, to the expulsion of those whose conduct had been grossly scandalous.

[1] See p. 284.

But the Senate did not rest satisfied with a merely negative control of legislation. It soon became accustomed to suggest to magistrates and tribunes subjects of legislation which these authorities were expected to bring before the Comitia or the Concilium Plebis in the form of bills. Thus, though the legal and constitutional initiative never passes out of the hand of the magistrates and tribunes, the Senate acquires a *de facto* initiative of great importance.

By the time of Tiberius Gracchus the vast majority of the Roman official world had come to regard the custom that a would-be legislator should, before making any proposal, get the consent of the Senate, as a custom of the constitution. The encroachment of that body on the powers of the magistrates had come by the time of Gracchus to be accepted by the mass of the Roman people as part of the natural order of things; but still it was obviously possible for anyone who dared to be bold to raise the question whether the custom was so established as to have become a part of the constitution.

The Senate's position with regard to the real legislative bodies of the state, the Comitia and the Concilium Plebis, was much less clearly defined. It had come by custom to exercise legislative powers, some of which, though, strictly speaking, unconstitutional, were not contested by public opinion, while others, though claimed and at times exercised, were never accepted by the Roman people.

The people generally had little or no desire to intervene in the foreign or domestic policy of the state, so long as they were efficiently conducted; and so matters which in early days had been brought before the people for decision came to be decided by the Senate. As far as the details of foreign policy, and indeed of domestic policy, were concerned, the passing of them to the Senate's control implied an increase of its powers at the expense of the magistrates rather than of the people; but it had always been the custom to bring the larger questions in these departments before the Comitia, and this custom was largely discontinued by magistrates who in time of war found it much more convenient to bring them before the Senate. There were, moreover, general reasons which made the encroachment of the Senate on the powers of the Comitia at this period a probable contingency. The Roman Assembly was an institution of a city state originating from a time when the state was small, and the population concentrated within such a small area that the citizens could attend its meetings without difficulty. But the effect of the conquest of Italy had been to scatter the body of citizens in communities in various parts of the peninsula, so that a very large number of them could never exercise the right of voting.

The population of Rome itself must have grown enormously in the century before Gracchus; but the increase was largely due to the influx of aliens from the provinces, attracted by the fame and wealth of the capital of the great empire. Even in Gracchus' day the Comitia was far from representative of the body of Roman citizens; and when such an Assembly ceases to be representative it loses prestige, and, consequently, power. Some fifty years later, when the whole body of Italians became citizens of Rome, the Comitia declined rapidly into such insignificance that Augustus, a statesman peculiarly anxious to disarm opposition, could all but ignore its existence. Its unrepresentative character had been very marked during the prolonged war period when thousands of the citizens were serving in the field. Apart from all this, it was a body ill adapted to the transaction of business calling for prompt decision such as arose again and again during the war period, whereas the Senate was a body which a magistrate could easily call together. Hence such cases as the prolongation of military command (prorogatio imperii) beyond the annual period came to be referred to the Senate, though, when first this practice was adopted, such extensions of office had always been voted by the people in Assembly. The people acquiesced because the times were anxious and pressing. In the same way the magistrates became accustomed to bring before it other matters connected with, or resulting from, the war, such as the settlement of terms of peace, alliances, the levy of troops, the annexation of provinces, and the lines on which they should be governed. The decisions of the Senate on such points were accepted by magistrates and people as final, so the resolutions of the Senate (senatus consulta) came to have in these departments the force of law.

There was, however, one power claimed by the Senate which the people never conceded to it, that of dispensing from the operation of the ordinary law, especially by the well-known formula, "Let the consuls see that the state takes no harm," a decree which, according to the senatorial view, placed the operation of the ordinary law in abeyance, and established a state of siege. The Roman citizen, knowing well that this meant the suppression for the time being of the law of appeal (provocatio), which he rightly regarded as the corner-stone of civil liberty, looked ever with suspicion, and sometimes with pronounced disfavour, on this arrogated right of the Senate.

The legislative powers acquired by the Senate were, as has been already seen, concerned with provincial and foreign affairs. The provincial empire sprang into being during the period of its domination, and, as the pre-existing constitution had not been constituted in such a way as to provide for the new circumstances brought into being by the growth of the overseas empire, it was more or less natural that its organisation and management should fall into the hands of the most powerful element in the working constitution of the time.

By Gracchus' day the senatorial order had become a close corporation of families. This class of "nobiles" had gradually closed its ranks so far as possible against all persons not in its social and official circle, so that it was very difficult for one from outside it to make his way into high office at Rome. This nobility was not, of course, a collection of patrician families; in fact, by the time of Gracchus the majority of the "nobiles" must have been plebeian in origin.

It was against these serried political ranks that any would-be reformer had to dash himself.

Tiberius Gracchus

In 133 Tiberius Gracchus brought forward a proposal for the allotment of the public lands (ager publicus) of the state. The proposer was a comparatively young man, peculiarly well instructed in the literature of Greece, and a student of that art of rhetoric which had in quite recent times become fashionable in the best-educated circles of the higher society of Rome. He had probably imbibed some liberal principles from his studies, and he belonged to a small coterie of progressives within the ranks of the senatorial order.[1] Sentimental modern historians whose sympathy Gracchus has attracted by his study of Greek, have ascribed his action to quasi-philanthropic motives. The Roman statesman and politician was often, judged by any standard, a very good man; but during the Republic the nearest approach he ever made in public life to the virtue of philanthropy was a mitigated severity.

The circumstances which Gracchus wished to meet by legislation, the depopulation of the country districts of Italy owing to the disappearance of the small farmer, and a consequent

[1] He belonged to the political body which Mommsen calls the "populares," a term which in this sense does not occur in extant literature till the time of Cicero. But Mommsen, owing to the way in which he speaks of this body, gives his readers the impression that the "populares" were a large party including large numbers of the proletariat. The Roman proletariat had no party politics. The "populares" or progressives of this period were no more than a coterie in the Senate opposed to rigid conservatism, who managed to win the support of the people when there was popular discontent with the inefficiency of the senatorial government. At other times the Roman people were quite willing to support the Senate. The word "party" is a most misleading term to apply to politics at Rome. It connotes a large number of persons committed to certain political views. Of political views in the ordinary sense of the term the mass of the Roman people had none.

shortage in the supply of the best human material for the Roman army, he proposed to meet by taking from those who held public lands under indeterminate leases all areas in excess of 500 jugera per head, and by settling thereon landless citizens drawn especially from Rome itself.

The public land in Italy (ager publicus) originated in the lands which Rome had confiscated from those communities which she had conquered. In the early days of Roman conquests, when the areas thus acquired lay near the city, and Rome, having but a small population, was anxious to increase the number of those whose property qualification fitted them for legionary service, the practice of the government had been to distribute such lands in lots to the poorer citizens. At a later stage, when her conquests became more extensive and more distant, the practice of selling the land to the highest bidder was adopted. In both these cases the land became the absolute private property of the new holder. But at a still later stage in her conquests in Italy, when the amount of land thus acquired became very large, the practice arose of distributing it to those who cared to take it up on indeterminate leases which the state could terminate at will, and on payment of a small rent (vectigal). This method was applied, not exclusively, but especially, to uncultivated lands suitable for pasture.

Inasmuch as these distributions were in the hands of the consul, it is not surprising that the magistrate tended to favour the senatorial class, into whose possession a large proportion of the land allotted passed accordingly from the very first. But it was alleged in the time of Gracchus that the large holders of these lands had in course of time ejected smaller holders from their property by arbitrary and forcible means, a most improbable political lie, inasmuch as the civil law of Rome was quite strong enough to protect any citizen, however humble. But two things had undoubtedly happened : the practice of paying rent had dropped owing to the state having neglected to collect it ; and the long-undisturbed tenure of what was really leasehold property had caused it to be regarded and dealt with as freehold to be bought and sold and left by will. By the time of Gracchus many of these tenures, perhaps most of them, had lasted for centuries. The holders, really " possessores," had come to regard themselves as " domini " (freeholders) of the land they held. How long this state of things had lasted is shown by the fact that the Licinian Laws [1] of two hundred and thirty years before the time of Gracchus had proposed to limit the size of tenements of public land in the same sense proposed by him.

The law introduced by Gracchus laid down that the maximum

[1] See p. 223.

of a holding on such lands should be 500 jugera, with certain additions in the case of a holder having sons; and that the surplus should be divided into inalienable allotments for the poorer citizens. Compensation was to be paid to those who were deprived under the law; and a Commission of Three (Tresviri) was to be established to put the law into operation.[1]

Roman law did not recognise long-undisturbed tenure (vetustas possessionis) as constituting a freehold right to landed property. But nevertheless it is easily comprehensible that the ejection of holders from property of which they had had undisturbed possession for centuries was regarded as an intolerable hardship.

The economic question as to the causes which had brought about the gradual disappearance of the small cultivator from Italy has been much debated. It has been alleged that one main cause had been that the importation of corn from Sicily and elsewhere had made it impossible for him to grow corn with profit, and that consequent ruin had driven him off the land. This is reading the economic conditions prevailing in England in the nineteenth and twentieth centuries after Christ into the history of Rome in the second century before Christ. The true analogy would be between England in Saxon times and Rome in the days of Gracchus. It is probable,—almost certain,— that the Italian farmer was not affected by the price of corn in Italy, for the very good reason that he had little or none to sell. He lived, like the Saxon agriculturist, on the produce of his farm; and, when that was done, there was very little left over to sell, not to say anything of the fact that the transport of that little to the nearest market would probably have been so expensive as to absorb all possible profits. It is not to the appearance of Sicilian corn in Italy that the disappearance of the small farmer from Italy is due.

It is probable that the modern world will never, owing to lack of evidence, know the whole truth of the causes of this economic position. The most efficient was probably the devastations of the Hannibalic period, when numbers of small proprietors must have been ruined, either owing to the depredations of armies or to the flight of the owners to safety. Even if at the end of the war the owners survived, they could not have the capital necessary to reconstitute the cultivation of their holdings, so that the best they could do would be to sell them to some large neighbouring owner for the best price they could get.

As to other possible causes, the growth of trade is one. The

[1] This last provision was made evidently under the expectation that if the carrying-out of the law was left to the ordinary executive, the consuls, it would be allowed to become a dead letter.

expansion of the empire in this and the previous century had led to thousands of Romans taking up trade in the provinces and in states bound by ties of friendship to Rome. Many of this new commercial class must have been persons drawn from the hard-working class of cultivators who were attracted by an employment which offered them something more than a bare means of existence.

The Lex Claudia of 218, which had practically excluded senators from participating in trade overseas, must have driven a large amount of senatorial capital into land. This would certainly result in the buying out of large numbers of small holders.

There can be little doubt that the motive which prompted Gracchus to make his proposals was a practical one, the desire to restore that efficiency of the Roman army which had fallen, or seemed to have fallen, so much below that of former times. The recent wars in Spain and Africa had disclosed defects of the gravest character, such as must cause alarm to anyone who realised that the maintenance of the empire was dependent on military efficiency. To the mass of the Roman people the empire overseas had become an interest so soon as it had become a source of profit, and so they were quite ready to support any measure which might reduce the danger of the situation, and to carry matters through in face of any opposition that might be offered. That the efficiency of the army had declined is quite certain ; but the story of the next thirty years was to show that the trouble really lay in the ineffectiveness of the Roman tactics of the time.

Inasmuch as the great landholders whose interests and property Gracchus was attacking were all members of the Senate, it was not unnatural that the Senate should be bitterly opposed to the Gracchan Agrarian Law. Gracchus therefore took the unusual course of ignoring the Senate and bringing the matter straight before the Concilium Plebis, a manœuvre to which the Senate replied by putting up one of his fellow-tribunes to veto the proposal. According to constitutional law, Gracchus had every right to bring the matter before the people without first getting the sanction of the Senate ; but at the same time, by so doing, he violated a custom which had been in existence for a century and a half.

The result of this action was disorder. Gracchus resorted to violence, removing Octavius from the tribunicial bench, and carrying the law in his absence, but in a form modified by the omission of the compensation clause. Gracchus then tried to stand for the tribunate of the following year. In the end he met the fate ordained for opponents of the Senate at this time : he was murdered.

SENATORIAL POWER

It has become commonly, though not universally, fashionable for historians of Rome to describe these events as a revolution which upset the predominance of the Senate. Gracchus certainly never started with the idea of posing as a revolutionary, still less of acting as one. He was driven by opposition into revolutionary violence. Constitutionally speaking, he did show that it was a tenable constitutional proposition that a magistrate or tribune might bring a law before the Comitia or the Concilium Plebis without consulting the Senate; but the Senate never accepted the proposition, nor did the people in this eighty last years of the Republic insist on it, though quite ready to act on it at times when the senatorial government showed marked inefficiency. As for the magistrates and tribunes who held office in the eighty-four years from 133 to the outbreak of the civil war in 49, the number of those who dared to defy the Senate on this point is very small.[1] In normal years the magistrates and tribunes are just as much the obedient servants of the Senate as they had been before Gracchus' time. But the fact that the principle on which Gracchus had acted was regarded as tenable led to a sort of anarchy in legislation during this eighty odd years, inasmuch as it was passed both with and without the consent of the Senate; and it all went into the statute book because there was no common agreement as to the necessity of senatorial consent. But there was nothing which can be called a revolution, unless the connotation of that term be extended beyond ordinary usage. It is also incidentally noteworthy that all the legislation of this period which is most directly responsible for the fall of the Republic is carried through without previous reference to the Senate. In point of fact, if the Republic was to last, the Senate must maintain its power, for the very good reason that in the Republic of Rome at this time there was no other element which could have taken over affairs, inasmuch as the people had neither the will nor the capacity for so doing, and magisterial supremacy would have meant a return to that magisterial tyranny which the people, during the struggle between the orders, had spent two centuries in overthrowing.

At the same time, there is no question that the action of Gracchus did shake the foundations of senatorial supremacy. Still, the edifice might have been repaired had not the senatorial order sunk into a close corporation of men in which the prevalence of inferior capacity made the man of first-rate capacity within its

[1] Of the 168 consuls of this period, Marius, Cinna, Pompeius and Crassus in 70, and Cæsar in 59; of the 840 tribunes, less than two per cent.

ranks an object of jealousy, dislike, and opposition, and the path to office for a man outside its ranks so thorny and so difficult that, if he won his way to it despite opposition, only a miracle could make him otherwise than hostile to the stupid bigotry of the order. The Senate, having no present, tried to live on a past reputation; and the supply ran out in 49 B.C. That it was conscious of the weakness of its position is shown by its reluctance to carry to extremes its opposition to laws passed after the fashion employed by Gracchus. It is always aware that its power is founded on the normal indifference of the mass of the Roman people with respect to political matters, and that to retain its normal supremacy it must yield to abnormal outbursts of popular feeling, with the satisfactory assurance that they will be passing phases. But, as far as the men who stirred up this feeling are concerned, it had no hesitation in bringing about their removal by assassination, having also the satisfactory assurance that the attachment of the people was to measures, not men. It would have been fatal to repeal a popular law; but there was little danger in killing the proposer. Politics at Rome had become too sordid to produce popular heroes. The law was the end which the people desired; the proposer of it was merely a means to an end which became obsolete when the end was attained. So his destruction caused no tears, and, at most, brief resentment.

Despite Gracchus' illegal action with regard to his fellow-tribune, Octavius, the Agrarian Law was accepted as law, and a commission composed of three sympathisers got to work. It must have acted with energy, for by 129 it had distributed all the public land belonging to the Roman people, and was proceeding to deal with that allotted to Italian communities, land whose possession was guaranteed to them by solemn agreements with the Roman people. The Roman retained in his most decadent days a superstitious regard for the sanctity of such agreements, so that the action of the commissioners shocked the conscience even of the progressives of the Senate, and the most prominent of them, Scipio Æmilianus, got the commission revoked. Its work was handed over to the consuls, who simply let the matter drop.

But the commission had done its work. Within twenty years the number of citizens qualified for legionary service had greatly increased. Not that this cured the ills of the military service, for their real nature had not been appreciated. It was left for Marius and Rutilius Rufus to do that.

Modifications of the law were made by subsequent legislation. The inalienable nature of the allotments, never popular with holders who would much rather have sold them and spent the proceeds in Rome, was revoked by a law of 121. In 118 the state began to charge a rent, which it abolished again in 111. After that the holders became freeholders.

The Socii

But before these things took place the progressives, disappointed at the discontinuation of the commission of 129, started in the next year or so what seemed on the face of it a very liberal agitation for the enfranchisement of the Italians, the real aim of which was to get hold of their ager publicus; for, if they became Roman citizens, their agreements with Rome would, *ipso facto*, come to an end, and their public land would be available for distribution. But the Roman people was becoming like the senatorial order, a close corporation in relation to the outside world, and was certainly not going to let others share the material advantages which Roman citizenship now offered. So the idea fell flat for the moment, and fell flatter still a few years later when Gaius Gracchus tried to revive it in the concrete form of legislation.[1]

Gaius Gracchus

If Tiberius had come, in spite of himself, to play the part of a revolutionary, there was nothing accidental about the part which his younger brother Gaius played. Elected tribune in 123, he deliberately set about using the office for the revolutionary purpose of completely overthrowing the senatorial supremacy, and transferring the constitutional control to the people, with the rich commercial class as a solid nucleus in a state democratic in fact as well as in form. There was for him no compromise with the men who had murdered his brother. The impossibility of the régime which he tried to establish is proof that he was either unstatesmanlike or merely actuated by a desire for revenge at any price. The history of the next seventy years showed unmistakably that, whatever the incompetence of the senatorial order, neither the rich commercial class nor the proletariat, nor both combined, could possibly have carried out the government of the Roman Empire.

His measures included laws for the distribution of government corn to the people at half price; for restricting the length of military service; for the substitution of a non-senatorial for a senatorial jury in the court established in 149 for the trial of cases concerned with maladministration in the provinces (Quæstio de Repetundis); for the putting up to auction of the

---

[1] I shall defer speaking of the claims of the socii of Rome to the franchise till I come to deal with the causes which led to the Social War of 90 B.C.

direct taxation of Asia ; laying down that the Senate should assign the provinces to magistrates before the persons concerned were actually elected ; for the grant of the full Roman franchise to the Latins and the Latin franchise to the rest of the population of Italy. It was indeed a comprehensive scheme affecting various sections of the population in various ways.

It was natural that the mass of the people should welcome the distribution of cheap corn and the relief from military service, of recent years a severe burden, especially in Spain. But they refused absolutely to extend the franchise, showing thereby that spirit which judged each measure on its merits, that is to say, on the material advantages or disadvantages which it offered to their personal interest, and ignoring the politics of the proposer. There was no party loyalty, because there were no parties. Theoretical politicians were confined to the Senate ; and even their views were not overloaded with theory. They were bidding for place rather than fighting for principles. Neither Gracchus nor any other statesman in Rome, with the possible exception of Cicero, had any permanent following among the voters. The Italian or country voters of Cicero's day come far nearer to the concept of a party than anything else in Rome.

Gracchus' other measures were mainly bids for the support of the rich commercial class,—measures to which the people gave a careless assent.

THE COMMERCIAL CLASS, OR "EQUESTRIAN ORDER"

Of the rise of this class there has already been occasion to speak ; but the legislation of Gracchus opens a new era in its history. In every state in which a commercial class of growing wealth exists side by side with an exclusive nobility, social jealousy is certain to animate it. Gracchus converted the ill-feeling and rivalry between it and the senatorial order from one of a social to one of a political type, by giving it a political standing in juries in the Quæstio de Repetundis. The class owed its wealth to two main sources : the one public, the farming of the indirect taxation of the empire, together with contracts for the construction of public works and the exploitation of public property such as mines, forests, and so forth ; the other private, banking and commercial enterprises on a large scale in the provinces.

The law which established this new form of jury seems to have laid down a property qualification of 400,000 sesterces as a qualification for jurymen, the same property qualification, as it so happened, as that for membership of the military body known as the Knights (Equites), the cavalry of the Roman army. But whereas the military equites were formed chiefly of the sons of senators, the law of Gracchus expressly excluded from the jurors all senators as well as their sons or near relations. Owing, as it would seem, to the identity of the property qualification (census), the new jurymen came to be called " equites " in popular parlance ; and they and the military equites are both included in the term Equestrian Order (Ordo Equester), which came into use after Gracchus' time. Thus the Ordo Equester of the first century before Christ really includes two categories of very different character and interests, to which the granting of the citizenship after the Social War added a third, those Italian country gentlemen who possessed the monetary qualification. As far as politics are concerned, it is the commercial element of the days of Gracchus which counts in the story of the struggle between the senatorial and equestrian orders.

The measure which handed over the juries in cases of extortion in the provinces to the new equites was either an abominable piece of political opportunism, the evil results of which for the provincials Gracchus or any other politician of the time could have foreseen, or a movement of political blindness due to the fury of personal revenge.

Tax-farming

The ancient world had neither the money nor the will to run a permanent government staff,[1] so that it farmed out such sources of revenue as were of a fluctuating character to tax-farmers who were accustomed to the intricacies of the particular system with which they had to deal. In most of the Roman provinces the direct annual taxation was a lump sum of unvarying amount ; and there the interposition of the tax-farmer was unnecessary. But in Asia and Sicily the tithe system, a heritage of Hellenistic days, though probably of ultimate Semitic origin, was in force, and there was nothing strange in the handing over of its working in Asia [2] to the Roman tax-farmer (publicanus).

In Sicily the tax-farmers were Greeks, for the Roman capitalist would not condescend to touch the system there because it did not allow the tax-farmer the uncontrolled freedom which he had in Asia. The Roman publicanus in Asia used the freedom for the grievous oppression of the provincials.

Gracchus' measure making the allotment of " provinciæ " anterior to all knowledge of who would hold them rendered it

[1] See p. 280.
[2] It seems probable that it had been recently reintroduced in Asia in place of a tribute at which the original taxation of the province had been assessed. It had prevailed there in pre-Roman days.

impossible for the Senate to arrange matters to the interest of its political friends, thus cutting away a good deal of ground from beneath senatorial patronage.

The author of these measures died the death of the pseudo-reformers of this period. He was killed in an uprising promoted by the senatorial order in 121.

His legislation had certainly weakened the position of the Senate; but it had not brought about that revolution at which he had aimed. The setting-up of the rich commercial class in a position of rivalry to the senatorial order was, from his point of view, an astute political move; but it was eminently disastrous to a state and constitution whose sole chance of salvation lay in the upper classes, especially in harmonious co-operation between the nobility and the upper middle class. The lower middle class had its attention concentrated on its personal interests, and government by the then decadent proletariat which resided at Rome would have meant anarchy and the destruction of the empire. Even at this time any weakness of the central government rendered it possible that some of the governors of the provinces might try to play the part which Alexander's generals had played in dismembering his empire.

Had the Senate of this time shown any capacity for government, the Roman people might have relapsed into its accustomed political passivity, when the voice of the would-be reformer would have been like that of one crying in the wilderness. But the last twenty years of the century were marked by inefficiency and disaster such as made the Roman people ready to attach itself to any leader who could save it from the perils of the moment.

The Jugurthine War

The trouble began in Africa. The kingdom of Numidia which lay east of the province of Africa had long been regarded by Rome as a client state. So, when in 118 troubles with regard to the succession arose between Jugurtha and Adherbal, Rome interfered in an attempt to accommodate matters by arranging for a division of the kingdom between the two claimants. The arrangement was pleasing to Rome because it set up two weak principalities instead of one strong kingdom on the borders of the African province; but Jugurtha accepted it with the obvious intention of breaking it at the first favourable opportunity. Within a very short time he overran the whole kingdom, driving out Adherbal, who appealed to Rome. The Roman government was so desirous of avoiding war that Jugurtha might have been left in possession had he not been misguided enough to commit an act which aroused the indignation of the

Roman people, the massacre of a large number of Roman traders after the capture of Cirta in 112. The Senate dare not defy the popular feeling thus aroused, and in that same year had to declare war on Jugurtha. The weakness and inefficiency of the government shown in the failure to protect the Roman trader abroad was exactly that form of inefficiency most calculated to arouse the masses from their political apathy.

The war went on for eight years. The details of it are wearisome. The outstanding features were Roman disasters, treaties made only to be cancelled, and a very disgraceful system of bribery carried on by Jugurtha in influential circles at Rome. The Roman army, badly led, and unfitted by nature to meet the mode of warfare adopted by the Numidians, suffered disgraceful defeats, which seemed to the Romans all the more disgraceful and disquieting in view of the fact that the Numidian kingdom was at most a second-rate power. The disasters also added to that anxiety for the safety of the empire which had been aroused by the military failures of the last forty years.

In 109 there appeared on the scene of war two men, Caius Marius and P. Rutilius Rufus, who as lieutenant commanders under the consul Metellus were acquiring experience which was to lead to a drastic and fatal change in the Roman army system. As year followed year and the war still dragged on, the people in their impatience took matters into their own hands, and in 107, in defiance of the Senate, appointed Marius to the command in Africa. By a strange fate he had L. Cornelius Sulla as his commander of cavalry. Even Marius, capable soldier as he was, had a hard fight; but he won the war. In 105 Jugurtha was defeated and executed.

The Roman government, following its usual policy, did not annex Numidia. It remained a client kingdom under Gauda.

The Jugurthine War had not yet come to an end, when the uneasy feeling it had created that something was wrong with the Roman military power was converted into a terrible certainty by events on the other side of the Mediterranean.

The Cimbri

Two powerful tribes, the Cimbri and Teutones, Celts by repute, but both probably containing Germanic elements, had appeared in Gaul about 106 from beyond the Rhine. Some years before that time, in 113, they had been on the Illyrian border, and had defeated Cn. Papirius Carbo at Noreia. They had then turned back north and west and invaded Gaul, where they raided the lands of various tribes; but, finding probably that there were more hard knocks than plunder to be got among their warlike Celtic brethren in that region, they turned south-

THE SECOND CENTURY, 200–100 B.C.

wards towards the richer regions of the Roman province and the territory of Massilia.

Gallia Narbonensis

The Roman dealings with southern Gaul after her conquest of Spain are obscure from lack of sure evidence. She had to use it as a passage to her Spanish possessions, for which purpose her friendly relations with Massilia, whose territory extended from the Alps to the Rhône, provided satisfactory accommodation as far as that river. How she dealt with the district between the Rhône and the Pyrenees is not known; but the discovery of numerous coins which must have been coined in Spain under Roman rule suggests that part at least was included in the province of Hither Spain. In 121 the powerful Gallic tribes of the Arverni and Allobroges, who had been threatening this important line of communication and been making themselves a general nuisance, were defeated and pacified; but the incident showed that the position, if allowed to remain as it was, would be insecure, and so Rome constituted the district between the Rhône and the Pyrenees as a province which came to be known as Gallia Narbonensis. Three years later, in 118, the town of Narbo was established as a Roman colony, the colonists, as early inscriptions from the place show, being drawn mainly from Umbria, a part of Italy where the Roman franchise had been very sparingly distributed. It is probable that very few of the colonists were Roman citizens before joining the colony. The Roman government was distinctly opposed to the permanent settlement of citizens outside Italy, inasmuch as it was desirable to keep the ruling race in the empire in a compact body ready to hand in case of trouble.

In 105 at Arausio, the modern Orange on the Rhône, a large Roman army tried to check the advance of the Cimbri. It was wiped out with a loss of 80,000 men. A series of disasters to the Roman arms so alarmed the Roman people that in 104 they elected Marius as consul for the second time so that he might take command in Gaul. In 103 the Cimbri had gone on an excursion into Spain, where their cousins the Celtiberi dealt so faithfully with them that they doubled back with intent to invade Italy. The Teutones first moved on Italy, but on their way thither they were in 102 defeated by Marius in a great battle at Aquæ Sextiæ. In the following year the Cimbri actually made their way into Italy to be utterly destroyed by Marius in the battle of the Raudine Plain.

The Marian Army

The army with which Marius won these two great battles was of a very different type from that which had been so disastrously defeated at Arausio only a year or two before. Never did an apparently small modification in one of its institutions have a more decisive effect on the fate of a people than the change in the conditions of service made in the Roman army by Marius in the two years which intervened between the close of the Jugurthine War and his victory at Aquæ Sextiæ. It brought into being an army of a type to which history cannot afford any exact parallel, that army of the last half-century of the Republic which, in order to distinguish its peculiar type, will be called hereafter the Marian army, and, as having been the weapon wherewith the Republic was destroyed, will be described now at the outset of its career in order to show its development in the course of the first century before Christ.

Marius did away with the property qualification which had hitherto been necessary for service in the legion—such a little change, but one which was to modify the history of the after-world!

He seems to have promulgated it on his own authority as commander of the army, without reference to the Senate or the comitia; but, though the Senate cannot have liked it, the times were so critical that it dare not oppose or attempt to reverse it subsequently; while, as for the mass of the people, they were only too glad to let the one trusted commander of the moment try any experiment which might possibly relieve a situation so bad that it could hardly be worse. Once made, the change was by its very nature, and owing to the circumstances of the time, irrevocable; and the success which resulted from it dispelled, or at any rate suppressed, any apprehension which foresighted men might have felt as to its ultimate effects. It is probable that the majority of the contemporary world in Italy regarded it as little more than a military reform of no political significance, and that such members of the Senate as distrusted it did so, not because they regarded it as dangerous to the state, but as threatening the supremacy of their own order.

The circumstances which brought about the change are easily traceable. In the Second Punic War Rome had been faced by armies drawn from the western region of the Mediterranean; and she had won through, though her victory was due rather to the mismanagement of the government opposed to her than to the virtues which she and her troops displayed in the long struggle. In the light of knowledge after the event it is clear that, in a military sense, the Roman army of the last years of the third century before Christ was but imperfectly adapted to face the methods of warfare of the wild peoples of the West. The victorious issue of the Second Punic War disguised, as has been already said, the real military position. The eastern campaigns of the first half of the second century B.C. tended to confirm the trust placed in the existing military institutions of Rome, though the prolonged struggle with the comparatively insignificant race of the Ligurians in north-west Italy might have suggested that not all was well with the Roman army and its methods. Yet in certain respects the army was founded on a sound basis. There was a property qualification for service, of which the practical effect was to impose the obligation on those classes which had a stake, even if a small one, in the country. This feature was, or had been, common to the military organisation of the city states of the Mediterranean ; and it did give practical expression to the theory that a citizen's burden of public service should be to some extent proportionate to the personal interest he had at stake in the defence of the state to which he belonged. But it is an unhistorical idealism which alleges that any such theory either originated the system, or was even a conscious force in its maintenance. It was to more practical considerations that the system was due. The original poverty of these city states rendered it impossible for them to provide the arms requisite for the equipment of an army ; and hence it was necessary to impose the cost of armament on the individual citizen, an expense which the poorer classes could not support.

The innate distrust which the ruling classes at Rome felt towards any pronounced development of the power of the proletariat caused this feature of the system to be maintained long after the financial necessity for its maintenance had ceased to exist ; and during the second century before Christ the Roman government was seeking to control a wide empire by means of an army whose formation and organisation was adapted rather to a restricted area of national defence. It was a situation which could not last if the empire was to last ; and it was complicated by economic causes.

Tiberius Gracchus, like all his contemporaries save the wilfully blind, had seen that something was radically wrong, and had tried to put matters right by re-establishing the class from which the best material for the army had in the past been drawn. But neither he nor anyone else at that time saw where the evil really lay.

At the bottom of all lay the fact that the Roman army as then organised, though it had proved itself equal to the conquest of an empire, was ill adapted for its maintenance. An army of citizens limited to those who had a property qualification which, though low, did imply that the person possessing it was an actual holder of property in some form or other—an army raised by levy, not by voluntary enlistment—an army, in short, typical of the city state of the old Mediterranean world—was adapted to the needs of the city state, that is to say to the defence of its territory, and to brief campaigns in the lands of near neighbours, but was not fitted for prolonged warfare in distant lands, for campaigns which kept the owner so long and so far from his work in life that his trade or property might go to ruin. It is true that this army had been used successfully in prolonged fighting in Asia and, too, in Africa; but then there had been rich plunder to be won from those centres of ancient and wealthy civilisations. Warfare in Spain, on the other hand, brought little save hard knocks, and had therefore always been unpopular. But, even so, in all these campaigns alike the soldier had served with the feeling that the war might, with luck, be over in a short time. But when after conquest it came to garrison duty in such lands as needed large garrisons, especially in Spain, the prospect of long detention away from home was certain. Spain was the special bugbear of the citizen soldier. It required a large army of occupation. Fighting, if such took place, brought no profits; and the distance and difficulty of communication with Italy made it impossible on the score of expense for the government to change the garrison at short intervals. In the second half of the second century evasion of the Spanish service became rife. The rich used bribery and influence. But the feeling of the less wealthy classes was such that magistrates who did not wish to bring their political careers to an end at the close of their year of office dared not insist on the literal enforcement of the levy, and sought to supply from the ranks of the socii the deficiency caused by the evasion of the citizen. It may seem strange that the government did not change the obviously anachronistic organisation of the army for some such system as Marius subsequently adopted; but the conviction of the need to modify institutions centuries old, especially those which have played a great part in the past, comes but slowly to men who have grown up under them; and besides, as has been already said, the Roman government seems to have been profoundly distrustful of any reform which would remove the centre of military gravity from the middle to a lower class. The future was to prove that the distrust was justified.

But another problem of a military nature had already arisen, and had, in a sense, been already solved. The Roman cavalry, the Equites, the members of which had been drawn from the highest class of the citizens, had never been of any great military value; and in the latter part of the second century its comparative uselessness had been accentuated by ill discipline. It had never been prominent in Roman warfare, partly because the lands in which the Romans had fought their battles were not adapted to its effective use, partly because both in quantity and quality the horses of that day were in most countries of the ancient world very inferior to those of the present time. Hence the legionary infantry had always been regarded as the "robur exercitus," the backbone of the army. The past inferiority of the Roman cavalry had been due to bad horses rather than bad men; but it was tolerated in an army which made little use of it, until in the middle of the second century its personnel became in the first place decadent, and as a natural sequel, mutinous. So, after the middle of that century, its services were practically dispensed with, and regiments recruited from Thrace and elsewhere took its place. It is in a sense an unexpected development in Roman military practice that foreigners should supply a branch of the army in which hitherto Roman citizens alone had served; but the branch was, for reasons already given, of inferior importance in the warfare of that age.

Rome entered on the last ten years of the second century without having done anything to remedy the defects apparent in that legionary service on which she mainly relied. The Italian socii had been ever more and more employed on unpopular military duties, so much so that thinking men began to consider whether they were not gaining a military experience from which the Roman was becoming more and more withdrawn. The socii themselves seem to have become conscious of the fact, for their demand for the rights of citizenship becomes more imperative with each repetition, and it is backed by some Roman politicians who, though they supported it from various motives, must some of them have been impressed with the necessity of including in the body of citizens men whose services became relatively ever more prominent in the armies of the state. But neither the Roman government nor the Roman proletariat would hear of any such thing, the latter influenced by the consideration that the share of each individual in the privileges and spoils of empire would be less if they were divided among a larger number. Such was the obstinacy of the time that it required one catastrophe to bring about the reform of the army, and another to force a recognition of the claims of the socii.

But whatever politicians might think and do, or leave undone, there were soldiers who were anxious to find remedies for the existing deficiencies. About the year 109 Rutilius Rufus introduced into the army a new drill in weapon tactics suggested by the practice of the gladiatorial schools. The motive for this change is not stated by Valerius Maximus, the author who records it; but it was natural that the scientific use of weapons should be carried to a high degree of development in such schools of training; and the very excellence of the system would be quite sufficient to suggest its adoption in the army. Still it must have been obvious to such an experienced soldier as Rutilius Rufus that its practical application to the existing form of service, when the soldier was merely called up for the campaign, would present great difficulties; and this suggests that the proposal was not merely made from a professional interest in an improved system, but because the practical circumstances of the time demanded a change. On the whole it seems probable that the experience of the existing system of weapon tactics had shown that it did not assure the Roman legionary of a superiority in combat with the races of the Spanish peninsula and of Gaul; and Spain was an endless source of trouble, while danger from Gaul was imminent. For the present purpose it is not the system but its results which are important.

The new drill was destined to promote a change such as began to come over Greek warfare about the close of the fifth century. In the last years of the Peloponnesian War the value of the peltast as a soldier came to be recognised; and the introduction of the type into Greek armies became merely a question of time. The character of the peltastic drill, much more elaborate than that of the hoplite, made it impossible for the Greek citizen soldiers to acquire it during their brief periods of service, apart from the fact that the Greek did not show any special aptitude for the kind of fighting it involved. Hence in the fourth century a change came over not merely the practice but the spirit of the whole Greek military system; and a race which had in the past set its face against the professional soldier, and had never employed the mercenary except under extreme stress of circumstances, found itself compelled to use a type of force which was both professional and mercenary.

The position of Rome in this year 109 was not quite the same as that of the Greek states in 400; but the difficulty was the same, though it was not destined to be solved on altogether the same lines. Rome had employed mercenaries in her cavalry and light infantry; but the professional soldier was as yet to come. It would be very interesting to know, but it is not known, how the new drill worked in the brief period between its introduction by Rutilius and the army reforms of Marius. It is probable, however, that it was then discovered that the period of service was too short for the purpose of learning it thoroughly; and that may well have been one of the main causes of the change in the conditions of service made by Marius three or four years later, in 106 or 105.

Marius did away with the property qualification for service in the legions, and threw the ranks open to all grades of the citizens. The qualification was so low, only 4,000 sesterces, before the change was made, that the change seems almost insignificant ; and yet its immediate results were striking, and the final results were fatal to the existence of the Roman Republic.

The need for some such reform had been obvious for half a century past ; and the Senate had, by omitting to adopt any measure of the kind, shown that its fear of the results it might have at home was greater than its hopes of any it might have abroad. But now disaster and danger due to the inefficiency of the government had roused the people ; and inefficiency was one of the two sins which the Roman masses, usually careless or even callous as to politics, would never forgive on the part of its rulers. So the Senate knew that its power would return to it if at such times it yielded,—even with a bad grace,—to the storm. What it really feared was lest, by showing too pronounced an obstinacy at times of popular discontent, it might create among the Roman proletariat an anti-senatorial party which would be a solid body in support of the so-called democratic politicians within the Senate itself. And so the act of Marius was allowed to stand.

The change introduced by Marius seems so small that anyone reading Roman history for the first time might well wonder why so much emphasis is laid upon it. It was well designed to meet the necessities of the moment ; but these necessities had existed, though not in so pronounced a form, for fifty years past ; and the fact that so obvious a remedy had not been adopted is a clear indication of the distrust with which the ruling classes within the Senate regarded it. Time was fated to show that this distrust was well justified, though the justification was to come in a form which could not have been anticipated at the time the change was made, inasmuch as certain elements of the dangers of the future were as yet in the future themselves.

The remedy sought in the first instance was concerned with the supply of adequate numbers for service, and of human material of better quality than that of the previous fifty years. Could Marius when he made the change have anticipated an adequate supply ? Or was he groping about in the dark for a remedy for an almost desperate situation ? There were as a fact certain features in the service of the previous age which must have encouraged him to anticipate that under the new regulations men would be forthcoming in sufficient numbers.

In contrast with the prevailing tendency to evasion which had in the recent past been a cause of anxiety to those who were interested in the efficiency of the army, there had sprung up a tendency on the part of some of those who had served in one levy to offer themselves for re-enlistment in the next, a phenomenon which showed that even in the propertied classes,—the qualification was indeed small,—there were those who regarded the rewards of military service as better than anything they could look for in other walks of life. The practice was contrary to the spirit, though not perhaps to the letter, of the Roman military system. But if such was the interest of men of small property, then that interest might be expected to be more prevalent among citizens of no property whatever. The anticipation proved to be correct ; and from the time of Marius onward the levy, though still retained as a power in reserve, was rarely employed, in so far as it is possible to form a judgment from the imperfect evidence relating to this last age of the Republic. Thus the forced levy was replaced for all practical purposes by voluntary enlistment ; and whatever may be the difficulties, and they are many, in applying customary military terms to this strange military phenomenon the Marian army, it can almost without reservation be called an army of volunteers, an army of enlistment.

But another change had been made. In the Roman army as previously constituted a man had been levied for a campaign, whereas in the new army he was enlisted for a war. This was necessitated by the fact that the training in the new drill, and especially in the elaborated weapon tactics of the gladiatorial schools, demanded a longer period of service. Thus the Marian army may be called a professional army. The professional element had indeed existed as a nucleus in the army of the previous years, consisting of those who offered themselves again for service, to whom those who were most responsible for the present change, Rutilius Rufus and Marius, belonged ; but, though it is impossible to say what percentage this professional element had formed in the pre-Marian army, yet it was probably small ; and it is certainly the case that the term professional would be inapplicable to that army in any general sense.

But the professional character of the Marian army went still further. The fact that the soldiers were henceforth drawn mainly from a class which had neither property, trade, nor profession to which to return at the end of the period of service, made those who enlisted look to the army as their profession. In any state in which such a type of soldier exists in large numbers and yet is not provided by the state with continuous employment during the period of his active life, together with an adequate pension on retirement, the soldier must form an ever-present peril to the whole constitution and economy of the state itself. It is in fact impossible to find in history any parallel to this extraordinary army—at any rate on the same scale. It is unique, not indeed in its individual features, but in its combination of them. In any military system the combination of

THE SECOND CENTURY, 200–100 B.C.

elements harmless in themselves may produce a dangerously explosive substance. This has been illustrated in the case of this army by one consideration of critical importance; but it may be illustrated by another almost equally striking to those at least who realise the nature of the Roman soldier.

In the Roman army the "sacramentum," the soldier's oath of obedience and loyalty, was sworn to the general in command of the army. The Roman was not peculiar among ancient peoples in his superstitious adherence to an oath of any kind. The average man of this ancient world had a wholesome dread of what might happen to him from the wrath of the gods if he broke his sworn word; and so the binding force of the sacramentum was of a strength hardly conceivable in an age where casuistry is apt to play a greater part than superstition in men's dealing with such contracts. Nevertheless, in pre-Marian times, when the Roman soldier was still a man with a stake in the country, there would be reasonable grounds for assuming that self-interest might get the better of superstition should any commander attempt to use his army against the constituted government. But under the new order of things the army was composed mainly of men who had no such interest as could tempt them to break their oath to their general; and, furthermore, however this might be, it was the fact that, so long as they obeyed their general, their sacramentum was not violated, even if adherence to it involved turning their arms against the government. It is strange that the government did not introduce some modification in the terms of the sacramentum such as would have transferred the allegiance of the soldier to the government rather than to his commander. It is still more strange that the government was stupid enough to adopt towards the Marian soldiers a policy which tended to make them more dependent on a general who looked after their interests than on a government which ignored them. Such were the causes, or some of the causes, which made the armies of the Marian type tools ready to the hands of any general for any enterprise however disloyal to the state.

Various terms of a military nature have been applied or misapplied to this army; and the very fact that authorities on the history of the time do not agree on their application serves to emphasise its unique character. It was not a mercenary army, for that term connotes the idea of the employment of foreigners in the army of a state, whereas the main, the legionary, element in this army was composed exclusively of citizens. It is true that in the last years of the Republic the spirit though not the letter of this rule was evaded. But, even so, there was no recruiting outside the provinces and client states; and the non-citizen so recruited was given, legally or illegally, the citizenship in order to make him formally eligible for the service.

Nor was the army a standing army, for that implies a permanent force in which the soldiers are serving during times of peace as well as of war. The Marian army was liable to disbandment at the end of every war; and actual disbandment, even if sometimes deferred, took place. It was not merely a question of getting rid of surplus troops; the whole army passed into civil life at the end of the war for which it had been enlisted; and if such were the circumstances that part or the whole of it could be re-enlisted forthwith by some commander for another war, that was essentially an accident, and not in any sense a feature of its organisation.

The intermittent existence of the army was, politically speaking, the fatal defect of the system. Augustus, whose practical wisdom was at least as great as that of any statesman who appears in history, saw that the extreme danger to the state involved in the Marian system lay in the fact that the government of the last fifty years of the Republic had never recognised the necessity of converting it into a standing army. He took that step at the very outset of his organisation of the empire.

The Marian army is an anomaly incapable of being defined by any of the terms customary in military history. It is a citizen force; but it stands in strong contrast to the typical citizen army. Its soldiers make war their profession, and live by it; but it is not a mercenary army. It is an army of the state; and yet to the state as such it swears no formal allegiance. Lastly, many of its most important features are wholly incompatible with the concept of a standing army.

It was its anomalous character which made it fatal to that government which, though it had not created it, had passively acquiesced in its creation.

The psychological development of the Marian soldier is as strange as the nature of the army itself. His mentality developed towards political evil; but the evil was not due to inherent depravity, but rather to external causes, many of which were preventable had the Roman government of the time shown the commonest foresight and the will to act upon it. But the government of this last half-century of the Republic is cursed with an inertia which makes it seek to kill realities by ignoring them, to stem the inevitable by raising difficulties, and to decrease its liabilities by not paying its debts.

The Marian soldier made fighting his profession; and, like other professional soldiers, he expected to get something from it. The bonds by which he was bound to the state were of the slightest. It was officially responsible for his pay, and for nothing else. Had the government been wise it would have recognised the advisability of accepting a moral, or at any rate a political, responsibility towards the personnel of the various armies which were raised for the defence of the state within this last age of the Republic; but, as far as such things were concerned, it never made any concessions to common sense until it had carried its refusal so far as to endanger its own existence. It was singularly consistent in its folly. The soldier soon found that he had nothing to look for from the government save his pay, and that, after the particular war for which he was engaged was over, the government, left to itself, washed its hands of all responsibility for his future. But the government was not left to itself. Its hand was forced by the generals under whom he had served; and thus it became apparent to the men that justice, at any rate as they regarded it, would only be done to them if they gave their commander unflinching support. Such a tie between general and soldier was obviously a danger to the state; yet the attitude of the Roman government of this period was eminently calculated to strengthen rather than weaken this dangerous combination of interests. Is it strange that under the circumstances the Roman soldier developed into a man who had no patriotism but only a profession? These inherent features of a bad system were emphasised by accidental circumstances. The service was outside Italy, to which after years abroad the soldier returned like a stranger, without those home interests which would have been created by the possession of property in his native land. His outlook on his return depended on whether another war was afoot. If it was, he could, if not too old for service, re-enlist for another quite indefinite period, the length of the new war; and by a further term of absence from Italy become still more a stranger to home ties,—if indeed he can be said to have had any,—and to home sympathies,—if of these he retained any remnant. But if on his return from one war no impending war offered a chance of re-enlistment, then his position became almost desperate. With a folly which seems almost inconceivable to those who with the light of knowledge of the event can see the inevitable results of it, the government showed no disposition to acknowledge that the disbanded soldier had any claims on the state; and, even when such claims were urged from outside, if it did not actually oppose them, it raised difficulties such as robbed ultimate concession of any claim to gratitude.

Not that there were not genuine difficulties which, though varying in their specific nature, according to the nature of the solutions which either were, or might possibly have been, proposed for the serious defects of the military system, culminated in one question, the amount of money available from the income of the state. The public income from the provinces did not show any large surplus. Some of them cost more, some less than they brought in; and the general balance, never large, was but too apt under adverse circumstances, such as the expenses of a war, to be on the wrong side.

Recourse was had to an expedient which, as every one must have known, could only solve the difficulty for the moment, with the certain prospect of its recurrence at some not far distant date. Even the commanders of armies, such as Sulla and Pompeius, had no better expedient to suggest than the grant of lands to disbanded soldiers; and the government, though it might oppose such proposals, had no alternative of its own to put forward. This expedient was faced by the difficulty that the Gracchan measure had absorbed practically all the lands available for distribution in Italy, so that whatever was appropriated to the soldiers had to be purchased out of the public funds; and there were practically no such funds available save such spoils as the army had won in the previous war—money badly needed for the payment of war expenses. Thus the resistance made by the Senate to such proposals, stupid as it may seem in view of the palpable dangers of resistance, was not without justification on financial grounds. There was the alternative of providing lands in the provinces; but it was contrary to the whole policy of the Roman government to give official encouragement to any scheme which involved the settlement of Roman citizens in large numbers outside Italy. The proposal of transmarine colonies had in the past been accounted outrageous; and doubtless before the full citizenship was granted after the Social War to all Italians south of the Padus it did involve a real danger in that it meant the removal from Italy of large numbers of that comparatively small body of citizens on whom the maintenance of the empire depended. Even after that war the inadvisability of such a measure was an article of the Roman political creed.

The only sound solution of the difficulty would have been that eventually adopted by Augustus, the creation of a standing army. But the financial difficulties of agrarian settlement would have been as nothing compared with those involved in the maintenance of a standing army of the size required by the empire of that day. It was from the provinces that the money for the purpose would have had to come; and there was very little money coming from them. Nor could much more be expected so long as the systemless methods of public finance prevailed with regard to them, so long in fact as they were looked on as sources of profit to the individual rather than to the state. It is the same tale in every department of the government of the last century of the Republic: remedies are wanted here, remedies are wanted there, but there is no money wherewith to carry them out. The roots of the failure of the Roman Republic are planted deep in financial incapacity.

The acquisition of financial resources necessary for the maintenance of a standing army would have meant a revolutionary change in the relations with the provinces, a change which the government of that time was incapable of making, incapable of desiring, and perhaps even incapable of conceiving. Its incapacity for good was unlimited.[1]

THE DEMOCRATS

At the close of the Cimbrian War Marius, the successful general who had saved Rome from catastrophe, the man of the people who had put to shame the incapacity of the senatorial commanders of armies, was the hero of the hour. The masses had shown their appreciation of him by electing him to the consulship year after year. The pseudo-democratic agitators regarded him as designed by providence to promote their professedly popular, but really self-interested policy. Here was a man, so it seemed to them, who by birth, by education,—or the lack of it,—by all the incidents of his recent career, by his high place in popular favour and by his military prestige, would be not merely a declared, but also a powerful opponent of the Senate, a champion indeed of those popular rights on which these pseudo-democrats proposed to insist.

Pseudo-democrats they were. Sallust describes their origin in his opening to the story of the Catilinarian conspiracy of forty years later. A greatly increased luxury of living due to the increase of the empire and the expansion of trade in this century had strained the finances of some of the great Roman families, all of whom had tried to go the pace, with disastrous results for some of them. As is usual under such circumstances those who had ruined themselves were anxious to restore their shattered fortunes at the expense of those who had not; and it was by the path of political change that they hoped to attain this end. The Gracchi, or at any rate the elder of the two brothers, seem to have acted from a sincere desire to reform defects and abuses; but, when the supporters of the Senate despatched them to another world, on whomsoever their mantle had fallen, it was certainly not on the agitators of the first century who professed

[1] I have thought it well before entering on the story of the first century before Christ to anticipate the history somewhat by indicating the enormous effect which this creation of the last years of the second century had on the course of events which in the next century led to the downfall of the Republic.

to be carrying on their task, men to whom that "popular" cause, which the experience and fate of the Gracchi had shown to have no sentimental or practical hold on the normal indifference of the mass of the Roman people, was merely a cloak for an economic revolution which might divert wealth from the hands of the prudent into those of the reckless. Their democratic sentiment was a sham. Altruism was a virtue which they never professed because they did not know it.

But they had much of the astuteness of the politically dishonest; and they showed it in a fatal recognition of that fatal fact that from henceforth in the Roman political world the last word was with the military power. So they enlisted Marius on their side. Marius had lived the life of a soldier all his days, and he knew that life and its teachings well; but he knew no other. He may have been according to his light a man of rough honesty; but his political inexperience, combined with a not groundless dislike of the senatorial order, made him the easy dupe of those who wished by contesting the authority of the Senate to reduce Rome to that social and political anarchy in which they sought private salvation. Thus the agitators of the time thought they had found in him exactly the man they wanted, a person of great political influence whom, owing to his ineptitude and inexperience, they might use for their own ends.

In the year 100 two of these agitators, Saturninus and Glaucia, having formed an alliance with Marius, got elected to the tribunate and the prætorship respectively. Marius, who had conceived political ambitions which, from the very nature of his past experience, could only develop on anti-senatorial lines, was ready to accept what he regarded as the leadership of the reform section.

The events which followed, though exciting and disturbing for the actors in them and for those who suffered from them, had no permanent influence on the future; so they may be dismissed in a few words. Saturninus' programme was an inferior copy of that of Caius Gracchus: to free the magistrates from dependence on the Senate, and to reduce the latter to its old position as a merely deliberative body. But, like Gracchus, he had the lack of foresight to tack on to these designs a proposal for the extension of the franchise to Italy and even beyond its limits. This wrecked him and his plans. Not even the popularity and influence of Marius could back successfully a measure which proposed to dilute so largely the privileges of the existing body of citizens. In the Appuleian Laws of that year the way was paved for these designs by proposals for transmarine colonies, and by measures bidding for the support of the equites and the proletariat. But the franchise cat was out of the bag; and

Marius, finding that support of such a policy meant for him the waning of popular favour, began to waver. Saturninus and Glaucia resorted to violence, and a senatorial candidate for the consulship was murdered, whereon the Senate called upon the wobbling Marius as consul to restore order, and the senatorials themselves slew Saturninus and Glaucia, probably to the relief of the disillusioned Marius. So once more the Senate recovered its supremacy until such time as another glaring example of inefficient government should rouse the mass of the people.

Social and Intellectual Life

The social and intellectual changes which passed over Roman life in this second century before Christ were greater than in any other period of Roman history. They were due to that intimate acquaintance with Hellenism which was brought about by Roman conquests beyond the Adriatic. Up to the end of the third century the influence which the Greek had exerted on the Roman world had been largely, though not wholly, material, relating to trade and its products, especially works of art, things which did no doubt modify the Roman character by enlarging the limits of its somewhat stereotyped experience, and by toning down its hard materialistic view of life. This influence had come to Rome mainly through the Greek cities of the Italian coast, cities which had once been among the greatest intellectual centres of the Greek world, but by that time had fallen far below the intellectual centres of the Hellenistic world such as Athens, Rhodes, and Alexandria. But though the influence of the Greek world of the third century had given birth to the beginnings of a Latin literature, yet by the end of the century the Roman had as yet but essayed to make third-rate copies of second-rate Greek originals.

This was all changed when in the second century the Roman came into direct contact with those eastern Hellenistic centres of culture which had included the literature of the great days of Greece in the somewhat miscellaneous literary matter which they preserved, produced, read, studied, and taught.

In Rome the influence made itself felt at first in the high social circles of the leisured noble class which came to devote itself with avidity to the study of literature and learning such as opened before it an intellectual world far more attractive than the material world of past experience. The Roman noble of the days of the Third Punic War, in the middle of the second century, is a very different person from his predecessor of the days of the Second Punic War. He has both gained and lost on him. He has become more civilised, more humane, more refined ; but he has in so doing lost some of that rigidity of character which had, whatever its merits or demerits, won for Rome that great place which she held in the world. He has acquired something of the religion of humanity, and lost some of the religion of God, a loss greater perhaps than it would be reckoned by one who regarded the mere formalism of the official cult and forgot that personal religion which was to some extent associated with, to some extent independent of it. In the Greek world the old faith was dead ; and, tied to the body of this death, the faith of the cultured Roman died also. Thus far the intellectual influence of Greece had been destructive. But as the second half of the century opens, the introduction of the various philosophic systems of ideas and life, especially the Stoic and the Epicurean, began to fill up the spiritual vacuum which earlier influence had created in the Roman mind. Adherence to the one or to the other of these forms was largely dependent on whether the Roman who sought such culture abided by the old stern moral system of the race, or whether he had acquired a taste for the less rigid morality and the greater luxury of that life which the Roman was learning from the eastern world. To the rigid conservative moralist Stoicism made an appeal owing to its inculcation of a system of life which had many points of similarity with the traditional morality of the Roman. To the modernist the less severe creed of the Epicurean was more adapted to the life which he had chosen. For these philosophies were no longer speculative. They had become creeds with sterotyped articles of faith, practical guides to life which had been so formulated that the adherents of them had merely to follow without being called upon to think.

In the lower social world of Rome Greek influence appeared in a different form. To it philosophy, had it appealed at all, would have appealed in vain. Its spiritual yearnings were confined to that longing ever present in the life, however rude, of the ancient world to acquire some satisfying solution of the mystery of death. Satisfaction came indeed in strange fantastic forms ; but human nature has ever regarded hope, however ill-founded, as better than blank despair. The Greeks of the lower classes who resorted to Rome in this century brought with them from Asia Minor and from Egypt many mystic superstitions which professed to give a more or less hopeful solution of the eternal problem ; and even the unintellectual Roman was ready to grasp at such straws on the sea of uncertainty. Unfortunately this mysticism was associated in many cases with a debased morality. The Roman government, a body of men brought up in a world which was in a religious sense absolutely tolerant, because its religious outlook was so alien to intolerance that it could not form such a concept, was not inclined to interfere with foreign cults even when they appeared in Rome and made converts among the citizens, provided always that they did not detach their citizen devotees from conformity to the national worship, that they were not associated with physical immorality or inhuman rites, and that they were not suspected of political tendencies subversive of the security of the state. If any one of these features showed itself, however, the Roman government could act with terrible and wholesale severity against those corrupted by such a cult, as it did in the case of the Bacchic orgiasts in the earlier part of this very century. But though there may be some uncertainty as to the amount of comfort which the Roman citizens of the lower classes derived from the mysticism of these rites, it is quite certain that the moral abuses connected with them had a very evil effect on their character.

The literary influence of Greece on Rome differs in the two halves of the century. In the earlier half the Roman is content to copy and translate Greek works, showing a strong preference for inferior rather than good models. In the latter half his taste becomes more educated, and his ambition is enlarged. He has come to admire and copy the best literature of Greece, and has furthermore conceived the idea of the creation of a native literature wherein only the purest Latin shall find a place. This is the beginning of that movement which produced the Latin of the golden age of a century later.

About the middle of the century the study of rhetoric became fashionable among the upper classes. In political life its value cannot have been very great, since the Roman who was judging of the acceptability of this or that proposal made to the Assembly had no appreciation of rhetoric as such, and did not want the facts obscured by elaboration of language. The success of the Gracchi, such as it was, was not due to their proficiency in the new study, but to the fact that they came forward to remedy defects due to the inefficiency of the government. In the Senate rhetoric won its way to popularity but slowly among senators who had been accustomed to look for businesslike brevity and clearness rather than adornment of language from those who addressed them. It was in the law courts that its value was first appreciated, and where those expert in it won their great successes.

CHAPTER X

THE FIRST CENTURY, 100-31 B.C.

THE suppression of Saturninus and his pseudo-democrats left the Senate, in so far as its powers in the home government were concerned, in its normal position of supremacy. The next disturbance was to come from another quarter.

Gaius Gracchus had done the empire an ill service when he made the commercial class, the Equites so called, the jurymen in cases of maladministration in the provinces, and gave it the right of farming the direct taxes of the wealthy province of Asia. He had sundered the interests of the two richest classes at Rome, the senators and the equites, so that their combination to resist would-be revolutionaries of the type of Saturninus had become almost impossible. This division of the solid interests in the state is one of the causes of the fall of the Roman Republic.

In the provinces the evils produced by the Gracchan measure were becoming so unbearable both for the governors and the governed that the political controversies of the first decade of the century centre almost completely on the effort of the senatorial order to free the court de Repetundis of equestrian control. In the provinces the equites were playing a most important part in three capacities, as farmers of indirect taxes everywhere, and of direct taxes in Asia; as bankers; and as moneylenders on a large scale, especially to provincial municipalities. The exercise of the first and the third of these capacities admitted of abuses which, if the position of the provincials was not to become unbearable, must be checked by the power of the governor. Yet under this Gracchan system that very governor was ever exposed to the peril of prosecution de Repetundis at the end of his year of office, with a trial to follow before an equestrian jury whose verdict was foredetermined in the case of a governor who had sought to restrain the evil doings of those equites who had operated in his province. As these evil doings were the rule rather than the exception, it came to this—that good governors were only too liable to prosecution and condemnation at the end of their term of office, while bad ones, who either winked at, or even abetted, the evil-doings of the equestrian financiers, came off scot-free. In this very decade Scævola and Rutilius set their faces against the extortion of the capitalists who were operating in Asia, with the result that Rutilius was prosecuted in 92 before the court de Repetundis, and his property was confiscated.

Not that many of the provincial governors were martyrs under this system : it was the provincials who played that part. The more or less haphazard and, in a sense, involuntary way in which the provincial empire had been acquired had made such organisation as had been applied to it haphazard and incomplete. Before ever the organisation had been accomplished the Roman official, the Roman financier, and the Roman trader had found that the provinces could be exploited for their individual profit, so that, had any amelioration of the system been attempted, it would, as implying a change in this lucrative situation, have met with opposition from all classes. The Roman character, severe or even ruthless, had nevertheless not been unsympathetic towards those who in early days had come under the power of Rome ; but with the acquisition of the control of the wealthy East commercialism had undermined it. The Roman thought he had found something which was worth getting in exchange for his soul. The rational conservatism of the abler Romans of early days had been replaced by an irrational opposition to all change, the opposition of that senatorial order which, once able enough to use its able men, was now stupid enough to prefer to be represented by its stupid men. It was wedded to many ideas which could not be accommodated to the circumstances of the time. Office at Rome, unpaid as it was, had become a financial burden which few could bear ; but the senatorial order, wealthy in itself, and, in so far as it did recruit its ranks, recruiting them mostly from men of wealth, would never have assented to, least of all proposed, that payment for office which would have thrown open the competition for magisterial positions to citizens of small or moderate means. Even within its own ranks, now that life was becoming for many of its members too dear to live, magistrate after magistrate ended his year of office in a state of bankruptcy for which there was no remedy save the profits which he could draw from subsequent provincial command. Is it strange if he became not very scrupulous as to how those profits were made ?

Provincial Administration

It is during this last half-century of the Republic that the scandals of provincial administration reach their highest point ; and it is therefore appropriate that this, one of the outstanding features of the story of the period, should be set forth at its outset.

It is possible to schedule these evils under two headings,

official and unofficial. It was in the eastern provinces that they were most prevalent, partly because they were the most wealthy, partly because the population was by nature, and to a certain extent, by past political education, accustomed to regard official oppression as a natural element in government. Two centuries of the rule of the successors of Alexander had crushed the old Greek spirit of independence. In the province of Asia, owing to the direct taxes of that province being farmed by equestrian publicani, the scandals reached their highest point.

Even had the official system of government been worked honestly, it was so defective in design that it would have been almost impossible to work it well. The governor, a proconsul or propraetor, had under him a quaestor who supervised the finance under the governor's direction. He had also a staff of lieutenants (legati) to whom he might delegate certain functions, especially those of a judicial character. But nothing in the system of apportionment guaranteed that the governor should have had any experience of provincial rule, still less experience of the people of the particular province he was sent to rule. He might indeed have been a quaestor or legatus in a province at an earlier stage of his political career; but that would have been a mere accident, not a feature of the system. The fact of his having been consul or praetor at Rome gave him what was practically an absolute claim to succeed to a provincial governorship quite regardless of whether he had or had not experience of Roman rule outside Italy. No such experience was demanded from his quaestor or legati; and the possibility of their having had it was even more remote. Even before Sulla a period of one year was the customary term for the tenure of a governorship, a custom which that statesman made a practical rule. It is true that it was departed from before and after Sulla's time in individual cases; but in the majority adherence to it meant that even the best governor was just beginning to have that experience of his province which would have made him really capable in his office at the very time at which he was forced to resign it. Indifferent means of communication made it impossible, especially in the case of the more distant provinces, for the Senate to exercise a proper control over governors, a consciousness of which fact made that body nervous as to the possibility of a governor who acquired a firm foothold in a province becoming disloyal to the central government. Before the time of Sulla it was necessary to give some governors a prolongation of their command simply because the number of consuls and praetors whose term of office at Rome came to an end at the close of each year was not sufficient to supply substitutes for the existing governors of provinces; but

Sulla by increasing the number of prætors at Rome provided the possibility of relieving every provincial governor of his command at the end of one year of office.

Apart from these political considerations the financial embarrassment in which so many consuls and prætors found themselves at the end of their term of office at Rome would make them impatient of being kept out of a lucrative governorship abroad by some one whose command had been prolonged beyond the usual year. From other save the financial point of view rule abroad was by no means universally popular, inasmuch as it withdrew the holder from the political and social centre of the empire.

There were certain formal restrictions on the power of the governor; but the means of enforcing them were so inadequate that evasion or violation of the legal position was only too common, because the profits from so doing were large, and the chance of escaping punishment in favour of the delinquent. The Lex Provinciæ of the particular province laid down the principles of taxation, in many cases those which had prevailed in the days before Roman rule, and scheduled the rights of the communities in the province. But to the latter, at any rate, a bad governor paid little attention, for all he had to fear in case he violated them was a prosecution for the recovery of damages (de Repetundis) before a court which, so long as the jury was senatorial, would be sympathetic, and whose sympathy, when the jury was equestrian, could be won by giving the publicani and business men of that order a free hand in their dealings with the provincial population.

But outside these formal restrictions the powers and discretion of the governor were almost unlimited. At the outset of his period of office he issued an edict laying down the principles of law which he would follow in deciding cases which came before him, an edict in the composition of which he had an absolutely free hand, though by this time it had become customary to borrow it mainly or entirely from that great body of case-made law which had grown up in the civil court of the prætor at Rome. But he need not tie himself down to this; so that even in this century governors' edicts varied in different provinces, especially in reference to the rules laid down for dealing with the equestrian publicani or private financiers, who were allowed much more freedom under the edicts of some governors than under those of others.

In respect to the official system of provincial government the main defects were the failure to guarantee experience and to enforce observance on the part of governors of those government regulations which protected the rights of the provincials.

The governor combined in his own person the chief military and judicial functions, so that it was only too easy to compensate for the defects of the latter by the exercise of the powers of the former. Unadulterated tyranny would have been preferable to the adulterated form which prevailed in the Roman provinces, because in the former case the tyrant would not have evaded personal responsibility by casuistic reference to a bad system which others had devised.

The legitimate burdens on the provincials, meaning thereby those permitted by law, were heavy. But their weight was increased by illegitimate use of them. A governor could levy troops within the province. During the Republic this burden was not so heavy as during the Empire, for the levies were but temporary, employed only in case of emergency and for the defence of the province, larger employment of them being discouraged by the fear which prevailed at the time of training any larger numbers of the provincials in the use of arms. And so under the Republic these provincial levies play but a small part in the Roman military system.

But in every province a governor had to have at his disposal a certain number of Roman troops for whom, inasmuch as no system of permanent camps had been established, quarters had to be found by billeting them on the municipalities of the province. The expense was great, and their misbehaviour still greater, so that the town communities of a province were ready to ransom themselves from this burden by large payments to the governor. It is probable that few even of the better governors failed to profit from this; and, as for the worse, they elaborated the whole arrangement into a system for extracting money far and wide from the towns of the province.

In judicial matters many of the communities had local jurisdiction guaranteed to them by the lex provinciæ; but outside these limits the governor's court dealt with legal matters. But, if a governor chose to disregard the rights of a community in this respect, there was no power on the spot which could stop him from so doing, and it was a far cry to Rome; while but cold comfort was to be derived from the possibility of calling him to account "de Repetundis" at great expense and with very uncertain prospect of success. It is, too, more than probable, judging from what took place in the contemporary courts at Rome, that the Roman citizens who sat as jurors in these provincial courts were faithful clients of anyone rich enough and willing to bribe them.

The decision of civil cases in the governor's court by Roman law had two results, in that it led in the first instance to the whole of the Empire becoming acquainted with a system of law which, when not corrupted in practice, was infinitely superior to any civil code which prevailed, or ever had prevailed, in the Mediterranean world, and later to the adoption of this code by provincial communities which had had a right of jurisdiction exercised originally under their own local code. There was hardly any deliberate policy of unification of the Empire under the Republic; but nevertheless, of all the ties which subsequently bound it together, that of a common code of civil law was one of the strongest.

In criminal matters there was no appeal from the decision of the governor, unless of course the accused happened to be a Roman citizen.

As to the dealings of the governor with the equestrian financiers who operated in his province, they may be considered in dealing with the operations of those gentry.

But even for the best governor the path of honesty was a rough one to tread. Honesty of dealing meant that he made friends of the uninfluential provincials, and enemies of his staff of legati and comites, all of whom expected to make something for themselves during his term of office, and none of whom were at all squeamish as to how it might be made: enemies of powerful members of the equestrian order both in the province and at Rome, all of whom regarded him as a debt-collector of debts which the unfortunate provincials had been obliged to contract mostly in order to meet the exactions of the governor and his staff. He was expected to billet soldiers on bankrupt communities, in fact to take every forcible means, legal and illegal, for the extraction of the monies due to the Roman money-lender. To an honest man like Cicero when governor of Cilicia the position was a hard one.

To discuss all the means not merely possible but employed for extortion from the provincials would take long. Even on his way to the province the governor could demand free entertainment from the cities of the provinces through which he passed; so could even unofficial Romans who journeyed through the Empire armed with what was called a "libera legatio," a travelling pass on an imperial scale issued by the Roman government.

Corn could be bought from the provincials for the sustenance of the provincial garrison at any price the governor cared to fix. Needless to say that if he fixed it at something less than the market price then current the persons from whom the demand was made were only too glad to pay him a percentage of the difference in order to get off the one-sided bargain. But if the seller had to sell, his troubles did not necessarily end there. He might be called on to deliver his corn at some place at the other end of the province, a sore expense in those days of bad communications. He would be only too glad to buy off the necessity by paying the governor a percentage of the cost of transport, only to see his corn used up in his own native place. This was a form of imposition which even the government of the Empire, keen as it was to abolish such abuses, was only partially successful in suppressing.[1]

But if there was some sort of limit to the official extortions of the senatorial governor and his staff, to those of the equestrian financiers there was practically none, save such as a good governor who dared to take his fate in his hands could impose on them. Unpaid debts increased by leaps and bounds under a system of compound interest such as would have made the mouth of a modern moneylender water. A community which had got into arrears with its tax payments had only one source from which to get the necessary cash, the equestrian financiers, for by the time the first century opens that powerful corporation of capitalists had practically cornered all the floating capital of the Mediterranean world. Moreover, it was far too well organised to permit between its members any cut-throat competition such as would have cheapened money.

In all the provinces members of the equestrian order farmed the indirect taxation, a department of their activities in which no notorious scandal occurred simply because the general system did not admit of much manipulation to the disadvantage of the trader. But, even so, their methods were unpopular, even in Italy. In Sicily, where the tithe system of direct taxation prevailed, the direct taxes were also farmed by publicani; but, as the system was one which Hiero of Syracuse had borrowed from Egypt, one under which the tax-farmer was so strictly supervised that profits could never be otherwise than small, the Roman publicani would not touch it; and the tax-farmers were all Greeks of moderate wealth.[2]

In the province of Asia, however, where the tithe system also prevailed in direct taxation, the principles of tax-farming there in operation had descended from the Seleucid kingdom in which the tax-farmer had been far more independent than under the Ptolemies. Hence the profits were potentially large inasmuch as the operations of the tax-farmers were less interfered with by government supervision. There the iniquities of a

---

[1] See Tacitus, "Agricola," ch. 19.

[2] Some historians of Rome speak of the tax-farmer in Sicily as though he were a Roman publicanus. This seems to be due to a misunderstanding of the language of passages in the Verrine Orations of Cicero, where the speaker does not go out of his way to explain facts well known to the jury he is addressing.

badly devised system reached their height. The Roman publicani had formed commercial companies (societates) which made contracts every five years for the direct taxes of the province, paying a lump sum for the right of collection during that period. It was thus to their interest to extract as much as possible from the taxpayer. The investment was nominally a speculation dependent on whether the harvest was good or not ; but, in point of fact, unless the governor checked their operations, a thing but few governors dared to do, they squeezed from the provincials quite enough to make up for any deficit due to a bad harvest. Most governors backed their arbitrary exactions by lending them soldiers for the purpose of collection ; and, if the governor would not help the unfortunate provincials, they had no one to whom to turn for protection or redress.

But the members of the equestrian order appeared in the provinces in another less public guise as bankers and moneylenders (negotiatores). Some were big men ; some were small ; and, while the big men drove hard bargains with the municipalities which required loans, the small did the same with the local traders. In some provinces many town communities were reduced to a state of bankruptcy, which meant that their inhabitants were incessantly harassed and robbed, often with violence, for the payments of debts contracted at an interest of as much as 48 per cent. Cicero [1] mentions that members of the town council at Salamis in Cyprus had been starved to death in the town building where they had been incarcerated till such time as the debt was paid.

The hatred with which the Roman came to be regarded in some at any rate of the provinces is shown by the wholesale murder of thousands of Romans in Asia when Mithradates invaded that province.

The evils of the Roman provincial government under the Republic were due to the fact that the individual Roman had been permitted to make individual gains from subject regions which the official government, having taken them over originally against its will, had never taken the trouble to organise either in the public interest as represented by itself or by the native inhabitants of the regions acquired, so that when a state of things arose which called for amendment and for reorganisation there were so many individual citizens of all classes interested in the maintenance of a pernicious system that the government dare not undertake so unpopular a task, even if it had had the ability to do so. The Roman people had to pass through the dread experience of a terrible civil war before it arrived at a

---

[1] "Epist. ad Att." v, 21 & vi, 2.

state of mind such as made reform possible even for the commander of the victorious legions. The story of the provinces in the last age of the Republic is sufficient in itself to justify the feeling that it would have been a pity if the Republic had not come to an end at the time it did, and a doubt as to whether the empire could have lived had not the Republic died. In this instance it was the life of the child, not of the mother, which was saved by the Cæsarian operation.

The Senate and the Equites in Rome

In politics at Rome during the first ten years of the century a triangular duel was going on between the senatorial order, the equestrian order, and the democrats. The senatorials were trying unsuccessfully to recover their place on the juries. The equestrians were resisting their endeavour, and taking vengeance on governors like Scævola and legates like Rutilius Rufus who had opposed their depredations in the provinces, while putting in a little time in condemning democrats who tried to disturb that peace so necessary for the happiness of the capitalist. The democrats were smarting under the defeat of Saturninus, and fully determined to get their own back again at the very earliest opportunity. This made the Senate nervous, a nervousness for which there would have been much more reason had Marius, the military friend of the democrats, been a more capable politician. One of the ablest members of the Senate, M. Livius Drusus, a genuine but enlightened member of the senatorial order, sought to bring about a reconciliation of interests by a series of laws which were to satisfy everybody, the senatorial and equestrian orders, the democrats, the mass of the citizens, and the non-citizen population of Italy. He succeeded in dissatisfying everybody. He proposed to reform the Senate, the last thing the Senate desired; to restore the jury courts to the Senate, which roused the fury of the equites; to give largesses of corn at the expense of debasing the coinage, a proposal naturally unpopular with the monied classes; to enfranchise the Italians, with whom the mass of the Roman citizens were determined not to share the franchise; to settle citizens in unallotted lands in Italy, which threatened the property of non-citizen communities throughout the country.

The laws were passed amid violent opposition; but were annulled on the ground of alleged informality in their passing. Many wished to murder Drusus; and somebody did so. So this reform movement had the sequel usual at the time.

But Drusus had fanned into flame a fire which had long been smouldering.

The Social War

For nigh forty years past the question of granting the citizenship to the Italian allies (socii) had been coming at intervals to the surface of politics like whiffs of smoke indicating the presence of a fire beneath.

There were general as well as particular grounds for the strong dissatisfaction with which the Italians regarded their position. At the end of the Second Punic War Rome had taken bitter and widespread vengeance on those Italian socii who had gone over to Hannibal during his occupation of south Italy. Large numbers of communities in that region had been deprived of all their political rights and of nearly all their civil liberty, regardless of the fact that this so-called disloyalty had been forced on them by the inability of Rome to protect them. These cities were now governed by præfects sent from Rome who exercised almost unlimited power over the lives and fortunes of the inhabitants. In the century which had passed since the close of the war little if anything had been done to mitigate the lot of these unfortunates. It is not strange that they were discontented with that lot, nor that their fellow-Italians sympathised with them.

A more widespread cause of discontent had been the war service which Rome had demanded from the socii during the latter half of the second century. The ever-growing indisposition of the Roman citizen to service in the army had driven the government into an ever-increasing employment of socii in the most unpopular forms of service. To the Italian it came to seem as if he was bearing all the burdens of empire while others were enjoying the fruits of it. But on the credit side of the consideration the Italians could not but take into account the fact that they were acquiring military skill and experience while the Roman citizens were losing it. The events of the last thirty years had been calculated to bring their discontent to a head. Their grievances had been used as a handy weapon in the political fights of the time. Democratic partisans had taken up their cause, not for philanthropic motives, for such things had no weight in the Roman politics of the time, but in the first instance in order to get hold of their public lands for distribution under the Gracchan Agrarian Law, and later with the hope that the Italians, when given the vote, would support those who had been instrumental in getting it for them. The failure of the first proposal had produced a revolt at Fregellæ in 125, which the Roman government had suppressed. The renewal of the proposal in a modified form by Caius Gracchus had cost that politician his temporary popularity with the Roman people, and possibly his life. The Roman citizens of the lower class had become a sort of imperial benefit club, which was determined not to reduce the benefits conferred by membership of it by admitting others to share them. Yet serious statesmen must have felt that the Italian question was a very serious one demanding settlement by concession. But, so far from adopting a policy of concession, the Roman government, backed in this by the mass of the Roman people, adopted a policy of ever-increasing stringency which culminated in the Lex Licinia Mucia of 95, forbidding the Italians even to seek attainment of the franchise. Livius Drusus has been represented in modern histories of Rome as a politician who was bidding on behalf of the Senate for the prospective Italian vote in the same way that the democrats had bidden for it in the past. But, taking into consideration Drusus' legislation as a whole, it is impossible to conceive of him as having been either an acknowledged or self-constituted political agent of the Senate. He appears rather to have been statesman enough to see the needs of the time, but not politician enough to devise practicable means of meeting them.

The Italians were ready for the rejection of his franchise proposal. They rose *en masse* in central and south Italy. The war which followed showed the extent of the danger involved in employing a large non-citizen force to fight the battles of the empire. On this occasion it was the Marian army which saved Rome. Had Rome had to fight the war with the pre-Marian army, there can be little doubt that the Italians would have won the day. The revolt broke out at Asculum, where the Roman prætor and all Roman citizens were murdered. The central tribes, the Pæligni, Marrucini, Frentani, and Vestini, were all up in arms; and the Samnites of the south joined them. The Etruscans and Umbrians held with Rome; and elsewhere, scattered throughout Italy, the Roman colonies, most of the Latin towns, and the Italian towns which enjoyed the most favourable political rights, remained loyal. The insurgents selected Corfinium as their capital, setting up there a government with Senate and Comitia on the same lines as the government at Rome. The first year of war was marked by many Roman defeats and few Roman successes, so that the insurrection spread more widely among that population of southern Italy which suffered so greatly from the severity with which it had been treated after the Second Punic War. By the end of 90 Etruria and Umbria were wavering; but here the situation was restored in favour of Rome by the grant of citizenship to all those communities which had been faithful to her. This had also a general effect in weakening the resistance throughout the peninsula, so much so that in 89 the Roman generals Strabo and L. Cornelius

Sulla broke the insurrection in the north and south respectively. But Rome had been taught such a lesson that she dare not revert to refusal of the citizenship. By the Lex Plautia Papiria of 89 the concessions made by the law of 90 were extended to all those, whether enemies or not, who cared to give in their names to a prætor at Rome within sixty days. Though resistance continued in the south for nearly two years, yet the final result of this legislation was that all free inhabitants of Italy from the Padus southwards became Roman citizens, while the Transpadanes received the Latin franchise.

The sudden addition of so large a body of new citizens to the number of enfranchised might have been expected to modify the whole character of the government and policy of Rome. In most respects it was the unexpected which happened. It is evident that the democrats had thought that the Italians, when they got the vote, would prove a radical anti-senatorial element in Roman politics; and that this anticipation was shared by others outside the democratic coterie is shown by the way in which the government proceeded to discount the votes of the new citizens. The number of tribes, raised to thirty-five a century and a half before, had remained stationary ever since. Thus the tribes gave thirty-five votes in the two chief legislative bodies of the time, the Comitia Tributa and the Concilium Plebis; and so, in order to nullify the effect of the new votes, the whole of the new voters were entered in eight tribes, with the result that their votes affected less than a quarter of the votes in those legislative bodies. No law was necessary for such an arrangement. The entry of the names of new citizens on the list (album) was part of the duties of the Censor, and thus distribution among the tribes was entirely at his discretion. Within a few years that anomaly was rectified by a redistribution of the Italian voters among a large number of the tribes, probably among thirty-one.[1] This may have been the work of Sulpicius.

It might have been expected that these new voters would prove bitterly hostile to that senatorial government which had ruled the state during that period when their claims to citizenship had been so bitterly opposed. It is at the same time probable that they knew that the real opposition had come from the mass of the Roman people. Be that as it may, the new voters proved themselves distinctly conservative in their views, quite ready to support the government of a senate which they had for two centuries past come to look upon as an earthly providence, the supreme disposer of the fate of the world as known to them. They were not inclined to contest the constitutional claims of a body which had ruled them and the rest of the empire from what

[1] New citizens were not put among the four original tribes of Rome.

was to them a time immemorial. They were also intensely proud of having become citizens of the great world-state whose greatness had been attained under senatorial control. Of the sordidness of public life at Rome at the time they had no knowledge; and they remained in ignorance of it right to the end of the Republic, pathetically sympathetic with a system which, originally good and effective, had hopelessly degenerated in the hands of those who had to carry it out.

Personal participation in the government of the empire was almost denied them by the fact that it was impossible for them, on the score of distance, to attend meetings of the Assembly at Rome. The fatal weakness of a non-representative democratic form of government came out here. A popular Assembly can only retain prestige and power so long as it is adequately representative of the whole body of the citizens, for it is on the personal interest of the citizens that its efficiency depends, an interest which cannot survive among those who cannot take part in its proceedings. The decline in the influence of the Assembly at Rome must have been going on for more than a century past, increasing ever as the body of the citizens became more and more scattered through the communities of Italy. But when with the grant of the citizenship after the Social War the whole of the free population of the peninsula south of the Padus came within the citizen body, the Comitia and the Concilium Plebis became so absurdly unrepresentative that they were, and were recognised as being, a mere travesty of popular government. Thus, when aristocracy failed to govern the empire, it was impossible to replace it by a restoration of democratic control, for the very good reason that the machinery of the constitution provided no means for its exercise. The Roman Assemblies became mere rump parliaments; and there was only one political refuge for the state, the protectorate of an autocrat. Even the cautious Augustus, ever formally concessive to such reality of republican power as survived the downfall of the Republic, had no hesitation in treating the Assembly of the Roman People as a practical unreality.

THE DEMOCRATS AND SULLA

While the Social War was drawing to its close political trouble was again rampant in Rome itself. On this occasion the author was a certain P. Sulpicius Rufus. He made a series of proposals significant at the time, and of the time, but unimportant in general history because, owing to the action of Sulla, their life was brief. The chief of them were two, one of which excluded from the Senate all those members who were in debt beyond a certain sum, and another which gave the vote to freedmen. For somewhat complicated reasons the opposition of the government, especially to the first of the proposals, was violent. The expenses of the life fashionable at the time were ruining many noble families which had scions in the Senate. Their opposition was natural. But these bankrupts, being usually debtors to wealthier members of the order, were so much under the control of their creditors that they formed a series of coteries in the Senate which voted according to the orders of that member of them who had played the part of money-lender to the rest. So Sulpicius' proposal was not likely to meet with the approval of the financially sound.

Events took the course chronic at the time,—violent opposition, violent proceedings, and violent passing of the laws. For security's sake there was tacked on to the proposals a further one that Marius should take over from Sulla the command of the army in south Italy. Those who made this proposal did not as yet know Sulla.

Of moral character Sulla had but little; of moral courage and determination he had enough and to spare. He knew his own mind; and he was minded to support the rule of that noble society of which he was a distinguished and peculiarly aristocratic member. Ignoring his supersession in the command, he, after a little difficulty with the officers, persuaded his army to march on Rome. Thus for the first time it was shown how a man with a Marian army at his back could defy, or even overthrow, the government. Marius and Sulpicius fled, the latter being subsequently caught and executed.

The judgments which have been passed on Sulla in modern times have tended to be extreme in appreciation or depreciation according as the writer favoured or disliked his political methods. Those methods were drastic. It was an article of faith fashionable at the time that it was well to put over-zealous political opponents out of the way; but this, at any rate, must be said for Sulla, that he did not on this, the first period of his power at Rome, put it into practice on a large scale.

The man himself is somewhat of an enigma. The very times in which he lived are, historically speaking, also somewhat of an enigma, partly because the evidence is inadequate, partly because the times themselves were, fortunately, unique.

Lucius Cornelius Sulla had had a career which must have been exceptional in an age in which long service in the army was not popular in those ranks of the higher nobility to which he belonged. He had been commander of the cavalry in the Jugurthine War; a lieutenant of Marius in the war against the Cimbri; had seen fighting when governor of Cilicia in 92; in 91 and 90 had been lieutenant-commander, and in 89 and 88 commander of the army of the south against the revolted socii of south Italy. He had been consul at the time of the disorders which accompanied the passing of the Sulpician Laws; and it was his experience on that occasion, when he and his colleague narrowly escaped with their lives, which now brought him back with his army to settle affairs at Rome.

He had proved himself an able, even a brilliant, soldier. In politics he was an out-and-out supporter of senatorial supremacy. It was the Senate, not the democrats, which had now got the military power on its side.

Sulla's Legislation of 88

Taking the legislation of Sulla both on the present occasion and seven years later, as a whole, it is difficult to say in some cases exactly what he did, still more difficult to say how much of it he did in this year 88. But all his legislation on both occasions had one end in view, to make the position in the constitution which the Senate had won by the growth of constitutional custom a position based on statute law, so that anti-senatorial politicians should not from henceforth have that base for attack on the Senate's position which was afforlded them by the uncertainty as to whether this or that power ctaimed by it had become established as a custom of the consitution.

The one measure which can safely be attributed to his legislation of 88 is a law forbidding the introduction into the Concilium Plebis of any bill not previously sanctioned by the Senate. This was, of course, nothing more than the legal enactment of a custom which had prevailed for nigh two centuries past. It is perhaps needless to say that the Sulpician Laws were annulled. Three hundred new members were introduced into the Senate from among the original military element in that now very miscellaneous body the Equestrian Order. It is probable, too, that a maximum rate of interest was imposed, and possible that the old preponderance of the higher property classes in the Comitia Centuriata was re-established.[1]

Mithradates

For some time past the state of things in Asia had called urgently for the intervention of the Roman armies on a large scale. Roman authority beyond the Ægean was dead, for the whole of Asia Minor had been overrun by Mithradates of Pontus; and he was now threatening Rome's European possessions and allies on the near side of that sea. The delay in meeting the danger had been caused by the desire of each of the warring

[1] See p. 114.

political sections at Rome to secure for their own nominee the command of the large army which would have to be employed. The events just narrated had secured it for Sulla; and so in 87 he departed for the East. He can hardly have thought that he had rendered the political interests of the Senate secure in Rome; but he can hardly have failed to have the assurance that, if things did go wrong in his absence, he could with his great army settle accounts with his enemies at Rome after he had settled accounts with Mithradates. He could repeat the political dose of 88.

THE CINNAN INTERLUDE

During the years of Sulla's absence in the East, Rome was a prey to disorder the like of which it had never known before. There reigned a political chaos, the details of which may fascinate those who love blood-curdling tales, but need not be set forth in full in a history mainly concerned with those events which had a sensible influence on future historical development.

Causes of grievance and discontent were indeed existent. The bankrupt members of the nobility were anxious to restore those fortunes which they themselves had shattered. The freedmen, a numerous class, were angry at being deprived of the franchise which the Sulpician Laws had given them. The Transpadanes were not satisfied with the Latin franchise in view of the fact that their friends south of the Padus had been given the franchise in full. But all these discontents might have remained in cold storage had not the mass of the Roman people been profoundly moved by the position in Asia. It was the old tale. The masses had been stirred from their wonted political passivity by the inefficiency of the government, which had once more imperilled the existence of the empire, and had led to the loss of thousands of Roman lives, and of hundreds of thousands of Roman money in Asia. The discontent of the masses was, as aforetime, the opportunity of the democrats;—and they seized it!

The consuls for 87 were Cinna, a democrat about whose origin nothing is known; and Octavius, a senatorial. Cinna revived the proposals of Sulpicius; but when the new voters turned up in large numbers to vote, Octavius with an armed band slew hundreds of them. Cinna flew to the army in Campania, which, like other Marian armies, was ready to follow any leader to a war where something might be gained; and, with the aid of Marius, now returned from exile in Africa, he put down all senatorial opposition in Rome. Marius celebrated his return by a wholesale massacre of opponents, affording thereby a terrible precedent for the action of Sulla some years later. But his end was near. He died early in 86, just after taking up his seventh consulship; and from that time till Sulla's return Cinna held the consulship year after year by the simple expedient of nominating himself as his own successor, together with a colleague of like views. In a sense the action was not unconstitutional; but it was a violation of the practice of centuries.[1]

But over there beyond the Adriatic was Cornelius Sulla, a substantial ghost who ever haunted the exponents of democratic happiness. Every effort was made to get together some kind of force which might face that terrible Asiatic army of his when it came back with him from Asia. Attempts were made to supersede him by sending out Valerius Flaccus in 86, and allowing Fimbria in 84 to take over the command in Asia; of whom Flaccus was murdered by his own troops, and Fimbria was crushed by Sulla, set free by a peace concluded with Mithradates in 85 to deal with troublesome democrats in Asia and at home. Early in 83 Sulla landed at Brundusium with 40,000 veteran soldiers and a band of émigré nobility who had fled from proscriptions at Rome.

The War in the East

Mithradates of Pontus ruled that kingdom on the south shore of the Euxine which had for two centuries or more existed side by side with the Seleucid kingdom in Asia. He seems to have been an awesome individual with a reputation fit to frighten all the nurseries in Asia for several centuries to come. But however much his fictitious reputation may have served to scare the naughty children of the future, his actual exploits gave the Romans of the present more solid grounds for alarm. His nature was of that kind which is typical among the successors of Alexander, eager in pursuit of the learning of the day, but capable of the most inhuman cruelty when faced by opposition. His kingdom stretched from Pontus on the north coast of Asia Minor round the east shore of the Euxine to include that ancient Bosporan realm in the Crimea and its neighbourhood. Rumours of troubles at Rome and of the weakness shown in the Jugurthine and Cimbrian wars had doubtless raised in his adventurous mind the hope of ejecting the Romans from Asia. He tried experiments first with the acquisition of Cappadocia and Paphlagonia; but Sulla, the then governor of Cilicia, taught him such a lesson that he was glad to make peace in 92. He had been backed in these proceedings by Tigranes of Armenia, who in 91 caused further trouble in Cappadocia and Paphlagonia. Meanwhile Mithradates was biding his time, busy with the establishment of a large army and fleet. In 88 he broke out with a huge force. The weak local levies of Rome were over-

[1] See p. 58.

powered, so that within a very short time he was on the shores of the Ægean, and ready to cross over into Europe. The Asiatic provincials of Rome welcomed him as a saviour from those abuses of provincial government which had been at their worst in the province of Asia. The Romans resident in the province, to the number of 80,000 it is said, were murdered at the bidding of Mithradates, victims of a hatred which they had doubtless done much to deserve. The Social War was still smouldering; and the struggle with Sulpicius prevented the Roman government from taking any measures to stem this eastern torrent which was now flooding northern Greece. But in 87 Sulla, having settled affairs at Rome, landed in Epirus with an army of 30,000 men and proceeded to clear the Greek mainland of the Pontic invaders. In 86 Sulla's own position became embarrassed. He was cut off from supplies and reinforcements from Italy now that his political foes held Rome. The Ægean was swept by the Mithradatic fleet; and just at this moment a new Pontic army three times as large as his own arrived in Greece. This he wiped out in a great battle at Chæronea. Shortly after this Valerius Flaccus, sent out by the democrats, appeared on the scene with a new Roman army and a commission to supersede him. Sulla was not going to take orders from Cinna and his crew, nor were Sulla's soldiers going to take orders from Flaccus; so the latter prudently marched through Macedonia and Thrace to Asia, leaving Sulla to look to himself. In Asia his troops murdered him. In 85 a third Pontic army arrived in Greece. This met its fate at the hands of Sulla in a great battle at Orchomenos.

In Asia, meanwhile, the proceedings of Mithradates had convinced the inhabitants that the rule of a semi-cultured barbarian was not preferable even to that of Rome. Serious risings took place, especially in Galatia, the home of the ever-turbulent Celt. Meanwhile Fimbria, who had succeeded to the command of Flaccus' army, was pressing Mithradates so hard that Sulla, to whom it was just as important to checkmate the democrat Fimbria as to defeat Mithradates, crossed over to Asia, aided by Lucullus, who had brought up from Syria a fleet which could deal with that of Mithradates. Mithradates, having had enough of it for the time being, concluded a peace on the terms that he should evacuate all the territory he had occupied. As for Fimbria, his army came over to Sulla, and he himself committed suicide.

Sulla's settlement of Asia can only be excused on the plea that he was anxious to get back to Rome, where his presence was so badly needed in the senatorial interest. His army had treated Greece and Asia as though hostile territory, and now to complete the misery of the Asian province a war indemnity was imposed on it of such magnitude that nearly the whole of the town communities, compelled to borrow from Roman capitalists the money to pay the fine, fell miserable victims to the rapacity of those pitiless money-lenders. The proceedings of the army had been characteristic of a force composed of soldiers of fortune who had thrown in their lot and staked their all on the success of a commander who had declared against the government. They were the outward expression of the very nature of the Marian army. To such an army the weal or woe of the provinces, save as sources of plunder, was a matter of indifference. The severities of Sulla himself, though ill-judged, were the natural outcome of the resentment of a Roman at the murder of so many of his fellow-countrymen.

SULLA IN ITALY

Before he landed in Italy in 83, Sulla had let the Cinnan government know exactly what it had to expect from him. It had consequently collected a large force; but these hastily gathered levies were not fit to meet the veteran army from Asia. In that same year the consul Norbanus was defeated at Mount Tifata, and Scipio's army deserted *en masse* to Sulla. In the next year, 82, he defeated the younger Marius at Sacriportus. Though Sulla was checked for a moment by Carbo, his lieutenant, Metellus, defeated Carbo in the Padus valley; and after that Carbo's army dissolved of its own accord. The final battle took place at the Colline Gate; after which Sulla entered Rome, and Præneste, a stronghold of the democrats, surrendered. It was in this war that Pompeius made his name as a lieutenant of Sulla. After serving in Italy, he won Sicily for him that same year, and Africa in 81. In 81, also, Spain submitted to the champion of the Senate.

The curious personality of Sulla comes out in that brief period of his life which follows the battle at the Colline Gate, during which he was absolute master of the Roman world. He was a lazy, able man who could be roused to great and effective energy by the force of circumstances. He was a cynic of a class of cynics produced among the Roman nobility of the age by the dislocation of politics and society on the one hand, and by adherence to a philosophy which attached no value to moral values. In the life resultant from such experience and such teaching scruples played no part.

There can be little doubt that he might, had he so wished, have anticipated the rôle of a Cæsar, but a Cæsar without Cæsar's humanity and without his faith in the possibilities of human nature. He might have kept the world in order, though the process in his hands would have been a terrible one. But that was not his idea of life. He was prepared to establish machinery for the maintenance of order, but he was determined to impose on others the responsibility for its working, while he himself enjoyed life in his own way. So he regulated the world after his own fashion, and then retired into private life, leaving his own senatorial order to carry on the task. So long as he lived his enemies were careful not to wake the drowsy lion.

He signalised his victory by a murder grim and great. His political opponents now reaped the fruits of the example they had set. Four thousand seven hundred persons were put to death, and their property confiscated, of whom 2,600 are said to have been members of the financial section of the Equestrian Order. Gracchus had set them up in opposition to the Senate; and such was the result of his work. Under the circumstances of the time, which demanded the close association of all those who were interested in law and order, this action of Sulla was a mistake which becomes apparent in the history of the next thirty years. The same lack of foresight was shown by his severity to those communities, especially in Etruria and Samnium, which had taken sides against him in the civil war. Property was confiscated far and wide through Italy, with the result that many of those Italians who regarded senatorial rule as the natural order of things, but had been forced to join the armies of the democrats quartered in their districts, were converted, for a time at any rate, into enemies of that Senate which they had every intention to support.

Sullan Constitution

Sulla had demanded from the Senate a dictatorship not limited to the ordinary six months' tenure of that extraordinary office. Had the Senate had the will to refuse, which it had not, it would not have had the power to resist the commander of the great Marian army. By a series of enactments the dictator then proceeded to set up a constitution the main object of which was to bring under legal control of the Senate those other elements in the constitution which had in the past been under its customary, though recently disputed, control.

As the tribunate of the Plebs, owing to its extraordinary powers, had been the main instrument employed by those who for the last fifty years had assailed the position of the Senate, he deprived the office of its right of veto on legislation, reducing the right of intervention to its original proportions, the protection of the civil liberty of the citizen from the arbitrary exercise of magisterial power. Already in 88 he had made it necessary for the tribunes to obtain the sanction of the Senate before introducing legislation into the Plebeian Assembly.

The office was further prejudiced by the holder of it being disqualified for any future magistracy. On the question of the magistracy generally, he knew well that, if the Senate, as he intended, was to be supreme, the very large Constitutional powers of the magistrates must be reduced in practice if not in theory. Consecutive tenures of the same office by the same person, such as the repeated tenures of the consulship by Marius and Cinna, had been really an infringement of a law of 342 B.C., which laid down an interval of ten years between two holdings of the same office by the same individual. An annual magistracy tended by reason of its temporary nature to become weak by the side of a permanent Senate; but that would not apply to a magistrate who held repeated and continuous office. So he re-enacted the law of 342.

But with respect to the magistracy there was a constructive as well as a restrictive side to his policy. The administration of criminal law had always been cumbersome and unsatisfactory at Rome. The courts of the first instance had been those of the magistrates; but the law of appeal provided that in cases where the penalties of death or the loss of civil rights were involved, an appeal lay to the Comitia Centuriata, a body far too large to be a suitable court. Appeal in such cases had become so much a matter of course that the magisterial courts had become accustomed to pass them on without further ado to the Comitia, which had therefore to take up the trial from the beginning, a function for which it was but ill adapted. In the earlier half of the second century recourse had been had in cases of peculiar difficulty or of an extraordinary character to the appointment of a special commission (quæstio extraordinaria) to try such cases, a commission proposed by the Senate and composed of members of the Senate, but formally established by a resolution (lex) of the Assembly. Such commissions had been originally appointed *ad hoc*, that is to say, for the trial of one particular case. It was in 149 that the idea of establishing a permanent commission (quæstio perpetua) for the trial of a particular class of cases, namely, those concerned with extortion in the provinces, was embodied in a law. To this Caius Gracchus added a perpetual commission for the trial of cases of bribery and murder. Sulla extended, or even completed, the system by setting up a series of such commissions designed to deal with every form of crime. This was the most useful reform which he introduced. The Roman lawyers invented with reference to these courts the interesting legal fiction that, inasmuch as the Assembly of the People had assented to their establishment, they were courts of the people, and therefore there could be no appeal from them to the Comitia; but those who were interested in the maintenance of their competence were very careful to avoid doing anything which might raise this delicate question ; and so these courts did not proceed to the extreme measure of inflicting the death penalty, lest the mass of citizens might be roused to claim the old right of appeal to the Comitia.[1] A sentence of exile or outlawry was regarded as equivalent to the penalty of death.

The pattern for the constitution of these criminal courts was taken from the civil courts of the Prætor Urbanus and Prætor Peregrinus, in which the cases were tried by a prætor, acting as judge, assisted by a judex. Sulla abolished the equestrian juries in quaestiones, restoring the senatorial juries which had acted in them before the time of Caius Gracchus.

The establishment of these new quæstiones had an important effect on the functions of the magistracy. To provide a prætor to preside over each of them, the number of prætors had to be raised from six to eight, an increase which would tend to weaken the power of the magistracy in face of the Senate. But a far more important result was that no prætor was now available for government in the provinces, since all the eight had duties which kept them at Rome during their year of office. The consuls were indeed free to take up commands in the provinces if they desired so to do ;[2] but the business at Rome had so increased with the growth of the empire that it was very inconvenient, and always difficult, for a consul to absent himself from the city. The effect of this was that the government of the provinces passed into the hands of proconsuls and proprætors. It had been necessary for a long time past to adopt this mode of government because the number of magistrates had not been sufficient to fill all the offices at home and abroad ; but from the time of Sulla onward it becomes the all but universal rule that the magistracy is exercised in Rome and the promagistracy abroad.

This was destined to settle the fate of the Republic ; and Sulla has been blamed for want of foresight in establishing a state of things which led to such a result. It may be said with-

---

[1] The practical abolition of the death penalty in the courts of the later Republic has been ascribed to the growth of humanitarianism among the Romans. The idea is refuted by the fact, which is so obvious in the story of the time, that never was Roman life held more cheaply by the Romans themselves than in this last age of the Republic.

[2] It used to be alleged that Sulla made a law definitely forbidding the consuls and prætors to leave Rome during their year of office. It is now recognised that no such law is traceable in the evidence, and the retention of the prætors, and the usual presence of the consuls in Rome after this time, was due to circumstances, not to any express legislation.

out further ado that it was not the Sullan system which was responsible for the disaster, but the perversions and evasions of it by those fools whom he left as trustees of his political will, and revisions of it brought about by his political adversaries. Sulla himself did all that a man could do to make the system fool-proof, a task perhaps impossible in view of the folly of its political supporters, and the blind recklessness of its subsequent assailants.

The main charge commonly made against Sulla is that he set up a rule in the empire in which the central government in Italy was left without military support in face of its nominal subordinates in the provinces, the proconsuls and propraetors, all of whom had bodies of troops at their command, and that he thus exposed the state to the danger of its central government being overthrown by a disloyal provincial governor.

It is true that after Sulla's time one proconsul *might* have overthrown, and one *did* overthrow, the government of the Republic; but Pompeius and Cæsar were exactly the type of proconsul against which Sulla had carefully provided. It was not Sulla nor the Sullan system, it was the opponents of Sulla and the Sullan system who brought *them* into existence. The Sullan provincial governor was a very different individual. He was practically the nominee of the Senate, and therefore personally loyal to its government. He ruled one province, and one only; and therefore controlled under normal circumstances but a small military force. Even if abnormal circumstances demanded the employment of a large force, such a nominee could presumably be trusted. Lucullus with his great army against Mithradates was never a danger to the Senate and its government. Pompeius had been Sulla's own lieutenant before the Senate gave him his extraordinary command in Spain against Sertorius; and, while never wholly disloyal to the Senate, might have remained wholly loyal save for the Senate's unwisdom in the years 71 and 70. Again, by an express law of Sulla a governor could be superseded at the end of one year of office by the mere expedient of despatching his successor to the province. A year was too short a period in which to attain to predominant and dangerous influence in any province. By neglecting to make use of this proviso of Sulla's, the Senate gave its enemies a precedent for the establishment of proconsular power in an obviously dangerous form. Finally, would it have been in any way likely that Sulla, who, whatever he was, was not a fool, would have failed to make that Senate which he proposed to establish firmly in the supreme power in the empire safe from the possibility of being overthrown by such a military *coup d'état* as he himself had brought about against the Cinnan government?

THE FIRST CENTURY, 100–31 B.C.

Of course, the military position of the government was weak in Italy. This has been ascribed before now to the fact that it would have been contrary to the custom of the constitution to maintain an armed force in a land now inhabited by Roman citizens. But the action of Cinna's government in providing an army to meet Sulla on his return from Asia shows that such a constitutional sentiment, if it existed, was of no real force. The real difficulty was that the government had no money wherewith to maintain in Italy a standing army powerful enough to ward off the attack of any proconsul with unusual military power at his command.

The Sullan constitution was a very intricate piece of political machinery which would fail in working if any single part of it got out of order. It could not be worked by careless or stupid workmen such as those who composed the senatorial order of the time. Had that order shown itself watchful in maintaining both the spirit and the letter of that constitution, it is difficult to say where any force could have been found in the Roman state, as then constituted, to overthrow it. Sulla had put an elaborate tool into the hands of the clumsy. Had the users been skilled, they had at their disposal in the Sullan constitution the means of crushing the most desperate effort of those,—and they were many,—who had suffered at the hands of Sulla. The failure of this constitution is due in the first instance and above all to the incapacity of those who had to work it ; secondly, to its having degraded that power of the tribunate on which the masses of the Roman people set such store ; and thirdly, to the terrible disorders in the empire in the decade after Sulla, disorders which accused the Senate of that sin of inefficiency which was in the eyes of the mass of the people unforgivable, and prevented them from sinking down into a passive acceptance of senatorial rule after the grievances and disabilities of the tribunate had been removed.

The less important features of Sulla's legislation were the establishment of a legal for what had hitherto been a customary rule that a man could not stand for any grade in the magistracy unless he had passed through the lower grades by successive steps (certus ordo magistratuum), and the restoring of the control of the priestly colleges to the nobility. It is probable, too, that he revived the ancient practice of legislating through the more aristocratically constituted Comitia Centuriata instead of making use of the Comitia Tributa or the Concilium Plebis. Having carried through his reactionary reforms, Sulla retired into private life, and died three years later, in 78 B.C.

The decade which followed the promulgation of Sulla's constitution was marked by a strong political reaction. The forces of discontent at home were powerful, the children of those who had been proscribed by Sulla, the surviving members of the financial section of the equestrian order, and above all the mass of the Roman people, nervous at the degradation of the tribunate, and incensed at the state of things in Italy and the provinces. The situation was indeed one hard for men of capacity to meet; and the controlling element in the senatorial order was bankrupt in that respect.

SERTORIUS IN SPAIN

Spain had submitted to Sulla after his victory in the civil war, and Quintus Sertorius, the democratic general, had to fly for his life. But in 80 he was back again, a desperate and an able man, determined to make Spain a refuge for the democratic émigrés, and, if necessary, a realm independent of Rome. Sertorius is the one personality among the prominent democrats of the day whose character is such as to provoke sympathy with the misfortunes of that political section, most of whose members had taken up the so-called democratic cause from motives of self-interest. Like Hannibal in the past, he had that peculiar capacity, which is usually the gift of an honest man, for dealing with semi-civilised races, so that for years after his death his name was one to conjure with in Spain, as Cæsar, his political descendant, was to find thirty years later. During 80 and 79 several defeats of the government generals sent against him had given him time to organise affairs on lines which showed clearly that he was aiming at the establishment of a principality independent of the Roman Empire. In 77 the Senate, finding that its general, Metellus, could accomplish nothing, sent Pompeius, Sulla's brilliant lieutenant, not as yet thirty years old, with an extraordinary command to Spain. For nearly four years the war went on with varying success; but defeats in the year 74 reduced Sertorius to despair, though not to submission. He tried to get help from Mithradates, who was then turning Asia Minor upside down. Either late in 73 or early in 72 Sertorius was treacherously murdered by two of his officers; and, though the insurrection was not immediately crushed, yet by the end of the year its dying embers had been stamped out, and Pompeius and Metellus returned to Italy, leaving behind them a Spain ruined by years of warfare, and a Gaul exhausted by requisitions for the army.

MITHRADATES IN ASIA

There had been a temporary renewal of trouble with Mithradates of Pontus in 83, after Sulla had made peace with him. But this was patched up; and Mithradates used the time during which the Romans were engaged in the civil war in Italy for the reorganisation of his army and fleet.

In 75 the last king of Bithynia left his kingdom to Rome, which accepted the legacy perforce as there was no one on the spot to set over it. This, so it is said, alarmed Mithradates, though there is no doubt that in any case he would soon have attacked the Roman dominions. In that same year he broke out in invasion of Cappadocia, Paphlagonia, and Bithynia, so that in 74 the consul Lucullus went against him with 30,000 men. For seven years he and Mithradates fought in Asia, a war distinguished by Lucullus' success in winning victories and failure in waging war. After various set-backs, Lucullus was able in 73 to invade Pontus itself and to overrun the king's home territory. Mithradates had taken refuge with Tigranes, king of Armenia ; and by 70 it must have seemed as if the war was over. The Senate at Rome would have been glad of a settlement of affairs in Asia, such a settlement as might have been made, had not Lucullus, acting in defiance of instructions, demanded from Tigranes the surrender of Mithradates, and, on his refusal, carried the war into Armenia, the most difficult of all countries surrounding the Roman world. That step was fated to prolong the war far into the next decade.[1]

REACTION AGAINST THE SULLAN CONSTITUTION

While these things were going on in Spain and Asia, things in Italy were not standing still. So long as the fierce, relentless Sulla lived, the opponents of the Senate dare not move a finger. That would have meant swift death. But his corpse was hardly cold ere they began to stir. A certain young man named Julius Cæsar, scion of one of the greatest and oldest families of Rome, was becoming known among the democrats as one who was likely to go further. It is difficult to say which was the most prominent trait in his character, his discretion in public, or his indiscretion in private affairs. He displayed the former quality at this, the outset of his public career, by holding aloof from the ill-judged attempt made by Lepidus, consul for 78, to recover power for the democrats by private means. Lepidus got up an insurrection in Etruria ; but, after a defeat at the Campus Martius outside Rome, he was crushed by the youthful but experienced Pompeius, whom the Senate had sent against him.

Sulla had been the creator rather than the establisher of order in Italy. The settlement of his veterans on the confiscated estates of the proscribed had met with that ill-success which might have been expected from an attempt to induce soldiers of fortune to turn the sword into a ploughshare. They sold their

[1] For the continuation of this war, see p. 424.

lots to capitalists, and with the proceeds embarked on brief but monumental sprees at Rome, after which, if they survived, they resorted to brigandage as a means of livelihood. Brigandage became so fashionable that even the slaves took to it as a relaxation, especially in those wide, wild Apulian pastures where evasion of consequences was easy. As no consequences resulted, they gathered courage, and broke out into a formidable rising under Spartacus, a gladiator. For two years Spartacus with 70,000 men slew Roman citizens and Roman armies in south Italy, until in 71 the prætor Crassus leapt into fame by crushing the rising.

The Consulship of 71 b.c.

So in 71 the Senate had on its hands two generals, Pompeius and Crassus, both of whom had done great service to the state; both of whom were quite aware of the fact; and both of whom were anxious to know what the Senate was prepared to do for them, having also a clear idea of what they wanted, the consulships for the next year, 70. Two capable young employés may be an embarrassment to an old-established firm. The case of Crassus did not present much constitutional difficulty; but that of Pompeius did, inasmuch as he had never held any lower magistracy whatever, and was therefore ineligible under the Sullan law prescribing successive gradations in tenure of office and a certain age for him who stood for the consulship, and indeed for the lower magistracies. This was all very well and very legal as an argument; but it meant that Pompeius, though by far the most distinguished Roman of the time, would have to begin at the bottom of the tree of public life just like any young noble who had never won any distinction whatever. Moreover, Pompeius knew,—everybody knew,—that the Senate could, if it liked, exercise its much-disputed claim to exempt from the operation of law. Cæsar saw his opportunity of winning back the alliance of the military power for the democrats, though, if he hoped to win Pompeius permanently for them, he must have been subsequently disappointed. But it was at any rate quite certain that Pompeius' disgust at the way in which the Senate had treated him would make him a ready instrument for anti-senatorial legislation. So he was illegally elected consul for 70, the Senate not daring to oppose the man who had an army at the gates of Rome.[1] Crassus was elected to the other consulship. A Marian army had given Sulla the opportunity for carrying through his constitution; and another Marian army gave Pompeius the opportunity for

[1] The Senate seems to have at the last moment exempted him from the operation of the law. Cic. pro Leg. Man. 21. 62.

THE FIRST CENTURY, 100–31 B.C.

undoing much that Sulla had done. Its very indifference to politics made this army a terrible political weapon.

The legislation of this year 70 included a law reinstating the tribunes in their old position; another abolishing the purely senatorial juries in the law courts and substituting a mixed panel of equal numbers of senators, equites, and tribuni ærarii, the last being apparently all persons with a property qualification of 300,000 sesterces. The Senate, too, was purged by the expulsion of the more disreputable partisans of Sulla.

The decade which begins with the year 69 is the last period of consciousness in the life of free institutions at Rome. In the next they are in that unconsciousness which precedes death. Decay at the heart of the body politic, the Senate, and moral disease in the body itself, the citizens which represented the state in the Comitia, had left Rome without any element in its constitution sufficiently efficient to make the maintenance of the existing political institutions either possible or desirable. The Republic had done its work in a life of four and a half centuries, —a great work, even if its latter days had not been worthy of its youth and middle age.

The Decade 69–60 b.c.

Before entering on the story of this most important decade, it may be well to estimate the forces, individual and corporate, which played a part in the last scene of the tragedy of the Republic.

The Senate and the senatorial order, composed of men who had learnt nothing that they should have learnt, and forgotten nothing that they should have forgotten, maintained claims to government which had at any rate this justification, that if they could not govern the state, there was no one else who could. The average magistrate is still content to obey the wishes of a body to which he himself belongs, and to which he will return in a private capacity. At times the Senate seems to be recovering its power; and then all the ground made up is lost by some act of political stupidity.

The financial equestrians pursue the tenor of a financial way which has been made very uneven by the past and present disorders of the empire. They have been soured by the cruelties of the Sullan time, and are resentful of the disastrous incompetence shown in the government of the empire as represented by the Senate, while on the other hand distrustful of that band of ruined men which form the backbone of the democratic coterie, anarchists with a would-be anarchist programme.

The better men, that is to say, the majority among the mass of citizens, long for a dawn after that long night of inefficiency through which the government of the empire has been passing, ready to retire to that life of personal endeavour and gain when that night has vanished when no man can work by reason of insecurity and the necessity of wasting on politics time which they would much rather have spent on their private affairs.

The democrats had in all probability for thirty years past at least consisted of two sections, men who had an honest desire to restore the government of the state to efficiency, and others who were merely out for a change, since any change could not but better the condition of financial ruin in which they found themselves. The general aims of the two sections were sufficiently similar to keep them together, though in this decade they parted company on the question as to how those aims were to be attained.

But overshadowing all these political sections was the military power, resident at this time in the person of Pompeius.

Some modern historians who have admired the Prussian method of government have never been able to forgive Pompeius for not having taken into his own hands the reformation of the Roman state, for not having anticipated the part which Cæsar played later. He has been represented by them as a man of little save military capacity, of no moral courage, and, generally speaking, weak in character. The exaggerations of the picture are plain on the face of it. The man who in 62 made off his own hand a settlement of the Asiatic problem of the empire, the main features of which lasted for some centuries, was certainly not a political incapable. But Pompeius is in his way, like Cicero is in his way, and other men of the time in their way, a figure strangely isolated amid its surroundings, a man who did not sympathise with the times in which he lived because there was so much which he disliked in the life of the day. Cicero tried to make the best of a world with which he had lost sympathy; but Pompeius never made any such attempt. He was ready to serve the state when it asked him to do so; but, if it did not want him, it might go to the devil its own way, that which, indeed, it seemed to have every inclination to do.

To a man who had so far spent his life in a world of military discipline, who had, while still well under the age of forty, gained as a commander a position and a reputation in the empire far higher than that of any living man, the sordid political life of the time, where advancement had to be sought by bribery and canvassing the now degraded population of the city of Rome itself, must have been repellent. Pompeius neither sought nor attained after his consulship of 70 any political position into which he was not forced by circumstances; and he was not successful in those into which he was forced, partly because he disliked them, partly because he had a contempt for the undisciplined political life of the time. If he had an ambition other than military, it was to be an unofficial chief of the state to whom the regular magistrates of the Republic should look for support and guidance. Of disloyalty to the government he does not appear to have dreamed, for he had not that ruthlessness of disposition which was bred in so many of his contemporaries by a long and close association with politics at Rome such as he, Pompeius, had never had the time to experience.

Cæsar, who knew by heart the seamy side of the politics of the day, though socially humane for his time, was politically ruthless in his conviction that the Republic could not reform or restore itself. But till the closing years of this decade he is, on the surface, merely the clever politician who is fostering the interests of the better class of the democrats, watchful for an opportunity of getting affairs into his own hands, an end for which he worked with all the more security because his contemporaries and political rivals had not as yet realised how supremely clever and how very able he was.

Cicero was a man who hoped from the world of his day far more than it had to give. An Italian rather than a Roman of the time, he was, like the race from which he sprang, more Roman than the Romans. Like the Italians who refused to be cured of their faith in the Senate by the cruelties which Sulla had perpetrated in the Senate's name, he himself, though his political ambition had been opposed at every step by that senatorial order which disliked the entrance of an upstart (novus homo) into the ranks of the higher magistracy, clung pathetically to the belief that the Senate, supported by the citizens throughout Italy, might still save Rome. He died a bankrupt in his ambitions, public and private, a grievously disappointed, but never disillusioned, man. But at the time at which this decade opens Cicero was climbing the first rungs of the ladder of office. He had already made a great reputation in the law courts as one of the greatest speakers of the day, and had thereby acquired a great influence with the Italian voters, who were proud of the success of a man sprung from their own ranks. He was one of the few who had ever dared to tickle that old lion Sulla with an oratorical straw. Altogether he was looked on as a rather bold man, a reputation which he to a certain extent deserved. He had, too, helped to shake the position of the post-Sullan régime by his attack on Verres, the most scandalous governor who had ever governed Sicily or any other province. He had, in fact, been a good deal before the public eye, and was doubtless regarded as a coming man. In private life he belonged to a literary circle which, judging from his letters and those of his friends, must have contained many brilliant men of wit, above all his correspondent Cælius, one of the greatest humorists of the ancient world. It is extraordinary how, from the days of Alexander the Great onwards, such literary circles are found embedded in political worlds whose acts tend ever to barbarity, and whose political ideas show no trace of refinement.

Crassus is the remaining prominent figure of the decade. Success in finance, which had made him the richest man of his day, seems to have given him an exaggerated idea of his own gifts. His political qualifications were so various that they must have been hard to reconcile. He was a member of the Senate, the leading financier of the day and therefore powerful with the equestrian order, and patron of those democrats of which a section was openly anarchist in its views on property. He was like a chameleon which had exhausted its powers of imitation in a successful effort to imitate some particularly gaudy pattern. But, in point of fact, very little is really known of the man save this, that his influence was very largely due to the fact that many prominent politicians of the day were up to their necks in debt to him.

The first two years of the decade, 69 and 68, passed quietly enough. Pompeius, contemptuous, no doubt, of a commonplace political career, did not take a provincial governorship after his consulship. But in 67 trouble began. The state of affairs in the East was such that Italian trade was suffering by land from Mithradates, and by sea from those pirates with whom he had always a close connection: nay, the latter had become so bold that they were cutting off the import of corn into Italy and raiding the Italian coast. The two main causes of the recrudescence of piracy in the eastern Mediterranean were that Rome, probably on the score of expense, had never maintained a fleet in commission, and had also shown herself for nearly a hundred years past peculiarly lax in her attention to affairs in the East. The Senate was sitting still doing nothing. But, instigated by the other classes at Rome, the tribune Aulus Gabinius introduced in 67 a law giving Pompeius a command against the pirates which was to last three years and to give him authority superior to all governors of provinces. Within three months of the time when he was first prepared for action Pompeius had cleared out the nests of pirates from Cilicia and the south coast of Asia Minor.

There remained Mithradates to be dealt with. Under Lucullus the war was taking a stereotyped form of resultless victories. The entry of Armenia into the field had made the task of the Roman armies much harder.

ARMENIA

This kingdom was destined to play a somewhat important part in the history of Rome during the next century and a half. It had won its independence when in 189 the Romans defeated the Seleucid Antiochus at Magnesia. Later in the second century its existence was threatened by the advance of the Parthians, who, after having robbed the Seleucid kingdom of the provinces of Media and Mesopotamia, had in 95 B.C. defeated the Armenian king and annexed his southern territories. But these were soon recovered, and, more than that, in 83 Syria was overrun and annexed as far as the borders of Judæa. Even the Roman sphere of influence in Cappadocia and Cilicia was threatened. By 70 Tigranes was cherishing schemes of driving the Romans out of Asia. But his rule was of the old Assyrian type, in which cruelty and oppression held together a miscellany of races so long as, and just so long as, no power from outside could interfere. He was in reality no match for Rome. In 69 Lucullus invaded his territory, and, after defeating utterly two unwieldy armies which the king sent against him, captured Tigranocerta, the royal city. In 68 Lucullus advanced on Artaxata, the old Armenian capital, a move which drew Tigranes and Mithradates after him, only to be defeated a third time. But Lucullus never got to Artaxata. His troops were becoming discontented and mutinous, resenting the severe discipline which he imposed on them. In 67 things took a bad turn for the Roman arms, so that by the end of the year the irrepressible Mithradates was once more in possession of his kingdom, while Tigranes was invading Cappadocia, unafraid of a Roman general whose troops had refused to fight.

It was under these circumstances that the Lex Gabinia was followed in 66 by a Lex Manilia giving Pompeius the command against Mithradates, a command so wide as to include in his province the whole of the Roman East. The step was a fatal necessity and a fatal precedent.

The Gabinian and Manilian Laws

The attitudes adopted by political sections at Rome towards the Gabinian and Manilian Laws were such as might have been expected. The Senate was obstructive and furious, incensed at the power given to one whom it regarded as a political traitor; nervous as to the possibility of his proving a second Sulla,— but on the other side,—when he came back with his army. The equestrian order supported the laws, since piracy was ruining trade, and Mithradates that Asia from the exploitation of which they had drawn their chief profits. The mass of the Roman people supported the laws for the same reasons, and also on the general ground of the inefficiency of the government, and the interruption of the corn supplies of Italy. The attitude of the democrats was curious. In 70 they had believed that they had won over to their side the military power in the shape of Pompeius. Since that time nothing had happened to upset that belief, though Pompeius had certainly not done anything to confirm it. But opposition to the laws meant a definite break with him, which they neither wished nor dared to risk. Yet his attitude to politics since 70 had been so disappointingly neutral that they were obviously nervous as to whether he might not on his return from Asia climb down on the wrong side of the political fence.

During the years of Pompeius' absence in Asia all thinking men at Rome but one were under a cloud of apprehension as to what he might do on his return, convinced that he would be able to do anything that he liked. Cicero alone displayed no nervousness, for he alone seems to have had the foresight or the insight to gauge the psychology of the great man, especially in relation to politics, sufficiently, at any rate, to feel confident that he would not be a danger to the constitution. But all alike had learned from past experience that political talk was mere vapouring, and political power a mere shadow, in face of one who had a Marian army at his back. And so for the next few years after Pompeius' departure the politicians at Rome are living under the shadow of a great fear, trembling at the thought of what Pompeius may do with the army when the war is over. The senatorials have naught to comfort them except the vague hope that the old lieutenant of Sulla may return to the senatorial fold. The more level-headed among the democrats, Cæsar and Crassus, are seeking to set up a military power outside Italy, another Marian army, to counterbalance that of Pompeius. Cæsar, the craftiest and most far-sighted statesman of the time, had made up his mind that the centre of gravity in the empire had shifted outside Italy, while the stupid leaders of the anarchist section of the democrats were under the delusion that, if they seized Rome, they could control the Roman world. And so the two sections of the democrats are sundered in their policy for the next few years. The equestrians are prepared to support the man who may restore their shattered finances, and to take the risk of what he may do when he returns as potential master of all. The mass of the Romans, in so far as it thinks at all, thinks only of the benefits to be attained by the restoration of the security for life and the gains of life.

There is evidence, which is not convincing, that in the very year in which the Manilian Law was passed, the year 66, the democrats formed what is called the First Catilinarian Conspiracy, of which the alleged design was to overthrow the consuls of 65; to appoint Crassus as dictator, with Cæsar as his lieutenant (Master of the Horse), and to send Piso to Spain as an external support. But the secret is said to have got out, so that no move was attempted.

In 65 the democrats did certainly make a move. Crassus, who was Censor that year, proposed to enrol the Transpadanes on the list of citizens. This implied that they had by law received the citizenship. It is quite evident from the action of Crassus' colleague in the censorship in vetoing this proposal for enrolment, as well as from a significant remark in a letter of Cicero of much later date,[1] that the possession of full citizenship by the Transpadanes was at the time, and later, a disputed question between the senatorials and the democrats. The conjectural explanation is that the Cinnan government had passed a law raising them from the Latin franchise given them after the Social War to the full Roman franchise; but that the law had been abrogated by the Senate on the ground of some informality in its passing. Be that as it may, the veto of Crassus' colleague put an end to a design to win Transpadane support for the democrats. The next democratic move, made in 65 or 64, was a proposal that Cæsar should be sent with an army to restore order in Egypt. This would have given him a very strong position as master of that land on which Italy was mainly dependent for its corn supply. But this proposal was rejected.

CATILINARIAN CONSPIRACY

In 64 was hatched the great, sometimes called the Second, Catilinarian Conspiracy. Its leader, Catiline, and another democrat, Antonius, were candidates for the consulship of 63. Antonius was elected. Cicero, who was also elected, owed his success to his Italian supporters, aided by the Senate, which backed him on the principle that, though respectability might be inferior to nobility, it was preferable to anarchy.

In the earlier part of the year 63 the moderate section of the democrats made another bid for power. The tribune Rullus was put up to propose an agrarian law, the least important part of which were its agrarian proposals, and the most important a commission of ten which was to be set up with large powers such as would make it possible for it to raise an army to counterbalance that of Pompeius. But this strange scheme was dropped.

The next democratic move aimed at winning the favour and support of the mass of the Roman citizens by reviving that judicial power of the Comitia which had been practically annulled by the establishment of the quæstiones. But the principle was illustrated on the present occasion by a farcical piece of archaism, the trial of a certain Rabirius, who thirty-seven years before had killed Saturninus. This somewhat silly scheme was also dropped.

[1] Cic. Letters, Ad Att. v 11 (Watson 31).

As the moderate section of the democrats had already in this year twice tried its hand and twice failed, the extreme section, led by Catiline, a bankrupt pre-eminent among the bankrupt nobles of the time, made preparations to overthrow the existing government. The plot was disclosed to Cicero in the autumn of the year. Backed by the Senate, he took such prompt measures to meet it that Catiline had to fly from Rome to join in Etruria the band of desperadoes of all sorts which the conspirators had got together from the discontented sections of the rural population of Italy, especially those veterans of Sulla who had been settled on confiscated estates,[1] which they had either sold in order to squander the proceeds, or spoiled through inexperience of agriculture. Even the former owners of these properties joined the strangely assorted company. In rural Italy Sulla's benefactions had been almost as ruinous to the benefited as his spoliations to the despoiled. At Pistoria, in Etruria, Catiline and his band met their death in a desperate fight with the government troops, while the conspirators at Rome were summarily executed by Cicero on the strength of a senatorial decree.[2] Cicero regarded himself as the saviour of the country; and said so. The senatorial and equestrian orders were quite ready to recognise his services in any form which did not demand any sacrifice on their part. His Italian friends probably hovered between relief at being saved from the anarchy threatened by Catiline and a certain uneasiness at the anarchy of Cicero in executing prisoners without trial, an action which might serve as a precedent for all sorts of high-handed proceedings. Cicero, elated for the moment at his own success and at a popularity which he certainly overestimated, was to learn in the next few years that, however divided the views of the Italian voters might be on the arbitrary methods he had employed, the old Roman citizens in Rome and elsewhere were so scandalised at this violation of that charter of their liberties, the Law of Appeal, that he had by his action closed for ever on himself the door to further election to the magistracy. The Italians gradually forgot what he had done; but the masses at Rome neither forgot nor forgave.

And then, in 62, Pompeius landed with his great army at Brundusium, while all save Cicero held their breath. Both in

[1] See p. 419.
[2] That Crassus or Cæsar were in the conspiracy is most improbable. They must have known that the design, even if momentarily successful, must be crushed by Pompeius and his army. They knew that Italy was no longer the centre of power. Crassus, the great financier, was not likely to lend himself to a declared attack on property. Finally, Cicero, who would have liked to ruin the reputation of both of them, living or dead, never charges them with complicity in the conspiracy.

THE FIRST CENTURY, 100–31 B.C.

a political and a military sense Pompeius had done his work in Asia well.

Pompeius in Asia

Just before Pompeius' arrival in Asia, in 66, Mithradates had quarrelled with Tigranes of Armenia, a circumstance which simplified Pompeius' task. He got together a large army mainly from the discharged soldiers of Lucullus and from the communities of the province of Asia. A little later large levies from Cilicia joined him. In this same year 66 he invaded Pontus and defeated Mithradates in a great battle at Nicopolis, which decided, though it did not end, the war. Tigranes, having quarrelled with Mithradates, and being pressed by the Parthians on the south, was glad to make peace, resigning all his Cilician and Syrian conquests, and ceding Sophene and Corduene to Rome. Mithradates fled to his northern kingdom, where he tried to collect a new army from a very unwilling population which turned against him. He committed suicide at Panticapæum in 63. After sweeping up the remains of the war in the Transcaucasian region, Pompeius in 64 turned southwards to Syria, where he brought to an end that Seleucid kingdom which for two centuries and a half had dominated west Asia, and for the last century had endured because Rome had not desired to annex it. He also annexed Judæa, not without some severe fighting with Jewish fanatics, which had its aftermath in various revolts which were not really suppressed till 54.

His settlement of affairs in Asia was drastic, and, tried by the test of time, masterly. The province of Cilicia was enlarged, and new provinces were formed out of Bithynia, Pontus, Syria, and Crete. Client kings were established in Cappadocia, Commagene, and Lesser Armenia, and a more peaceful civilisation was promoted by the foundation of new cities, especially in the old semi-civilised kingdom of Pontus.

Affairs at Rome, 62–60 b.c.

To the amazement of all, Pompeius disbanded his army at Brundusium on his arrival there in 62. Consequently, those who had hitherto feared him got the impression, common among men under such circumstances, that they might ignore, or even treat with contempt, the man who had refused to be their master. This was an egregious mistake, as the immediate future was to show; but the grievous results of the error were not due so much to Pompeius himself as to the fact that there were at the time two men, Cicero and Cæsar, who were not so profoundly stupid as their contemporaries, but were quite aware that Pompeius, properly directed, was potentially an overwhelming force in politics. No doubt Pompeius had no wish to be directed ; but the folly of the Senate smoothed over the difficulty for one of his would-be directors, while wrecking the plans of the other.

Though Cicero seems to have been the one prominent man at Rome who did not look forward with apprehension to Pompeius' return, he was probably surprised at the disbandment of the army. To Pompeius himself he was disposed to be very friendly, in the expectation that the great man would congratulate him as the saviour of his fatherland. But when Pompeius, who had himself hoped to play that part on his return, found the rôle already taken and the play over, he showed not the slightest inclination to recognise the services of Cicero. That the latter bitterly resented this he shows in some of his letters. But he had been so alarmed by the threat from the forces of disorder that he determined to pocket his resentment and to win over Pompeius for a plan of his own.

The Catilinarian affair had united Senate and equites in bonds of interest, though hardly of affection, for the first time for sixty years. Cicero conceived the idea of making them the nucleus of a union which should include all respectable citizens (boni), that is to say, his friends the Italian voters, together with Pompeius as representing that military power so necessary for the support of any policy at Rome. All might have gone well with the plan, had not the unspeakable Senate committed what amounted to political suicide by quarrelling both with the equites and Pompeius,—with the former by refusing to listen to any proposal for a revision of their tax contract for Asia, which, owing to the war, had resulted in severe losses ; with the latter by refusing to confirm his settlement of Asia, on the ground that, as it was made without consulting the Senate, it was illegal—which was, strictly speaking, true. Cicero was furious, but defeated. But Cæsar had now got his chance.

In 61 he was serving as prætor in Spain, where he acquired some military experience and reputation, as well as sufficient money to pay his debts. Shortly after his return the above-mentioned action of the Senate had reduced the political situation to a tangle which Cæsar thought he might unravel by getting hold of the ends of the skein, all the more so as the Senate had put the coping-stone on its ineptitude by refusing to provide lands for Pompeius' disbanded soldiers. With Crassus he already had political ties. He proceeded to win over Pompeius, who was at the moment ready for any anti-senatorial policy. Through Crassus he got the support of the equites, though they cannot have required much persuading. He tried to build upon a wider foundation by getting Cicero to come in and to bring with him the support of the Italian voters. It was to be a quattuorvirate of all the leading men outside the confirmed senatorials. But Cicero refused on principle,—a creditable excuse for a practical error.

Thus was formed what was called the First Triumvirate.

The First Triumvirate

The secret of the immediate and unquestioned success of what was practically, though not theoretically, a revolutionary measure, was that disbanded army of Pompeius which could be called again into existence at the slightest sign from its old commander. When it was too late the politicians at Rome came to see it in its true light, a horrible vision of dry bones which it needed no miracle to call to life.

In forming the triumvirate Cæsar had arranged that he was to have the consulship in 59, to be followed by the proconsulship of Gaul. That year 59 saw all other powers and influences in the state bowed beneath the power of the triumvirate. The mass of the people, utterly weary of senatorial mismanagement, was ready to support Cæsar, so that he had no difficulty in carrying through the legislation expected of him,—the ratification of the settlement in Asia, the provision of lands for Pompeius' soldiers, and the revision of the contract for the taxes of Asia. There was, of course, no consultation of the Senate; nor did Cæsar pay any attention to his senatorial colleague's attempt to block legislation by alleging that he was watching for omens in the sky. A tribune was also put up to propose that Gaul and Illyricum should be Cæsar's provinces for the next year. Cisalpine Gaul was so near to Rome that he could watch events from there; and the state of things in Transalpine Gaul called for military interference, which meant a great army, and possibly a great reputation.

Cicero had been making himself a nuisance to the triumvirs by his opposition; so it was determined to get rid of him. Clodius, a tribune of peculiarly worthless character, was put up in 58 to attack him on the ground of his having executed the Catilinarian conspirators without trial. Cicero knew by this time the feeling of the mass of the Roman people on this question, and so went into exile before the actual sentence of outlawry was passed. Pompeius, however, soon found that Clodius was that kind of instrument which leaves the hands dirty, and so allowed the sentence to be recalled in the next year, 57.

It was through the Italian voters that the sentence had been reversed. Cicero regarded the recall as a personal triumph. This emboldened him to resume once more his political war on the triumvirs. Whether his attitude gave new heart to the Senate, or whether that body began to perceive that Pompeius was too little interested in the vulgar politics of the day to take the trouble to control them, it is certain that in that year other people besides Cicero were trying to overthrow the triumviral authority. But whatever Pompeius might think or do, Cæsar was quite determined not to put up with this state of things, and so called his two colleagues to a conference at Luca, at which they made such arrangements that they may be said to have shared the near future between them. Pompeius was to have the two Spains for five years, from 54 to 50 ; Crassus was to have Syria Cæsar was to have his command prolonged for five years, making ten years in all, and to be allowed to increase his legions to ten. It was also agreed that he should have the consulship of the year 48. Had the agreements entered into at this epoch-making conference been abided by, the Republic might have continued to exist with a modified constitution. It was the failure of Pompeius to keep faith with Cæsar which led to the Civil War and the fall of the Republic.

The conference scared all opponents, especially Cicero, who, seeing himself in danger, made a speech in favour of the allotment of provinces arranged at Luca. It was a bitter degradation to him, on which he put a bold face in public, but about which he made no secret in a letter to his friend Atticus. From this time forward, however, things went from bad to worse. Life at Rome became almost unbearable from the rioting and disorder of political clubs, of one of which Clodius was the leader. Cæsar was so busy in Gaul that his senatorial opponents thought it safe to move heaven and earth to break down the triumviral coalition, all the more so as his military successes were making Pompeius jealous of his reputation. From the time when Crassus was killed at Carrhe in battle with the Parthians in 53, the end of the political partnership was in sight. Pompeius allowed himself to be drawn into the net of senatorial politics and to be used as a half-hearted means of bringing Cæsar to ruin. It is plain that he did not like the part he was expected to play ; and so he made a feeble effort to half undo that which he had been persuaded to do.

The Question between Cæsar and the Senate

It was all-important for Cæsar that he should hold his province of Gaul till he entered on his consulship on January 1, 48, a consulship to which he was practically certain of being elected. If any period intervened between his proconsulship and consulship, his enemies were certain to prosecute him on some ground or other ; and even if he were not eventually found guilty, yet the mere fact of his being under a charge (reus) was by law a bar to his standing for office, so that he would not be able to stand for the consulship of 48. Had the constitutional custom existent at the time when, in consequence of the arrangements made at Luca, he received a second period of five years' command in Gaul, not been altered, he would have held his proconsulship till December 31, 49, for his successor would have been one of the consuls of 49, whose period of office at Rome would not terminate till the last day of that year.

In 52 Pompeius was sole consul at Rome, a wholly unconstitutional position into which he had been thrust by the senatorials, who, seeing that he had practically broken with Cæsar and was jealous of him, were anxious to use the great man as a military shield against any attack which Cæsar might make. Constitutional custom was further violated by Pompeius, who was proconsul in Spain, and received this very year a five years' extension of that command, being allowed to govern his province through lieutenant governors (legati).

In this year Cæsar got the tribunes to propose a law allowing him to stand for the consulship during his absence from Rome, a proposal which was actually supported by Pompeius. But later in the year Pompeius was persuaded by Cæsar's enemies to introduce a law (Lex Pompeia de jure magistratuum) making new regulations as to the magistracies and governorships of provinces, among which was a general clause practically annulling the leave recently given to Cæsar, and a much more important clause laying down that an interval of five years must elapse between the holding of a magistracy at Rome and the tenure of a provincial governorship, which meant that Cæsar would not be succeeded in Gaul by a consul of 49, but by some ex-magistrate who had held office at least five years before 48, and would therefore not be prevented by the calls of office at Rome from superseding Cæsar at the earliest possible date. The date would be March 1, 49, because that had always been the *technical* date on which a proconsul or proprætor was supposed to take up his provincial command. But that date had hitherto been purely technical, because, since long-established custom had laid down that a magistrate of one year should pass the next year to the command of a province, it had not been possible for the magistrate to take up his provincial governorship on the technical date, but at the end of his year of office at Rome, that is to say, on the 1st of January of the succeeding year, or ten months late. Thus when Cæsar's second period of five years in Gaul began on March 1, 54, he knew that, though it would end technically on March 1, 49, his successor, who would be by custom one of the consuls of 49, could not actually take it over till January 1, 48. He could thus look to passing straight from proconsulship to consulship without any interval in which, owing to his being a " private " person (privatus), his enemies could prosecute him on any charge they cared to bring against him. But all these anticipations had been upset by the Lex Pompeia, for by it a consul of 49 could *not* succeed to Gaul, and therefore his successor, whoever it was, would not be detained at Rome in the usual way for ten months after the technical date for his succession to a province, in other words, would be able to supersede Cæsar on March 1, 49 ; and thus from that date till January 1, 48, there would be an interval of ten months in which Cæsar would not be holding public office, and would therefore be liable to prosecution ; and, as has been said, even if the charge were bogus, it was certain to be brought at such a date that Cæsar should be "reus" in July, 49, the time of the consular elections for 48, and be thus ineligible as a candidate.

The result was a complicated series of negotiations in which each side tried to put the other in the apparent, if not the real, wrong. Cæsar, knowing well that his own constitutional position was weak, tried to get his opponents to weaken their own by some unconstitutional action. It was not that he himself would have shrunk from such action had circumstances called for it, but he wanted to have public opinion in Italy as far as possible on his side. He had certain tribunes acting in his interest. To the senatorials nothing was more irritating than the tribunicial veto ; and Cæsar knew that its exercise was peculiarly calculated to drive them into illegalities. The plan succeeded ; for when two tribunes proposed to veto certain drastic measures proposed against Cæsar, they were expelled from the Senate and took refuge with their patron. Popular liberty had been violated in the person of the tribunes ! Early in 49 Cæsar crossed the Rubicon.

The Gallic War

He himself had made a great reputation by his conquests in Gaul ; and the army which he brought with him was probably the most efficient, and certainly one of the largest, that had ever been set on foot by Rome. Cæsar's object in choosing Gaul as his province had been attained. He had made a great reputation and a great army.

The state of Gaul at the time when, in 58, Cæsar took over the governorship, was such as to cause anxiety. The Roman province (Narbonensis) had had a fairly peaceful existence since the Cimbrian War ; but just outside its borders the very powerful tribes of the Arverni, Ædui, and Allobroges had by their internecine quarrels made peace precarious. Rome had interfered on the side of the Ædui, an action which had alarmed the tribes of middle and northern Gaul lest Rome should interfere with them also. They had accordingly established relations with the Germans beyond the Rhine, some of whom had crossed that river. The general tendency of the Germans at the time was to press southwards. But the Gauls soon found that they would like to be saved from their new friends. Ariovistus, a German chief who had crossed the river, was treating the Gauls in his neighbourhood as subjects rather than allies, while others of his compatriots were pressing so hard on the Helvetii, who inhabited the west part of the modern Switzerland, that in 59 they began to move westward into mid-Gaul with a view to settling there. As this would have set all Gaul in ferment, and certainly have endangered the peace of the Roman province, the movement had to be stopped. Thus Cæsar had at the outset two tasks on hand, to bar the passage of the Helvetii, and to prevent Ariovistus from establishing himself in Gaul. The first he accomplished with difficulty, owing to his being hardly prepared for war on a large scale; but, after preventing the would-be migrants from crossing the Arar (Sâone), he drove them back into their own territory. Later in the year he defeated Ariovistus in southern Alsace, a victory which gave his Marian soldiers a confidence which they had not previously had in his leadership. He had, in fact, had the greatest difficulty in getting them to face the terrible Germans.

From this time forward Cæsar used the German tribes on the near side of the Rhine as a screen against any attempted advance of their countrymen from beyond the river. Middle Gaul was now for the moment pacified. In the next year, 57, after much critical fighting, he brought into subjection the Belgæ of northern Gaul, a tribe of Celtic origin, but in some way which cannot be determined differing racially from the other Gauls. It is possible that Germans had mingled with them. The next year, 56, was spent in two operations, the reduction of the Veneti, a maritime race in Brittany which controlled the trade with Britain, and the subjugation of the Iberians south of the Garumna (Garonne) by Publius Crassus, Cæsar's lieutenant. In 55 an expedition was made by Cæsar himself across the Rhine, not with any idea of permanent conquest, but with intent to show the Germans what would happen to them if they interfered in Gaul. Then came the celebrated expedition to Britain, repeated in 54, the intent being apparently to teach the Britons the same lesson which the Germans had been taught in 55. At this time Gaul seemed to have been pacified. But that turned out to be a delusion, for in 53 a widespread insurrection broke out in northern Gaul which caught the Romans all unprepared, their army being dispersed throughout the region. The Gauls tried to take it in detail; but a defeat of the Nervii enabled Cæsar to reverse the plan by taking the tribes themselves in detail, to their prompt discomfiture.

In the next year an insurrection on an equally large scale, and more formidable, because more ably engineered by its leader Vercingetorix, broke out in western and middle Gaul. The campaign was marked by sieges of various of those hill cities which were so conspicuous a feature of the Celtic settlement both in Gaul and Britain. It ended with the capture of Alesia, where Vercingetorix had been blockaded by the Roman army. With his capture all serious resistance ceased; and the next two years were spent in minor operations for the pacification of the territory which had been won. Cæsar had given the western empire that frontier on the Rhine which was, save for a brief interval, to remain its frontier for several centuries. He thus laid the foundations of that definite frontier system which was elaborated under the Empire. The Republic had never devised anything of the kind: it may even be doubted whether it had ever conceived of such a thing.

The First Civil War

It was with the great and magnificent veteran Gallic army of nine legions, 50,000 men in all, together with German and Noric cavalry, that Cæsar invaded Italy; and so began the Civil War. He had sacrificed two legions to Pompeius in the endeavour to preserve peace, one of them a legion of his own, the other a legion which he had borrowed from his rival. They had been demanded from him by the government; and he had given them up on demand.

The Roman government had committed its fortunes to Pompeius. They were not very valuable; but it had little else to commit to him. There was no military force in Italy except one which would certainly have been wiped out of existence had it attempted to face Cæsar's veteran army; so it was Eastward-ho! for Pompeius and his friends, for in the East the fame of Pompeius might summon legions from the soil. Thus Pompeius and his new senatorial clients evacuated Italy. Cæsar, who could be as ruthless as any Roman where non-Romans were concerned, showed peculiar clemency in Italy such as won him grateful recognition from a population which had experienced one Sulla, and was agreeably surprised not to find a second in him. So he now held Italy and Gaul. His opponents held the rest; and, what was more important, they could in the eastern part of the empire raise a fleet which would command all the passages of the Mediterranean. Apart from his influence in the East, Pompeius' name was great in Spain, both as former commander in the war against Sertorius, and in more recent years as governor of the two Spanish provinces. Moreover he had seven legions there.

The task before Cæsar might have been the despair of a lesser man. It was however plain that he could not venture on any decisive move eastwards until the Spanish legions were prevented either by defeat, or by being kept busy in Spain, from falling on his back. The native Spaniards had at any rate a grateful memory of Sertorius; and he, Cæsar, was a political heir of that great man.

Meanwhile the departed and departing senatorials were forwarding Cæsar's cause in Italy by breathing forth threatenings and slaughter such as recalled to the Italian mind the proscriptions of Sulla.

One curious incident in Cæsar's occupation of Italy casts light on the strange mentality of the Marian soldier—Cæsar's immediate incorporation in his own army of all the prisoners he had taken in the peninsula. Later he does the same after Pharsalus. Pompeius also had in his army a legion of Cæsar's and another which had served under him. The confidence which the two commanders showed in trusting to the fidelity of soldiers who had been in the enemy's service proves that they were convinced that the soldier had no patriotism and no politics, but merely a superstitious loyalty to the commander to whom he had sworn his latest sacramentum.

For the operations in Spain Cæsar had collected on the Rhône nine legions and 6,000 horse. The Pompeian army of seven legions was commanded by two able officers, Afranius and Petreius. They had intended to defend the passes of the Pyrenees; but, being anticipated there by Cæsar's troops, had fallen back to the general line of the Ebro (Iberus). The campaign lasted from late in June to early in August, ending with the capitulation of the Pompeian army on August the second, and the passing of Hither Spain into Cæsar's power. Shortly afterwards Further Spain followed suit. The native population had declared emphatically in favour of Cæsar.

Massilia, that ancient Greek colony, formerly an outpost and now sole remnant of Greek freedom, had taken sides against Cæsar owing to its having had relations with Pompeius when the latter marched against Sertorius twenty-eight years before. It was captured after a prolonged siege; and so ended its ancient greatness and its long-standing and faithful alliance with Rome. It lost a large part of its territory.

Sardinia and Sicily had been occupied by lieutenants of Cæsar. In Africa, however, Cæsar's lieutenant Curio was destroyed with all his army by Juba, king of Numidia, who was aiding what he expected to be the winning side.

But Cæsar's bitterest enemies, the *émigré* nobility, now gathered at Thessalonica, were proving his best friends by scaring the population of Italy by threats of what they would do when they came back as victors, and by hampering Pompeius with interference and advice as stupid as themselves. Even that senatorial monomaniac Cato came to dread the possible victory of his own side.

Pompeius had now raised a large army with the troops brought from Italy as a nucleus, and legions raised in various parts of the eastern empire. He had prepared Dyrrhachium (Durazzo) as a base for the attack on Italy, it being situated at the west end of that Via Egnatia which had been made through the only convenient passage of the Pindus chain, and formed the sole line of land communication between east and west. But he nearly lost Dyrrhachium. Cæsar by eluding the Pompeian fleet managed to slip across the Adriatic from Brundusium to a remote landing-place on the inhospitable shore of the Acroceraunian mountains. The Pompeians were just in time to save it from the attack of Cæsar's six legions. For months the situation at Dyrrhachium was stalemate ; but all the time the position of Cæsar's army was becoming more and more desperate from lack of supplies. He was temporarily saved by Marcus Antonius, who managed to come to his relief with four legions. But a very critical time once more supervened. After a failure to capture Pompeius' camp, Cæsar was compelled to retreat. Various complicated operations in the mountainous region to the north-west and west of Thessaly ended in Cæsar crossing the Pindus by the Metzovo Pass into Thessaly. Hither Pompeius, under the impression that the war was won, followed him, and with an army twice as large as Cæsar's attacked him at Pharsalus on August 9, 48, only to be utterly defeated. The effect of the battle was tremendous. All the client states of the East sent in submission to Cæsar. Of the *émigré* nobility the moderates, such as Cicero, made terms with him, and the rest scattered to the four winds. The eastern provinces followed the example of the client states. For two years longer the war dragged on. Pompeius fled to Egypt, where he was murdered by a Roman military tribune in September, 48. Thither Cæsar had followed him with a small force, evidently recking little of any resistance to be faced in Egypt. But a rising in Alexandria proved so formidable that had he not been rescued by a scratch army got together in Asia Minor by Mithradates of Pergamum his career might have come to an end there. By the spring of 47 Egypt was pacified. Cæsar then went to Asia Minor, where things had been going unfavourably, and restored the situation by defeating Pharnaces of Lesser Armenia at Ziela in August, 47. Meanwhile the shattered remnants of the senatorials had been collecting in Africa, where Juba of Numidia had been lording it ever since the defeat of Curio. The detention of Cæsar in the East gave them the time to collect an army of fourteen legions, large indeed in numbers but poor in quality. Cæsar's operations against this new concentration were delayed by that mutiny of his troops in south Italy which has become ever famous by reason of his having brought it to an end by addressing the men as "quirites" (civilians).[1] By October, 47, he was in Africa; but it was not till after various critical happenings that he defeated the senatorial army at Thapsus in April, 46. There was trouble in Spain; but that was later suppressed. Thapsus indeed left Cæsar absolute master of the Roman world. The Roman Republic was dead, and with it died Cato, self-slain, the one supporter of its last years who possessed those qualities which had made it great.

The Legislation of Cæsar

While the history of the Civil War is easy to follow in the contemporary evidence, that evidence is very fragmentary and uncertain with respect to the legislation by which Cæsar sought to establish a new constitution and a new policy for the empire, and very deficient with regard to the concept which he formed of the general lines on which reconstruction should proceed. It is not known whether Cæsar designed to rule as a monarch of the old Roman type. Certain actions of his point in that direction; while other considerations, especially the persistent traditional unpopularity of the kingship with the Roman people, render the idea improbable. Two things are certain: that he did not intend to re-establish the Republic in its old form: that he was not going to be hampered in his acts by restrictions arising from the nature and details of the old constitution.

Given the legality of his appointment to office, the offices he held at the time of his death gave him a power so absolute that all other powers in the state were absolutely subordinate to his. The dictatorship, originally conferred on him in 49, was gradually extended until in 44 it was granted to him for life. A life tenure of the censorship was conferred on him in 44. The tribunicial power was granted to him for life in 48; and in 46 the title of Imperator was conferred on him. And so it seems almost superfluous to record that after holding the regular office of consul in 48, that magistracy was conferred on him first for five, and then for ten years.

A question which has been much debated by modern historians of Rome is as to the extent to which his ideas and his

[1] The effectiveness of the taunt shows the divorce between the Marian soldier and civilian life.

acts formed the foundation and pattern of that constitution of the empire which Augustus elaborated within twenty years of Cæsar's death. The difficulty arises from the fact that many of the Roman historians of the earlier centuries of the empire were wont to ascribe to Julius imperial institutions which cannot, on any evidence which can be called contemporary, be attributed to him.

The Julian and the Augustan Systems

But there are certain general features of his policy which were also essential features of the imperial system of government.

Years before he became dictator he had recognised that the rule of the empire rested, and must rest, on military power ; and that, as a corollary, the centre of gravity in the empire lay in the provinces outside Italy. It is also the case that no one knew better than he those peculiarities of the professional soldiers which would render their presence in large numbers in Italy a danger to the very government, whether personal or otherwise, which they were designed to uphold. Augustus sought diligently to camouflage the fact that the imperial power rested on the army : that the principate was ultimately a military autocracy ; but it came out again and again under him and his immediate successors, while under the Flavian emperors no pains were taken to conceal it. It seems also fairly clear that Julius, in so far as moral and political support was concerned, looked for it from the provinces rather than from Italy ; and this is a marked feature of the policy of the emperors. The reliance on provincial support led both Cæsar and his successors to adopt towards the provinces a policy in great contrast to that of the Republic. The empire had been run as a profit-making machine for that body of Roman citizens into which a native of the provinces could hardly obtain entrance. But Julius showed by his grant of Latin rights to Sicily, by his foundation of colonies of Roman citizens outside Italy, and by his grant of the citizenship to a non-Roman town, Gades in Spain, that he was prepared to contemplate under certain conditions the wide extension of Roman citizenship through the provinces, a citizenship which, though nominally of Rome, should be in reality a citizenship of the empire. Nor is it hard to recognise the conditions, for they are written large in history from this time onwards. The test of qualification was to be civilisation, a Latin civilisation in the West, a Greek in the East ; and the foundation of Roman colonies in the provinces was intended to promote its attainment. Under Augustus the policy indicating an intention to make the attainment of the citizenship widely accessible to the provincial population suffered a set-back, for that cautious statesman was of more conservative origin than his relative and predecessor. The Octavii from whom Augustus was sprung were one of those upper middle-class families of Italy which had, ever since Italy was granted the citizenship, shown a conservative pride in its possession, and a conservative tendency to support the impressive but empty majesty of the Senate. They did not know its emptiness, for they had not lived in that inner circle of politics at Rome to which the great patrician family of the Cæsars belonged as a natural right. Cæsar knew the rottenness of senatorial politics; and, acting on that knowledge, treated the Senate with scant courtesy. Augustus, partly from policy, partly no doubt from genuine respect, restored to the Senate at any rate the outward dignity, and some of the real power, it had lost. Of the body of the citizens Cæsar cynically represented himself as the representative; but he did not regard them as a chosen people for whom the privileges of the empire should be strictly reserved. Augustus on the other hand had been brought up in all the pride of a class which had won a great privilege, and was intent on hedging that privilege about with a ring fence. Cæsar knew the worthlessness of the masses at Rome itself, and had found the Italians respectable but unsympathetic. He looked therefore to find better human material in the provinces. Augustus inherited a faith, not altogether ill-founded, in the Roman citizen in Italy outside Rome.

It is also a question of the sentimental basis on which the two great men respectively determined to found their rule. Cæsar knew that the support of the masses at Rome was valuable only for election purposes, and valueless when he had attained a position in which election could no longer play a part. He had attained to an autocracy for life. The real sympathy of the rural population of Italy he had never won. The best it had to give him was a negative gratitude for his forbearance in his treatment of it. In the recent civil war it had suffered but little, for the fighting had been carried on outside Italy; and it did not therefore feel that intense personal relief at the establishment of peace which it felt after the second civil war had brought home to it the misery of the sufferings of war. Augustus appeared to it as a saviour; Cæsar as a master. But even in the case of Augustus it might seem that towards the end of his reign he was becoming conscious that the Romans of rural Italy were forgetting the benefits he had conferred on them : that a generation had sprung up which no longer associated the Republic with war and the Empire with peace, and was consequently prepared to regard the continuation of the empire as an open question. It is not likely that either of these very able men would fail to realise that those who had benefited by the change would be supporters of the change from Republic to empire, whereas those who had lost, or conceived themselves to have lost, by it would welcome the re-establishment of the old order of things. And so from the latter part of Augustus' reign onwards there is an ever-growing tendency for the emperors to rely more and more on the support of the population of the provinces, a tendency which, though faint at first, becomes definitely marked in the reign of Claudius, and a definite policy under the Flavian emperors. In this respect Cæsar's policy becomes eventually that of the Principate, more from the force of circumstances than from choice, since it was the only policy which could ever ensure a peaceful maintenance of the imperial power. There was of course the terrible power of the army as a last resort; but the emperors were wise enough to keep that in the background as a resort, rather than in the foreground as a threat, knowing well that the most powerful government is asking for trouble if it does not seek to win the sympathy of at least a large element in the governed.

But apart from such dynastic reasons as weighed with Cæsar or with the emperors who succeeded him, the very security of the empire as an empire called for a new policy which might convert it from a loose agglomeration of states into a unity. The very men who saw that this new policy was necessary had in their own personal careers illustrated the dangers to which an empire was exposed formed of provinces so loosely bound to the central government that the officials sent out to govern them might under favourable circumstances not merely break loose from the empire but overthrow the central government itself. They did not require a prophet to interpret to them the doom of such an empire written on the walls of fate. The new policy must aim at an imperial unity such as the Republic had never tried to realise. It must create an empire held together at the outset by a central government armed with a strength superior to that which any portion of the whole could display, not a government whose weakness tempted the man of ambition to grasp at overweening power, and whose incompetence incited the man of ability to take forcible measures to remedy the defects and injustice of its rule. In this respect also the policy of Cæsar was the policy of the rulers who succeeded him.

But when it comes to the form devised for this powerful central authority it is plain that that indicated by Cæsar is not that adopted by his great successor or by those who in turn succeeded him. It may be said,—it is indeed almost certain,—that Cæsar did not live to elaborate a permanent form for his power. But he went far enough to show that it would have been something very different from the cleverly disguised autocracy devised by **Augustus**. He forgot that, if a few feet of steel may make an empire, a few inches of steel may unmake an emperor. From his fate Augustus learned a lesson which he never forgot. When the details of the Augustan régime come to be considered it will be found perhaps that the position which Augustus designed for himself was a realisation of the ambitions of Pompeius rather than those of Cæsar.

Yet it is probable that if the mind of Cæsar at the opening of the civil war were known it would be found that he did not then dream of the position in which that war eventually placed him, master of a world which had no possible master save himself. He had fought to save himself from ruin. But in the very act of saving himself he had placed himself in the position of having to save the world. And how short was the time which fate allowed him for such a task! He lived for a little more than five years after the beginning of the civil war, of which more than three were occupied with the war itself.

The most striking feature of his peace policy was a clemency towards political opponents such as amazed a generation which regarded proscriptions and political murders as natural features in political life.

His legislation designed to meet immediate needs is more remarkable in the spirit than in the letter. He restored to their rights the children of those whom Sulla had proscribed. If his old anarchist associates among the democrats expected a financial revolution as a set-off against that of Sulla they were disappointed. The allotment of lands to his soldiers was carried out without the spoliation of any owner or holder of land. The law against clubs (collegia) was put into force so that the riotous bands which had disturbed Rome in the years before the civil war were suppressed. The system of corn doles was restricted to genuine poverty at Rome, while poverty in the rural districts of Italy was relieved by the establishment of transmarine colonies at Carthage and Corinth. His economic measures were not in the end wholly successful; but the spirit of justice and sympathy was apparent in them.

That unification of the empire which was so sorely needed was promoted by the drastic plan of concentrating under his own control all the government of the provinces and all relations with foreign powers. There were to be no more great proconsuls. Cæsar was the one proconsul, and the acting governors of the provinces were his lieutenants (legati) appointed or removed at his will. This policy was, in a modified form, adopted by the Principate.

There were conspicuously unpopular elements about these arrangements, necessary as they were at the time. The perpetual dictatorship reminded men of Sulla and his works. The absorption of the provincial governorship robbed the Roman nobility of its most lucrative prizes. The general amelioration of the government of the provinces was disliked by all classes whose gains from the provinces had been largely dependent on misgovernment.

Meanwhile the old constitution went on working, passing laws, and electing magistrates; but the laws were such as Cæsar approved, and the magistrates had only such power as he allowed them. Respect for constitutional tradition was shown when convenient, ignored if inconvenient; in fact it was made quite clear that the old institutions existed only on sufferance and might at any time be replaced by new. The Senate was humiliated by the introduction of freedmen and Gallic provincials into its ranks.

The whole general tendency was to make the surviving elements of the old constitution merely applicable to Rome in order to municipalise them, in fact to reduce them *at once* to that position which they only attained *gradually* under the empire. The treatment of the Senate was viewed with sullen discontent by that old nobility which Julius was prepared to defy, Augustus anxious to humour. It was a mistake in that it meant personal danger to its author.

The grant of the citizenship to Italy forty years before had never been followed by a readjustment of the many forms of municipal constitutions, implying originally various rights, which prevailed throughout the country, a manifest anachronism and inconvenience under the new order of things. The reorganisation and simplification of the now meaningless system was carried out by Cæsar's law, the Lex Julia Municipalis [1] of 45 B.C.

It is not definitely known, but it is almost certainly the case, that the government of the provinces by Cæsar's legati was free from the corruptions of the old system. Cæsar had already shown a sympathy for the provincials by a law passed in his consulship of 59 restricting the power of governors to make extortionate exactions from the subject populations.

Cæsar was murdered in March, 44. Until the very last years of his life he had shown remarkable ability in calculating the value of the factors present at every moment of his long and perilous political career. But in these last years he underrated the strength of the feeling aroused in the ranks of the old nobility of Rome by their practical exclusion from power under the form of government he had established. His murderers were members of that comparatively small section of the senatorial nobility

[1] It established a form of municipal government which was later applied under the empire to the municipalities of the provinces.

which had supported him in the recent struggle, but had evidently expected his reconstruction of affairs to proceed on lines different from those which the great man adopted. And so they killed him from what was at best a mistaken patriotism, or at worst disappointed self-interest.

Various were the feelings which his death excited. Cicero, to whom he had shown peculiar consideration and courtesy, could never forgive him for having overthrown that senatorial government which, despite those defects which Cicero knew so well, he had worshipped as a sort of political fetish. And so on the death of the tyrant he sang a song of victory which jars somewhat on the ear of anyone who reads even Cicero's own tale of the advances which Cæsar had made to him. But there were others who felt and expressed a real sorrow at the death of a great man who at the height of his power had ever sought to reconcile rather than to crush his political foes. The letter written by Matius [1] in answer to one which Cicero had sent him rejoicing in the " tyrant's " death, is one of the most beautiful compositions preserved in ancient literature. It is all but a poem.[2]

---

[1] Cic. "Epist. Ad Fam." ix, 28.
[2] The finer passages, when translated, fall almost naturally into verse:

" I know full well how men since Cæsar's death
　Reproach me, and count it as a sin
That I lament the death of him, my friend,
And wrathful am that he, the man I loved,
　Has perished.
　　　　　Yes, they say indeed
That patriotism is a thing to place
Before one's friendships,—just as if they had
Proved that our country profited
　By Cæsar's death.
　　　　　　　But I,
I will not use evasion, but confess
That such philosophy attains a height
That I have never reached.
　　　　　　　In the late civil war
I did not follow him ; but ne'ertheless,
Although I liked it not, did not desert
My friend. Nor did I e'er approve
The war itself, nor even that dispute
Which led to it : nay, rather did my best
To stifle it at birth.
　　　　　　　And so, when victory came
To him who was my friend, I was not caught
By the delights of office or of wealth,
Rewards which others, men of less account
In influence with him, immeasurably abused.

The band of nobles who had murdered Cæsar posed as the liberators of their fatherland. Thus they posed; but the people generally were dismayed at an act which could only mean the renewal of civil war. Cicero dreamed for a time that the Republic could be restored, and that he could restore it. But he soon found that words were of no avail in a situation which must be decided by the sword. Cæsar had left four men in positions such as might afford them some hope of attaining supremacy in the state. Marcus Antonius, his trusted and able lieutenant in the Gallic and Civil Wars, was sole consul, and, as such, titular head of the state. But he had no army at his disposal. Lepidus was governor of Hither Spain and Narbonensis, a great noble, but not a great man. Sextus Pompeius, the outlawed son of the great Pompeius, of desperate courage and great ability, had got control of Further Spain.

Last but not least was a youth of nineteen, Gaius Octavius, great-nephew and heir of Cæsar. Cautious, astute, and able, he bided his time, building up his influence with the army and the people, while avoiding any quarrel with Antonius. Both he and Antonius now began to manœuvre for position, which meant the control of an army. Antonius had late in 44 openly declared himself against the murderers of Cæsar, and had attacked Decimus Brutus in Cisalpine Gaul. Octavius, with more judgment than sentiment, declared against the would-be avenger of his uncle, winning thereby the approval of the Senate, which granted him the command against Antonius. In April, 43, Antonius was defeated in Cisalpine Gaul. Had the Senate shown any common sense, it might have attached Octavius to its side; but, misled by Cicero, it transferred the command to Decimus Brutus, and refused to make Octavius consul. It was irreparable folly to alienate the sympathy of the man to whom, as Cæsar's heir, Cæsar's veterans looked. Octavius, marching on Rome with eight legions, arranged affairs to his own liking. But mean-

> That mercy should be shown to vanquished foes,
> To fellow-citizens, I ever urged
> As though I worked to save myself.
>   Can I
> Who wished to save the lives of all, not feel
> A righteous wrath that he from whom I won
> That grace of mercy should have died the death?
> —And this the more that they whose lives he spared
> Are those that got him hated, got him killed.
> And now these murderers say to me, 'Ah, you!
> You shall be punished, since you even dare
> To fail to laud the deed which we have done.'
> O arrogance unheard of! Some may even boast
> Their shameful deed, while others may not e'en
> Show trace of grief, lest vengeance fall on them!"

while Antonius had formed relations with Lepidus and various other governors of western provinces. It might have come to a collision between their army and that of Octavius, had not Marcus Brutus and Cassius been at the time collecting an army in the East to champion the cause of the Senate and the Republic. Thinking that, as matters stood, a conference would be more useful than a battle, Octavius, Antonius, and Lepidus met near Bononia (Bologna) and formed a compact which resulted in their being appointed by the terrified people of Rome a commission of three (triumvirate) for a term of five years " for the purpose of reorganising the state." Then ensued a reign of terror for some months, in which Cicero paid with his life for having attacked Antonius in the famed Philippics. The proscription is a regrettable incident in the career of Octavius, though it was perhaps to Antonius that this orgy of blood was mainly due. But it is also necessary to take into account the fact that, as the murder of Cæsar had shown, there was danger in sparing the lives of political opponents who, in the exasperation of the times, were but too apt to become political assassins.

The triumvirs were not, however, by any means masters of the Roman world. Sextus Pompeius with a great fleet commanded the western Mediterranean, and held Sicily and southern Spain, while Brutus and Cassius were for the time masters of the eastern empire. In 42 took place that campaign of Philippi which might have had so different a conclusion had Marcus Brutus been left to himself. As it was, it ended in disaster and death to him and Cassius. After the battle Antonius went off to a settlement of that East where great reputations were so easily won and lost, while Octavius returned to Italy to deal with Sextus Pompeius and affairs at Rome. This is the first step in that path of events which led to Octavius posing as the champion of the West against the East.

In Italy Octavius' high-handed proceedings in providing land for veterans led to a very dangerous situation. Lucius Antonius, a brother of the triumvir, took up the cause of the dispossessed, and, incidentally, of the Senate. But in January of the year 40 he was captured at Perusia, so that Octavius was left master of Italy, with, however, the near prospect of trouble with Marcus Antonius, who was likely to resent his brother's fate. In the West the provinces of Spain and Numidia had been assigned to Octavius, while Gaul and Africa had been allotted to Antonius, to Lepidus being given the rule in Italy. It was by now evident that that high-born but somewhat indolent nobleman was not equal to the task in Italy; and so Octavius shelved him to Africa, Antonius' province. If this left any doubt as to his having broken with Antonius, that doubt was dispelled by his seizing for himself Antonius' other province of Gaul. Meanwhile Sextus Pompeius was carrying on piracy on an imperial scale in the western seas, so much so that it was apparent that Italy would be starved unless a stop were put to his proceedings. To this intent Octavius appointed Marcus Vipsanius Agrippa, that able man who was to play such a notable part in the later establishment of the empire, with a commission to drive him out of Sicily.

But Antonius had now to be reckoned with. After a couple of years spent after the fashion of one who has yielded to the charms of the East and of a Cleopatra, he was goaded to action by the proceedings of Octavius, and so landed at Brundusium with intent to try conclusions with him. Octavius might have crushed him offhand on land; but feared that his fleet, and he himself, if he escaped, might join Sextus Pompeius, in which case the position in Italy would become desperate. So in the autumn of this year 40 the two rivals concluded the famous treaty of Brundusium, whereby a new partition of the empire was made among the triumvirs, to Antonius being assigned the lands east of the Adriatic, to Octavius the West, while the negligible Lepidus played the part of the little dog to whom were given the bones of Africa to pick. A treaty concluded at Misenum pacified Sextus Pompeius for the time; and so Octavius went off to organise Gaul, while Antonius was called to troubles in the East.

Brutus and Cassius had during their brief control of the East formed an alliance with the Parthian king Orodes. That monarch bided quiet after the defeat of his allies, having a certain dread of Antonius. But when he found that that gentleman was much more concerned with his interest in Cleopatra than with the interests of the empire, he took courage and invaded the eastern provinces with such effect that by the end of the year 40 he was master of all as far as the Ægean. He had been advised by renegade Roman partisans of Brutus and Cassius, who had reckoned on civil war in Italy. The treaty of Brundusium upset these calculations. The work of driving Orodes back was committed by Antonius to an excellent soldier, Ventidius Bassus. By the middle of 38 the Parthians had retired east of the Euphrates. The next year or two were spent by Octavius in organising the West; by Antonius in disorganising himself. Only once again before Actium did the two triumvirs meet. In 37 Antonius made a call on Octavius with 300 ships. The caller was not well received; but, as on the previous occasion, the quarrel was patched up,—chiefly by the skill of that Mæcenas who was to be associated with Agrippa as a trusted adviser of the future emperor. The triumvirate was renewed for another five years.

By the middle of 36 Octavius, who had got 120 ships from Antonius, was ready to tackle Sextus Pompeius. The treaty of Misenum had broken down. An attack on Sicily, in which Octavius' forces suffered preliminary reverses, was finally successful owing to a great defeat which Agrippa inflicted on Pompeius' fleet off Naulochus in September of that year. Sextus escaped with a few vessels. Then Lepidus seemed likely to make an attempt to restore his position in the Roman world; but his great army of twenty-two legions melted like wax before the solicitations and seductions of Octavius; and he spent the remaining twenty-five years of his life in exile.

In 35 Sextus Pompeius, who had taken refuge in the East, was captured and executed by legates of Antonius. His death brought peace to the West. Octavius had now the opportunity for restoring to Italy that peace which had been disturbed by piracy, brigandage, and the other accompaniments of civil war. The success which he, seconded by his able ministers Mæcenas and Agrippa, attained in the settlement of the West, marked him out in the minds of men as a future ruler of the empire. He also rectified that most dangerous frontier of Italy on the northeast by the pacification of the hill tribes of Illyria and the defeat of the Pannonians, a powerful tribe living west of the middle Danube. The Savus (Save) became the new imperial frontier. But his work here could not be brought to completion, for by 33 it became plain that Antonius was preparing to contest with him the supremacy in the empire.

Antonius' proceedings meanwhile, having been dictated by the caprices of the fair and ambitious Cleopatra, had not brought to the Roman East that peace which the West had enjoyed. In 36 he undertook that attack on Parthia which he had long advertised; but, after penetrating into Media, he returned towards the close of the year with only a fragment of the great army he had taken with him. In 34 he won somewhat cheap glory by a successful invasion of Armenia.

It was in the winter of 34-33 that startling developments took place in the East. Cleopatra, who had reduced the amorous Antonius to a condition of maudling obedience, got him to proclaim her " Queen of Kings "; to assign five Roman provinces to her reputedly legitimate sons, and to proclaim Cæsarion, her natural son by Cæsar, as heir to that great man.

The infatuation of love cannot excuse the insensate folly of Antonius in assenting to a policy which must give the western Roman world the impression that he was prepared to subordinate it to the East—a policy more calculated than any other to unite the whole of the western empire in support of Octavius against himself and all he represented. He had also reason to know, better perhaps than any living man, the military superiority of the West when matched against the East. He had elevated Octavius into the position of champion of Roman against Greek civilisation by threatening the Italian with the domination of the despised Hellene. Even senatorial elements, hitherto sullenly hostile to Octavius, now rallied to him. The one thing in favour of Antonius was that, in 32, when he broke out he was better prepared for war than was Octavius. The wealthy East provided at the moment resources which the financially exhausted West could not supply. But Antonius, having crossed with army and fleet to Greece, delayed there all through the winter of 32–31, thus giving Octavius time to complete his preparations. In the spring of 31 he was ready.

ACTIUM

The fleet and army of Antonius were at the mouth of the Ambraciot Gulf. While he was dallying time away at Patræ, Octavius,—which really means Agrippa,—occupied the promontory north of the narrow entrance of the gulf opposite to that promontory of Actium which was to give its name to the great battle; while the fleet under Agrippa blockaded the entrance. Weeks passed in a position of stalemate which did not inconvenience Octavius, who could get supplies from Italy, but meant scarcity and semi-starvation to Antonius, whose communications with Egypt and Asia were interrupted by the flying squadrons of Octavius. The time came when Antonius had to force his way out or lose both army and fleet. In his attempt to win safety the great naval fight of Actium took place off the entrance of the strait. The big ships of Antonius were almost helpless against the attack of the light Liburnian galleys of Agrippa, which could inflict damage without coming to close quarters. Fire completed the ruin of the great fleet, though the Egyptian squadron escaped with the disillusioned lovers aboard. Actium decided not merely the history of the Roman Empire, but that of Europe up to the present day.

In the next year Antonius and Cleopatra committed suicide; and Egypt was at last annexed to the Roman Empire.

CHAPTER XI

THE EMPIRE, SOMETIMES CALLED THE PRINCIPATE, 31 B.C.—A.D. 138.

THE JULIO-CLAUDIAN FAMILY

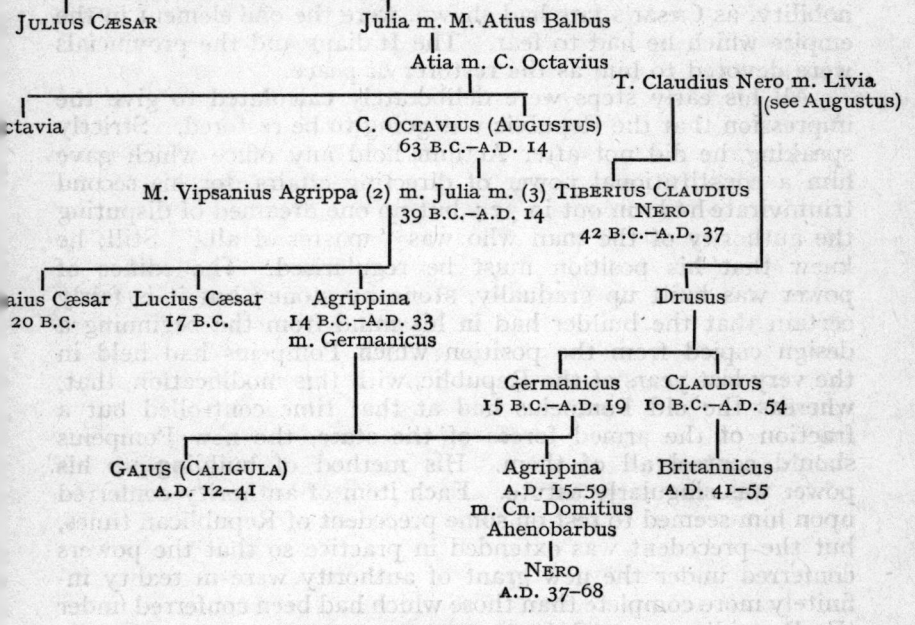

```
JULIUS CÆSAR                    Julia m. M. Atius Balbus
                                         │
                                   Atia m. C. Octavius
                                         │
                                         │                    T. Claudius Nero m. Livia
                                         │                                  (see Augustus)
   Octavia          C. OCTAVIUS (AUGUSTUS)
                         63 B.C.–A.D. 14
         ┌───────────────────┴───────┐
  M. Vipsanius Agrippa (2) m. Julia m. (3) TIBERIUS CLAUDIUS
           39 B.C.–A.D. 14                      NERO
                                           42 B.C.–A.D. 37
  ┌──────────┬──────────┐                         │
 Gaius Cæsar  Lucius Cæsar  Agrippina           Drusus
  20 B.C.      17 B.C.    14 B.C.–A.D. 33         │
                          m. Germanicus           │
                              │                   │
                          Germanicus           CLAUDIUS
                        15 B.C.–A.D. 19      10 B.C.–A.D. 54
              ┌───────────────┴─────┐              │
        GAIUS (CALIGULA)       Agrippina       Britannicus
          A.D. 12–41           A.D. 15–59       A.D. 41–55
                             m. Cn. Domitius
                              Ahenobarbus
                                   │
                                 NERO
                              A.D. 37–68
```

REIGNS OF THE EMPERORS

Augustus, Triumvir, 42–32 B.C.
           Absolute but irregular power, 32–27 B.C.
           Princeps, 27 B.C.–A.D. 14.
Tiberius, A.D. 14.
Gaius (Caligula), A.D. 37.
Claudius, A.D. 41.
Nero, A.D. 54.
Galba, A.D. 68.
Otho, A.D. 69.
Vitellius, A.D. 69.
Vespasian, A.D. 69.
Titus, A.D. 79.
Domitian, A.D. 81.
Nerva, A.D. 96.
Trajan, A.D. 98.
Hadrian, A.D. 117–138.

IN taking measures for the re-establishment of the government of the empire, every step in which was a disguised advance towards monarchy, Octavius started with two advantages: that he issued from the war not merely as one who had crushed a rival, but as one who had championed the cause of the West against the East, and maintained the unity of the empire; that he possessed in the treasure of Egypt the means of restoring almost immediately the ruinous financial situation in Italy.

He had now to determine the form which the government should take. On the mere question of his personal safety undisguised autocracy was out of the question. The Republican nobility, as Cæsar's fate had shown, were the one element in the empire which he had to fear. The Italians and the provincials were devoted to him as the restorer of peace.

All his early steps were deliberately calculated to give the impression that the Republic was going to be restored. Strictly speaking, he did not after Actium hold any office which gave him a constitutional power of directing affairs, for his second triumvirate had run out in 32; but no one dreamed of disputing the authority of the man who was "master of all." Still, he knew that his position must be regularised. The edifice of power was built up gradually, stone by stone; but it is fairly certain that the builder had in his mind from the beginning a design copied from the position which Pompeius had held in the very last years of the Republic, with this modification, that, whereas the old Pompeius had at that time controlled but a fraction of the armed forces of the state, the new Pompeius should control all of them. His method of building up his power was singularly astute. Each item of authority conferred upon him seemed to rest on some precedent of Republican times, but the precedent was extended in practice so that the powers conferred under the new grant of authority were in reality infinitely more complete than those which had been conferred under the Republican precedent.

Settlement of 27 B.C.

On the first day of the year 27, the opening day of his seventh consulship, he announced his intention of handing back the government to the Senate and the people. But this dramatic scene had undoubtedly been rehearsed beforehand. He received back at the same time from the Senate and the people power which really gave him the control of the state. He was given the imperium for ten years, and the government of certain provinces, namely, a selected list of those which lay either on the frontiers of the empire or which had not been completely pacified under the Republic, every province, in fact, in which any military force of any appreciable size was required. As, according to this first settlement of the permanent form which his power was to take, he seems to have contemplated basing it mainly on the holding of the consulship, it is plain that, so far as precedent was concerned, he relied on that of Pompeius, who governed Spain by legati (lieutenants or deputies) while consul at Rome.

But both Dio Cassius and Strabo are said to assert that at the time at which the above powers were conferred on him, there was also conferred on him the sole command of all the armies of the state, and the exclusive rights of levying troops, of making war and peace, and of concluding treaties.[1] Were this so, it would be necessary to suppose that in one most important respect Augustus departed from that concealment of realities which was the foundation of the diplomacy by which he established his power on a legal footing. It would have been useless to disguise under precedent the main powers which he acquired had the command of the army been given to him in so bald and direct a form. Nor does Dio's evidence really support such an account of what happened,[2] for that author expressly attributes the acquisition of that command to Augustus' artfulness in arranging the division of the provinces between himself and the Senate in such a way that he took all the frontier provinces where a military force was required, leaving to the Senate those provinces which were not exposed to direct external danger, and were sufficiently pacified to require no more than a small armed force. He thus acquired a *de facto* control of the whole Roman army; and all that he and his successors (if any) had to do was to see that the distribution of the provinces was always maintained on this principle. The right of levying troops followed as a matter of course. With respect to the making of war and peace and the concluding of treaties, the governors of the outlying provinces had had in Republican times to provide for their defence. Invasions could not be warded off by mere reference to the government at Rome, a process which took a long time. They had had to make war on their own responsibility; and, when the time came, to settle the war by agreement with the enemy. There was plenty of precedent for this kind of thing; and the stretching of an old precedent was less likely to excite resentment than the establishment of a new one. The claim of Augustus to re-establish the Republic would have been an undisguised sham had he allowed such power to be voted to him *en bloc*. Time and custom would soon convert his *de facto* position into a constitutional one. All he had to do for the moment was to arrange the division of provinces with discretion.

[1] Dio. liii, 12. Strabo, p. 840.
[2] Cf. Pelham, "Outlines of Roman History," p. 368.

All this camouflage was adopted with a view to his personal safety in Rome itself, especially from the old Republican nobility. It gave them the impression that they were merely dealing with a second Pompeius, a chief of the state (princeps civitatis), whose position might or might not be maintained during his lifetime, but would certainly die with him. But to the population of rural Italy and the provinces Augustus seemed to be the monarch of the world.

SETTLEMENT OF 23 B.C.

And so things went on for four and a half years, at the end of which, in June of the year 23 B.C., Augustus sprang on the world a surprise which alarmed it. He resigned the consulship, which, as every one knew, meant the resignation of the constitutional supremacy of the state. The world stood aghast at the prospect of a re-establishment of that old evil order of things in which a government at Rome was faced by the power of a great proconsul abroad, for the proconsular authority he still maintained. But there was no genuineness about the renunciation. Augustus could reckon that that would happen which did happen. He was offered all sorts of compensatory powers, and, after refusing many, finally accepted an arrangement by which his power (imperium) at Rome was made superior to that of the consuls. The proconsular power had been exercised by Pompeius *from* Rome; but never before had it been exercised *in* Rome. That Augustus sought such change was due to the inconvenience he had felt in having beside him at Rome the other consul whose power was technically equal to his own; that he accepted power in an unprecedented form was a novel feature in his new policy. But for the practical exercise of authority within Rome itself he still made use of that tribunicial power (tribunicia potestas), granted to him in 36, which gave him the right of veto and regularised his relations with the Senate. Still the old Republicans could hope, for those powers, with the exception of the tribunicia potestas, which was given him for life, were only voted for definite periods.

THE SUCCESSION

There was no provision either expressed or implied that these powers would be conferred on any successor; still less was there any outward appearance of the foundation of a hereditary dynasty. Nor did the principate ever become hereditary in theory, or even a constitutional permanency. In theory it was always an open question whether on the death of an emperor the power which had been conferred upon him should be conferred on some one else, and whether that some one else, if adopted, should be a member of the family of his predecessor. Augustus knew exactly how far it was safe to go in predetermination of affairs, and that there were other ways of securing a succession than the insertion in a constitution of clauses which might exasperate formidable elements in the state, such as the Republican nobility at Rome. The means adopted by him and by subsequent emperors was to raise the successor they desired to such a high position that on their death no other candidate would have much chance against him; and, as to his actual succession,—well,—that was dependent on the skill with which he managed to play his cards with the army. A law of succession would have been a scandal to the Republican nobility, and a dead letter against the military power. That is why Augustus never dreamt of making one, though his supremacy in the last years of his reign was so complete that he might have safely done so had it been worth his while. On the whole the practical method of succession which he indicated by his action in raising Lucius and Gaius Cæsar, and, after their death, Tiberius, to high positions, worked, if not well, at least fairly effectively, in spite of the influence of the Prætorian Guard and the provincial armies. The most important qualification for the principate was that the princeps should either be a distinguished soldier, or the son of one, for the soldier is at all times inclined to let his affections run on family lines. This it was which tended to keep the early principate within the Julio-Claudian house, and this despite the fact that of the first five emperors two were unspeakable fools. That it was which secured the Principate for the upstart Flavian family. Taking the circumstances on the whole, there was far more method than want of method in Augustus' apparently unmethodical way of dealing with the succession. It worked out in the end in this way,—that the Senate conferred on each new successor to the imperial power the prerogatives originally voted to Augustus; but it had no real choice as to the person on whom it conferred that power. That was settled beforehand by the method adopted by Augustus, and sealed by the overwhelming power of the army. It is probable that the method worked out after his death very much on the lines on which he anticipated. It is quite certain that under the circumstances no other method could have been more practically effective.

In thus looking forward to the working out during the first century and a half of the empire of a principle established in the days of Augustus, the plan which will be followed in dealing within a necessarily limited space with the story of this one hundred and fifty years has been anticipated. Emperors come and emperors go; but during the whole of the period the various parts and institutions of the empire are developing on lines which are hardly affected by the changes in the person of the supreme ruler. The fact is that the organisation which Augustus established was so able and so thorough that in the case of a feeble emperor it worked by itself, and able, energetic emperors recognised that it was best and easiest for them to carry on the work on the lines laid down by the system they found in operation. It was on the life of the city of Rome itself that the person of the emperor had most effect. Plots and executions of the Republican nobility varied according as the character of the emperor rendered them more or less common. The official relations between emperor and Senate varied according to the whim of the emperor of the moment. Court and society scandals maintained a high level of frequency in the high social circles of the Julio-Claudian house, though less common in the more respectable middle-class family which succeeded it. But varied as were the domestic, social, and political experiences of the different emperors in Rome itself, in Italy and the provinces their actions, save for certain follies committed by Caligula and Nero, aimed at the welfare of the population. It became, indeed, more evident each year that the sentimental foundation of the Principate was in the provinces; and that the financial welfare of the state depended on the provinces; and so the central government at Rome had the interest of the provinces at heart, at any rate in the first two centuries of the empire.

The fifty years during which Augustus was the dominating personality in the world of western civilisation are in some respects the most remarkable in history. He appears on the scene as a mere lad of nineteen at a moment when it is all in wild disorder, when the fate of the empire is hanging in the balance, and the scale seems likely to incline towards a chaos of disruption which must bring misery unspeakable to the many millions of dwellers round the Mediterranean. He, a mere novice in war, takes up the sword against one of the most experienced soldiers of the day, and against the desperate son of the great Pompeius. It has been said of Octavius that he was not a great commander in war such as his predecessor Cæsar had been. Yet he brought that second civil war to a victorious conclusion, starting on his task from a situation more desperate than that of Cæsar at the outset of a first civil war, for the mere boy Octavius had not at his disposal a great veteran army, the best of its time, nor had he that great prestige of past success which might win the confidence and fidelity of the fickle Marian soldier. His success has been ascribed to Agrippa. It is always possible to decry the reputation of any great commander by attributing his successes to some officer who is in a position equivalent to that of a modern chief of the staff. Did Cæsar owe nothing to Marcus Antonius when he rescued him from his perilous position at Dyrrhachium?

It is without doubt the case that Augustus had the advice of men of very great ability both during the period of the civil war and in the critical early years of his reign, when a false step might have been fatal. But it is a part of ability to recognise in subordinates that ability which may be of value in a given situation.

ECONOMIC REFORM

When the civil war was over Augustus was faced by two tasks, the settlement of the future constitution, and the economic restoration of affairs within the empire. The first was difficult; the second was appalling in its magnitude. For a century and a half the government of the empire had been economically bad. Whatever merits the provincial government of the Republic had possessed, they had not been financial; and its *laissez-faire* attitude or impotence in respect to the public and private exploitation of the provinces and the financial oppression of the provincials had accentuated greatly the evils due to the neglect to establish any sound financial system of public administration. Rome had, indeed, in the first instance given the world a peace which it, and especially the eastern part of it, sorely needed after the wars and confusions of the third century; but when in the middle of the second century the efficiency of the senatorial government broke down, there began a period during which almost every region of the empire suffered from the devastation of war or disorder. The catalogue of disasters is terrible. Italy suffers from the ruin caused by the Hannibalic War and from the bad political and economic conditions resulting from it. The Social War with its devastation undoes whatever Tiberius Gracchus had done to restore its economic position. The Gladiatorial War brings temporary ruin to a large area in the south after Sulla's proscriptions had done the same for various parts of the peninsula. The trade of Italy and the empire is paralysed by piracy. Then come the two civil wars, in the course of which every corner of the empire suffers more or less loss. Of the woes of the individual provinces it would take too long to tell; but the Jugurthine and Civil Wars brought disaster to Africa, the Sertorian War to Spain, the thirty years' War with Mithradates to Asia,—to cite merely the most notable examples of the sufferings of some of the richest and most important areas of the empire during the last century of the Republic. That was the world which Octavius found on his hands after Actium. Forty years later he bequeathed it to his successor in a political and economic position such as made the first two centuries of the Christian era the happiest period through which the population of the Mediterranean region has ever passed. It was a wonderful work; and the man who did it cannot have been other than a very wonderful man,—perhaps, judged by results, the ablest man in history. Economic tasks seem so commonplace in the telling. They do not excite the neurotic admiration which is called forth by the fire and fury of war. But success in them is hard,—very hard,—and rare,—very rare;—and those who have been successful in them on a large scale belong to a very limited first class in the school of ability. Though the evidence for the time does record some of the main features of this marvellous work of reconstruction, yet some of them have passed into an oblivion from which there is no prospect of their being recalled. And so much of the plot of what would have been the greatest story in the economic history of the world has perished.

Dyarchy. The Assemblies

In modern times the name of dyarchy has been given to the division of power in the empire which Augustus established between himself and the Senate. It may be said here, once and for all, that as participants in the government of the empire the Roman people in the Assembly pass quickly out of the picture. Augustus, ever anxious to disguise inward facts by outward appearances, claimed that he himself represented the commons of Rome. In point of fact he recognised their political existence as subjects whose interests had to be considered, but ignored them as a power in the constitution. It was safe for two reasons to do so. They regarded his power as the best guarantee of peace; and, as the majority of them could not, and for half a century had not been able to, take part in the meetings of the Comitia and Concilium Plebis, it was to them a matter of indifference whether these assemblies continued or ceased to form working parts of the constitution. Having become ever more and more unrepresentative during the last two centuries of the Republic, they had come to have less and less hold on the affections of the mass of the citizens, mere gatherings of that least reputable element of the citizen body which was resident at Rome.

Augustus used their vote to give the appearance of popular confirmation to the powers conferred on him; and after that let them die the death of exhausted prestige. They had become anachronisms in a constitution which was to be no longer that of a city state but of a unified empire.

The tale of the final disappearance of the Assemblies of the people is a brief one. Under Cæsar's dictatorship they were suspended for months together, there being no legislation and no elections. Under the Second Triumvirate they elected consuls and prætors who had no power when elected. Under Augustus, after having been called upon to confirm the powers granted to him, there are rare traces of their having passed actual laws; but all the great questions of imperial policy, such as war and peace, are in the hands of the emperor. In the reign of Tiberius the election of magistrates was transferred to the Senate, and the Assembly rarely if ever called upon to legislate. After his reign certain laws were passed by Claudius through the Concilium Plebis at a time when that emperor was on bad terms with the Senate; but that is the only case in which any form of Assembly acts in a legislative capacity, except when, on the occasion of the accession of a new emperor, the comitia is called upon to confirm the powers voted to him by the Senate, an act which becomes a mere formality in which no one takes any particular interest.

SENATE

Thus the new constitution started practically as one of three elements operating in two departments, the emperor in the one, the magistrates and Senate in the other. Nominally the Senate and magistrates have exclusive control of Rome, Italy, and the interior provinces of the empire, while to the emperors are left the frontier provinces. How nominal was the partnership in power may be seen immediately from the fact that has already been mentioned, that the control of the frontier provinces gave the emperor the control of the army. Furthermore the authority of the emperor had been made superior to that of any regular magistrate, so that, just as under the Republic a consul could, if he would, interfere in the government of any province, so the emperor might interfere in the provinces allotted to the Senate. Augustus seems to have used this power sparingly, only perhaps in case of some notorious scandal in provincial government. Tiberius professed to dislike to use it. But his reserve is not maintained by most of the emperors; and under and after the rule of the Flavians the general superintendence of the government of all the provinces is openly assumed by the emperor. This was partly due to the growing subservience of a Senate which prejudiced its own rights by referring to Cæsar matters which were not really in his department.

Thus from the first the professed equality of partnership between the emperor on the one hand and the Senate and magistrates on the other was never a reality. Furthermore, by a process which was gradual, but was not slow, the imperial was ever encroaching on the senatorial department of the government. The very composition of the Senate rendesed some such process practically inevitable. At the outset of his rule Augustus, certainly from policy, and perhaps also from a respect due to his Italian origin, restored the dignity of the Senate by purging it of those lower social elements, home and provincial, which Julius had introduced into it, and by confining it as of old to members drawn from the noble families of Rome. Haunted as he was in the early years of his reign by the ghost of that Cæsar whom the Republican nobility had murdered, he was ever anxious to propitiate it as a class lest he himself should be sent to Hades by the same agency. Thus his original Senate was to a certain extent a body with an independent opinion, containing, as it did, many men who felt that they owed nothing to the emperor save a loss of power and, in a sense, of social position. These were not the senators of a hundred, or even fifty years later, who looked on the emperor as not merely the arbiter of their official destinies but as their social superior. To many, if not to most, of the senators in the years which followed Actium Augustus was merely the scion of a socially second-rate family which had had the good fortune to marry into the great family of the Cæsars, a young man who had attained to a position to which their own ancient lineage gave them as good if not a better claim. But the composition of the Senate began soon to be modified by dilution in the imperial interest; though up to the time of Nero's death it remained,—but to an ever-decreasing degree,—a rallying-point of the Republican opposition.

The extraordinary power to which the Senate had attained in the practical working of the Republican government had been due largely to the divided power of the magistracy. Face to face with one supreme magistrate, it sinks back into what is little more than its original constitutional position of a purely advisory body. And yet to all outward appearance it had gained power by the virtual disappearance of the Assembly; by its resolutions coming to have the force of law; by the transference to it of magisterial elections; and by becoming a court for the trial of important criminal cases. The appearance would have represented reality except for one fact: in the performance of these functions it acts on the dictation of the emperor. It appears to exercise some independent authority on the death of an emperor, because authority was represented as reverting to it and the consuls. But the military power, represented either by the Prætorian Guard or the great provincial armies, treated such a prerogative as non-existent, so that all that was left to the Senate was to ratify the choice of the soldiers by conferring on their candidate the customary constitutional powers.

The ever-growing subserviency of the Senate was due to its becoming ever more and more filled with imperial nominees. Under the Republic entrance into it had been granted by the choice (adlectio) of the censors, modified, or almost abolished, at least from the time of Sulla onwards, by recognition of the right of entrance in the case of all who attained to the quæstorship. The old censorial power was used, at first sparingly, but later much more frequently, by the emperors for filling up the ranks of the Senate with those whom they favoured. Only on three occasions did Augustus cause it to be conferred on himself; but Tiberius exercised it more frequently. Vespasian and Domitian held the power for life. After their time, as the use of it by the emperors had become so customary, the successors of Domitian acted in virtue of their power as principes without troubling about any formal vote of the old censorial power. The censorial authority included also the power of expelling members from the Senate; but it seems to have become customary at quite an early age in the Principate to confer this power on the emperors by an annual resolution. Nor was the emperor's control over the composition of the Senate much less complete in reference to those who qualified for membership by attaining the quæstorship. Under the Republic the nomination and recommendation of candidates had always been the rule; and it will be easily understood that a candidate nominated or recommended by the emperor was not likely to be opposed. Augustus rarely employed nomination, though he seems to have had no hesitation in recommending candidates for election. Other emperors used both practices freely.

By the time half the century after Christ had run the Senate had become a body composed mainly of direct or indirect nominees of Cæsar.

But it was by no means free in the performance of its functions, for the emperor when at Rome sat in it; and it is needless to say that any opinion he expressed on a question prevailed. Even when away from Rome he would communicate with it by rescripts, written opinions which carried the same weight as if he had given them by word of mouth. In the early days the Senate did not like this method of communication, though it was regarded as excusable when an emperor was absent on business in the provinces, but resented as somewhat arrogant when employed as Tiberius employed it when he was sulking out his last years in self-chosen retirement at Capreæ.

But the Senate as an institution was useful in various ways to the holders of imperial power. Its existence disguised the ever-growing autocracy. Again, though the majority of the emperors left it but little freedom and independence of action, there were some who, like Tiberius in the first, and Marcus Aurelius in the second century A.D., were anxious to shift some of the burden of government on to its shoulders; and others who, like Claudius and Nero, had spasmodic impulses that way. But to all the emperors its main value lay in its being a means ready to hand for doing unpopular things—for the passing of laws such as might be unpopular with certain classes, and for other work of an invidious kind.

Its judicial activities may be left for consideration in connection with the general administration of justice which was organised and developed under the early emperors; but here also the emperor sat as member of the court, and his opinion was practically decisive. Finally by the possession of the tribunicial power the emperor could veto any act of the Senate.

Extension of the Emperor's Power

Encroachment by the imperial upon the senatorial department began at an early date. The utter lack of organisation or of any attempt at organisation in the municipal administration of Rome, even in the last age of the Republic, is almost incredible.[1] It is not strange therefore if the administration under the revived machinery of the Republic left something to be desired. The ordered mind of Augustus could not put up with this state of things. In his reign the department of the corn supply (annona) of Rome and Italy was handed over to a præfect of Cæsar, and a proper control of fires at Rome was organised under another Cæsarian præfect (Præfectus Vigilum). At various periods in his reign a Præfect of the City, also an imperial officer, was put in general charge of municipal affairs at Rome, an office which became permanent under Tiberius. Thus before Augustus' death a large slice had been cut out of the Senate's administration of Rome and Italy.

The office of City Præfect, originally charged with the duty of maintaining order, developed greatly under the early emperors. A certain criminal jurisdiction of the first instance grew more or less naturally out of it, which by Domitian's day had become so enlarged as to include cases which would fifty years before have come before the regular criminal courts (Quæstiones); and by the end of the first century A.D. the jurisdiction extended beyond Rome over a considerable part of Italy. In the end this præfect became the great judicial authority in criminal cases in Rome and Italy.

This illustrates the way in which officials of the emperor absorb powers originally resident with the officials who had come down from the old Republic. The tendency is ever the same in all cases.

Augustus found it necessary to take over the management

---

[1] Mommsen gives a vivid description of it towards the end of the last volume of his history of Rome.

of the corn supply so early as 22 B.C. He worked it first through curators; but in the last years of his reign a præfect was set over it. The importance of the office was so great that by the reign of Domitian it was regarded as the great prize open to men of equestrian rank. An office of more sinister significance which is superimposed upon, not cut out of, the senatorial administration of Rome, is the præfecture of the Prætorian Guard established early in the reign of Tiberius. The presence of a standing body of troops at Rome was a novelty which was cordially disliked, so that the office of præfect was so unpopular that, though he was an officer who must necessarily have intimate relations and influence with the emperor, the one attempt to give it political importance, made in the case of Sejanus under Tiberius, aroused such resentment that other emperors of the first century did not attempt any further experiments in that direction; and the influence of a Burrus under Nero was due to personal relations, not to political position. But in the second century, beginning with the reign of Trajan, this præfecture develops in a great and unexpected way into a great judicial office owing to Trajan and his successors using the præfect as their deputy in the emperor's court of appeal, the highest court of the empire.

During the lifetime of Augustus also other departments of administration were placed under officials of Cæsar, such as the roads in the neighbourhood of Rome and the aqueducts of the city, both of which were put under imperial curators.

Thus by the end of the reign of the very first of the emperors the original department of the Senate in Italy has been shorn of much of its importance.

In the provincial department the process of absorption was not so rapid. Open interference in that was much more likely to cause resentment than the taking over of unremunerative jobs in Rome and Italy. The provincial system of government was subjected to such drastic reorganisation that, though the names of the old offices remain, though the officials perform the same functions, yet the circumstances under which they perform them are so different as to amount to a radical change of system. That such a change was badly needed a consideration of the working of the system under the Republic has already shown. But much of the provincial reorganisation was dependent on a fundamental innovation made by Augustus in the civil service of the empire.

THE SENATORIAL AND EQUESTRIAN CIVIL SERVICES

The new system was designed especially with a view to provincial administration. One great defect of the old system had been that it made no provision that those sent out to responsible posts in the provinces should have had any previous experience of such administration. Stated briefly, the new system substituted the professional for the amateur in this great branch of administration, or at any rate provided against the possibility of an amateur being placed in a position of any importance. The provincial civil service was to be manned by members of the senatorial and equestrian orders, a hard-and-fast line being drawn between the posts for which members of the two orders were respectively eligible. This distinction was rigidly maintained. Not even under the plea of necessity was a senatorial put into an equestrian post, or vice versa. This strict proviso was due to the policy of the emperors whereby they sought to placate the feelings of the old nobility by giving them an exclusive claim to the positions of great power and dignity in the government of the empire, and to build up out of the richest and most influential class a body of persons whose interests would bind them to the existing order of things.

There was thus a senatorial career and an equestrian career; and the careers did not overlap. The general principle was maintained in both cases that the first qualification a man should possess, and his first step in an official career, should be service in the army, a proviso which seems to have been made by Augustus in consequence of the widespread evasion of military service which had prevailed among the higher classes during the last century of the Republic, apart from the practical consideration that the governor of a Cæsarian province would have troops under his immediate command. In each career, but more especially in the senatorial, the steps through which a man passed were much the same in every case, that is to say every individual career tended to conform to type; but whereas the senatorial career was one in which certain parts of it were passed in the senatorial, and others in the Cæsarian department of administration, the equestrian was, under the early emperors, at any rate, passed entirely in the department of Cæsar. In dignity, and, during the first century, in power, the senatorial career was much superior to the other; but developments, easily traceable in the first century, were ever increasing the practical power attached to certain posts held by the equestrian order, until they became some of the most influential positions in the service of the empire; and, apart from that, the growth of the autocratic power of the emperors tended to promote the influence of that order, the equestrian, which was peculiarly attached to the Cæsarian department of government. By the second century A.D. three-quarters of the real work of the empire was done by that order, whereas the senatorial service was tending to become more ornamental than useful.

The senatorial career consisted of alternate strata of posts at home and abroad; that is to say, after holding magisterial office at Rome, a man was qualified for, and usually proceeded to, a post of correspondent dignity in the provinces. The quæstorship might indeed be served either in a senatorial province or at Rome, according to the allotment at the time of election. The prætorship qualified a man for the governorship of some province of second-class importance, generally one of the Cæsarian provinces. After holding the consulship he would be qualified for the governorship of a province of the first class, the custom being for him to receive a first-class Cæsarian province, and then, if he was a very distinguished man, the governorship of one of the great senatorial provinces, Africa, or Asia,[1]

The equestrian career tended to take a less sterotyped form than the senatorial; and only a few of those engaged in it ever arrived at the highest posts open to it. But more or less typical features were the preliminary military service; the command of a regiment of auxilia of the Roman army; the procuratorship of a province, a financial office which in the Cæsarian provinces meant the control of the provincial finances, and in a senatorial an unofficial position as agent for the private property of the emperors in that province. There were special prizes in the career to which a peculiarly lucky individual might rise, especially the præfecture,—really governorship,—of Egypt, or the procuratorships,—also governorships,—of Rætia or Noricum, as well as the præfectures of the corn supply or of the Prætorian Guard at Rome.

A very important practical result of the system was that every official of any importance in the empire came at some stage or stages of his official career under the personal command of the emperor, the senatorial whenever he held a post in the Cæsarian department, the equestrian from the day that he entered the public service to the day he left it. The " certus ordo magistratuum " which had been adhered to in the later times of the Republic was maintained with even greater rigidity during the empire, though the steps in an official career were more numerous. Thus the emperors could bring a senatorial

[1] The following is a more or less typical example of the chief steps of a senatorial career:
Agricola (second half of the first century) (see Tac. "Agric."): Tribunus Militum in Britain (Cæsarian province); quæstor in Asia (senatorial province); tribune of the Plebs at Rome; prætor at Rome; commander (legatus) of the XXth Legion in Britain; governor of Aquitania (second-class Cæsarian province); consul at Rome; governor of Britain (first-class Cæsarian province); declined governorship of Syria (Cæsarian province).

career to a full stop by refusing to appoint the person concerned to a post in the Cæsarian provinces, not to say anything of the control they exercised over elections to magistracies at Rome. And they did exercise this power in the case of officials who had shown themselves tyrannous or incompetent, as well as in the case of those of proved or suspected disloyalty. It was rare for a queer fish like Varus, the hero of the disaster in Germany in A.D. 9, to slip through the fine meshes of the imperial net.

The invention of this system of civil service is one of the most remarkable products of the amazing ability of its designer. It was an effective system for the government of the empire, how effective is shown by the smoothness with which the machine worked for two centuries until patchwork modifications and additions made by inferior brains corrupted it. Never in history was a great empire better governed, relatively to the time, than the Roman Empire during the first two centuries of the Principate.

Knowledge after the event makes it possible to say that its eventual ruin was brought about by an ever-growing tendency to over-centralisation due to the desire of certain emperors to do that which the second-rate man in high position is ever wont to try to do,—to control a great undertaking in detail as well as in general,—to a failure, arising sometimes from over-conscientiousness, sometimes from some meaner motive such as jealousy, to recognise that management on a large scale, if it is to be successful, must leave details to well-chosen subordinates. The letters exchanged between Pliny and Trajan show that the mania for personal interference may afflict even the best men.

Apart from the effect of this tendency towards over-centralisation, an apparently small change made in the reign of Claudius was destined in the end to bring about the economic ruin of the population of the empire. The procurators who were responsible for the collection of taxes in the Cæsarian and, at a later period, in all the provinces, were given jurisdiction in disputes relating to taxation. This ended in taxation revolving in a vicious and ever-enlarging circle from which the unfortunate taxpayer could not escape. In the western empire at any rate it ended in the cultivators being reduced to the position of slaves to a government to which they were ever in debt. In the northern provinces they welcomed the Goths as liberators when those northern barbarians broke into the empire.[1]

[1] Hieronymus ("Epist." 182, 17) says of the old Roman provincial population under barbarian rule : " Time dried their tears : save for a few old folk, all those born in servitude and captivity regretted not a

But these defects and evils were later excrescences on what was originally a most effective system.

FRONTIER SYSTEM

In preparation for these measures of provincial reform which both the state of the provinces and the policy of unifying the empire called for so urgently, Augustus carried out two great tasks, the establishment of a frontier, and a survey (census) of the resources of the provinces. The government of the Republic had not known such things as frontiers, partly because it had never taken the trouble to define lands which it had not originally desired to possess, partly because it preferred to have, where it could, a client state between its territory and outer barbarism, partly because it had no money to spend on wars for the conquest of poor but fierce peoples who were not divided from its territory by any definite limits, limits which they would not have accepted save under compulsion. Hither Spain faded away in the northwest into the lands of unsubdued tribes. No one could have said where Macedonia ended on the north. But the absolutely haphazard character of the policy of the Republic is best realised by the fact that the tribes of the southern valleys of the Alps were unsubdued, although they had again and again raided Transpadane Gaul.

The process of carrying the conquests of the Republic to their physical and logical conclusion was spread over a considerable number of years. On the south Egypt had been annexed in 30 B.C., and in 25 B.C. the kingdom of Numidia had been taken over; while to the west of the latter Mauretania acknowledged the suzerainty of Rome. On the east Rome was now in contact with Parthia, a kingdom whose power was exaggerated and needlessly dreaded in consequence of the defeat at Carrhæ in 53 B.C., emphasised by the invasion of 40, and by Antonius' futile expedition of 36. But this apprehension died away, to be revived in the reign of Nero. Pompeius' settlement of Asia had made a fairly satisfactory adjustment of affairs on this frontier, so that Augustus, who was on it in 20 B.C., did not make any notable change.

On the northern fringe of the empire the position was far less satisfactory. Italy, the empire's centre, was in immediate contact with barbarism, and therefore directly exposed to bar-

liberty which they had never known." From Salvian ("Gubern. Dei," v, 8) we learn the deep-rooted evil of the later Roman system of administration, which brought the peasant to despair, and drove him from hearth and home. This class actually welcomed the dominion of the Visigoths in Gaul and Spain, for among the Goths the great could not with impunity oppress the small.

barian attack. Also the position differed from that in the East owing to the fact that there were no powerful or properly organised states which could, in the form of client kingdoms, serve as buffers between civilisation and barbarism. Had they existed, Augustus would most certainly have made use of them, for he shared that indisposition, which was so marked a feature of the policy of the Republic, to bringing under the direct rule of Rome any lands which could as client kingdoms maintain peace within and on their own borders. So in this northern region there was much to do ere a satisfactory position could be attained : and it took a long time to do it. After a campaign in 15 B.C. Rætia and Noricum were added to the empire. Mœsia had been subdued in 29 B.C. ; but it did not really come into line as an organised province till A.D. 6. Nor was it till after the suppression of the great Pannonian rising of A.D. 6–9 that Pannonia became really a part of the empire.

In the eastern section of the northern boundary the Danube was designed to be the frontier line ; and a very unsatisfactory one it proved until Trajan by his conquest of Dacia remedied matters on the lower river. Later, in A.D. 180, after the Marcomannian War, Marcus Aurelius formed the design of carrying the frontier forward to the Carpathians ; but he did not live to carry it out.

In the western section Augustus seems to have been won over to the idea of carrying the frontier forward from the Rhine to the Elbe. Campaigns carried out beyond the Rhine by his stepsons Drusus and Tiberius between 13 B.C. and A.D. 6 reduced the region between the rivers to such apparent obedience that all the blessings and curses of provincial administration, a permanent garrison, bridge-building and road-making, administration and taxation, had been introduced into it before the Germans rose in A.D. 9 against the tyrannies of that Varus who made the mistake of supposing that the Germans could be treated in the same high-handed manner as the passive resisters of the Syrian East. The annihilation of him and his army shook the nerves of an old emperor who had been sorely tried by fifty years of fighting, reconstruction, and rule in a vast empire. Augustus renounced the idea of an Elbe frontier, and withdrew to the Rhine.

The completion of the conquest of the Spanish peninsula was effected by Agrippa early in the reign of Augustus after eight years of warfare.

FINANCE

The other great work of Augustus in the general organisation of the empire was the drawing up of a survey and valuation (census) of the resources of the provinces, on which might be based a system of taxation less haphazard than that which had prevailed under the Republic, a system in which the amount demanded by the government might bear some real relation to the resources of each region. It need hardly be said that this was an enormous benefit to the provincials. He also replaced those miscellaneous imposts of republican times, which had been so easy to manipulate for the purposes of extortion, by two great direct taxes, the land tax (tributum soli) and the tax on personal property (tributum capitis). These reforms put the finance of the empire on a business-like basis which was a benefit alike to the government and to the taxpayer.

The defects of provincial government under the Republic had lain partly in the system or want of system, partly in the incompetence or dishonesty, or both, of the officials, partly in the vicious nature of the proceedings of the publicani and private financiers (negotiatores).

The expenses of office at Rome had been largely responsible for the grasping spirit which governors and their subordinates had shown in their dealings with the provinces. But under the empire these expenses were greatly reduced by the fact that office was no longer gained by courting popularity with the mob by the exhibition of enormously expensive shows, but by nomination by the emperor and election by the Senate. Furthermore the burden of office had been greatly reduced in consequence of so much of the administration having been taken over by the emperor's department, so that it was no longer necessary to maintain so large a household for the transaction of clerical business. Furthermore it became increasingly common for consuls and prætors at Rome to hold office without having any department of administration assigned to them.

The financial position of governors of the provinces was also greatly ameliorated,—in the case at least of honest men,—by the assignment of an adequate salary to the office. To the dishonest, no doubt, this meant a loss, because most of the requisitions which a governor legally might, and illegally could, levy were done away with.

The organised careers of officials now guaranteed that those who got posts in the administration should be persons of experience in such offices ; and it seems even to have been the case that the government tried as far as possible, in selecting men for the higher posts in a province, to choose those who had had some experience of that province in their previous official career,—a very desirable policy in an empire composed of so many different races of mankind.

Save under the insane Gaius or the frivolous Nero merit and

demerit in the public service met their due reward. Whatever the other emperors might be or do in Rome itself, they were so profoundly convinced of the necessity of maintaining good and efficient government in the provinces, that an official who showed himself incapable or corrupt found his public career come to a sudden end, whereas a really capable governor of a province might be kept in office far beyond that term of one year which had been the custom under the Republic. In the Cæsarian provinces the extension of command became customary as early as the days of Tiberius. In the senatorial provinces, though at first it was found politic to abide by the old rule in order that as many of the nobility as possible might attain to these coveted offices, this consideration began early to be outweighed by the obvious undesirability of withdrawing a good and efficient governor from a province just at the time when he was beginning to become familiar with its needs. The general effect of the new system was to put all but the very worst on their best behaviour.[1]

The activities of the financiers in their capacity as publicani was restricted by confining them to the indirect taxation of the empire, especially the customs duties, and to the leasing and working of public property such as forests and mines. And in their capacity as bankers and moneylenders their operations, though not technically restricted, must have been in practice much reduced by the results of the imperial census, that is to say by a proper apportionment of the burdens of taxation on individual communities. Even under the empire communities such as the tribe of the Iceni in Britain might get into difficulties and have to resort to a loan from some Roman banker—nay, more, might be driven into rebellion by harsh measures taken for the exaction of payment; but such cases of hardship must have been infinitely more rare under the scientific finance of the empire than under the haphazard system of the Republic. But in the poorer, and especially in the more outlying provinces such as

[1] The governor of a senatorial province came to be known as proconsul, and that of a Cæsarian as a proprætor (Legatus Cæsaris pro Prætore). The financial officer in a senatorial province is a quæstor: in a Cæsarian province a procurator. Procurators are also stationed in senatorial provinces, but merely as agents for the emperor's property in those provinces, and, later, for the collection of the 5 per cent. death duties (vicesima hereditatum) which went to the imperial as distinct from the senatorial treasury. Otherwise such procurators have nothing to do with the management of the province in which they are stationed. Two of the Cæsarian provinces, Raetia and Noricum, were for special reasons not governed by proprætors but by procurators. Egypt was treated rather as a domain of the emperor than as a province. It was under an imperial præfect.

THE EMPIRE

Britain, the burden of taxation, though comparatively light, was severely felt, probably owing to the scarcity of currency and the consequent dearness of money, and above all to the difficulty of exchanging the surplus produce of regions far removed from the great markets of the then world for such money as was available. The immense cost of transport would deter buyers from making offers for any form of produce the bulk of which was large in proportion to its value. The government might accept a certain percentage of payment in kind where the stuff could be used for local purposes, such as corn for the provincial garrison ; but it had to demand a certain proportion of payment in transportable cash for the purposes of the central government at Rome ; and it is not difficult to realise that the inhabitants of regions such as middle and northern Britain must have had difficulty in obtaining the necessary cash.

GOVERNMENT BUREAUX IN ROME

The machinery of provincial administration was set in working early in the days of Augustus ; but that of the central administration at Rome took more than a century to elaborate. Time had to break down a very strong barrier of social prejudice ere it was possible to evolve a really satisfactory civil service in Rome itself. The contrast is due to the fact that whereas under the Republic the provincial administration had been associated with the highest ranks of society, the clerical business of government at Rome had been transacted by the slaves and freedmen of the household of the magistrate. Augustus when he came to power had to take over the direct control of more than half the business of the empire without having at hand any form whatsoever of permanent offices at Rome through which the routine business could be transacted. He had to do everything through his own household (domus), just as any magistrate of the Republic had had to do, which meant that slaves and freedmen had to be the instruments, for no free Roman who could possibly have been employed on such a task would have accepted a post associated from time immemorial with the servile class. So the household of Cæsar went on, enormous and ever-growing, as the only form of permanent civil service at the centre of government, till by the time of Claudius its importance had increased to such an extent that the heads of various of its departments, though mere freedmen, were some of the most important, and certainly, by fair means or foul, the richest officials in the empire. Men like the head of the exchequer (libertus a rationibus) or the imperial secretary (libertus ab epistolis) had more real power, influence, and patronage than any Roman of the highest rank outside the imperial family. The senatorial ranks of society loathed the prominence of the despised freedman. The equestrian ranks loathed him too ; but began to consider whether a social exclusiveness which forbade them to accept these lucrative posts was not too severe and too expensive a form of self-denial. Gradually, very gradually, they came in. The emperors wanted them, because they were keenly alive to the fact that there was little sense in working on unpopular lines a great institution which might be worked on lines far more popular. Members of the equestrian order accept the higher posts in that service in the brief stormy reign of Vitellius. This infiltration of the equites into the government offices at Rome goes on under the Flavian emperors and their successors until, under Hadrian and from his time onwards, the equites have absorbed all the higher posts in this central government office.

FINANCE

Its most important functions were concerned with the management of that part of the public income which was connected with the Cæsarian department of administration. This part of the revenue was entirely under the control of the emperor, and always remained so ; in fact until the days of Claudius it was regarded in the light of the private income of the emperor of the day, and spoken of as " Cæsar's property " (res Cæsaris). Under Claudius that aspect of it is weakened by its reorganisation under the title of " fiscus," which is henceforth the imperial as distinct from the senatorial treasury (ærarium), so that it has from that time more of the appearance of a part of the public income. But a very large proportion of it was contributed by the estates of the imperial family which were to be found in almost every province of the empire, and were of enormous value.

The fiscus had a heavy financial burden to bear, the weight of which was chiefly due to its providing for the support of the whole army of the empire, because that army was practically confined to those provinces of which the emperor was governor. It had also to meet the other expenses in the administration of those provinces, and the expenses of the emperor's department of the central administration at Rome. The burden became greater when the emperor took over the supervision and management of the corn supply and of certain aqueducts and roads.[1] Furthermore under the early emperors the senatorial treasury (ærarium) was continually getting into financial difficulties so that the emperors had to help it by grants from the fiscus. The general tendency as time went on was for the fiscus to become ever richer, and the ærarium ever poorer, partly because newly created

[1] See p. 462.

imposts were allotted to the fiscus, partly because the less efficient administration of the senatorial provinces had the general effect of creating a financial situation in them which seldom improved and often deteriorated, while the Cæsarian provinces advanced rapidly in wealth. Thus the emperors were called on ever more and more to assist the senatorial treasury, so much so that by the second century, though it continued to exist in name, its management had practically passed into Cæsar's hands, so that the whole financial management of the empire was in reality merged in the emperor's department.

At the outset of the empire the two divisions of the public income were drawn from the Cæsarian and senatorial provinces respectively. But, as has been said, the income from the Cæsarian provinces was from the first supplemented enormously from the great personal income which the emperors drew from their private estates throughout the empire, and from that Egypt which was treated as an imperial domain. Other sources of revenue were added gradually to the fiscus, such as the confiscated property of condemned persons, the five-per-cent. death duties, and so forth, while the personal property of the emperors received huge accessions owing to the value of the legacies left to them by private persons. But even so, the military expenses, ordinary and extraordinary, were so great that it was difficult for the emperors to make both ends meet; and any tendency to extravagance of living on the part of an emperor was very upsetting to the public balance sheet. To the credit of the majority of the emperors of the first two centuries be it said that they showed anxiety to keep their private expenditure within such limits as would not make it embarrassing to the state, and were ready to contribute freely from what was their own personal income towards the demands of the state expenditure.

The civil service which sprang up at Rome became rapidly very skilled in financial management; but in one department, that of indirect taxation, especially customs duties, it took long to create a skilled staff which could take this department over from the tax-farmers (publicani) who had companies of underlings trained by long experience in the business. But these publicani have no longer the dignity of membership of the equestrian order. Augustus had purged that order of the purely financial element which Caius Gracchus had introduced into it. It was not till the second century A.D. was well advanced that the tax-farmers ceased to operate in the collection of indirect taxation.

There is one more department of civil administration which calls for consideration before passing on to the great military organisation which Augustus founded.

Judicial Administration

Under the Republic the judicial administration on the civil side had grown up gradually in the courts of the prætor urbanus and the prætor peregrinus, resulting in a great body of case-made law the like of which the Mediterranean world had never known. Even under the Republic principles of civil law had been established which still, after the lapse of two millenniums, form the basis of the civil law in many states of modern Europe. Moreover these principles of law had been introduced into the provinces owing to the practice of governors to adopt *en bloc* the body of law in the prætorian courts at Rome as the code under which they would decide cases in the courts of the provinces. Thus Roman civil law became so familiar to the provincials as to render that policy of unification of the empire which is introduced under the Principate more easy to carry out than it would otherwise have been.

The merits of the administration of civil justice under the Republic had been so obvious that those clear-sighted men who founded the imperial system allowed it to go on without any express modification, though by a process of gradual evolution the emperor's Court of Appeal did acquire a great and commanding position in the administration of civil law.

In criminal justice the practice under the Republic until the time of Sulla had been primitive and clumsy. His establishment of a large series of perpetual courts (quæstiones) for the trial of various forms of crime had greatly improved matters, though it had not produced an ideal state of things. The defects in their working seem to have been due on the one hand to a congestion of business owing to the number of comparatively minor cases which came before them, and on the other to the uncertainty of justice being done when the accused happened to be a person of wealth and influence. These defects Augustus remedied by setting up a series of lower courts of similar form but with juries composed of men with a lower property qualification for the trial of minor offences, and by the transfer of cases involving men of rank to the Senate. The republican nobility in the Senate would prefer to be tried, if tried at all, by its own class; and the people generally did not care by whom the old republican nobility were tried; so nobody was likely to object to the new arrangement. On the whole, owing to the presence of the emperor in the Senate, the plan worked well. The members of that august body had had every sympathy with those accused of extortion in the provinces under a system which encouraged it; but were quite ready to condemn those who were foolish enough to try the same game under a system which made it dangerous.

Originally the court of appeal to Cæsar was a mere survival

of a provincial court under the Republic in which the governor sat to hear appeals from decisions either of his legati or of the native courts of the province. As all the governors of Cæsarian provinces were merely legati of the emperor, an appeal lay from their courts to his central court at Rome. But it was as it were in the very nature of things that a court so constituted would widen its jurisdiction with the growth of the power of the emperors ; and so it came to be customary for the emperors to call into their own court even such appeals from the senatorial provinces as they wished to hear, though strictly speaking these should have come before the Senate. But the powers of the emperor were not limited to such action as he might take in his own court of appeal, or as presiding over a case tried before the Senate, but also included the right of veto which was attached to his tribunicia potestas, a right which enabled him to quash the decision of any court.

On the whole the system generally worked well. It was at any rate a great improvement on that of the Republic, which was always clumsy, and frequently corrupt.

The civil reforms of Augustus are, relative to the time at which they were made and to the system which they superseded, the most remarkable work of political organisation which the world has ever seen. They brought infinite blessings to that great empire which was affected by them.

Army under the Principate

But all this civil organisation would have been a mere house of cards had it not been supported by an army system effective for the defence of the empire against external attack and internal disruption.

No one had better reason than Augustus to know that the government of the Republic had been brought to ruin by the nature of the army which it employed, that Marian army of the last half-century of its existence. For nearly four centuries, ever since the close of the Peloponnesian War, the Mediterranean world had been cursed with a floating population of soldiers of fortune which was at the disposal of anyone who was discontented with the existing order of things, a world of chaos into which even the great power of Rome had never been able to introduce a lasting order. The mercenary armies of the Greek states of the fourth century had been succeeded by the armies of Alexander, followed in their turn by those bands of land pirates which posed as the armies of Alexander's successors. And when they came to an end the Roman army was declining towards a ruin from which it was only saved by those reforms of Marius which converted it into a force still more dangerous to the peace of the world than those which had served the Macedonian and the Seleucid kings, or the Ptolemies of Egypt.

By converting the Marian army into a standing army Augustus changed its character. Soldiering became a permanent instead of a casual profession. No longer was the soldier to return in time of peace to a civil life which he did not know how to live, and in which he could not make a living. No longer would he be the willing tool of any would-be revolutionary who was ready to give him employment and a more or less legitimate excuse for plundering a peaceful world.

It is true that the great army which Augustus found on his hands after the victory of Actium was not of the pure-blooded Marian type. The number of soldiers required by the various commanders in the civil war had been so large that it could not be supplied by voluntary enlistment, so that for the first time since the reforms of Marius it had been necessary to resort to the levy on a great scale. But there was a large enough percentage of the Marian element in the armies of 31 B.C. to make their future disposal a very critical question. When the war came to an end Augustus had to deal with at least fifty legions, of which more than half had belonged to the army of Antonius. The peculiar psychology of the Marian soldier made it quite unnecessary to treat Antonius' soldiers as enemies; indeed it would have been dangerous to do so. Augustus knew well that they would be faithful to him now that the defeat of their old master was assured. But the maintenance of a great army such as this was neither requisite nor indeed possible, for the financial resources of the empire could not have borne the expense; so he reduced it in the first instance to twenty-five legions and disbanded the rest. But he made it clear from the first that this army was to be a permanent force existent in peace as well as in war. Apart from the general advisability of the change, the defence of the empire and the maintenance of his own personal power demanded an army whose existence should be continuous.

One of the main difficulties connected with the armies of the last age of the Republic had been the question of dealing with the discharged soldier, a question which had been peculiarly difficult owing in general to financial difficulties, and in particular to the dislike of the Roman government for any scheme which removed Roman citizens from residence in Italy. On this latter point Augustus had no particular prejudice. The necessity recognised by the Republic for keeping the citizens concentrated as far as possible in Italy no longer existed now that a great standing army was to be maintained; and, though Augustus was not prepared to proceed more than slowly with the work of unifying the empire, yet it was a definite policy of his which might be promoted by the settlement of ex-soldier citizens in communities scattered through the provinces such as might educate the provincials gradually in that civilisation which they must attain before they could be fitted to receive full citizen rights. Moreover the provision of land for veterans was much more easy in the provinces than in that Italy where the public lands once available had been appropriated under the law of Tiberius Gracchus.

The next question was the distribution and disposition of the army. This was determined by two decisive considerations, the necessity for defending the frontier provinces, and the undesirability of having large bodies of troops in Rome or Italy where mutiny or discontent would mean immediate danger to the emperor and the central government, and where their presence would advertise that fact which Augustus was anxious to disguise, that his rule was a monarchy, and, more than that, a military monarchy. So from the very beginning of the empire was laid down the enduring policy of keeping the legions far from Rome. Thus they became strange to the city of Rome, and the city of Rome to them—how strange is shown by the account which Tacitus gives of the relations between the citizens and the legionaries in 69 A.D. when, for the first time for exactly a century, the latter appeared in the eternal city. Mutual amazement, contempt, and antipathy were the feelings excited on both sides.

But the military policy of the Principate had to be further elaborated on the side of precaution. The ultimate reliance on the military power could not long remain a secret from the soldiery. The army would soon learn that it could overthrow that which it supported; and thus it was necessary so to distribute it throughout the empire as to isolate the larger masses of troops from one another, in such a way that a certain rivalry rather than sympathy might spring up between the armies of different parts of the empire, so that, in case one army became disaffected, the others might be used against it. The armies of Spain, Africa, Egypt, and Syria were isolated by nature; but on the great northern frontier of the Rhine and the Danube, where the bulk of the troops had to be stationed, the legions of the Rhine had to be separated from those on the Danube by artificial means. This was provided for by excluding legionary troops from the provinces of Rætia and Noricum on the upper Danube, a policy so strictly observed that, when in the reign of Vespasian it became advisable to place legionary troops at Carnuntum and Vindobona, those towns and their regions were transferred from Noricum to Pannonia. It was not till the reign of Marcus Aurelius in A.D.

180 that legionary troops were stationed for the first time in the Norican province, at Regina on the upper Danube.

Precautions of a similar nature were taken with regard to the commands in different parts of the empire. The story of the last age of the Republic had shown the danger of allowing the control of any large body of troops to fall into one hand. This led to the establishment of two policies, one of a general, the other of a particular nature. The proprætor of a Cæsarian province was in immediate command of the troops stationed in his province, though the emperor was the ultimate commander to whom the sacramentum was sworn. Though the number of troops in a province would depend on the military requirements of the region, yet it was always provided that the number under the control of any one governor should be limited. Thus if, owing to the growing extent or importance of a province, it became necessary to increase the garrison permanently, it was customary to divide the province into two. Hence, early in the Principate, Pannonia is divided from Illyricum, and later Mœsia Superior from Mœsia Inferior, while later still Pannonia itself is divided into an upper and a lower province. Such was the policy in normal times. But in abnormal times, when some serious war called for a large concentration of troops, the command of such an army was, under the early emperors, committed to some member of the imperial house, such as Tiberius and Drusus under Augustus, and Germanicus under Tiberius, while from the time of the Flavian emperors onwards it became customary for the emperor to take over such a command in person, as Domitian did in the war against the Dacians, and Trajan in the war against the same people.

It is impossible for human ingenuity to devise a policy which shall fit all the varying circumstances of the life of a great state; but on the whole the policy of isolating the various imperial armies worked effectively and well. It broke down when, as in A.D. 69, the question of the succession to the supreme power became, owing to the dying-out of the Julio-Claudian house, an open one. Then the tendency was for each of the great armies to put forward its own candidate,—generally its own commander, —with the result that the aspirants to power fought out a civil war on the same lines and for the same end as that which the members of the Second Triumvirate had fought out with one another. But though in the later history of the western empire armies such as that of Britain made and unmade emperors, the part which the army played in the succession during the early Principate was, save in A.D. 69, that of assenting to the succession of him who stood highest in the regard of the army generally. On the negative side, at any rate, it soon became clear that

THE EMPIRE

supreme power could not be held against the will of the army. The legions of the Republic had always been in name, and for the most part in fact, an army of citizens. In the middle period of its existence the contingents from the socii of Italy had played a part of ever-increasing importance. With the change to the Marian army the qualification of citizenship is still maintained for the legions; and, shortly afterwards, the grant of full citizenship to the socii brings completely to an end their existence as a separate branch of the service. But there can be no doubt that from the time of Marius onward the qualification of citizenship for the legions was maintained rather in the letter than in the spirit, to this extent at any rate, that commanders of armies conferred the citizenship on provincials with a view to qualifying them for legionary service. At the same time, this power seems to have been used with discretion, in that it was only exercised in the case of persons who were members of civilised communities in the provinces, for it was a power which a commander could only exercise by special resolution of the people,—a power which would have been certainly cancelled had it been used too indiscriminately for the enlistment of the less civilised populations of the empire. Marius received the right for the Cimbrian War, and used it largely; but chiefly, it would seem, for the enlistment of the civilised population of Cisalpine Gaul. During the first civil war, partly owing to the confusion of the time, partly to the enormous demand for troops, all restrictions were ignored, and "legiones vernaculæ," composed entirely of non-citizens, were raised by both sides, though Cæsar seems to have been careful to draw on the civilised populations of such regions as Transpadane Gaul. But in the war of Philippi and in the wars of the Second Triumvirate all restrictions were cast to the winds, and commanders enlisted in their legions any whom they could get, whether citizen or not, whether civilised or barbarian.

Augustus restored the strict qualification of citizenship for the legions; but it is doubtful whether it was found possible to retain its strictness for any length of time. It is almost certain that under the early emperors the practice of giving a man the citizenship in order to qualify him for legionary service came once more into use. Under the Flavian emperors that was certainly done, owing to a change which came over the recruiting areas at that time.

All citizens were still liable to be called out by levy for service in the legions; but, as a fact, save under extraordinary circumstances, voluntary enlistment supplied the numbers required, so that when authors mention that a levy for the legions was held in a certain year in a certain province or certain provinces, it means little more than that recruits were enlisted from those regions at that particular time. The burden of supplying the numbers requisite for the legions lay lightly on the empire. In the year A.D. 9, for instance, the legionaries in the west part of the empire numbered about 110,000 men. On the basis of an average of twenty-five years' service, and allowing for deaths, the number of recruits required annually would be about 6,000, a number which Italy alone could easily have supplied. But from the beginning of Augustus' reign recruiting for the western legions was by no means confined to Italy, but was carried out largely among the civilised populations in such provinces as Bætica and Gallia Narbonensis. The same principle was observed in the recruiting of the eastern legionary army, Egypt and the civilised provinces of Asia Minor being the recruiting regions.

All this suggests the tendency which is ever growing under the empire, to substitute the qualification of civilisation for that of citizenship in legionary recruiting. The empire comes to be divided up into the civilised provinces in which recruiting for the legions is carried on, and the less civilised provinces in which the recruiting for the non-citizen branch of the army (the auxilia) takes place. Within the official area of Narbonensis lived the tribe of the Vocontii, a people more backward than the rest of the population of the province. And so their territory is a recruiting ground for the auxilia, whilst recruiting for the legions takes place throughout the rest of the province.

The extension of the legionary recruiting even by Augustus to regions outside Italy is probably part of that general policy by which the emperors looked for more moral support from the provinces than from Italy itself.

Up to the time of Nero the Italians are largely represented in the legions, though the better paid service in the Prætorian Guard was more attractive. In the year of the civil war, 69, Tacitus contrasts the Italianism of the Guard with the provincialism of the Rhine legions.[1] But still, in Nero's time the number of Italians in the legions is considerable.[2] But under Vespasian there comes a change, for which there were both general and particular reasons. The Italians in the legions were undoubtedly unpopular with the provincial element owing to the airs they gave themselves as the ruling race of the empire. They had also shown after the death of Nero a disposition to claim that the imperial throne was in their gift. When Vespasian and his legions had shown them the futility of this attitude, they revenged themselves by treating the family of the Flavii with as much social contempt as they dare show. To the Roman of Italy it

[1] Tac. Hist. ii, 21.
[2] Cf. the monuments of soldiers of the Eleventh Legion at Vindonissa *temp.* Nero.

was indeed a startling novelty to find himself for the first time in a history eight centuries old governed by a man who had no connection whatever with the old Roman nobility, the son of a father who, born of a humble family of rural Italy, had spent his life as a money-lender in Gaul.

All this tended to emphasise that reliance on provincial support which had been a feature of the policy of even the members of the Julio-Claudian house. They had sought it as a counterpoise to the jealousy of the old ruling families; and now the Flavii had to seek it as a counterpoise to the arrogance of the old ruling race. There is no trace of any measure abolishing recruiting in Italy. The practice is simply dropped; and henceforth the legions are composed of dwellers in the provinces.[1]

In the general recruiting system of the legions a dividing-line between East and West is generally, though not rigidly, observed from the very first. It originated, doubtless, in the recognition that the fighting material to be obtained from the Greek East was inferior in quality to that of the Latin West. It foreshadows the creation of an eastern and a western army, and of an eastern and a western empire. Under the early emperors the dividing-line is not fully developed; but even in their day it runs, generally speaking, as it did when developed, along the frontier between what came to be the provinces of Upper and Lower Mœsia: between Illyria and Dalmatia on the one hand, and Macedonia on the other; and then down the lower Adriatic to the frontier between Africa and Cyrenaica.[2]

A later very important development in recruiting under Hadrian was due to the system of standing camps which Augustus had established. These were the necessary outcome of a standing army, and of the policy of stationing the legions in the frontier provinces. The existence of such camps would be certain to tend to stabilise the distribution of the army; and that tendency becomes more and more apparent as time goes on. Even under the early emperors, except during some important war, the quarters of a legion are rarely shifted, such movements involving great expense. Legio VI Victrix is in Spain from the time of Augustus till Nero's death; and III Cyrenaica in Egypt from the reign of Augustus till that of Hadrian; and these are only two examples of others that might be cited. Such large changes as take place are due to the shifting of danger points on the imperial frontier. Under the early emperors the line of the Rhine is the dangerous section on the north; and so up to the time of Vespasian eight

[1] The Prætorian Guard is still largely Italian.
[2] Under the early emperors the Dalmatian, and probably the Mœsian legions, contained elements recruited from Asia Minor. In A.D. 65 Asia was still drawn upon for recruits for the Illyrian legions. Tac. Ann. xvi, 13.

legions are quartered there. But under the Flavian emperors the Danubian section becomes the more dangerous area; and by the time of Trajan the Rhine garrison has been reduced to four legions, while there are ten in the Danubian provinces.

Hadrian's main endeavour was to stereotype the frontier defence, for which purpose he established fortified lines on various parts of the imperial frontier where natural features did not provide some form of protection. The great wall from the Solway to the Tyne, part certainly of the great palisade which cut off the re-entering angle between the upper Rhine and the upper Danube, and perhaps some of the fortified lines the remains of which are to be seen in the old province of Dacia and in the modern Dobrudscha, were his work. From his time onward legions tend to remain, like Legio XX Valeria Victrix in Britain, not merely for years, but for centuries in the same station. This led to legions being recruited, not as aforetime by levies made in various provinces, but rather within the province in which they were stationed. The stationary camps grew into towns; the soldiers were allowed to marry; and the tendency of their children to enter the service began to make soldiering a hereditary profession till a time arrived later in the empire when the town-bred soldier was no longer capable of facing the wild hordes which assailed it, and emperors were compelled to recruit their legions from the ranks of barbarism.

THE AUXILIA

The legions were but about half of the standing army which Augustus established. He was determined that the non-citizen as well as the citizen should contribute to the defence of the empire; and so he put on a permanent basis what had been a temporary service in the days of the Republic, that of those provincials whom a governor might call out for the defence of the province. But these " auxilia " of the army of the empire bear far more resemblance to the contingents of the socii of Italy of the days before the Social War, as is shown by the borrowing of the terms " ala " and " cohors " from the old Italian for this new provincial service.[1]

This great body of non-citizen but regular troops was, as far as can be reckoned, about equal in number to the legions; and, generally speaking, their distribution in particular areas depended on the distribution of the legions. In levying them

[1] " Cohors " was used of a regiment of infantry both in the old Italian and the new provincial service. " Ala " was used in this new service of a regiment of cavalry. In the old Italian service it had merely implied a body of allied troops stationed on one of the wings, the customary place for the regiments of socii in line of battle.

two general principles were adhered to : they were raised as a rule in those provinces which were not called upon to furnish legionary recruits ; and they were levied especially from the best fighting races of the empire.

The system became eventually a grievous burden against which the provincials were wont to raise bitter complaints ; but it is probable that the hardships which it entailed were chiefly due to a modification in the original policy of the government towards these provincial regiments. Up to the time of Hadrian the principle was maintained of confining the personnel of each regiment to one race, so that, for instance, a Cohors Britannorum, even if not serving in Britain, would have its numbers maintained by drafts sent from that province. From Hadrian's time onwards, however, the principle of local recruiting which became applied to the legions came to be applied to the auxilia also, so that by the end of the second century a Cohors Hispanorum in Britain was probably composed mainly of Britons ; and so on in other provinces. But before Hadrian's time the burden and unpopularity of this service had been increased by a change which the Roman government had found it necessary to make.

The general but by no means universal policy of Rome under the earliest emperors was to employ the regiments of auxilia in the provinces in which they were raised. Thus the employment of Pannonian auxilia in Pannonia had given to large numbers of the natives a military training which made them very formidable in the great rising of A.D. 6–9. In the same way Gallic alæ and cohortes had been employed on the Rhine, as well as the Batavian auxilia which proved so disloyal at the time of the rising of Civilis in 69 and 70. It is fairly clear that after the Pannonian rising Augustus sent all Pannonian auxilia to garrison other provinces, and imported into Pannonia auxilia drawn chiefly from Spain. A similar measure was taken on the Rhine after the events of 69 and 70 ; and, in fact, after that time the employment of local levies in the provinces in which they were raised is rare. For the provincials the change implied this hardship,—that numbers of them were forced to serve during the best years of their lives in distant lands among strangers. Most of those called on were lost for ever to their relations and friends, condemned to what was practically, and often in reality, a lifelong exile ; for many of them, when their period of service was over, did not care to return to a land they had forgotten and which had forgotten them, but settled down in the province in which they had taken their discharge. This grievance was remedied from the time of Hadrian onwards by the growth of local recruiting. By that time the romanisation of the provinces had gone far enough to kill the more dangerous elements of nationalism among the subject races.[1]

Such are the chief institutions of the empire as they were formed or reformed by Augustus; and such are the *main* lines on which they were modified up to the time of the death of Hadrian.

CÆSAR-WORSHIP

No policy which Augustus adopted, or rather permitted, shows more clearly his desire to bring about a unification of the empire into one state than the encouragement of that cult known as Cæsar-worship as a bond of religious union between all its races. In the mind of the ancient world the association between religious unity and political unity was so intimate that the concept of political unity could never have been complete unless a religious unity was associated with it. One state, one worship, was to that world an idea as old as time. There must be an imperial religion if there were to be an empire state; a religion superimposed on, but in no way superseding, the local cults of the races of the empire. Nor was there any reason to anticipate that such a policy would meet with opposition from them. Religion in the Mediterranean world had always taken, as elsewhere, the form of worship of powers seen or unseen; and only among the Jews had these powers been concentrated in the personality of one spiritual being. Among the other races each power was represented by a god; and, if it occurred to some one of them to form the conception of some new power, that meant merely the addition of one more deity to the local pantheon. So the races of the empire, if convinced that there was really a new power to be propitiated, would not require much persuasion to accept it as an object of worship. And they needed no convincing of the reality of the power of Rome and Augustus!

Nor had the idea of the worship of power been limited in the ancient mind to the inanimate world. Ancestor-worship, like nature-worship, is found among the Mediterranean peoples at the very dawn of history. It implied, no doubt, a belief in the occult influence of the dead; but it implied more than that, a reverence for the power the dead had wielded, and the things they had done, during their lifetime. From that it was a short step first to hero-worship, a common cult in the Greece of the fifth and earlier centuries; and secondly, to the worship of a living individual, such as Lysander, who had attained to great place and power in the world. If such a cult could arise among the Greeks, it is not surprising that it became common among those

[1] The history and organisation of the Auxilia is well told in " The Auxilia of the Roman Imperial Army," by G. L. Cheeseman.

Asiatic peoples who had for centuries bowed passively under the power of their rulers. The kings who succeeded Alexander,[1] and Roman generals such as Sulla and Pompeius, had been deified by the peoples of the East. In that part of the empire the cult of the emperors would have sprung up naturally without any official encouragement. Only the Jews showed any opposition to it,[2] and the Christians too, when later that sect sprang into being.

In the western provinces there was no obstacle to its acceptance. The emperor took his place side by side with the numerous deities, local and national, which the western races worshipped. To them it was little more than a test of loyalty leading to social advantages small and great; but not, in so far as is known, associated with that marked superstition which was attached to it in the East.

To Augustus any extravagance of superstition attached to the cult was distasteful; and, though he had to accept the grosser form which it took in the East, because there was no human means of checking this enthusiasm and its manifestations in that part of the world, he did all that he could to keep it in other parts of the empire within the bounds of a spiritual and impersonal acknowledgment of the imperial power. He preferred to pose as the personification of a divine principle rather than as the deity itself. Any other attitude, in Rome and Italy at any rate, would have been repugnant to him. But Cæsar-worship, even if in Augustus' own lifetime it took in the provinces exaggerated forms which he disliked, served its purpose as a political bond of unity in the empire. Its altars at Tarraco, Lugdunum, Colonia (Cologne), and elsewhere were monuments of loyalty to the empire at which the provincial magnates testified that loyalty by worship and sacrifice to the master of all. In that Cæsar-worship attained the end for which it was designed. For the rest, the Senate granted to Augustus, Tiberius, and Claudius, after their death, that honour of deification which they had never sought during their lives, but denied this posthumous gift to those two members of the Julio-Claudian house, Caligula and Nero, whose imbecility had tempted them to claim the honour during their lifetime. Under the Flavian emperors, deification of the head of the empire, whether living or dead, became a matter of customary etiquette, to the educated meaningless save when it was omitted, to the uneducated a part of the routine of religion and of loyalty.

But, though a clearer view of the imperial system may be obtained by thus following the developments of these institutions during the first century and a half of the Principate, and

[1] See p. 326 f. [2] See p. 524.

though such a treatment of the story of the period is justified by the fact that its main features as determined by its great founder were so durable that they were but little affected by the neglect of such emperors as Caligula and Nero, and were maintained in reality, though not always in detail, by the more diligent of his successors, yet the personalities of these early emperors did at times and in some respects permanently affect the evolution of the Augustan system. That growing tendency towards centralisation to which reference has been already made is not an inevitable, though a probable, development in such a monarchy; but it was undoubtedly promoted by the deliberate policy of the Flavian emperors. It is therefore necessary to make a brief survey of the personalities of the emperors themselves, of such members of their families as played a part in making history, and of that high society at Rome whose doings and undoings loomed so large on the local history of the centre of the empire.

To the greatness of Augustus the account of the great political fabric he devised is testimony more convincing than any words of eulogy.

Tiberius

His successor Tiberius was a soured and disappointed man ere ever he reached the throne. He was the residual product of an imperial favour which had been given to others at a time when it was denied to him. He was fifty years of age when in A.D. 14 he succeeded to the imperial power. He had commanded armies and governed great provinces; and in all that he had done he had shown himself a man of remarkable ability, so that he possessed unrivalled qualifications for the carrying-on of the work of Augustus. Though not of the family of the Cæsars, being but a step-son of Augustus by his mother's second marriage, he belonged to the Claudii, a family equal to the Cæsars in social standing, and perhaps superior to them in the fame of its members in the past history of Rome. It was a family which had often offended others by its reserve and apparent pride; and this, its last great representative, inherited, so his contemporaries thought, the family failing. To anyone who tries to realise the situation, the accession of this able, soured, reserved man to the mastership of the world may seem one of the greatest tragedies recorded in the history of any individual life. He had seen great things: he had done great things; but the great things he had seen and the great things he had done had been wiped off the slate of remembrance by that fate which had robbed him of his brother Drusus and by that policy which had separated him from his well-loved first wife, Agrippina, whom he had been compelled by

Augustus to put away in order for dynastic reasons to marry the emperor's daughter Julia.

Troubles arose soon after his accession. The armies of the Rhine and Danube, dissatisfied with the conditions of service, broke into mutiny in A.D. 14; but were pacified by concession. But the conspiracy of Libo Drusus in A.D. 16 showed him where the real danger lay, that danger which had made even Augustus so anxious to give monarchy the guise of republicanism. In his very desire to avert the danger Augustus had in a way made it greater for his successors by representing the Principate as a potentially temporary office which might be discontinued, or, if continued, might be held by anyone on whom the state chose to bestow it. Augustus lived long enough to show the Republican nobility that the Principate might develop into an autocracy, a development which they might unwillingly tolerate in his person, but were quite determined to resist in the person of any other. The conspiracy of Libo embittered a mind already disillusioned by past experience. From this time to the end of his reign the noble families of Rome, whether guilty of conspiracy or not, had good cause to regret that the suspicion of a disappointed man had been roused against them. There began a series of attacks and executions which was destined within about half a century to bring about the practical extermination of their class. They found Tiberius a grim enemy; and they gave vent to their exasperation in memoirs which formed the evidence on which Tacitus blackened the memory of a man whom he never understood. Yet the tale of the reign is very similar to those of the reigns of the other early emperors,—society in Rome suffering many grievous things by reason of its ill-advised ambitions at the hands of autocrats who are keen and capable in promoting the interests of all who will submit to their rule. Under Tiberius the provinces, the army, and the finances were managed with a justice and efficiency in great contrast to the mismanagement of Republican times. Even Tacitus has to admit the excellence of his government during the early years of his reign, especially as shown in his expressed, and probably real, desire to share its burdens with the Senate. But conspiracy, real and suspected, at Rome made the city distasteful to him; and so he spent the last years of his life in a retirement at Capreæ so impenetrable that his enemies could safely attribute to it all the invented horrors of the unknown. He died in 37.

Gaius or Caligula

Tiberius, disheartened by the death of his son Drusus in 23, had not made those definite arrangements which Augustus had made to determine his successor. All that he had done was to leave the half of his fortune to Gaius (Caligula), son of Germanicus, and grandson of his brother Drusus. While the two first holders of the Principate had owed their position largely to the fact that they had been the successful commanders of great armies in great wars, Gaius' only claim to recognition by the army was that he was son of that Germanicus who had commanded the Rhine army under Tiberius. The popularity of his father with the soldiers was sufficient, in the absence of any competitor of great military reputation, to assure the assent of the army to the nominee of the Prætorian Guard.

There is no reason to dwell at length on the reign of one of the greatest fools who ever attained to a great position. He began by seeking a cheap popularity founded on an expressed determination to reverse the methods of his able but unpopular predecessor. But it was not long ere Rome came to look back with regret to the reign of the gloomy Tiberius. This spoilt child of his ambitious mother, Agrippina, the granddaughter of Augustus, determined his policy by childish whims; plunged into reckless expenditure which he sought to defray by wholesale executions of the wealthy; insulted the Senate he professed to respect; carried out military picnics with the professed intention of invading Britain and Germany; introduced disorder into any province in which he had the fancy to interfere; and in fact did all that he could to make the Principate a laughing-stock, and to endanger the empire. That no great disorder resulted from his proceedings was due partly to the brevity of his reign, partly to the solidarity of the system which Augustus had established. He was assassinated at Rome in January of the year 41.

CLAUDIUS

In the absence of any obvious successor to Gaius, the Senate began to discuss that which it had always desired, the restoration of the Republic. Its members, apart from their natural ambitions, had suffered severely under the severities of Tiberius and the murderous whims of Gaius. But the real key to the situation was that no one else had suffered very much. The army had doubts as to its own fate under senatorial rule, and the Prætorian Guard no doubts whatever. So the latter seized on that ungainly antiquarian Claudius, uncle of the late emperor, a man already fifty years of age, who had hitherto spent a life of deliberate retirement in the pursuit of low company and high learning, and carried him off to their own camp, an unwilling prisoner to be made into an unwilling emperor. In view of the attitude of the Prætorians the senatorial discussions on the restoration of the Republic had been postponed *sine die*.

Judged by actual performance during his reign, Claudius does not seem to have been quite such a fool as contemporary authors, especially the venomous Seneca, made him out to have been.

It is true that he did various silly things in a silly way; but, when all is said and done, his policy left its mark, mostly for good, on the later history of the empire. Whether he was a deliberate imitator of Julius Cæsar cannot be said; but it is certain that some of the main items of his policy bear a much closer resemblance to that of Julius than to the more cautious policy of Augustus. Augustus had inherited from the Republic a preference for the client state over the province; whereas Claudius thought the time had come for the direct rule of Rome throughout her great sphere of influence, and so converted Mauretania, south Britain and Judæa, and reconverted Thrace, into provinces. Augustus had refused to adopt the liberal policy of Julius with regard to the extension of the citizenship, preferring to keep the Italians, for the time being, at any rate, as the privileged race of the empire. Claudius was lavish of the grant of the franchise, and even admitted the chiefs of the Gallic Ædui to the Senate; moreover, he sought to romanise and civilise the backward provinces on the Danube.

BRITAIN

Various reasons have been suggested for his undertaking the conquest of Britain: the reputed wealth of the island; the wish to strike at the roots of Druidism. It may be taken as certain that a century's intercourse with the island had taught the Romans that it was not the El Dorado which it had been supposed to be in the days of Cæsar. As for Druidism, its influence in Gaul does not appear to have been very great; and, such as it was, it could have been effectively crushed there without any great expedition to Britain. It is probable that Claudius' enterprise was undertaken for dynastic reasons, to give him that military reputation which was so important to the holder of a monarchy whose power rested on the support of the army. It was in Britain that such a reputation could at the time be won most cheaply and at the least risk.

He carried out many important public works in Italy in relation to aqueducts, roads, and the port of Ostia, all of which were of great benefit to the country. Under him the " domus Cæsaris," which had played the part of a permanent civil service at Rome, was organised into what it became thereafter, the great home civil service of the empire; and in connection with this the revenue of the Cæsarian department of government was put on a more businesslike footing under the name of " fiscus."

These are not the works of an incapable. It is in his works, not in contemporary literature, that the real Claudius lives.

NERO

In 54 he died. The later years of his life had been disturbed by the rivalry and intrigues of his wife Messalina and the younger Agrippina, daughter of Germanicus and sister of the late Caligula, each of whom wanted to secure for her own son the succession to the empire at Claudius' death. In view of the exclusion of women from public life under the Republic, it is very remarkable how great an influence the women of the imperial house exercised under the early empire. Augustus and Tiberius had been strong enough to hold their own against such influence, but the childish Gaius, the weak Claudius, and the trifling Nero were, except during periods of imperial tantrums, pliant to the wills of those strong and fierce women, viragoes of the type of those who had now and again played havoc in the courts of Alexander's successors. Claudius, who seems to have made up his mind that the best way to get a quiet life was to yield to the more violent of the two, sacrificed his wife Messalina for the ruthless Agrippina, and renounced the succession of his own son Britannicus in favour of Agrippina's son Nero. Clothed with the proconsular power before Claudius' death, the latter was indicated as the successor to the throne; and by the time Claudius died Agrippina had got the Prætorian Guard on her side by influence of the præfect, Burrus.

Nero would have been more at home on the stage of a music-hall than on the throne of the Cæsars. Still, under the joint tutelage of Burrus and the philosopher Seneca, the first five years of his rule went well enough. But from 59 onwards his reign was tragedy both for himself and for the Roman world; and the impression of disaster conveyed to contemporaries was heightened by accidental occurrences, such as an earthquake at Pompeii and the great fire at Rome. The youth who had been so popular in his early years died loathed by all save the two least respectable elements in the population of the empire, the feckless lower classes at Rome, and the decadent population of Greece. Even in that age his family life was a scandal. In 59 he removed his too competent mother by murder. Burrus died in 62; and even Seneca, whose life and disposition were not quite so virtuous as his philosophy, had to throw up the part of bear leader to so vicious a cub. In 62 his wife Octavia died the death of the inconvenient, and he married Poppæa, a lady of a more than usually criminal disposition among women with whom criminality was fashionable. She died in 65, and was deified by request. In 65, too, a conspiracy of the old Republican nobility, led by Piso, inflamed his anger against that somewhat depleted body to the further depletion of its ranks.

Tired of his reckless extravagance and of the cruel exactions by which he sought to supply the means for it, the armies of the western provinces of the empire rose against him. He hurried back to Rome from a triumphal progress through Greece to find that Galba was marching on the city, and that the game was up. To escape a worse fate, he committed suicide on June 9 of the year 68.

It is a singular tribute to the perfection of the imperial system of this age that while Rome was full of horrors, and Italy of oppression from the exactions of Nero, the life and administration of the provinces ran smoothly. Even when the armies of the West rose against him, it was because they felt that his egregious folly was imperilling an institution, the monarchy, which gave them benefits which they could not have looked for from any other form of government, an institution which the civilian population of the provinces regarded as the sole effective barrier against anarchy.

The wild confusion of the year which followed Nero's death has been told in what is perhaps the most brilliant prose work in any literature of any language, the Histories of Tacitus.

The Four Emperors

With Nero the Julio-Claudian house came practically to an end, for Britannicus had died thirteen years before. But the revolt of the armies had revived that situation which had been fatal to the Republic and had always been a potential danger under the empire, where a provincial governor found himself in command of a military force with which he could hope to overthrow the constituted government. With Nero's death the succession to the imperial throne became an open question, which, in the absence of any claimant with obvious claims, could only be decided by force of arms. While the Julio-Claudian house lasted the policy of separating the armies of the empire both geographically and administratively had tended towards peace and security. But the division of interest, which had worked well so long as the loyalties of the armies met in the person of an emperor who was heir to Augustus, made each army, now that such a centre of loyalty no longer existed, anxious to promote in its own interest that of its commander.

The first movement against Nero had been promoted by C. Julius Vindex, a Gaulish chief of high rank, who was in the year 68 serving as governor of Gallia Lugdunensis. But he had no legions behind him, and his hastily raised Gallic levies were no match for the legions of the Rhine, which, though at the time quite ready to be disloyal to Nero, had no mind to ignore what looked like an attempt at the restoration of the national independence of Gaul. By May, 68, the rising was over, and Vindex dead.

But Vindex had stirred to action a much more formidable rebel, Galba, governor of Hither Spain, a man sprung from the highest ranks of the old Roman nobility. The Spanish legions declared for him, which encouraged him to make formal claim to the succession. By October, 68, he was in Rome, accepted by the Senate, and apparently by the armies generally. But he was an old man. He had long and honourably borne the cares of provincial administration; but the cares of empire, when he came to face them, somewhat dismayed him; so in January, 69, he adopted L. Capurnius Piso as his designated successor. But there was a fly in the ointment. The Prætorian Guard disliked the accession of a nominee of a provincial army, and Otho, the governor of Lusitania, who had supported Galba and accompanied him to Rome, saw his way to obtain the imperial power for himself. At his instigation, Galba and Piso were murdered, whereupon an obsequious Senate voted him the usual imperial powers. Otho's position was much strengthened by the acquiescence of the Illyrian and Syrian legions in his succession. But the armies of the Rhine were of a different mind. They claimed the throne for their commander, Vitellius, marched on Italy and defeated Otho's army at Bedriacum. Otho committed suicide, and Vitellius entered Rome, where the appearance and behaviour of his wild troops caused considerable consternation. But the Syrian and Illyrian legions were not minded to accept the dictation of those of the Rhine, and were angered at the death of Otho, so that by July the armies of Egypt, Syria, and the Danubian provinces had declared for Vespasian. By December, 69, the Danubian legions were in Rome; Vitellius had been slain; and the Senate had voted the powers of emperor to Vespasian.

VESPASIAN

With Vespasian begins the line of the Flavian emperors, a line which, though brief, was destined to leave a permanent mark on the empire and its administration. The high birth and splendid traditions of the Julio-Claudian house had made it possible to leave the powers of the Principate, especially with respect to the succession, undefined, with the assurance that the prestige of the family would guarantee their development along the lines desired. But the Flavians, a family of humble birth, could not reckon on anything of the kind. Moreover, the camouflage of political colouring matter with which Augustus had disguised the monarchy had been rubbed off in the late civil war, so that it was apparent to the meanest intelligence that the Principate was in reality a military autocracy. But of drastic open change under the Flavians there is nothing. Reality takes the place of appearance. Vespasian knew he was an autocrat : was quite determined to act as such ; and was indifferent to whether people recognised the fact or not ; just as he was ready to ignore the sneers of noble families which did not rule at a low-born family which did. The phase would be a passing one. The position of the Flavian family would have to be recognised sooner or later. To expedite the recognition he adopted the name Cæsar as an official title ; and so it remained while the empire lasted. But furthermore, this title was henceforth conferred on the natural or adopted son who was destined for the succession, a more clear-cut method of securing that succession than that which had prevailed in Julio-Claudian days ; and, moreover, the hereditary nature of the imperial power was further emphasised by the custom of citing in official acts the name of the previous emperor as father of the reigning Cæsar, whether any blood-relationship existed or not. Republicanism was dead as a political force, killed partly by the lapse of time, partly by the gradual disappearance of the old Republican families. It continued to exist as an academic fad among those intellectuals to which Tacitus belonged. Perhaps they would not have yearned for it had it been realisable. The Senate, too, filled largely by provincials and Italians of inferior birth, was no longer the formidable body that it once had been. Nominees of Cæsar, men chosen by reason of their success in the law, in finance, and in public administration, were placed in the Senate without ever having attained the rank of quæstor, forming a new nobility attached to the monarchy by the tie of dependence, and by pride in that social position which it was in Cæsar's power alone to bestow. Its members are drawn from all over the empire, socially resplendent and imposing, especially in their provincial homes ; but practically powerless.

Such remnants of senatorial authority as survived in the old senatorial department of government were either swept away or made directly subordinate to the master of all. The consuls no longer ruled even in Rome itself, where all real authority had passed to the præfects of the city and of the Prætorian Guard. Even judicial matters which had formerly come before consuls and prætors now come before these officers of Cæsar. Such legislation as was carried through the Senate was suggested or controlled by the emperor ; and, after the time of Hadrian, the Senate ceases practically to be a legislative body. All the power is with the emperor and the imperial bureaucracy. And that bureaucracy whose power had been disclosed in the reign of Claudius, is now organised and reorganised until it becomes an all too efficient machine of centralised government. The senatorial career as devised by Augustus retains its offices and its dignity; but in actual power the senatorial administrators are being ever more and more supplanted by the hard-working officials of the equestrian order. The governors of senatorial provinces become little more than figure-heads in view of the increasing powers and activities of the imperial procurators, who, nominally appointed to supervise the interests of Cæsar, have got control of all the public interests in the provinces, just as under the *ancien régime* in France the middle-class "intendants" reduced the noble governors of the French provinces to dignified impotence. The equestrian order, too, essentially the service of the emperor, is gradually introduced *vice* the freedmen into the great positions in the central bureaux at Rome, and from the time of Hadrian onwards controls them.

Even from the time of Augustus it had been customary with the emperors to consult on questions of policy a body of advisers chosen by themselves. This body ever tended to become more stereotyped into the form of an official privy council, and its decisions to become equivalent to resolutions of the Senate. By Hadrian it was given an official position as Council of the emperor.

These modifications in the government and methods of administration begin in the days of Vespasian. Originally they seem to have worked well; but they led by a gradual process of evolution to that over-centralisation which was to be the ruin of the imperial system.

On the purely practical side of government Vespasian's greatest work was the restoration throughout the army of that discipline which had fallen into disorder during the confusion of the civil wars.

Titus

The new arrangement with regard to the succession worked smoothly in the case of Titus. Educated with Claudius' son Britannicus, he had a social training such as his father had never had. A seeker after popularity, he squandered money on unworthy objects, human and otherwise, to the depletion of the imperial treasury. To the immense gain of the dishonest official, the strict financial supervision which Vespasian exercised had no attractions for him. And so, taking all in all, it was fortunate for the empire that this "darling of the world"[1] passed in 81, after a brief reign of two years, to another world where his merits would be more accurately appreciated.

---

[1] Tacitus: " deliciæ humani generis."

Domitian

He was succeeded by that brother Domitian whose character the authors of his day have drowned in the blackest ink. Like Tiberius, and for similar but less justifiable reasons, he was a soured man when he succeeded to the throne. During his father's reign he was kept in the political background in order to bring Titus more into public relief. Titus, when emperor, also repressed his ambitions, though he knew so well that Domitian must be his successor that he tried to marry his daughter Julia to him. But Domitian, preferred an illigitimate to a legitimate union.

Courteous and cautious at first in his relations with the Senate, his attitude towards it changed so soon as success in a war in Germany had made him feel more secure in his power. From that time onward it became manifest that he was determined to sweep away the small remnants of competitive power which that body still retained. In most other respects his rule resembles that of Tiberius, a hard-headed and efficient administration of the empire which was callous to the traditions of the past and to the foibles of the present. When the Senate's opposition was aroused he showed quite plainly that he was fully prepared to use the army to crush all opposition, thus brutally disclosing the indecent truth which had been treated as the secret of imperial power. Whether owing to this candid exposure of the autocratic character of the monarchy, or to the personal dislike with which he was regarded, various of the nobility, old and new, began to think that it would be a very good thing if Domitian were sent to sleep with his fathers, and the rule of the empire passed into other hands, preferably their own. The movement was supported by the Stoic intellectuals, who contributed literature of veiled doctrinaire Republican tendencies which, combined with personal attacks, still more veiled, exasperated Domitian, and were fatal to the authors. From the time when, early in 88, Saturninus, the aristocratic governor of Upper Germany, revolted with two legions, a revolt which was promptly crushed, Domitian was haunted by plots, real and imaginary, ghosts which he sought to allay by the wholesale execution of actual or alleged conspirators. So the last years of his reign became a reign of terror, during which practically all the remnants of the old nobility, together with many others, perished. But these murders begat more conspiracies of an unquestionably genuine nature, for even those who had in the past been innocent came to see that no man's life was safe so long as the tyrant lived. He was assassinated in a palace conspiracy in September of the year 96.

If the good had reason to hate Domitian, so had the bad. Never did human nature display greater contrasts in the person of a single individual. Of his care in the government of the empire there has already been occasion to speak; but this was accompanied by an equal desire and determination to restore a healthy public morality by punishing the moral debaucheries of the time, and to re-establish the national religion by suppressing the unwholesome cults which had made their way into Rome from the East. He may have felt that he had just cause for resentment against those who sought to kill him ere his work was done. To rule in the Rome of that day, a world of idealists and decadents, was not an easy task, especially for one who regarded the idealism as foolishness, and the decadence as crime, —and was perhaps not far wrong in so doing.

NERVA

The assassins of Domitian had previously arranged that the succession should fall on Nerva. Considering that the army had no say in the choice of the new emperor, his succession was extraordinarily peaceful. The Senate adopted him as its own candidate, and thus for the first time a nominee of the Senate sat on the imperial throne. A jurist by profession, Nerva showed an unusual respect for the old Republican forms, so that in his short reign of two years the Senate recovered temporarily the position it had lost since the days of Augustus, and played a real part in the government of the empire. Even the Comitia was called out of oblivion for the purpose of legislation. Nerva's kindly and merciful disposition, a pleasant contrast to the savagery of his predecessor, carried him successfully through the two years of his reign. But it may be doubted whether such qualities would have assured him success in a more prolonged rule of a world for whose government cruder qualities were necessary.

TRAJAN

Before his death he had designated M. Ulpius Trajanus, the governor of Upper Germany, as his successor, and had caused him to be given those titles and powers now commonly voted to the heir-presumptive of the empire.

It is a sign of the change in the times, a sign, above all, of the disappearing pre-eminence of Italy and the Italians in the empire, that the new emperor, the first non-Italian to ascend the imperial throne, was tacitly accepted by the whole Roman world. It was perhaps expected that Nerva's chosen successor would follow in the footsteps of his predecessor; but, if so, that expectation was disappointed by this ambitious soldier and painstaking administrator who wanted to do things, and great things, by himself without the interference of senatorial or other authority. Outwardly courteous to the Senate, he kept it, as far as the administration of the empire was concerned, in a state of dignified idleness. As a strategist he did some wise things, such as the conquest of Dacia ; but also some risky things, such as his Asian campaigns, which were hardly justified by success. As an administrator he had that conscientiousness which misleads those in charge of a great office to try to deal with minutiæ which an abler man would leave to subordinates. Pliny, as governor of Bithynia, dare not decide without reference to the emperor matters which would now be left to the discretion of a town-surveyor.

Yet he has a great place in the history of the Principate, and would have had a much greater one had not so much that he did been undone by a successor in whose mind the mental rigidity of a drill-sergeant was combined with the caution of an elderly lady.

Trajan died in 117, without having made before his death those clear-cut arrangements by which, since Vespasian's time, the emperors had been wont to designate their successors ; but he had in a general way indicated his second cousin, P. Ælius Hadrianus, as the man he would choose.

HADRIAN

Hadrian had not only seen a good deal of military service in the Dacian and eastern wars, but had shown himself capable in subordinate commands. His chief characteristics were a restless curiosity in learning fostered by an education in Greek literature, and a cosmopolitanism instilled into him partly by his education, partly by his keenness for foreign travel and sight-seeing. By spreading his mind in dilettante fashion over many branches of learning, he acquired many ideas in conflict with those begotten of the rugged common sense of the more able of his predecessors, and a conviction of their rightness which nothing could shake. It was quite certain that under so novel an emperor imperial policy would take novel form.

With him organisation was a mania. So wide and so minute were his activities in this respect that it was, humanly speaking, inevitable that in his measures of reform the wise should be mingled with the unwise.

It was doubtless to the benefit of the administration that the chief posts in the imperial offices at Rome should be taken finally out of the hands of freedmen and put into those of members of that equestrian order which, since the days of Vespasian, had been gradually losing its prejudice against employment in tasks associated with the labour of ex-slaves.[1] It is from this time forward that the importance of this order grows at the expense of the higher senatorial officers in the government of the empire. Under him it becomes common for the emperor, when absent from Rome, to delegate jurisdiction either to the præfect of the city or to that of the Prætorian Guard.[2] Under Hadrian, too, the last faint traces of senatorial independence in administration vanish, and the supremacy of the emperor in all departments of government becomes a theory as well as a fact. In all these respects Hadrian's reign marks the consummation of tendencies which have been developing since the very beginning of the Principate, all leading to one end,—the concentration of power in the hands of the man who controls the army.

His frontier policy has left on the map of Europe traces which may still be seen in the form of the remnants of those great fortified lines with which he sought to strengthen the weaker parts of the frontier. He had no sympathy whatever with that enterprise of Trajan which had added Dacia, Armenia, the Mesopotamian region, and parts of Arabia to the empire; and he took drastic measures to rectify a policy which, as he thought, had added to the empire responsibilities heavier than it could bear. On the general question he was right; but in certain details both the past and future showed that he was wrong. He did not renounce the conquest of Dacia; but he showed his dislike to it by removing the superstructure of the great bridge which Trajan had thrown over the Danube at Drobetæ (Turn Severin). Yet the past had shown, and the future was to show yet more distinctly, that the holding of Dacia was necessary for the securing of the Balkan Peninsula against the raids of the Sarmatæ, Roxolani, and other wild tribes of south Russia. It might have been wise to retain Armenia as an outpost against the East. But he renounced it. On the other hand, Mesopotamia, which he also renounced, would have been a source of military weakness rather than of strength to Rome. Arabia Petræa he retained.

On the frontiers everything was organised to such an extent that it took a stereotyped form which both in general and in detail lasted for ages. Legions tend henceforth to have the same headquarters, and auxiliary cohorts and alæ the same stations for centuries, so that the Roman army becomes what it had been under the Republic, a series of armies of provinces rather than a single army of the empire, a tendency promoted still more by the practice of local recruiting, the natural corollary of such a stabilised system. The results were bad in two ways. The legionary soldiers became too domesticated by married life

[1] See p. 471.   [2] See p. 463.

in legionary camps which grew into towns with a large civilian population, with the result that their fighting qualities declined ; and the sentiment of the soldiers became associated with the province in which they lived, and of which an ever-increasing number of them were natives, which resulted in the patriotism of the armies tending to become local rather than imperial at the very time when civilian sentiment throughout the empire was tending to become Roman rather than national. The empire, becoming ever more united in the sentiment of the majority, became disunited in that of the most important minority.

Hadrian tried to include the empire in an impenetrable ring fence ; but he dealt with the material of it in such a way that it was bound to decay in all too short a time.

Social Life in Rome

In dealing with the diverse effects of the characters of the various emperors of the first century and a half of the Principate it has been necessary to touch on their relations with society both high and low in Italy. But these incidental lights illuminate but a small part of the life of that society.

Of the lower ranks in the city itself it may be said that they lived much as they had lived under the last age of the Republic, a life of semi-employment eked out by government charity in the form of doles, or more permanent government relief in the form of cheap corn : a life corrupted by association with an ever-increasing servile and ex-servile population, and by the influx into the capital of the empire of very undesirable immigrants from the provinces, who brought with them vices and superstitions destructive of the old Roman morality. Rome would have been a dangerous, or even impossible, residence for the emperors had not the presence of the Prætorian Guard instilled into its population a wholesome fear of the consequences of disorder.

In Italy economic development tended towards a decrease in its rural population owing to an increase of large estates worked by slave labour. The economists of the time deplored the change, partly because it was a change, partly because the idea that a land should feed its own people was the most important principle they recognised, and the tendencies of cultivation on these large estates implied a large decrease in the native corn supply. It was in Italy in the first century after Christ, as it had been in Greece in the sixth and fifth centuries before the Christian era. The application of capital to land had made it possible to institute cultivation of the vine and olive, which the poor cultivator of Attica in the early sixth century, and the small farmer of Italy in the centuries before Christ, had never had the capital to institute, though much of the land of both countries was better suited to such cultivation than to that of cereals. It made both countries more dependent on imported corn; but, probably in the case of Italy, as certainly in that of Attica, the new cultivation permitted of the purchase of far more corn than ever the lands converted from cereal cultivation could have produced. "Large estates ruined Italy," said the Roman economist; but then he was so anxious about the maintenance of the ruling race in sufficient numbers, and about the strategic importance of a large local supply of cereals, that his judgment on the purely economic question may have been exaggerated.

Of actual life in Rome much is told by the authors of the first two centuries of the empire; but of the life in Italy they say but little. Still, the little that is told of that rural life leaves the impression that it was much happier than that in the capital, where poverty and wealth, misery and delirious amusement, presented that contrast of extremes in the scale of existence which is not conducive to human happiness. Even the Roman who could afford at times to leave the city found in the rural life of Italy enjoyment more sober but more real than that which he found in Rome. Even the old Roman nobility found in their country seats something which led them to forget for the time that loss of political power of which everything in Rome reminded them only too vividly. The life in the municipalities of Italy seems to have been a happy one where local ambitions could be satisfied with the dignity of municipal offices which had not become, as they afterwards became, intolerably burdensome.

Of the fate of the old nobility under the Principate it has already been necessary to speak. Could it have forgotten the pride, power, and ambitions of the past, and have accepted the inevitable, it might have survived as a social class of great influence in the empire. It made the mistake of making itself feared by the all-powerful; yet, though its blindness to the hard facts of the time may be deplored, its refusal to give a passive acceptance to defeat calls for a certain admiration. But with the growth of the Principate there grows up a new nobility which plays an ever-increasing part in the higher social life in Rome, composed of men tried by years of administration in all parts of the empire, capable men, and honest men, even if their honesty is sometimes due to fear of consequences.

Of the private life of this high society at Rome under the earlier emperors but little is known save the gloomy side of it which is pictured in Tacitus' accounts of its sufferings under the grim Tiberius, while of the happier side of its life under later emperors some glimpses are caught in Pliny's letters.

Its wilder extravagances are depicted in the satires of various authors; but it would seem that they are characteristic rather of the *nouveaux riches* among its members than of the old nobility which sought in the austerities of the old-fashioned life of the past a somewhat gloomy compensation for the ills of life in the present, or of that part of the new element which had been sobered by the responsibilities of administrative office. But under the empire the richer classes of Rome, with minds less taken up with public life, less occupied with wars and rumours of wars, had more time to think, or to try to think, out the problems of individual existence. Their women-folk might be attracted by novel religions and superstitions, and seek comfort therein; might become devotees of Jehovah, of Isis, and other deities which the educated male world regarded as the playthings of uneducated minds; men of education wanted a creed which could come as near as possible to satisfying the intelligence, and they found it in one of the now systematised philosophies which the Greek world had evolved, above all in a Stoicism which narrowed severely the limits of "the good," or perhaps in an Epicureanism which had a more catholic creed. The letters of Pliny imply a society of kindly cultured men whose wit has been sharpened by mutual intercourse. Even the bitter Tacitus loses his acidity when he comes to speak of life under Nerva and Trajan.

But the political state of the world of the Mediterranean had from the time of Augustus onwards been infinitely more happy than ever it had been before; for it had been ruled in the interests of the many, not as aforetime, in the interests of the few; and the few who had suffered had been for the most part the few who had resented this government, and had tried to overthrow it in order to restore the old evil state of things. With the exception of Caligula and Nero, and perhaps of Titus, the emperors had been men who had the welfare of the empire as a whole at heart, so that they cannot be utterly blamed for their severity to those who would have destroyed them and their work. Some of the friends of Tacitus, whose fate under Domitian caused that historian to paint that emperor's character and actions in the blackest colours which language can produce, had rushed on their own fate by covert attacks on a man whose nerves had been set on edge by conspiracies which had not stopped at words. The academic republicanism of that day may have represented little more than the eternal dissatisfaction of humanity with the present, whatever it be; but its expression could hardly fail to be taken seriously by emperors against whose predecessors the more genuine Republicans of the past had plotted.

The Provinces

But while the life of the upper classes at Rome passed through all these vicissitudes, the life of the provinces pursued a course more peaceful than those lands had ever known.

Of the various ways in which their general government and condition had been ameliorated under the empire, there has already been occasion to speak. It remains to say something of their individual histories and development.

As under the Republic, the real basis and the real unit of administration in the provinces was not so much the province itself, but the units, usually municipal, but in some cases tribal, which were grouped together to form a province. As under the Republic, a province meant nothing more than a certain number of small political units grouped together for either physical, ethnical, or administrative reasons, under one superintendent governor. Even at the close of the first century A.D. the communities scattered through the provinces presented many varieties of local institutions and rights. In the second century a good deal of assimilation takes place ; but even when it comes to a close much variety still exists. The towns in the provinces with full Roman rights had of course similar institutions wherever they might be situated. Provincial towns which received those Latin rights which were regarded as a step towards Roman citizenship had constitutions similar in form to the Roman towns, and were, like them, under Roman law. In the other provincial towns all sorts of local law might prevail, Celtic law in Gallic towns, Greek law in the towns of the East ; for even under the government of the empire, with its mania for uniformity, the emperors were chary about interfering with those local rights which the subject communities valued so highly. But the imperial officials exercise an ever-growing supervision over the exercise of these rights lest they conflict in working with the duties which the communities owe to the empire. Points of difficulty and doubt are referred to the emperors, whose decisions grew into a body of rescripts which built up gradually a code of municipal law applicable to the whole empire, superseding the old local institutions.

This centralising tendency did much to weaken municipal life by robbing the communities of that semi-independence in which they took a pride. Its effect on that life was bad in three ways : municipal office became unpopular when the officers came to find themselves little more than the executors of orders in the framing of which they had played no part ; local needs were not recognised by a central government which had at best second-hand knowledge of the circumstances ; and finally, a spirit of

THE EMPIRE

weak dependence on the central government began to prevail, which weakened the resisting power of the empire to foreign aggression.

But in the first century of the empire, and indeed to a great extent during the second century, the policy of respect to local institutions and of regard for local conditions leads to great variety of treatment in the organisation of the various provinces.

Spain

Spain was one of the older provinces of the empire wherein the emperors found an organisation, nigh two centuries old at the time of the foundation of the Principate, into municipal districts, or, where no town existed, into rural regions. It was the customary form of institution in the empire, and so Augustus saw no reason to modify it.

In two respects the organisation of Spain contrasts with that of the Three Gauls : in the establishment of municipal districts wherever the presence of a town rendered that possible ; and in the breaking up of the tribal unit into small districts, whether rural or town communities. The policy of Augustus in allowing the large tribes of Gaul to continue their existence as communities under Roman rule was one to which the government of the Republic would never have assented.

But Augustus' completion of the conquest of the peninsula led to a reorganisation of the provinces. Hitherto there had been but two, Hither and Further Spain. With the new additions to the Roman territory Hither Spain would have become an area larger than the imperial government was wont to place under one command. Even so early as 49 B.C. Pompeius had separated Lusitania from Bætica. Augustus stereotyped this threefold division with slight modifications, keeping Hither Spain, henceforth called Tarraconensis from its new capital Tarraco, and Lusitania under his own command as provinces which required garrisons, and handing over Bætica, by far the most civilised region of the peninsula, to the Senate.

In the general organisation of Spain under the empire one feature stands out with extraordinary clearness, the effect of the great system of roads constructed by the government on the civilisation and development of the country ; and this may be taken as the text for the discussion of a policy which changed the face of the world.

Road System of the Empire

Under the Republic Italy had been covered with a network of roads constructed for the purpose of maintaining military control of the peninsula. But the state into which many of these roads had lapsed by the time of Augustus shows how difficult the government had found it to meet the expense of maintaining them in good repair. Outside Italy the Via Egnatia, leading from Dyrrhachium to the East, and the great road through Gaul to Spain, were the only made roads of any length outside Italy. It was the establishment of a standing army under the empire which made the extension of the imperial road system possible. The soldiers had to be paid in peace as well as in war; and employment in time of peace was necessary in order to keep them out of mischief such as idleness is wont to beget. They were therefore employed on public works of a military character: on the building of permanent camps, and above all on the making of roads necessary as lines of military communication. The improved finance under the empire, combined with what was, under the circumstances, unpaid labour, made it possible to construct through the provinces a network of lines of military communications connected with Italy by arterial highways. These roads were an asset of not merely military value. The increased rapidity of communication which they afforded rendered it far more easy for the central government to maintain control over the outlying parts of the empire and their governors, and tended in every way to facilitate that unification of the empire which was the main policy of the Cæsars. Though not made for purposes of trade, there can be no question but that they not merely increased but multiplied its volume many times; and, though the roads of the early empire were constructed with the military end in view, it is plain that in those provinces which became peculiarly wealthy, such as Gaul, from at least the second century onwards roads were constructed, sometimes by local enterprise, for purely trade purposes. Another benefit which they conferred on the ancient world was the possibility which they afforded of conveying to famine-stricken regions supplies from outside.

Spain (continued)

Augustus had promoted the romanisation of Spain by the founding of numerous settlements, especially in the wild north-west, whose names betray their founder.[1]

The Spanish provinces are remarkable among the provinces of Rome for the enormous wealth which the Roman government drew from the mines. Spain was by far the richest mining region of the ancient world, producing appreciable quantities of gold and silver, and enormous quantities of copper and iron, even as at the present day.

[1] Augustobriga in Celtiberia; Asturica Augusta and Lucus Augusti in Galicia; Emerita Augusta and Pax Augusta further south.

Of the three provinces, Bætica was the richest and the most civilised. During the Carthaginian rule it was that part of the peninsula into which the Semitic civilisation had penetrated most deeply. Though all the three provinces assimilated Roman civilisation rapidly under the empire, in no one of them was the process so rapid and so thorough as in Bætica. Ere the first century after Christ has come to an end Spain is a rival to Italy in the field of Latin literature. Bætica produces Lucan and Seneca ; Tarraconensis Martial and Quintilian. Moreover, the first provincial consul and the first provincial emperor were both of Spanish blood. Roman dress and the Roman language became so customary that Spain became almost more Roman than Italy itself.

Gaul

North of the Pyrenees Gaul presented a far more complicated political problem. There Augustus had two questions to face, differing according to the different nature of the regions concerned. The old province of Narbonensis was divided from the rest of Gaul by the range of the Cevennes and the mountains of Savoy, which, taken together, form at this point the boundary between the two climatic belts of Europe known as the mid-European and the Mediterranean. In climate and products it contrasted with the rest of Gaul. For nearly a century before the time of Augustus the greater part of it had been a Roman province ; and in 49 B.C. Cæsar had annexed to it the greater part of the old Greek colony of Massilia, leaving that former ally of the Roman people but a small region in the neighbourhood of the town itself. The romanisation of the old province had been carried far before the days of Augustus, partly owing to deliberate policy, partly owing to the settlement of large numbers of Italians in a land with a climate like that of their old home. Julius did much to promote the romanisation of the region, the only part of his task of organisation in Gaul which he was able to bring to completion before his death. He founded colonies at Forum Julii, Arelate, Arausio, and Bæterræ, endowing these cities with lands taken from Massilia. To the north he left the tribe of the Vocontii in a position which it held for several centuries, that of a state federated with Rome. Still further north the large territory of the Allobroges was all made into the municipal territory of the town of Vienna (Vienne). Many towns in the province were granted Latin rights ; and in fact Cæsar's policy in Narbonensis was but a special example of his general policy of promoting civilisation with a view to the spread of Roman citizenship throughout the empire. All the south part of the province became a sort of second Italy.

33

In strange contrast with the Roman civilisation of the rest of the province, the land of the Vocontii between the rivers Isara (Isère) and Druentia (Durance) preserved for many years its native Gallic customs and character. In this remote corner of the world the tribe lived on for centuries a life undisturbed by the wars of the empire, and but little influenced by the developments of periods of peace. It went on living its own life, speaking its own language, worshipping its own gods, and holding its own festivals, protected by the great power of Rome, which was quite ready to leave it alone to live out that life in peace so long as it paid its imperial taxes, and contributed its quota to the auxilia of the army. The records which have survived of the Vocontii present what is probably a typical picture of the life of those more out-of-the-way parts of the empire which appreciated that protecting power of a great and well-ordered government which gave them a peace that they had never known before.

North of Narbonensis lay that Gaul which, when Augustus undertook its organisation, had been but recently reduced by Cæsar. Such organisation as its conqueror imposed was determined by the expediency of the moment, and cannot be regarded as representing the final form which he would have given it had he lived. In 50 B.C. the whole of it was placed under one command. In 44 it was divided into three provinces: Belgica, containing Celtic (mainly Belgic) and Germanic elements; Celtica, wholly Celtic; and Aquitania, to the south of the Garumna (Garonne), whose population was almost wholly Iberian. When Augustus came to organise the country he did not like this division, mainly because it blocked together in one province of Celtica a Celtic population so large as to be a danger in case of a national rising; and therefore, though he retained the triple division, he cut off from north-west Celtica the three important tribes of the Lingones, Sequani, and Helvetii, and included them in Belgica, while in the south the Celtic tribes between the Liger (Loire) and the Garumna (Garonne) were added to Aquitania. Moreover, Celtica was known henceforth as Lugdunensis.

But by far the most important feature of his organisation was his acceptance of the tribe as the unit of division within each province, though he was careful to break up those tribal confederacies into which powerful tribes had been able to force their weaker neighbours. Thus the land of Gaul was not, as in most of the provinces, divided into units which formed the territory of some municipality,[1] but the tribal capital within the unit was merely part of the unit and not, as it were, the possessor of it.

---

[1] E.g., as has been mentioned, the territory of the Allobroges in Narbonensis was not dealt with as the territory of that tribe, but as the municipal territory of Vienna.

The result of this is shown in the nomenclature of modern France, where, in that part of it which was formerly within the territory of the Three Gauls, the town names are not derived from the names those towns bore in Roman days, but from the names of the tribes of whose territories they were the capitals; whereas in what was formerly Narbonensis, in which the municipal system prevailed, the modern town names are derived from the names the towns themselves bore in Roman times.[1] The foundation of Roman colonies, so marked a feature in the policy observed in Narbonensis, is almost entirely omitted in the Three Gauls. Lugdunum was the only such colony in Lugdunensis; and there were only two such colonies in Belgica up to the time of the Flavian emperors. In Aquitania there were none. It is very strange that Augustus did not in the case of the Three Gauls adopt that customary method of promoting Roman civilisation; and his failure to do so has been criticised as a sign of weakness. But what his reasons were for the omission is not known. As regards the tribal " civitates," loyalty was rewarded and encouraged by giving some of them the position of states " federated " with Rome, enjoying thereby superior rights guaranteed to them by treaty (Fœdus). At the end of the first century A.D. there were numerous " liberæ civitates " (free states) in Gaul, tribes which enjoyed a second grade of privileges. Thus in Gaul Rome maintained the principle of differentiating rights with a view to dividing interests. Altogether there were in Gaul sixty-four " civitates."

But owing to the large army required on the Rhine, and, at that time, probably in Gaul itself,[2] the then prætorian governors of these provinces seem to have been placed under the command of trusted friends of Augustus, such as Agrippa, or of princes of the imperial house, such as Tiberius, and perhaps Drusus.

The defeat of Varus in A.D. 9 brought about the evacuation of the region between the Rhine and the Elbe, which resulted in the establishment of a military frontier district on the Rhine,

---

[1] Cf. in Belgica: Durocortorum, Capital of the Remi, now Rheims; Lutetia, Capital of Parisii, now Paris; Andematunnum, Capital of the Lingones, now Langres; etc., etc. N.B.—Towns which were not Capitals of the tribal civitates have names derived from the Roman names, e.g. Tullum (Toul), Virodunum (Verdun), etc.

In Lugdunensis: Juliomagus, Capital of the Andecavi, now Angers; Cæsarodunum, Capital of the Turones, now Tours.

In Aquitania: Mediolanum, Capital of the Santones, now Saintes; Elimberrum, Capital of the Ausci, now Auche.

But in Narbonensis: Nemausus (Nîmes), Arelate (Arles), etc.

[2] Up to the time of Augustus' residence in Gaul (16-13 B.C.) the permanent camps of the legions seem to have been, to a certain extent, at any rate, not on the Rhine, but in southern Belgica.

converted later into the provinces of Upper and Lower Germany. But though the Three Gauls were administratively separate provinces, Lugdunum (Lyons) was in a sense the capital city of all three of them, where Cæsar-worship was established, in connection with which a meeting (concilium) of Gallic nobility was held. This council had the right of making to the central government at Rome representations on matters connected with the three provinces. This worship and this council were the sole bonds which bound the Gallic tribes together. In all other respects the policy was to keep the Gallic " civitates " as far as possible isolated from one another.

For a century after Cæsar's conquest the Gaul proved a restless subject of Rome. Revolts on a small scale were frequent. But there were three on a much larger scale, all of which aimed at the recovery of Gallic independence. The first, that of Julius Sacrovir, took place in A.D. 21, caused by the burden of imperial taxation. It was put down by the local Roman legions.

In the year A.D. 68, Julius Vindex, who was governor of Lugdunensis, raised a revolt on a large scale, in word against Nero, indeed with a view to the recovery of Gallic independence. He got together a native army large in numbers but ill armed and ill disciplined, no match whatever for the legions which Virginius Rufus, the governor of Upper Germany, brought against it.

In the next year, 69, another rising, which began in the German province, but spread later to Gaul, was, partly in itself, partly owing to its taking place when the main Roman armies were occupied in the war between Vitellius and Vespasian, much more formidable than that of Vindex. This was due to its being originally a mutiny of the various auxilia which served in the Rhine armies, regiments recruited from the neighbouring regions, from various of the tribes of Belgica, and above all from the German Batavi on the lower Rhine.

Rome had made the mistake of allowing this large force of natives, commanded for the most part by their own nobility, to serve in the region from which they were drawn. It was almost inevitable that what was originally a mutiny should become a national movement. The legions on the Rhine were at the time little more than skeleton forces, inasmuch as large numbers of the best troops had been withdrawn for the civil war in Italy. Civilis, the leader, was a Batavian. At first the revolt was confined to the Batavi and their neighbours in the Rhine delta, especially the Frisii. It was then joined by eight Batavian cohorts from Moguntiacum (Mainz). In the next year, 70, the Treveri joined in ; and then the movement was declared as aiming at an empire of the Gauls. The capture of the legionary camp at Vetera led to the legions on the Rhine joining in the movement. So far all had gone well with the rebels; but now arose two awkward questions which eventually ruined the enterprise; one for the Germans, as to whether submission to a Gallic would be preferable to subjection to the Roman Empire; and the other for the Gauls, as to what tribe should have first place in the new dominion.

Vespasian, now master of the world, was free to send Petilius Cerialis with a large army, before which the movement, once so formidable, promptly collapsed. From that time forward Gaul remained for long loyal and apparently contented under Roman rule.

The rapidity and completeness of the romanisation of the Three Gauls has been much debated by modern authors, whose conclusions are biassed either by modern Gallic patriotism or by anti-Gallic feeling. One fact, namely, that the modern French language is almost exclusively Latin in origin, and that even the few Celtic words which survive in it had almost certainly made their way into the Latin of Gaul long before the evolution into French had taken place, would suggest perhaps to the unprejudiced mind that the romanisation of Gaul was eventually complete. To the extreme north and to the out-of-the-way regions of Iberian Aquitania, Latin civilisation came later than to the rest of the land. In these exceptional regions, old cults, old customs, and the old language died a slow death; in fact, it is probable that throughout Gaul the native cults survived until they were superseded by Christianity.

From the very beginning of the days of subjection to Rome the natives had taken kindly to Latin civilisation, though not to Latin dominion; but when matters settled down after the rising of Civilis, Gaul became one of the most advanced centres of Latin civilisation; and the Celtic schools or universities became some of the most famous of the empire.

Germany

The Roman relations with Germany beyond the Rhine were of brief duration. Of the original design of Augustus to make a frontier on the Elbe there has already been occasion to speak. Under him the campaigns of Drusus and Tiberius between 13 B.C. and A.D. 6 had that end in view; and from the time when, in 9 B.C., Drusus reached the Elbe, the organisation of the region between that river and the Rhine in the form of a province had been carried forward towards completion. A campaign against Maroboduus, the king of the Germans of Bohemia and Moravia, planned in A.D. 6, would have completed the frontier design, had not the great rising in Pannonia in that year diverted the armies to that region. And then the defeat of Varus in A.D. 9 brought the whole scheme to an end, so that the

Elbe frontier was renounced, and Rome practically evacuated the land between the two great rivers. All that she retained on the far side of the Rhine was a partial dominion over the Batavi and the tribes of modern Holland; a strip of land a few miles broad, denuded of population, on the far bank of the lower and middle river, bordered by a military highway, no doubt the official frontier of the empire which no German could pass without a special permit; and the region of the Taunus in the angle between the Main (Mœnus) and the Rhine. The re-entering angle between the upper Rhine and the upper Danube, consisting mainly of the modern Baden, and called in the first century A.D. the Agri Decumates (Tithe Lands), is spoken of by Tacitus as a land " of doubtful possession." It seems to have been cleared of its German population, and to have been a No Man's Land. It is uncertain as to when the region was definitely annexed, though it is probable that this took place under one of the Flavian emperors. Under either Trajan or Hadrian, probably the latter, its northern boundary was fortified by an artificial line of defence similar to, but not exactly the same as, the Roman wall of north England. For the rest, the activities of Rome beyond the Rhine consisted of brief expeditions either in consequence of disorder threatening the peace of the empire, or due to a wish to keep the German tribes in a wholesome state of fear.

On the near side of the Rhine a new and restricted Germany was organised after A.D. 9. Parts at least of this region had belonged to the German province beyond the river, for Colonia (Cologne) had been selected as the centre for Cæsar-worship in the German province as originally designed.

The first arrangement after A.D. 9 seems to have been to create two districts of Upper and Lower Germany, in each of which the commander of the army in the district acted as military governor, while civil administration was exercised by the governor of Belgica. But this was apparently a temporary arrangement; and the two Germanies became provinces of an ordinary kind with governors exercising both civil and military powers.

Britain

The conquest of Britain, undertaken in the first place by Claudius in A.D. 43, was a dynastic rather than a strategic measure.[1] An excuse for invasion was furnished by the fact that since the expeditions of Cæsar, one hundred years before, some of the chiefs of the south-east part of the island had been allies of Rome. They had become accustomed to appeal to Cæsar when circumstances at home went against their interests. A somewhat large commerce existed between the island and

[1] See p. 489.

Gaul through which the Britons had learnt and acquired some of the elements of Roman civilisation, a process furthered by the fact that the Celtic tribes of the south part of the island were closely related to the tribes of Gaul itself. Brythonic Celts had by this time overrun the whole of what is now England except perhaps the Cornish peninsula, where a Gaelic remnant of the earlier Celts may have survived. In Wales the population seems to have been mainly Gaelic, though it later adopted a Brythonic tongue. In South Wales however the Silures seem from the description of Tacitus to have been a survival of that Iberian race which still formed the foundation of the population of the western shores and hinterland of Europe. Nor can there be much doubt that throughout what is now England an Iberian race survived in subjection to the Celts, though not perhaps in so large a proportion as it did in Gaul. The hill cities of Britain, now called camps, so similar to the hill cities of Gaul in Cæsar's time, indicate the military domination of a superior over an inferior race.

The trouble in Britain in A.D. 43 was due to a certain Caractacus who was known to be hostile to Rome, and had lately succeeded his father Cunobelinus in the rule of the south-eastern part of the island. He was likely to interfere with Roman trade and murder Roman traders. At any rate in A.D. 43 the expedition crossed over and captured Camulodunum (Colchester), the capital of Caractacus. Aulus Plautius seems, before his command came to an end in 47, to have conquered the whole of the south-east up to a line from Exeter to Lincoln; and perhaps the Akemann Street is an earlier, and the Fosse Way a later frontier road which he made for the purpose of securing the territory he had won.[1] Ostorius Scapula, who succeeded him, seems to have conquered the west Midlands between the Trent and the Severn. In A.D. 50 he defeated Caractacus, who had taken refuge with the western tribes; and then he attacked the Silures in South Wales.[2] After Ostorius' death in 52 there was no real advance for six years. The Roman hold on the south-east was being consolidated. Camulodunum (Colchester) became a Roman colony: Verulamium (St. Albans) a municipality; and Londinium was becoming a centre of population. In 61, when Suetonius Paulinus was governor, took place the revolt of the Iceni (Norfolk) under Boudicca (Boadicea). The destruction of Camulodunum, the sacking of Londinium and Verulamium,

[1] The existence of these two Roman roads is difficult to account for on any other supposition.
[2] It is probable that that so-called part of the Watling Street which runs south from Church Stretton in Shropshire into Herefordshire was a frontier road made at this stage in the conquest of Britain.

show the critical nature of the position in which the Romans were placed. After its suppression affairs remained *in statu quo* during the reign of Nero and the brief period of the civil war. But under the Flavian emperors operations were renewed with vigour. Between 71 and 77 half of Wales was subdued, and the Roman frontier in the north pushed forward into Yorkshire. Then came the governorship of the great Agricola, under whose command the conquest of Wales was completed. In the north his predecessors Cerialis and Frontinus had done something to break the power of the Brigantes, a great tribe in north England and south-east Scotland. In a series of campaigns Agricola reached the isthmus between the Forth and Clyde estuaries, where he established a chain of forts. He penetrated north of this into the Highlands of Scotland, where he fought a great battle at Mons Graupius, possibly the Ochil Hills; but the country to the north of the Forth and Clyde seems never to have come under permanent Roman occupation. South Scotland remained in the hands of the Romans till the days of Trajan, when it was temporarily lost in consequence of a great native rising. Hadrian seems to have acknowledged the loss by building the great permanent line of wall and forts from the Solway to the Tyne. Under Antoninus Pius south Scotland was temporarily recovered, and the Clyde-Forth isthmus was provided with a turf wall and forts.

Britain never became one of the wealthy provinces of the empire. Of the life of its inhabitants under Roman rule little is really known, though the discoveries at the great military centres in the north and west throw a good deal of light on the lives of those who formed its garrison.

THE ALPINE TRIBES

Between Gaul and Italy lay the lands of those Alpine tribes which had enjoyed under the Republic a life of independence which they brightened by raids on the rich plain of the Padus. Augustus exterminated some of them, and reduced the rest; after which he organised their territories in the western Alps as two small præfectures, of one of which, that of the Cottian Alps, he allowed its native chief Cottius, a loyal friend of Rome, to act as præfect. Under Claudius the præfecture was enlarged, and its native præfect given the rank of king; and under Nero the præfecture was converted into a procuratorship.

RÆTIA AND NORICUM

Of Rætia and Noricum most of what need be said has been said already in relation to the Roman army.[1] Conquered by

---
[1] See p. 477.

Tiberius and Drusus in 15 B.C. they became Cæsarian provinces governed, for reasons already stated, not by propraetors but by procurators, essentially second-class provinces whose garrisons were composed entirely of auxilia. Of the details of their history under the early emperors very little is known, save that there was a certain contrast in their respective development. Before the Roman conquest Noricum, under the influence of Roman traders from Emona and Nauportus, had shown much zeal for the acquisition of Roman civilisation, a zeal which was not quenched by the subsequent conquest. In the first century and a half of the empire numerous Roman towns sprang up within its area. Rætia seems on the other hand to have remained somewhat backward. The only town in it which became important was Augusta Vindelicorum (Augsburg), which Tacitus describes as a place of some,—probably relative,—magnificence.

THE DANUBIAN PROVINCES

The provinces of the middle and lower Danube, Pannonia, Mœsia, together with the strategically dependent Dalmatia, and that Dacian province which Trajan added to the empire, become of the greatest importance when, from the time of the Flavian emperors onwards, this eastern part of the northern frontier becomes the most dangerous part of the imperial boundary. The whole of the middle and lower Danube basin and the lands north of it were occupied by peoples various in race, but uniform in disposition, which was, from the point of view of Rome, bad. Illyrian races in Pannonia and Dalmatia, Celtic tribes such as the Scordisci in the Save basin, Thracians in Mœsia and Dacia, Iranians such as the Iazyges in Hungary, and the Sarmatæ and Roxolani north of the Carpathians, not to say anything of the Germanic Bastarnæ, formed an agglomeration of peoples with whom Rome's experiences and dealings were frequent, often troublesome and often unpleasant. Of these the most formidable were the Dacians, because they were the most capable and best organised; but as a general nuisance to Roman peace the Sarmatæ and Roxolani competed with them in persistent raids into the Balkan Peninsula.

Of the Dacians the Greeks of the classical period knew nothing, unless the Agathyrsi of Herodotus,[1] in whose land there was gold, are to be identified with them or with former dwellers in what was afterwards Dacia. But in the third century there are traces of a lively trade in gold between the Dacians and the mine-owners of Thasos, and also of trade intercourse by the Save valley between Dacia and the Greeks who had pushed up the

---

[1] Hdt. iv, 49.

Adriatic to Black Corcyra.[1] In Cæsar's time Dacia became united under a king Burebista, who made himself so sore a trouble to Rome by raids into the Balkan Peninsula that Cæsar planned a campaign against him. If all the tales of the time be true both Octavius and Antonius regarded the Dacian power as potentially a serious factor in the Second Civil War.

But when that was over the Dacian question became merged in the larger question which was then occupying the mind of Augustus, the pushing forward of the imperial frontier to the Danube. Still in 29 B.C. Marcus Crassus was sent to carry on a campaign on the lower Danube against the Dacians whose raids south of the river had been frequent and destructive. This campaign resulted in the reduction of Mœsia. Later, in A.D. 5, Lentulus invaded Dacia itself, and transported a large number of its people to the south side of the river. From this time for about eighty years the power of Dacia was under an eclipse.

But before this time came Augustus had begun his work on the middle Danube. In 12–10 B.C. Tiberius reduced Pannonia, —officially as far as the Danube, in fact probably not much beyond the Drave, for Pœtovio on that river became the legionary centre; and it is not till the time of Vespasian that legionary troops are found on the Danube above Singidunum (Belgrade), at Carnuntum and Vindobona. Still regiments of auxilia may have been stationed on the river before that reign. Legionary troops at Singidunum and Viminacium show that Mœsia was converted into a province early in Augustus' reign. The great Pannonian rising of A.D. 6–9 was a serious setback to arrangements on this frontier; but on its suppression matters remained very much *in statu quo*, though raids across the lower Danube severely harassed Thrace, which Augustus had left as a client kingdom under the princes of the Odrysæ, the most powerful tribe of the country.

Under Tiberius the old province of Illyricum, in which Pannonia had been included after conquest, was divided into two provinces, Pannonia and Dalmatia; and it was to Tiberius in the first instance that the road system of Dalmatia and Mœsia was due. Under him, too, Thrace was converted into a province in A.D. 21, only to be re-established as a vassal kingdom by the idiotic Caligula. Claudius however made it once more into a province.

DACIA

Frontier troubles on the middle Danube in the form of raids made it necessary in the days of Nero for the governor

---

[1] Coins of Thasos and Dyrrhachium (Epidamnos) are frequently found in Transylvania, the ancient Dacia.

of Mœsia to carry out a campaign north of the river. They were due to the inadequacy of the garrison of Mœsia, only two legions; and when during the civil war of 69 even these were withdrawn, raiding went on unchecked, so much so that when Vespasian succeeded to power he found it necessary to send Mucianus his right-hand man to clear the province and punish the invaders, a task which he performed most effectively. It was this chronic raiding which must have caused Vespasian to push forward the Pannonian legions to the river itself.

But while this was going on a new life was being put into the Dacian kingdom by a certain Decebalus, a second Burebista. He was not a mere land pirate or robber chief, but an able man who was determined to make a great kingdom, and had clear ideas as to the way to do it. In order to face the Romans he introduced among his own people the Roman military organisation. To Rome he was dangerous as the professed champion of the Thracians in Roman territory south of the river. In 86 he invaded Mœsia and defeated and killed the governor. Domitian found it necessary to move, and himself went to take charge of the Dacian War, though he left the actual command in the first instance to Cornelius Fuscus, who perished with his army, and then to Julianus, who was so successful in an invasion of Dacia that the jealous Domitian recalled him and his army and made peace in 91 on what were really disadvantageous terms.

It was somewhere about this time that Mœsia, probably owing to the large number of troops which had to be concentrated in the province, was divided into two, Upper and Lower Mœsia.[1] In the reign of Trajan Pannonia was similarly divided into an upper and a lower province, and for a similar reason.

It was left to Trajan to avenge the humiliation which Dacia had inflicted on Rome in the days of Domitian.

The history of the Roman empire has suffered irreparable loss in the disappearance of the sources for the history of the reign of Trajan; and consequently the story of his Dacian campaigns can only be pieced together from very fragmentary and uncertain evidence.

After annulling Domitian's treaty he collected a large army of legionaries with probably an equal number of auxilia. He prepared for the advance by carving a road along the cliffs of the great defile of Kazan by which the Danube breaks through between the Carpathians and the Balkans. The inscription which marked the exploit survives at the present day cut in the living rock on the south side of the river.

In his first campaign the attack was from the west by way of the Eiserne Thor Pass which debouches into the valley where

[1] For this policy, see p. 478.

stood Sarmizegethusa, the Dacian capital. But the result of
the campaign was certainly indecisive, and probably favourable
on the whole to the Dacians, for in the next winter of 101-2
they invaded Lower Mœsia in company, as it would seem, with
the Sarmatæ and Roxalani from the plains of Russia.

Early in 102 Trajan opened the second year's campaign
with a victory over the Sarmatæ near Nicopolis. He then
invaded Dacia, on this occasion from the south side through the
Rothethurm Pass. But it was not till the next year, 103, that
any decisive success was obtained. After that Decebalus made
peace on the best terms he could get, a peace which, as the sequel
showed, he had no intention of keeping. Nor apparently had
Trajan; for by 105 he had built the great bridge at Drobetæ
(Turn Severin). In this year the war began again. Decebalus'
plans for a great coalition against the Romans miscarried, and
in 107 Dacia was annexed by Rome. Colonists from various
parts of the empire settled in the country, which for nearly one
hundred and eighty years remained a Roman province, though
Hadrian would have evacuated it had he dared to do so.

The Balkan Peninsula

To the Balkan provinces of Rome the possession of Dacia
proved an unmixed blessing. The passage between the Eastern
Carpathians and the marshes of the Danube delta became so
dangerous for the former raiders from south Russia now that
a Roman garrison lay on its flank that the raids ceased. The
great natural fortress of Transylvania had always been a necessary
complement of the Danube line of defence.

Macedonia's history under the empire is not marked by incidents of supreme importance. In the division of provinces
under Augustus it was allotted to the Senate, probably because
the operations on the Save were regarded as having secured
it on the north. The towns retained their native constitutions;
but Thessaly, which formed part of the province, had its own
provincial council at Larissa distinct from that of the northern
part of the province, which met at Thessalonica. In the Principate of Tiberius Macedonia was amalgamated with Achaia and
transferred to the Cæsarian category of provinces; but Claudius
separated the two provinces once more, and restored it to the
Senate. Greece was economically speaking a ruined land whose
pitiable condition had been brought about in the first instance
by the follies of its own people in the fourth and third centuries
B.C., a ruin consummated by the wars with Rome and of Rome
in the first half of the second century. Pictures of its desolation
may be found in the famous and most pathetic letter of sympathy
which Sulpicius Rufus wrote to Cicero in 45 B.C. on the death of

his daughter Tullia, and scattered through the pages of Pausanias who traversed the land from end to end towards the close of the second century after Christ.

But though the wars and commercial rivalry of Rome under the later Republic had brought ruin on Greece, the Roman government under both the Republic and the empire treated the non-commercial Greek with extraordinary consideration and with but half-deserved respect. The Greek of the first century after Christ was living on the capital of an ancestral reputation, heir to an intellectual wealth which he only appreciated for the glamour it cast upon him in the eyes of those who attributed to him the intellectual capacity of a far-off ancestry. Having lost the creative ability of his forefathers, he maintained his reputation by discussion and rediscussion of the ideas which they had created, and by the invention of futile intellectual novelties, a " seeker after some new thing," as St. Paul sarcastically called him. But the Roman who had borrowed Stoicism and Epicureanism from him did not recognise that the source which had supplied those systems had run dry. Moreover the Roman regarded the Greek as politically harmless; and, whatever respect he had for his intellectualism, he regarded his politics, tested by their hopeless failure, as utter foolishness. He owed some things to the Greek; but naught on the political side.

So to Athens was left the position of a free federate state; and to various other towns, Tanagra, Delphi, Sparta, and others, the same freedom was allowed. Even the revolt of such communities, if it ever came to that, could never be more than a temporary annoyance. Patræ and Corinth were made Roman colonies, while the rest of Greece, with the exception of the northwest, formed the province of Achaia. North-west Greece was made into a free state under Nicopolis, the town Augustus had founded in commemoration of the victory of Actium. For the first century and a half of the Principate the Greeks enjoyed a fussy local life varied by the visits of Nero with his concert party and of that inveterate tourist Hadrian.

The Asiatic Provinces

The history of the Asiatic provinces during this period was, owing to the presence of the Parthian kingdom beyond the frontier, not devoid of excitement.

The basis of imperial organisation in the East was the settlement made by Pompeius in 62 B.C. The basis of imperial policy was an exaggerated fear of Parthia. Alexander had conquered western Asia because the Persia of that day had accepted pitched battles with European armies at times when the latter were not in difficulties due to their nature being ill adapted for war in the large desolate spaces of the Near East. Crassus and Antonius had failed because the Parthian of their day avoided such battles save when the circumstances were, as they were bound to be at times, overwhelmingly in his favour. Scared by their experiences, the Roman forgot that the case would be different if the Parthian were the invader, and had to fight the Romans on ground of the Romans' own choosing.

Of all the provinces of the empire the old province of Asia profited most from the changes in provincial administration made under the Principate. The farming of the direct taxes by the equestrian order of the days of the Republic, with all the abuses which had been connected with it, was done away; and the strict supervision of the acts of governors and their subordinates was a special blessing to a land whose wealth had always been a temptation to the impecunious or greedy administrator. It was a peaceful province permeated with Hellenic civilisation; and so it was allotted to the Senate. It became one of the wealthiest regions in the Roman world, a land of cities of great splendour.

To the Senate also was allotted the province of Bithynia, which included Pontus. Here civilisation was far more backward; and so the government did all that it could to promote the hellenisation of the region. The other old Republican province in Asia Minor, Cilicia, was at first administered as part of the Cæsarian province of Syria.

For the rest Augustus, adhering to the policy of the Republic, left in existence various client kingdoms which served as buffers between the empire and the outside world. The kingdom of Galatia, then ruled by Amyntas, a Celtic island in the midst of Hellenic or semi-Hellenic civilisation, which included the non-Celtic regions of Pisidia, Lycaonia, Isauria, and western Cilicia, continued to exist till the death of that king in 25 B.C., when it was converted into a Cæsarian province, except that Pamphylia, which had belonged to it, was made into a separate province. Hellenised under the empire, it became a wealthy region, though it was never free from the attention of the brigands who lived in the neighbouring mountains.

Cappadocia remained under Augustus a client kingdom, to be converted into a province under Tiberius. On the south-east shore of the Euxine about Trapezus and Colchis a Pontic kingdom continued in existence, as also a kingdom of Little Armenia, and various principalities of small size in Paphlagonia. The latter were absorbed in 7 B.C. On the north of the Euxine the now small kingdom of Bosphorus in the Crimea was a Roman dependency; and the Greek cities on that coast looked to Rome for a protection which they were fitfully accorded. Commagene, a kingdom on the upper Euphrates, was not finally included in the provincial system till the time of Vespasian, in A.D. 72, though it had been made a province by Tiberius, only to be restored to the position of a client state by Caligula.

In Syria the old province was made Cæsarian because a large army had to be maintained there as a protection against Parthia. Farther south Palestine had a variegated administrative history under the early empire. Julius Cæsar, with whom the Jews, for some reason not known, enjoyed peculiar favour, had made the Jews of Palestine all but free. After his death a period of confusion arose. When Augustus came to power Herod, supported by Rome, had made himself king of Judæa, in which position Augustus confirmed him. So Judæa settled down into a client kingdom. When he died in 4 B.C. he left his kingdom divided among his three sons, an arrangement which Rome confirmed. But as troubles resulted, Augustus in A.D. 6 converted Judæa into a province of the second rank under a procurator, the rest of Herod's kingdom surviving in the form of principalities. Under Claudius the procuratorship of Judæa was abolished, and it was handed over, together with Samaria, to Herod Agrippa, grandson of the first Herod. But in 44 he died, and the procuratorship was restored.[1]

PARTHIA

The Parthian kingdom which Rome feared as a danger to her eastern possessions was in a sense a revival of the old Persian monarchy; but, though the Parthians were Iranians like the Medes and Persians, they were traditionally members of the Scythian branch of that family of nations which had come from the north and won an empire over their kinsmen in west Asia, supplanting the Seleucids, and posing as the legitimate successors of the Persians. It was in the time of the Gracchi that Parthia extended its rule to the Euphrates at the expense of the Seleucid monarchy. At its greatest extent, in the time of the Julio-Claudian emperors of Rome, the Parthian kingdom extended from the Euphrates to the Indus, and perhaps beyond the latter river into India. How far north the kingdom stretched is uncertain.

As the Parthians had played a part in the struggles of the First Civil War, it was Cæsar's intention to conduct a campaign against them, a plan never realised in consequence of his assassination. In 41 B.C. the Parthians invaded Syria, defeated the governor, and overran the Roman possessions in Asia, but were driven out by Ventidius Bassus two years later, in 39. Of the

---

[1] For Rome's general policy towards the Jews, see p. 522.

Parthian expedition of Antonius in 36 B.C. there has already been occasion to speak.

When Augustus came to the throne he renounced all idea of conquest beyond the Euphrates at the expense of Parthia, but showed a firm determination to uphold Roman influence in Armenia, which was henceforth regarded as the strategic key to the relations between the two monarchies. The difficulty at the time, and later, was that the Armenians were much more predisposed in favour of the Parthians than of the Romans, and that any troubles of Rome in Armenia were sure to lead to trouble with Parthia also. For a few years all went well. Rome had installed Tigranes, a nominee of her own, as king of Armenia; and Parthia had restored the standards taken at Carrhæ. But on Tigranes' death the Parthian party in Armenia asserted itself, with the result that for some years there was confusion. But matters were settled in 1 B.C., and Parthia ceased to interfere in Armenia. A new nominee of Rome was set up as king of the country. Then he died, and another nominee, Vonones, was installed. And so the game went on, Rome setting up her nominees, and the Armenian people either pulling them down, or offering an unwilling obedience combined with intrigue with Parthia.

In the last years of Tiberius' reign Artabanus the Parthian king, mistakenly supposing that the old emperor was played out, got his son appointed king of Armenia; to which Rome replied by persuading the wild peoples of the Caucasus and beyond to make much trouble in Armenia itself, while she fomented trouble for Artabanus in his Mesopotamian possessions with such effect that with the aid of her Syrian legions she was able to place Tiridates, a nominee of her own, on the Parthian throne. But in A.D. 36 Artabanus was back again in so submissive a mood that Rome made peace with him. Caligula, with his usual genius for blundering, lost hold of Armenia; but Claudius restored Roman influence there,—all the more easily as there was civil war in Parthia at the time. Rome tried to set up a nominee of her own in Parthia, whom the Parthians, when they came to know him, treated with the contempt he deserved. Affairs in Armenia were naturally favourable to Roman policy so long as trouble reigned in Parthia; but on the accession of Vologasus, an able and cautious man, to the Parthian throne in 37, troubles began again.

The dreary story of these relations between Rome and Parthia under the early Principate suggests to the mind of him who reads it that Rome and Parthia were needlessly afraid of one another; and that, but for this mutual fear, occurrences in Armenia would have been a matter of indifference to both empires. This at any rate is certain, that, could they have been persuaded to leave Armenia alone, no other real cause of quarrel would have existed between them, since Rome certainly, and Parthia almost certainly, was quite ready to acquiesce in a frontier at the Euphrates, each empire having found that attempts at conquest on the side of that river farthest from them were apt to lead to disaster.

In 52 the usual dynastic quarrels began in Armenia. The king of the Iberians, a brother of Mithradates king of Armenia, wished to set up his son Rhadamistus as king of the latter country. Mithradates was murdered after being handed over to his rival by the commander of the Roman garrison in Armenia. The Roman governors of Cappadocia and Syria cared for none of these things, thinking it best to let the Armenians settle their own affairs their own bloody way; and, after they had cynically acknowledged Rhadamistus as king, all might have gone happily, as happiness was understood in those parts, had not Vologasus of Parthia invaded Armenia and placed his son on the throne. The Roman government now made up its mind that this process of pulling feathers out of the tail of the Roman eagle had gone far enough, and so sent Gnæus Domitius Corbulo, a man with the best military reputation of his day, to command in Cappadocia. This in the year 54.

Both the military and the political situation were curious. Corbulo found the Syrian legions a worthless army, and said so; while the Roman government, so far from wishing to do anything drastic, was quite ready to recognise Tiridates, Vologasus' son, as king of Armenia, provided that he would do homage to Rome. Which things being so, Corbulo could do nothing but negotiate with Parthia an accommodation which lasted till such a time as Tiridates showed plainly that he had no intention of carrying it out. In 58 Corbulo invaded Armenia with an army which he had rendered fairly efficient. At the same time the Iberians invaded that land from the north. Unable to get help from his father, who had troubles of his own on hand, Tiridates had to fly from Armenia after making a good show in an unequal fight. By the year 60 Armenia was in Roman hands. Again things might have gone well had not the new Roman nominee as king of Armenia, Tigranes, thought well to attack Parthian territory, an act which brought the Parthian king once more on the scene, with whom Corbulo, who was convinced that Rome would be well rid of the Armenian question, made an agreement which the Roman government would not ratify. And so it came once more to war. The war which followed brought more disaster than glory to Rome; but Vologasus was so weary and anxious that he conceded that his son should receive the

Armenian crown in Rome, provided Rome would accept him as king of Armenia. This agreement was carried out in 66.

Under the Flavian emperors the relations of Rome with Parthia were frequent but friendly, and so continued till the days of Trajan. Then trouble began again over the succession in Armenia. There ensued a war of which the main result was to show that the power of Parthia had greatly declined in strength, and emphasised the fact which had come to light in the days of Corbulo, that the Roman legions of the East had become so decadent as to be a danger rather than a defence to the empire. Yet with an army of very miscellaneous quality, and in a series of campaigns between 115 and 117, in which disaster played an almost equal part with success, Trajan was able to overrun rather than subdue Armenia and Mesopotamia; and, with a policy which did more credit to his ambition than to his statesmanship, to annex them as provinces of the empire. And then he died.

The cautious Hadrian, who had a narrow-minded wisdom in details, renounced Mesopotamia, and converted Armenia once more into a vassal kingdom of Rome.

Of Judæa and its administration it has been necessary to speak. But the relations of the Roman government with the Jews themselves both in Judæa and in other parts of the empire are far more interesting and important.

The attitude of the Roman government both under the Republic and under the empire was a tolerance such as might be expected in a world which hardly knew what intolerance meant. The Roman attitude in the matter is therefore nothing more than the expression of the feeling of a world in the mind of which religion and nationality were intimately associated; but, like the rest of that world, its religious prejudice was aroused when Roman citizens became devotees of some foreign cult to the neglect of the national worship. On the purely moral aspect of religion, however, the Roman government took its own line in that it resented the presence in Rome or Italy of any cult with which immoral practices were, or were suspected to be, associated; which accounts for the severity shown to the Bacchic cult in Italy in the first half of the second century before Christ. In the provinces it displayed absolute toleration towards the religions of provincials, except when they were associated with some barbarous practice, such as human sacrifice, inimical to civilisation, or tended to promote an anti-Roman nationalism among some race within the empire.

The Romans from the time of the first contact with the Jews were aware of two anomalous and disquieting features in the Jewish religion: a belief in the coming of a Messiah who should free them from the foreign dominion, and a proselytising tendency which spread the religion beyond the bounds of the Jewish race, not to speak of a religious fanaticism and belief which caused certain practical inconveniences in regard to the demands made on the subjects of Rome, military service, the performance of secular duties on the Sabbath, and, later, conformity to that worship of Cæsar which was to bind the empire together.

They soon found however that this superstition with regard to the Messiah was not really dangerous among a people which set far more store by religious rather than political independence so long as the ruling government respected, as the Seleucids had done, their national religion, and conceded those exemptions from secular service which the practice of that religion demanded. But the extension of these privileges by proselytism, and the extension of proselytism to Roman citizens, were inconveniences which might become dangers; and so the exemptions seem to have been limited to persons of Jewish birth, and did not apply to Jews who had become Roman citizens, while the proselytism at Rome was checked, and, under Tiberius, the practice of the religion in the capital was suppressed on various excuses other than the true grounds. Under Claudius all Jews were expelled from Rome, on what pretext is not known.

But, though severe towards Judaism in Rome, remarkable concessions were made to it in the provinces by the licensing of synagogues,[1] exemption from military service, and so forth, a liberality shown most prominently by Julius Cæsar, owing either to policy or to his cosmopolitanism, and imitated by the emperors.

In Judæa itself the government, ever anxious to avoid aught which might disturb the peace of the provinces, preserved a strict attitude of non-interference with religion until the silly Caligula outraged it by setting up his statue in the temple. To this was added some misgovernment of Roman officials, all of which led to the terrible war which ended in the capture of Jerusalem by Titus in 70, and the disappearance of the Jews from the officially recognised races of the empire, though in other respects the practice of their religion was allowed to go on the same as before.

The last bid which the Jews made for liberty was in the reign of Trajan, at the time when he was occupied with the troubles in Mesopotamia. In all the provinces in which they were numerous, Cyprus, Cyrenaica, Egypt, Mesopotamia, and Palestine, they suddenly rose in a rebellion marked by wholesale massacre and bloodthirsty cruelty. They met with their reward. In Egypt they were all but exterminated by the Greek population. From

---

[1] They came under the law of associations (collegia), which were not allowed to exist except on licence.

Cyprus they were henceforth excluded. In the other provinces large numbers of them perished.

Intimately connected at first with the Jewish question was that of Christianity in the empire. The connection was due to an error on the part of the governing class who regarded it as a sect of Judaism, till the troubles which arose between the Jews and Christians, and the rapid spread of Christianity among the Gentiles of the empire, undeceived them on this point. It then became an enigma to the Roman official because, though it claimed to be a religion, it had characteristics which the ancient mind did not associate with religion, above all a comprehensiveness which paid no regard to those differences of nationality which the ancient world looked upon as implying a natural difference of worship. The Jewish proselyte became to all intents and purposes a Jew : the Christian became nothing in particular. To the Roman this seemed contrary to the very nature of religion ; and he came to look on Christianity as a political conspiracy masquerading under the guise of religion, a view which seemed to be confirmed by the refusal of the Christian to take part in Cæsar worship, and by that hostility to the social manners of the day which cut him off from the social life of the time, an attitude which the world, as Tacitus says, put down to " hatred of the human race." Its spread among the servile class made it still more suspect with the authorities. The natural tendency of the Christians to form exclusive communities, and, owing to the hostility of their fellow-citizens, to hold their gatherings in secret, all went to confirm the idea that they were members of a secret political society aiming at the subversion of the existing political and social order of things. The Roman government had from time immemorial set its face against unauthorised societies of any kind as constituting a political danger, a view which might be justified by the circumstances of all ages of the world ; and so it is not strange that it sought to suppress by what has been called persecution an unauthorised society which seemed more formidable than any that had come into being up to that time. There are traces in the letters of Pliny and Trajan of the growth of a less mistaken view of the nature of Christianity ; but the suspicion with which the Christians were regarded by the Roman government died a very lingering death.

Egypt

To the Hellenic and Hellenistic worlds and to the world of the days of the Roman Republic Egypt had represented a source of corn supply so important that, had it been cut off, the margin of safety in respect to food would have ceased to exist in many of the countries on the north shore of the Mediterranean. Never

THE EMPIRE

perhaps was its importance greater in this respect than in the age of the Roman Principate. A third part of the corn necessary for the consumption of Rome was drawn from it. And so under the empire the government continued to show fear lest the control of the country should get into the hands of the disloyal, a possibility evaded under the Republic by the refusal to make it a province, and provided against in a special and peculiar way in the arrangements made by Augustus. Though it had now come under the direct rule of Rome, and though Augustus himself spoke of it with his usual diplomatic deceit as a province, its government, administration, and revenue were really organised as though the land were part of the private domain of the emperor. Though by far the most important of the provinces [sic], the emperors did not govern it through a proprætor of senatorial rank, but through a præfectus of the equestrian order, an official belonging essentially to their own department of administration. Their caution went even so far as to exclude from the country all men of senatorial rank who were not given special permission to visit it.

As a source of revenue for the Cæsarian side of the administration it was all-important, because it contributed more than any other region to the sources from which that revenue was drawn. This was due to a local financial system which was better organised than that of any other part of the ancient world, one having its roots in the days of the Pharaohs, and infinitely improved by the financial genius of the Ptolemies.

Nor was the personal rule of Cæsar in the country limited by the existence within it of numerous towns of Greek origin with a certain amount of local autonomy such as were scattered thickly through Asia Minor and Syria. Only two Greek cities existed in the country, Alexandria and Ptolemaïs. The other districts (nomes) had each its own town centre; but they were towns which had always been under the direct rule of the central government.

And so Egypt during the first centuries of the Empire went on living its immemorial life, " a land where all things always seemed the same," a land isolated from the rest of the world by nature, by customs, and by administration, and therefore undisturbed by the storms which passed over the other lands of the empire.

CYRENAICA

Cyrenaica had been made into a Roman province in 74 B.C. The island of Crete had been added to it. In the partition of the provinces at the beginning of the empire it had been assigned to the Senate. It had a large Jewish population which joined in the fierce Jewish rising of the reign of Trajan, displaying that same bloodthirsty cruelty which it showed in other lands affected by the same rebellion. Otherwise the history of the province was uneventful.

AFRICA

Under Julius Cæsar the old Republican province of Africa had been increased by the addition of Numidia, while it extended eastwards to the innermost corner of the Greater Syrtis. Westward of Numidia Mauretania, in the days of Augustus a client state to which he had appointed Juba as king, stretched to the shores of the Atlantic Ocean.

Augustus' policy in the whole of this region was exceptional in two respects : in Africa, though it was a province allotted to the Senate, he was obliged to allow a legion to be stationed,[1] owing to its southern frontier being exposed to the attacks of the nomad tribes of the desert ; in Mauretania, though it was a client kingdom, he established, with a view to civilising the country, colonies which were independent of the rule of Juba.

In Africa Rome had found a Punic civilisation tinctured by Greek influence. Following her usual policy she had adopted its main features in her organisation of the province, especially that Phœnician town community which was very similar to the town community of Italy. In respect to prosperity this part of the African continent attained to a height it has not known since. Nowhere perhaps may the blessings which Rome conferred on the Mediterranean world be more fully realised than in Tripoli, that land of proverbial desolation, where the remains of great irrigation schemes carried out under Roman rule, and of

[1] In many Roman histories this African legion is spoken of as having been under the command of the senatorial governor of Africa. The significance of the statement depends on the connotation of the term " command " as thus used. If it is intended to imply the sort of command which a Roman governor under the Republic exercised over the troops in his province, then I think the term is used mistakenly. I have no space wherein to elaborate the argument ; but I may state briefly two reasons for disagreeing with this view : (1) that it would have been contrary to the most important of all the principles of Augustus' policy to leave the command of an army to any governors save his own deputies in his own provinces; (2) that any difficulty arising from the fact that an army was required in this senatorial province could have been got over easily by resorting to that practice, prevalent in the days of the Republic, by which the governor of one province in cases of emergency placed troops at the disposal of the governor of another province. Those troops were a loan, not a gift. They were at the temporary disposal of him to whom they were lent ; but they were not his troops. That was, I take it, the position of the troops in Africa as between the emperor and the governor of the province. They were the emperor's troops ; and the commander of the legion (legatus legionis) was really responsible to Cæsar.

the cities to which they gave birth, are found in regions which are now once more part of the great realm of the sands of the Sahara.

Carthage, after its restoration by Cæsar, became once more the capital of the region, attaining eventually under Roman rule a size three times as great as that of Phœnician days. The remains of such cities as Lambæsis are eloquent of a life to which the modern world of Tunis has neither the wealth nor the wit to attain. The history of the province of Africa under the empire was on the whole unexciting.

In the region generally certain important changes were made in the reign of Caligula : the suppression of the client states of Mauretania, which were later divided into two Cæsarian provinces ; and the withdrawal of the African legion from the disposal of the senatorial governor of Africa by setting up Numidia as a sort of province which seems to have been under the control of the legionary legate. Under Claudius a rising in Mauretania took some years to suppress. It was on its suppression in A.D. 45 that the division of Mauretania into two provinces was finally carried out.

Of the two island provinces of the western Mediterranean, Sicily on the one hand and Sardinia and Corsica on the other, little need be said.

SICILY

When Augustus came to power Sicily was little if at all inferior to Italy in civilisation. Once the storm centre of the Mediterranean world, it lapsed under the empire into a peaceful province without a history ; and it was allotted to the Senate in the partition of provinces. Sardinia and Corsica were what the former has remained till the present day, lands of ill-repute, Corsica by reason of its inhabitants, Sardinia by reason of both its inhabitants and its climate. The emperors found the latter useful for expediting the departure of political exiles to another world. In 27 B.C. this island province was allotted to the Senate ; but in A.D. 6 Augustus had to take it over by reason of the attacks of pirates, which rendered it necessary to station troops there. Under Nero it was restored to the Senate, only to be reincluded among the Cæsarian provinces under Vespasian.

At the time at which this story closes, the end of the reign of Hadrian, the ancient world of southern Europe was passing through the second century of a life in which the happiness and prosperity of its peoples reached a level never attained in these lands at any other age in history. The spring of civilisation in the Mediterranean had been a stormy one ; but its summer was under the rule of Rome of a nature such as made life a joy, and of a duration such as has no parallel in the history of Europe. Perhaps, too, the enjoyment was heightened by its contrast with that life of those fiercer times before the Christian era during which it had brief experiences of the blessings of peace and prolonged sufferings from the horrors of war. The change was due to the magnificent fabric of government which Augustus established, a fabric so strong that it could not be ruined by the follies of a Caligula or a Nero, and so admirable that it encouraged his successors whatever their ability, whatever their character in private life,—and some of them were both able and good,—to make a conscientious endeavour to maintain it both in principle and in practice, a blessing to the millions of a world to which such a blessing had never come before. Looking back on the past there is only one period of Mediterranean history which can in that respect compare with that of the first two centuries of our era, the last three-quarters of the fifth century before Christ in the history of the Persian kingdom; and that is far more restricted both in respect to time and space in the benefits which it conferred on the peoples round the great inland sea. It is too the happiness of lethargy, rather than of active life. The Greek was formed by nature to contribute to the happiness of others rather than to attain to it himself. His was a delirious life of extremes. In art alone, not in life, did he attain that mean which he defined and sought. He failed where failure is irremediable,—in politics. Largely as the Roman borrowed from him in the world of philosophy and literature, he rejected utterly his political ideas as unpractical and unworkable. The enduring character of the Roman state system was due to the fact that the Roman world was governed by what were on the whole the best and most experienced practical intellects which the race could produce, whereas the ephemeral existence of governments in the Hellenic world was due to their policy being guided in the main by a mass of popular opinion which was necessarily inexperienced and too often ignorant. The condemnation of Greek political ideas is written in letters of blood in the history of the fourth and the third centuries before Christ. The Roman came far nearer than ever did the Greek to the realisation of those social ideals which are set forth in that great essay of Thucydides known as the Funeral Speech of Pericles.

Popular political enthusiasm when undirected is a danger; when misdirected is a catastrophe. The cheques which the intelligentzia draws on human nature have eventually to be referred to the drawer; for, though the dreamers have been able to provoke crises in the history of nations, they have never been able to control them.

Those political institutions which have been of most lasting beneficence in the history of the world have not been the outcome of popular movements or of the imaginings of dreamers, but of the ability of great men who have either originated them, or have, by their capacity for distinguishing the nature of the end which it is desirable to attain and the best means to its attainment, directed popular impulses towards a rational solution of political questions.

The reading and writing of any long period of history is apt to be destructive of those day dreams which men cherish of a victory of the good in human life won by the strength of the good itself. The abstract good cannot fight its own battles. They have to be fought by those who are prepared to risk their lives in its defence. Even the best ideas have to be backed by force in a world in which there are always those who are ready to fight for material advantages, to reap where they have not sown, to enjoy the fruits of the labour of others. It is the men with the best weapons and the best determination to use them who can inflict their ideas, good, bad, or indifferent, on the world of their day. The ideas may not be necessarily their own; they may have been adopted from others: but it is they who are in a position to put them into practice. The Roman state passed through three stages of political morality. Under the early Republic its people fought for liberty against internal oppression and external aggression. Under the later Republic, tainted by the new commercialism, they fought to maintain those gains and advantages which had come to them by dint of war. Under the government and direction of the emperors they fought to maintain a peace which should be a blessing to themselves and to the population of the empire. But whatever their aspirations, high or low, they attain them by fighting for them, and, to come to the crudest but most effective factor in their history, by the possession, in the form of the Spanish sword, of the most effective weapon of their time. It was on the point of that sword that Roman ideas were handed down to the modern world, even as Greek ideas had been thrust upon the world of western Asia on the point of the Macedonian spear.

The lessons which history teaches are almost brutal in their simplicity; and those to be drawn from the story of the ancient world are such as no author can disguise without falsifying the story itself.

INDEX

Acarnania, 187, 193, 194
Achæan League, 332; constitution, 335 f., 339 f., 341, 356
Achæans, 21 f.; institutions, 23 f.; in Crete, 28; colonies in Italy, 64 f.
Achæmenids, 84; Alexander, 274
Acragas, Agrigentum, 67
Actium, 450
Ægina, 126, 164
Ætolian League, 332; constitution, 332 f., 340
Africa, 359; first Civil War, 439; under the Principate, 526
Agrarian Legislation, 366 ff., 371 f.
Agriculture, Greece, 95 f.; Rome, 301 f.
Agrippa (Marcus), 449; Actium, 450
Alcibiades, 201 ff.
Alcmæonids, 97; medism, 132
Alexander the Great, 268 ff.; policy and administration, 273 ff., 275; campaign in the East, 274 f.; organization of empire, 276 ff.
Alexandria, 273, 326
Alyattes, 14 n., 104
Amasis, 109 f.
Amphipolis, 177, 198, 256
Antalcidas (Peace of), 246
Anthology (Greek), 41 n., 44 n., 49, 76 n.
Antipater, 276
Antonius (Marcus), 438, 446 f.; the second Civil War, 446 ff.
Appian, 53 n., 116 n.
Aquitania, 13 n., 435, 506
Aratus, 332 ff.
Arcadia, 158, 232, 251
Archidamus, 188
Argos, 70 n., 101, 120 f., 126, 137, 158, 202
Aristides, 133, 145, 150, 155, 157
Aristocracies, 52
Aristotle, the Politics, 239; the Ethics, 263 f.
Armenia, 82; and Mithradates, 419, 424 f., 429, 438; time of the Principate, 520 f.
Armies (see Warfare), Marian Army, 377 ff., 437; Augustan, 453; under the Principate, 475 ff.; in A.D. 69, 491 f.; under Hadrian, 498; decadence of Syrian Legions, 521–2;

army in Africa under the Principate 526 and n.
Artaphernes, 123, 128
Asia (Roman Province), taxation, 400; Mithradates, 411; Sulla's settlement, 411; under the Principate, 517 f.
Asia Minor, general topography, 3 f.; ethnography, 15 f., 52
Assyria, 53, 79, 80 f.; fall, 81 f.
Ἀθηναίων πολιτεία, 74 n., 93 n., 94 n., 170 n., 213
Athens, 73; sixth century, 91; parties in fifth century, 116 ff.; Ionian Revolt, 123 f.; party history, 510–490 B.C., 128 ff.; Marathon, 127 f., 130 ff.; party history, 490–480 B.C., 132 f.; party history, 478–462 B.C., 153 f.; beginnings of Empire, 158 f.; War, 459–446 B.C., 162 f.; Unemployment, 170 f.; the Empire, 173 f.; citizenship, 177; Thirty Years' Peace, 177; Peloponnesian War, 184 ff.; parties, 187; the Ten Years' War, 191 ff.; politics, 431–421 B.C., 200 f.; Sicilian Expedition, 204 ff.; mutilation of the Hermæ, 205 f.; Revolution of the Four Hundred, 212 f.; tyranny of the Thirty, 219 f.; constitutional changes, 230 f.; second confederacy, 248 f.; Philip of Macedon, 257 ff.; Alexander the Great, 269, 319, 517
Augustus Cæsar, family origin, 440; ideas, 441 f.; the Imperial system, 441 f., 446; the second Civil War, 446 ff.; organization of the government of the empire, 452 ff.; arrangements of 27 B.C., 452; settlement of 23 B.C., 454; census, 468 f.
Auxilia in the Roman Army, 482 f.

Babylonia, 83 f.
Bithynia, Bithynians, 16; province under the Principate, 518
Bœotia, 137, 177, 191, 248
Brasidas, 192, 193, 198 f., 199 and n.
Breitenbach, Hellenica of Xenophon, 253 n.

531

Britain, Cæsar's expedition, 435 ; Claudius' expedition, 489 f. ; as a province, 510 f.
Bury, Prof., 64 n., 92 n.
Byzantium, 176, 243, 215
Caligula or Gaius, 487 f.
Cappadocia, 16, 80, 429 ; under the Principate, 518
Carchemish, 16
Carthage, 17, 53, 86, 110, 152 f., 220 f., 302 ff. ; Constitution, etc., 304, 359 f.
Caria, 16, 124
Catiline, 427 f.
Cavaignac, M. Eugene, 13
Celts, in West Europe, 6 ; in Italy, 225, 292, 308, 309 n. ; in Greece and Asia, 321, 323, 329 ; in Gaul and Britain, 436
Censorship (at Rome), p. 169
Chalcis, 64, 65 ff.
Cheeseman, Mr. G. L., 484 n.
Christianity, 524
Cicero, letters, 401 n., 423 ff. and passim to 445 ; letters, 423, 427 n. ; Pompeius, 426, 430 ; the Triumvirs, 430 ff. ; exile, 431 ; Cæsar's death, 445 ; letters, 445 n. ; after Cæsar's death, 446 ; death, 447
Cimbri, 376
Cimmerians, 79 ff.
Cimon, 156, 161, 177
Cinna, Cinnan Government, 409
Civilization, types, 2 ; Hellenistic in the East, 277–8 ; in Italy, 316, 331 f. ; in Roman policy, 298 ; Hellenistic, 342
Claudius (Emperor), Bureaux at Rome, 471 ; the Fiscus, 472 f. ; as emperor, 488 ; general policy, 489 ; Britain, 489
Cleisthenes, 70 ; constitution, 97
Cleomenes, 123, 125 ff.
Cleon, 195, 199
Colonization, Greek, 559 ff.
Comitia (at Rome), 57, 113 f. ; Tributa, 169 ; especially Tributa, 252 f. ; Senate, 364 ; decline in prestige, 406 ; Centuriata, 414, 417 ; under the Principate, 458
Commagene, under the Principate, 518 f.
Communications, effect on life, 31 ff. ; under the Principate, 503 f.
Concilium Plebis, 116, 168, 283 f., 285, 408 ; under the Principate, 458
Consuls, form of choice, 58
Corcyra, colonies, 63, 66, 184 ff., 193, 194
Corinth, Corinthians, colonization, 65, 66, 101 ; at Salamis, 144, 145, 163 f., 178, 185 f.
Corn Supply, Egypt, 4 ; Troy, 29 ; Rome, 61 f., 186

Corsica, ethnography, 7 ; under the Principate, 527
Crassus, 420, 424, 428 n., 430 ; Carrhæ, 432
Crete, Minoan civilization, 8 ff. ; civilization in Asia Minor, 50
Crœsus, 104 f.
Curiæ, Comitia Curiata, 56 f., 282
Cyprus, Cretan settlement, 19 ; Assyria, 81, 124, 177
Cypselus, 68
Cyrene, 68 ; under the Principate, 525 f.
Cythera, 195
Cyrus, 103 ; Lydia, 105, 106
Cyrus (the younger), 216

Dacia, 497, 498, 513 ff.
Darius, 121 f. ; 134 f.
Dates, Oriental history, 78 ; Hellenistic monarchies, 281 ; Roman Emperors, 451
Decelea, 210, 211
Delian League, 185 ; removal of Treasury from Delos, 174
Delphi, Crœsus, 105 ; in 480, 137, 142 ; the snake pillar, 152
Demetrius Poliorcetes, 319 ff.
Democrats (at Rome), from 366, passim
Demosthenes (general), 192, 194 f., 199 n., 209
Demosthenes (orator), 257 ff., 269, 276
Dickins, Mr. Guy, 99 n., 100 n., 101 n.
Dionysius of Halicarnassus, 54
Dionysius of Syracuse, 221, 261 f.
Dionysius of Syracuse (the younger), 262
Domitian, as emperor, 495 f.
Dorians, 29 f. ; in Caria, 52
Draco, code, 74 and n. and 93 f.
Dyrrhachium, 438

Egypt, general topography, 4 f. ; corn supply, 5 ; attacks on, 19 ; Greeks, 84 f., 162 f., 273, 318 ff., 325, 327, 358 ; Cæsar and Pompeius, 438 ; Antonius and Cleopatra, 448 ff. ; annexation by Rome, 450 ; under the Principate, 524
Elis, 202 f.
Epaminondas, 248, 250, 251, 253
Epicurean Philosophy, 344 ; in Rome, 392, 501
Equestrian Order, 373 f., 380, 394 f., 400, 413, 421, 424, 430 ; under the Principate, 463 f. ; in the bureaux at Rome, 472 ; financial element expelled, 473 ; Hadrian, 497 f.
Eretria, 64, 124, 130 f.
Etruria, Etruscans, 6 ; origin, 20 f., 46 ; rule in Rome, 87 ff., 224, 292

INDEX

Eurymedon, political significance of the battle, 154, 156, 159, 171
Euxine, Greek colonies, 62–3
Ezekiel, 82 and n.

Farnell, Dr., 36 n.
Frontier System, Rome, 467 f., 498, 512
Fustel de Coulanges, 27 n., 40 n.

Galatia (see Celts), under Principate, 518
Galba, 492
Gardner, Prof. P., 172 n.
Gaul, Gauls, Celts in, 6 n., 46, 54, 222; Narbonensis, 377; the Gallic War, 434 ff.; organization under the Principate, 505 ff.
Gelo, 153
Germany, Germans, Ariovistus, 435; Province of, 468, 509 f.
Gnossos, 8 f.; fall, 18 f.
Gracchus (Tiberius), 366 ff.
Gracchus (Gaius), 372 f.
Granicus, battle, 271
Greece, Ethnography, 9 ff.; first invasion from the north, 18 f.; early communities, 51, 117, 227, 245; relations with Rome, 308, 330, 339, 350, 353; reduced by Rome, 354, 356; under the Principate, 517
Greeks, original home, 21; origin of name, 64 f. and n.; in Egypt, 109 f.; Alexander, 277 f.; democratic constitutions, 287 f., 331; Hellenistic culture, 331
Greenidge, Dr. A. H., 70 n., 169
Gyges, 78 ff.

Hadrian, military organization, 482; local recruiting, 482; changes in the Auxilia, 483; imperial officials, 494; as emperor, 497 f.
Hannibal, 309 ff.; relations with Philip of Macedon, 341
Hellas, Hellenes, origin of name, 64 f.
Hellenism, in the East, 331 f.; in Roman life,
Herodotus, 11 and n.; tomb of Alyattes, 14 n.; Phœnicians, 18; the Etruscans, 20; tyranny, 74; Assyria, 81; Media, 83 f.; Egypt, 85, 109 n. n., 110 and n.; the Ionian Greeks, 122 f., 127; Marathon, 128; Themistocles, 133, 144, 146; autopsy, 138 n.; Thermopylæ, 141; Salamis, 142 f., 145; Platæa, 150 and n. ff.; as a historian, 228 f., 513
Hiero (the second), 303 f.
Hieronymus, 466 n.
Himera, battle, 153
Hippias, 97, 129

Hittites, 16, 52
Hogarth, Dr. D. G., 14 n., 15 n.
Holroyd, Mr. M., preface
Homer, Iliad, 11 n., 24, 26 and n.
Hortensia, Lex, 284 f.

Iberians, in West Europe, 5 f.
Illyria, Illyrians, Illyricum, 21, 514
Ionian Greeks, possible origin, 12 ff.; settlement in Asia, 47; Lydia and Cyrus, 104, 105; culture, 107 f.; Ionian Revolt, 122 ff.
Ionian War, 210 ff.
Isocrates, 239 f.
Issus, battle, 272
Italians (see Socii), municipalities, 444; in the legions of the Principate, 480 f.
Italy, ethnography, 61; early, 46; the Alpine tribes under the Principate, 512

Jeremiah, 83 and n.
Jews, 326, 429; Palestine under the Principate, 519; Rome and the Jews, 522 f.
Jugurthine War, 375
Julius Cæsar, 423, 426; Catiline, 428; in Spain, 430; First Triumvirate, 431; the Senate, 432 f.; Gallic War, 434 f.; Civil War, 436 ff.; Legislation, 439 f.; Ideal of government compared with Augustus, 440 f.; methods of government, 442 f.; as a statesman, 443 f.

Latins, 226 f.
Leaf, Dr. Walter, 29
Lepidus, the second Civil War, 446 ff.
Leuctra, 250 f.
Ligurians, general distribution, 6
Livius Drusus, 402
Livy, 54
Long Walls, 165, 190, 252 n.
Lydia, Lydians, 16; Tomb of Alyattes, 14 n., 52, 77, 104 f.
Lysander, 216, 241 f.

Macan, Dr. R. W., 138 n.
Macedon, Macedonians, 254 ff., 318, 320, 322, 333, 335, 350 f., 354, 355; under the Principate, 516
Mæcenas, 449
Malta, 7
Mantinea, 202 f., 253
Mardonius, 127, 146, 148 ff.
Marius, 376, 377 ff., 389 f., 402 ff., 407, 409
Massilia, 54, 62, 67, 87, 112; Julius Cæsar, 437
Mauretania, 526
Medes, Media, 82, 83, 103 f.

Mediterranean Region, physical characteristics, 2
Megara, colonies, 63, 163, 177, 186, 191
Melos, 203 f.
Mesopotamia, 16
Messenia, 77, 251 f.
Metics, 134 and n.
Miletus, colonization, 63 f. and 79; Egypt, 86
Military Developments (see War, Art of), 89
Miltiades, 122, 129, 131
Mithradates, 408 f.; wars with Rome, 410 ff., 424 f., 429
Mœsia, 468, 514
Mommsen, 462 n.
Mycale, 152
Mycenæ, 9 f., 23; culture, 23 f.
Mysia, Mysians, 16
Mytilene, 199

Nahum, 82
Naucratis, 110
Naupactus, 162
Navigation, 48
Naxos, 123, 159
Nero, as emperor, 490
Nerva, as emperor, 496
Nicias, Peace of, 199, 203, 205 f., 209
Nisæa, 95, 192
Noricum, 468, 512
Numidia (see Jugurthine War), Juba, 439; made a province, 467, 526

Oeniadæ, 193
Otho, 492

Pannonia, 449, 468, 513
Parthia, 330, 448, 449, 467, 519 f.; in time of the Principate, 522
Patricians, at Rome, 113
Pausanias (author), 14 n., 75 n., 516 f.
Pausanias (Spartan), 148 ff., 155, 158
Pelasgi, 11 f.
Pelham, Prof. H., 57
Perdiccas, 186, 198
Pergamum, 323, 329, 330, 341, 352, 358
Periander, 68
Pericles, 161, 177 f.; strategy, 188
Persia, Persians, 84 f., 103, 159; Peace of Callias, 177, 211, 242 f,. 252, 270 ff.
Pharnabazus, 211 ff.
Pharsalus, battle, 438
Philip of Macedon, 254 ff.
Philippi, battle, 447
Philistines, 19
Philopœmen, 341 f.
Phocæa, colonization, 67, 111
Phocis, 256
Phœnicia, Phœnicians, in the Ægean, 17 f. and 50
Phrygia, Phrygians, 16, 52 f., 79

Pisistratus, 95 ff.
Placentia, 311 n.
Platæa, 125; battle, 148 ff., 191
Plato, 60; political philosophy, 235 f.
Pliny, letters, 466; in Bithynia, 497, 500
Plutarch, Solon, 92–3, 147, 162, 170 n.
Polybius, 288
Pompeius, 418 ff.; character and aims, 422 f.; command in Asia, 425 ff.; settlement of Asia, 429; Cicero, 430; First Triumvirate, 431 ff.; Civil War, 436 ff.
Pompeius, Sextus, 446; Civil War, 447 f.
Pontus, 323, 518
Principate, the, 451 onwards, succession, 454 f., 493
Proconsulship and Promagistracy, 300, 415, 470 n.
Property in Land, 26
Provinces (see Rome), government under Cæsar, 444; under the Principate, 463, 465 f., 467 f., 502 ff.
Psammetichus, 85–6
Pteria, 16
Ptolemies, 318 ff.
Punic Wars, first, 302 ff.; second, 309 ff.; third, 359 f.
Pyrrhus of Epirus, 293, 294, 322
Pythagoras, Pythagoreans, in S. Italy, 102

Quæstiones, 414 f., 474

Raetia, 468, 512
Religion, 36 ff.; association with politics, 39 ff.; ancestor worship, 40 ff.; Alexander the Great, 273; at Rome, 317; king worship, 326 f.; Cæsar worship, 484 f.; Domitian, 496
Republicans, under the Principate, 452, 456, 460, 487; Nero, 490; academic, 493; Domitian, 495, 500, 501
Rhetoric, 183 ff.
Rhodes, 319, 324 f., 338, 352, 358
Roads, 33 ff., 503 f.
Rome (see Senate, Comitia, etc.), foundation and early history, 54 ff.; early Republic, 112 ff., 167 ff., 222 ff.; Licinian Laws, 223; imperialism, 224; magistracy, 280 f.; mos majorum, 286; characteristics of the lower classes, 289 f.; imperialism, 293 f.; organization of conquests, 295; army, 299; imperialism, 307 f.; relations with Greece, 308; trade, 316; provincial government, 345; war with Macedon, 351; war with Persius of Macedon, 354; commercialism, 356;

INDEX

provincial government, 357; increase in number of magistrates, 362 n.; Lex Claudia of 218, 369; the Democrats, 389 f.; provincial government, 395 f.; the First Triumvirate, 431 f.; Conference at Luca, 432; First Civil War, 436 ff.; Second Triumvirate, 447; government bureaux in Rome, 471 f.; finance under the Principate, 468 f., 472; judicial administration under the Principate, 474; social life under the Principate, 499 f.
Rostovtseff, Prof., 63 n., 79 n.
Rutilius Rufus, 381 f.

Salamis, 95; battle, 141 ff.
Salvian, 466 n.
Samnites, 167, 224, 226 f., 291 f.
Samos, Polycrates, 106; revolt, 179
Sardinia, ethnography, 6–7, 307; under the Principate, 527
Saturninus, 390
Scipio, 314
Scythians, 79; expedition of Darius, 122, 258
Seleucids, 318 ff., 429
Senate at Rome, 58, 88, 285, 360 ff.; power after time of Gracchus, 370 ff., 402, 408; new members, 408; B.C. 69–60, 421 ff., 430; under Cæsar, 444; under the Principate, 459 ff.; encroachments on the senatorial department, 462 f.; senatorial civil service, 463 f.; judicial powers under the Principate, 474; Tiberius, 487; under the Flavians, 493; Domitian, 495; Nerva, 496; Trajan, 497
Sicily (see Western Greeks), ethnography, 7; colonization, 66; intellectual development, 181, 196 f., 220 f.; Carthage, 306, 345; tax-farming, 400; under the Principate, 527
Sicyon, 101
Slaves, Slave Labour, 117, 170
Socii in Italy, 348, 372; Social War, 404; as Roman citizens, 405, 430
Socrates, 244
Solon, 91 f.
Spain, ethnography, 5 f., 45, 54, 112, 222, 309, 314, 346, 347, 359; Sertorius, 418; in the First Civil War, 436 f.; under the Principate, 503, 504
Sparta, policy, 29; cultural development, 30, 76; Pisistratids, 97; sixth century, 98 ff.; policy in the fifth century, 119 f.; before Platæa, 148, 158, 160; revolt of the Helots, 161, 163 and n.; Peloponnesian War, 187, 202 f.; Lysander's policy, 218; politics, 240 ff., 243, 246 f.; Philip of Macedon, 260, 274 n., 333, 336; Cleomenes, 336 f.; battle of Sellasia, 337
Stoic Philosophy, 343; in Rome, 392, 501
Sulla, 376, 406 ff.; legislation of, 88 B.C., 408 and 413; constitution, 413 f.; reaction against constitution, 419 f.
Sybaris, 64
Syracuse, 66, 196 ff., 204 ff.
Syria, general topography, 3; Pompeius, 429; under the Principate, 519

Tacitus [Agricola], 400 n., 493, 501, 511
Taras, Tarentum, 66, 292
Tax Farming, 374 f.
Tempe, 139
Thasos, 161
Thebes, 247 f., 260
Themistocles, 133 f., 139, 140 n.; at Salamis, 143 f.; as political leader, 147, 156 f., 158, 202
Theramenes, 214, 218, 219 f.
Thermopylæ, 139 ff.
Thessaly, 70, 137, 139, 252, 256
Thrace, 122, 514
Thucydides, the Etruscans, 20 and n., 61 and n., 144 and n., 160 n., Bk. I, ch. 103, 160 n., 183; causes of the Peloponnesian War, 187 n., 190 n., 195 n. 2, 197 n., 199 n., 201, 204; Syracuse, 205, 208, 209 n.; as a historian, 229
Tiberius, as emperor, 486 f.
Timoleon, 262
Tiryns, 10
Tissaphernes, 211 ff.
Titus, as emperor, 494
Trade, Greek, 61 f., 301; Roman, 301, 316 f.; Rome, 348
Trajan, centralization, 497; distribution of the legions, 482; as emperor, 496
Tribunate, at Rome (see Rome), 285, 363, 413 f., 421
Troy, Trojan War, 22 n.
Tyrants, 74 f.
Tyre, siege of, 272

Unity of Hellas, 135 f., 240

Valerio-Horatian Laws, 168
Veneti (Italy), 6
Veneti (Gaul),
Vespasian, recruiting for the army, 480, 492
Vitellius, 492

Wace and Thompson, 14
Warde-Fowler, Dr. W., 36 n.

536 A HISTORY OF THE GREEK AND ROMAN WORLD

Warfare, Art of, Greek methods, 189 f., 194; naval, 210 f.; changes, 233 f.; Leuctra, 250; Macedonia, 255; Macedonian, 271; Rome, 294; Roman and Carthaginian naval, 305; Roman and Carthaginian armies, 312; general, 352 f., 377 ff.

Western Greeks (*see* Sicily), 102, 152, 166, 261, 292, 302; influence on Italian civilization, 316

Xenophon, 243, 244; his works, 253
Xerxes, 135

Printed in Great Britain by Butler & Tanner Ltd., Frome and London

METHUEN'S GENERAL LITERATURE

A SELECTION OF
MESSRS. METHUEN'S PUBLICATIONS

This Catalogue contains only a selection of the more important books published by Messrs. Methuen. A complete catalogue of their publications may be obtained on application.

PART I. GENERAL LITERATURE

Armstrong (Anthony) ("A.A.")
WARRIORS AT EASE. WARRIORS STILL AT EASE. PERCIVAL AND I. HOW TO DO IT. *Each* 3s. 6d. *net.*

Ashby (Thomas).
SOME ITALIAN SCENES AND FESTIVALS. With 24 Illustrations. *Crown 8vo.* 7s. 6d. *net.*

Bain (F. W.)
A DIGIT OF THE MOON. THE DESCENT OF THE SUN. A HEIFER OF THE DAWN. IN THE GREAT GOD'S HAIR. A DRAUGHT OF THE BLUE. AN ESSENCE OF THE DUSK. AN INCARNATION OF THE SNOW. A MINE OF FAULTS. THE ASHES OF A GOD. BUBBLES OF THE FOAM. A SYRUP OF THE BEES. THE LIVERY OF EVE. THE SUBSTANCE OF A DREAM. *All Fcap. 8vo.* 5s. *net.* AN ECHO OF THE SPHERES. *Wide Demy 8vo.* 10s. 6d. *net.*

Balfour (Sir Graham)
THE LIFE OF ROBERT LOUIS STEVENSON. Twentieth Edition. In one Volume. *Cr. 8vo. Buckram,* 7s. 6d. *net.*

Barker (Ernest)
NATIONAL CHARACTER. *Demy 8vo.* 10s. 6d. *net.* GREEK POLITICAL THEORY: Plato and his Predecessors. Second Edition. *Demy 8vo.* 14s. *net.*

Belloc (Hilaire)
PARIS. THE PYRENEES. *Each* 8s. 6d. *net.* ON NOTHING. HILLS AND THE SEA. ON SOMETHING. THIS AND THAT AND THE OTHER. ON. *Each* 6s. *net.* FIRST AND LAST. ON EVERYTHING. ON ANYTHING. EMMANUEL BURDEN. *Each* 3s. 6d. *net.* MARIE ANTOINETTE. 18s. *net.* A HISTORY OF ENGLAND. In 5 vols. Vols. I, II, III and IV. 15s. *net* each. HILLS AND THE SEA. Illustrated in Colour by Donald Maxwell. 15s. *net.*

Birmingham (George A.)
A WAYFARER IN HUNGARY. Illustrated. 8s. 6d. *net.* SPILLIKINS. SHIPS AND SEALING-WAX. Two Books of Essays. *Each* 3s. 6d. *net.*

Budge (Sir E. A. Wallis)
A HISTORY OF ETHIOPIA: NUBIA AND ABYSSINIA. Illustrated. In 2 vols. £3 13s. 6d. *net.*

Chandler (Arthur), D.D.
ARA CŒLI. 5s. *net.* FAITH AND EXPERIENCE. 5s. *net.* THE CULT OF THE PASSING MOMENT. 6s. *net.* THE ENGLISH CHURCH AND REUNION. 5s. *net.* SCALA MUNDI. 4s. 6d. *net.*

Chesterton (G. K.)
THE BALLAD OF THE WHITE HORSE. 3s. 6d. *net.* Also illustrated by ROBERT AUSTIN. 12s. 6d. *net.* CHARLES DICKENS. 3s. 6d. *net.* GENERALLY SPEAKING. ALL THINGS CONSIDERED. TREMENDOUS TRIFLES. FANCIES VERSUS FADS. ALARMS AND DISCURSIONS. A MISCELLANY OF MEN. THE USES OF DIVERSITY. THE OUTLINE OF SANITY. *Each Fcap. 8vo.* 6s. *net.* A GLEAM-

MESSRS. METHUEN'S PUBLICATIONS 3

ING COHORT. *Fcap. 8vo.* 2s. 6d. net.
WINE, WATER, AND SONG. *Fcap. 8vo.* 1s. 6d. net.

Clutton-Brock (A.)
WHAT IS THE KINGDOM OF HEAVEN? ESSAYS ON ART. SHAKESPEARE'S HAMLET. *Each* 5s. net. ESSAYS ON BOOKS. MORE ESSAYS ON BOOKS. ESSAYS ON LIFE. ESSAYS ON RELIGION. ESSAYS ON LITERATURE AND LIFE. MORE ESSAYS ON RELIGION. *Each* 6s. net. SHELLEY, THE MAN AND THE POET. 7s. 6d. net.

Cottenham (The Earl of)
MOTORING WITHOUT FEARS. Illustrated. 2s. 6d. net. MOTORING TO-DAY AND TO-MORROW. Illustrated by A. E. HORNE 5s. net.

Crawley (Ernest)
THE MYSTIC ROSE. Revised and Enlarged by THEODORE BESTERMAN. Two Vols. *Demy 8vo.* £1 10s. net. STUDIES OF SAVAGES AND SEX. Edited by THEODORE BESTERMAN. *Demy 8vo.* 10s. 6d. net.

Dolls' House (The Queen's)
THE BOOK OF THE QUEEN'S DOLLS' HOUSE. Vol. I. THE HOUSE, Edited by A. C. BENSON, C.V.O., and Sir LAWRENCE WEAVER, K.B.E. Vol. II. THE LIBRARY, Edited by E. V. LUCAS. Profusely Illustrated. A Limited Edition. *Crown 4to.* £6 6s. net.
EVERYBODY'S BOOK OF THE QUEEN'S DOLLS' HOUSE. An abridged edition of the above. Illustrated. *Crown 4to.* 5s. net.

Dugdale (E. T. S.)
GERMAN DIPLOMATIC DOCUMENTS, 1871-1914. Selected from the Documents published by the German Foreign Office. In 4 vols. Vol. I, 1871-90. Vol. II, 1891-8. *Demy 8vo.* Each £1 5s. net.

Edwardes (Tickner)
THE LORE OF THE HONEYBEE. Thirteenth Edition. 7s. 6d. net. BEEKEEPING FOR ALL. 3s. 6d. net. THE BEE-MASTER OF WARRILOW. Third Edition. 7s. 6d. net. All illustrated. BEE-KEEPING DO'S AND DON'TS. 2s. 6d. net.

Einstein (Albert)
RELATIVITY: THE SPECIAL AND GENERAL THEORY. 5s. net. SIDELIGHTS ON RELATIVITY. 3s. 6d. net. THE MEANING OF RELATIVITY. 5s. net. THE BROWNIAN MOVEMENT. 5s. net. *Write for Complete List of books on Relativity.*

Erman (Adolph)
THE LITERATURE OF THE ANCIENT EGYPTIANS: POEMS, NARRATIVES, AND MANUALS OF INSTRUCTION FROM THE THIRD AND SECOND MILENNIA B.C. Translated by Dr. A. M. BLACKMAN. *Demy 8vo.* £1 1s. net.

Fouquet (Jean)
THE LIFE OF CHRIST AND HIS MOTHER. From Fouquet's "Book of Hours." Edited by FLORENCE HEYWOOD, B.A. With 24 Plates in Colours. In a box. *Crown 4to.* £3 3s. net.

Fyleman (Rose)
FAIRIES AND CHIMNEYS. THE FAIRY GREEN. THE FAIRY FLUTE. THE RAINBOW CAT. EIGHT LITTLE PLAYS FOR CHILDREN. FORTY GOOD-NIGHT TALES. FAIRIES AND FRIENDS. THE ADVENTURE CLUB. FORTY GOOD-MORNING TALES. SEVEN LITTLE PLAYS FOR CHILDREN. *Each* 3s. 6d. net. OLD-FASHIONED GIRLS. Illustrated by ETHEL EVERETT. 7s. 6d. net. A SMALL CRUSE, 4s. 6d. net. THE ROSE FYLEMAN FAIRY BOOK. Illustrated by HILDA MILLER. 10s. 6d. net. A GARLAND OF ROSE'S: COLLECTED POEMS. Illustrated by RENÉ BULL. 8s. 6d. net. LETTY. Illustrated. 6s. net. A PRINCESS COMES TO OUR TOWN. Illustrated. 5s. net. A LITTLE CHRISTMAS BOOK. Illustrated. 2s. net.

Gibbon (Edward)
THE DECLINE AND FALL OF THE ROMAN EMPIRE. With Notes, Appendixes, and Maps, by J. B. BURY. Illustrated. Seven volumes. *Demy 8vo.* 15s. net each volume. Also, unillustrated. *Crown 8vo.* 7s. 6d. net each volume.

Glover (T. R.)
THE CONFLICT OF RELIGIONS IN THE EARLY ROMAN EMPIRE. POETS AND PURITANS. VIRGIL. *Each* 10s. 6d. net. FROM PERICLES TO PHILIP. 12s. 6d. net.

Graham (Harry)
THE WORLD WE LAUGH IN: More Deportmental Ditties. Illustrated by "FISH." Seventh Edition. 5s. net. STRAINED RELATIONS. Illustrated by H. STUART MENZIES and HENDY. 6s. net. THE WORLD'S WORKERS. Illustrated by "FOUGASSE." 5s. net.

Grahame (Kenneth)
THE WIND IN THE WILLOWS. Nineteenth Edition. *Crown 8vo.* 7s. 6d. net. Also, illustrated by WYNDHAM

MESSRS. METHUEN'S PUBLICATIONS

PAYNE. *Small 4to. 7s. 6d. net.* Also unillustrated. *Fcap. 8vo. 3s. 6d. net.*

Hadfield (J. A.)
PSYCHOLOGY AND MORALS. *Seventh Edition. Crown 8vo. 6s. net.*

Hall (H. R.)
THE ANCIENT HISTORY OF THE NEAR EAST. *Seventh Edition Revised. Demy 8vo.* £1 1s. *net.* THE CIVILIZATION OF GREECE IN THE BRONZE AGE. Illustrated. *Wide Royal 8vo.* £1 10s. *net.* A SEASON'S WORK AT UR OF THE CHALDEES. *Demy 8vo. 15s. net.*

Herbert (A. P.)
HONEYBUBBLE & CO. 6s. *net.* MISLEADING CASES IN THE COMMON LAW. With an Introduction by LORD HEWART. 5s. *net.* THE BOMBER GIPSY. 3s. 6d. *net.* LIGHT ARTICLES ONLY. Illustrated. 6s. *net.* THE WHEREFORE AND THE WHY. "TINKER, TAILOR . . ." Each illustrated. 3s. 6d. *net.* THE SECRET BATTLE. 3s. 6d. *net.*

Hind (A. M.)
A CATALOGUE OF REMBRANDT'S ETCHINGS. Two Vols. Profusely Illustrated. *Wide Royal 8vo.* £1 15s. *net.*

Holdsworth (W. S.)
A HISTORY OF ENGLISH LAW. Nine Volumes. *Demy 8vo.* £1 5s. *net each.*

Hudson (W. H.)
A SHEPHERD'S LIFE. Illustrated. *Demy 8vo.* 10s. 6d. *net.* Also, unillustrated. *Fcap. 8vo. 3s. 6d. net.*

Hutton (Edward)
CITIES OF SICILY. Illustrated. 10s. 6d. *net.* MILAN AND LOMBARDY. THE CITIES OF ROMAGNA AND THE MARCHES. SIENA AND SOUTHERN TUSCANY. VENICE AND VENETIA. THE CITIES OF SPAIN. NAPLES AND SOUTHERN ITALY. Illustrated. *Each,* 8s. 6d. *net.* A WAYFARER IN UNKNOWN TUSCANY. THE CITIES OF UMBRIA. COUNTRY WALKS ABOUT FLORENCE. ROME. FLORENCE AND NORTHERN TUSCANY. Each illustrated. 7s. 6d. *net.*

Inge (W. R.), D.D., Dean of St. Paul's.
CHRISTIAN MYSTICISM. (The Bampton Lectures of 1899.) *Sixth Edition. Crown 8vo. 7s. 6d. net.*

Kipling (Rudyard)
BARRACK-ROOM BALLADS. 246*th Thousand.*
THE SEVEN SEAS. 180*th Thousand.*
THE FIVE NATIONS. 143*rd Thousand.*
DEPARTMENTAL DITTIES. 111*th Thousand.*
THE YEARS BETWEEN. 95*th Thousand.*
Four Editions of these famous volumes of poems are now published, viz. :—
Crown 8vo. Buckram, 7s. 6d. *net. Fcap. 8vo.* Cloth, 6s. *net.* Leather, 7s. 6d. *net.* Service Edition. Two volumes each book. *Square Fcap. 8vo. 3s. net each volume.*
A KIPLING ANTHOLOGY—Verse. *Fcap. 8vo.* Cloth, 6s. *net* and 3s. 6d. *net.* Leather, 7s. 6d. *net.* TWENTY POEMS FROM RUDYARD KIPLING. 458*th Thousand. Fcap. 8vo.* 1s. *net.* A CHOICE OF SONGS. *Second Edition. Fcap. 8vo. 2s. net.*

Lamb (Charles and Mary)
THE COMPLETE WORKS. Edited by E. V. LUCAS. A New and Revised Edition in Six Volumes. With Frontispieces. *Fcap. 8vo. 6s. net each.*
The volumes are : I. MISCELLANEOUS PROSE. II. ELIA AND THE LAST ESSAYS OF ELIA. III. BOOKS FOR CHILDREN. IV. PLAYS AND POEMS. V. and VI. LETTERS.
SELECTED LETTERS. Chosen and Edited by G. T. CLAPTON. *Fcap. 8vo. 3s. 6d. net.* THE CHARLES LAMB DAY BOOK. Compiled by E. V. LUCAS. *Fcap. 8vo. 6s. net.*

Lankester (Sir Ray)
SCIENCE FROM AN EASY CHAIR. SCIENCE FROM AN EASY CHAIR : Second Series. DIVERSIONS OF A NATURALIST. GREAT AND SMALL THINGS. Illustrated. *Crown 8vo. 7s. 6d. net.* SECRETS OF EARTH AND SEA. Illustrated. *Crown 8vo. 8s. 6d. net.*

Lodge (Sir Oliver)
MAN AND THE UNIVERSE (*Twentieth Edition*). 7s. 6d. *net and* 3s. 6d. *net.* THE SURVIVAL OF MAN (*Seventh Edition*). 7s. 6d. *net.* RAYMOND. (*Thirteenth Edition*). 10s. 6d. *net.* RAYMOND REVISED. 6s. *net.* MODERN PROBLEMS. 3s. 6d. *net.* THE SUBSTANCE OF FAITH (*Fifteenth Edition*). 2s. *net.* RELATIVITY (*Fourth Edition*). 1s. *net.*

Lucas (E. V.)
THE LIFE OF CHARLES LAMB. 2 Vols. £1 1s. *net.* EDWIN AUSTIN ABBEY, R.A. 2 Vols. £6 6s. *net.* THE COLVINS AND THEIR FRIENDS. £1 1s. *net.* VERMEER THE MAGICAL. 5s. *net.* A WANDERER IN ROME. A WANDERER

MESSRS. METHUEN'S PUBLICATIONS   5

IN HOLLAND. A WANDERER IN LONDON. LONDON REVISITED (Revised). A WANDERER IN PARIS. A WANDERER IN FLORENCE. A WANDERER IN VENICE. Each 10s. 6d. net. A WANDERER AMONG PICTURES. 8s. 6d. net. E. V. LUCAS'S LONDON. £1 net. INTRODUCING LONDON. INTRODUCING PARIS. Each 2s. 6d. net. THE OPEN ROAD. 6s. net. Also, illustrated by CLAUDE A. SHEPPERSON, A.R.W.S. 10s. 6d. net. Also, India Paper. Leather, 7s. 6d. net. THE JOY OF LIFE. 6s. net. Leather Edition. 7s. 6d. net. Also India Paper. Leather. 7s. 6d net. FIRESIDE AND SUNSHINE. CHARACTER AND COMEDY. Each 6s. net. THE GENTLEST ART. 6s. 6d. net. And THE SECOND POST. 6s. net. Also, together in one volume. 7s. 6d. net. HER INFINITE VARIETY. GOOD COMPANY. ONE DAY AND ANOTHER. OLD LAMPS FOR NEW. LOITERER'S HARVEST. CLOUD AND SILVER. A BOSWELL OF BAGHDAD. 'TWIXT EAGLE AND DOVE. THE PHANTOM JOURNAL. GIVING AND RECEIVING. LUCK OF THE YEAR. ENCOUNTERS AND DIVERSIONS. ZIGZAGS IN FRANCE. EVENTS AND EMBROIDERIES. 365 DAYS (AND ONE MORE). A FRONDED ISLE. A ROVER I WOULD BE. Each 6s. net. URBANITIES. Illustrated by G. L. STAMPA. 5s. net. YOU KNOW WHAT PEOPLE ARE. Illustrated by GEORGE MORROW. 5s. net. THE SAME STAR : A Comedy in Three Acts. 3s. 6d. net. LITTLE BOOKS ON GREAT MASTERS. Each 5s. net. ROVING EAST AND ROVING WEST. 5s. net. PLAYTIME & COMPANY. 7s. 6d. net. Mr. Punch's COUNTY SONGS. Illustrated by E. H. SHEPARD. 10s. 6d. net. "THE MORE I SEE OF MEN . . ." OUT OF A CLEAR SKY. Each 3s. 6d. net. See also Dolls' House (The Queen's) and Lamb (Charles).

Lucas (E. V.) and Finck (Herman)
TWELVE SONGS FROM "PLAYTIME & COMPANY." Words by E. V. LUCAS. Music by HERMAN FINCK. Royal 4to. 7s. 6d. net.

Lynd (Robert)
THE GREEN MAN. OLD FRIENDS IN FICTION. THE GOLDFISH. THE PLEASURES OF IGNORANCE. Each 5s. net. THE LITTLE ANGEL. THE BLUE LION. THE PEAL OF BELLS. THE MONEY BOX. THE ORANGE TREE. Each 3s. 6d. net.

McDougall (William)
AN INTRODUCTION TO SOCIAL PSYCHOLOGY (Twenty-first Edition). 10s. 6d. net. NATIONAL WELFARE AND NATIONAL DECAY. 6s. net. AN OUTLINE OF PSYCHOLOGY (Fourth Edition). 10s. 6d. net. AN OUTLINE OF ABNORMAL PSYCHOLOGY. 15s. net. BODY AND MIND (Sixth Edition). 12s. 6d. net. CHARACTER AND THE CONDUCT OF LIFE (Third Edition). 10s. 6d. net. MODERN MATERIALISM AND EMERGENT EVOLUTION. 7s. 6d. net. ETHICS AND SOME MODERN WORLD PROBLEMS (Second Edition). 7s. 6d. net.

Mackenzie (W. Mackay)
THE MEDIÆVAL CASTLE IN SCOTLAND. (The Rhind Lectures on Archæology. 1925-6.) Illustrated. Demy 8vo. 15s. net.

Mallet (Sir C. E.)
A HISTORY OF THE UNIVERSITY OF OXFORD. In 3 vols. Illustrated. Demy 8vo. Each £1 1s. net.

Maeterlinck (Maurice)
THE BLUE BIRD. 6s. net. Also, illustrated by F. CAYLEY ROBINSON. 10s. 6d. net. DEATH. 3s. 6d. net. OUR ETERNITY. 6s. net. THE UNKNOWN GUEST. 6s. net. POEMS. 5s. net. THE WRACK OF THE STORM. 6s. net. THE MIRACLE OF ST. ANTHONY. 3s. 6d. net. THE BURGOMASTER OF STILEMONDE. 5s. net. THE BETROTHAL. 6s. net. MOUNTAIN PATHS. 6s. net. THE STORY OF TYLTYL. £1 1s. net. THE GREAT SECRET. 7s. 6d. net. THE CLOUD THAT LIFTED and THE POWER OF THE DEAD. 7s. 6d. net. MARY MAGDALENE. 2s. net.

Masefield (John)
ON THE SPANISH MAIN. 8s. 6d. net. A SAILOR'S GARLAND. 6s. net and 3s. 6d. net. SEA LIFE IN NELSON'S TIME. 5s. net.

Methuen (Sir A.)
AN ANTHOLOGY OF MODERN VERSE 147th Thousand. SHAKESPEARE TO HARDY : An Anthology of English Lyrics. 19th Thousand. Each Fcap. 8vo. Cloth, 6s. net. Leather, 7s. 6d. net.

Milne (A. A.)
TOAD OF TOAD HALL. 5s. net. NOT THAT IT MATTERS. IF I MAY. THE SUNNY SIDE. THE RED HOUSE MYSTERY. ONCE A WEEK. THE HOLIDAY ROUND. THE DAY'S PLAY. Each 3s. 6d. net. WHEN WE WERE VERY YOUNG. Eighteenth Edition. 189th Thousand. WINNIE-THE-POOH. Seventh Edition. 96th Thousand. NOW WE ARE SIX. Fourth Edition. 109th Thou-

sand. THE HOUSE AT POOH CORNER. Second Edition. 86th Thousand. Each illustrated by E. H. SHEPARD. 7s. 6d. net. Leather, 10s. 6d. net. FOR THE LUNCHEON INTERVAL. 1s. 6d. net.

Milne (A. A.) and Fraser-Simson (H.)
FOURTEEN SONGS FROM "WHEN WE WERE VERY YOUNG." Twelfth Edition. 7s. 6d. net. TEDDY BEAR AND OTHER SONGS FROM "WHEN WE WERE VERY YOUNG." 7s. 6d. net. THE KING'S BREAKFAST. Third Edition. 3s. 6d. net. SONGS FROM "NOW WE ARE SIX." Second Edition. 7s. 6d. net. MORE SONGS FROM "NOW WE ARE SIX." 7s. 6d net. Words by A. A. MILNE Music by H. FRASER-SIMSON. Decorations by E. H. SHEPARD.

Montague (C. E.)
DRAMATIC VALUES. Cr. 8vo. 7s. 6d. net.

Morton (H. V.)
THE HEART OF LONDON. 3s. 6d. net. (Also illustrated, 7s. 6d. net.) THE SPELL OF LONDON. THE NIGHTS OF LONDON. Each 3s. 6d. net. THE LONDON YEAR. IN SEARCH OF ENGLAND. THE CALL OF ENGLAND. IN SEARCH OF SCOTLAND. Each illustrated. 7s. 6d. net.

Oman (Sir Charles)
A HISTORY OF THE ART OF WAR IN THE MIDDLE AGES, A.D. 378–1485. 2 Vols. Illustrated. Demy 8vo. £1 16s. net. STUDIES IN THE NAPOLEONIC WARS. Crown 8vo. 8s. 6d. net.

Oxenham (John)
BEES IN AMBER. Small Pott 8vo. 2s. net. ALL'S WELL. THE KING'S HIGHWAY. THE VISION SPLENDID. THE FIERY CROSS. HIGH ALTARS. HEARTS COURAGEOUS. ALL CLEAR! Each Small Pott 8vo. Paper, 1s. 3d. net. Cloth, 2s. net. WINDS OF THE DAWN. 2s. net.

Perry (W. J.)
THE ORIGIN OF MAGIC AND RELIGION. THE GROWTH OF CIVILIZATION. Each 6s. net. THE CHILDREN OF THE SUN. £1 1s. net.

Petrie (Sir Flinders)
A HISTORY OF EGYPT. In 6 Volumes.
Vol. I. FROM THE 1ST TO THE XVITH DYNASTY. 11th Edition, Revised. 12s. net.
Vol. II. THE XVIITH AND XVIIITH DYNASTIES. 7th Edition, Revised. 9s. net.
Vol. III. XIXTH TO XXXTH DYNASTIES. 3rd Edition. 12s. net.
Vol. IV. EGYPT UNDER THE PTOLEMAIC DYNASTY. By EDWYN BEVAN. 15s. net.
Vol. V. EGYPT UNDER ROMAN RULE.
By J. G. MILNE. 3rd Edition, Revised. 12s. net.
Vol. VI. EGYPT IN THE MIDDLE AGES. By STANLEY LANE POOLE. 4th Edition. 10s. net.

Ponsonby (Arthur), M.P.
ENGLISH DIARIES. £1 1s. net. MORE ENGLISH DIARIES. 12s. 6d. net. SCOTTISH AND IRISH DIARIES. 10s. 6d. net.

Raleigh (Sir Walter)
THE LETTERS OF SIR WALTER RALEIGH. Edited by LADY RALEIGH. Two Vols. Illustrated. Second Edition. Demy 8vo. 18s. net. SELECTED LETTERS. Edited by LADY RALEIGH. 7s. 6d. net.

Smith (C. Fox)
SAILOR TOWN DAYS. SEA SONGS AND BALLADS. A BOOK OF FAMOUS SHIPS. SHIP ALLEY. ANCIENT MARINERS. Each, illustrated, 6s. net FULL SAIL. Illustrated. 5s. net. TALES OF THE CLIPPER SHIPS. A SEA CHEST. Each 5s. net. THE RETURN OF THE "CUTTY SARK." Illustrated. 3s. 6d. net. A BOOK OF SHANTIES. 6s. net.

Stevenson (R. L.)
THE LETTERS. Edited by Sir SIDNEY COLVIN. 4 Vols. Fcap. 8vo. Each 6s net.

Surtees (R. S.)
HANDLEY CROSS. MR. SPONGE'S SPORTING TOUR. ASK MAMMA. MR. FACEY ROMFORD'S HOUNDS. PLAIN OR RINGLETS? HILLINGDON HALL. Each illustrated, 7s. 6d. net. JORROCKS'S JAUNTS AND JOLLITIES. HAWBUCK GRANGE. Each, illustrated, 6s. net.

Taylor (A. E.)
PLATO : THE MAN AND HIS WORK. Demy 8vo. £1 1s. net. PLATO : TIMÆUS AND CRITIAS. Crown 8vo. 8s. 6d. net. ELEMENTS OF METAPHYSICS. Demy 8vo. 12s. 6d. net.

Tilden (William T.)
THE ART OF LAWN TENNIS. SINGLES AND DOUBLES. Each, illustrated, 6s. net. THE COMMON SENSE OF LAWN TENNIS. MATCH PLAY AND THE SPIN OF THE BALL. Illustrated. 5s. net.

Tileston (Mary W.)
DAILY STRENGTH FOR DAILY NEEDS. 32nd Edition. 3s. 6d. net. India Paper. Leather, 6s. net.

Trapp (Oswald Graf)
THE ARMOURY OF THE CASTLE OF CHURBURG. Translated by J. G. MANN. Richly illustrated. Royal 4to. Limited to 400 copies. £4 14s. 6d. net.

MESSRS. METHUEN'S PUBLICATIONS 7

Underhill (Evelyn)
MYSTICISM (*Eleventh Edition*). 15s. net.
THE LIFE OF THE SPIRIT AND THE LIFE OF TO-DAY (*Sixth Edition*). 7s. 6d. net. MAN AND THE SUPERNATURAL. 7s. 6d. net. CONCERNING THE INNER LIFE (*Fourth Edition*). 2s. net.

Vardon (Harry)
HOW TO PLAY GOLF. Illustrated. 19th Edition. *Crown 8vo.* 5s. net.

Wand (J. W. C.)
THE DEVELOPMENT OF SACRAMENTALISM. *Fcap. 8vo.* 6s. net. A HISTORY OF THE MODERN CHURCH. *Crown 8vo.* 7s. 6d. net.

Wilde (Oscar)
THE WORKS. In 17 Vols Each 6s. 6d. net.
I. LORD ARTHUR SAVILE'S CRIME AND THE PORTRAIT OF MR. W. H. II. THE DUCHESS OF PADUA. III. POEMS. IV. LADY WINDERMERE'S FAN. V. A WOMAN OF NO IMPORTANCE. VI. AN IDEAL HUSBAND. VII. THE IMPORTANCE OF BEING EARNEST. VIII. A HOUSE OF POMEGRANATES. IX. INTENTIONS. X. DE PROFUNDIS AND PRISON LETTERS. XI. ESSAYS. XII. SALOME, A FLORENTINE TRAGEDY, and LA SAINTE COURTISANE. XIII. A CRITIC IN PALL MALL. XIV. SELECTED PROSE OF OSCAR WILDE. XV. ART AND DECORATION. XVI. FOR LOVE OF THE KING. (5s. net.) XVII. VERA, OR THE NIHILISTS.

Williamson (G. C.)
THE BOOK OF FAMILLE ROSE. Richly Illustrated. *Demy 4to.* £8 8s. net.

PART II. A SELECTION OF SERIES

The Antiquary's Books
Each, illustrated, *Demy 8vo* 10s. 6d. net.

The Arden Shakespeare
Edited by W. J. CRAIG and R. H. CASE. Each, *wide Demy 8vo.* 6s. net.
The Ideal Library Edition, in single plays, each edited with a full Introduction, Textual Notes and a Commentary at the foot of the page. Now complete in 39 Vols.

Classics of Art
Edited by J. H. W. LAING. Each, profusely illustrated, *wide Royal 8vo.* 15s. net to £3 3s. net.
A Library of Art dealing with Great Artists and with branches of Art.

The Connoisseur's Library
With numerous Illustrations. *Wide Royal 8vo.* £1 11s. 6d. net each vol.
EUROPEAN ENAMELS. FINE BOOKS. GLASS. GOLDSMITHS' AND SILVERSMITHS' WORK. IVORIES. JEWELLERY. MINIATURES. MEZZOTINTS. PORCELAIN. SEALS. MUSSULMAN PAINTING. (£3 3s. net.) WATCHES. (£2 2s. net.)

English Life in English Literature
General Editors: EILEEN POWER, M.A., D.Lit., and A. W. REED, M.A., D.Lit. Each, *Crown 8vo*, 6s. net.
A series of source-books for students of history and of literature.

The Faiths: VARIETIES OF CHRISTIAN EXPRESSION. Edited by L. P. JACKS, M.A., D.D., LL.D. Each, *Crown 8vo*, 5s. net each volume. The first volumes are: THE ANGLO-CATHOLIC FAITH (T. A. LACEY); MODERNISM IN THE ENGLISH CHURCH (P. GARDNER); THE FAITH AND PRACTICE OF THE QUAKERS (R. M. JONES); CONGREGATIONALISM (W. B. SELBIE); THE FAITH OF THE ROMAN CHURCH (C. C. MARTINDALE); THE LIFE AND FAITH OF THE BAPTISTS (H. WHEELER ROBINSON); THE PRESBYTERIAN CHURCHES (JAMES MOFFATT); METHODISM (W. BARDSLEY BRASH); THE EVANGELICAL MOVEMENT IN THE ENGLISH CHURCH (L. ELLIOTT BINNS); THE UNITARIANS (HENRY GOW).

The Gateway Library
Fcap. 8vo. 3s. 6d. each volume.
Pocketable Editions of Works by HILAIRE BELLOC, ARNOLD BENNETT, E. F. BENSON, GEORGE A. BIRMINGHAM, MARJORIE BOWEN, G. K. CHESTERTON, A. CLUTTON-BROCK, JOSEPH CONRAD, J. H. CURLE, GEORGE GISSING, GERALD GOULD, KENNETH GRAHAME, A. P. HERBERT, W. H. HUDSON, RUDYARD KIPLING, E. V. KNOX, JACK LONDON, E. V. LUCAS, ROBERT LYND, ROSE MACAULAY, JOHN MASEFIELD, A. A. MILNE, C. E. MONTAGUE, ARTHUR MORRISON, EDEN PHILLPOTTS, MARMADUKE PICKTHALL, J. B. PRIESTLEY, CHARLES G. D. ROBERTS, R. L. STEVENSON, and OSCAR WILDE.

A History of England in Seven Volumes
Edited by Sir CHARLES OMAN, K.B.E., M.P., M.A., F.S.A. With Maps. *Demy 8vo.* 12s. 6d. net each volume. ENGLAND BEFORE THE NORMAN CONQUEST (Sir C. OMAN); ENGLAND UNDER THE NORMANS AND ANGEVINS (H. W. C.

MESSRS. METHUEN'S PUBLICATIONS

Davies); England in the Later Middle Ages (K. H. Vickers); England under the Tudors (A. D. Innes); England under the Stuarts (G. M. Trevelyan); England under the Hanoverians (Sir C. Grant Robertson); England Since Waterloo (Sir J. A. R. Marriott).

The Library of Devotion
Handy editions of the great Devotional books, well edited. *Small Pott 8vo. 3s. net and 3s. 6d. net.*

Methuen's Half-Crown Library
Crown 8vo and Fcap. 8vo.

Methuen's Two-Shilling Library
Fcap. 8vo.
Two series of cheap editions of popular books.
Write for complete lists.

The Wayfarer Series of Books for Travellers
Crown 8vo. 7s. 6d. net each. Well illustrated and with maps. The volumes are:—Alsace, Austria, Czecho-Slovakia, The Dolomites, Egypt, French Vineyards, Hungary, The Loire, Morocco, Portugal, Provence, Pyrenees, The Seine, Spain, Sweden, Switzerland, Unfamiliar Japan, Unknown Tuscany, The West Indies.

The Westminster Commentaries
Demy 8vo. 8s. 6d. net to 16s. net.
Edited by W. Lock, D.D., and D. C. Simpson, D.D.
The object of these commentaries is primarily to interpret the author's meaning to the present generation, taking the English text in the Revised Version as their basis.

THE LITTLE GUIDES
Small Pott 8vo. Illustrated and with Maps
THE 65 VOLUMES IN THE SERIES ARE:—

Bedfordshire and Huntingdonshire 4s. net.
Berkshire 4s. net.
Brittany 5s. net.
Buckinghamshire 5s. net.
Cambridge and Colleges 4s. net.
Cambridgeshire 4s. net.
Cathedral Cities of England and Wales 6s. net.
Channel Islands 5s. net.
Cheshire 5s. net.
Cornwall 4s. net.
Cumberland and Westmorland 6s. net.
Derbyshire 4s. net.
Devon 4s. net.
Dorset 6s. net.
Durham 6s. net.
English Lakes 6s. net.
Essex 5s. net.
Florence 6s. net.
French Riviera 6s. net.
Gloucestershire 5s. net.
Gray's Inn and Lincoln's Inn 6s. net.
Hampshire 4s. net.
Herefordshire 4s. 6d. net.
Hertfordshire 5s. net.
Isle of Man 6s. net.
Isle of Wight 4s. net.
Kent 6s. net.
Lancashire 6s. net.
Leicestershire and Rutland 5s. net.
Lincolnshire 6s. net.
London 5s. net.
Malvern Country 4s. net.
Middlesex 4s. net.
Monmouthshire 6s. net.
Norfolk 5s. net.
Normandy 5s. net.
Northamptonshire 4s. net.
Northumberland 7s. 6d. net.
North Wales 6s. net.
Nottinghamshire 6s. net.
Oxford and Colleges 4s. net.
Oxfordshire 4s. net.
Paris 5s. net.
Rome 5s. net.
St. Paul's Cathedral 4s. net.
Shakespeare's Country 4s. net.
Shropshire 5s. net.
Sicily 4s. net.
Snowdonia 6s. net.
Somerset 4s. net.
South Wales 4s. net.
Staffordshire 5s. net.
Suffolk 4s. net.
Surrey 5s. net.
Sussex 5s. net.
Temple 4s. net.
Venice 6s. net.
Warwickshire 5s. net.
Westminster Abbey 5s. net.
Wiltshire 6s. net.
Worcestershire 6s. net.
Yorkshire East Riding 5s. net.
Yorkshire North Riding 4s. net.
Yorkshire West Riding 7s. 6d. net.
York 6s. net.

METHUEN & CO. LTD., 36 ESSEX STREET, LONDON, W.C.2.

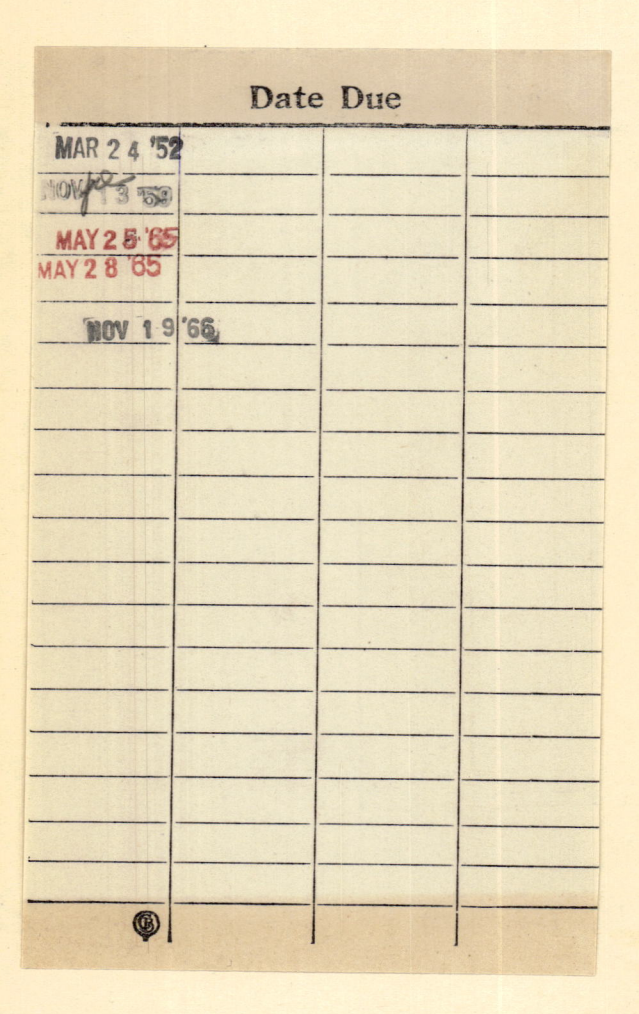

Date Due			
MAR 24 '52			
NOV 3 '59			
MAY 25 '65			
MAY 28 '65			
NOV 19 '66			